Sports Finance and Management

As the sport business continues to evolve, so too does sport finance and management. The first version of this book took an in-depth look at changes in the sport industry, including interconnecting financial issues between teams and their associated businesses, the nature of fan loyalty influences, and the impact of sponsorship on team revenues. This second edition updates each of these elements, introduces relevant case study examples in new chapters, and examines the impact of changes in facility design, media opportunities, and league and conference policies on the economic success of teams, the salaries earned by professional players, and the finances of collegiate athletics.

Jason A. Winfree, PhD, is an Associate Professor at the University of Idaho, Moscow, USA.

Mark S. Rosentraub, PhD, is the Bruce and Joan Bickner Endowed Professor of Sport Management in the School of Kinesiology at the University of Michigan, Ann Arbor, USA.

Brian M. Mills, PhD, is an Assistant Professor in the Department of Tourism, Recreation, and Sport Management at the University of Florida, Gainsville, USA.

Mackenzie P. Zondlak is the Manager of the Center for Sport and Policy in the School of Kinesiology at the University of Michigan, Ann Arbor, USA.

Sports Finance and Management

Real Estate, Media, and the
New Business of Sport

Second Edition

Jason A. Winfree, Mark S. Rosentraub,
Brian M. Mills, and Mackenzie P. Zondlak

Routledge
Taylor & Francis Group

NEW YORK AND LONDON

First published 2019
by Routledge
711 Third Avenue, New York, NY 10017

and by Routledge
2 Park Square, Milton Park, Abingdon, Oxon, OX14 4RN

Routledge is an imprint of the Taylor & Francis Group, an informa business

© 2019 Jason A. Winfree, Mark S. Rosentraub, Brian M. Mills, and
Mackenzie P. Zondlak

Library of Congress Cataloging-in-Publication Data
A catalog record for this book has been requested.

ISBN: 978-1-4987-0526-4 (hbk)
ISBN: 978-1-138-34181-4 (pbk)
ISBN: 978-1-315-11966-3 (ebk)

Typeset in Sabon
by Deanta Global Publishing Services, Chennai, India

Sports Finance and Management

Real Estate, Media, and the New Business of Sport

Second Edition

Jason A. Winfree, Mark S. Rosentraub, Brian M. Mills, and Mackenzie P. Zondlak

NEW YORK AND LONDON

First published 2019
by Routledge
711 Third Avenue, New York, NY 10017

and by Routledge
2 Park Square, Milton Park, Abingdon, Oxon, OX14 4RN

Routledge is an imprint of the Taylor & Francis Group, an informa business

Library of Congress Cataloging-in-Publication Data
A catalog record for this book has been requested.

ISBN: 978-1-4987-0526-4 (hbk)
ISBN: 978-1-138-34181-4 (pbk)
ISBN: 978-1-315-11966-3 (ebk)

Typeset in Sabon
by Deanta Global Publishing Services, Chennai, India

Dedication

While this book was written, Mila Rae Glimcher, my 10th grandchild, grew to be a toddler. This book is for her, and the nine other grandchildren who, each day, give me faith in the future. This book is also dedicated to my wife, Karen, and our four children and their spouses. I am not sure what we did "right," but our days are bright because of the contributions to society each makes every day. This one is for Sabrina (Danny), Natalie (Jason), Alexa (John), and David (Jenny). Karen and I are so very proud of each of you. On behalf of the two of us, I hope this book gives you 1 percent of the pride we feel when we look into each of your eyes.

Mark S. Rosentraub, Ann Arbor, Michigan, August 2018.

To my family, who should certainly receive some of the credit for this book. Without their dedication and support, I would not have been able to contribute to this second edition. My wife, Nikki, has always provided encouragement and any help that was needed, while Max and Grace provided the motivation.

Jason A. Winfree, Moscow, Idaho, August 2018.

To Caitlin, who has been a bedrock of support every step of the way.

Brian M. Mills, Gainesville, Florida, August 2018.

To my family. Mom, Dad, Allyse, Brendan, Harper, and Josie – thank you for your love and support.

Mackenzie P. Zondlak, Ann Arbor, Michigan, August 2018.

Contents

Figures

Tables

Preface

This second edition of *Sport Management and Finance* benefitted from the research opportunities afforded to the authors by several teams and cities. We are grateful to Sterling Project Development, Olympia Development, the Green Bay Packers, the Cleveland Indians, the Ottawa Senators, the Calgary Municipal Land Corporation, Bedrock Management, the Children's Museum of Indianapolis, the New York Racing Association, the Tampa Bay Lightning, the University of Nevada Las Vegas, the Oakland Raiders, and St. Lucie County. We benefitted from each of these organizations and their extraordinary staff. From each of these projects, we learned a great deal about the sport business, real estate development, and the ways in which teams engage with fans, the media, and the entertainment industry.

Each of us has colleagues that we rely upon to discuss ideas and concepts that improved this book. This list of friends and colleagues includes Ed Blumenfeld, David Blumenfeld, Michael Brown, Paul Dolan, Jim Dunn, Daniel Glimcher, Ken King, Barry Klarberg, Ed Policy, Matt Rossetti, Janet Marie Smith, Jeff Wilpon, and Susan Veres. While confidential topics were left unsaid, what is imbedded throughout are the insights and first-hand knowledge you were willing to let novices understand.

We are extremely grateful to the journal, *The Physical Educator*, for permitting the use of some of the data that appeared in a 2019 (Volume 76) article written by Michael B. Cantor, Sierra R. Bain, and Mark S. Rosentraub. Michael Cantor and Sierra Bain also wrote Chapter 13.

Sierra Bain began her work with the Center as an undergraduate student and became a full-time staff member in 2017. Dr. Michael Cantor left the Center in 2013 to pursue his career with Sterling Project Development and the New York Mets. Before relocating, he was a driving force in building and shaping the University of Michigan Center for Sport and Policy's philosophy.

Madelaine Moeke, another former Center for Sport and Policy staff member, also worked on several of the projects from which we learned a great deal. Ms. Moeke left the Center in 2018 to pursue a new position with ROSSETTI Architects. We are grateful for the insights generated by her research.

This second edition brings two new authors to *Sports Finance and Management*. Professor Brian Mills – who worked at the University of Michigan Center for Sport and Policy as a doctoral student before joining the faculty at the University of Florida – added much to the new elements that define this volume.

Mackenzie Zondlak, the second new author, was the driving force behind the completion of this book. She was responsible for rewriting and reorganizing several chapters, and her research is an integral part of those and all others. Mackenzie, on behalf of your coauthors, we thank you for all that you did that made it possible for this book to exist. Without your efforts, this book would not have appeared in 2018. We are grateful for all of work.

Lastly, we are indebted to the numerous students who provided comments and reactions to the first edition. Your comments helped to make the second edition better. We hope we have not failed the new readers of this book.

Chapter 1

Redefining the Sport Business Industry

Introduction

The sport business continues to be defined by dramatic changes, which means *Sport Finance and Management* is far different today than it was just a few years ago. Indeed, the sport business has changed so quickly that a second edition of this book is warranted to ensure students have the insights, skills, and knowledge needed to compete for jobs in the industry. For example, in 2017 *Forbes* concluded that every National Football League (NFL) team was worth at least $1.6 billion and the league-wide average was more than $2.52 billion; just four years earlier, the average value of an NFL team was $1.17 billion. *Across a period of 48 months, the value of the average NFL team more than doubled.* In 2017, *Forbes* valued 18 of the National Basketball Association's (NBA) 30 franchises at or above $1 billion, and the league's average franchise value was $1.36 billion, which is more than double what it was just three years earlier. In the summer of 2015, the National Hockey League (NHL) required an expansion fee of $500 million for its newest franchise, the Las Vegas Golden Knights. The commissioner noted in 2017 that if another team, the Carolina Hurricanes, for example, was to be sold, the selling price should also be approximately $500 million. Finally, the United States' fifth major professional sport, Major League Soccer (MLS), has reportedly sold franchises for $150 million.

This book is designed to provide extensive insight into the changes that are driving the explosion in team values and the impact of those asset prices on athletes and every other aspect of the business of sport. Our goal is to give students and practitioners the knowledge needed to succeed in this rapidly shifting business world. This second edition provides greater coverage of business areas that even a few years ago were just emerging or were far less dominant than they are today.

The financial returns from sport have always been a function of the ways in which owners could use their franchise to leverage or "activate" different revenue streams. What began as a business that sold only tickets for admission and beer (initiated by the Cincinnati Red Stockings, North America's first professional team, now the Reds) now includes various premium seating products (suites and club seats or seating in other club areas), social seating (non-fixed seating in areas of a venue that look more like a neighborhood pub or restaurant), other new seating options and accommodations for fans with young children, numerous naming and advertising opportunities, real estate development (inside and adjacent to a venue), non-sport (entertainment) and non-team (other games or matches) events at a venue, and the 24/7 delivery of content through various media platforms. These changes are not limited to the four or five major sport leagues in North America. The financing of collegiate sport has also undergone substantial shifts and that has created new opportunities and issues for universities. It was reported in 2016 that the Big Ten Conference distributed $32.4 million to its 11 oldest members; this financial success convinced the universities of the Big Ten Conference to give the conference's executive director a $20 million future bonus payment (Berkowitz, 2017).

The magnitude of these financial gains illustrates the insights and skills that students need to compete for jobs in the rapidly changing industry. Students need to have a greater understanding of the ways in which teams, universities, and cities benefit from the leveraging of sport and the venues used by teams. In many ways, the changes in the sport world that have led to the enhanced value of teams and university athletics (for some conferences) are a result of the business philosophy pioneered by the Disney Corporation and Walter O'Malley at Dodger Stadium in Los Angeles.

So, what was this new, innovative business philosophy? As will be discussed in the sections and chapters that follow, the Disney Corporation and the Dodgers designed their attractions to appeal to vastly different fan or market segments to ensure everyone visiting had a great experience. For the Dodgers, this meant that fans would leave the ballpark having had a great time even when the team lost a game (Podair, 2017). *Disneyland* (1955), and then *Disney World* (1971), as well as Dodger Stadium at the Chavez Ravine (1962), were designed to provide those families and individuals with distinct preferences, with specialized amenities capable of making each visit a great one. This commitment to the fan experience now defines every aspect of the sport and hospitality business. The targeted approach to fan segments is evident in today's venues' diverse seating areas and the various experiences offered to both casual and committed fans. It is also demonstrated by teams' usage of an almost endless list of media platforms and the different types of content used to connect each fan segment with the players and franchise. Today's newest venues, as will be discussed in later chapters, feature several different clubs, restaurants, and exhibits to ensure every game is an exciting, varied, and valuable experience for all visitors. The success of this business philosophy has contributed to the elevation of professional sport franchise values across the board.

Today's team executives must understand that while many fans attending games are intently focused on the playing action, this is just one segment of a team's expansive fan base. Other fans may want to enjoy the game while also spending time mixing with their friends in a social atmosphere, sometimes referred to as social seating. An extreme example of redesigning a venue to appeal to different fan segments is illustrated by the University of Central Florida's (UCF) decision to offer fans "beachfront" seating at its stadium (UCF Knights, 2015). UCF's provision of beachfront seating, for fans interested in social seating options, is an example of how a team or athletic department can design one part of its stadium to appeal to the needs of a specific fan segment. The Cleveland Indians are another example. In 2015, the team opened clubs with non-fixed seating that look similar to what is available at neighborhood sports bars, restaurants, and pubs, replacing what had previously been several large and unappealing sections of outfield seating.

Some might think appealing to more casual fans, such as families, would be unorthodox, if not blasphemous, but nothing could be further from the truth. Today's teams must be proactive in creating unique and varied experiences for each of their fan segments – casual or otherwise – in order to compete with fans' alternative option: to watch games from the comfort of their homes in extreme clarity (with the help of ever-improving HD television technology). Young adults with children are interested in entertainment options that accommodate their kids while also saving parents' money on babysitters. One way to get these fans to a venue is by providing a children's play area that is fun for the kids and provides parents with a place where they can watch both their children and the game. The San Diego Padres were pioneers in this effort with the placement of a giant sandbox beyond the right center field fence and special seats allowing parents to watch both their children playing and the game. The Cleveland Indians also turned several suites into daycare and play areas for young children (known as the Kids Clubhouse) to attract families to games. Many teams now routinely provide families with various smaller-scale amusement and other family-friendly options, just as the Disney Corporation has mixed low-impact rides for younger children into the Magic Kingdom.

Teams also offer special spaces and amenities to appeal to businesses that utilize teams, games, and events as vehicles for marketing their services and products to clients, or to reward employees. Private suites with space for meetings and for entertaining clients and employees have been included in the design of venues since the 1980s. Club seat sections were added in the late 1980s and 1990s. These areas have a reserved club area where a firm's clients and employees can be entertained around tables in an area adjoining special seating areas. The newest venues now include opera- or theatre-style seating (private booths with four to six seats) adjacent to a private dining area. The newest venues also include several club and social seating options to appeal to different segments of a team's fan base.

Disneyfication and the Battle for Discretionary Income

There is an urban legend regarding Walt and Roy Disney's business approach to entertainment. It is said that when the brothers saw the real estate development around *Disneyland* and the amenities that other (outside) developers offered to visitors to their Magic Kingdom, they decided if they built another park they wanted enough real estate to offer all of the activities people enjoyed when they visited their anchor amenity. The Disney brothers wanted to offer every visitor to *their* theme park(s) (specifically, any visitor in any segment of their overall customer base) the full range of amenities that could complement their vacation or day-trip. The vision was to have enough Disney-owned real estate – it's always about the land – to offer different segments of consumers anything and everything they could enjoy: hotels, retail centers, meeting spaces, evening entertainment, numerous other entertainment parks, etc. In a sense, the Disney brothers wanted to turn the *Disneyland* concept into a *Disney World* of activities. *Walt Disney World Resort* (Orange and Osceola Counties, Florida) was the fulfillment of that vision, and so began the concept of integrating a full set of amenities across a large "footprint" of real estate anchored by a major attraction. This management strategy became identified as the Disneyfication of entertainment experiences.

At the *Walt Disney World Resort*, these other amenities were positioned as new experiences and were anchored by an even larger Magic Kingdom than the one built in Anaheim. The Walt Disney Corporation changed the scale and focus of the hospitality industry by concentrating on every visitor's total experience before, during, and after a visit. In essence, the corporation's vision was the blueprint for the entertainment districts and neighborhoods that are now part of real estate strategies anchored by arenas, ballparks, and stadia across North America and Europe. These new districts have involved as much as 50 or more acres of new development and real estate investments of more than $1 billion. What has been developed is similar to what has been employed by the Disney Corporation. Where the Disney Corporation is focused on serving tourists on vacations or those attending conventions with their families, team owners use the excitement of sport to create districts that capitalize on people's interest to live, work, or "play" at businesses and restaurants surrounding a sport venue. In effect, the goal is to create a Wrigleyville – the neighborhood surrounding the legendary home of the Chicago Cubs – around every new venue. Sport districts have now become a goal for many teams, and these new neighborhoods or developments include residential spaces, park areas, retail establishments, and offices for businesses that want to benefit from the proximity to an arena, a ballpark, or a stadium. The focus on residential development is an effort to capitalize on people's desire to live and work in the neighborhoods where events take place. These neighborhoods are designed to offer residents a place to live that has a constant "buzz" or vibe.

While the Disney Corporation set the pace for creating a total "fan" experience, credit must also be given to Walter O'Malley and the attention to detail he applied to the design of Dodger Stadium. When it opened, Dodger Stadium was the most expensive privately financed sport venue ever built. To attract a large number of fans to every game, even when the Dodgers were not successful on the field, Mr. O'Malley made sure everyone had a great day at the ballpark. He focused on the total experience from the time someone parked their car until they left the area. At a time when the sport business was primarily focused on attracting the "true fan," Walter O'Malley was busy redefining the sport business by attending to even the most casual observers of Los Angeles' newest attraction, Major League Baseball (Podair, 2017).

There were other entrepreneurs who understood that expanded amenities and a focus on the visitor's experience were what separated successful from unsuccessful hospitality and entertainment businesses. Expanded amenities and unparalleled unique experiences are magnets that have the potential to attract larger portions of consumers' discretionary income. At the same time that the Walt Disney Corporation was redefining the ways to be visitors' preferred destination, other entertainment businesses were providing team owners with examples of the ways to attract people to sport venues. Casino and resort owners in Las Vegas transformed their tourist and gaming economy with mega-resorts hosting special entertainment events on a daily basis. The extraordinary hotels and resorts in Las Vegas were designed to compete with the far smaller casinos on Indian reservations that offered similar games of chance but could not match the adjoining amenities and events available at the MGM Grand, Caesar's Palace, the Bellagio, and the Venetian (complete with its own canal). Not be outdone, the Paris hotel included an Eiffel Tower and *New York, New York* added a roller coaster that thrills visitors with a brisk ride along its faux New York skyline.

Las Vegas' initial success and profitability was a function of the effective monopoly on gaming in the United States and Canada. But as numerous other states and provinces approved the construction of casinos, it became possible for people to gamble closer and closer to where they lived. Despite the fact that gaming is legal in 37 states and provinces across the United States and Canada, Las Vegas and its mega-resorts was able to attract a record-breaking 42.9 million visitors in 2016 (LVCVA, 2017). Las Vegas' entrepreneurs have taught team owners a valuable lesson. Providing amenities that cater to the needs of specific communities or segments of visitors (fans) will attract larger numbers of visitors. Teams need to create their own set of amenities that will attract and retain their unique communities of fans. When fans can access sport at home, at work, or in neighborhood restaurants and pubs through a variety of devices, unique experiences are needed to bring people to venues.

Enhancing fan experiences at existing venues has required substantial changes to Progressive Field (Cleveland Indians), the Bankers Life Fieldhouse (Indiana Pacers), Alltel Stadium (Jackson Jaguars), Amalie Arena (Tampa Bay Lightning), Coors Field (Colorado Rockies), Fenway Park (Boston Red Sox), Wrigley Field (Chicago Cubs), and Dodger Stadium (Los Angeles Dodgers). Large-scale renovation projects have taken place at each of these venues to create additional new and exclusive amenities. Teams that fail to focus on the use of both in-facility real estate and the real estate surrounding a venue to enhance fan experiences will not be as financially successful as those that do.

Teams are now embracing the business and management philosophy of Walter O'Malley and the Dodgers, *Walt Disney World*, and Las Vegas' mega-resorts and hotels. As noted, we can date this change back to 1962 with Dodger Stadium's opening. Another important milestone, however, was the opening of Oriole Park at Camden Yards and the incorporation of an urban street setting into the ballpark in 1992. Eutaw Street offered fans a new amenity that created a reason to come to games earlier and then stay for a while afterwards. On non-game days, Eutaw Street is part of Baltimore's entertainment infrastructure. In 1998, the Anschutz Entertainment Corporation (AEG) enhanced the ideas of what could be built near a sport venue with its L.A. LIVE complex adjacent to the Staples Center. In San Diego, John Moores' Ballpark District surrounding PETCO Park created an entire new neighborhood. The building of that neighborhood began with the construction of the ballpark in 2001 and was completed several years later. These models of success redefined the sport business and real estate development.

Real estate development, additional amenities, and expanded entertainment offerings define *Sport Finance and Management*. The preceding examples highlight the knowledge base and perspectives students and professionals need to be successful. Teams, universities, leagues, and college conferences are now part of a sport world redefined by media, the hosting of entertainment events, and real estate development initiatives. Students interested in careers in the sport business must navigate within the horizontally and vertically integrated corporations that are now integral parts of the sport business. Some might be confused by the use of the term "real estate" to discuss the electronic or media footprint now involved with sport. As will be discussed, the digital footprint of sport is indeed related to the real estate over which signals can be sent and consumed. For example, the New York Yankees' YES network cannot broadcast games in the market area of the Detroit Tigers. In effect, Major League Baseball allocates the real estate over which teams can distribute their games regardless of demand. Leagues that distribute their games across the Internet also have to adhere to the laws of each country that govern the space in which digital contact is delivered to residents.

Teams not taking advantage of these new and expanding business opportunities miss out on revenue streams and fail to offer to their fans new experiences. When those experiences are not available, attendance levels can sag. When teams and universities fail to capitalize on these possibilities, fewer financial benefits are produced for host communities as well. When events are held at Progressive Field and Quicken Loans Arena, the City of Cleveland receives revenues that would otherwise accrue to suburban cities. Similarly, L.A. LIVE has anchored a renaissance of development in downtown Los Angeles. The new residential and commercial properties built and renovated generate property tax revenues for the city and the school district. It is possible that some of that development could have been built elsewhere in Los Angeles, but it is far more likely the development would have taken place in adjacent suburban cities; if new venues are built in the suburbs, the City of Los Angeles loses property taxes. These are just a few brief examples of how a commitment to Disneyfication and the fan experience can make it possible for both team owners and cities to benefit from the development of new sport facilities.

Challenges Facing Sports Managers Today

This book is about understanding the new business opportunities that, if anchored to sport, can elevate team values while also helping cities. For students who dream of a career in what Robert Lipsyte called *SportsWorld* (1977), it is necessary to understand the management principles that elevate the value of franchises while also enhancing the economy of host cities.

While the opportunities that exist for teams are somewhat unique because of the nature of sport, the phenomenon of rapidly changing market conditions and opportunities is not limited to the sport business. Every business is challenged to keep pace with increasingly dynamic and rapidly shifting market conditions. While examples abound of how corporations must adapt or face dramatically declining revenues, the news and information business provides stark evidence of how quickly a marketplace can change. While many people had grown accustomed to living in metropolitan areas with only one major daily newspaper, few envisioned a time when even the print version of even one daily newspaper would be an economically obsolete concept. The ability to access news and information through the Internet has made print journals less relevant for generations either raised on computers or accustomed to accessing information through smartphones, tablets, and notebook computers. The media world is being redefined by the delivery of content and games on social media platforms (e.g., Twitter, Facebook, etc.). Those changes have led to losses in market share by cable operators and the platforms that relied on the delivery of content on cable or over-the-air stations.

To remain viable, newspapers have dramatically increased their web presence. ESPN, to reduce costs and refresh its image, has eliminated certain programming and released announcers. And leagues are now experimenting with the delivery of games through Facebook and other platforms. These are just some of the examples of how every business must adopt and adapt to emerging technologies and customer preferences. The ability of customers to more easily select sport and entertainment products from a wide-ranging set of alternative platforms has increased the pressure on teams to be relevant to each fan segment. The Internet makes the cost of accessing an unlimited number of substitutes for almost every product and amenity practically zero. This level of competition to manufacture, package, and deliver products and content with appropriate pricing is nothing new for any enterprise. What is new, however, is the rate of change and how quickly businesses and their managers must (1) adapt their financing and management skills to meet consumers' expectations; (2) identify new revenue streams and opportunities; (3) carefully evaluate the profitable potential of these new revenue streams, products, and methods of delivery; and (4) respond to the expanding range of choices made available by the Internet. Those businesses and managers that are unable to innovate and adapt to the real-time age of the Internet and the various other demands of consumers for enhanced experiences will be less financially successful.

Some might be tempted to believe the business of sport is insulated from these pressures. For example, some believed that college sport were isolated from changing preferences of students and alumni. After all, what was more iconic or a more ingrained ritual than to be at a football game on a fall afternoon? What several universities have found is that students, too, have found other ways to enjoy their team. The student-consumer can be found at tailgate parties on campus, or at the local sports bar. Athletic departments have found that they must also compete for the interest of students.

Empty Seats, Fewer Donors?

By Jake New
(This article originally appeared in *Inside Higher Education*)

Game day. For many college alumni, the phrase alone is enough to conjure autumnal memories of watching football while surrounded by cheering student sections, marching bands, and brisk fall air.

But an increasing number of students, researchers say, now see the experience a little differently. For them, attending a football game more likely means sitting outdoors for hours in chilly weather, with little or no access to cellphone reception and alcohol. Once the tailgate party has ended, why not just cheer on the home team from a bar down the street? There are probably some cheap game-day specials, and there may even be free Wi-Fi.

Student attendance at major college football games is declining across the country. By how much varies greatly at each institution, but a recent *Wall Street Journal* analysis of turnstile data at 50 public colleges with top football programs found that average student attendance is down more than 7 percent since 2009.

In 2013 the University of Georgia's designated student section was nearly 40 percent empty. The University of California at Berkeley has sold about 1,000 fewer student season tickets this season than last year – a season that already saw a decline from the previous one. Since 2009, student attendance at the University of Florida has dropped 22 percent. Three-fourths of the University of Kansas' student tickets went unused last season.

The students who do still attend games tend to arrive later and leave earlier, said Richard Southall, director of the College Sports Research Institute, which can be an embarrassing headache for athletics programs.

"Fundamentally, students are part of the show, and that's something that folks don't always recognize," Southall said. "If you watch a college sports telecast, where do the cameras go for in-crowd shots? The cameras are in the student section. If that section is not there, it's like having a movie without enough extras to walk in the background of the shots. I always joke to my students, 'You understand you're paying to be extras. You're just there for the show, so everyone else can keep consuming it.'"

Today's uninterested students, athletic directors worry, could easily become tomorrow's uninterested alumni. "Current students are not that important [to ticket sales], per se," said Dan Rascher, a sports management professor at the University of San Francisco. "But you're trying to turn those current students into former students who are still fans decades later. You want students, when they become alumni, to have that attachment and come back for the games, and that's what's concerning athletic departments."

A possible link between athletics – particularly success in athletics – and alumni giving has been debated for decades. Older studies are split about the issue, but more recent research argues that there is a connection, especially between football and donations to athletic programs rather than a university's general fund.

The culprits for the downward trend in student attendance are not difficult to identify, said Mark Nagel, a professor of sports and entertainment management at the University of South Carolina. Tickets are getting more expensive, nonconference games are less evenly matched, and – thanks to lucrative and far-reaching broadcast contracts – it's never been easier to watch games from the comfort of just about anywhere else. Students can often watch their college's team play not just on television, but also on their computers, smartphones, and tablets.

The more difficult question to answer, Southall said, is what can colleges and universities do to slow or halt the decline. "Students are showing that they're consumers like anyone else," he said. "As college sports have become more and more commercialized, they're having to compete with that home experience like the NFL and everybody else."

Some institutions are hoping that part of the solution lies in replicating aspects of watching the games on television. Last year the Big Ten Conference announced that its colleges could now show an unlimited number of replays at any speed on stadium video boards, mirroring the multiple, slow-motion replays commonly featured in game broadcasts.

Previously, stadiums were allowed to show just one replay at only 75 percent of the actual speed. "Our goal on game day is to blend the best parts of an in-stadium experience with the best parts of an at-home experience," Jim Delany, the Big Ten's commissioner, said at the time.

More commonly, universities are trying to attract student fans by adding more amenities to stadiums and transforming the game day experience into something that can't be found at a bar or in someone's living room.

More than half of Division I FBS institutions plan on spending more than $10 million on facility investments over the next year, according to a recent survey conducted by Ohio University's Center for Sports Administration and stadium designer AECOM. The top three priorities for that spending – enhancing food and beverage options, premium seating, and connectivity – all focus on the experience of fans, rather than the players.

This book is organized around nine major issues or elements that have irrevocably changed sport finance and management. The implications and meanings of these shifts are then explored through the various components of the sport industry for teams, universities, and international organizations.

Change Number 1: Ownership Models

In the past, individuals, families, and partnerships were the dominant forms of ownership models. Today, each league still requires the designation of a principal owner. In the NFL – given the large valuation of teams – at least one individual must own at least 10 percent of the team. In other leagues, one individual is required to own at least 51 percent of the team. The percentage controlled by a principal owner is not what makes ownership models different today. What has fundamentally changed is that individual owners are now frequently linking teams directly to a set of other business initiatives. Teams are now often part of a conglomerate that, at its center, could be a media, entertainment, food services, or real estate business. The team then becomes an integral part of the "empire" and the owner leverages the unique value of sport and the team's identity for the benefit of the conglomerate.

Against that framework of teams linked to large-scale business organizations or plans, there are still a small number of franchises owned by sole proprietors or limited partnerships that are not also focused on other businesses. The Green Bay Packers have a unique community-based ownership model that, while "grandfathered" into the NFL, is not permitted for any other city. The other major sport leagues also do not allow teams to be owned by a community. There are, however, Minor League Baseball (MiLB) teams that are owned by the public sector, including the Wisconsin Timber Rattlers (Milwaukee Brewers' Class A MiLB affiliate); the Harrisburg Senators (Washington Nationals' Double A MiLB affiliate); the Memphis Redbirds (St. Louis Cardinals' Triple A MiLB affiliate); and the Toledo Mud Hens (Detroit Tigers' Triple A MiLB affiliate).

Another business institution has also become part of sport world (if only as a minority partner): hedge funds. A hedge fund is an investment partnership where a managing partner becomes a limited partner of the fund and is expected to secure a favorable return on funds committed by individuals. The term "hedge fund" comes from the expectation of high rates of return, regardless of the performance of the stock market. To "beat the performance of the stock market," the fund's managing partner targets securities or other high-value investment vehicles. The rapid appreciation of the value of sport teams has made ownership a potentially valuable asset for a hedge fund, but a partnership of investors in a hedge fund cannot be the managing partner of a franchise. There are, however, instances where a hedge fund owns 49 percent of a team. In the second chapter, *Ownership and the Emergence of Team Sports*, each ownership type is defined and discussed, and the implications of the involvement of hedge funds in ownership models is also considered.

Foreign investors have also bought teams. The first non-American to buy a controlling interest in a team based in the United States was Mr. Hiroshi

Yamauchi, who purchased the Seattle Mariners in 1992. Today there are American entrepreneurs who own Premier League soccer teams in England and franchises in Israel. Russian billionaire Mikhail Prokhorov purchased a majority position in the Brooklyn Nets and now also owns the team's home arena, the Barclays Center (as this edition is being written, there have been indications that Mr. Prokhorov may be considering the sale of the team or the arena, or both). Foreign ownership makes it easier for leagues to connect with and market in different countries. The impact of the internationalization of the leagues and cross-ownership (owning teams in more than one country) is explored in Chapter 2.

Some teams have also sold shares that were publicly traded (Boston Celtics, Cleveland Indians, and the Florida Panthers). The Green Bay Packers have issued stock, too, but those shares do not have any financial value. As noted earlier, the Green Bay Packers are community-owned in the sense that its management board is linked to a community-based organization, the Sullivan Post of the American Legion. If the team is ever sold, the proceeds accrue to the Sullivan Post to build a memorial for soldiers from the area. This management structure was created – the board is in essence self-perpetuating – to ensure the team would never leave Green Bay and would be managed by individuals committed to its presence in Northeast Wisconsin. The management committee was initially established in the 1920s. This ensures a level of continuity, but also restricts the "public ownership and management" to an elite group that, in turn, appoints the professional managers.

MSG, the Madison Square Garden Corporation, is listed on the New York Stock Exchange (MSG). MSG's lead shareholders (the Dolan family) also own the New York Knicks and the New York Rangers, making the teams part of a large entertainment conglomerate. Shares of the Simon Property Group (SPG on the New York Stock Exchange) are publicly traded, and the Simon family also owns the Indiana Pacers. This ownership model makes the Pacers part of a retail development corporation. There are many other examples of this form of ownership (teams as part of larger conglomerates), including the Boston Red Sox, Cleveland Cavaliers, Detroit Pistons, Detroit Red Wings and Tigers, New York Mets, and New York Yankees.

Two North American teams underscore the different approaches taken by two owners. Mark Cuban purchased controlling interest in the Dallas Mavericks from income earned in his other businesses. The basketball team was not going to be part of his past businesses nor would the team anchor a new set of initiatives. Mr. Cuban owns the team because of his love for basketball. As a result, the Mavericks' business model can be classified as "traditional," with a focus only on the team and the classical revenue streams: tickets, the leasing of rights to broadcasters, in-facility advertisements, etc.

At the other end of the spectrum, Ted Turner purchased the Atlanta Braves and used the franchise to advance another major business, the cable

network TBS. Mr. Turner used the Braves as the center of his programming for the station and the team's games helped attract millions of viewers to TBS. The team, as part of a cable television station that became a regional and then a national presence, substantially extended the Braves' fan base and built a sort of "Braves Nation" across the United States. The Braves helped advance the Turner broadcasting empire and that empire, in turn, helped to build the Braves' national image and brand. TBS brought baseball to fans living in markets without a franchise and scores of cable subscribers began demanding Turner's station so they could follow the Braves.

Universities and their intercollegiate sport operations represent another unique form of ownership. The different ways in which athletic departments are financed, the returns (value) produced by collegiate sport, and the economic tensions that lead to the issues that athletes, universities, coaches, and athletic directors must address are also considered in Chapter 2.

Change Number 2: Sport, Entertainment Complexes, and Real Estate Development

As already noted, and as will be underscored in several of the chapters in this book, most team owners link teams to entertainment complexes, media outlets, and new neighborhoods. There are three factors driving this interest. First, enhancing revenues and the value of a franchise is the top priority for professional staff on the business side of a team's operations. Second, the quality of the at-home experience for fans since the advent of large-sized HD televisions has meant that new and unique experiences must exist at a venue to attract fans. Without those additional experiences, fans could decide to stay home to enjoy what many have described as "the best seat in the house" for each and every play in a game: the couch. The experiences in or near a venue are often linked to the use of real estate inside and adjacent to a venue. Several teams have party decks that would rival anything available from sport pubs. Several teams, as already noted, have different clubs within their venues, each providing varying experiences. Jerry Jones' 60-yard television, suspended over the football field at AT&T Stadium, elevated the era of huge in-facility video displays. These extraordinary video displays offer fans the same HD view of the action and replays available to them at home while also putting the fans themselves on the "big screen" during breaks in the action. Every new venue now contains an unimaginably large and crystal-clear LED screen(s). Auburn University, Texas A & M University, and the University of Texas (in 2015) claimed to have the largest video screens in college football. The newest arenas and those that have been renovated have also installed very large video displays. Whether or not these large video displays add to or subtract from a venue's appeal will be discussed later in this book.

Third, the popularity of sport has made it possible to build new urban neighborhoods complete with residential, entertainment, and commercial properties anchored by arenas, ballparks, and football stadiums. How does a venue contribute to the creation of a desirable neighborhood in which to live, work, and play? The crowds that attend games and entertainment events at these venues create a demand for restaurants, pubs, and other attractions that produce unique urban environments. Their excitement also creates a sort of "vibe" that gives the area a sense of excitement. These neighborhoods attract the growing number of younger professionals who seek a very different living experience from the one available in suburban areas. As older couples complete their child-rearing responsibilities, they too seek an urban lifestyle. These growing demographic cohorts are attracted to the crowds and experiences that can be produced by urban neighborhoods anchored by a sport venue. These development opportunities, underscored by the popularity of sport, can create new revenue streams for team owners. This change in a venue's role means that students interested in a career in the sport business need to understand aspects of real estate financing, urban design, and architecture.

Change Number 3: Young Fans and Their Loyalties

The need to focus on new experiences at venues or in adjoining neighborhoods has also been driven by the spectacular increase in the popularity of fantasy teams. In the past, fans were laser-focused on the win/loss records of their favorite teams. Today, many fans are more interested in the performance of the collection of players on their "fantasy" teams. Watching two teams play at a venue is not as attractive as watching several games at home or at a pub, where one can watch the performance of the players on their fantasy teams. Teams now have to offer amenities and in-facility experiences that accommodate the loyalties fans have to their fantasy teams and compete with the draw and convenience of fans' homes or local pubs where they have the ability to watch several games at once. The first fantasy baseball league began in 1979. It is likely the idea, known as the Rotisserie League, created by Glen Waggoner and Daniel Okrent, was viewed as a passing fad. However, fantasy sports have forced the owners of real teams to rethink how they compete for attention and loyalty from their fans, who are now the "owners" of their own fantasy teams. Recently, some team owners have bought an interest in "E-Sports," or have agreed to sponsor an E-Sport team. These investments are yet another example of horizontal integration.

Change Number 4: A New Media World

As televisions became an integral part of everyone's living room in the 1950s and 1960s, many wondered if the telecasting of games would have a negative effect on revenues and attendance. There was even a time when the National Collegiate Athletic Association (NCAA) limited the number of games of each university's football team that could be televised in a single season (two). There was a belief that an overexposure of the sport on television would lead to lower levels of aggregate revenue. There was also a fear that if the games of the most popular college teams were all televised, college football fans would not support teams at other, less popular universities. The idea that televised games would convince fans to stay home led NFL owners to "black out" the local telecast of home games even if games were sold out. In later years, the blackout rule was relaxed.[1] What seems strange to fans today was the blackout rule even applied to championship games. The legendary 1958 game between the Baltimore Colts and New York Giants was not broadcast in the New York metropolitan area. The earliest Super Bowls were not televised to fans living in the host market.

With fan resentment at a fever pitch over blacked-out NFL games (even when games were sold out weeks or months in advance), no fewer than 20 different pieces of legislation were introduced in the early 1970s in Congress to force the NFL to change its policies. Some of the proposed laws threatened to severely reduce the NFL's control of broadcast rights; others would have regulated relationships between the league and networks. With broadcast revenue growing at extraordinary rates, team owners wanted the NFL to be exempt from any regulatory agency (Hochburg, 1973). The NFL avoided oversight by implementing its own anti-blackout policy. As introduced and sustained since 1973, any game that is sold out 72 hours in advance of kick-off is televised in the local market. In addition, a team can petition to have the 72-hour guideline reduced to 48 or 24 hours. Many teams have exercised that option, and in most markets, there have been few, if any, games that have not been telecast. Teams also are allowed to give away a certain number of tickets to community organizations and those tickets can count toward the definition of a "sellout."

During the recent economic recession when fans might have needed to reduce their spending – especially for teams that were not successful – some games were not televised. This took place in Jacksonville and Detroit. In other markets, there have been times when local businesses bought unsold tickets to distribute to community organizations, permitting games to be telecast in the team's home market. In late 2014, the Federal Communications Commission ruled that if a local station did not broadcast a game, it could be made available to a cable system's subscribers through the transmission of the game by a station located in a city outside of the blacked-out market area if that station was part of the package of stations available to cable customers.

Colleges have also dramatically expanded the telecast of games. Today all of the football and basketball games of the most popular college teams are telecast by one of the numerous networks created by the universities themselves or through contracts with commercial networks. Many of these games are also available online or on a subscription basis. On any given weekend, a football fan can watch a dozen or more games from the comfort of their living room or at sport-themed restaurants.

There has been a decline in attendance at college football games and for some professional teams. What is germane at this point, however, is that overexposure created by games on television has not led to lower interests in teams or sport. When attendance declines, it is probably more related to the quality of the fan experience in or near a venue than a team's performance. What is also evident, however, is that communications and the media are now among the most important revenue streams for teams. Sport has become synonymous with media exposure and that connection has contributed to the escalating value of teams.

The past 20 years have witnessed a dramatic shift in the role of the media and the finances of teams. Dozens of new networks have been created, and several collegiate conferences have their own networks or have formed new ones with media corporations. Fox Sports Net (FSN) was born from the buyout of the Prime Network and now there are at least 19 individual regional networks that form FSN (together with five affiliated or co-owned companies). In total, the FSN umbrella includes at least 24 networks serving numerous regions across the United States. ESPN (Entertainment and Sports Programming Network), the pioneer in the creation of sport-devoted media, is comprised of 20 different networks serving 150 countries with programming in 15 different languages. The ESPN family of networks broadcasts the games of numerous professional leagues in North America, Europe, and Asia.

The importance of these networks for the sport business is most easily understood by looking at outcomes from the Big Ten Network (BTN) after only a few years of operation. The value of television rights was made abundantly clear in 2016 when the Big Ten Conference sold rights to Fox Sports for $250 million per year. Fox bought the rights to those games not broadcast by ABC/ESPN. And if neither ESPN or Fox want to telecast a game, BTN would have the right to telecast the game. In 2015, the total amount of money received by the members of the Big Ten Conference for the telecast of football games was $21.5 million per university. There was even a projection in 2014 that 12 of the 14 universities in the Big Ten Conference would receive revenues in excess of $44 million each year beginning in fiscal year 2018 (Fornelli, 2014). The BTN provides television programming to cable and satellite television networks serving more than 70 million homes (Hyland, 2009). Reaching 21 of the 22 largest markets in the United States, the network's programming reaches more than just the region of the Big Ten.

Not to be left behind, the NFL and MLB each created their own networks and MLB launched a nightly show to compete with ESPN's *Baseball*

Tonight. MLB's advanced media corporation, MLBAM, has become the gold standard for the production and delivery of content to fans across the globe on its platform and app. Indeed, the application, *At Bat*, has become one of the most popular sport apps. Comcast joined the "create your own network" mania to capitalize on its vast cable delivery systems. It bought the Outdoor Life Network and signed agreements to telecast individual college football games, NHL games, and other sporting events not covered by other networks (NBCSN). Comcast also acquired NBC in 2011, adding a new network and new levels of sport programming to its inventory. In 2015, the NHL decided to join with MLBAM to explore even more ways to deliver its games to fans.

Beginning in 2016, social media networks entered the fray and now compete for the right to stream games. The new presence of sport content delivered to fans by Facebook, Twitter, Amazon, and Yahoo has led to a decline in cable television subscriptions and led ESPN to dramatically decrease the number of broadcasters they employ. In 2017, ESPN even reduced its highlight shows given the presence of content now available online.

While the NFL has released a great deal of information about its national media contracts, individual teams do not. The NFL's collective bargaining agreement stipulates that approximately 55 percent of all national media income be used for player salaries, presumably because those contracts account for the majority of most teams' media income. *Forbes* also provides some insight into each team's total media revenue (including local contracts).

In addition, important evidence of the impact of media rights on team values was provided by the recent sale of the Los Angeles Dodgers and the Los Angeles Clippers. In 2012, the Dodgers were sold for $2.15 billion, and that sale was driven by the potential for the team to anchor a sport network in the very large Southern California media market. Then, in 2014 the Los Angeles Clippers were sold for $2 billion. Again, the expectation is that the NBA will be able to sell the rights to games for a substantial amount of money. The Clippers could also be a vital part of any network serving the large Southern California market and in the development of a new sport district that includes the new stadium for the Los Angeles Rams and a renovated Forum which is part of the planned residential development in Inglewood.

This brief history on the technological improvements leading to new ways to deliver games to fans has dramatically changed the world of professional and collegiate sports. Understanding the sport business in real time requires an appreciation for how quickly the dynamics of the relationship between sport and television, and sport and the Internet, has changed. In turn, these changes have had and will continue to have profound economic consequences for teams, leagues, and universities.

Change Number 5: The Real Estate Management Issues within Venues

Today, sport venues are far different from those built in the 1960s and 1970s, which were designed as homes for both baseball and football teams. New York's Shea Stadium opened in 1964 and was considered the most innovative dual sport venue because some of the seats on the first level could be moved along tracks to enhance sight lines. The movable seats were positioned behind home plate and near the first- and third-base lines for baseball. For the football season, these seats moved along a track that permitted their placement between the 30-yard lines on both sides of the football field. This technological innovation was not included in the multiuse facilities that were built in Cincinnati, Houston, Minneapolis, Philadelphia, Pittsburgh, St. Louis, Oakland, and San Diego. Upper deck outfield seats for baseball sometimes provided the best views of a football game but were located a considerable distance from the sidelines. In short, one team's best seats were distant from the playing field and that meant less ticket revenue could be generated, as fans were not willing to pay high fees for seats that were located far from the playing field.

The exception to the pattern of building dual-use facilities took place in Kansas City. Facing demands for a new ballpark from Charles Finley, who threatened to move his Athletics to Oakland, California, Jackson County voters in 1967 supported a tax increase to pay for a bond of more than $102 million (approximately $700 million in 2017 dollars) to build a ballpark for the Athletics and a stadium for the Kansas City Chiefs. The public support for this bond package secured a new baseball franchise after the Athletics moved to Oakland (the Kansas City Royals began play in 1969). Arrowhead Stadium, the home of the Chiefs, opened in 1972, and Kaufmann Stadium, the home of the Royals, opened in 1973.

Separate venues meant far better sight lines for fans, and most responded positively when these better seats meant higher ticket prices. With a wave of new stadiums having just been built, the widespread acceptance of the need for and desirability of separate facilities would not re-emerge until events contributed to Baltimore's building of its baseball-only facility for the Orioles. When Oriole Park at Camden Yards was planned, the Colts had already relocated to Indianapolis and, as a result, there was no need for a venue that could be home to both a baseball and football team.

Before focusing on the game-changing characteristics of Oriole Park at Camden Yards, it is important to understand how dramatic a change in sport management and finance for franchises and fans it was to move from shared to separate facilities. From 1921 through 2010, baseball and football teams in 25 different metropolitan areas shared facilities for varying lengths of time (Table 1.1). The Miami Marlins relocated from Sun Life Stadium (now Hard Rock Stadium), a facility they shared with the Miami

Table 1.1 The Era of Shared Professional Baseball and Football Facilities

Teams	Years of Dual Use	Year New Facility Built (Year Old Facility Built)	
		Ballpark	Stadium
Baltimore Orioles/Colts	1954–1983	1992 (1953)	1998 (1953)
Boston Red Sox/Patriots	1963–1968	1912	1971, 2002 (1912)
Chicago Cubs/Bears	1921–1970	1916 (1893)	1971, 2003 (1916)
Cleveland Indians/Browns	1946–1995	1932, 1994 (1910)	1999 (1932)
Detroit Tigers/Lions	1938–1974	2000 (1912)	1975, 2002 (1912)
Kansas City Royals/Chiefs	1969–1972	1973 (1923)	1972 (1923)
Los Angeles Angels/Rams	1961–1997	1966 (1925)	1995 (1966)
Minnesota Twins/Vikings	1961–2009	1982 (1961)	1982 (1961)
New York Yankees/Giants	1956–1973	2009 (1923)	1976, 2010 (1883, 1923)
Oakland Athletics/Raiders[1]	1968–1981, 1995–2010	1968	1966 (1922)
Seattle Mariners/Seahawks	1976–1994, 1995–1999	1999 (1976)	2002 (1976)
Toronto Blue Jays/Argonauts	1959–1989, 1989–2010	1989 (1959)	1989 (1959)[1]
Atlanta Braves/Falcons	1966–1991	1997 (1965)	1992 (1965)
Cincinnati Reds/Bengals	1970–1999	1970, 2002 (1912)	2000 (1970)
Colorado Rockies/Denver Broncos	1993–1994	1995	2001 (1948)
Florida Marlins/Miami Dolphins	1993–2010	1993	1987 (1937)
Houston Astros/Oilers[2]	1968–1996	2000 (1965)	2002 (1965)
Los Angeles Dodgers[3]/Rams[4]	1958–1961	1962 (1913, 1923)	1966, 1995 (1923)
New York Mets/Jets	1964–1983	2009, 1964 (1891, 1911)	2010, 1964 (1911)
Philadelphia Phillies/Eagles	1940, 1942, 1944–1957, 1971–2002	2004, 1971, 1938 (1895)	2003, 1971 (1938, 1895)[5]
Pittsburgh Pirates/Steelers	1933–1963,[6] 1970–2000	2001, 1970 (1909, 1891)	2001, 1970 (1909)
St. Louis Cardinals/Cardinals	1960–1987	2006, 1966 (1920, 1892)	2006 (1966, 1958)[7]
San Diego Padres/Chargers	1969–2003	2004 (1967)	1967 (1915)
San Francisco Giants/49ers	1971–2000	2000, 1960 (1891)	1971 (1922)
Washington Redskins[9]	1930–1997	–	1997 (1961, 1921)[10]

Notes:

[1] The NFL's Raiders anticipate a 2020 move to a new stadium in Las Vegas.

[2] The Oilers moved to Tennessee when a new facility was not built.

[3] The Dodgers initially played games at the L.A. Coliseum before Dodger Stadium was built.

[4] The Rams moved from the L.A. Coliseum to Anaheim Stadium, which they shared with the Angels before moving to St. Louis. The team moved back to the L.A. Coliseum in 2016, sharing the facility with the USC Trojans football team as they awaited their new stadium to be built in Inglewood.

[5] During some periods, the Eagles played home games at the University of Pennsylvania's stadium while also sharing facilities with the Phillies in other years.

[6] The Steelers also moved to collegiate facilities in some years while in others they shared facilities with the Pirates.

[7] The football Cardinals moved from Chicago to St. Louis and then to Phoenix. They shared facilities in Chicago and St. Louis with baseball teams.

[8] The Washington Nationals initially played in Montreal where there was an older facility and then a newer domed facility.

[9] The Washington Redskins shared facilities with the Washington Senators, who moved to Minnesota. The second Washington Senators franchise became the Texas Rangers, leaving the Redskins as the major tenant in RFK Stadium.

[10] The Redskins played initially in facilities built for both baseball and football teams. Those facilities were built in 1921 and 1961.

Dolphins, to Marlins Park in 2012. With the NFL's Raiders' anticipated 2020 relocation from the Oakland Coliseum (shared with the Oakland Athletics) to a new football-only venue in Las Vegas, there are no longer any professional baseball and football franchises sharing facilities in the United States.

Why is it better for baseball and football to be played in venues built for each sport? The action in baseball and football is concentrated in two very different physical spaces. Football's action takes place within a 120 by 53⅓-yard rectangle. While there is a degree of concentration of the action near the end zones, plays occur across the entire expanse. The substantial level of play across such a large area means higher-level seats can offer valuable panoramic views. In addition, with play occurring within a large rectangular space, seats located along the entire length or between the 20-yard lines (a 60-yard expanse) provide excellent views of play. The design that produces the largest number of seats with excellent sight lines involves two crescent-shaped seating areas from goal line to goal line with somewhat lower seating areas built behind each end zone.

Baseball's action is concentrated in a 30 by 30-yard diamond, and the best views for fans result when the vast majority of seats are concentrated along the baselines and behind home plate. Even when balls are hit to the outfield, the action that results as runners and the batter try to advance from base to base occurs in the 900-square yard diamond infield. To provide the largest number of seats with the best views of the action in baseball and football, two very different physical designs are needed. The profitability of a baseball and football team is enhanced if the seating patterns align with the distribution of play on the field.

Oriole Park at Camden Yards – a baseball-only facility – opened on April 6, 1992, and was an immediate "game changer" on several levels. The new ballpark for the Baltimore Orioles enjoyed strong political support as the community had lived through the loss of its storied football franchise, the Colts.[2] After the Colts left Baltimore, and with no NFL team in town (the Browns did not relocate from Cleveland to Baltimore to become the Ravens until three years after Oriole Park opened), the Orioles had the luxury of being supported in their quest for a baseball-only facility (Miller, 1990; Rosentraub, 1999).

These factors created an opportunity for the Orioles to come forward with an entirely new vision for a ballpark. That vision would benefit from the lessons learned from the Royals' Kaufmann Stadium and would have a profound, immediate, and dramatic effect on sport management and finance. Camden Yards combined a design that paid homage to the ballparks of the early twentieth century with the improved sight lines offered by Kaufmann Stadium. Even more, added into the design of Camden Yards was a unique retail space and luxury seating; both amenities were innovations in the design of ballpark and had the potential to generate more spending by offering fans new choices relative to what could be enjoyed when attending Orioles games. The new designs created a focus on the real estate *inside* a venue. Revenue per square foot – a concept familiar to retailers – became part of facility management for every sport executive. The Orioles' addition of a unique area for the sale of food and beverages (Eutaw Street) adjoining the venue and the inclusion of other retail outlets in what was a warehouse for freight trains created an immediate tourist attraction. Overnight, Oriole Park at Camden Yards became the benchmark for every team. The team's ownership had hired its own urban design expert, Janet Marie Smith, and after rejecting the initial designs provided by architects, what emerged resembled the smaller facilities of the 19th and early 20th centuries. The much-improved sight lines (from those available in Memorial Stadium where the Orioles had played since 1953) commanded higher ticket prices that fans were only too eager to pay. Janet Marie Smith and Orioles team president Larry Lucchino worked together to revolutionize sport management and finance through the building of Oriole Park at Camden Yards.

The Orioles' success sent a message to every team owner. Nostalgia sells, unique retail settings generate more revenue, and good sight lines sustain elevated ticket prices. How successful was this complex concept? Table 1.2 summarizes attendance at Orioles games before and after the opening of Camden Yards. The opening of the new ballpark produced a 42 percent increase in attendance compared to the next to last season played by the Orioles at Memorial Stadium. In Camden Yards' second season, attendance increased by more than 50 percent. To be sure, there were years when attendance levels were less robust, but even when the team finished no higher than third in its division, attendance levels were often far larger than they had been at the aging Memorial Stadium (which opened in 1950). The message was clear: build a new ballpark with improved sight lines and other revenue-generating outlets (restaurants, for example) and attendance (as well as revenues) will increase. In a relatively short period of time, every team tried to have, and most succeeded in having, new facilities built. When the new home of the Miami Marlins opened in 2012 and the Atlanta Braves moved into SunTrust Park, 24 of MLB's 30 teams were playing in post–Camden Yard facilities (Table 1.3).

The new real estate management in a sport facility includes luxury seating. Just as Oriole Park at Camden Yards was not the first baseball-only facility, it also was not the first to offer luxury seating. What it did do is illustrate fans' interest in paying for more luxury and the resulting revenue growth that would exist if a facility had suites, club seats, and other high-end amenities. Luxury and even a degree of lavishness began to dominate facility design. These amenities substantially bolstered revenues.

Table 1.2 Attendance at Baltimore Orioles games, 1954–2006

Season	Finish	Wins	Losses	Attendance	Average Ticket Price[1]	Ticket Revenue
1954	7th AL	54	100	1,060,910	–	–
1955	7th AL	57	97	852,039	–	–
1956	6th AL	69	85	901,201	–	–
1957	5th AL	76	76	1,029,581	–	–
1958	6th AL	74	79	829,991	–	–
1959	6th AL	74	80	891,926	–	–
1960	2nd AL	89	65	1,187,849	–	–
1961	3rd AL	95	67	951,089	–	–
1962	7th AL	77	85	790,254	–	–
1963	4th AL	86	76	774,254	–	–
1964	3rd AL	97	65	1,116,215	–	–
1965	3rd AL	94	68	781,649	–	–
1966	1st AL	97	63	1,203,366	–	–
1967	6th AL	76	85	955,053	–	–
1968	2nd AL	91	71	943,977	–	–
1969	1st AL East	109	53	1,062,094	–	–
1970	1st AL East	108	54	1,057,069	–	–
1971	1st AL East	101	57	1,023,037	–	–
1972	3rd AL East	80	74	899,950	–	–
1973	1st AL East	97	65	958,667	–	–
1974	1st AL East	91	71	962,572	–	–
1975	2nd AL East	90	69	1,002,157	–	–
1976	2nd AL East	88	74	1,058,609	–	–
1977	2nd AL East	97	64	1,195,769	–	–
1978	4th AL East	90	71	1,051,724	–	–
1979	1st AL East	102	57	1,681,009	–	–
1980	2nd AL East	100	62	1,797,438	–	–
1981	Split[2]	59	46	1,024,247	–	–
1982	2nd AL East	94	68	1,613,031	–	–
1983	1st AL East	98	64	2,042,071	–	–
1984	5th AL East	85	77	2,045,784	–	–
1985	4th AL East	83	78	2,132,387	–	–
1986	7th AL East	73	89	1,973,176	–	–
1987	6th AL East	67	95	1,835,692	–	–
1988	7th AL East	54	107	1,660,738	–	–
1989	2nd AL East	87	75	2,353,208	–	–
1990	5th AL East	76	85	2,415,189	–	–
1991	6th AL East	67	95	2,552,753	$8.04	$20,524,134
Oriole Park at Camden Yards Opens for the 1992 Season						
1992	3rd AL East	89	73	3,567,819	$9.55	$34,072,671
1993	3rd AL East	85	77	3,644,965	$11.12	$40,532,011
1994	2nd AL East	63	49	2,535,359	$11.17	$28,319,960
1995	3rd AL East	71	73	3,098,475	$13.14	$40,713,962
1996	2nd AL East	88	74	3,646,950	$13.14	$47,920,923
1997	1st AL East	98	64	3,612,764	$17.02	$61,489,243
1998	4th AL East	79	83	3,684,650	$19.77	$72,845,531
1999	4th AL East	78	84	3,432,099	$19.82	$68,024,202

(continued)

Table 1.2 Continued

Season	Finish	Wins	Losses	Attendance	Average Ticket Price[1]	Ticket Revenue
2000	4th AL East	74	88	3,295,128	$19.78	$65,177,632
2001	4th AL East	63	98	3,094,841	$18.23	$56,418,951
2002	4th AL East	67	95	2,655,559	$18.23	$48,410,841
2003	4th AL East	71	91	2,454,523	$20.15	$49,458,639
2004	3rd AL East	78	84	2,744,018	$22.53	$61,822,726
2005[3]	4th AL East	74	88	2,624,740	$22.53	$59,135,392
2006	4th AL East	70	92	2,153,250	$22.53	$48,512,723
2007	4th AL East	69	93	2,164,822	$22.45	$48,600,254
2008[4]	5th AL East	68	93	1,950,075	$23.85	$46,509,289
2009	5th AL East	64	98	1,907,163	$23.42	$44,665,758
2010	6th AL East	66	96	1,733,018	$23.42	$40,587,282
2011	5th AL East	69	93	1,755,461	$23.90	$41,955,518
2012	2nd AL East	93	69	2,102,240	$23.89	$50,222,514
2013	3rd AL East	85	77	2,357,561	$23.89	$56,322,132
2014	1st AL East	96	66	2,464,473	$24.97	$61,537,891
2015	3rd AL East	81	81	2,320,590	$24.97	$57,945,132
2016	2nd AL East	89	73	2,172,344	$29.96	$65,083,426
Memorial Stadium Avg		84	74	1,307,045	–	–
Camden Yards Avg		77.12	82.1	2,686,915	$20.14	$51,851,384

Notes:
[1] Consistent ticket price data are not available prior to 1991. However, 1991 does represent the last year of Memorial Stadium.
[2] Split – Refers to MLB's only split season format used after a labor dispute that led to the cancellation of numerous games.
[3] Washington Nationals begin play at RFK Stadium in downtown Washington, D.C.
[4] Washington Nationals open their new ballpark.

The building of luxury seating now meant that teams had to market different "seating products" to differing communities of fans. The improved seats in non-luxury areas (usually referred to as *the deck*) were the seats upon which most of the business management literature of the past has been focused. That work focused on the value of charging fans slightly lower ticket prices to encourage more consumption of food and beverages in the venue. Luxury seating is attractive to the corporate sector and higher income households.

In the new facilities, for both luxury and general seating, team owners were able to capitalize on fans' desire for more comfortable seats and wider concourses that made it easier for retail activity, and to enjoy games, while being surrounded by amenities that were increasingly part of their homes and offices. Suites were designed to offer fans the amenities usually found in their homes or in executive offices.

Overnight, teams that played in facilities without these amenities were at a financial disadvantage when it came to profitability and enhanced revenue streams. Oriole Park at Camden Yards was built with 72 suites, and every venue built since has included suites and club seats. The number of suites

Table 1.3 Year Old and New MLB Ballparks Built

Teams	Former Ballpark	New Ballpark
Atlanta Braves	1965, 1997	2017
Arizona Diamondbacks	1998	–
Baltimore Orioles	1953	1992
Boston Red Sox	1912	–
Chicago Cubs	1914	–
Chicago White Sox	1910	1991
Cincinnati Reds	1970	2002
Cleveland Indians	1932	1994
Colorado Rockies	1995	–
Detroit Tigers	1912	2000
Houston Astros	1965	2000
Kansas City Royals	1973	–
Los Angeles Angels	1966	–
Los Angeles Dodgers	1962	–
Miami Marlins	1987	2012
Milwaukee Brewers	1953	2001
Minnesota Twins	1982	2010
New York Mets	1964	2009
New York Yankees	1923	2009
Oakland Athletics	1966	–
Philadelphia Phillies	1971	2004
Pittsburgh Pirates	1970	2001
San Diego Padres	1967	2004
San Francisco Giants	1960	2000
Seattle Mariners	1976	1999
St. Louis Cardinals	1966	2006
Tampa Bay Rays	1990	–
Texas Rangers	1965	1994
Toronto Blue Jays	1989	–
Washington Nationals	1977	2008

included in each facility generally depends on the team owner's assessment of the demand for this product in the local market. Today, it seems, there has been a shift toward building fewer suites in venues. This does not necessarily mean that there is less demand for suites; rather, owners may be increasing the exclusivity of their luxury products by including fewer suites and club seats. The factors contributing to that change are addressed later in this book and underscore the need for managers to understand how the market for different seating products matures and shifts. How a manager deals with the changes in fans' preferences is also a new element included in this edition.

There are, however, some markets where the demand for suites remains robust. The Dallas Cowboys' AT&T Stadium in Arlington has 300 luxury suites on four different levels and more than 15,000 club seats. The New York Jets and Giants' Met Life Stadium in New Jersey is also still able to satisfy a high demand for suites at 218. Little Caesars Arena opened in 2017 to serve as the new home for the NHL's Detroit Red Wings and NBA's Detroit Pistons. The new arena has but 60 suites – substantially fewer than what existed at the Detroit Pistons' former home, which opened in 1988 with 180 suites.

There are also design and real estate issues that need to be considered when an arena is built. For example, a basketball court is much smaller than an ice hockey rink. A venue designed *only* for basketball can offer fans much closer views of the court at each level if all of its seating is designed around the shape and length of a basketball court. However, if hockey is also to be played in an arena, the second and third levels need to be set back further so that fans in those seats can see both nets at the end of the rink. Since a basketball court is 94 feet long, but an NHL rink is 200 feet long, the higher-level seats cannot be as close the playing surface if both basketball *and* hockey are to be played in the same arena.

The Barclays Center in New York faces this particular issue, which has led to the NHL's Islanders' decision to leave the venue. Barclays was designed to be the home to the NBA's Brooklyn Nets. After the venue opened, the New York Islanders signed a lease to relocate from the Nassau Coliseum to the Barclays Center. When the Islanders play their home games at the Barclays Center, the arena actually becomes the second smallest in the NHL; it has 17,732 seats for basketball but just 15,813 for hockey. Some critics have noted that there really are fewer than 13,000 seats in Barclays that have unobstructed views of the rink. Regardless of the number of seats being sold, the basic issue for design is that a basketball-only arena can be designed to place more fans closer to the court, as compared to a venue built for both hockey and basketball.

Change Number 6: League Policies

It is possible that the interests of a team may not always align with those of the entire league. The majority of these conflicts arise due to the simple fact that some teams operate in large markets, while others serve fans in much smaller metropolitan areas. Further, certain markets are much wealthier than others. For example, there are more (and wealthier) people living in the San Francisco–San Jose region than there are in Jacksonville or even metropolitan Atlanta. The resulting unequal distribution of wealth provides teams in the larger and wealthier regions with the potential to earn more money than those in smaller areas. Those differences may give incentives for a variety of league policies. Simply put, the question for each league is whether to transfer some money from high revenue teams to those who earn less in an attempt to equalize profits, or let each team operate as an individual entity. If teams win more with higher payrolls, then how often will large market teams dominate in the absence of league policies, and will that hurt long-run demand for the league? The answer to that question also is at the heart of policies debated by each league.

Chapter 12 focuses on league and conference policies and their relationship to competitive balance and team popularity. Briefly, however, revenue sharing requires owners of teams in larger markets to share some of their income with owners of teams in smaller markets. While this might be done in an attempt to create more balance within the league, the actual impact of revenue sharing on competitive balance is in question. To avoid more revenue sharing, some leagues have restricted the amount of money players can earn (salary cap), thereby assuring greater opportunities for team owners in smaller markets to enjoy profitable operations. Of course, the players' unions argue against restricting player salaries. This ongoing conflict between players and owners even led to the cancellation of the entire 2004–2005 NHL season.

Along the same lines, another issue some sport business managers are faced with is the extent to which an individual player should receive a larger share of the revenue his or her play produces for the league and franchise. For example, Pittsburgh Penguins forward Sidney Crosby, earned only $10.9 million in 2017. His impact on team and league revenues, however, is arguably far greater in terms of additional tickets sold and team merchandise purchases. One assessment of LeBron James' impact on the Cleveland Cavaliers estimated that his presence encouraged the sale of more than 3,000 tickets per game. With even more fans watching him play on television, advertisers also pay more, which increases his team's revenues even further. The revenue LeBron James generated for the Cavaliers franchise, and the league, was arguably far more than what his $31 million salary (2017) provided (Rovell, 2014).

Salary caps divide the financial pie between owners and players, but managers also need to understand how and why a salary cap could lead to lower revenues for both players *and* owners. There are always short- and long-term implications to changes in the distribution of funds between players and owners. In the chapters that follow, we explain that it is possible that various policies can elevate revenues for both players and owners and that agreements to "cap" players' salaries can lead to higher or lower league-wide revenues. In the case of the NHL, for example, it is possible the salary cap might help the players in the long run if it increases fans' interest in the league by creating more parity. Even if this did happen, it might be that a specific group of players benefit, while some players similar to Sydney Crosby could actually be worse off. Given the number of multi-year, million-dollar contracts enjoyed by players in the NHL, an argument could be made that enhanced parity has elevated the amount of money earned by players.

There are other interesting outcomes from league policies. For example, each year when it becomes clear that a very talented player will be eligible for a league's draft, some fans will create websites urging their team to lose games to ensure a high draft pick. How can a league devise a player draft so that teams do not want to lose games in these situations? Interest in this issue peaked in 2017 when the owner of the Dallas Mavericks, Mark Cuban, told Yahoo Sports, "Once we were eliminated from the playoffs we did everything possible to lose games" (Dwyer, 2017). If teams actually did try to lose games, then fan interest in attending or watching those contests might decline, reducing the revenue earned by teams and the league.

While revenue sharing does give money to small-market teams, does the policy really help competitive balance? If a luxury tax helps competitive balance, is that good for the league? Under what conditions would owners be against a salary cap? These questions are addressed in the chapters that follow, as are the effects of the policies. For example, economic incentives given by revenue sharing are very different than what most fans believe. While revenue sharing can help the bottom line of small-market teams, the use of this strategy does not necessarily ensure that small-market team owners will actually spend their additional revenue sharing-generated money on players.

Another interesting issue is the role of sustained dominance by a few teams on overall league revenues. For example, the NFL has the highest level of revenue sharing, and there is also a firm salary cap. Despite those protections – put in place to ensure competitiveness – several teams continue to be dominant (New England Patriots, the Pittsburgh Steelers, the Dallas Cowboys, and Green Bay Packers). Along the same lines, another group of NFL teams has had a long legacy of misfortune (e.g., Cleveland Browns and the Detroit Lions).

All major professional sports leagues have a player draft. The teams that finish with the fewest wins are the first to choose players. It would seem that this would help the smaller-market teams or the teams that typically finish poorly. The draft, however, will not help bad teams get better if an owner believes fans will not pay higher prices for a team that wins more games. If teams in the largest markets will ultimately attract and retain the best players (because of their value to what a team in a larger and wealthier market can charge for tickets and advertising), then a draft accomplishes little. A player draft, however, does decrease the pay of players in the short run. Why? A team that drafts a player has the rights to that player for a specific amount of time, eliminating the ability of the athlete to auction his or her services among competing franchises. The lack of an auction lowers salaries.

Managers have to remember that revenue sharing means that large market teams share their income with others that cannot or do not earn as much. This means that on net, money will be going from larger-market teams to franchises in smaller markets. Economic models, however, illustrate that it is the players who lose the most when revenues are shared. Why? Since teams must give away part of their revenue, this reduces the incentive to earn more. That, in turn, reduces the willingness to invest in talent. In effect, a disincentive exists for teams to invest in players. As a result, all teams will reduce their payrolls and possibly their investments in their stadiums, depending on which revenues are shared. If all teams invest less in players, it is not clear that balance will improve. Again, it does seem clear that this will reduce player salaries since teams are investing less. The Pittsburgh Pirates are a perfect illustration of these deductions. In 2010, their financial documents were leaked to the public. Some fans and pundits were outraged because even though the Pirates were spending a minimal amount of money on player salaries, they were making a profit. It is easy for fans to ask, why aren't they spending that money on talent? The answer is simple. Spending the money from revenue sharing on player talent would not generate more revenue for the team given the size of the market and the wealth in the region. The complexity of this situation, where better players do not necessarily mean a team can earn more, will also be discussed.

Change Number 7: The Globalization of Sports

The sport business, just like so many others, has gone global. In one sense, the business of sport was always global, given the existence of the Olympics and the worldwide appeal of soccer, tennis, golf, racing, gymnastics, ice-skating, ice hockey, basketball, skiing, and rugby. What has changed is the ways in which the North American sport leagues are interacting with the rest of the world and the extensive televised presence of England's Premier League matches in North America.

The NHL and NBA have permitted their players to participate in the Olympics since the International Olympic Committee (IOC) decided to permit professionals to compete. Yet, prior to the 2018 Winter Games, the NHL and the IOC could not agree on revenue sharing policies. As a result, the NHL refused to permit its players to represent their home countries in the 2018 Olympic Games. The issue of a league's players competing in international games will also be discussed in later chapters of this book. Attention will also be directed to explain why MLB and the NHL decided to host their own world cup competitions. FIFA's World Cup and the European Championship are some of the most valuable tournaments and many of those players do not compete in the Olympics. Perhaps MLB and the NHL are trying to send the same message to the IOC – the Olympics are not necessarily valuable to team owners.

Each of the four major North American sport leagues has begun playing games in foreign countries. The finances, benefits, and costs of these games will also be explored. The auction of players from foreign leagues also is discussed and is very critical for MLB, given the increasing presence of players from leagues in Japan, Korea, and South America. The NHL and the NBA also draft players from foreign leagues, and those same leagues compete for players who could also play in the NBA or NHL. The future of sport finance and management entails an understanding of international issues ranging from player development academies and player posting fees (United States and Japan) to the expansion of leagues into Europe and Central America. The wide range of issues that now defines the globalization of sport is considered in a separate chapter.

Change Number 8: Teams and Public/Private Partnerships

In an effort to lure the Dodgers to Los Angeles, the city made land available for a privately funded ballpark. Years before the Dodgers ever dreamed about relocating to Los Angeles, more than 1,000 families were evicted from the area to permit a public housing project to be built on the land that was subsequently traded to (or given) to the Dodgers. Tragically, the evicted families were never allowed to return to their neighborhood even in the years before the Dodgers relocated from Brooklyn and when it was clear the anticipated public housing project would not be built. In preparing for other uses for the land, the public sector invested several million dollars into the area. The entire tract of land was then traded to the Dodgers for the ballpark and land where a minor league team played. The Dodgers purchased the minor league team (the Los Angeles Angels) and their ballpark so that they could exchange that smaller parcel for the land where Dodger Stadium was built. The Dodgers exchanged the older ballpark and the land on which it was built for the 315 acres known as the Chavez Ravine. The deal had to be approved by voters, and with a plurality of approximately 25,000 votes, the partnership between the Dodgers and the public sector was ratified (Becerra, 2012; Masters, 2012). Milwaukee was also interested in attracting an MLB team and in 1950 began to build a new ballpark. In 1953, the Boston Braves relocated to Milwaukee, where the city had established its first public/private partnership with a sports franchise. These post–World War II actions began an era of public sector participation in the financing of venues for professional teams.

The help both teams received from local governments initiated a series of public/private partnerships across North America to attract and retain professional teams where the proportion of the public sector's investment was far larger than the return it received. Increased public investment in sport venues reached its zenith in the 1990s. Each time one of these public/private partnerships was created, there was opposition from some taxpayers and voters. In almost every instance, what teams wanted in exchange for either staying in a city or relocating elsewhere was eventually offered. Numerous studies and books published in the late 1990s bemoaned the largesse conveyed on teams and the imbalanced nature of the public/private partnerships. Rosentraub (1999) described a corporate welfare system that turned cities into *Major League Losers*. Noll and Zimbalist (1997) added their own assessment to the work of many others in noting that at the regional level there was no evidence of any economic benefit justifying the public sector's investment of tax dollars in venues for professional sports teams. The academic community was in agreement that the returns at the regional level were undeserving of the public sector's investment. Unanimously, independent public policy expects urged local governments to be extremely cautious when considering a partnership with a team for a new arena, ballpark, or stadium.

These cautionary notes and proclamations did not reduce interest in attracting and retaining teams and ensuring that the needed venues were built. The largesse that ensued eventually produced a level of opposition that demanded real public value from the use of taxes to pay for part or all of a facility. The situation was so contentious that if the public sector was to invest in a venue, experts advised that public/private partnerships vastly different from those negotiated in the past must be created (Rosentraub, 2014).

There are ways to build effective partnerships producing financial benefits for teams and cities. Those professionals preparing for careers in sport finance and management must be able to advance a team's interests while also ensuring that real economic benefits exist for the public sector. One chapter in this volume details the ways in which a team and city can make prudent investments that produce positive financial returns for each partner. The task for today's sport manager is to create partnerships that ensure a team and the public sector both receive fair market returns on their investments in a venue.

Change Number 9: The Landscape of Collegiate Sport and NCAA

The last several years have also seen an extraordinary set of changes in college sport. At one level, the most successful athletic conferences, several individual universities, and the NCAA itself are generating a substantial amount of money from media contracts, ticket sales, donors, and tournaments. At another level, some student–athletes believe they are not being fairly compensated for the revenues they produce while college coaches and athletic directors earn salaries that eclipse those earned by most if not all faculty members and university presidents. The NCAA argues that amateur status is needed to maintain a level of parity, but that relationship is not necessarily obvious (Mills & Winfree, 2018).

These issues led student athletes from Northwestern University to attempt to form a union. While their efforts were not sustained, the NCAA did respond by allowing individual conferences to increase the support given to athletes. That decision created a greater schism between what some schools offer their athletes and what others are able to afford to do for their students.

There has also been an increase in the public's knowledge of sex-related issues involving athletes and entire programs. Domestic abuse has become an issue for many athletic programs, and Penn State University was shaken by the news that a pedophile had been an integral part of its football program for several years. His behavior went unchecked by the university's administration and the school's legendary coach, Joe Paterno. Similarly, the University of Louisville's basketball program was at the center of an investigation in 2017 into the use of escorts and bribes to lure players to the school's basketball team. These revelations led the university to fire the coach, Rick Pitino. Countless scandals have ensnared other legendary programs as well, including those at Michigan State University, the University of North Carolina, The Ohio State University, and the University of Southern California. One university's football team, Southern Methodist, received the unofficial "death penalty," which meant the school was prohibited from playing all games for an entire year. The university then sanctioned itself and suspended play for two years.

At the same time that these issues were swirling around college sports, NCAA revenues soared as media outlets showered money on several conferences. To maximize revenues, several athletic conferences have expanded. The Big Ten Conference added schools located on the east coast (Maryland and Rutgers) and in the Midwest (Nebraska). The Pac12 has now added members from the Rocky Mountain region. Notre Dame football is no longer truly independent, as it "partially" joined the Atlantic Coast Conference (ACC). The traditional NCAA basketball powerhouse conference, the Big East, is now quite different from what it was a short time ago.

Meanwhile, student attendance at football games has decreased as university athletic departments compete with broadcasts and the comfortable viewing of games at home. Some have attempted to improve attendance and elevate revenues by serving alcoholic beverages inside the stadium. There is a delicate balance between revenue maximization and long-term relationships that must be considered in the context of college sports.

The relationship between athletic departments and each university's academic mission requires careful attention to ensure the alignment of responsibilities and expectations. Understanding these challenges is critical to the education of any future sport manager. The changes in college sports are the subject of one of the chapters in this book.

Sport Finance and Management in Real Time

The extraordinary scale of these changes establishes the need for a book that includes a basic toolkit of skills with an assessment of the management issues that shape the sport business world. Along the way, various management "myths" need to be exposed. This book accomplishes these goals by providing you with the professional skills needed to realize the economic and social benchmarks that define success and profitability. The changing face of sport finance and management is probably best illustrated by the Boston Red Sox having a senior vice president for economic development and the Baltimore Orioles having their own urban planner. The Mets have experts in real estate management throughout their organization, and media managers are now part of the operations of numerous teams that own part or all of their own networks. Two decades ago, expertise in these areas was seen as exotic. Today those skills define success and profitability, and people with the needed expertise are as integral to an organization's profitability as an eighth inning set-up man.

This book is designed to help you understand various aspects of the dynamic world of sport finance and management. Traditional topics, such as ticket pricing and player valuation, are covered, as are the tax implications of player depreciation. Added to the array of materials usually found in sport finance books are sections dealing with the complex web of team ownership arrangements, real estate development, entertainment, media, and the Internet. Revenue-sharing models are also analyzed together with a complete assessment of the cross-pressures created by the different prices owners have paid for a franchise.

As each topic is explored and analyzed, data are presented in the context of pricing or revenue-enhancement activities entered into by specific teams. In this manner, financing and management are joined with practical applications. We analyze several management decisions made by different teams and the outcomes from those choices.

In addition to updating several statistics and figures, this revised version of our book adds two application chapters. The first looks at seven recent sports and economic development efforts that involved a new venue for the Detroit Red Wings; the relocation of the Oakland Raiders to Las Vegas and the St. Louis Rams to Los Angeles; the expansion of the NHL to Las Vegas; and the building of new arenas in Calgary, Edmonton, and Ottawa for NHL teams. The second application chapter looks at spring training baseball, the emergence of Arizona as a major competitor to Florida, and the financing and economic development initiatives surrounding the public sector's investment in complexes for the 30 MLB teams.

Notes

1 In a similar vein, many predicted that movie audiences would dwindle when home VCRs became common. After all, why would somebody go to the movies when they could watch the movie at home? Even though fans of sports and movies can watch their favorite entertainment at home, people still want to go out and see sports and movies in public. There could be many reasons for this, but it appears that various forms of consumption of movies and games are a good profitable opportunity for owners and a desired and valued experience for consumers and fans.
2 Robert Irsay moved the Colts to Indianapolis because that city had just built a football-only domed stadium as part of an expanded convention center. Indianapolis had no illusions about its ability to host an MLB team, and site design constraints (railroad tracks) made it impossible to build a dome that would be capable of hosting baseball and football games.

References

Becerra, H. 2012. Decades later, bitter memories of Chavez Ravine, *Los Angeles Times*, April 5. Retrieved from http://articles.latimes.com/2012/apr/05/local/la-me-adv-chavez-ravine-20120405 (accessed February 8, 2015).

Berkowitz, S. 2017. Jim Delany, Big Ten commissioner, earns $20 million bonus, *USA Today*, May 12. Retrieved from https://www.usatoday.com/story/sports/college/2017/05/12/jim-delany-big-ten-conference-20-million-bonus/101591564/(accessed July 30, 2018).

Dwyer, K. 2017. Mark Cuban: "Once we were eliminated from the playoffs, we did everything possible to lose games," *Yahoo! Sports*, May 17. Retrieved from https://sports.yahoo.com/news/mark-cuban-eliminated-playoffs-everything-possible-lose-games-174335008.html(accessed July 30, 2018).

Fornelli, T. 2014. Big 10 schools projected to make $45 million with new TV deal, *CBS Sports*. Retrieved from http://www.cbssports.com/collegefootball/eye-on-college-football/24540002/big-ten-schools-projected-to-get-45-million-with-new-tv-deal (accessed September 9, 2015).

Hochberg, P. R. 1973. Second and goal to go: The legislative attack in the 92nd Congress on sports broadcasting practices. *New York Law Forum* (180): 841–896.

Hyland, T. 2009. The Big Ten network: It's here to stay, *About.com Guide to College Football*, March 12. Retrieved from http://collegefootball.about.com/b/2009/03/12/the-big-ten-network-its-here-to-stay.htm, (accessed September 23, 2009).

Las Vegas Convention and Visitors Authority (LVCVA). 2017. 2016 Las Vegas year-to-date executive summary, *Stats & Facts*. Retrieved from http://www.lvcva.com/stats-and-facts/visitor-statistics/ (accessed July 30, 2018).

Masters, N. 2012. Chavez Ravine: Community to controversial real estate, *Social Focus, KCET Public Television*. Retrieved from http://www.kcet.org/updaily/socal_focus/history/la-as-subject/history-of-chavez-ravine.html (accessed February 8, 2015).

Miller, J. E. 1990. *The baseball business: Pursuing profits and pennants in Baltimore.* Chapel Hill, NC: The University of North Carolina Press.

Mills, B., & Winfree, J. 2018. Athlete pay and competitive balance in college athletics. *Review of Industrial Organization* 52: 211–229.

Noll, R., & Zimbalist, A, eds. 1997. *Sports, jobs, & taxes: The economic impact of sports teams and stadiums.* Washington, DC: The Brookings Institution.

Podair, J. 2017. *City of dreams: Dodger Stadium and the birth of modern Los Angeles.* Princeton, New Jersey: Princeton University Press.

Rosentraub, M. S. 1999. *Major league losers: The real cost of sports and who's paying for it.* New York: Basic Books.

Rosentraub, M. S. 2014. *Reversing urban decline: Why and how sports, entertainment, and culture turn cities into major league winners.* Boca Raton, FL: CRC Press/Taylor & Francis Group

Rovell, D. (2014). What is LeBron James' real value? *ESPN*, July 5. Retrieved from http://www.espn.com/nba/story/_/id/11168967/nba-lebron-james-real-value (accessed July 30, 2018).

UCF Knights. (2015). The Carl Black & Gold Cabana, *UCF Exposure*, September 16. Retrieved from https://ucfknights.exposure.co/cbgc (accessed July 30, 2018).

Chapter 2

Ownership and the Emergence of Team Sports

Introduction

Today's ownership models are shaped by the changing revenue opportunities of the sport business. For example, large-scale, mixed-use real estate development projects are now being anchored by arenas and ballparks more frequently than ever before. That change has attracted owners of real estate development corporations to purchase teams. In other instances, media, entertainment, or food service corporations have made teams part of their business plans. Before focusing on the legal description of ownership types, there is value in understanding how teams and leagues emerged. While today's teams are valued at upwards of $1 billion and are commonly pieces of much larger conglomerates, we must appreciate that teams and leagues originally began as risky and very speculative enterprises.

Emergence of Team Sports

Sport existed long before it became a commercial enterprise with professional athletes. Different societies have used sport as a tool to socialize people to understand American culture and the organizational value of teamwork for enhancing industrial output (McCormack & Chalip, 1988; Levine, 1993). The creation of professional sport leagues in the United States was a result of the demand for at least two different phenomena: (1) enhanced entertainment options related to growing consumer wealth and available leisure time, and (2) a socializing element that satisfies societal or corporate needs. Let's focus first on the economic factors that convinced entrepreneurs to invest in teams and create professional leagues.

The market for spectator sport, and the creation of a business model that today is evident in the demand for tickets, did not exist when the United States was formed. There was no real market for spectator sport until consumers had earned enough money to have discretionary income (money in excess of what is needed to meet living expenses) and the leisure time to attend entertainment events. Only among the elite was there sufficient leisure time to engage in extensive recreational pursuits (Hannigan, 1998).

These barriers lessened in the decades after the Civil War when the industrialization of the economy created more wealth for a middle class as well as a concentration of people in densely populated urban centers (creating markets of potential consumers).

In the last decades of the 19th century, spectator sport became one of the most popular forms of entertainment for the emerging middle class. Coinciding with rising levels of income was an increase in free time for workers to enjoy their slowly increasing wages. The industrial workweek shrank to six days, then to five and a half, and finally to the more standard five days that many enjoy today. The emergence of paid vacation periods, holidays, and weekends created a supply of hours that could be filled with entertainment. The United States' population also increased dramatically during this time, producing a number of cities with large concentrations of workers with discretionary income. These population centers established prime locations for teams, which in turn formed leagues in order to compete with other teams. Not surprisingly, it was in the early years of the 20th century that there was enough demand to support two professional baseball leagues and justify the creation of the first championship series, dubbed "The World Series." As illustrated in Figure 2.1, personal consumption soared into the trillions in the 1970s and continued to grow through the onset of the Great Recession in 2008.

In its early years, however, spectator sport had to compete with other forms of entertainment for the rising discretionary income of America's industrial workers. Each of these new entertainment businesses was fraught with financial risk for investors, causing many enterprises (and teams) to shutter their doors or declare bankruptcy. Teams also floundered as investors experimented with different ownership models and business practices. As with any emerging industry, businesses were plagued with failure until sustainable business models emerged. With help from favorable antitrust

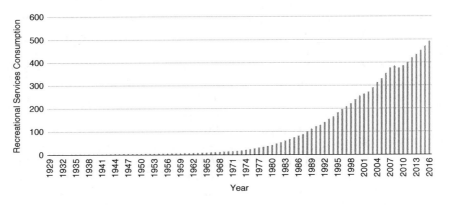

Figure 2.1 Personal Consumption Expenditures by Year, 1929–2016 ($billions).

treatment from the U.S. Supreme Court and Congress (limiting the ability of competing leagues to establish themselves), a league structure with defined market areas for each franchise became the most prominent and most successful model for professional leagues in the United States and Canada. The franchises created by each league would eventually settle into the largest and fastest-growing regions. Once unsuccessful were teams disbanded, profitability was sustained and stability resulted.

At the same time that professional teams and leagues were emerging, burlesque attracted large audiences and "nickelodeons" opened in many cities, offering short movies for a small price (one penny and up to a nickel). The growing popularity of nickelodeons and then-theaters that showed movies attracted the interest of a commercial artist in Kansas City. That artist, Walt Disney, began his journey and ultimately redefined both the entertainment and sport industries (Hannigan, 1998; Gottdiener, 2001; Gabler, 2007). In later years, there would be a merging of sport and entertainment into integrated business syndicates, but in the 1920s and through the 1970s, professional sport leagues competed with mass entertainment for consumer dollars. In addition, the competition with other forms of entertainment would prove to be a persistent issue for many smaller metropolitan areas that sought to add some level of professional sport to the package of amenities available to their residents. When professional teams are added to the range of amenities available in smaller metropolitan areas, there may be too few discretionary income dollars to support all of the entertainment options available. When this occurs, consumers can choose between many entertainment amenities, increasing the chance that some businesses will lose attendance and no longer be profitable. Currently the number of entertainment options and the financial viability of these options is still an issue that community leaders and investors in several regions must address (Columbus, Indianapolis, Jacksonville, Miami, metropolitan Phoenix, Tampa/St. Petersburg, etc.).

In the course of the evolution of the sport business, some cities that wanted to be home to a team had too few consumers to make a franchise financially viable. Relocations from smaller to faster-growing and larger markets were relatively common. For example, Fort Wayne, Indiana was a very successful manufacturing center through the 1950s and 1960s and hosted one of the NBA's initial teams. In the 1950s, the team's owner, Fred Zollner, relocated his Zollner Pistons to Detroit (where they dropped his name, becoming the Pistons). Syracuse, another early home to an NBA team in another then-successful industrial center, was abandoned for Philadelphia (76ers). The nearby Rochester Royals relocated to Cincinnati, and later, Kansas City. Today that franchise is the Sacramento Kings.

In several instances, competitive leagues were formed by different groups of investors, often because those investors were denied franchises in the existing leagues. Some of these competitive leagues were successful enough to pressure the more established league to merge or include teams from the "startup" league. Some mergers led to larger metropolitan areas having more than one team in the same sport. For example, New York City had three teams in MLB for a period of time (the Yankees were the team from the start-up American League) and Chicago, Boston, and St. Louis each had two teams. The Boston Braves (the older team from the National League) moved first to Milwaukee and then to Atlanta. The St. Louis Browns (from the start-up American League) became the Baltimore Orioles. The Dodgers and Giants (from the older National League) relocated to Los Angeles and San Francisco, and in the 1960s the Mets were created, leaving New York with just two teams.

Relocations took place in the NFL, too. The Chicago Cardinals left the market to the Bears and for decades called St. Louis home. When the Cardinals' owner could not find a stadium deal to his liking in St. Louis, he relocated the team to the Phoenix metropolitan area. After the first year of operation in the American Football League (AFL), the Los Angeles Chargers moved south to San Diego. In 2017, after a referendum for a new stadium was defeated in San Diego, the Chargers returned to Los Angeles. This was not the homecoming some might have expected as the Rams (originally from Cleveland) returned to Los Angeles after playing first in Anaheim and then in St. Louis. The Dallas Texans (of the upstart AFL) relocated to Kansas City (as the Chiefs), ceding the Dallas/Fort Worth area to the NFL's Cowboys.

While entrepreneurs experimented with different ways to organize leagues, it is important to keep in mind the social changes that created the market for new *commercial* products (fans as ticket-buying consumers, professional athletes as paid labor, and entrepreneurs as team owners). Spectator sport has existed for centuries. Most of the athletic events that preceded the late 19th century involved individuals competing against each other. For example, the first inaugural Olympic Games featured individual athletic events. While some team games were included, the gladiatorial games held across the Roman Empire were dominated by events involving individuals that fought against each other. There is some evidence that team sport were part of the life of North, Central, and South American native populations, but it is not clear if those forms of athletic competitions involved spectators as paying customers. Team sport, as they are practiced today, are a product of the 19th century and the changes wrought by industrialization and urbanization (Mandelbaum, 2004).

The second factor that drove a societal interest in sport, beyond its commercial properties, was its socializing impacts and social value. Team sport provide object lessons on the value of coordinated activities among several people to achieve success. Such activity was necessary for the success of factories and the emerging economies of the 19th and 20th centuries. In contrast, economic activities of the 17th and 18th centuries largely involved individuals working alone (agriculture, or in small-scale activities with just a few workers) and were thus less reliant on teams of workers for success. As people moved away from closely knit villages to more impersonal cities, teams also became a source of identity with fellow workers (Branscombe & Wann, 1991; Wheeler, 1978).

The industrial revolution created the need for coordinated activities or teamwork among groups of workers. Team sport mirrors the need for coordinated activity and replicates the success (or profitability) that can occur when all individuals work as a collective. Baseball, basketball, cricket, football, hockey, and soccer required groups of individuals to perform their roles and execute their work in a timely manner to win. Throughout the 20th and 21st centuries, sport metaphors have become integral parts of workday life and normal conversations: hit a home run, cross the goal line, throwing a "Hail Mary," doing something in the ninth inning, etc. Through language and the accomplishments of sport-like teams organized for business, there was soon an inexorable link between the corporate world and athletic competitions on the court, field, pitch, or rink.

As discussed, there was a large-scale shift of people from rural areas to rapidly expanding cities in both North America and across Europe. In many instances, these cities did not have the infrastructure to support the large number of new residents; living and working conditions were both unsafe and unsavory. While larger population bases provided larger pools of consumers, overcrowded cities created new tensions, which, in many instances, led to large-scale riots. Sport became a diversion from the drudgery of labor and urban life.

As larger numbers of immigrants entered the United States (1880 through 1920), sport assumed a vital role as a socializing institution promoting stability. To be sure, there were long periods when discriminatory practices reduced this democratic function within sport (the exclusion of black athletes first from leagues, then from certain positions, and then from management and ownership roles), but across the decades these have slowly eroded. With its emphasis on performance and skill, sport demonstrates that success is egalitarian. Immigrants gained a level of "Americanization," if not acceptance, through their success in sport. As waves of different ethnic and racial groups migrated to cities and were permitted to play in each of the professional sports leagues, Jewish, Irish, Italian, and then African-American individuals began a climb through strata of American society after decades of discrimination and exclusion (Levine, 1993). There is, however, with regard to ownership and administrative and managerial positions, very limited inclusion of racial minorities and women.

Another socializing aspect of sport results from the concept of allowing set rules, applied impartially by unbiased referees, to govern play. The growing popularity of soccer in Europe, for example, was at first subject to disdain from governments, as the game was quite brutal and played without referees or structured rules. Rules and officials were seen as unnecessary to regulate a game played by "gentlemen." Gentlemen recognized infractions and would admit to their occurrence and allow the other team to offset any disadvantage resulting from a foul (this was also characteristic of baseball in the early years of the sport after the Civil War.) When the game became popular among the working class, violence was rife. The establishment of rules and penalties made the game more civilized and also provided lessons on the extent of physical confrontation that would be tolerated (before penalties were assessed). These lessons and the value of teamwork fit well into the emerging factory life that also required adherence to rules and cooperation with others.

The socializing aspect of sport to reduce labor unrest was at the heart of the interest in creating factory and community teams in North America and Europe. These teams created diversions from the dreariness of manufacturing jobs. In the absence of these diversions, it was feared political or social protest could result, or workers could become less productive (McIntosh, 1971; Riess, 1980; Thompson, 1981). These many positive outcomes from sport meant that community leaders were eager to ensure that teams were part of the social infrastructure of communities.

The role of sport in maintaining and advancing social stability meant that governments were often eager to ensure that teams enjoyed a special status or were treated differently than other businesses. In the United States, for example, there was a critical U.S. Supreme Court decision that exempted MLB from antitrust laws to ensure its continued existence in its current form in the early 20th century. Part of the justification for the exemption was the special characteristics of sport that made it different from a business. That logic, while arguably flawed, would sustain baseball's exemption, which then led to restrained wages for players. For decades Congress never saw fit to change MLB's status, inferring that the social benefits from baseball made it something more than a business. In another example, President Theodore Roosevelt recognized the value of football for colleges but was troubled by the violent injuries in the sport. His threat to abolish the sport unless it was better regulated led to the creation of the National Collegiate Athletic Association (NCAA).

Four Major Leagues in North America

Major League Baseball

The first professional team – the Cincinnati Red Stockings – began play in 1869. This team played community teams, creating games that were part of a barnstorming circuit. The Red Stockings' success in playing games against community teams created interest from other entrepreneurs. The stronger clubs formed the National Association of Base Ball Players, a rather loosely organized association, in 1871. The National League of Professional Baseball clubs was then created in 1876 to replace the older league, which was seen as too corrupt, lacking central authority, and having too many members to sustain a consistent format for the game. The new organization was formed with the Boston Red Stockings (which became the Braves), Chicago White Stockings (now the Chicago Cubs), Cincinnati Red Stockings, Hartford Dark Blues, Louisville Grays, New York Mutuals, Philadelphia Athletics, and St. Louis Brown Stockings.

When the National League refused to admit other teams, the rejected investors formed the American League in 1901. The upstart league placed teams in Baltimore, Boston, Chicago, Cleveland, Detroit, Milwaukee, Philadelphia, and Washington. The Baltimore Orioles would relocate to New York to become the Yankees. The Philadelphia Athletics would relocate to Kansas City and then to Oakland. The Washington Senators would relocate to Minneapolis (Twins), and the Milwaukee Brewers would relocate to St. Louis to become the Browns before relocating again to Baltimore (Orioles) in 1954.

In 1903, the two leagues merged to short-circuit a bidding war for players that had been escalating player salaries. The teams played games only against the members of their respective league, with the first-place team from each league playing in a World Series, beginning in 1903. There was no World Series in 1904 as the New York Giants refused to recognize the American League and its champion, the Boston Americans. The Series would again be played in 1905 and every year since except for 1994, when labor strife lead to the cancellation of a substantial portion of the season and the World Series.

National Football League

In 1920, a group of professional football teams met in a car dealership in Canton, Ohio to form the Professional Football Association. The teams were concentrated in the Midwest with one team from Rochester, New York. At the time the league was established, they selected Jim Thorpe to serve as president. In 1922, however, the league chose a new president with more business acumen: Joe Carr, who owned the team in Columbus. There were other events in 1921 and 1922 that would bring more definition to the league, which was renamed the National Football League in 1922. Before the 1921 season began, the team in Green Bay folded, but the franchise was purchased for $50 by Curly Lambeau. To ensure its fiscal stability, a group of local business leaders formed a nonprofit corporation to operate the team and provide Curly Lambeau with $2,500.[1]

By the 1930s, there were just eight teams remaining in the NFL. Franchises were granted to teams in Pittsburgh and Philadelphia that would change names (and owners) and eventually became the Steelers and Eagles.

The Portsmouth (Michigan) Spartans were sold and relocated to Detroit and became the Lions. In the post–World War II years, the league would be stabilized into the cities with teams that are recognized today, but there were still relocations. For example, the Chicago Cardinals relocated to St. Louis, and then would move to Arizona. The Cleveland Rams would move to Los Angeles, and then to Orange County, California, then to St. Louis, and then back to Los Angeles again.

As football became more popular in the post–World War II years, a competitive league formed: the All-America Football Conference. That league operated from 1946 to 1949, and as player salaries rose because of the bidding for talent, three of the teams from that conference were admitted to the NFL: the Baltimore Colts, the Cleveland Browns, and the San Francisco 49ers. Another competitor league emerged in 1959, the American Football League. In 1966, all of the franchises in the AFL were admitted to the NFL. In January 1967, the first championship between the two leagues was played; that game was renamed the Super Bowl and today is North America's most watched athletic event.

National Basketball Association

The Basketball Association formed in 1946 to challenge the nine-year old National Basketball League. But by August 1949, after competing with each other for players, the Basketball Association of America and the National Basketball League merged to form the National Basketball Association. There were 11 teams that joined the new NBA, but by 1953, the league had only eight franchises: New York, Boston, Philadelphia, Minneapolis, Rochester, Fort Wayne, the Tri-City Blackhawks, and the Syracuse Nationals. Tri-City would relocate to Milwaukee and then to St. Louis before settling in Atlanta as the Hawks. The Rochester Royals would move to Cincinnati, Kansas City–Omaha, Kansas City, and then settle in Sacramento (Kings).

The American Basketball Association emerged as a competitor in 1967. The league introduced the 3-point shot, and while it began play with a 30-second shot clock, it quickly switched to the 24-second clock used by the NBA. Professional basketball was not immune to the battles between competitor leagues and established ones that plagued baseball and football; escalating player costs led to the NBA and ABA's merger in 1976. Four of the ABA's teams – the Indiana Pacers, New York Nets, Denver Nuggets, and San Antonio Spurs – were admitted to the NBA. Owners of other franchises received compensation for the loss of their team. Increasing demand for basketball has led to a stable league of 30 teams with interest from other cities, including Seattle, for an expansion franchise.

National Hockey League

The NHL was formed in 1917 with teams in Ottawa and Quebec, two in Montreal and two in Toronto. However, the modern era for the league begins in 1942 with six franchises in Boston, Chicago, Detroit, Montreal, New York, and Toronto. The league would remain with just six teams through 1967. Six teams were added for the 1968 season, and two more joined in 1970,1972, 1974, and 1978.

The World Hockey Association was formed in 1972, and while a total of 26 franchises were part of the league during its eight years of existence, when it merged with the NHL in 1979 there were only six that remained. In 1979, the New England Whalers, Winnipeg Jets, Quebec Nordiques, and Edmonton Oilers joined the NHL. The Whalers would become the Carolina Hurricanes. The original Winnipeg Jets relocated to Phoenix, and the Nordiques became the Colorado Avalanche. Today the NHL has 31 teams with the Las Vegas Golden Knights joining the league in 2016.

The very brief histories are provided to illustrate the similar process that each league underwent; the common story of creation, consolidation, stability, expansion, and then competition with an upstart league. There is then a consolidation with the newer league to reduce player costs, and then after another period of stability, further expansion. This process is now playing out with soccer, as Major League Soccer has achieved stability and is seeking to expand. There are issues to be settled between Major League Soccer, the North American Soccer League, and the United Soccer League. History may predict that some of the teams from those leagues (or the owners) will become part of MLS. Currently as the MLS seeks to expand, the cost of a franchise is approximately $150 million, a figure that just a few years ago seemed far-fetched.

There are many other professional sport leagues in North America, including women's hockey, arena football, and lacrosse; the expanding population size of cities in the United States and Canada make it possible for other niche leagues to form. The experience of the four more dominant leagues suggests that some of these other leagues will succeed, some will fail, and within each there will be teams that are successful and others that will need to cease operations. The pattern of what takes place is what sport management students must understand and appreciate.

Textbook Definitions of Ownership

The three most common forms of business ownership structures are sole proprietorships, partnerships, and corporations. While the sport industry has many examples of these three types, sport is somewhat unique in that it also has other types of structures. Because of sport's public nature, communities can also own teams, but this is limited to the minor leagues. With the exception of the Green Bay Packers, there is no public ownership of a major league team (in the sense that a city owns the team) in the United States. When we describe public ownership, it refers to the few examples where a city owns a minor league baseball team. There have also been instances where shares of stock in an individual franchise have been sold, but when that has happened in North America, shareholders have not had substantial voting roles in team operations and thus have had little power in team decision making.

There does exist, however, public ownership of some very valuable sport properties. By this we refer to the teams operated by numerous universities, some of which have gross revenues that rival those of professional franchises. College sport have emerged with their own unique ownership structure, which requires its own discussion, but which largely falls under the umbrella of a nonprofit organization (discussed later in this chapter). Football clubs in Europe have varied ownership structures; Kuper and Szymanski (2012) provide the best summary of those arrangements. Given this diversity, the sport industry has become an impressive laboratory in which to study different and unique business ownership structures.

Sole Proprietorship – A Changing Breed

A sole proprietorship is when one individual owns a business. There are many individuals who own teams and, thus, are sole proprietors. Far more common, however, are arrangements when a dominant majority partner functions as a sole proprietor but, when making decisions, refers to other, silent minority owners who have made important financial investments in the team. This is generally described as a limited partnership. There are many advantages to a sole proprietorship, including low organizational costs, easy decision making, secrecy, and independence. Sole proprietors rarely have to answer to anybody. This can be crucial in the sport industry because, as noted, sport is becoming part of more complex entertainment conglomerates. A single owner has the opportunity to utilize the team as he or she envisions and can fit the team into a long-term strategic plan for a conglomerate of firms. While the rewards can be high with a sole proprietorship, so is the risk. A sole proprietor has unlimited liability, meaning the owner's total wealth is at risk to pay off creditors.

Divorce American Style: Sole Proprietors and Community Property States

Sole proprietorships do not exempt ownership from the community property laws that guide divorce settlements in numerous states. The complications that can arise when an individual who owns a team seeks a divorce from his/her spouse have been vividly illustrated when John Moores (San Diego Padres) and Frank McCourt (Los Angeles Dodgers) each separated from their wives. Settlements in the many millions of dollars ensued and ultimately led to sales of each team. In addition, large ownership shares can create estate (inheritance) issues, which have been concerns for at least two families where patriarchs had been the sole owners (Pittsburgh Steelers and Buffalo Bills). There were also complications regarding the inheritance of the Indianapolis Colts when its owner Robert Irsay died. Mr. Irsay had remarried and there were severe tax issues, but ultimately his son from his first marriage was able to retain ownership of the team.

The NFL has very strict ownership rules, and while partnerships are permitted, it does require that somebody own at least 10 percent of the team (down from 30 percent in 2004). However, it is increasingly difficult for a single individual to own a large proportion of a team. Given the increasing value of NFL teams (in 2017, according to *Forbes*, no team is worth less than $1.6 billion), if the league still required one individual to own at least 30 percent of the team (as was required as early as 2004), a minimum investment of $480 million would be required. For the average team in the NFL, this 30 percent ownership stake would mean an investment of more than $700 million.

Partnerships/Syndicates and the Single-Entity Ownership Model

The initial team owners were usually individual entrepreneurs or partnerships that often recruited many other partners to create a syndicate (a group of individuals who owned a single team). The formation of syndicates – a widely used ownership strategy today – spread the risks of ownership across many investors. With several investors involved, any needs for operating cash are spread across more individuals. In addition, the extraordinary cost of acquiring a team sometimes requires a group of investors to pool their resources. Today, as in the past, one of the members of the syndicate is designated as the managing partner who essentially is the "owner" for all matters involving the team and its relationship with the league. The most obvious drawback to having a team owned by two or more people is that there might be disagreements among the owners. The advantage of a partnership is that any risks are shared. If a team must raise cash, for instance, each partner can contribute. Of course, while risks are shared, profits are as well.

While partnership structures are generally used for individual teams, some partnerships have been created to form single entity leagues, where a group of individuals owns all of the teams. This ownership structure is used by Major League Soccer (MLS), with each individual owning a percentage of the entire league. While owners might run just one or two teams, all profits are divided among the partners, and all business decisions about teams and the league are made by the entire partnership. Player contracts are negotiated through the league – not with an individual owner.

This structure permits the league to assign a player to the team for which the most revenue will be generated. This does not mean that the best players will always be on the teams in the largest markets, though some suggest doing so would likely generate the most profits.

Ultimately, the single-entity league ownership model can create the impression that decisions are made to ensure that the teams in the largest markets have the greatest collection of talent. Larger markets have a greater potential for generating more returns, and if each owner benefits from the revenues generated in the largest markets, then it would make sense for decisions to be made to ensure success of teams in New York and Los Angeles. As will be discussed further in later sections of this chapter, the other major sport leagues do not permit ownership of multiple teams in the league.

Corporate Ownership: Subsidiaries and Cross-Revenue Sharing (or Not)

Corporations are legal entities with all of the rights of citizenship (except for the right to vote). They are, in essence, "artificial beings" created by law and given all of the legal rights in business that individuals enjoy. Corporations account for approximately 5 percent of the businesses in the United States and 62 percent of the revenues generated by private sector entities (Lundeen & Pomerleau, 2014).

A board of directors oversees the work of a corporation. Shareholders – those who own stock in the corporation – each own a portion of the corporation (measured by the proportion of a firm's total shares that they own). Shares can be held by a small group of family members, a group of unrelated individuals, or by many people. The shares themselves can be publicly traded on a stock exchange, or the company may elect not to be listed on any of the stock exchanges. If a company is not listed, then the shares cannot be publicly traded; they can, however, be privately traded among individuals.

Stockholders benefit by receiving profits in the form of dividends from the corporation. While a corporation might retain some current profits to increase investments and future profits, the goal of most corporations is to maximize the value of depreciated dividends. The board of directors, elected by shareholders, makes the general policies for the firm and addresses the issue of the use of profits. Also, corporations typically have a treasurer in charge of financial activities and a controller in charge of accounting activities.

The benefit of a corporation over other ownership structures is that it limits owner liability. Investors can lose their investment, but they are not legally liable for any fiscal losses of the company and cannot be held financially responsible in any lawsuits against the corporation. There are also many types of corporations, which provide variations on the issue of liability for financial responsibilities in the event of a failure.

Some teams are owned by corporations and act as subsidiaries of the larger corporations, but there is far less use of this ownership model than one might expect. As will be discussed later in this chapter, the NFL does not allow corporate ownership. In that sense, each team is an independent corporation or partnership that is not owned by another company. The NFL has a preference for each team to be controlled by one person. That individual is expected to be the one person from the ownership group whose attention is completely focused on the NFL, the team, and the game of football. Another concern about this ownership structure is that if a league were to permit corporate ownership and the stock of that company was public traded (or listed on a stock exchange), then the team might suffer as a result, and some of its decisions and deliberations would have to be disclosed to the public. The leagues are always protective of the internal finances of each of their teams.

While it is not common in North America, a few teams have sold stock that has been publicly traded. No team is currently trading its stock on any of the exchanges. In the past, however, the Boston Celtics and Cleveland Indians each sold shares of stock. The Indians were taken private in 2000 and the Celtics went private in 2002 when the team was sold.

Corporate ownership is more common in other countries. These teams are typically part of a larger conglomerate and, in some instances, known by their corporate sponsor. Many Japanese teams are not known by the city, region, or province in which they play (the typical naming pattern in North America) but by the corporation that owns them. For example, Nippon Ham, a food processing company, owns the Nippon Ham Fighters baseball team. Similarly, in Korea, the Samsung Lions are one of the more recognizable teams for those who own a Galaxy smartphone.

Public Ownership

There are a total of 123 major league teams (146 including MLS); only the Green Bay Packers have a degree of public ownership. Chapter 1 illustrates the uniqueness of the ownership structure of the Green Bay Packers, but they are not the only sports entity with a unique community-based ownership structure. Displayed in Table 2.1, there have been quite a few minor league teams that have been community-owned. The exact ownership structure is not the same for these teams, but all of them are or have been controlled by a local government, usually a city or county. Interestingly,

Table 2.1 Minor League Baseball Teams, Currently or Formerly Community-Owned

Team	Classification	League
Columbus Clippers	AAA	International League
Rochester Red Wings	AAA	International League
Syracuse Skychiefs	AAA	International League
Toledo Mud Hens	AAA	International League
Memphis Redbirds	AAA	Pacific Coast League
Harrisburg Senators	AA	Eastern League
Beloit Snappers	A	Midwest League
Burlington Bees	A	Midwest League
Wisconsin Timber Rattlers	A	Midwest League
Auburn Doubledays	Short-Season A	New York-Penn League

community-owned teams do not perform very well in terms of attendance, but it is not clear if this is because public agencies operate the teams poorly or if local governments purchase teams where demand is low to ensure the team's continued presence.

Fan Participation in Team Operations

Ebbsfleet United, an English football (soccer) team, is unique in that it allows fans to make key decisions regarding team operations. Since 2008, a web community, "My Football Club," has managed the club. Fans pay a fee to join and members are allowed to make proposals and vote on various policies. Although Bill Veeck tinkered with the idea of letting fans vote on critical game decisions for one of his MLB teams, the structure in place for Ebbsfleet United allows fans to set team policy and select personnel. Since this concept was implemented, other teams across the globe have experimented with similar ideas. Soccer fans around the world, through the Internet and their "global ownership group," can now have a role in running a team. They can even claim to be a part owner. Perhaps this is a form of fan participation and ownership that will become a new type of fantasy sport, with entrepreneurs forming teams in a league that allows fans to actually trade players and establish starting lineups (Heffernan, 2016).

Nonprofit

Another type of ownership structure found in sport is the formation of a nonprofit firm. Athletic departments at universities operate as nonprofit organizations, but nonprofits are seen outside college sport as well. Several high-profile organizations in the United States are nonprofits, such as the NFL and the United States Olympic Committee (USOC). While they are both considered nonprofits, there are many differences between the NFL and the USOC. The NFL is a nonprofit organization because it distributes all of its earnings to teams (for-profit entities) and its employees (both of whom pay taxes on income earned). The USOC, on the other hand, uses its income to support various programs that enhance the success of athletes in the Olympic Games or to choose cities that will compete against cities from other countries to host the Games. The USOC receives revenue from donations and sponsorships and for hosting competitions for Olympic teams. College athletic departments use the revenue generated by high-profile teams (e.g., football, men's basketball, etc.) to fund other varsity sport fulfilling the requirements to be defined as a nonprofit organization.

It should be noted that even though the goal of these organizations is not to make a profit, the financial decisions are not much different when compared to for-profit businesses. Nonprofit organizations still must generate revenue and maintain solid financial situations; the difference is that any excess money will be invested back into the organization to provide services for its stakeholders (young athletes, Paralympic athletes, etc.). Still, nonprofit status will certainly impact the tax status of the organization, since nonprofit organizations generally pay little or no taxes. The justification is that they are providing services for the public, whose tax payments would otherwise go to support in lieu of their nonprofit status. There has been some discussion of disallowing professional sport organizations similar to the NFL to claim nonprofit status. And while Congress has not changed the internal revenue code to prohibit the classification of major sport leagues as nonprofit organizations, the NFL recently decided to drop its tax-exempt status after coming under considerable scrutiny in 2015.

Observations on Individual Sports

Individual-sport athletes (e.g., golf, tennis, swimming) can incorporate or operate as a sole proprietor. These athletes control their business operations without the involvement of others, although their sponsors might make demands or participate with the athlete in making decisions. In contrast, players in the four major leagues are part of unions that negotiate the contracts that outline what is expected of the players and the rules that govern employment. These critical elements are not made by individual-sport athletes. In golf or tennis, for example, the athletes must adhere to rules of the associations that operate tournaments, but they have far more control over the terms of sponsorships and the delivery of content related to their participation in the sport.

Just as there are limits placed on athletes playing for teams (negotiated in the collective bargaining agreements), there are limitations or requirements that are enforced by the Professional Golf Association and the United States Tennis Association. Those organizations operate or sanction competitions or events and establish the rules for participants. As each organization has numerous sponsors for every tournament and owns the distribution rights for the images from the competition, individual athletes cannot cross-compete or engage in ambush marketing with competing sponsors.

Golf

Another example of various ownership structures in the sport industry is golf courses. For example, golf courses are not only owned by sole proprietors, partners, and corporations, but there is also public ownership of golf courses. Similar to minor league teams, there are many municipal golf courses that are owned by cities or sometimes counties. Presumably cities own golf courses because they feel they provide some public benefit. Sometimes cities feel they have an obligation to provide cheaper outdoor recreation for residents. In these cases, any financial analysis should take these public benefits into account. This does not mean that the golf course should make bad financial decisions, but that financial profitability may not be the only objective of the course.

Another factor that makes golf course ownership similar to team ownership is that golf courses are often part of a larger investment. For example, there is often high demand for houses next to a golf course, so housing developers often create a golf course in housing developments. In this case, it might be perfectly acceptable if the golf course loses money, as long as that loss is not large enough to negate the gains in home sales. This is analogous to a baseball team creating a valuable media network or a college football team boosting enrollment at a university.

There are other forms of sport that are not part of this book. The financing and management of auto racing, tennis, horse racing, yachting, lacrosse, soccer, European football, and others would require additional chapters. This volume focuses on the four major sport leagues in North America. While many of the issues identified and discussed in this chapter regarding the four major leagues can be applied to other games, readers are reminded that the structure of every sport is different and that the financing, management, and economics of each sport will vary.

College Sports "Ownership"

Faculty Governance in Collegiate Sport

Another unique ownership structure is college sport. Collegiate teams are part of athletic departments, which function within a larger college or university. The university's athletic director (AD) oversees each team's finances, even though the college or university is ultimately responsible. The AD is essentially the chief operating officer of each of the university's athletic teams and reports, in most instances, to the university's president or board of regents.

As with professional sports, knowing some of the history can shed light on the current state of governance of college sports. Many fans might know that college sport have a long tradition, but it is also important to know that it has also long been big business. While the financial numbers have been increasing over recent decades, college sport have had large fan bases for a century. In the 1920s, Notre Dame played some of their games at Soldier Field with estimated crowds well over 100,000 people. In fact, the NFL started to gain legitimacy in the 1920s by signing well-known college football stars. Because these sporting events rose to prominence with the association of universities, universities have had a long history of governing sport. The fact that college students enjoy playing and watching sport has created an odd ownership structure for universities in charge of big-time athletics.

When analyzing the ownership structure or financial performance of college athletics, it is critical to understand that while many people associate universities with athletics, athletic departments are typically a small part of a university's bottom line. A university's athletic budget is typically around 5–10 percent of the university's total budget (Fort & Winfree, 2013). This means that any financial decisions made by the athletic department should consider the impact on the rest of the institution, which may be substantial. This also means that many different people have a stake in what happens with college athletics.

The importance of college sport to different stakeholders makes its governance and oversight a challenging administrative task. Students, alumni, faculty, coaches, and boosters each have their own visions of the role and importance of collegiate sport. Balancing the interests of these different constituencies is a demanding responsibility.

As the popularity of college sport soared and the revenue possibilities increased, management was professionalized. Some have described this professionalization as a system that is insulated from and increasingly independent of the management system used elsewhere in universities. There have been many instances across the past decades when this professionalized staff has run afoul of university expectations. That said, at many universities there is a more positive and supportive relationship between the academic and athletic sides of a university. That success requires affirmative management and clear-set agreements on standards and expectations.

When an AD cannot manage the contributions and involvement of these different constituencies, severe difficulties can ensue. For example, the illegal activities by supporters of Southern Methodist University's football program in 1987 led to the university's suspension of the team for two consecutive seasons. There have also been instances at other universities where student athletes received credit for classes that never met, or where the requirements for a particular class taken by an athlete were actually fulfilled by work produced by other students or staff members.

Many universities have had to consider whether or not to admit student–athletes with academic records that are below those of non-athletes. When this happens, student athletes are sometimes unable to compete in the classroom with other students. Therefore, ADs must balance the interests of coaches who want to recruit students with relatively weak academic records (accompanied by great athletic prowess) with their university's academic standards and reputation. ADs and coaches are not formally charged with the responsibility of approving admission to a university, but informal pressure has created tensions in a number of universities.

Financing Collegiate Sport

There is an obvious overlap between governance and the financing of college athletics because of the role of donors in achieving financial stability. In this section, we want to draw attention to the issues when an athletic department cannot produce enough revenue to sustain the entire athletic program.

The unique "ownership" and stakeholder groups of college sport do allow for different types of financing. For example, alumni and other friends of the university and its athletic department can frequently be counted upon to make donations to support teams and their operations. This revenue stream complements the traditional sources of income that include ticket sales, media rights, income from naming and advertising, profits from the sale of food and beverages, and income from the sale of athletic apparel. Some universities may require that income from several of these sources be shared with the academic sector. At many universities, students are assessed a compulsory fee that is used to support teams. This revenue stream generates a considerable amount of opposition from students and faculty members at some universities. Some schools also receive support from local governments for sport venues and a few have built facilities with professional sport teams (or use venues built by organizations that own a professional team).

A great deal of the data to understand the issues facing athletic departments is available from the NCAA.[2] In addition, most public universities publish the financial reports of their athletic departments.[3] The important element to discern from the data is the extent to which an athletic department is able to pay for all of its own costs from gifts, tickets, media contracts, sponsorships, and the sale of apparel. For those programs that cannot, the university has to pay some of the costs from its other revenue sources, including the fees paid by students.

Why would universities make the decision to spend money for intercollegiate sport? That question has been at the center of thorny conversations on many campuses. Proponents point to the benefits athletics provide for campus life and the college experience. Some have suggested that games create an opportunity to "pitch" donors. Other proponents suggest that there will be far more students applying for admission if a university has a great campus life and sport programs. Those who are opposed to a subsidy for university athletics focus on the problems generated when coaches seek to win and attract athletes regardless of their academic prowess. Those in opposition also point to the fact that universities were originally created to provide educational opportunities, and athletic programs do not contribute to schools' pursuit of the true objective of higher education. Arguments of this nature convinced the University of Chicago, a founding member of what is today the Big Ten Conference, to abandon its athletic programs.

There is no simple answer to the appropriate amount of support universities should provide their athletic programs. Universities have a long history of cross-subsidizing academic programs. For example, some universities transfer revenue from law or business schools to support the university's less profitable academic programs. Proponents for collegiate athletic programs suggest this policy could be applied to athletic departments as well. Sport managers must understand the perspectives of those opposed to subsidies for athletic programs and also ensure that the athletic department makes sufficient contributions to a university and its campus life to warrant the support provided.

Each of the financial decisions made by an athletic department has an impact on the university's academic units. A student fee for intercollegiate athletics reduces the flexibility to increase tuition. It is possible that a donor's generosity to a university's athletic department could mean a smaller commitment to its academic mission. Any illegal activities by donors or supporters reflect poorly on the entire university. It is also possible that a successful athletic program attracts more students.

While the goals for athletic programs might differ from those of a professional team, a college or university still wants its athletic programs to operate as efficiently as possible relative to established goals. Those goals include support from alumni and donors and using the popularity of sport to attract students. Some faculty members belittle the use of sport for those goals and, to be sure, mistakes are made that lead to adverse publicity for the university. Some have suggested that academic institutions have sacrificed their principles to ensure their teams win. But if athletics does help a school attract more students, faculty, and philanthropic contributions, these contributions can have a positive effect on a college or university.

For a school's leadership, the issue is the optimal level of focus on athletics, relative to the university's mission. Think about the problems that several universities have faced in the past several years. Baylor University has been under scrutiny since 2014 from a series of sexual assault scandals. The university was found to have failed to ensure that athletes accused of sexual assault were investigated and that victims were protected. Those failings led to the dismissal of the university's president and football coach and the resignation of the AD. A set of child abuse cases linked to a football coach shook the foundations of the Pennsylvania State University. More recently,

Michigan State University had a somewhat similar scandal. The University of North Carolina has been involved with a scandal involving the falsification of academic achievements by athletes. These are just some of the issues and crimes that have marred intercollegiate sports, prompting many to ask, "what is the best way to govern collegiate sport?" This is an issue that everyone involved with sport management must address, and it is certain to remain in the discussion among the public, universities, and the media.

There is also a unique revenue sharing issue in collegiate sports. Before turning to the salaries paid to college coaches, universities use the excess revenue produced by football and basketball (and sometimes hockey) to fund teams that attract far fewer fans. Of course, if an athletic department's only priority were ensuring fiscal stability, it would only field teams where fan interest is sufficient to meet costs. The decision of how many sports will be played, however, is made by a university's board of regents (and informed by Title IX restrictions).

The Rise of the Collegiate "Super Coach" and Salary Escalation

The unique rules and finances of college sports have led to dramatic increases in coaching salaries. Since athlete compensation is limited and largely in the form of free tuition, many athletes do not get paid their full value. Large differences between the value of an athlete and the payment to an athlete can happen when the labor market is not competitive, in other words, when there is monopsonistic power. A monopsony is sometimes referred to as a buyer's monopoly – a single buyer controls a large portion of the market and drives prices down. The NCAA certainly qualifies as having monopsonistic power because the NCAA controls most of this particular labor market.

The question becomes, if college athletes do not receive all of the revenue or value that they generate, then where does that revenue go? The answer to this is more complicated than most cases of monopsonistic power. In most monopsonies, the excess revenue would simply become profit for the owner. But because universities do not make "profit," the answer is less straightforward.

First, since directly paying the athletes is not allowed, the value goes to the people who are able to obtain the athletes. For example, suppose the expected marginal revenue productivity (MRP) of a college prospect is $1 million of revenue generated, relative to the cost to the athlete. If a coach is able to recruit that athlete, the coach's value just jumped up $1 million. To put it another way, college coaches are more valuable than they otherwise would be because they also have the job of recruiting athletes. We can see this as evidenced by data.

According to the Department of Education's numbers, the average revenue that came from football for NCAA Division I-A schools in 2013 was

$27.8 million. This ranges from $4.1 million at Louisiana-Monroe to $112.5 million at the University of Texas. Meanwhile, according to *USA Today*, the salaries for head coaches for these schools in 2013 averaged $1.7 million and ranged from $288,268 (Todd Berry at Louisiana-Monroe) to $5.5 million (Nick Saban at Alabama). While we do not have all the data for all of the schools, on average coaches earned 7.2 percent of the revenues that came from the football team. As a percentage, Brian Kelly at Notre Dame actually earned the least at 1.4 percent of football revenues, while Tommy Tuberville's salary was 21.6 percent of football revenues at Cincinnati.

To be sure, NFL head coach salaries are higher than head coach salaries in college. Again in 2013, the average head coach's salary in the NFL was $4.6 million, with a range from $2 million to $8 million. However, according to Forbes, the average revenue is $299 million. On average, head coaches in the NFL only earn 1.6 percent of revenue, which means that college head coaches make 4.7 times what NFL coaches as a percent of revenue.

The point here is that one would expect the contribution on the field (the marginal product) of the head coach to be similar for college football and the NFL. And given that the revenues in the NFL are more than ten times that of revenues from college football, we might expect the salaries of head coaches to be about ten times higher. Instead, we find them to be 2.6 times higher, and as many football fans know, major colleges often compete with NFL teams for coaches even though the revenues from football for major colleges are much less than NFL revenues.

There are many caveats with this analysis. Perhaps the data is not perfect, and as earlier described, direct revenues are not the only thing the football team generates. We also have to think about additional tuition and merchandise revenue. There could also be some differences in the coach's labor markets in college and professional sports, as well as differences in the way that winning affects revenues. However, given the magnitude of the differences of percentages of revenue that go to coaches, this is evidence that they are simply different jobs with different marginal products.

This all implies that coaches are more valuable in college than they are in professional sport, which is consistent with economic intuition. If athletes cannot be paid their full value, then the factor of production that can get the athletes will be more valuable. In other words, when athletes are not paid, recruiting becomes valuable.

Coaches are not the only thing that becomes more valuable when athletes are not paid. Anything that can lure the athletes becomes more valuable. Often assistant coaches are heavily involved with recruiting. Also, facilities can make a difference in recruiting. A new gym, practice facility, or stadium can be a valuable recruiting tool. Therefore, the more athletes are compensated, the more one would expect to see a decrease in coach's salaries and facilities.

Ownership and Expansion

An excellent history of the ownership of professional teams in North America is contained in an appendix to Quirk and Fort's *Pay Dirt: The Business of Professional Team Sports* (1992). There are several key points from a reading of the entertaining history of the humble beginnings of what became the multi-billion-dollar sport industry of the 21st century.

As teams became more financially successful, they were often sold as owners capitalized on their team's elevated value. While today we are accustomed to announcements that teams are sold for a billion dollars or more, there were still some extraordinary sales in the late 19th and early 20th centuries. For example, a Baltimore baseball franchise was sold in the 1890s for $40,000 (around $1 million in today's dollars). In 1909, the Phillies were sold for $350,000, or about $9.1 million in today's dollars. The value of franchises was rapidly escalating in the nation's largest markets. What must have appeared as a princely sum for a baseball team was shattered by the $500,000 paid in 1915 for the Cubs ($12.2 million in today's dollars). Most revealing in terms of the value of sport franchises in the early part of the 20th century was the $1,092,000 sale price of the New York Giants in 1919 ($15.5 million in today's dollars).

In the initial years of operations, owners and leagues learned other valuable lessons that are reflected in today's league policies. For example, when the leagues began, it was possible for individuals to be involved with the ownership of more than one team in the same league. When this occurred, players could be easily moved from one team to another to maximize revenue gains for the owner. When that took place, fans were unsure of an owner's commitment to fielding a winning team. Instead, with owners allowed to move players among two or more teams, it was clear that the owner was focused on maximizing revenue for one team at the expense of another team's success.

Limiting an individual's ownership to one team in each league helps to sustain the impression (or, as cynics would argue, the illusion) that each investor will try his or her best to field a competitive team focused on winning as many games as possible. The owners in each league, looking at the possibility of one individual owning multiple teams, concluded that ownership should be restricted to one team so that it would appear that owners were competing with each other to win championships. As discussed, owners in the NFL, NBA, NHL, and MLB are restricted to just one team per league (MLS is the exclusion).

To sustain a league and each team, owners were also required to respect the territorial market of every other franchise, agreeing not to play games with any team that was not part of the league. In practical terms, this has meant that each owner agrees not to play games in another team's market area (except for those that are part of the schedule approved by the league) or to relocate their team into the metropolitan region where other teams play their home games. For example, the Kansas City Royals cannot play games in New York that are not part of the approved schedule. Furthermore, requests for relocation cannot be within the agreed-upon market area of another team. For years, the Oakland As have wanted to relocate to San Jose. That area, however, was ceded to the San Francisco Giants by MLB in the 1990s, and as a result a relocation to San Jose has not taken place. When the New York Islanders wanted to relocate from Nassau County to the city of New York, the New York Rangers had to agree to their request as the city is part of the Rangers' primary market area.

Al Davis and the Los Angeles County Commission challenged these geographic exclusivity rules when he relocated the Oakland Raiders to Los Angeles without the approval of the league in 1982. It was his belief that the league's rules, requiring a vote of all owners to approve the relocation of a team to a market that was not already served by an NFL team, violated U.S. antitrust laws. No other owner has ever tried to move into a region without a league's approval. Eventually, when the Raiders and local governments in Los Angeles could not agree to renovate the Los Angeles Coliseum, the Raiders returned to Oakland in 1995. In 2020, the Raiders will begin their tenure as the Las Vegas Raiders, a relocation approved by 31 of the league's 32 teams.

Relocation within a team's market area does not generate the same level of scrutiny from the league. The Dallas Cowboys, for example, relocated from Dallas to the adjacent city of Irving (Texas Stadium), and then to Arlington (another suburban city in the Dallas/Fort Worth metropolitan area) without the need for any substantial review by the NFL. That move, as well as the recent move of the Detroit Pistons from Auburn Hills to downtown Detroit, were reviewed and approved by their respective leagues. Those decisions generated far less debate than when the NFL voted to allow the Rams to relocate to Los Angeles, the Chargers to move from San Diego to Los Angeles, and the Raiders to move from Oakland to Las Vegas.

To make it more difficult for a competitive league to be established or to establish its legitimacy by playing games with teams from the more established league, owners of each league have agreed not to play games against any team that is not recognized by the league. For example, prior to the merger of the NFL and AFL, NFL teams could not and did not play any sort of game (competitive or a friendly exhibition) against AFL teams. Teams do play games, on occasion, with college teams (baseball) or national teams. But when that occurs, the league must sanction the game.

Each league has expanded by adding teams in growing markets or regions, but this has been a very slow process, leaving many areas underserved. In the past, that unwillingness to move quickly created openings for competitive leagues. In the early 20th century, the American Baseball League was able to establish a secure foothold with teams in Chicago (National League had a team in this city), Cleveland (National League had decided to abandon this market), Detroit (no baseball team in the city), and New York City (in its second year of operations even though the National League had two teams in that city). The AFL was able to achieve a level of financial success in the 1960s because the NFL had failed to aggressively expand into cities that could sustain a professional football team.

The leagues' reluctance to expand is rooted in the very small incremental fiscal returns that accrue to existing owners when a new franchise is added. Adding a new team means that existing owners' portion of shared revenues declines. Suppose a league has 30 members and earns $1 billion dollars from its national media contract per year. Prior to adding a 31st team, each franchise receives $33,333,333. The existence of a 31st team reduces that share to $32,258,064. To offset this loss of more than $1,000,000 per year for each team, the existing team owners will charge a franchise fee that, in essence, represents their assessment of the present value of the future shared revenues the new team owner will receive. That fee has to be larger than the present value of the foregone revenues to existing owners. When the NHL decided to approve a new franchise to be located in Las Vegas, the new owner had to pay $500 million to join the league. A fee of that magnitude ensured that every existing owner would make a tidy profit, at least in the short term, as the fee was far larger than the value of shared revenues.

In one instance, the threats of legal action against a league by a city and state for allowing a team to relocate did create the need for an immediate expansion. In 1995, Cleveland Browns owner Art Modell requested and was granted permission by the NFL to relocate his franchise to Baltimore (where the team was renamed the Ravens). Cleveland's mayor and members of Ohio's Congressional delegation threatened legal action against the NFL; legislation was then introduced in the Congress to investigate the NFL and its practices. A new law could have set a precedent where a league could have been compelled to expand so that the region losing a team would have the right to a new franchise. However, rather than risking any interference with its business practices, the NFL's owners decided to support the creation of new franchise for Cleveland.

The potential attractiveness of the Los Angeles market for an NFL franchise had been a popular topic for conversation for years. In 2015, Rams owner Stan Kroenke decided not to renew his stadium lease in St. Louis and in 2016 the team returned to the Los Angeles Coliseum. A new, privately funded stadium will open in 2020. When the voters in San Diego decided not to support a proposed new venue for the Chargers, that team received permission to join the Rams in Los Angeles. Each team believes it can earn more money than was possible in St. Louis or San Diego. While each team believes there is greater potential for in-facility revenue in Los Angeles, there may not be much new value for the league from media contracts as the league's media partners already deliver NFL games to the market, even without the presence of a team. Football fans likely already watch games, and as a result, the presence of local teams in the Los Angeles region may not translate into a substantial shift in viewership levels for the league as a whole. The movement of the St. Louis Rams back to Los Angeles for the 2016 season suggested that the owners believed there was potential in the region. The confidence in the market's ability to generate revenue for a team is underscored but also threatened by two teams' interests in locating in the market. The presence of both teams will likely reduce the earnings that would accrue to the Rams if they were the only franchise.

In terms of overall expansion, there have been only a handful of additions in recent decades, though expansion has taken place more quickly than in the first half of the 20th century. The NFL added the Houston Texans in 2002 after returning a franchise to Cleveland in 1999. The Jacksonville Jaguars and Carolina Panthers began play in 1995. And despite the interest in American football in the United Kingdom, the NFL has decided to play one-off games in London between existing franchises, rather than expanding internationally.

The Tampa Bay Rays and Arizona Diamondbacks were the last teams added by MLB (1998). Five years earlier, the Colorado Rockies and the Florida (now Miami) Marlins joined the league. The Washington Nationals relocated from Montreal (Expos) in 2005. Some have also argued that MLB would benefit from the placement of a franchise in Mexico or Havana if relations are fully normalized with the United States and the Cuban government.

The NBA and the NHL have considered expansion back into the Seattle market. The NBA last expanded in 1995, extending its footprint to the Canadian markets of Vancouver and Toronto. In 2016 the NHL added the Las Vegas Golden Knights; the league began to play with 31 teams for the 2017–2018 season. Meanwhile, the Arizona Coyotes (formerly Winnipeg Jets) who began play in downtown Phoenix in 1996 have not been financially successful in a number of seasons; relocation may be one option for the franchise that has been successful for other teams in the league. The Atlanta Thrashers relocated to Winnipeg in 2011. In 2000, the league added the Columbus Blue Jackets and the Minnesota Wild. The latter franchise replaced the North Stars that had relocated to Dallas in 1993. Expansion to Seattle is anticipated in the next few years.

Profit Maximizers and Welfare Maximizers

Many believed that an NHL team in Las Vegas would have a market value that was less than the $500 million expansion fee the league required. There was, however, an investor willing to pay the fee. So ... why would anyone pay more than the value of an asset? Peter Sloane (1971) addressed this issue when he argued that those who own professional sport franchises could be welfare maximizers. Profit maximizers are easy to understand: someone who seeks the most tangible wealth from an asset wants the greatest possible financial return on their investment. These individuals will seek to reduce labor and other costs to the point where profit levels are the highest.

Achieving that point of profitability is easy to pinpoint theoretically but far more difficult to achieve in reality, as the owner must carefully estimate the quality of players needed to win a sufficient number of games to please fans. One might assume that the best way for teams to maximize profits is by winning 100 percent of their games and winning the league championship. However, fans in certain markets value winning more than others. In other words, it may not be in the best interest for some teams to strive for a perfect winning record; some profit-maximizing owners understand this concept and take this into consideration during drafts and in player trades. Many owners will tell you, finding the perfect combination of wins to maximize profitability is a convergence of both a science and art. It is assumed that quality players are more expensive, but it is not clear how much more a high-quality player will contribute to generating more wins from a player that is slightly less talented. Many have tried to measure that phenomenon with a statistic known as WAR (wins above replacement). An owner can use WAR to help fine tune a team's payroll in an effort to maximize profits, assuming that data can be arrayed to predict fan spending as the number of wins increases. A profit maximizing owner also prices tickets and other elements according to market demand.

Welfare maximization, on the other hand, is described as placing a higher value on winning, even if the resulting cost of players will lead to lower profits. That could occur if fans in a particular market will not pay the ticket prices necessary to afford the players needed to win more games. If an owner receives intangible benefits from more wins or a championship and has sufficient wealth to absorb any losses, that individual would be described as a welfare maximizer.

Every owner is somewhere on the continuum between profit and welfare maximization. Some lean towards welfare as opposed to profit maximization. Some lean in other direction. Typically, fans' welfare is maximized if the owner of their team is more of a welfare maximizer. In that instance, a team is likely to win more games even if the owner is not made much wealthier by ownership.

Business Acumen and Sport: Changes in Team Operations

Teams have always been in the "business" of providing entertainment to fans. What began with the selling of tickets to people interested in games has evolved into a business that delivers games through various media to fans. In addition, the fan experience inside sport venues has changed to fit the ways in which different groups of fans consume games. Some fans attend games to carefully watch all of the action on the field, court, or ice.

For other fans, the game is secondary to networking with business associates or connecting with friends and family. Some fans attend games to enjoy the identity it gives as they support their teams. It is not uncommon to find some fans in elaborate costumes that proclaim their identity as "rabid" supporters. And yet other fans attend for a mixture of reasons. Every team now seeks to tailor in-facility experiences to provide each fan segment with an experience that will encourage them to continue attending games.

Because they are serving these different fan segments, teams essentially behave as entertainment companies, providing food, beverage, retail, and seating options at varied price points and levels of quality. For example, some attendees like to eat food at their seats; others prefer to sit in clubs; and still others prefer drink rails (loge standing or seating areas) where they can enjoy food and beverages while watching a game. Decades ago sport venues were designed to attract as many fans as possible while allowing all seats to have the best possible view of the playing surface. Today, many fans want an extreme set of luxury amenities and upscale food and beverage services. Many owners have also learned that a scarcity of seats can increase the rate of pre-game ticket purchases as fans fear there will be fewer tickets available on game day. As such, today's ballparks are noticeably smaller in terms of seating capacity than older venues. Arenas built for basketball and ice hockey have generally not changed in terms of seating capacity; most offer seating for approximately 19,000 spectators. While AT&T Stadium (home of the Dallas Cowboys) can seat more than 90,000 spectators, football stadia are also a fair bit smaller than older venues.

As discussed in Chapter 1, many venues also include separate spaces for families and young children. Some teams have hired counselors to supervise play areas for young children, a service that allows parents to attend and enjoy games. These spaces are usually separated from the areas built for other fan segments. Other venues have created club spaces that make it possible for entrepreneurs with tighter budgets than the traditional luxury fan to have an area to entertain their clients at a lower cost. Many venues now also feature museums, halls of fame, games of skill such as batting cages, football passing, baseball pitching machines, and other attractions. Each is designed to enhance the fan experience for teams' unique fan segments.

However, the focus on entertainment is not limited to ensuring unique experiences for teams' fan segments. Venues are now also being used more frequently to host other sport and non-sport events. As a result, venues are being designed to facilitate both the sport of the home team and a wide range of other events, improving the efficiency of these facilities. This has not been a particularly innovative approach but is now far more ubiquitous.

The original Yankee Stadium, for example, hosted boxing matches, college football games, and religious events. There is now more emphasis on facility designs with excellent views of the action for the primary team while also offering the flexibility to host other events, concerts, and meetings.

These changes mean that ownership groups have begun to include entertainment divisions as part of their business. Some teams might expand their management to include an entertainment department with employees knowledgeable in that field. Others have subcontracted the operation of in-facility entertainment options to other firms more equipped to handle such operations.

Several teams are now anchors or principal parts of large entertainment corporations. The Detroit Red Wings and Detroit Tigers are vital to the operations of Olympia Entertainment (OE). The New York Knicks and New York Rangers are part of the Madison Square Garden Corporation (MSG). The Los Angeles Kings and Los Angeles Lakers, whose owners built L.A. LIVE (an entertainment, residential, and commercial complex across from the teams' home) and the STAPLES Center have created a new entertainment destination. The Edmonton Oilers and their new arena, Rogers Place, are part of the Oiler Entertainment Group. Before relocating to Detroit's new Little Caesars Arena (also home to the Red Wings), the Detroit Pistons were an integral part of Palace Sports and Entertainment (PSE). PSE and Olympia Entertainment have since merged as both teams use the same venue.

These new and expanded business opportunities have led to changes in the management structures of the corporations that own franchises. Organizations routinely have managers (or several vice presidents) who are responsible for real estate development and its ongoing management, media, communication, marketing, entertainment, network operations, internet, and web-based applications (also linked to their individual leagues). These are in addition to the usual mix of staff responsible for player development and the team itself.

To help explore the structure and changing patterns of ownership, Tables 2.2 through 2.5 identify the majority owners of each franchise from the four major sports leagues and their principal business (the source of wealth generated to acquire the team, or related businesses developed with the team as the anchor). In only a few instances is the principal business interest "sport," which means the team itself and its direct operations alone are not the central business of the owner. While there exist some teams that were initially purchased to be the main or sole business interest, some of these owners have also expanded into the real estate, media, or entertainment businesses.

For example, George Steinbrenner focused almost entirely on the Yankees for much of his ownership tenure. However, the family owns 34 percent of the highly successful YES television network. The Yankees, therefore, are focused on baseball and leveraging the team for the success of their media investment. Alternatively, the Rooney family (which founded the Pittsburgh Steelers), has not created a television network, as the NFL pools each team's regular season games in the national package.

Table 2.2 MLB Team Owners and Related Business Interests

Franchise	Majority Owner	Related Business Interest/ Source of Wealth
Arizona Diamondbacks	Ken Kendrick	Software, education, banking
Atlanta Braves	Liberty Media	Media
Baltimore Orioles	Peter Angelos	Law
Boston Red Sox	John Henry	Sports, entertainment
Chicago Cubs	Ricketts family	Financial services, media
Chicago White Sox	Jerry Reinsdorf	Real estate and sports franchises
Cincinnati Reds	Robert Castellini	Food services
Cleveland Indians	Lawrence Dolan	Cable television
Colorado Rockies	Charles & Richard Monfort	Food services
Detroit Tigers	Christopher & Marian Ilitch	Sports, entertainment, food services
Miami Marlins	Jeffrey Loria	Sports, new real estate project
Houston Astros	Bruce Sherman	Financial services
Kansas City Royals	David Glass	Retail
Los Angeles Angels	Arturo Moreno	Billboards, real estate
Los Angeles Dodgers	Guggenheim Partners	Financial services
Milwaukee Brewers	Mark Attansio	Financial services
Minnesota Twins	James Pohlad	Mixed business conglomerate
New York Mets	Wilpon family	Real estate
New York Yankees	Steinbrenner family	Sports, media
Oakland Athletics	John Fisher	Retail
Philadelphia Phillies	David Montgomery	Sports, syndicate
Pittsburgh Pirates	Robert Nutting	Media and resorts
San Diego Padres	Ron Fowler & Brian O'Malley	Sports, financial services
San Francisco Giants	Charles Johnson & Peter Magowan	Sports, financial services
Seattle Mariners	John Stanton	Nintendo
St. Louis Cardinals	William DeWitt, Jr.	Sports, real estate
Tampa Bay Rays	Stuart Sternberg	Financial services
Texas Rangers	Ray Davis	Energy
Toronto Blue Jays	Rogers Communication	Media
Washington Nationals	Theodore Lerner	Real estate, entertainment, media

The far more common outcome is for owners who have accumulated wealth from other enterprises to add a team to their holdings. The shift to teams as part of real estate development efforts, entertainment corporations, or media corporations is vividly illustrated in Tables 2.2 through 2.5. It is easier to appreciate this shift against a backdrop of the types of ownership structures that existed prior to the changes in the sport business. We turn to those next before refocusing on the role of teams in real estate development, entertainment, and the media in subsequent chapters.

Table 2.3 NFL Team Owners and Related Business Interests

Franchise	Majority Owner	Related Business Interest/ Source of Wealth
Arizona Cardinals	William Bidwell	Sports
Atlanta Falcons	Arthur Blank	Retail, sports
Baltimore Ravens	Stephen Bisciotti	Business services
Buffalo Bills	Terry & Kim Pegula	Energy, real estate
Carolina Panthers	Jerry Richardson	Food services
Chicago Bears	McCaskey family	Sports
Cincinnati Bengals	Michael Brown	Sports
Cleveland Browns	Jimmy Haslam	Energy, real estate
Dallas Cowboys	Jerry Jones	Oil, sports, entertainment
Denver Broncos	Patrick Bowlen	Oil, sports
Detroit Lions	Martha Firestone Ford	Automobile
Green Bay Packers	Shareholder owned	Public with vested control
Houston Texans	Robert McNair	Energy
Indianapolis Colts	James Irsay	Sports
Jacksonville Jaguars	Shahid Khan	Automobile
Kansas City Chiefs	Lamar Hunt family	Oil, sports
Miami Dolphins	Stephen Ross	Real estate
Minnesota Vikings	Zygi Wilf	Real estate
New England Patriots	Robert Kraft	Business conglomerate
New Orleans Saints	Thomas Benson	Financial services
New York Giants	John Mara & Steve Tisch	Entertainment
New York Jets	Woody Johnson	Pharmaceuticals
Oakland Raiders	Mark Davis	Sports
Philadelphia Eagles	Jeffery Lurie	Entertainment
Pittsburgh Steelers	Art Rooney	Sports
Los Angeles Chargers	Alex Spanos	Real estate
San Francisco 49ers	Denise & John York	Retail/shopping malls
Seattle Seahawks	Paul Allen	Computer software
Los Angeles Rams	Stan Kroenke	Sports, real estate
Tampa Bay Buccaneers	Malcolm Glazer	Business syndicate
Tennessee Titans	Kenneth Adams IV	Energy, ranching, real estate
Washington Redskins	Daniel Snyder	Advertising

Mergers, Acquisitions, and Integration

Firms can increase their size by acquiring or merging with other businesses. Often when teams merge with other businesses, it is a strategic decision related to how a team can be leveraged to benefit other assets, and vice versa – to enhance franchise ownership value. Teams are becoming more adept at leveraging various parts of their business to increase revenue. One of the major reasons ownership structures are becoming more complex in the sport industry is because teams are becoming more integrated, both horizontally and vertically.

Table 2.4 NBA Team Owners and Related Business Interests

Franchise	Majority Owner	Related Business Interest/ Source of Wealth
Atlanta Hawks	Tony Ressler	Financial services
Boston Celtics	Wycliffe Grousbeck	Financial services, medical information
Charlotte Hornets	Michael Jordan	Sports
Chicago Bulls	Jerry Reinsdorf	Real estate and sports franchises
Cleveland Cavaliers	Dan Gilbert	Financial services
Dallas Mavericks	Mark Cuban	Information technology
Denver Nuggets	Stan Kroenke	Real estate, business syndicate, media
Detroit Pistons	Tom Gores	Financial services
Golden State Warriors	Joseph Lacob & Peter Guber	Venture capitalism, entertainment
Indiana Pacers	Herbert Simon	Shopping malls, real estate
Houston Rockets	Tilman Fertitta	Restaurants
Los Angeles Clippers	Steve Ballmer	Technology
Los Angeles Lakers	Buss family	Sports, real estate, media, entertainment
Memphis Grizzlies	Robert Pera	Technology
Miami Heat	Micky Arison	Tourism
Milwaukee Bucks	Wesley Edens & Marc Lasry	Financial services
Minnesota Timberwolves	Glen Taylor	Manufacturing
Brooklyn Nets	Mikhail Prokhorov	Oil and gas
New Orleans Pelicans	Tom Benson	Auto dealerships, investments
New York Knicks	James Dolan	Cable television
Oklahoma City Thunder	Clay Bennet	Oil, financial services
Orlando Magic	Richard Devos	Retail sales
Philadelphia 76ers	Joshua Harris & David Blitzer	Financial services
Phoenix Suns	Robert Sarver	Banking, real estate
Portland Trail Blazers	Paul Allen	Software
Sacramento Kings	Vivek Ranadive	Software
San Antonio Spurs	Peter & Julianna Holt	Manufacturing
Toronto Raptors	Lawrence Tanenbaum	Finance, construction
Utah Jazz	Gail Miller	Auto dealerships, media
Washington Wizards	Ted Leonsis	Software

Horizontal Integration

Horizontal integration implies that firms are buying their competition. Most leagues prevent individuals from owning multiple teams within the league, rendering horizontal integration impossible. However, teams do compete for fans with franchises in other sport leagues in the same area. If an individual owns more than one team that serves the same market

Table 2.5 NHL Team Owners and Related Business Interests

Franchise	Majority Owner	Related Business Interest/ Source of Wealth
Anaheim Ducks	Henry & Susan Samueli	Communication equipment
Arizona Coyotes	Andrew Barroway	Financial services
Boston Bruins	Jeremy Jacobs, Sr.	Sports, entertainment
Buffalo Sabres	Terry & Kim Pegula	Computer services
Calgary Flames	N. Murray Edwards	Sports
Carolina Hurricanes	Tom Dundon & Peter Karmanos, Jr.	Software, computer sales
Chicago Blackhawks	William Wirtz	Food services, real estate, banking
Colorado Avalanche	Stan Kroenke	Real estate, sports, media
Columbus Blue Jackets	John McConnell	Manufacturing
Dallas Stars	Tom Gaglardi	Hotels and restaurants
Detroit Red Wings	Christopher & Marian Ilitch	Food services, entertainment
Edmonton Oilers	Daryl Katz	Pharmaceutical sales, real estate
Florida Panthers	Vincent Viola	Financial services
Las Vegas Golden Knights	Bill Foley	Financial services
Los Angeles Kings	Phil Anschutz & Edward Roski, Jr.	Entertainment, real estate
Minnesota Wild	Craig Leipold	Financial services
Montreal Canadiens	Geoff Molson	Food services
Nashville Predators	Thomas Cigarran	Healthcare services
New Jersey Devils	David Blitzer & Joshua Harris	Financial services
New York Islanders	Jonathan Ledecky & Scott Malkin	Retail, financial services
New York Rangers	James Dolan	Media, entertainment
Ottawa Senators	Eugene Melnyk	Pharmaceuticals
Philadelphia Flyers	Comcast Spectacor	Media
Pittsburgh Penguins	Mario Lemieux & Ron Burkle	Retail, manufacturing, sports
San Jose Sharks	Hasso Plattner	Software
St. Louis Blues	Tom Stillman	Beer
Tampa Bay Lightning	Jeff Vinik	Financial services
Toronto Maple Leafs	Lawrence Tanenbaum	Finance, construction
Vancouver Canucks	Francesco, Roberto & Paolo Aquillini	Real estate
Washington Capitals	Ted Leonsis	Computing services
Winnipeg Jets	Mark Chipman	Automobiles, entertainment, investments

(the Detroit Tigers and Detroit Red Wings, for example, are both owned by the Ilitch family), there is a level of horizontal integration that can be achieved.

Horizontal integration can also be achieved in sport business with its application to entertainment; because spectator sport is a form of entertainment, franchise owners can incorporate their team into a set of other amusement options. As described earlier, Olympia Entertainment Madison Square Garden, and the recently created Oak View Group are each examples of horizontal integration between teams and entertainment companies.

There are several reasons for owners to pursue horizontal integration strategies. The classic reason is to eliminate competition within and between the spectator sport and entertainment businesses. If the same firm owns multiple teams and entertainment venues in an area, they can increase the firm's profits by raising ticket prices. With fewer competitors in the area, this can be done without fear that competitors will reduce the price for entertainment in their own venues.

Another reason for owning multiple teams is that there may be some efficiency gains. For example, when buying a second team (in another sport), a firm is more knowledgeable about the product and may be able to use some of the same resources already being used for their first team (venue, game-day staff, marketing team, sales staff, etc.).

A third reason for owning multiple teams might be to minimize risk. It is not uncommon for markets to have more than one professional team. Of course, fans would prefer for all of their city's teams to be the best in the league. Unfortunately, it is almost impossible for each of the market's teams to dominate their respective leagues at the same time. When this occurs (often), some fans limit their interest to the city's best-performing team, which puts the lower-performing teams at financial risk. The risk of becoming unprofitable would then encourage ownership to make a change to restore stability. However, if the same people own all the teams, ownership need not be as concerned with profitability if one of their teams' performance begins to decline – as long as at least one of their franchises remains successful.

Horizontal Ownership and the NFL

The NFL does not allow individuals with a share of ownership of an NFL team in one market to own part of teams from another sport in the same market area. This issue of cross-ownership in the same market is not part of the governance issues for the other sport leagues. As a result, if an NFL owner wants to own another team from another sport, that franchise cannot be in the same market as the NFL team. For example, Paul Allen owns the Seattle Seahawks (NFL) and the NBA's Portland Trailblazers, which is in a different market that does not have an NFL franchise. Similarly, Stan Kroenke owns the Los Angeles Rams (NFL), the Denver Nuggets (NBA), and the Colorado Avalanche (NHL).

Vertical Integration

Vertical integration means a firm owns various parts of its supply chain or other firms related to the business. There are many ways for teams to vertically integrate. For example, several food and beverage distribution companies own teams so their products can be sold at the venue and competitors' products can be excluded. Part of the justification for naming Toronto's MLB team the Blue Jays resulted from their initial ownership by the Labatt Blue Brewing Company. The Blue Jays (players, coaches, game broadcasts, and other charity and public relations events) were the equivalent of an advertisement for the company. Similarly, Anheuser-Busch beers are sold at St. Louis Cardinals games, which are played in a stadium that is also named after the company. While several beer companies have paid for the *naming rights* to venues (e.g., Miller Park in Milwaukee, Coors Field in Denver, etc.), this comes at a heavy cost if they do not have an ownership stake in the team.

Teams can also vertically integrate with media corporations. Because the importance of media revenue is rapidly increasing, some franchises choose to allow the same company to run the team and its affiliated media outlet. As a result, teams and leagues have begun creating their own television networks. Each of the four major leagues have their own television networks (NFL Network, NBA TV, NHL Network, MLB Network). Similarly, the Big Ten Conference has the Big Ten Network (BTN), which typically showcases football and basketball games not broadcast as part of NCAA contracts, as well as other sports and shows produced by Big Ten universities.

At the franchise level, the Cleveland Indians, Boston Red Sox, New York Mets, and the New York Yankees have each created their own networks (the Indians' owners later sold Sports Time Ohio). While there is a trend of teams creating networks, existing media outlets have also purchased teams. The Dolan family used its fortune from Cablevision Systems in New York City to purchase the New York Rangers and Knicks and then to merge all of their assets into the MSG Corporation. The Disney Company, which owns ESPN, owned the Anaheim Ducks for a brief time and the Fox Entertainment Group also owned the Los Angeles Dodgers. Disney and Fox Entertainment have since decided to focus on the delivery of content instead of teams, simplifying their own business models.

The question of whether a team or league should have the same ownership as a media outlet can be a complicated one. While some might think that it makes sense to be integrated, there are reasons not to. The most common explanation is that it is sometimes more efficient to have separate owners. Sport companies might be more effective than media firms at operating teams and vice versa. In these cases, it makes more sense to have a contractual relationship. For example, the Southeastern Conference (SEC) created its own network, but unlike the Big Ten Network, the SEC Network is owned and operated by ESPN. The SEC's member universities decided it was in their best interest not to run the network.

One other way teams can vertically integrate is by owning their minor league teams. This is not possible for the NFL because it does not have a minor league system, but MLB and the NHL have extensive minor league systems, and the NBA has a developmental league with 26 teams. It may surprise some to know that most minor league baseball teams are not owned by their major league affiliate. Most minor league teams have, instead, "player development contracts" with major league teams. This means that the major league team is in charge of everything that happens on the field or ice, but the minor league owner is in charge of the facility and promoting the games.

Sometimes there are cross-marketing benefits if a major league team owns its minor league affiliate. This can be done by strategically deciding where the minor league affiliates are placed. For example, in the past MLB teams tried to have minor league affiliates throughout the country to develop a national fan base. This has changed more recently since it is easier to move players between the major league team and the minor league affiliates if there is a high degree of geographic integration. The Cleveland Indians have their AAA affiliate in Columbus (2.5 hours from Progressive Field) and their AA team in Akron (1 hour away). The New York Yankees have their AAA affiliate in nearby eastern Pennsylvania. Several hockey teams now have their minor league affiliates playing their home games in the same arena as the NHL team. The geographic concentration may also help to excite the local fan base as a new prospect moves through the minor leagues, establishing player interest before they even reach the big leagues.

Strange Bedfellows in Minor League Baseball

Some minor league teams are owned by their major league affiliate and some are not, but there is a notable case involving the minor league team in Vero Beach, Florida. From 1980 to 2006, the Los Angeles Dodgers owned and operated the Vero Beach Dodgers in the Class A Florida State League. Vero Beach had been the home of the Dodgers' spring training facility and was part of the Dodgertown complex. But in 2006 the Tampa Bay Rays took over operations of the team on the field and renamed the team the Vero Beach Rays. For many minor league teams, players are under contract with the Major League team but the venue and related entertainment offerings are owned by another company. The unique situation in Vero Beach is that the Tampa Bay Rays hire the players but the Dodgers still own the team, which means their company operates the stadium. The Dodgers also receive revenues from the team.[4] It is difficult to know if the Dodgers were rooting for or against the Vero Beach Rays (Shelley, 2006), but the team was ultimately sold to Ripken Baseball and moved to Port Charlotte to become the Charlotte Stone Crabs.

In summary, what has changed the sport business has been the merging of teams into conglomerates that seek to leverage the media, entertainment, and real estate development. Fewer and fewer teams are "just teams," and this means that those seeking careers in the sport business world have to be as familiar with the changing entertainment, media, and real estate markets as they are with the metrics used to evaluate players' performance.

Notes

1 The Green Bay Packers, today, are still controlled by an executive board that is directly connected to the group of business leaders who originally saved the team.
2 For more information, see http://www.ncaapublications.com/p-4443-division-i-revenues-and-expenses-2004-2015.aspx
3 The University of Michigan is one example of a public university that publishes their Athletic Department's financial reports; see http://finance.umich.edu/reports/2016/financial-statements/
4 More details can be found at http://dodgers.scout.com/2/586774.html

References

Branscombe, N. & Wann, D. L. 1991. The positive social and self-concept consequences of sports team identification. *Journal of Sport and Social Issues* 15 (2): 115–127.

Fort, R., & Winfree, J. 2013. *15 sports myths and why they're wrong*. Stanford, CA: Stanford University Press.

Gabler, N. 2007. *Walt Disney: The triumph of the American imagination*, 2nd ed. New York: Alfred A. Knopf.

Gottdiener, M. 2001. *The theming of America: American dreams, media fantasies, and themed environments*, 2nd ed. Boulder, CO: Westview Press.

Hannigan, J. 1998. *Fantasy city: Pleasure and profit in the postmodern metropolis*. London: Routledge.

Heffernan, C. 2016. The Ebbsfleet United fan ownership experience, *These Football Times* March 9, 2016, https://thesefootballtimes.co/2016/03/09/the-ebbsfleet-united-fan-ownership-experiment/ (accessed August 1, 2018).

Kuper, S., & Szymanski, S. 2012. *Soccernomics*. New York: Nation Books

Levine, P. 1993. *Ellis Island to Ebbets Field: Sport and the American Jewish experience*. Oxford: Oxford University Press.

Mandelbaum, M. 2004. *The meaning of sports: Why Americans watch baseball, football, and basketball and what they see when they do*. Cambridge, MA: Perseus Books Group, Public Affairs.

McCormack, J. B. & Chalip, L. 1988. Sport as socialization: A critique of methodological premises, *The Social Science Journal* 25(1): 83–92.

McIntosh, M. 1971. Changes in the organization of thieving. In *Images of deviance*, ed. S. Cohen. Harmondsworth, U.K.: Penguin.

Lundeen, A., & Pomerleau. 2014. "Corporations make up 5 percent of businesses but earn 62 percent of revenues, *Tax Foundation*. Retrieved from http://taxfoundation.org/blog/corporations-make-5-percent-businesses-earn-62-percent-revenues (accessed September 15, 2015).

Quirk, J. P., & Fort, R. D. 1992. *Pay dirt: The business of professional team sports*. Princeton, NJ: Princeton University Press.

Riess, S. A. 1980. Sport and the American dream: A review essay. *Journal of Social History* 14: 295–303.

Shelley, B. 2006. No more Vero Dodgers? Not entirely! Message posted November 4 to http://dodgers.scout.com/2/586774.html (accessed May 10, 2011).

Thompson, E. P. 1981. *Protest and survive*. London: Monthly Review Press.

Wheeler, R. F. 1978. Organized sport and organized labour: The workers' sport movement. *Journal of Contemporary History* 13: 191–210.

Chapter 3

Financial Statements, Revenues, and Costs

Financial Statements

This chapter examines the financial statements and sources of revenues and costs for different types of teams and businesses. As Chapter 2 made clear, because of the various ownership structures, teams often indirectly affect various revenue streams of a larger entertainment or media company. This implies that the full value of a team may not be found on a team's financial statements. Nonetheless, this chapter focuses more on direct revenues and the costs of operating a team. Financial statements provide the raw data that is vital to understanding the financial health and growth of a firm. It is understandably difficult to obtain financial data on teams. Publicly traded companies, like those on the New York Stock Exchange or the NASDAQ, are required to periodically file with public agencies four different financial statements: balance sheets, income statements, statements of cash flow, and statements of retained earnings.

Financial statements should be used to examine the health of a company, identify its financial shortcomings, and focus its leaders' attention on remedial steps. The financial statements of publicly traded companies are typically used to ensure that stock prices are appropriate. Financial statements give investors the knowledge to discover a company's value. In professional sport, however, it is far more difficult to determine the strength of a team's finances.

Although teams do give those financial statements to their league, privately held teams are not required to file these documents with regulatory agencies. While analysts do not have access to the financial statements for most teams, these documents are sometimes made available to sport-related businesses, such as Nike or Callaway Golf. Teams' financial documents are occasionally made available to the public as well, such as when the Arizona Coyotes' income statement became public when the team filed for bankruptcy in 2009. Some of the Green Bay Packers' financial data are also disclosed because the franchise is owned by a community institution.

While financial statements for professional teams are difficult to come by, these documents are easier to come by for college athletic programs.

In the case of collegiate sport, the athletic departments of public universities must disclose their financial documents. This permits insight into the magnitude of various revenues and costs for different universities and even for different sports. Athletic departments, however, are part of a university, and the total contribution of an athletic department to its university, or the contribution the university may make to its athletic program, is not easy to detect. However, financial statements from athletic departments do offer insight into where college teams get a majority of their revenue.

Of course, financial statements rarely tell the whole story about a firm. Industry knowledge is also useful. For example, financial statements of a team do not describe its impact on other holdings of the company. It is also very easy to transfer profits within a conglomerate. For instance, if a team is owned by a food or beverage company, the team could simply "overpay" for concession rights. This is not a common practice, but it shows the ease with which the financial statements can be manipulated. Furthermore, sometimes owners will pay themselves or family members a salary. That salary item appears as an expense and lowers the reported profits. There are various ways teams can change the profit levels described to fans. As Paul Beeston, former vice president of baseball operations for the Toronto Blue Jays, once said,

> Anyone who quotes profits of a baseball club is missing the point. Under generally accepted accounting principles, I can turn a $4 million profit into a $2 million loss, and I can get every national accounting firm to agree with me.
>
> (Millson 1987, 137)

Casual observers might wonder why teams would have an incentive to manipulate financial statements. One reason might be taxes. If there are different tax rates for various holdings of a company, owners will want to move profits to where the tax rate is the lowest. This concept is discussed further in Chapter 12. It should also be noted that when teams release their financial documents, the documents are often used in negotiations. These negotiations can be between the players and owners trying to set parameters for payrolls or between an owner and a local government being asked to provide a subsidy for a new facility. It can be beneficial for teams to obscure profits in order to present as strong a case as possible for government support for arenas, ballparks, and stadiums, or for lower salary demands. Because of these circumstances and the sport industry's elevated public profile, the financial statements that are released are often done to sway voters, fans, or the media – meaning it may not be appropriate to take their findings at face value.

So, even though there is some financial data available for teams, it is easy to manipulate these figures to advance political positions. Nonetheless, in this chapter, we examine some of the available statements. Even if the financial statements might not tell the whole story, they do provide useful data in terms of revenue sources and other key aspects of the sports industry. It also is important that all future sports managers have the skill to interpret and understand these documents.

Balance Sheets

Balance sheets illustrate a firm's assets and liabilities. A firm's assets are essentially anything the firm owns, including payments owed. Liabilities are the firm's debt (anything the firm owes directly) or the equity financing (the investment made by the owners). If a firm has more assets than liabilities, the difference is stockholder's (or owner's) equity. Another way of looking at it is if the firm or team ceased operations, the value to the owners would equal its assets minus its liabilities.

$$\text{Stockholder equity} = \text{Assets} - \text{Liabilities}$$

It is important to note that the balance sheet is a snapshot in time. It essentially shows the current wealth of a firm, team, or department. Because the Green Bay Packers are "publicly" owned, their balance sheets are available. As an example, Table 3.1 shows their balance sheet for 2016 and 2017. It is easy to get a basic idea of a team's financial health from its balance sheets. We will look at financial ratios later in the chapter, but one can tell that the Packers are, financially, quite secure.

Balance sheets generally divide assets and liabilities into groups relative to liquidity. In other words, there are short-term assets known as *current assets* and short-term liabilities known as *current liabilities*. Something is usually considered a current asset if it can be converted into cash within one

Table 3.1 Green Bay Packers' Balance Sheet, 2016 and 2017 ($thousands)

	2016	*2017*
Assets		
Cash and investments	357,697	397,166
Unamortized signing bonuses, net	88,489	95,070
Property and equipment, net	327,303	340,695
Other	54,024	83,006
Total assets	827,513	915,937
Liabilities and Equity		
Debt	111,063	103,803
Compensation liabilities	46,575	47,382
Other liabilities	136,849	150,598
Equity	533,026	614,154
Total liabilities and equity	827,513	915,937

year and a current liability if it needs to be paid within one year. Current assets are generally items such as cash, inventory, and accounts receivable (money owed to the company). Current liabilities are accounts payable, notes payable, and accruals. Fixed assets are long-term assets, usually things like automobiles or buildings. Long-term liabilities are things that do not need to be paid within one year.

It is also instructive to know that in 2017, Titletown, a mixed use real estate development with numerous amenities for public use (ice skating rink, snow slide hill, and public football field) opened directly across from Lambeau Field (the Packers' home stadium). Titletown is an independent entity and its revenues and profitability would not be included in documents related to the team.

Table 3.2 shows balance sheets for Nike Inc. from 2013 to 2017. Since Nike is a publicly traded company, this is a slightly more traditional balance sheet. In addition to assets and liabilities, it includes some information regarding preferred and common stock. Notice that for each year the total assets must equal total liabilities and shareholder equity. Nike's total assets far outweigh their total liabilities, and the firm's equity seems to be increasing at a robust rate.

Income Statements

An income statement provides a financial summary of a firm across a period of time, typically a year or quarter. The income statement lists the firm's revenues, costs, and profits. Some detail regarding the firm's taxes and any earnings or dividends per share if the firm is publicly traded is also included. Fortunately, many more income statements are available for sports teams than balance sheets. The Green Bay Packers' 2016 and 2017 income statements are presented in Table 3.3.

Income statements are available for other teams as well, but we turn next to the income statement for Nike. Table 3.4 shows revenues and expenses for Nike but does not go into detail regarding various revenue streams or types of costs. Instead, it provides details regarding financing and taxes. While Nike did not always make interest payments, it should be noted that interest payments are deducted from profits before taxes. After the taxes are taken out, the earnings are shown per share (EPS). As this shows, income statements from publicly traded companies typically do go into detail regarding financial data.

Table 3.5 illustrates the revenues and expenses of the ten largest athletic departments in 2016. These data are also available for specific teams, such as football, men's basketball, and women's basketball. Each of the athletic departments in Table 3.5 are profitable, though it is quite common for even large athletic departments to run cash-negative.

Table 3.2 Nike's Balance Sheet, 2013–2017 ($millions)

End of Fiscal Year	05/2013	05/2014	05/2015	05/2016	05/2017
Assets					
Current assets	–	–	–	–	–
Cash	–	–	–	–	–
Cash and cash equivalents	3,337	2,220	3,852	3,138	3,808
Short-term investments	2,628	2,922	2,072	2,319	2,371
Total cash	5,965	5,142	5,924	5,457	6,179
Receivables	3,117	3,434	3,358	3,241	3,677
Inventories	3,434	3,947	4,337	4,838	5,055
Deferred income taxes	308	355	389	–	–
Prepaid expenses	802	818	1,968	1,489	1,150
Total current assets	13,626	13,696	15,976	15,025	16,061
Non-current assets	–	–	–	–	–
Property, Plant, and Equipment					
Gross property, plant, and equipment	5,500	6,220	6,352	7,038	7,958
Accumulated Depreciation	–3,048	–3,386	–3,341	–3,518	–3,969
Net property, plant, and equipment	2,452	2,834	3,011	3,520	3,989
Goodwill	131	131	131	131	139
Intangible assets	382	282	281	281	283
Deferred income taxes	993	1,651	2,201	2,439	2,787
Total non-current assets	3,958	4,898	5,624	6,371	7,198
Total assets	17,584	18,594	21,600	21,396	23,259
Liabilities and Stockholders' Equity					
Liabilities	–	–	–	–	–
Current liabilities	–	–	–	–	–
Short-term debt	178	174	181	45	331
Accounts payable	1,646	1,930	2,131	2,191	2,048
Taxes payable	290	636	245	244	280
Accrued liabilities	1,572	1,993	3,375	2,445	2,347
Other current liabilities	240	294	402	433	468
Total current liabilities	3,926	5,027	6,334	5,358	5,474
Non-current liabilities	–	–	–	–	–
Long-term debt	1,210	1,199	1,079	2,010	3,471
Deferred taxes liabilities	1,292	1,544	1,480	1,770	1,907
Total non-current liabilities	2,502	2,743	2,559	3,780	5,378
Total liabilities	6,428	7,770	8,893	9,138	10,852

(continued)

Table 3.2 Continued

End of Fiscal Year	05/2013	05/2014	05/2015	05/2016	05/2017
Stockholders' Equity					
Common stock	–	–	–	–	–
Additional paid-in capital	5,184	5,868	6,776	7,789	8,641
Retained earnings	5,695	4,871	4,685	4,151	3,979
Accumulated other comprehensive income	274	85	1,246	318	−213
Total stockholders' equity	11,156	10,824	12,707	12,258	12,407
Total liabilities and stockholders' equity	17,584	18,594	21,600	21,396	23,259

Table 3.3 Green Bay Packers' Income Statement, 2016 and 2017 ($thousands)

	2016	2017
Revenue		
National	222,555	243,978
Local	186,156	197,424
Total Revenue	408,711	441,402
Expenses		
Player costs	165,671	192,507
Team	43,339	47,698
Sales and marketing	51,783	56,612
Operations and maintenance, net	27,152	30,046
General and administrative	45,742	49,187
Total expenses	333,687	376,050
Profit from operations	75,024	65,352
Net income	48,941	72,772

Statement of Retained Earnings

Statements of retained earnings report the profits that firms keep, as opposed to making a distribution to shareholders in the form of dividends. The statement typically reconciles how much of the profits go to preferred stockholders[1] and common stockholders, and how much the company retains against future losses or for future investments. This statement can give some useful information to investors or analysts. Some may think that if a company is not offering the highest possible dividends to shareholders, then it is not successful. If the statement of retained earnings shows that the company is retaining profits, however, it could be a sign that the firm's leadership places a high value on quick access to funds for future investments or to protect against future losses. Retained earnings could be a sign that a firm's leadership

Table 3.4 Nike's Income Statement, 2013–2017 ($millions)

End of Fiscal Year	05/2013	05/2014	05/2015	05/2016	05/2017
Revenue	25,313	27,799	30,601	32,376	34,350
Cost of revenue	14,279	15,353	16,534	17,405	19,038
Gross profit	11,034	12,446	14,067	14,971	15,312
Operating Expenses					
Sales, general and administrative	7,780	8,766	9,892	10,469	10,563
Total operating expenses	7,780	8,766	9,892	10,469	10,563
Operating income	3,254	3,680	4,175	4,502	4,749
Other income (expense)	18	-136	30	121	137
Income before taxes	3,272	3,544	4,205	4,623	4,886
Provision for income taxes	808	851	932	863	646
Net income from continuing operations	2,464	2,693	3,273	3,760	4,240
Net income from discontinuing ops	21	–	–	–	–
Net income	2,485	2,693	3,273	3,760	4,240
Net income available to common shareholders	2,485	2,693	3,273	3,760	4,240
Earnings per Share					
Basic	1.39	1.52	1.90	2.21	2.56
Diluted	1.35	1.49	1.85	2.16	2.51
Weighted Average Shares Outstanding					
Basic	1,795	1,767	1,723	1,698	1,658
Diluted	1,833	1,812	1,769	1,742	1,692
EBITDA	3,767	4,312	4,824	5,164	5,465

anticipates the emergence of valuable future investment opportunities and is setting aside money to take advantage of those possibilities. For Nike, the statement of retained earnings is essentially a subset of the income statement. For example, we know from the income statement that their (diluted) earnings per share in 2017 were $2.31 and their dividend was $0.74. This implies that they retained $1.57 per share or 67.9 percent of earnings.

Statement of Cash Flows

As the name would suggest, this document reports cash flows across different time periods. The statement reports cash flows from operating, investment, and financing activities. Operating cash flows need to be positive; if negative, a business may not be viable. The cash flow report identifies

Table 3.5 Revenues and Expenses of the Ten Largest Athletic Departments, 2016 ($millions)

	Texas A&M	Texas	Ohio St	Alabama	Michigan	Oklahoma	LSU	Florida	Tennessee	Auburn
Revenues										
Ticket sales	$47.8	$60.9	$61.4	$40.1	$49.6	$39.7	$45.2	$27.7	$36.8	$32.1
Contributions	$75.5	$42.2	$33.1	$29.7	$37.6	$46.6	$33.5	$43.1	$34.1	$35.7
Rights/ Licensing	$57.9	$75.0	$60.4	$66.3	$62.7	$55.1	$57.1	$62.2	$61.5	$54.4
Student fees	$0	$0	$0	$0	$0	$0	$0	$2.4	$1.0	$5.0
School funds	$0	$0	$0.8	$7.9	$0.3	$0	$0	$1.9	$0	$1.9
Other	$13.3	$9.9	$15.8	$19.9	$13.7	$8.9	$5.8	$4.0	$7.1	$10.9
Total revenues	$194.4	$188.0	$170.8	$164.0	$163.9	$150.4	$141.7	$141.4	$140.4	$140.0
Expenses										
Coaching/ Staff	$40.7	$58.6	$61.8	$49.6	$56.2	$43.5	$41.3	$50.8	$41.7	$45.6
Scholarships	$9.7	$11.7	$19.2	$15.5	$23.2	$12.5	$15.3	$13.4	$13.7	$15.6
Facilities/Overhead	$39.5	$32.8	$42.2	$25.3	$30.6	$27.2	$23.0	$21.2	$31.2	$23.6
Other	$47.2	$68.3	$43.6	$54.8	$47.9	$44.1	$44.2	$35.9	$41.4	$40.0
Total expenses	$137.1	$171.4	$166.8	$145.3	$157.9	$127.3	$124.0	$121.3	$128.0	$124.9

Source: USA Today.

operating profits after payment of all taxes and allowances for capital depreciation and changes in inventories and accounts receivable or payable. Investment cash flows deal with buying and selling various investments, such as assets and business interests. Financing cash flows are any cash flows that deal with either debt or equity financing. An example of a cash flow statement appears in Table 3.6.

Notice from the income statement that net income in 2017 was $4.24 billion, which carries over to the statement of cash flows. There are, however, other things, such as deferred taxes, that are included from operating activities. In 2017, Nike's investing cash flows were negative, but this is from investments for capital items. Their cash from financing activities is also negative, but much of that includes dividends given to shareholders. Overall the company's cash flows were positive, but it is not always clear that net cash flow should be too positive. After all, the goal of a company is to give shareholders their dividends, which decreases the cash available to the company. Nike's management apparently believed that by increasing cash flow slightly in 2017 they would be able to maximize future dividends.

Table 3.7 is the statement of cash flows for the Texas Rangers for 2008 and 2009. Prior to their sale, the team had been placed into bankruptcy to facilitate the transaction. Without addressing the legal issues and benefits from the bankruptcy filing to expedite the sale, the data illustrate that the previous owner, Tom Hicks, had implemented policies and practices that led to extremely poor financial performance. For the calendar years ending in 2008 and 2009, losses in excess of $10 and $11 million were reported. To operate the team, the owner had to invest $36 million in 2008 (capital contributions). By 2009, the team had more than $7.4 million in cash on hand. For an organization as large as a Major League Baseball team, however, that is a meager amount.

Analyzing Financial Statements

There are many different ways to use and analyze financial statements. When trying to identify the health of a company, an analyst can compare it with other firms or analyze the data across years or quarters. Cross-sectional analysis involves comparing a firm with others for the same years or quarters, and a time-series analysis looks at trends over time. Table 3.5 offers a cross-sectional view of large collegiate athletic programs, while Table 3.3 and Table 3.4 are time series assessments of the Packers and Nike, respectively.

Various analytical techniques can be used for a cross-sectional analysis when comparing firms from the same industry. Many different statistical techniques exist to better understand if a firm is using appropriate practices and policies. Benchmarking is a popular technique where similar firms are compared with each other. A shortcoming, however, is that there are often very few firms that are similar to each other, and that can limit the available

Table 3.6 Nike's Statement of Cash Flows, 2013–2017 ($millions)

Period End Date	05/2013	05/2014	05/2015	05/2016	05/2017
Cash Flows from Operating Activities					
Net income	2,485	2,693	3,273	3,760	4,240
Depreciation and amortization	513	632	649	662	716
Deferred income taxes	21	−11	−113	−80	−273
Stock-based compensation	174	177	191	236	215
Accounts receivable	142	−298	−216	60	−426
Inventory	−197	−505	−621	−590	−231
Prepaid expenses	−28	−210	−144	−161	−120
Accounts payable	41	–	–	–	–
Other working capital	–	525	1,237	−889	−364
Other non-cash items	−124	–	424	98	−117
Net cash provided by operating activities	3,027	3,003	4,680	3,096	3,640
Cash Flows from Investing Activities					
Investments in property, plant, and equipment	−636	−880	−963	−1,143	−1,105
Property, plant, and equipment reductions	14	3	3	10	13
Acquisitions, net	786	–	–	–	–
Purchases of investments	−3,702	−5,386	−5,086	−5,217	−5,928
Sales/Maturities of investments	2,499	5,058	5,871	5,310	6,046
Other investing activities	−28	−2	–	6	−34
Net cash used for investing activities	−1,067	−1,207	−175	−1,034	−1,008
Cash Flows from Financing Activities					
Debt issued	986	–	–	981	1,482
Debt repayment	−49	−77	−26	−113	−61
Common stock repurchased	−1,674	−2,628	−2,534	−3,238	−3,223
Dividend paid	−703	−799	−899	−1,022	−1,133
Other financing activities	400	590	669	721	993
Net cash provided by (used for) financing activities	−1,040	−2,914	−2,790	−2,671	−1,942
Effect of exchange rate changes	100	1	−83	–	–
Net change in cash	1,020	−1,117	1,632	−609	690
Cash at beginning of period	2,317	3,337	2,220	3,852	3,138
Cash at end of period	3,337	2,220	3,852	3,243	3,828
Free Cash Flow					
Operating cash flow	3,027	3,003	4,680	3,096	3,640
Capital expenditure	−636	−880	−963	−1,143	−1,105
Free cash flow	2,391	2,123	3,717	1,953	2,535

Table 3.7 Texas Rangers' Statement of Cash Flows, 2008 and 2009 ($thousands)

	12-31-09	12-31-08
Cash Flows from Operating Activities		
Net income	$(11,981)	$(10,435)
Adjustments to reconcile net loss to net cash used in operating activities:		
Depreciation and amortization	5,822	11,574
Amortization of player contracts	13,268	12,071
Earnings from investments in unconsolidated entities	(5,179)	(410)
Return on investments in unconsolidated entities	2,000	(1,165)
Non-cash interest, net	(149)	153
Provision for bad debt expense	(581)	145
Loss from player transactions, net	207	110
Deferred tax benefit	–	(90)
Changes in other assets and liabilities:		
Accounts receivable	(3,490)	7,796
Merchandise inventories	(398)	(98)
Prepaid expenses, other assets, and deposits	23,307	(19,616)
Restricted cash	(588)	638
Deferred compensation and signing bonuses	(8,128)	(26,943)
Unearned revenue	1,473	(1,727)
Accounts payable and accrued expenses	388	4,443
Other liabilities	(823)	(197)
Net cash used in operating activities	15,146	(23,751)
Cash Flows from Investing Activities		
Additions to facilities, property, and equipment, net	(7,450)	(8,259)
Net cash provided by investing activities	(7,450)	(8,259)
Cash Flows from Financing Activities		
Proceeds from the issuance of debt	765	–
Capital lease payments	1,620	(639)
Repayments of debt	(2,344)	(3,364)
Net borrowing on lines of credit, net	17,300	–
Capital contributions/distributions	(17,599)	36,000
Net cash provided by financing activities	(258)	31,997
	7,439	(13)
Cash and cash equivalents, beginning of year	3	16
Cash and cash equivalents, end of year	$7,441	$3
Supplemental Disclosure of Cash Flow Information		
Cash paid for interest	$4,381	$3,735

comparisons. For example, suppose you were charged with analyzing the financial affairs of the Chicago Blackhawks. You could compare their profit or cash flow with all Fortune 500 companies, but this would seem rather useless since there is no reason to believe the profit of the Blackhawks should be comparable to a Fortune 500 company. A more reasonable approach would be to compare their data with other teams. You could choose to compare the Blackhawks' financial practices with teams that have the most in common with them, which might be other NHL teams, but some of those play in much smaller markets. Or, you could decide to compare the Blackhawks to other teams in Chicago. While a thorough analysis might involve several different comparisons, it is not obvious which one would be most valid and produce the best insights. If regional concerns are the most important, then the Blackhawks should be compared with other teams in Chicago. If, however, profits are usually league-dependent, it might make more sense to compare the Blackhawks to other NHL teams.

Time-series analysis is useful for identifying trends. Basic time-series analysis might entail calculating growth rates to try to predict future outcomes. For example, if the Blackhawks' profits are consistently increasing 7 percent per year, there might be reason to believe that that would continue if nothing dramatically changed. Some data, however, tend to oscillate. If a firm has a large growth in revenue one year, it is possible that the firm should expect growth to slow the next year. If many years of data are available, this type of change in the data can be tested.

The most helpful analytical technique might well be panel data analysis. Using panel data means that the analyst is looking at multiple firms across numerous time periods. This framework gives the analyst the advantages of more observations, and the assessment is less likely to be flawed because it is not dependent on any one firm or a year in which a single event could have impacted numerous firms. When using cross-sectional analysis, there could be an anomaly during any one year. There also could be something unique about one particular firm when using time-series analysis. If one wants to find a trend for a particular firm, the uniqueness of the firm might be lost in a large cross-section of data. An analyst has to weigh the extent to which any observation can be generalized to the performance of the firm in future years.

Ratio Analysis

Having examined some financial statements, several basic analyses can be performed and financial ratios calculated. Financial ratios are basic statistics that can be calculated from the financial statements. Financial statements actually have much in common with player statistics. It is virtually impossible to settle a debate about which player is best by using one statistic. Even though *sabermetricians* are getting better at providing one statistic that is an overall metric of a player's ability, there are still disagreements and methodological problems. First, when it comes to players, it is always a challenge to calculate the most appropriate measure of performance or quality. Is a higher batting average the most important, or would each player's on-base percentage be the most accurate measure of quality? Second, there will always be intangible qualities that are impossible to quantify. How does one measure leadership or the value of a player to his teammates? Financial ratios are similar. Although some measures such as profit margin or even profits are crucial to a firm, there is always more information required to provide an accurate picture of a firm's performance. Regardless, financial ratios can be very useful in understanding growth rates or in diagnosing a current or emerging problem. Ratios can answer important questions, such as *Is the firm's efficiency increasing or decreasing?* or *Does the firm have enough cash for its short-term needs?*

One important ratio is the *current ratio*. The current ratio gives an indication of how able the firm is to meet its short-term obligations. If the current ratio is high, it implies that the firm can easily pay off short-term debts. It is possible, however, that a firm will not want this ratio too high if they would rather make long-term investments as opposed to having a large amount of current assets.

The *quick ratio*, or the acid test, is similar to the current ratio, but it does not include inventory in the current assets as a firm's inventory is not always a liquid asset. Some types of firms can hold inventory for a long time. As a result, they may not want to include inventories when determining if they can meet their short-term financial obligations. The current ratio and quick ratio are considered measures of a firm's liquidity.

Debt ratios can be very important to teams. Debt ratios give an indication of how much a firm is using other people's money for its operations. One of the more common debt ratios, the aptly named *debt ratio*, simply calculates the ratio of total liabilities and total assets. Another common debt ratio is the *times interest earned ratio*, which is the ratio of earnings before interest and income taxes and interest. Some financial analysts suggest that this ratio should be at least 3; otherwise, the firm might have difficulty making interest payments if profits decrease.

Profitability ratios are also clearly important. The *gross profit margin* calculates what percentage of sales are gross profits. Note that gross profit only includes the costs of the goods sold. The *operating profit margin* is similar, except that it uses operating profits instead of gross profits, which means operating expenses, such as administrative, selling, marketing, and depreciation expenses are subtracted from the gross profit figure. The *net profit margin* again is similar, but it includes interest payments, taxes, and any other expenses in the costs.

Current Ratio = Current Assets / Current Liabilities

Quick Ratio = (Current Assets - Inventory) / Current Liabilities

Debt Ratio = Total Liabilities / Total Assets

Times Interest Earned Ratio = Earnings before Interest and Taxes / Interest

Gross Profit Margin = (Sales - Costs of Goods Sold) / Sales

Operating Profit Margin = Operating Profits / Sales

Net Profit Margin = Earnings / Sales

It is useful to analyze gross profit margin, operating profit margin, and net profit margin together. That way, if there is a large jump in the percentages, an analyst can tell if the change is a result of the costs of goods sold, changes in operating costs, or other financial cost alterations. If a firm is publicly traded, earnings per share is also a very common profitability ratio. Another group of ratios is *activity ratios*, which measure how fast things like inventory, accounts receivables, and sales turnover are changing across a specified time period. While this might be important for some sport-related businesses, this is not usually crucial for teams. Teams sell entertainment (through games played), so inventory is not as vital. Also, there are market ratios, such as the price/earnings ratio, but again those are used for publicly traded companies, so they are rarely available for sports teams.

Table 3.8 illustrates some ratios from Nike's balance sheet. Nike's current ratio is quite robust, implying that the company can easily sustain its short-term debts. Most firms have a current ratio greater than 1. While a value under 1 can sometimes be a concern, it does depend on the time constraint on both the current assets and liabilities.

Table 3.9 examines ratios from Nike's income statements. Nike didn't have any interest payments until 2010, and after that the obligations were still small. Nike's gross profit margin is approximately 45 percent. This means that when someone buys a Nike product, 55 percent of the price supports the actual costs of producing the goods. Nike's costs include marketing, which is similar to those faced by teams, but also includes research and development, costs that are typically not part of a team's business operations. Nike's operating profit is fairly consistent, ranging from 13 to 14 percent. The company's net profit margin was 12 percent in 2017.

Table 3.8 Basic Financial Ratios for Nike from Balance Sheets

Ratio	2013	2014	2015	2016	2017
Current	3.47	2.72	2.52	2.80	2.93
Quick	2.60	1.94	1.84	1.90	2.01
Debt	0.37	0.42	0.41	0.43	0.47

Table 3.9 Ratios from Nike's Income Statements

Ratio	2013	2014	2015	2016	2017
Gross profit margin	0.44	0.45	0.46	0.46	0.45
Operating profit margin	0.13	0.13	0.14	0.14	0.14
Net profit margin	0.10	0.10	0.11	0.12	0.12

More sophisticated financial analyses will be done later in the book. This chapter provides some essential financial concepts that need to be fully understood. While financial statements can sometimes be misleading, they do give some indication of wealth from the balance sheet and income from income statements. A firm or team's wealth and income give an indication of its location and a trajectory of its financial well-being. Furthermore, financial statements tell a story about what the company keeps and what exactly shareholders or owners are taking out of the company. The financial statements also might allow comparisons across firms or provide a sense of the firm's recent history.

Revenues and Costs

We now turn attention to the changes in team revenues and costs. Managers need to understand how these basic building blocks of financial statements have been changing for teams across the years. For example, it was noted in Chapter 1 that revenues from media sales had dramatically increased for the NFL and many teams. Facility-generated income has also increased. On the cost side, player salaries have increased as the athletes have tried to gain a share of the rising revenue streams.

Between 2008 and 2009, the Texas Rangers enjoyed a 9.9 percent increase in income from the broadcast of the team's games, from $62.6 million to $68.6 million, but as a percentage of team revenue, media-related income accounted for about the same proportion, 41.9 percent (Table 3.10). Then, in 2010, the franchise announced a new contract with Fox Sports and will receive $80 million a year for each of the next 20 baseball seasons. The dramatic increase in income from media affords numerous options for the franchise's leadership. On the other hand, NHL teams earn far less, as illustrated in Table 3.11. In addition, the NHL franchises had a combined loss of more than $270 million for the 2002–2003 season.

Stadium Revenue

Although stadium revenues have not grown at the same rate as those from media contracts, they are core components of income for most teams, and they too are growing as a result of luxury seating, improved sight lines, and enhanced retail operations. One reason these funds are so important is that each team is required to share far less with other clubs. For example, in the NFL, teams share only part of their stadium revenue, while all revenue from the league's media contracts are divided into equal shares. The importance of these agreements for managers is that an individual team can do very little to increase their share of the media revenue, but there is a lot they can do to increase their stadium revenue. As a result, team managers are keenly focused on enhancing income from in-facility operations.

While ticket sales are an important part of stadium revenue, as discussed in Chapter 1, many new revenue sources have emerged. Anyone entering a new

Table 3.10 Texas Rangers' Income Statement, 2008 and 2009

Texas Rangers Baseball Partners and Subsidiaries

Consolidated Statements of Operations (Unaudited) for the 12 months ended December 31, 2009 and 2008 ($thousands)

	12-31-09	12-31-08
Revenue		
Net ticket sales	$46,875	$39,978
Television and radio	68,797	62,583
Concessions	10,523	8,627
Stadium suite rentals	5,629	4,766
Parking	4,253	3,497
Advertising	13,261	14,074
Merchandise sales	7,807	5,817
Other, net	10,224	10,120
Total revenue	167,368	149,462
Operating Expenses		
Player salaries	75,948	70,671
Trade settlement costs	–	–
Other direct team costs	18,095	18,465
Player development	11,211	10,814
Scouting	7,736	7,026
Ballpark operations	13,102	11,374
Ticket office	2,384	1,852
General and administrative	10,481	7,793
Marketing	16,016	16,752
Merchandise cost of sales	4,319	3,184
Parking	1,726	1,192
Revenue sharing, net	(5,495)	(23,129)
Amortization of player contracts	13,268	12,071
Loss from player transactions, net	207	110
Loss on impairment of intangible assets	–	6,638
Depreciation and amortization nonplayer	5,822	5,005
Total operating expenses	174,818	149,818
Operating income (loss)	(7,450)	(356)
Other Income (Expense)		
Income from unconsolidated entities, net	5,179	410
Gain/(loss) on sale of net assets	–	–
Interest expense	(9,795)	(9,545)
Interest income	21	24
Income tax benefit	63	(968)
Net income	$(11,982)	(10,435)

Source: Deadspin.com

facility is immediately greeted with myriad choices and ways to spend money. For one thing, concession sales and parking revenue can be very substantial. Naming rights deals have become extremely common. For some teams, naming rights sponsorships can generate $20 million per year. The New York Mets, for example, sold the naming rights to their new ballpark, Citi Field,

Table 3.11 Summary of Operations, Combined League-Wide Tabulations for the 2002–2003 Season ($millions) for all NHL franchises

Revenues	Season	Playoffs	Total
Gate receipts	886	111	997
Preseason and special games	50	–	50
Broadcasting and new media revenues	432	17	449
In-arena revenues	401	14	415
Other hockey revenues	82	3	85
Total revenues	1,851	145	1,996
Player Costs			
Salaries and bonuses	1,415	14	1,429
Benefits	64	1	65
Total player costs	1,479	15	1,494
Other Operating Costs			
Other player costs	28		28
Team operating costs	259	23	282
Team development costs	69	2	71
Arena and building costs	138	7	145
General and administration	116	1	117
Advertising, marketing, public relations, and tickets	126	6	132
Total operating costs	736	39	775
Total costs	2,215	54	2,269
Operating loss (excluding depreciation, amortization, interest, and taxes)	−364	91	−273

Source: Levitt Report, Appendix I, 2004.

Note: From elsewhere in the document, 19 teams lost money; combined loss = $342.4 million; 11 teams had a combined profit of $69.8 million. The net is the same as here, namely, a loss of $272.6 million (rounds to $273 million).

for $400 million. The 20-year deal began in 2009. Table 6.8 (see Chapter 6) contains the annual revenue produced by naming rights for select sport venues.

Furthermore, facilities are used to host many other entertainment events. While indoor facilities have a clear advantage relative to generating income from non-sport activities, ballparks and stadiums also are used to host concerts, shows, and games involving sports and teams from other sports. For example, in 2016, MetLife Stadium in New Jersey (Giants and Jets) sold 540,852 tickets to non-NFL games. Gillette Stadium (New England Patriots) sold 411,089 tickets for non-NFL games. AT&T Stadium (Dallas Cowboys) sold 216,085 tickets to events that did not involve the team. Table 3.12 shows some of the top venues for the entertainment events at venues that also serve as home to a team. As many would suspect, the most popular U.S. venue is Madison Square Garden with ticket sales of more than 1 million for entertainment events. The Barclays Center in Brooklyn sold 757,487 tickets for entertainment events in 2016. Table 3.12 uses data from Pollstar, an event tracking information website, to project the number of annual events

Table 3.12 Tickets Sold for Entertainment Events at Selected Venues, 2016

Arenas

Arena	Location	Ticket Sales
Madison Square Garden	New York, New York	1,053,675
Barclays Center	Brooklyn, New York	757,141
Air Canada Center	Toronto, Ontario	702,516
American Airlines Arena	Miami, Florida	627,026
Bridgestone Arena	Nashville, Tennessee	591,954
Oracle Arena	Oakland, California	577,090
Staples Center	Los Angles, California	574,048
Bell Centre	Montreal, Quebec	571,770
Prudential Center	Newark, New Jersey	515,143
Verizon Center	Washington, DC	509,473
Madison Square Garden	New York, New York	1,053,675

Stadia & Ballparks

Arena	Location	Ticket Sales
MetLife Stadium	East Rutherford, New Jersey	540,852
Gillette Stadium	Foxboro, Massachusetts	411,089
Fenway Park	Boston, Massachusetts	374,675
Wrigley Field	Chicago, Illinois	290,323
Soldier Field	Chicago, Illinois	252,114
Lincoln Financial Field	Philadelphia, Pennsylvania	236,782
AT&T Stadium	Arlington, Texas	216,085
Levi's Stadium	Santa Clara, California	182,505
Ford Field	Detroit, Michigan	166,882
Citi Field	Queens, New York	162,009

at arenas across North America. While franchise owners do not disclose the income earned from the hosting of entertainment events, it is not unreasonable to expect that in venues selling thousands if not millions of tickets, there is meaningful additional revenue. The various in-venue revenue streams available to teams will be discussed, in detail, in other chapters of this book.

NFL In-Stadium Revenue

It is useful to look at variances of in-stadium revenue for the NFL. The NFL divides more revenue among all its member teams than any other league. Each team owner, however, can retain most in-stadium revenue. As a result, there is a management focus on maximizing income from that source, and there is a surprisingly high degree of variation. This highlights for future sport executives why facility design is so important.

Because NFL clubs do not distribute information on their earned revenues, three different estimates were developed. First, *Forbes* magazine does an annual estimate of team revenues from their facilities, and this was included. Second, a fan cost index is developed by other organizations reflecting the average amount of money people spend at games, and that figure was multiplied by the total number of tickets sold to provide a second estimate of in-stadium revenue. Third, the total number of tickets sold was multiplied by the average price to provide the most conservative measure of in-stadium revenues, as it does not include spending for food and beverages. As illustrated in Figure 3.1, regardless of which estimate is used, the Dallas Cowboys earn far more money, and there is indeed substantial variance in the amounts each team earns. There is a clear "bunching" of high revenue teams and lower revenue earners. What is essential is that there is far more variability than many would expect, illustrating the management opportunity to enhance a team's bottom line by expanding fans' spending.

NBA In-Facility Revenue

In-facility revenue is very critical to NBA teams because the income from national television contracts is lower than what exists for NFL franchises. In 2014, the NBA accepted a $24 billion, nine-year deal with ESPN and Turner (Prada, 2014). On average, this means the league can divide $2.67 billion among its 30 teams each year. Despite this agreement, NBA teams also rely on in-venue revenue streams to enhance their profitability. There is substantial variation in earnings, as illustrated in Figure 3.2.

Media Revenue

The growth of media and its importance will be discussed in Chapter 7. Before looking at the media revenue earned by the four major sports leagues, however, some other points should be underscored. First, there are two different types of contracts: national contracts negotiated by the leagues for all franchise owners and local contracts entered into individually by each team. Revenue from the national contracts is typically shared equally by all franchise owners regardless of the size of their local market (at least in the United States). There is no revenue sharing of money earned from local contracts.

There are two major factors that determine the magnitude of these television contracts. The first issue is simply the demand for watching sports on television. The rising demand for televised games is one explanation for the increasing revenues paid to leagues, conferences, and teams. The other major factor that affects television contracts is bargaining power. Today there are many more media outlets and a limited number of leagues and games available to televise. This means that leagues tend to have more leverage in their negotiations with television networks.

Consider the importance of "football Sundays." For millions of Americans, a major staple of fall afternoons is watching professional

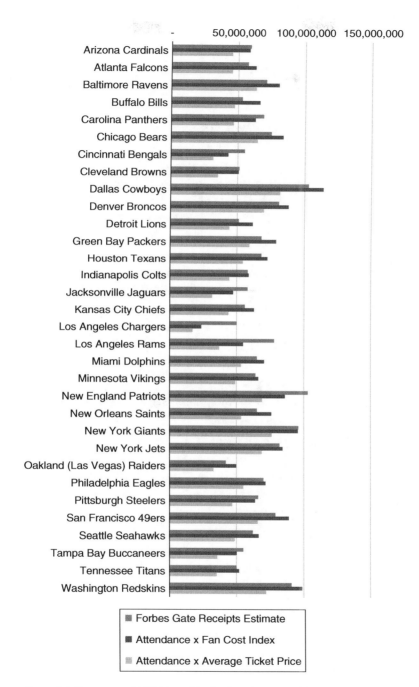

Figure 3.1 Estimates of NFL Teams' In-Stadium Revenue, 2016.

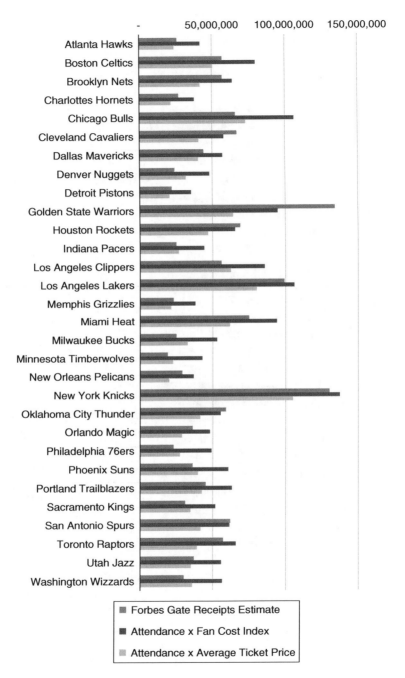

	-	50,000,000	100,000,000	150,000,000

Atlanta Hawks
Boston Celtics
Brooklyn Nets
Charlottes Hornets
Chicago Bulls
Cleveland Cavaliers
Dallas Mavericks
Denver Nuggets
Detroit Pistons
Golden State Warriors
Houston Rockets
Indiana Pacers
Los Angeles Clippers
Los Angeles Lakers
Memphis Grizzlies
Miami Heat
Milwaukee Bucks
Minnesota Timberwolves
New Orleans Pelicans
New York Knicks
Oklahoma City Thunder
Orlando Magic
Philadelphia 76ers
Phoenix Suns
Portland Trailblazers
Sacramento Kings
San Antonio Spurs
Toronto Raptors
Utah Jazz
Washington Wizzards

- Forbes Gate Receipts Estimate
- Attendance x Fan Cost Index
- Attendance x Average Ticket Price

Figure 3.2 Estimates of NBA Teams' In-Arena Revenue, 2016.

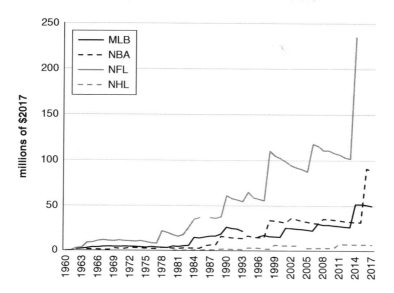

Figure 3.3 Per Team Revenues from National Media Contracts, 1960–2017.

football. But, if a network wants to put professional football on its Sunday schedule, it has to go through the NFL. There are three networks (CBS, Fox, and NBC) that have NFL games on Sunday. Given that there is one major professional football league and multiple networks, this gives the NFL an advantage. Although there are multiple sports leagues, they play in different seasons and fans are often sport-specific. Since the number of networks is increasing at a much faster rate than sports leagues, this gives leagues an advantage in bargaining power. The size of the national media contracts for each league and the rate of increase between 1960 and 2017 is illustrated in Figure 3.3.

Player Costs

As the income statements show, there are many different costs incurred by teams. Things such as marketing costs, administrative costs, travel costs, and interest payments can certainly add up. Leagues like the NHL and MLB can also have significant player development costs. The biggest cost for most professional sports teams are their players. As Table 3.5 shows, this is not the case for universities because there are restrictions on paying college athletes. But in a more competitive labor market such as professional sports, players will receive a large percentage of revenues because they produce the entertainment fans want to see. In other words, players get paid a lot because their performances sell tickets and attract viewers. We will explore how league policies affect the competitiveness of the labor market later in

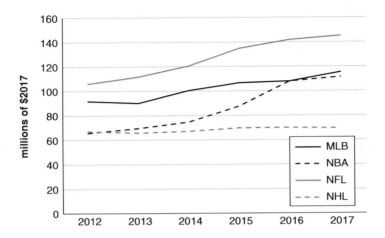

Figure 3.4 Payroll Costs.

the book, but Figure 3.4 shows how payrolls for major sports leagues have changed in the past few years.

The changes over the past few years are certainly not as dramatic as the changes over the last few decades. Team payrolls are still increasing in real terms. If we compare Figure 3.4 with Figure 3.3, it can be seen that national media contract revenue exceeds NFL payroll costs by nearly $90 million, but, in other leagues, national media contracts do not even come close to covering payrolls. The variance of team payrolls is very different depending on the league.

The Payoff from College Bowl Games

One of the most valuable games to college teams is the bowl played at the end of each regular season. For 2016–2017, the Big Ten received more than $130 million from the appearance of their teams in different bowl games (Figure 3.5). In that year, Ohio State was in the championship play-off series, and Penn State played in the Rose Bowl. Each of those games had substantial payoffs.

Notice that each of the Power Five Conferences earned more than $80 million, with three earning at least $100 million. Each conference has rules describing the distribution of these funds. Those teams that did not participate in any bowl do receive a share of the revenue received. Each of the bowl games is sanctioned by the NCAA, but they are owned and organized by independent non-profit organizations. Each of those organizations uses money from media and game-day revenue streams to pay participating teams.

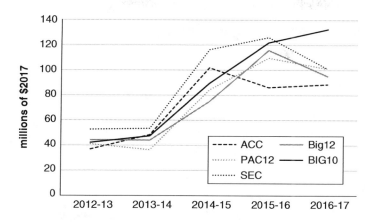

Figure 3.5 NCAA Football Bowl Payouts.

Note

1 Preferred stockholders get paid a fixed periodic dividend before any profits are given to common stockholders.

References

Millson, L. 1987. *Ballpark figures: The Blue Jays and the business of baseball.* Toronto: McClelland & Stewart.

Prada, M. 2014. NBA to announce 9-year, $24 billion TV deal with ESPN, Turner, *SBNation*, October 5. Retrieved from https://www.sbnation.com/2014/10/5/6916597/nba-new-tv-deal-espn-turner-24-billion (accessed July 31, 2018).

Chapter 4

Placemaking, Sport Venues, and the Fan Experience

Introduction

The selection of players and their development is regarded by many fans as the most important investment made by an owner. However, the design and placement of the arena, ballpark, or stadium are also vital decisions for the profitability of the team. These venues and their adjoining amenities enhance fans' experiences and create extraordinary business opportunities for team owners. The sport business has always been defined by the extent to which the games played and the athletes playing can be leveraged to enhance revenue. In early years, team owners debated the wisdom and profitability of beer sales; the issue was settled in the late 19th century when the Cincinnati Red Stockings were readmitted to the National League in 1889. The team had been expelled from the league in 1880 in part because they sold beer at their home games. After eight seasons in the American Association – a league formed in 1880 that permitted beer sales – the Red Stockings rejoined the National League and each team was permitted to sell beer.

The next phase in the process of using teams to leverage other revenue streams involved signage – sport's first taste of advertising – which was initially limited to outfield fences. Signage then spread to scoreboards and then, in the early 20th century, to telegraph lines which were used to bring game action to listeners at home; those descriptions were also sponsored. The first ballgame was telecast in the 1930s. By the end of World War II, the widespread telecast of games was debated and monetized by every league.

Today, every owner seeks to include many different amenities to leverage the benefit of owning a team. Sport managers are focused on creating enhanced sight lines and building in-venue clubs with premium food and beverage services. At the same time, there are numerous naming rights opportunities at games as well as live entertainment and other non-sport events. League-wide media issues are typically handled at both the league level and by individual teams in each sport. For example, the NFL sells the right to televise or webcast all of its regular and postseason games. Preseason games, for the most part, are distributed by the teams. In the other leagues, there are national and international contracts for many games, but individual teams have some rights to sell broadcast rights for games that are not part of the league-wide television package or web-based distribution systems that are increasingly common (MLB.com, etc.).

While some complain about the increasing cost of attending games, fans have shown themselves to be more than willing to pay the higher prices *if* upgraded amenities exist. Those amenities include wider seats, improved sight lines, and access to expanded food and beverage options. Most venues now also include a variety of different luxury seating and club areas. If a team fails to offer these amenities, attendance can decline – even if a team is winning games. The best example of a team winning on the field but failing to offer fans the amenity packages desired has been the Tampa Bay Rays. For several years, the team had an extraordinary winning percentage, but average attendance levels never exceeded 23,200 (per game). In years when the team challenged for the American League pennant and appeared in the World Series, overall attendance levels were 700,000 below the league's average. The failure to have the right mix of amenities – despite winning – attests to the value of the overall experience fans demand if they are to purchase tickets and attend games. If the experience at a venue or in the adjoining real estate is not satisfying, fans will watch a successful team on television (or their favorite video device) instead of visiting a venue altogether.

Relative to designing the fan experience, a venue should be treated as a large-scale real estate project. Team management must visualize the different ways to generate acceptable levels of revenue per square foot just as they would for any other retail space. Every team must design, package, and sell the various "locations" and square footage within their venue to properly leverage the asset. Failure to do so will result in fans voting with their feet: deciding to stay home or visiting restaurants and pubs to follow their favorite team instead of the venue. Fans want competitive teams. Once that is achieved, however, they also want amenities that enhance their experience. Those teams able to offer the most satisfying mix of amenities tend to have the greatest ability to attract fans and tend to be more financially successful than those that do not.

As has been discussed, team owners have focused on developing real estate adjacent to their venues since the late 1990s. In several instances, entirely new neighborhoods have been developed. Team owners are now actively engaged in "placemaking." Placemaking refers to the design of buildings, parks, and entertainment spaces to create a unique experience for visitors and residents. Across the past 20 years it has become common to see teams create arena, ballpark, and stadium districts in the neighborhood around their venues. The venues are then completely integrated into the overall real estate development plan. The focus on placemaking usually leads to the presence of unique retail outlets and several entertainment activities, as well as parks and public spaces. Some of these districts have also included commercial spaces as numerous businesses have found it valuable to locate near sport venues.

This chapter's two primary focuses are on (1) the venue design and the market dimensions that define the range of amenity options available and (2) placemaking activities involving adjacent real estate. It has long been realized that some fans are willing and able to pay higher admission prices to secure access to seats that offer the best available sight lines. As a result, seats closer to the playing surface have always cost more than those located elsewhere. Fans will also pay more money for more comfortable (wider) seats. Building a facility with more comfortable seats, however, reduces the total number that can be offered, as wider seats take up more space. How many wide seats should a team build at the expense of having fewer seats to sell? What is the appropriate balance between higher and lower priced seats given the distribution of income in the region and the amount of discretionary income that consumers can spend?

As discussed in Chapter 1, venues have also become far more family friendly in an effort to ensure young parents are able to enjoy a game. Numerous teams also offer play areas for young children. Some of these areas are built with additional space that offers parents a chance to see the games from the play areas. All of the play areas are staffed with counselors to entice young families to attend games and to make visits to the venue part of their go-to family entertainment activities.

This chapter will also discuss the impact of building several facilities in a single region on the aggregate demand for entertainment given existing levels of discretionary income. The importance of this last point is underscored by the recent trend of building football stadia that can host other sport and entertainment events as well as conventions. The expanding supply of days on which events can be held (hereafter, event days) has a direct effect on the revenues available to franchises. In New York, for example, where there are several all-purpose arenas, the Yankees announced in 2010 that they would begin hosting a college bowl game (Pinstripe Bowl) and consider hosting other football games, too. With the Mets' hosting of concerts at Citi Field and the Giants/Jets' hosting of concerts and other athletic events at MetLife Stadium in the Meadowlands, the New York market area suddenly had a plethora of event days available with every facility competing for a portion of the region's discretionary entertainment dollars. How much demand is there in any region for sport and entertainment, and what happens when the supply of entertainment increases faster than demand? The recent bankruptcy of the Arizona Coyotes and the financial problems encountered by the arena in which the team plays (Glendale, Arizona's Gila River Arena) have elevated a concern that some regions may have overbuilt their entertainment infrastructure. The issue of event days and balancing the supply and demand for entertainment are also considered in this chapter.

Facilities: The Early History

The original facilities used by teams were built as spectator sport began to rise in popularity in the early part of the 20th century. Team owners paid for these facilities with little or no investment by local governments. Fenway Park and Wrigley Field, built before World War I, are still the home fields for the Chicago Cubs and Boston Red Sox, and while both have been renovated several times, they are the only remaining examples of older venues built near the nexus of local public transportation systems. Most early 20th century venues were nestled into urban neighborhoods to take maximum advantage of the emerging population densities in America's cities. The need to fit venues into urban neighborhoods gave many "quirky" characteristics. Some had very short home run porches (Ebbets Field, Brooklyn; left field at the Polo Grounds in New York; right field at Yankee Stadium, and "Pesky's Pole" in Boston); very high walls to offset the short distances (Fenway Park's "Green Monster"); overhanging third decks that caught home run balls before they could fall into outfielders' gloves (Briggs/Tiger Stadium, Detroit); inclines in the outfield (centerfield at Crosley Field, Cincinnati); or overly expansive center fields (Polo Grounds, New York). The facilities with overhanging upper decks sometimes obstructed the view of the flight of the ball for fans in the lower deck. All facilities had poles to support the upper decks and those created obstructed views for some fans as well. Most of the amenities that are commonplace in today's venues did not exist. Concourses were narrow, leaving little space for retail sales. There were no clubs, suites, or any option similar to the social seating that is now seen as vital to attract younger fans. Family-friendly facilities did not exist, nor did comfort stations for women. Even in the very large stadia with seating for upwards of 60,000 spectators (the original Yankee Stadium and Municipal Stadium in New York, and Cleveland's "Mistake by the Lake"), fans found little more than seats all arranged as if they were in a theater.

Often remembered as "jewel boxes," these urban venues and their unmistakable oddities became part of the romantic folklore defining sport in the early part of the 20th century (Smith, 2001):

- The original Yankee Stadium, Bronx (1923);
- The New York Giants' Polo Grounds, Manhattan (1883);
- Crosley Field, Cincinnati (1912);
- Comisky Park, Chicago (1910);
- Ebbets Field, Brooklyn (1913);
- Briggs/Tiger Stadium, Detroit (1912).

While jewel boxes have been romanticized in folklore, in truth these ballparks provided little comfort or convenience for fans. Indeed, even after renovations, the cramped aisles and concourses and obstructed views stood in stark contrast to the romanticized view many held of these original venues. With these facilities aging and professional football emerging as another outdoor sport of increasing popularity in the 1960s, attention turned to the building of dual purpose facilities that would minimize land consumption and maximize facilities' event dates. Cincinnati, New York, Philadelphia, Pittsburgh, and St. Louis each built saucer-like facilities that were home to both baseball and football teams. To accommodate both sports, a circular venue was built; unsurprisingly, most were architecturally uninspiring destinations.

The sight lines for fans of either sport were also compromised in these circular stadia, given the need to fit both a diamond and rectangle into a round structure. For baseball, the majority of the action is concentrated within the 8,100 square feet defined by the infield diamond. Even balls that are hit to the outfield inevitably involve action within the infield. The best seats are the ones located between first and third base that circle around home plate. Football's action occurs across a space that is 100 yards from goal line to goal line and 53⅓ yards across. The best seats are at the 50-yard line with the stands pressed as close to the field as possible to ensure that those seats between each 10-yard line still offer a great view of the action. The two very different geometric shapes of the playing fields – a diamond and a rectangle – are not conducive for maximizing sight lines for fans if both games are played in the same venue. The compromises made to fit both playing fields into a single facility inevitably meant that the fans from one sport or the other were farther from the action on the field, and that meant lower revenue levels as fans would likely be reluctant to pay higher prices for compromised views of the field. The reduced revenues led to keen interest in building separate venues for baseball and football. The first region with separate facilities for baseball and football teams was Kansas City (1970s).

Since the opening of the Chiefs' Arrowhead Stadium (1972) and the Royals' Kaufman Stadium (1973), separate venues for baseball and football have been built in every major market. With the NFL's Chargers relocating to Los Angeles and the Raiders moving to Las Vegas (2020), there will be no venues shared by MLB and NFL teams.

Arenas followed a similar history in terms of initially being built and maintained by franchise owners or other entrepreneurs. In later years, several local governments made investment in new arenas. A number of new arenas in the largest markets, however, have been largely privately financed. As discussed in Chapter 2, one of the first public investments in an arena was the War Memorial Coliseum in Fort Wayne, Indiana. The venue, built by Allen County, was meant to serve as the new home for the Fort Wayne Zollner Pistons (NBA). After just a few seasons, team founder Fred Zollner decided to move the team to Detroit, leaving the county to find another tenant and other entertainment events to generate sufficient revenues to repay the bond sold to build the War Memorial Coliseum.

Arenas were initially designed solely for basketball and entertainment events. However, many venues eventually added the machinery needed to maintain a sheet of ice, making it possible to host a hockey team and other entertainment events as well. Basketball-only arenas are able to place upper level seating closer to a basketball floor. If a hockey team uses the same arena, the upper deck or second seating level must be further from the playing surface to accommodate the greater length of an ice rink for hockey. An NBA basketball court is 94 feet long and 50 feet wide. An NHL rink is 200 feet long and 85 feet wide. With an additional 53 feet at each end of the court, fans in the upper decks might not see the net as well as they would if the deck were placed closer to the playing surface as exists in the basketball-only venues. Similar blind spots could exist if an arena was constructed for basketball and that team's owner wanted to ensure fans were as close to the court as possible. For an arena to accommodate both basketball and hockey, the upper deck must have a greater setback (distance from the playing surface) to ensure both goals (for hockey) are visible from every seat.

Some hockey teams in regions with basketball franchises sought their own venues and found willing partners in Glendale, Arizona, and St. Paul, Minnesota. In Detroit, the Pistons built their own arena (Palace of Auburn Hills) in the region's northern suburbs, though its design would permit a hockey team's presence without any obstructed views of the goals. No hockey team ever joined the Pistons at the Palace; the team eventually decided to return to downtown Detroit when the owner of the Detroit Red Wings entered into a public/private partnership to build Little Caesars Arena (opened in 2017). In their decision to play in Little Caesars Arena with the Red Wings, the Pistons joined a growing number of NBA franchises that have made the decision to share venues with NHL teams. In most areas with both an NBA and NHL franchise the teams play in the same facility (e.g., Boston, Chicago, Dallas, Los Angeles, New York City, Washington, D.C.). Later in this chapter, the implications for a region having separate arenas for basketball and hockey teams will be explored.

Chapter 2 explored the relationship between private- and public-sector funding of sports venues. It discussed leagues' ability to control the supply of teams and what happened when that control was combined with the growing popularity of sport and increasing levels of consumer wealth: team owners could and did make demands that convinced the public sector in many regions to invest in facilities. If those investments were not forthcoming, the usual threat was that the team would relocate to a city that would invest in a venue. The commitment of tax money for venues reduced owners' costs, creating the opportunity for greater profits. In this chapter, we uncover that there may be an appropriate reason for the public sector to make an investment in sport facilities.

The Constrained Supply of Franchises

In the early years of professional sport in the United States, teams fell into bankruptcy or ceased operations at about the same rate as other start-up businesses (Scully, 1995). These failures, despite the success of numerous other teams, convinced franchise owners to form leagues that would facilitate profitability. There were several benefits to owners from joining a league. Of paramount importance was the establishment of exclusive market areas for each team and the assurance that no league member would schedule games with a team from a competing league. These arrangements allowed each owner to develop a fan base and ensured that, even if another league formed, teams from the original league would not participate in activities that would grant the new league legitimacy.

In the United States and Canada, the supply of teams is restricted, while demand tends to coincide with population and the amount of discretionary income available. In the wake of the baby boom and the post–World War II years, professional sport saw a proliferation of demand. Sport fans in cities without teams yearned for a franchise, and professional teams became *the* amenity North American cities wanted to offer their residents. Many community leaders recognized that the failure to have this amenity could result in the loss of talented human capital to other cities. If the leagues would not create new expansion teams, the next best strategy for cities was to offer to build a new venue in exchange for a team owner's willingness to seek permission to relocate. The draw for cities taking this approach was the idea of exclusivity: host cities could maximize their return (on the subsidy they provided teams) because no other city could have the asset; no other city could offer that amenity to its residents. Cities were guaranteed this because the leagues would limit competition through designated market areas and by refusing to recognize or play against new leagues' teams.

In addition to "major league status" and the appeal of exclusivity, evidence suggests sport venues can produce benefits for host cities through positive economic effects on real estate development and their ability to relocate regional economic activity (Feng & Humphreys, 2012; Cantor & Rosentraub, 2012; Tu, 2005; Weidner, 2016). Each study had limitations, and others have found instances where venues for professional teams might not have elevated property values or led to a relocation of regional economy activity (Noll & Zimbalist, 1997). Despite opposing theories, it is important for sport managers to understand cities' motivations for providing subsidies to fund sport venues. In most instances, whether voters or city councils are asked to support a public investment in a professional sport venue, the vast majority of proposed investments are approved (Gerretsen, Rosentraub, & Bain, 2018).

The 1950s saw the relocation of four baseball teams and, in each instance, a new facility in an untapped market for professional sport was the lure. Wisconsin's Milwaukee County launched the modern era of public support for sport facilities, paying 100 percent of the cost a new ballpark that lured the Braves, who left Boston to their American League rivals (Red Sox). Years later, Atlanta would offer the Braves another new facility and a larger population base. Baltimore paid 100 percent of the cost of the ballpark that brought the Browns from St. Louis. The team left that market to the Cardinals and assumed the name of Baltimore's original baseball team, the Orioles. The original Orioles had left Baltimore to become the New York Highlanders in 1903. The Highlanders later changed their name to the Yankees and moved from Manhattan to the Bronx.

The 1950s also saw the Dodgers leave Brooklyn for Los Angeles. Los Angeles's offer of land upon which a privately financed ballpark could be built was far more attractive than New York's interest in a having the team play its home games at the World Fair site in Queens. After agreeing to relocate to Los Angeles, a public vote on the transfer of land to the team had to be held and several law suits settled. Ironically, the location in Brooklyn, preferred by the Dodgers, would eventually become the site of the Barclays Center. That venue was built to allow the Nets to return to New York State from New Jersey. The Giants also moved west, and San Francisco was more supportive of the plan to ensure that Candlestick Park would became that team's home until 1999 when the team moved again to AT&T Park (closer to downtown San Francisco). The Giants shared Candlestick Park with the city's other professional team, the NFL's 49ers. The 49ers, in 2014, moved to a new stadium in Santa Clara (south of San Francisco). To entice MLB back to New York, after threatening to form a third major league, New York City agreed to build a new home for an expansion franchise (the Mets). Shea Stadium, which would also serve as home to the New York Jets, was built on land Robert Moses offered the Dodgers, in Flushing Meadow Park. Adjacent to one of the region's major highways, Moses' plans called for a new ballpark that would be convenient for those arriving by car and two mass transit lines (the NYC subway system and the commuter rail line, the Long Island Railroad).

The rise of competing leagues also affected cities' decisions to subsidize venues. Cities that were not granted teams by more established leagues found hosting a team from a new league was another way to ensure the presence of professional sports. For example, in 1900, the National League of Professional Baseball contracted, eliminating teams in Baltimore, Cleveland, Louisville, and Washington, D.C. The American League was created then as a competing major league in 1901 and placed teams in Baltimore, Boston, Cleveland, Chicago, Detroit, Milwaukee, Philadelphia, and Washington, D.C. In the 1960s, the American Football League battled the NFL and brought football teams to cities the older league had ignored. Similarly, the American Basketball Association brought professional basketball to

Denver, Indianapolis, Louisville, and Long Island (New York) – markets the NBA had left unfulfilled.

The building of facilities to lure teams continued into the 1980s. Indianapolis built the Hoosier Dome as part of its new convention center with substantial financial support from a local foundation. Ostensibly created to enhance the city's ability to attract conventions, the community's leadership was hardly secretive in its willingness to offer the facility and very generous lease terms that included retention of all income from suites to any NFL team willing to relocate to Indianapolis. The inclusion of luxury seating in facilities was, at the time, a novelty, and their inclusion of this asset in the Hoosier Dome was a clear incentive to pique the interest of an NFL team owner who wanted to enjoy an immediate boost in revenues. Robert Irsay owned the Baltimore Colts and when he could not secure a financial commitment from Baltimore for a new stadium, he chose to move the legendary franchise to Indianapolis. Numerous other communities would also respond to the scarcity of franchises by offering to pay for facilities. Chicago and Illinois feared the White Sox would move to Florida and increased their investment in a new ballpark in 1992. Ironically, the White Sox threat was to move to St. Petersburg where the Tampa Bay Rays now play. The Rays have had attendance problems for years, and questions remain unanswered as to the long-term viability of this region as a market for baseball. Had the White Sox moved, they too would have encountered some of the same challenges that have plagued the Rays' efforts to attract fans. Far fewer people live in the Tampa/St. Petersburg region (2.8 million) than live in the Chicago metropolitan area (9.6 million) (U.S. Census Bureau). Even if half of the Chicago region's fans support the Cubs, the White Sox would enjoy a market of at least 4.8 million people, considerably larger than what exists in Tampa/St. Petersburg.

Cleveland and Cuyahoga County feared the Indians would relocate to Florida, especially after MLB's commissioner said the franchise would be supported in its efforts to move if a new ballpark was not built in Cleveland (Rosentraub, 1999). As a result, Cuyahoga County's voters agreed in 1990 to an investment in a new ballpark, which opened in 1994. Cleveland then lost the Browns to Baltimore (the team changed its name to the Ravens) when Maryland offered to build a new stadium for the franchise without requiring an investment by the team's owner or any substantial rental fees. Baltimore and Maryland responded to the loss of the Colts by offering a facility just as Indianapolis had done. After Browns owner Art Modell announced the Browns would relocate to Baltimore, Cleveland rallied political support and convinced the NFL to immediately offer the city an expansion franchise, with the stipulation that Cleveland and Cuyahoga County had to secure financing for a new stadium before the new Cleveland Browns could begin play. A detailed list of the early set of capitulations to ensure teams would move to a city or stay is available in Cagan and deMause's

Field of Schemes (1998); Judith Grant Long's 2002 dissertation, *Full Count: The Real Cost of Public Subsidies for Major League Sports Facilities*; and Zimbalist and Long's (2006) journal article, "Facility finance: Measurement, trends, and analysis."

The examples noted above show that no city is free from the threat of relocation. What is perhaps more intriguing is that host cities are at even greater risk of losing their teams to cities within their own region. The leagues' established market areas limited (in the lightest of terms) teams' ability to move from one region to another, but intraregional moves have been left completely uninhibited. As a result, host cities often face competition with other cities within teams' designated market areas. For example, the NFL's Cowboys played their home games in Dallas before moving to Irving in 1971. In 2009, the team moved further west to a new stadium in Arlington, for which taxpayers invested $325 million. They could do so without opposition from the NFL as the league assigns the entire Dallas/Fort Worth region to the team. With a final cost in excess of $1 billion, the team's investment was more than twice as large as that made by taxpayers. It was, however, Arlington's willingness to provide the subsidy that convinced the team to relocate from Irving.

The 1990s were a watershed period when dozens of facilities were built. The public sector, in many instances, paid a substantial portion of the construction costs associated with the building of arenas, ballparks, and stadiums. In several cities, the public sector also assumed a large portion of the responsibility for ongoing maintenance costs. These annual maintenance costs, after the initial few years of operations, frequently amounted to several million dollars if the facility was to remain attractive and state-of-the-art relative to amenities and revenue production. This term, *state-of-the-art*, found its way into numerous contracts between teams and local governments and became a standard for defining what was meant by appropriate maintenance of a facility.

As cities attempted to use teams and their venues as tools to further the redevelopment of downtown areas, there was even more pressure to retain or attract teams. As described by one former U.S. senator, when St. Louis lost its NFL team, the Cardinals (to Phoenix), the general feeling was that the city's best days were behind it because it was no longer home to the team (Rosentraub, 1999). Many feared that the loss of the team would be seen as further evidence of St. Louis' decline. The fear of a loss of stature – major league status – when a region is no longer home to a major team has allowed franchise owners to become the beneficiaries of large public investments in venues. In addition, legal challenges (by cities) to the leagues' ability to control the supply of teams have been unsuccessful. Furthermore, the U.S. Congress, even when urged by various federal courts to restrain the power of the professional sports leagues, has been unwilling to pass laws that would have created an economic environment in which competitive leagues could flourish (Grow, 2015). As a result, an environment continues to exist in which cities encounter substantial challenges to attract and retain teams, and a great deal of innovative policies, practices, and politics are needed to ensure the subsidies granted to owners and players also serve as prudent investments with financial benefits for host cities.

The magnitude of public sector investments led to a series of analyses highly critical of the relations between teams and their host cities. In a variety of ways, researchers noted that the payments by local governments for facilities were a direct result of the constraint placed on the number of franchises by the major sport leagues. Zimbalist (1992) tackled this issue by noting the potential for more high-quality teams to exist as a result of the growth in the supply of high-quality athletes and the population base of various markets. He concluded that in 1903, when the American League was independent and challenging the National League for fans and players, there was one ballplayer for every 250,000 people. Given today's population of the United States and the number of teams that exist, the ratio is larger, not smaller. Today there is one ballplayer for every 400,000+ people in the United States. To be sure, there are more leagues (the NBA and the NFL, for example), and one could then argue that there has been a diminution of the talent available for baseball teams despite this impressive ratio. The obvious response, of course, is that MLB in the 21st century draws players from a much larger pool of human capital than did owners at the beginning of the 20th century. For example, in the early part of the 20th century, MLB did not include African-American players; as a result, Zimbalist's ratio for 1903 included a large segment of the population that was excluded from participation. In reality, the ratio was probably closer to 200,000 people for every ballplayer than it was to 250,000. Today there are also substantial numbers of MLB players from Central America and a score of other countries, meaning there is far more talent for MLB teams to capture. The population has increased so much that there is no deficiency in the supply of people with the ability to play MLB. The expanded supply of potential ballplayers is more than sufficient to support a larger number of teams than currently exist, meaning that Zimbalist's point remains valid.

If the supply of ballplayers is sufficient, that leaves the question of whether there is enough demand and consumer spending available to support more teams. With constant and very high attendance levels for MLB and minor league baseball, there is ample evidence that fans would support more teams. Of course, if there were more teams, prices might decline, as supply would increase. That might well be in the interest of fans, but it might not be in the best interest of team owners or local governments that have invested in facilities. The value of these investments – owning or hosting a team – lies in the artificial scarcity that has been created. After all, if every city that wanted a team had one, then being home to a team would no longer be unique or special, and the amenity would become less valuable.

Owners have an incentive to restrict supply. Similar to Zimbalist's work, Rosentraub (1999) used the growth in the United States' population to illustrate that more NFL and MLB teams could exist without overstressing markets. At the time of the study, the Dallas/Fort Worth, New York, and Los Angeles regions had grown sufficiently large that each could comfortably support additional NFL or MLB franchises. The population base in the Dallas/Fort Worth and Los Angeles regions had more than doubled since teams were originally placed in each. That population growth suggested additional teams would have little, if any, impact on the profitability of some existing franchises. Of course, the Los Angeles Rams joined the city's list of professional teams in 2016. In just a few years a sufficient amount of time will have passed to determine whether Los Angeles' other teams' revenues have been negatively impacted by the Rams' presence.

When demand increases faster than supply, prices rise, and consumers are often asked to pay more to ensure a team's presence via the contribution of tax revenues toward venue construction and renovations. With demand growing faster than supply, cities continue to present bids to convince teams to remain in or come to their region. The bids typically consist of pledges from businesses to purchase luxury seating, commitments from both businesses and individuals to buy season tickets, and an investment by the public sector in a playing facility for the team. These public investments reduce the cost of operating a team and profits are enhanced.

Placemaking and the Fan Experience

We have already discussed the ability of facility designs to contribute to both the host cities' identities and the attraction of human capital. However, of equal importance are two of the key factors cities and teams must consider in the decision-making process: (1) the extent to which a professional sport venue aligns with citywide development plans and (2) whether the venue design will contribute to an iconic exterior design that will help to define its urban space.

The image benefits for a city or region of such an external design are clear. Later in this chapter, we will discuss why an iconic external design can lead to higher revenue for a team from the hosting of other events. Before turning to that issue, it is necessary to focus on "internal" design issues that must be considered to maximize revenue generation. That discussion is anchored in what has been labeled the Disneyfication of sport, tourism, and entertainment. Understanding these changes are critical for sport managers because these new design elements have created extraordinary new revenue sources to improve teams' financial positions.

As noted in Chapter 1, the term Disneyfication is used to refer to the building of facilities that include a wide set of complementary activities that fans or visitors are likely to engage in when they attend a game or event.

That experience begins when a fan or visitor enters the area in which the venue is sited and includes the amenities both inside and outside the venue. The concept grew from Walt Disney's conclusion after seeing the hotels and activities that other entrepreneurs built surrounding the *Disneyland* complex in Southern California. Walt Disney declared that, when he built a new park, it would be large enough to include all of the activities and amenities visitors consumed from other entrepreneurs when visiting his park. Such a park would require a great deal of land so that numerous hotels, restaurants, and even other parks and attractions could be built by Disney and controlled by his corporation. After rejecting a location in the St. Louis region, Walt Disney and his team chose land in the Orlando area to build *Disney World*. Today *Disney World* includes 25 hotels; more than 700,000 square feet of ballroom, convention, and meeting spaces; four golf courses, four theme parks, and scores of restaurants and retail outlets. *Disney World*'s facilities cover more than 40 square miles (a land area approximately the size of the city of San Francisco). The total land mass controlled by the Disney Corporation is 25,000 acres.

As discussed in Chapter 1, some credit for the concept of fan experiences beyond the game itself should also be given to Walter O'Malley and his design for Dodger Stadium. Regardless if it was the lessons learned from the Disney Corporation or from the work of Walter O'Malley, the focus of sport managers today is on the fan experience.

What Does This Mean for the Fan Experience?

Fans can easily choose to watch games at home or at pubs and restaurants, so venues must create a level of excitement that makes it *the* place fans want to see a game. The focus on fan experience has led to sport venue footprints expanding to include the full set of amenities a fan or visitor might enjoy on a game day or while attending an entertainment event. Controlling land adjacent to the venue makes it possible to begin the experience before the visitor enters the building. The possible amenities include restaurants, pubs, retail spaces, residential areas, public parks and plazas, and other activities that one can enjoy before and during a game or show. Because businesses use sport and entertainment to facilitate connections with their clients and to reward their employees, additional space is needed to host visitors in suites or club areas. Playing fields have not changed sizes (and, in numerous instances, there are fewer seats in the newer facilities than in older venues to afford better sight lines), but the newer, fan experience-oriented venues tend to be far larger than older venues. In fact, some sport venues anchor 60 or more acres of development.

For example, the new Yankee Stadium has almost twice the retail square footage of the old ballpark and 13 restaurants and pubs, compared to the four that operated in the original, 1923-built (1970s-remodeled) facility.

The new Yankee Stadium has 56 luxury suites and 410 party suites (which can be rented for individual games). The older facility had just 19 suites. The new Yankee Stadium is 63 percent larger than the size of the facility it replaced even though the playing fields in both facilities were identical. Another example, Lucas Oil Stadium (the current home of the Indianapolis Colts) covers 12 acres with 522,720 square feet of space. It replaced the 7.25-acre RCA Dome that included just 315,820 square feet of space. The new facility is 65.5 percent larger than the one it replaced even though the size of the playing surface is unchanged. The new facility includes 148 retail sites compared to 85 in the older one, and more suites and space within each suite for added amenities. As unbelievable as this might sound, and as large as Lucas Oil Stadium is, it could be placed *inside* AT&T Stadium, which serves as the home of the Dallas Cowboys. The Cowboys' new home can seat 35,000 more fans than their former home, Texas Stadium (80,000, with the ability to accommodate as many as 100,000 spectators for football games), and has 800 retail and restaurant points and 2,900 video screens. AT&T Stadium covers 73 acres, making its footprint six times that of Lucas Oil Stadium. Citi Field has 15,000 fewer seats than the stadium it replaced; the Mets' new home is far larger than Shea Stadium and includes a rotunda as well as several clubs, restaurants, and numerous points for retail sales. Citi Field was also sited to anchor a 60+ acre new neighborhood that will be built across the next several decades. The Tampa Bay Lightning's owner also acquired more than 50 acres around the Amalie Arena to build a new arena district. Little Caesars Arena is the anchor for a $1.2 billion plan in The District Detroit. US Bank Stadium, the new home for the Minnesota Vikings, has 1.75 million square feet; the venue it replaced had just 900,000 square feet of space, and Mercedes-Benz Stadium in Atlanta (Falcons) has 1.6 million square feet of space (300,000 more than in their previous home, the Georgia Dome).

Just as Walt Disney greatly expanded his concept of *Disneyland* to encompass the total experience of an amusement park, team owners now seek designs that encourage fans to enjoy their pre- and postgame activities at the facility or at an adjacent real estate district, which provides space for entertaining friends or clients and numerous points of sale for merchandise, food, and beverages. With fans spending far more time at facilities and/ or adjoining districts, advertising, sponsorships, and naming rights have become more valuable as there is more time for people to see the messages and products of different companies. Each of these changes creates opportunities for sport managers to maximize team revenue.

However, in order to build a facility and adjacent entertainment district with ample space for each of these amenities, a sizeable amount of land must be assembled. To fully maximize revenue potential, a new arena requires a building site of approximately 10 acres. Ballparks and stadiums, as the example of the Colts, Cowboys, and Yankees illustrate, can utilize anywhere from approximately 15 to 73 acres. The first issue in building a facility, then, is to ensure that enough land is available to maximize all the revenue streams that can be built into a facility. The next issue to consider is convenient fan access, and that varies quite a bit between the sports.

Where Should a Facility Be Built?

The availability of land is one of the most important issues when choosing a location for a new facility. If an appropriate amount of land is available in more than one location, and one of those locations is closer to a region's central business district, that option will typically be a more profitable location for ballparks and arenas. Football teams also might find such a location attractive, but the nature of their product offers locational options with minimal risk. For baseball, basketball, and hockey teams, with their longer schedules and the high proportion of weekday games, locations farther from central business districts, mass transit nodes, and employment centers carry more risk. Most NFL games are played on Sunday, allowing football teams to be successful at suburban locations. However, several venues have been built in downtown areas (e.g., Atlanta, Indianapolis, and Minneapolis) and their teams have remained financially stable and successful. Sites near cities' central business districts also tend to be more accessible from various modes of public transportation, adding value to a downtown facility option. Land and location, then, are the two main factors that should guide the selection of a site, but other factors inevitably enter into the process.

Sport managers must also factor in the issue of fans' consumption costs. Consumption costs, as they relate to attendance at a sporting event, refer to the cost of tickets and transportation to and from games, as well as the amount of time the fan invests in attending the event. The game and the related experiences must be sufficiently valuable to fans to convince them to invest their time and money to attend a game. Executives who forget the entire range of consumption costs borne by fans jeopardize a team's attendance base. This issue is most important to baseball teams, since each season they host more home games than do hockey, basketball, or football teams. With 41 home games each season, the issue of consumption costs is also critical to management of basketball and hockey teams. Even with fewer home games, NFL teams are also concerned with enhancing the fan experience, in part because ticket prices usually exceed those charged at other sporting events. That financial cost is offset somewhat by convenience of weekend games. There are then fewer games, and the games are typically played at times that are more convenient for fans; fans might attend as many as eight regular season home games and up to three playoff games, played across five months. That is very different from the commitment fans of any of the other major sport must make if they acquire season tickets. Basketball and hockey teams, as a result of the playoff systems in each of those leagues, can host as many as 57 regular season and playoff home games. While some fans might decide to attend most or all games, baseball, basketball, and hockey teams must also provide half- and quarter-season ticket packages to keep other, less engaged fans entertained for shorter periods of time.

Simply put, there is greater risk for professional hockey, basketball, and baseball teams to locate their facilities too far from central business districts. After a day of work, commuting a long distance to a game and then having to return home increases consumption costs. Building facilities near business centers maximizes convenience for those fans and businesses. Downtown areas often offer this type of concentration even in decentralized areas (e.g., Dallas, Los Angeles, Phoenix) where there may be more than one business center. Downtown areas are often located at the nexus of public transportation, roadways, and large concentrations of parking structures. The latter is an important asset as the existence of these structures can reduce the need for building new parking lots. The transportation and parking advantages in downtown areas minimizes congestion, making attendance even more convenient.

Given the changing consumption demands from fans, teams in aging venues often prefer to build new venues over renovating existing facilities. However, for some teams playing in historic venues, choosing another location for a new venue is unrealistic due to fan and public outcry. Senior leadership at the Chicago Cubs and Boston Red Sox assessed the potential for new venues, but each team settled for renovations to their historic parks. While teams may prefer "new builds" over renovations to existing facilities, extensive renovations are almost always undertaken as venues age. Five of the latest renovations have involved Madison Square Garden (Rangers and Knicks, 2013); Bankers Life Fieldhouse (Indiana Pacers, 2015); Progressive Field (Cleveland Indians, 2016); EverBank Field (Jacksonville Jaguars, 2016); and Hard Rock Stadium (Miami Dolphins, 2016).

Relative to the ability of teams and venues to relocate economic activity and enhance an area's vibrancy (noted earlier in this chapter), the public sector has an interest in deciding where a venue is located, and there have been instances where the public sector has used incentives to be part of those discussions. The public sector is frequently interested in enhancing the economic vitality of aging downtown areas. Sometimes teams may be interested in relocating to other locations within a region; in these instances, cities have used incentives to encourage teams to remain in or relocate to their preferred sites (often to sites that produce the greatest benefits for central cities). The San Diego Padres, for example, played their home games in a suburban facility controlled by the NFL's Chargers. Its sight lines were far from ideal for baseball, but they were not as terrible as those in some other dual use facilities. The Padres preferred a suburban location for a new ballpark, but the City's interest in a new facility and their willingness to invest in it was tied to a downtown location. In the end, the Ballpark District was built on the location chosen by the City. The resulting partnership led to more than $3 billion in new residential and commercial real estate development in the Ballpark District. Similarly, the State of Michigan provided $250 million for the building of a new arena for the Detroit Red Wings in downtown Detroit. The Ilitch Family responded with a commitment to invest more than $900 million in the downtown area.

Changing a Downtown's Image: Edmonton and Rogers Place

In 2016, the City of Edmonton and the NHL's Oilers opened Rogers Place. The new venue replaced the aging Rexall Place. The new venue anchored the revitalization of a section of downtown Edmonton. What is notable is the design of the venue and the resulting contribution to the city's architecture. Rexall Place, built in the 1970s, was a circular concrete venue which added little to the city's brand image. In contrast, Rogers Place has sweeping lines surrounding public plazas and a set of new buildings, each with its own unique architecture, that help to define downtown Edmonton.

The arena's development and the new buildings in the downtown area were the result of a ten-year planning and building process. During the process, a deal was negotiated that involved the use of a property tax increments (a Community Revitalization Levy or CRL, also known as a TIF or Tax Increment Financing District in the United States) to support the public sector's investment in the venue. Initially there was opposition to the plan, the scale of the public sector's investment, and the limited investment by the team's owner in the new arena. There was also criticism of the City of Edmonton's agreement to rent a substantial proportion of one of the buildings developed by the team's owner in the Ice District. The Ice District is a mixed-use real estate project that is anchored by the arena. Within a year of the arena's opening, the Edmonton Tower (27 stories) opened, as did 300,000 square feet of multi-level retail, including restaurants, cafes, and commercial and entertainment space (Ice District, n.d.). Construction of the Stantec Tower began in 2016 and the JW Marriott will open in 2019 (3CBC News, 2017). The success of the Ice District has meant that sufficient real estate taxes were produced to support the CRL and the public sector's commitment to the arena. There is concern, however, that there has not been sufficient growth in the region's population to avoid the fear that the Ice District has simply transferred some development from one part of the downtown area to another (a substitution effect).

Design and the Competition for Discretionary Income and Time

After location and the consideration of linkages to business and population centers, the next decision a team must make involves a venue's overall capacity and the appropriate mix of luxury and other seating options. There are certain size issues that have become benchmarks relative to sight lines. For example, ballparks with seating for approximately 45,000 have been found to maximize sight lines and offer fans the best range of seating options. Facilities of this size maximize the number of seats between first and third base and then along the foul lines, but beyond the bases. Larger ballparks that offer more seating capacity must place extra seats in more expansive upper decks in the outfield. Including more seats is sometimes not desirable, as many would have a restricted or distant view of the field and tickets for these seats would need to be sold for a reduced price. Further, if the team has an unsuccessful season, those seats tend to remain unsold. While it is usually considered better to play games without too many vacant seats, there is another very important reason not to build too much excess capacity. When fans know that there will always be tickets available, they are reluctant to make advance purchases. This leaves teams dependent on large walk-up crowds on the day of a game and vulnerable to the possibility that at the last moment people might decide not to attend a game. When fans are concerned that good seats for a particular game they want to see may sell out, they are more likely to make an advance purchase. Owners benefit from advance ticket sales as the team not only has use of the cash for longer periods of time, but there is far less or no need to hire staff to sell tickets on the day of a game. When deciding on how big a facility to build, it actually is far more beneficial to have too few seats than too many. To avoid the chance that people might not attend, building a facility that creates an impression of scarcity actually is in the owner's best interest. For this reason, it is not uncommon to find that newer facilities are smaller than a team's older home (see Table 4.1).

The seating capacity of all ballparks and the date the facilities were built or renovated are detailed in Table 4.2. The convergence on seating capacities for ballparks of approximately 42,000 for those built in the 1990s or later is evident. Differences in the demand for baseball from market to market explain the variations in this figure. As would be expected, Yankee Stadium has more seats than the league average. At the same time, the New York Mets, intent on building a facility more similar to the jewel box-era ballparks, chose a smaller capacity. The two Florida franchises, given the challenges they have had in attracting fans even in successful years, chose designs with fewer than 40,000 seats. What is critical to understand in terms of the seating capacity at a ballpark is that with less than 45,000 seats, there

Table 4.1 Smaller Is Often Better: Creating a Sense of Scarcity and Urgency in Buying Baseball Tickets

City	Former Facility	Former Facility Opened	Former Facility Capacity	New Facility	New Facility Opened	New Facility Capacity	Ballpark Useful Lifespan
Atlanta	Turner Field	1997	49,586	Sun Trust Park	2017	41,500	20
Miami[1]	Sun Life Stadium	1987	47,662	Marlins Park	2012	37,442	25
Minneapolis	Metrodome	1982	56,144	Target Field	2010	38,871	28
New York	Yankee Stadium[2]	1923	67,377	Yankee Stadium	2009	49,642	86
New York	Shea Stadium	1964	57,333	Citi Field	2009	41,922	45
St. Louis	Busch Stadium	1966	46,048	Busch Memorial Stadium	2006	43,975	40
Philadelphia	Veterans' Stadium	1971	62,418	Citizens Bank Park	2004	43,651	33
Detroit	Tiger Stadium	1912	52,416	Comerica Park	2000	41,297	88
Houston	Astrodome	1965	54,816	Minute Maid Park	2000	41,676	35
San Francisco	Candlestick Park	1960	59,000	AT&T Park	2000	41,915	40
Cleveland	Municipal Stadium	1931	73,200	Progressive Field	1994	35,225	63

[1]   The Miami Marlins played their home games at the football stadium used by the Miami Dolphins until Marlins Park opened in 2012.
[2]   The original Yankee Stadium opened in 1923 with 58,000 seats. When the third deck was completed, the capacity grew to 67,337. After being remodeled in the 1970s, the capacity declined to 56,866.

are a large number of high-value seats with good sight lines. Larger capacities mean the inclusion of more low-value seats, and this should only be done when market demand assessments indicate those seats, too, will be sold on most game days.

There is even more convergence in the seating capacity for arenas. The venue with the largest seating capacity in the NBA can be found in Philadelphia at the Wachovia Center where 21,600 seats are available for 76ers' games. The Sacramento Kings play in a facility with a capacity of 17,500. The average for basketball-only arenas is 19,272. Given the larger playing surface for hockey, seating at hockey-only arenas would be expected to be less. The average for NHL teams is 18,441. The Montreal Canadiens' Molson Centre can seat 21,273 fans for hockey games. The decision on seating capacity for an arena is driven by the same factors that shape the conversations regarding the capacity for ballparks. As discussed, including

Table 4.2 Seating Capacity at MLB Ballparks

Team	Facility	Seating Capacity	Year Opened or Renovated
Arizona Diamondbacks	Chase Field	48,519	1998 (2009)
Atlanta Braves	SunTrust Park	41,500	2017
Baltimore Orioles	Oriole Park at Camden Yards	45,971	1992 (2016)
Boston Red Sox	Fenway Park	37,731	1912 (2017)
Chicago Cubs	Wrigley Field	41,268	1914 (2017)
Chicago White Sox	Guaranteed Rate Field	40,615	1991 (2016)
Cincinnati Reds	Great American Ball Park	42,319	2003 (2015)
Cleveland Indians	Progressive Field	35,225	1994 (2016)
Colorado Rockies	Coors Field	50,398	1995 (2017)
Detroit Tigers	Comerica Park	41,297	2000 (2015)
Miami Marlins	Marlins Park	37,442	2012 (2016)
Houston Astros	Minute Maid Park	41,676	2000 (2017)
Kansas City Royals	Kauffman Stadium	37,903	1973 (2017)
Los Angeles Angels	Angel Stadium of Anaheim	43,250	1966 (2017)
Los Angeles Dodgers	Dodger Stadium	56,000	1962 (2014)
Milwaukee Brewers	Miller Park	41,900	2001 (2015)
Minnesota Twins	Target Field	38,871	2010 (2015)
New York Mets	Citi Field	41,922	2009 (2016)
New York Yankees	Yankee Stadium	49,642	2009 (2017)
Oakland Athletics	Oakland Alameda Coliseum	63,132	1966 (1996)
Philadelphia Phillies	Citizens Bank Park	43,651	2004 (2012)
Pittsburgh Pirates	PNC Park	38,362	2001 (2017)
San Diego Padres	Petco Park	40,162	2004 (2015)
San Francisco Giants	AT&T Park	41,915	2000 (2015)
Seattle Mariners	SAFECO Field	47,943	1999 (2015)
St. Louis Cardinals	Busch Memorial Stadium	43,975	2006 (2017)
Tampa Bay Rays	Tropicana Field	31,042	1990 (2017)
Texas Rangers	Globe Life Park in Arlington[1]	48,114	1994 (2013)
Toronto Blue Jays	Rogers Centre	49,282	1989 (2005)
Washington Nationals	Nationals Park	41,313	2008

[1] In late 2017, Arlington voters approved the use of up to $500 million toward the cost of a new ballpark for the Texas Rangers. The team anticipates playing in the new ballpark by 2020 or 2021.

more seats typically means some fans will be seated farther from the playing surface. These seats will command far lower prices unless the demand for tickets is relatively inelastic. In addition, when the team enjoys less success, tickets for these seats may be in relatively low demand, meaning there could be empty sections. The team also would become more dependent on walk-up sales (Table 4.3).

Table 4.3 Seating Capacity at NBA and NHL Arenas

Team	Facility	Seating Capacity	Year Opened or Renovated
Atlanta Hawks	Philips Arena	18,238	1999 (2016)
Boston Celtics, Boston Bruins	TD Garden	18,624	1995 (2014)
Brooklyn Nets, New York Islanders	Barclays Center	17,732	2012 (2015)
Charlotte Hornets	Spectrum Center	19,077	2005 (2017)
Chicago Bulls, Chicago Blackhawks	United Center	20,917	1994 (2015)
Cleveland Cavaliers	Quicken Loans Arena	20,562	1994 (2016)
Dallas Mavericks, Dallas Stars	American Airlines Center	19,200	2001 (2017)
Denver Nuggets, Colorado Avalanche	Pepsi Center	19,520	1999 (2013)
Detroit Pistons, Detroit Red Wings	Little Caesars Arena	21,000	2017
Golden State Warriors	Oracle Arena[1]	19,596	1966 (1997)
Houston Rockets	Toyota Center	18,055	2003 (2013)
Indiana Pacers	Bankers Life Fieldhouse	18,165	1999 (2015)
Los Angeles Clippers, Los Angeles Lakers, Los Angeles Kings	Staples Center	19,060	1999 (2016)
Memphis Grizzlies	FedexForum	18,119	2004 (2017)
Miami Heat	AmericanAirlines Arena	19,600	1999 (2016)
Milwaukee Bucks	BMO Harris Bradley Center[2]	18,717	1988 (2010)
Minnesota Timberwolves	Target Center	19,356	1990 (2017)
New Orleans Pelicans	Smoothie King Center	16,867	1999 (2013)
New York Knicks, New York Rangers	Madison Square Garden	19,812	1968 (2013)
Oklahoma City Thunder	Chesapeake Energy Arena	18,203	2002 (2014)
Orlando Magic	Amway Center	18,846	2010 (2013)
Philadelphia 76ers, Philadelphia Flyers	Wells Fargo Center	21,600	1996 (2015)
Phoenix Suns	Talking Stick Resort Arena	19,023	1992 (2014)
Portland Trail Blazers	Moda Center	19,441	1995 (2014)
Sacramento Kings	Golden 1 Center	17,500	2016
San Antonio Spurs	AT&T Center	18,418	2002 (2014)
Toronto Raptors, Toronto Maple Leafs	Air Canada Centre[3]	19,800	1999 (2009)
Utah Jazz	Vivint Smart Home Arena	19,911	1991 (2016)
Washington Wizards, Washington Capitals	Capital One Arena	20,356	1997 (2017)
Anaheim Ducks	Honda Center	18,900	1993 (2015)
Arizona Coyotes	Gila River Arena	17,125	2003 (2014)
Buffalo Sabres	KeyBank Center	19,200	1996 (2016)
Calgary Flames	Scotiabank Saddledome	19,289	1983 (2013)
Carolina Hurricanes	PNC Arena	19,722	1999 (2016)

(continued)

Table 4.3 Continued

Team	Facility	Seating Capacity	Year Opened or Renovated
Columbus Blue Jackets	Nationwide Arena	20,500	2000 (2016)
Edmonton Oilers	Rogers Place	18,641	2016
Florida Panthers	BB&T Center	20,737	1998 (2014)
Las Vegas Golden Knights	T-Mobile Arena	20,000	2016
Minnesota Wild	Xcel Energy Center	18,064	2000 (2015)
Montreal Canadiens	Bell Centre	21,273	1996 (2015)
Nashville Predators	Bridgestone Arena	17,113	1996 (2016)
New Jersey Devils	Prudential Center	18,711	2007 (2017)
Ottawa Senators	Canadian Tire Centre	17,373	1996 (2014)
Pittsburgh Penguins	PPG Paints Arena	18,087	2010 (2012)
St. Louis Blues	Scottrade Center	19,150	1994 (2016)
San Jose Sharks	SAP Center	17,562	1993 (2017)
Tampa Bay Lightning	Amalie Arena	21,500	1996 (2015)
Vancouver Canucks	Rogers Arena	18,910	1995 (2016)
Winnipeg Jets	Bell MTS Place	15,294	2004 (2014)

[1]   The Golden State Warriors anticipate moving to Chase Center in Mission Bay in 2019.
[2]   The Milwaukee Bucks anticipate moving to a new arena in 2018.
[3]   The Raptors' arena is anticipated to be renamed Scotiabank Arena in 2018.

Once finished with setting the overall seating capacity, sport managers must determine which and how many experiences will be offered to ensure that fans want to be at the venue. Today, teams must offer many different products and cater to various fan segments in order to maximize revenue. How teams' product offerings have expanded to meet different fan segments' preferences, as well as how teams measure the demand for luxury seating, will be discussed in detail in Chapter 6.

The Exterior Design of Facilities and Competing for Events

The decisions made regarding the exterior of a facility are as important as those made involving the number of luxury seats in a facility. The exterior of a facility becomes the "face" of the franchise and in some instances of the city itself. A venue's exterior establishes the essential linkages to the surrounding real estate development and creates an anchor for an entire neighborhood's development. A venue's appearance has the potential to help attract other sport events and even non-sports events to an area as well.

Iconic Design

Whether it's the Green Monster in Boston, the lattice-work façade and gold lettering that symbolizes Yankee Stadium, the fieldhouse vibe of the

Pacers' Bankers Life Fieldhouse, the arches that surround the Los Angeles Memorial Coliseum, or the striking exterior glass design of the Sprint Center in Kansas City that helped make it a venue of choice even in the absence of a major league team as an anchor, iconic designs and façades create an image for a team and city. These unique architectural statements can turn a facility into a tourist attraction and also create a special ambience that attracts fans to athletic and nonathletic events. When a new sport venue is built, teams and architects are given a unique opportunity (and as some may argue, duty) to contribute to a community's identity. Most importantly, a venue that creates an important visual statement for a city also creates a sense of excitement that brings fans and their consumption to the venue and the adjacent area.

While many facilities have added to their host city's skyline or contributed to building the city's image, the exterior designs of some older, circular facilities often lacked architectural appeal, and the views from seats of the surrounding landscape were generally non-existent. The contrast of Figures 4.1 and 4.2 demonstrates two of the extremes in exterior venue appeal. Minneapolis' U.S. Bank Stadium (opened in 2016) is an extraordinary architectural statement and creates an inviting environment. U.S. Bank Stadium's ability to reflect the skyline of downtown Minneapolis adds to its allure. In contrast, Rexall Place, former home of the Edmonton

Figure 4.1 Minneapolis' U.S. Bank Stadium.

Figure 4.2 Edmonton Oilers' Former Venue, Rexall Place.

Oilers, opened in 1974, and the lack of imagination in its design created a very different image for the city. Facilities built more recently tend to be far more iconic, a feature which adds to the value provided to fans and the community.

The unique design of a venue also increases its value to sponsors who want to affiliate their business, product, or service with the team and its home. The importance of design and architecture is best illustrated by the success of Target Field. Its success led the *Minneapolis Star Tribune* to declare the facility's architect, Earl Santee, the region's sportsman of the year. In describing the accomplishment, Jim Souhan concluded, "In one season, Target Field became for downtown Minneapolis what the North Star is to the night sky" (Souhan, 2010).

It is essential that any new venue includes design elements that allow for a stunning view to the local area. To do so is far more important when a new arena is built in a city that already hosts a successful venue. The Barclays Center in Brooklyn, for example, was built as a new arena for the Nets as well as a place to host concerts in New York City. However, because the Barclays Center would be entering the same market area as New York's Madison Square Garden (MSG), "the world's most famous arena," Barclays would require an incredibly unique and iconic design. This would be necessary if the new venue was to compete to host entertainment events in the New York Market, where MSG reigned "king." As a result, when Barclays was built in Brooklyn, it became an iconic testament to the city, tying together features from its past and future.

Monumental and Neighborhood Design Scales

While all venues should be designed as city-defining icons, there is flexibility in the way venues can be designed to fit in with (or stand out from) its surrounding area. Scale is one way to categorize different types of venue designs. Though many other types exist, this textbook describes two types of design scales: monumental and neighborhood design scale. A venue's exterior can be so dramatic that it transforms a place into a destination that attracts other events. For example, the spectacular scale and interior design of AT&T Stadium in Arlington, Texas has helped attract the Super Bowl, the NBA's 2010 All-Star Game, numerous college football and bowl games including the Cotton Bowl Classic, which relocated to AT&T Stadium from Dallas' Cotton Bowl Stadium, and the NCAA championship games for men's basketball and football. AT&T Stadium is an example of **monumental design**. The term monumental is used to describe something that dwarfs its surrounding environment. AT&T Stadium and Yankee Stadium (Figures 4.3 and 4.4, respectively) are each examples of monumental design.

In contrast, Little Caesars Arena in Detroit and Petco Park in San Diego were each designed to facilitate the development of new neighborhoods (see Figures 4.5 and 4.6). Each of these venues align with the **neighborhood design** concept and were built to "fit" into the neighborhoods in which they were built. Facilities built in neighborhood design scale tend to follow the guidelines of the jewel box ballparks built in the first half of the 20th century. These facilities were designed to fit comfortably into the design of an entire urban neighborhood, rather than dominate the area. Often there are nearby structures that actually are far larger in height than neighborhood scale venues. Venues designed in either monumental or neighborhood can be iconic, and, as Chapter 6 will discuss, both types of venues can serve as anchors for real estate development as well.

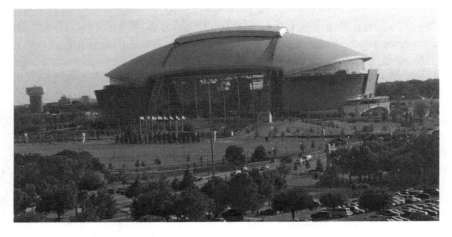

Figure 4.3 Monumental Design: AT&T Stadium.

Figure 4.4 Monumental Design: Yankee Stadium.

Figure 4.5 Neighborhood Design: Little Caesars Arena and The District Detroit.

Figure 4.6 Neighborhood Design: Petco Park.

Overbuilding Facilities and Market Saturation

Every new facility built in a region increases the supply of available dates on which sport and entertainment events can be hosted. When planning a new facility, it is necessary to study the effect of adding to the supply of event dates that exist in a region, as well as the demand for residential, commercial, and retail space that can surround these venues. In developing a business plan for a new venue and the real estate that could be built (discussed further in Chapter 6), absorption assessments should be performed. An absorption assessment is a critical review of the market that exists for events and new real estate in an area.

To maximize the financial success of an arena, for example, hosting more than 100 events each year is desirable. A football stadium might only host ten games and the occasional concert; generating sufficient revenue for a facility with an event schedule of that nature is a greater challenge and helps explain the reliance of higher ticket prices, luxury seating, and many other amenities at NFL games. Ballparks host 81 games and therefore have a greater opportunity to spread the costs of construction and maintenance across more event days. Over the past several years, however, there has been an extensive effort to increase the event days at ballparks and stadiums.

Two different sets of information are provided to consider these issues. Table 4.4 identifies the number of tickets sold for entertainment events in arenas used by NBA or NHL teams. There are a large range of events that are not included in this table. The data illustrate the pressure on facility managers to attract events, and that pressure can have a downward effect on rental fees if there are too many facilities in any region. Tables 4.5 and 4.6 illustrate the number of tickets sold for entertainment events held at venues used by NFL and MLB teams, respectively. These data illustrate the interest and revenue potential for teams hosting entertainment events in addition to what a team generates on game days.

Table 4.4 Event Days in Selected Arenas, 2016

Arena	City	Concert Event Days	NBA/NHL Game Days[1]	Total Event Days
Philips Arena	Atlanta, GA	69	39	108
TD Garden	Boston, MA	37	76	113
Barclays Center	Brooklyn, NY	91	83	174
Spectrum Center	Charlotte, NC	22	40	62
United Center	Chicago, IL	55	82	137
Quicken Loans Arena	Cleveland, OH	40	46	86
American Airlines Center	Dallas, TX	44	81	125
Pepsi Center	Denver, CO	54	84	138
Little Caesars Arena[2]	Detroit, MI	30	80	110
Oracle Arena[3]	Oakland, CA	69	42	111
Toyota Center	Houston, TX	48	38	86
Bankers Life Fieldhouse	Indianapolis, IN	52	42	94
Staples Center	Los Angeles, CA	64	116	180
FedexForum	Memphis, TN	24	44	68
AmericanAirlines Arena	Miami, FL	87	38	125
BMO Harris Bradley Center[4]	Milwaukee, WI	24	43	67
Target Center	Minneapolis, MN	58	41	99
Smoothie King Center	New Orleans, LA	33	47	80
Madison Square Garden	New York, NY	84	80	164
Chesapeake Energy Arena	Oklahoma City, OK	29	40	69
Amway Center	Orlando, FL	40	40	80
Wells Fargo Center	Philadelphia, PA	79	82	161
Talking Stick Resort Arena	Phoenix, AZ	66	38	104
Moda Center	Portland, OR	46	43	89
Golden 1 Center[5]	Sacramento, CA	51	38	89
AT&T Center	San Antonio, TX	46	37	83
Air Canada Centre[6]	Toronto, Canada	63	83	146
Vivint Smart Home Arena	Salt Lake City, UT	30	44	74
Capital One Arena	Washington, DC	56	85	141
Honda Center	Anaheim, CA	49	39	88
Gila River Arena	Glendale, AZ	11	41	52
KeyBank Center	Buffalo, NY	19	39	58

(continued)

Table 4.4 Continued

Arena	City	Concert Event Days	NBA/NHL Game Days[1]	Total Event Days
Scotiabank Saddledome	Calgary, Canada	25	41	66
PNC Arena	Raleigh, NC	14	37	51
Nationwide Arena	Columbus, OH	18	42	60
Rogers Place[7]	Edmonton, Canada	39	41	80
BB&T Center	Sunrise, FL	53	40	93
Xcel Energy Center	Saint Paul, MN	47	38	85
Bell Centre	Montreal, Canada	96	42	138
Bridgestone Arena	Nashville, TN	60	40	100
Prudential Center	Newark, NJ	72	37	109
Canadian Tire Centre	Ottawa, Canada	35	42	77
PPG Paints Arena	Pittsburgh, PA	54	43	97
Scottrade Center	St. Louis, MO	28	40	68
SAP Center	San Jose, CA	66	43	109
Amalie Arena	Tampa, FL	57	40	97
Rogers Arena	Vancouver, Canada	33	45	78
T-Mobile Arena[8]	Las Vegas, NV	49	0	49
Bell MTS Place	Winnipeg, Canada	51	43	94

Source: Pollstar.

[1] Accounts only for games held in the 2016 calendar year (end half of 2015–2016 season and first half of the 2016–2017 season). Includes postseason games.

[2] Events from Joe Louis Arena and the Palace of Auburn Hills have been combined and inserted for Little Caesars Arena; event totals for Little Caesars Arena are from FY2017 for a more accurate representation following the venue's late-2017 opening.

[3] The Golden State Warriors anticipate moving to Chase Center in Mission Bay in 2019.

[4] Event totals for the Golden 1 Center are from FY2017 for a more accurate representation.

[5] The Milwaukee Bucks anticipate moving to a new arena in 2018.

[6] The Raptors' arena is anticipated to be renamed Scotiabank Arena in 2018.

[7] Event totals for Rogers Place are from FY2017 for a more accurate representation.

[8] Event totals for T-Mobile Arena are form FY2017 for a more accurate representation.

College Venues and the Student Section

A great asset for attracting fans to college games is the excitement generated by students. Their verve creates a unique experience that is not only nostalgic for alumni but something that rarely exists for professional teams. There is value in creating venue designs that maximize the ways in which the student section is visible during telecasts. It is also important to design venues that ensure students arrive early and stay for the entire game. Too often college venues fail to capitalize on the contribution that students make to the unique aspect of collegiate sports.

College students are notorious for tailgating or attending "pre-game" parties. The challenge for many universities is to offer competitive entertainment that encourages students to arrive at venues earlier and inject

Table 4.5 Event Days in NFL Stadia, 2016

Arena	City	Concert Event Days	NFL Game Days	Total Event Days
AT&T Stadium	Arlington, TX	7	9	16
Mercedes-Benz Stadium[1]	Atlanta, GA	4	9	13
M&T Bank Stadium	Baltimore, MD	1	8	9
Bank of America Stadium	Charlotte, NC	1	9	10
Soldier Field	Chicago, IL	6	9	15
Paul Brown Stadium	Cincinnati, OH	3	9	12
FirstEnergy Stadium	Cleveland, OH	0	9	9
Sports Authority Field at Mile High	Denver, CO	0	8	8
Ford Field	Detroit, MI	4	7	11
MetLife Stadium	East Rutherford, NJ	31	16	47
Gillette Stadium	Foxborough, MA	10	8	18
University of Phoenix Stadium	Glendale, AZ	4	9	13
Lambeau Field	Green Bay, WI	0	9	9
NRG Stadium	Houston, TX	28	9	37
FedEx Field	Hyattsville, MD	1	7	8
Lucas Oil Stadium	Indianapolis, IN	1	8	9
EverBank Field	Jacksonville, FL	0	8	8
Arrowhead Stadium	Kansas City, MO	2	9	11
Los Angeles Memorial Coliseum	Los Angeles, CA	1	7	8
Hard Rock Stadium	Miami, FL	3	8	11
US Bank Stadium	Minneapolis, MN	2	7	9
Nissan Stadium	Nashville, TN	7	7	14
Mercedes-Benz Superdome	New Orleans, LA	5	8	13
Oakland Alameda Coliseum	Oakland, CA	0	8	8
New Era Field	Orchard Park, NY	0	9	9
Lincoln Financial Field	Philadelphia, PA	5	7	12
Heinz Field	Pittsburgh, PA	3	7	10
Levi's Stadium	Santa Clara, CA	8	8	16
CenturyLink Field	Seattle, WA	4	8	12
Raymond James Stadium	Tampa Bay, FL	2	7	9

Source: Pollstar.

[1] 2018 concert event dates were utilized for Mercedes-Benz Stadium to provide a more accurate estimate.

their enthusiasm into pre-game activities. This can be accomplished with live entertainment as well as food and (non-alcoholic) beverages (given that many students are under the age of 21) that can be competitive alternatives to other pre-game activities. All teams (college and professional) must compete with alternative entertainment options available to fans. The success of professional teams to attract fans to their "footprint" before

Table 4.6 Event Days in MLB Ballparks, 2016

Arena	City	Concert Event Days	NFL Game Days	Total Event Days
Chase Field	Phoenix, AZ	1	81	82
SunTrust Park	Atlanta, GA	0	81	81
Oriole Park at Camden Yards	Baltimore, MD	0	80	80
Fenway Park	Boston, MA	11	80	91
Wrigley Field	Chicago, IL	77	81	158
Guaranteed Rate Field	Chicago, IL	2	80	82
Great American Ball Park	Cincinnati, OH	1	80	81
Progressive Field	Cleveland, OH	0	81	81
Coors Field	Denver, CO	0	81	81
Comerica Park	Detroit, MI	1	80	81
Marlins Park	Miami, FL	1	80	81
Minute Maid Park	Houston, TX	3	81	84
Kauffman Stadium	Kansas City, MO	0	80	80
Angel Stadium of Anaheim	Anaheim, CA	3	81	84
Dodger Stadium	Los Angeles, CA	4	81	85
Miller Park	Milwaukee, WI	3	81	84
Target Field	Minneapolis, MN	2	79	81
Citi Field	Queens, NY	8	80	88
Yankee Stadium	Bronx, NY	2	81	83
Oakland Alameda Coliseum	Oakland, CA	0	81	81
Citizens Bank Park	Philadelphia, PA	5	81	86
PNC Park	Pittsburgh, PA	2	80	82
Petco Park	San Diego, CA	7	81	88
AT&T Park	San Francisco, CA	3	81	84
SAFECO Field	Seattle, WA	1	81	82
Busch Memorial Stadium	St. Louis, MO	1	80	81
Tropicana Field	St. Petersburg, FL	0	81	81
Globe Life Park in Arlington	Arlington, TX	1	81	82
Rogers Centre	Toronto, Canada	11	81	92
Nationals Park	Washington, DC	3	80	83

Source: Pollstar.

a game – and then to keep them onsite after – is part of the Disney philosophy. While professional teams have understood this business approach and increased in-venue spending levels, most college athletic departments are far behind. As a result, attendance at college football games has been dropping the last decade. Not only are in-facility spending levels reduced, but athletic departments also fail to fully capitalize on the unique excitement that students bring to events. The application of the plaza concepts that are now ingrained in the design of venues that host professional teams should be considered in the management strategy of collegiate athletic programs. A leading example of the incorporation of plazas to encourage fans to arrive early and create a new level excitement can be seen in the fly-through video of Mercedes-Benz Stadium in Atlanta (Mercedes-Benz Stadium, 2014).

References

Cagan, J., & deMause, N. 1998. *Field of schemes: How the great stadium swindle turns public money into private profit.* Monroe, ME: Common Courage.

Cantor, M. B., & Rosentraub, M. S. 2012. A ballpark and neighborhood change: Economic integration, a recession, and the altered demography of San Diego's Ballpark District after 8 eithers. *City, Culture, and Society* 3 (3): 219–226.

CBC News. 2017. Ice District gives sneak peek of downtown towers, *CBC News*, September 12. Retrieved from http://www.cbc.ca/news/canada/edmonton/ice-district-towers-construction-1.4286093 (accessed July 30, 2018).

Ice District. n.d. Ice District properties, *Ice District*. Retrieved from http://icedistrictproperties.com/ (accessed July 30, 2018).

Feng, X., & Humphreys, 2012. The impact of professional sports facilities on housing values: Evidence from census block group data. *City, Culture, and Society* 3 (3): 189–200.

Gerretsen, S., Bain, S. R., & Rosentraub, M. S. 2018. *Public choice theory as an explanation for public funding of sport venues.* Unpublished report, Ann Arbor: Center for Sport & Policy, the University of Michigan.

Grow, N. 2015. Regulating professional sports leagues. *Washington and Lee Law Review* 72 (2): 573–652.

Mercedes-Benz Stadium. 2014. Mercedes-Benz Stadium fly-through, *Mercedes-Benz Stadium*, August 24. Retrieved from http://mercedesbenzstadium.com/fly-through-mercedes-benz-stadium/ (accessed July 30, 2018).

Noll, R., & Zimbalist, A, eds. 1997. *Sports, jobs, & taxes: The economic impact of sports teams and stadiums.* Washington, DC: The Brookings Institution.

Rosentraub, M. S. 1999. *Major league losers: The real cost of sports and who's paying for it.* New York: Basic Books.

Rosentraub, M. S. 2010. *Major league winners: Using sports and cultural centers as tools for economic development.* Boca Raton, FL: CRC Press.

Scully, G. 1995. *The market structure of sports.* Chicago: University of Chicago Press.

Smith, C. 2001. *Storied stadiums: Baseball's history through its ballparks.* New York: Carroll and Graf.

Tu, C. C. 2005. How does a new sports stadium affect housing values? The case of FedEx Field. *Land Economics* 81 (3): 379–395.

Weidner, D. 2016. Pro football's return to Los Angeles hinges on a new stadium project that promises to enhance the economy and property values of the region,

Trulia. Retrieved from http://www.trulia.com/blog/trends/nfl-stadium/ (accessed June 29, 2016).

Zimbalist, A. 1992. *Baseball and billions: A probing look inside the big business of our national pastime.* New York: Basic Books.

Zimbalist, A., & Long, J. G. 2006. Facility finance: Measurement, trends and analysis. *International Journal of Sport Finance* 1: 201–211.

Chapter 5

Financing Sport Venues

Introduction

A great deal of attention has been directed toward the level of the public sector's investment in sport venues. In the classical sense, professional sport is a private good that should be produced by private companies and sold to its customers. When individual athletes earn more than $20 million a year and several teams are valued at more than $2 billion, is it really necessary for the public sector to help pay for arenas, ballparks, and stadia?

In the 1990s, one of the authors of this volume described most of the public sector's investments as helping to create a welfare state for professional sport (Rosentraub, 1997). That observation was similar to those made by others who were concerned with governments offering subsidies, tax abatements, and loans to build venues without a clear development strategy to produce financial benefits for the host city. The leagues, through their control of the number of franchises, created an artificial scarcity of teams in the United States. They were essentially operating a country-wide auction, with cities bidding wildly to secure a franchise. Team owners enjoyed economic rents and excess profits as a result of their market power.

Since then, there have been some major changes in the attitude of public officials regarding the use of tax dollars when they appear to be nothing more than a subsidy. Leaders in the public sector have begun to negotiate with teams in a way that allows for both private *and* public returns on investment. The extent to which the expenditure of tax dollars is a subsidy – or an investment – depends on the economic gains secured by the public investment for the host city.

This chapter explores the financing tools used to build and maintain venues by the public and private sectors. Before the various tools can be discussed, however, there are two other issues that should be considered. First, is it appropriate to consider teams and their venues as public goods? And, second, how can the public sector benefit from a team's presence and the building of a venue?

Teams and Venues as Public Goods and Strategic Investments

To describe what governments should pay for, James Buchanan (1965) and Richard and Peggy Musgrave (1973) developed the theory of public goods. Needed goods and services have characteristics of non-rival consumption. This means that consumption of the good or service by one individual does not affect the ability of another consumer to consume the good or service. For example, a street light generates benefits that, once used by one neighbor, do not reduce another neighbor's chance to also enjoy the light. Where consumption is non-rival, private firms will not produce goods or services unless there is a collective agreement to pay for the good or service. Where exclusion is not possible, public goods will also not be produced by the private sector. James Buchanan (1965) cited the example of a lighthouse with the light visible to all even if they do not pay. Since everyone can see the light and exclusion is not feasible, the private sector will not ensure that lighthouses are built even if they are needed. On the other hand, the private sector is more likely to produce products and services that can be provided exclusively.

Spectator sport and venues, on the other hand, might be considered private goods because non-paying individuals can easily be excluded from attending games. Consumption would also appear to be rival, given that if one person sits in a seat, someone else cannot. Furthermore, watching games on any media platform requires access to the internet or cable television. If an individual does not purchase tickets, internet services, or cable, they cannot enjoy games. For these reasons, it seems reasonable to classify sport as a private good. If sport is a private good, is there really a justification for the public sector to participate in financing a professional team's venue? There are additional elements to consider.

The public sector's involvement in the financing of any good or service rests on two theoretical points. First, if a good or service generates positive externalities to a third party that cannot be captured by market transactions, then private markets produce less of the goods or services than is socially optimal since the third party's preferences are not taken into account. Professional teams might create positive externalities to a community in the form of commentary, chatter, or exuberance among fans and residents of a region. As you may have experienced, people frequently talk about "the game" in the days after a matchup. If a team were not present, there would be less banter or conversations. As will be discussed, more than 1.3 million joined in a celebratory parade throughout the downtown area when the Cleveland Cavaliers won the NBA championship in 2016. Those can be considered positive externalities, and if a team were not present there would be fewer benefits.

The second theoretical justification is based on Charles Tiebout (1956) and work he did with Vincent Ostrom and Robert Warren (1961). Their public choice theory argues that communities differentiate themselves from others in their region by the mix of goods and services they offer to residents (households and businesses). Sport is an amenity, just like public schools or other conveniences a community could decide to collectively provide (e.g., swimming pools, community centers, golf courses, parks). Each of those amenities could be considered private goods, but if a community wanted to use those assets to differentiate itself from other towns and cities in a region, there could be residents who would pay more in taxes for those assets. For Ostrom, Tiebout, and Warren (1961), people are better off if there are choices in the mix of goods and services available to residents. People and businesses can then "vote with their feet" by choosing to live or work in the community that best conforms to their preferences. Within this perspective, a community might well invest in a venue for a professional team if leadership and residents believe such an investment would maximize the preferences of a desirable set of households and businesses. For example, if one region decides to publicly fund arenas and one region decides to not publicly fund arenas, mobile consumers can have the option of living in either scenario. Local governments also understand that teams can be tempted to relocate within their current markets. Arlington's decision to pay for half of the $1 billion cost of a new ballpark for the Texas Rangers in 2016 was likely an attempt to secure the team's presence in the city before it left for another within the region.

As will be discussed, there is a completely different train of thought that argues the investments made by the public sector in sport venues are a function of the artificial scarcity that the major sport leagues are empowered to sustain. With judicial and Congressional protections, the leagues can restrict the number of teams so that the value of owning a team is higher than it would be if more franchises existed.

Regardless of which perspective is most accurate, local governments have funded their investment in sport venues with property taxes, sales, and income taxes, taxes on rental cars and hotel rooms, and sin taxes on gambling activities as well as on alcohol and tobacco products. Sometimes teams receive favorable lease terms for the use of publicly owned venues. Owners often invest their own private funds to build new facilities – some of which have covered 100 percent of the cost. There are countless ways for teams and their host cities to negotiate financing plans for venues. We turn first to the decisions a team owner can make when a new venue is planned. We also deal with the focus on interest in real estate development that can enhance a team's financial viability.

Facility Financing: The Team's Share

The Team as a Financing Tool

There are generally two ways for businesses to pay for capital investments: debt financing or equity financing – though a combination of both can also be used. *Debt financing* refers to borrowing funds to pay for an investment, while *equity financing* means selling a percentage of the firm to investors.

Equity financing involves selling a percentage of the firm or leasing some of the team's future revenues to investors in exchange for a reduction in the capital that team owners must invest in the venue. When this is done, the team has better access to cash to invest in the venue in exchange for some of the future profits that will be realized from the new venue. For publicly traded corporations, equity financing means that the firm will sell shares of stock in order to raise funds. While there are few examples where shares of teams have been sold to pay for a facility's construction, there have been countless instances where a team's principle owner raised capital from those investors who owned smaller portions of the team. When that occurs, there may be no change in the number of shares that are owned by the team, but each individual owner increases their equity investment in the team.

Some may be tempted to note that the Green Bay Packers have issued "shares" to facilitate modifications to Lambeau Field. We do not refer to that as an example of increasing the number of shares to pay for an investment as that stock has no market value. In other words, when people buy shares of the Green Bay Packers, they are essentially making a donation to the team for the privilege of saying they are an owner. Those owners know, however, that they cannot sell their shares and acknowledge that their shares have no economic value.

Again, debt financing is the borrowing of funds to pay for capital investments. There are different forms of debt. Debt financing could mean a loan from a bank, a consortium, or an individual. A team could also issue a bond. Debt financing always involves borrowing money and then making payments to repay the principal and the associated interest charges (just like a car loan or a mortgage on a home). If a team decides to use debt financing to build a new facility, it could seek a loan from a bank; however, investments of the size needed to build a facility often involve issuing a bond. Because teams often use bonds to pay for facilities, managers need to understand the value of bonds. Typically, bonds require investors to pay a periodic payment equal to the face value of the bond multiplied by the contractual interest rate. They also pay a value at maturity (usually the face value) when the bond ends. Therefore, bonds have both a periodic payment and a future value.

An example is useful in understanding the typical cash flows of a bond. Suppose that a team wants to build a new facility and issues multiple bonds with a face or par value of $1,000, with an initial maturity of 20 years and a coupon rate of 5 percent. That means that the team would receive $1,000 for each bond as soon as it was sold. They would also have to pay the

Table 5.1 Cash Flows from a $1,000 Bond

Year	0	1	2	3	...	19	20
Cash Flow	$1,000	−$50	−$50	−$50	...	−$50	−$1,050

bondholder $50 (5 percent of $1,000) each year and an additional $1,000 at the end of the 20 years. Table 5.1 illustrates the cash flows of such a bond. Knowing the cash flow, however, does not reveal the actual value of the bond relative to the time value of money. The present value of the bond is what we need to understand.

First, as all financial analysts know well, money depreciates over time. Everyone would rather have a dollar today than the same dollar a year from today, in part because its purchasing power is likely to decline (inflation). A firm or team's depreciation rate might vary. If a team is indifferent between $1 today and $1.10 next year, then their depreciation rate is 10 percent. If we know a future cash flow and the depreciation rate, the net present value of that cash flow equals:

$$PV = \frac{CashFlow}{(1+r)^N}$$

In this equation, r is the depreciation rate and N is the number of periods (usually years) in the future when the payment is made. While a team's depreciation rate does not have to be equal to the interest rate, it should be close to the interest rate. For example, if the interest rate is 11 percent, then the team could loan $1 and receive $1.11 in a year. Thus, the team's depreciation rate should be close to that. If we go back to our bond example, we can calculate the present value of each cash flow. In other words, we can calculate what each of the payments is worth in today's money.

Table 5.2 shows that with a 6 percent depreciation rate, the present value of money received 19 or 20 years later is drastically lower than money received in the near future. Now we know the value of each of the cash flows. To find the value of the entire bond, we simply need to add up the present value of each cash outflow and compare this with the $1,000 inflow. Mathematically, the value of a bond is given by:

$$NPV_{Bond} = \frac{I}{(1+r)^1} + \frac{I}{(1+r)^2} + ... + \frac{I}{(1+r)^N} + \frac{M}{(1+r)^N} = \sum_{t=1}^{N} \frac{I}{(1+r)^t} + \frac{M}{(1+r)^N}$$

where I is the yearly interest payment and M is the face value that is paid at the end of the bond's maturity. While this formula for a bond helps us

Table 5.2 Present Value of the Cash Flows from the Bond (6 Percent Depreciation Rate)

Year	0	1	2	...	19	20
Calculations	$1,000	$-\$50/1.06$	$-\$50/(1.06)^2$	–	$-\$50/(1.06)^{19}$	$-\$1050/(1.06)^{20}$
NPV Cash Flow	$1,000	−$47.17	−$44.50	–	−$16.53	−$327.39

understand how to value a bond, it can be tedious to add up all of these values. This is where financial calculators become very useful. All financial calculators have five important buttons:

- PV = the present value
- PMT = a constant payment made every period
- N = the number of periods
- I/Y = the depreciation rate (in percentage terms)
- FV = the future value

If four of these values are known, the calculator will solve for the fifth. In our example, PMT = −50, N = 20, I/Y = 6, and FV = −1000. The calculator gives us a value of $885.30.[1]

It might seem odd that the coupon rate was different from the depreciation rate in this example. After all, when the bond is issued it would make sense that the coupon and depreciation rate both equal the market interest rate given the amount of risk involved. Because the coupon rate of a bond does not change over the life of the bond and the market rate does change over time, the value of the bond can change. This is important because bonds can be traded. As a result, the face value and present value of a bond are not always the same. If the coupon rate and the depreciation rate are, in fact, the same, then the present value is equal to the face value. If the depreciation rate is greater than the coupon rate, then the bond is said to have a discount. In our example, the bond had a discount of $114.70, because that was the difference between the face value and the present value. If the depreciation rate is less than the coupon rate, then the bond would be bought at a premium.

The coupon rate of the bond depends on the risk of defaulting on the loan. In the past, the Memphis Redbirds (a Triple-A minor league baseball team) could not make full payments on their bond agreement. It is the job of many financial analysts to judge the probability of an entity or seller defaulting on a bond. The three most popular bond rating agencies are Moody's, Standard & Poors, and Fitch Ratings. The AAA ranking is the highest, while a D ranking means the bond issuer is in default. Bonds with low ratings are considered junk bonds, and investors would demand a higher return on their purchase. The higher return demanded for lower-rated bonds reflects the greater risk to the investor that the borrower might not have the ability to repay the bond. During the Great Recession, there was profound questioning of the ratings issued by some of the agencies. If any skepticism remains, it is likely that investors are considering the possibility that the ratings might be too generous. If that is the case, then interest rates would be higher than when there is more confidence in the rating given to a bond.

There is a bond market that is based on the U.S. Federal funds interest rate. The difference between the bond's coupon rate and the U.S. Federal funds rate depends on how likely the firm or public entity can make payments across the life of the bond. If a firm has financial problems, any bond they offer to investors will have a low bond rating and a high coupon rate. Typically, when the Federal government issues bonds, it does not have to pay a high coupon rate as the U.S. government has never defaulted on a bond. As we will discuss later in the chapter, public entities are often able to issue bonds at a much lower rates than private companies or teams. The following example, written by Greg Kinney at the Bentley Historical Library at the University of Michigan, illustrates that bonds have been used to finance stadiums for a long time.

Financing the Stadium

Just as Fielding Yost made an extensive study of stadium design, he also thoroughly investigated methods of financing the stadium. A successful businessman himself, with interests in oil, coal, and real estate in Tennessee and West Virginia, Yost was impressed with the University of Pittsburgh's use of bonded debt to fund its stadium. He, in particular, wanted to make certain that the university not conduct a fund drive to finance the stadium as Illinois had done. The Board in Control had realized significant profits with the growth in football attendance in the 1920s. In fact, football receipts had enabled the board to completely pay the cost of Yost Field House in just three years. By all indications, a new stadium would quickly pay for itself. The problem was how to accumulate the initial capital to fund construction.

A plan was devised and approved by the Board in Control to finance stadium construction and the facilities called for in the Day Report through a $1,500,000 issue of 3,000 bonds at a par value of $500 at 3 percent interest. These financial instruments bearing the picture of a wolverine would fund not only the stadium, but all the facilities called for in the Day Committee Report.

To drum up support for his stadium proposal, Fielding Yost promoted the bonds to U-M Alumni and extended the offer to "any citizen of the State of Michigan." Yost was sure the alumni would look upon the stadium bonds as a good investment. As an added attraction, each $500 bond guaranteed the right to purchase two tickets between the 30-yard lines for a 10-year period. One person even argued that the right to purchase tickets alone was so valuable that the bonds would not have to pay interest. One-twentieth of the bonds were to be retired each year through a random drawing. The ticket privileges were guaranteed for 10 years even if a bond was redeemed. The stadium bonds went on sale August 20, 1926. A prospectus sent to each of the 63,000 alumni described the stadium and athletic building program and touted the bond's ticket buying privileges. "These bonds are reasonably certain to be taken in a very short time," football fans were warned. Bond no. 1 was purchased by former athletic director Charles Baird.

For the first 10 days, sales averaged less than 15 bonds per day. By October 1st, when it had been anticipated that the issue would be nearly sold out, Yost began to worry. The alumni were not responding; only 637 bonds had been purchased. Yost and publicity director Phil Pack feverishly developed promotional plans. A new prospectus was prepared for alumni and sent to all Michigan bank presidents and chambers of commerce as well. Pack targeted all Detroit households with incomes over $10,000, the membership of the Detroit Athletic Club, and high-income Highland Park households. Suggestions were made to raise the interest rate to 4 percent and extend ticket privileges to 20 years. In a confidential letter, Yost asked newspaper editors to cooperate in promoting the bonds to the general public. "Naturally," he added, "we do not want the public to know that the bonds have been going disappointingly slow." In a radio broadcast over WWJ, Yost tried to dispel the notion that a larger stadium meant no sellouts. The renewed appeal and warning succeeded as all bonds eventually sold before the 1927 season opener.

The contract for excavating a 230,000-cubic-yard hole for the stadium was issued to R. C. Merriam of Detroit in October 1926. By May, the site was ready for the Leck Construction company of Minnesota to start pouring concrete. At the same time, work was underway at Palmer Field, the women's athletic field house, and the intramural building. With Yost paying attention to every detail of construction and cost, Michigan Stadium was ready for the opening game against Ohio Wesleyan on October 1, 1927. An additional 15,000 wooden seats were erected for the dedication game against Ohio State. As Yost had predicted, all the "big games" were sold out.

The next step was to begin paying off the bonds. Between 1927 and 1930, the increased revenue from ticket sales provided the Athletic Department with ample funds to finance its regular operations, undertake additional construction, including the golf course, and to reduce its bonded debt. There were 550 bonds randomly selected for retirement by 1930. For the next six years, however, no bonds were redeemed. The onset of the great depression had significantly reduced ticket sales. The department managed a budget surplus, and never missed an interest payment in each of those years, but could not retire any bonds. Redemption of bonds resumed in 1937. By 1940, $625,000 in bonds had been retired. For many bondholders, the stadium bonds proved to be a good investment. By 1940 standards, 3 percent tax-free interest was an attractive rate. A growing number of holders whose bonds were randomly selected for retirement suggested that their bonds be returned to the pool. Eventually, many took advantage of an offer to have their bonds extended for five years at the 3 percent interest rate. The last of the stadium bonds were retired in 1951.

The $1.5 million in stadium bonds represents only a small portion of the money spent on the expansion of athletic facilities over the years. It was these bonds, however, that financed the facility that has given so much to Michigan including the revenue that has allowed Michigan to build some of the finest intercollegiate and intramural facilities in the nation (University of Michigan, 2007).

It is not common for teams to pay for large stadiums with a bank loan, but teams do sometimes get loans, which is another type of debt financing. This is more common with smaller enterprises. In the case of a bank loan, it is typically very different with regards to the cash flows compared to a bond. Instead of only paying off interest until maturity, as in the case of a bond, a loan is typically paid off with constant payments over time with no large payment at the end. While there are interest-only loans, generally the principal is paid off over time with each payment.

We can use a similar example for a loan as we did with a bond. Let us suppose that a team takes out a $1,000, 20-year loan with an interest rate of 5 percent. This means that the team would receive $1,000 cash inflow right away and then make periodic payments. To know how much the payments will be, we again can use a financial calculator. Because there is not an extra payment at the end of the loan, the future value is equal to zero. In this example, PV = 1,000, N = 20, I/Y = 5, and FV = 0, and the calculator gives us a value of –$80.24 for the payment.[2] Table 5.3 shows the cash flows of the loan.

Table 5.3 Cash Flows from the Loan

Year	0	1	2	...	19	20
Cash Flow	$1,000	−$80.24	−$80.24	−	−$80.24	−$80.24

Table 5.4 The First and Last Four Years of the Amortization Table

Year	Beginning-of-Year Principal ($)	Loan Payment ($)	Interest Payment ($)	Principal Payment ($)	End-of-Year Principal ($)
1	1,000.00	80.24	50.00	30.24	969.76
2	969.76	80.24	48.49	31.75	938.01
3	938.01	80.24	46.90	33.34	904.67
4	904.67	80.24	45.23	35.01	869.66
...	−	−	−	−	−
17	284.60	80.24	14.23	66.01	218.59
18	218.59	80.24	10.93	69.31	149.28
19	149.28	80.24	7.46	72.78	76.50
20	76.50	80.24	3.83	76.41	0.09

In this case, it is assumed that the interest rate is the same as the depreciation rate; therefore, the net present value of the loan is $1,000. Now that we know the cash flows associated with a loan, we can use an amortization table to calculate how much principal is left on the loan (Table 5.4).

The information in an amortization table is important. First, it shows how much the principal is at the beginning and the end of each year. This helps calculate a firm or team's wealth because it lets the organization understand how much is owed on the loan. Second, it divides the loan payment into the interest payment, which equals the principal multiplied by the interest rate, and the principal payment. The actual interest payment is important for taxes. Notice that at the beginning of the loan, a majority of the loan payment goes toward paying the interest, but at the end of the loan nearly all of the payment goes toward the principal. Appendix 1 at the end of this chapter gives much more detail on finding the present value of different cash flows.

Team Financing, Public Bonds

Every sport organization will look at its capital expenses a bit differently. What is germane, however, is that the team will seek to borrow money and, in doing so, will try to minimize its borrowing costs. Some suggest the easiest way to accomplish that objective is to have a unit of local government borrow the money so that the interest earned by the bond holders is not subject to the federal income tax. In many cases, even if the money for a venue has been borrowed by a unit of government, the team's owners are held responsible for repayment of the bond. If the public sector can borrow the money, the interest payment savings to a team, even if it repays the entire amount, can reduce the cost of the facility by tens of millions of dollars. The first objective in any sport facility financing plan is to determine if tax-exempt bonds can be sold. If they can be sold and there is a unit of government willing to extend its credit to secure the bonds, teams save a substantial amount of money even if they are going to pay the full cost of the building of a facility.

Another advantage of using public entities to issue bonds is that they can generally get lower rates because the probability of defaulting on the bond is much lower. In some cases, the public is not actually paying the bond, but they would have to if the team could not. One reason this is done is because the local government may have a higher bond rating. In other words, municipal bonds, which are bonds issued by local, state, or federal governments, offer a lower coupon rate than corporate bonds. As Table 5.5 shows, the average default rate for corporate bonds is roughly 100 times higher than municipal bonds. Therefore, the coupon rate would be substantially less if a sports arena were backed by a municipal government. But remember, although the public is not technically paying for the venue, they are responsible for bonds if they are the issuer. Care must be taken to ensure that the risk of default for the public sector is minimized. The details of aspects of facility financing plans are sometimes unclear to taxpayers.

Once the annual cost of the bonds (the mortgage for the facility) is determined, team leadership will look for new revenue streams that can be used to meet that obligation. A team might sell naming rights or other advertising packages and use that income to help repay any bonds that have been

Table 5.5 Cumulative Historic Default Rates (%)

Rating Category	Moody's		S&P	
	Muni	Corp	Muni[1]	Corp
Aaa/AAA	0.00	0.52	0.00	0.60
Aa/AA	0.06	0.52	0.00	1.50
A/A	0.03	1.29	0.23	2.91
Baa/BBB	0.13	4.64	0.32	10.29
Ba/BB	2.65	19.12	1.74	29.93
B/B	11.86	43.34	8.48	53.72
Caa-C/CCC-C	16.58	69.18	44.81	69.19
Averages				
Investment grade	0.07	2.09	0.20	4.14
Noninvestment grade	4.29	31.37	7.37	42.35
All	0.10	9.70	0.29	12.98

Source: U.S. Municipal Bond Fairness Act, 2008. (Monevator, 2010).

[1] Muni = Municipal Bond; Corp = Corporate Bond.

sold. It should come as no surprise that ticket prices usually increase when new teams move to new facilities. In part, this results from improved sight lines and the inclusion of new amenities. In one preliminary assessment, Mason and Rosentraub (2010) estimated the Edmonton Oilers would enjoy at least an additional $20 million in annual revenues when the team moved into its new venue.

Facility Financing: A Public Sector Investment

With teams negotiating to retain as much as possible from the new revenues generated by their facilities, the public sector's investment frequently involves a new tax, an increase in an existing tax, or an allocation from aggregate or total tax collections. Each of these has different impacts and implications, and some do not require residents paying more money. Indeed, some taxes are actually paid by the team. If, however, there are positive externalities generated, then it may be efficient and appropriate for residents to invest some of their money to ensure their desired returns or benefits are secured. There also are instances where tax revenues, collected for a set of purposes, have been dedicated to a sport venue and resulted in an opportunity cost. For example, some cities have a tax on hotel rooms and that money can be used for a project that advances tourism. A new facility could advance tourism, but so could many other investments. The impacts (who pays), the incidence (whose wealth is actually decreased), and the distribution (is the taxing method progressive?) are explained in the discussion that follows.

Ticket Tax

Several local governments have implemented a ticket or amusement tax that is calculated either as a percent of the ticket price or as a flat figure. This tax is added to the price of a ticket just like a sales tax on any purchase. The likely result of a ticket tax is to increase the ticket price. This increase should be less than the amount of the tax. Generally speaking, adding a ticket tax to the cost of a ticket will result in fewer fans attending events (due to increased cost). The magnitude of the change in price, and also the tax incidence, will depend on the slopes of the supply and demand curves. If fans are simply willing to pay the tax and still purchase tickets, then most of the tax incidence falls on them. If, on the other hand, fans are not willing to pay any more for tickets, then teams will actually pay the tax – in the form of receiving less revenue. While the team's financial burden depends on fans' willingness to pay, the net result of the tax is that teams receive less revenue and fans pay higher prices for tickets. The distribution of this tax depends on who exactly purchases the tickets. Lastly, as the tax does not impact nonusers, it is classified as voluntary because those who do not wish to pay the tax can decide not to attend games or events.

Parking Taxes

The same logic and effects apply to any parking taxes that are levied to offset the expense of paying for a facility. In the absence of a tax on parking, the owner of the parking lot or structure – the team or another entrepreneur – will charge what they think is the optimal price. If a portion of that fee must be transferred as a tax to the city, the price will increase. This tax is also voluntary in that only attendees who use the parking structure pay the tax. The distribution of the tax is also similar to ticket taxes.

In-Facility Sales

Additional sales or amusement taxes are sometimes placed on all transactions within a facility. Similar to ticket taxes or taxes on parking, additional amusement taxes raise the costs to fans, businesses that entertain clients, and those advertising at the facility. Prices for souvenirs, food, beverages, and advertising would increase. This tax is, again, voluntary. The tax can be avoided if fans refuse to buy things at the game or event or decide not to attend, but this would hurt the team.

Sales Taxes

A number of communities have financed their investment in sport facilities with revenues collected from a small increase in the general sales tax on all retail activities in a city, across several cities, in a county, or across several counties. Unlike the preceding three taxing tools, which were voluntary because payments were made by people attending an event, parking a car in the vicinity of a facility, or buying goods and services at a facility, the use of a general sales tax is relatively involuntary as it affects all retail sales. The only way for a consumer to avoid the tax would be to shop for all goods and services in an untaxed area. This tax affects nonusers of the sport venue, and, to avoid the tax, consumers must be inconvenienced (traveling and shopping in another city). If the majority of services are not subject to the tax by state and local laws, the sales tax is considered regressive. If all forms of consumption are taxed, then the tax would be described as proportional.

If that tax is involuntary and impacts nonusers, why do communities use this tool? There are three reasons. First, if there is a large volume of retail sales, the increase in the sales tax rate needed to finance an investment in a sport facility is usually quite small (frequently 1 percent or less). This small increment generally does not engender a great deal of political opposition. Second, the total amount of sales in a city, county, or region is quite large, so the small increment usually generates a large amount of money. Thus, the sacrifice for any one taxpayer is quite small, but the outcome is frequently large enough to support the public sector's investment in a facility. Third, if a city is home to a large regional mall that attracts shoppers from many cities, a substantial portion of the tax is actually paid by nonresidents. This "exporting" of the cost of an investment in a sport facility to nonresidents (in the form of their payment of the sales tax when they shop at the mall) attracts local political support as it gives the impression that a portion of the burden is shifted to residents of other cities, while the benefits are concentrated in the city where the facility is located. The possibility that others would pay for benefits that accrue in a city is an attractive political theme. However, even if consumers are nonlocal, the businesses are local. Since businesses are hurt by this tax, there is a local cost even when consumers are nonresidents.

The Impact of Arlington's Sales Tax for Two Venues

Arlington, Texas used an increment in its general sales tax to pay for its investment in AT&T Stadium (Dallas Cowboys) and for the Texas Rangers' new ballpark. The city is home to two major retail centers that serve residents of many different parts of the Dallas/Fort Worth region. Mills, Rosentraub, Winfree, and Cantor (2015) found that the addition increased monthly sales tax collections by $1.7 million. A large proportion was exported to residents in nearby cities. However, retail activity in Arlington, compared to growth in other cities, actually was less than would have been expected. The businesses in Arlington and its workforce suffered from less economic activity as a result of the sales tax increment. In addition, Arlington residents also pay more for taxed goods and services than do residents of other cities.

Property Taxes

Property taxes are paid by fans and non-fans, regardless of their interest in a team. The tax is not voluntary since it cannot be avoided if someone disagrees with a public investment in a sport venue. The attractiveness of the use of a property tax, however, is that a very small increase in the property tax rate will generate a large amount of money. Increases in property taxes are frequently opposed by homeowners – especially those living on fixed-incomes. Other opponents have objected to using property taxes for the facilities used by professional teams, arguing those taxes should support education and basic services provided by cities. However, there is also evidence that sport venues elevate property values. That work would suggest that using or taxing part of that increment would be appropriate as the owners benefit from the presence of the sport venue (Cantor & Rosentraub, 2012).

Tax Increment Financing (TIF) and Sport District Taxes

Many communities have also used a property tax tool, tax increment financing (TIF), to help pay for sport venues.[3] In a TIF district, the value of property in the designated area is established before the sport venue is built. The taxes that result from the growth in property values is then used to pay for the public sector's investment in the venue. Some might be tempted to suggest that there is a voluntary aspect to this sort of a plan; if someone does not want to have their property taxes used for a sport venue, they can build elsewhere. Of course, there is no way for a developer to avoid the property tax and the use of the funds if development does occur in the TIF district.

Unlike typical property taxes, TIF, CRL, and sport district taxes are voluntary in that whatever tax is collected is only paid by people who attend events or visit restaurants or other amenities in the district. TIF districts have clearly established boundaries, usually extending for several blocks. Taxes collected from consumption that takes place outside of the district is not used for the sport venue. As a result, people who do not want their tax dollars used for the sport venue simply can decide to avoid restaurants, pubs, and other amenities inside the district.

There are several elements to consider before a TIF district can be created to help pay for a sport venue. First, the establishment of the TIF district's boundaries are critical for ensuring that the venue is responsible for any increases in value. In some instances, TIF districts have encompassed areas that are so large that it is hard to argue that the all property value increments could be attributed to the venue(s) inside them. Care must be taken in setting the boundaries to ensure that the justification for the use of property increments is appropriate.

Second, the expectation is that the venue will be the catalyst for enhanced property values which in turn produce an increment in property taxes. That increment in valuation is what is "captured" by the local government agency selling the bond for the venue or the needed infrastructure. The base (value that existed prior to the building of the venue and the sale of the bond) is not dedicated to the repayment of the bond. Hence, only the incremental value of each parcel attributed to the venue is used to repay the public sector's investment. Public officials weighing the use of a TIF mechanism must be certain that the property values would likely not increase if the venue was not built. If the property values would have increased in any event, then the venue is not responsible for the creation of new taxes.

Third, TIF districts capture all local property taxes, not just those that would accrue to the city, so entities that depend on local tax revenues can be put at risk. For example, school districts are generally funded by property taxes, as are independent public library systems. In some cities, there are also independent park districts. Each of these public but independent entities loses the increment in property tax revenue that is captured by the TIF district. Since a TIF includes all of the taxes collected by each unit of government, any increases in value do not produce additional revenue for other public entities. There is often substantial concern that the implementation of a TIF could compromise a community's support for education. However, several TIF plans have provided specific protections to their local public school systems. For example, in Columbus, the City agreed to transfer any lost revenue from its general fund to the Columbus Public Schools. The State of Michigan also agreed to repay the Detroit Public Schools for any loss of revenue resulting from property taxes generated by the TIF district created for the Red Wings' and Pistons' new Little Caesars Arena and its associated real estate development. In Cleveland, the Gateway District is responsible for paying some of the property tax revenues lost by the Cleveland Public Schools even though the ballpark and arena are owned by the city and county and are therefore exempt from paying property taxes.

Fourth, when a TIF is used to repay a bond, there is risk in that the increment may be too small to satisfy the annual payments required to finance the venue. If that occurs, the government issuing the bond would have to use other funds to meet its obligation. Fearing that property value increments would not be sufficient, Columbus required Nationwide Insurance Company to be responsible for two-thirds of any annual shortfalls relative to the bonds sold for the Nationwide Arena (home to the NHL's Columbus Blue Jackets). Similarly, in exchange for public sector support for the building of a new ballpark for the San Diego Padres, the team's owner at the time guaranteed that at least $455 million in new property development would take place in the Ballpark District. If that level of property development did not occur, he personally would pay the taxes that would have been generated by that level of construction activity. The possibility that the tax increment is not produced should be part of any TIF plan.

Finally, while TIF programs have largely relied on property tax growth, it is possible to consider the use of an increment in a sales or income tax to finance a bond for a sport venue. A sales or income TIF program would require legislation similar to what states and provinces have created for property tax-based increment financing plans.

Income Tax

The use of an income tax to finance an investment in a sport venue facility has the same benefits and liabilities found in the use of the property tax. A small increment in an income tax will generate a large amount of money. The tax, however, is involuntary. The income tax is generally considered to be the most progressive of any of the taxing tools available to governments. Its use would mean the distribution of the burden could be progressive if higher-income people pay a larger portion of their income to repay the investment. Income taxes can be based on where one lives and/or works. The latter is referred to as an earnings tax, and, if that exists, suburbanites who commute to jobs in a city also would share the responsibility for an investment in a sports facility.

Tax Exporting and Tourist Taxes

If a community has a large base of businesses that sell their products to nonresidents, then a portion of their taxes can be exported to others, reducing the burden on residents. Tourist taxes (transient occupancy taxes) and other taxes paid by visitors are exported to non-residents. This occurs as businesses incorporate their total tax bill in the prices of their goods and services. As most businesses have clients from a variety of places within a region, state, or country, the cost of an investment in a sport facility can be partially exported to nonresidents. This is particularly true in cities where businesses account for most of the property taxes paid. If business property, for example, accounts for two-thirds or more of the total valuation of property, then at least two-thirds of the cost of the investment would be paid for through the sale of those companies' products. As property taxes are generally considered mildly progressive, use of this tax instrument – while sometimes politically inconvenient – does distribute the burden in a progressive fashion, with higher income individuals and businesses with more property supporting far more of the investment. One drawback is that it becomes harder to entice new businesses to come or to get existing businesses to stay.

Taxes on a region's tourists or business visitors typically engender less political opposition than some others because the immediate impact falls on nonresidents. As a result, taxes on hotel rooms and rental cars have been used to support the public sector's investment in sports facilities in several areas. The most recent example of this is Las Vegas, with their new football stadium. While tourist taxes make a good deal of political sense as a result of the lower levels of opposition from voters, from one perspective, their imposition may be inappropriate. In this perspective of tax efficiency, some believe that those paying a levy should be the same people who benefit from the existence of the good, benefit, or amenity the levy funds. In other words, residents are generally more likely to use sport venues on a regular basis (or at least more than tourists would), so residents should be the ones who pay taxes to support the venue. As a result, some argue that collecting taxes from those who do not benefit from the asset created (charging tourists taxes) is not appropriate. There is also the possibility that taxing tourists reduces their spending on other activities. However, it should be noted that in some instances the tourist tax increment is so small, given the number of visitors and hotel rooms in some markets, that its impact on overall consumption levels is negligible. In addition, as tourists frequently have higher annual income levels, the tax is being paid by those with more discretionary income. In the case of business travelers, the cost of the tax is actually borne by their employers. Lastly, the tax is voluntary; tourists or those on business can decide not to visit an area. Tourists might decide to reduce the number of nights they spend in an area or decide to stay with friends or family and avoid the tax.

Sin (Excise) Tax

Taxes on the purchase and consumption of alcohol and tobacco products are popularly described as sin taxes. These taxes are often seen as the least objectionable, since they increase the price of products considered unhealthy and, if abused or excessively consumed, dangerous. As a result, it is more politically desirable to impose a sin tax to help support the public sector's investment in a sport facility. Again, as with tax exporting, it may not be appropriate to ask those who do not benefit from an amenity to pay for it. In addition, sin taxes are frequently insufficient to repay substantial investments in facilities but can be part of a group of revenue streams to repay the public sector's investment. The sin tax is essentially a special form of a sales tax (limited to a single product or a group of products) and therefore is also properly defined as an excise tax.

Gaming Taxes and Lotteries

Maryland used proceeds from the state lottery to finance the investment in the new stadium that convinced Art Modell to relocate the Cleveland Browns to Baltimore (Ravens). While gaming taxes and lotteries are seen as voluntary, sufficient research exists to sustain the view that in operation these taxes are regressive (Mikesell, 2009).

Food and Beverage Taxes

A tax on the consumption of food and beverages sold at restaurants and pubs has emerged as a popular tax to support the public sector's investment in sports facilities. This tax is seen as voluntary (it does not apply to food purchased at markets for consumption offsite) and it is either proportional or progressive given the clientele at restaurants and the prices at more exclusive restaurants.

Facility Financing: Who Really Pays?

The relationship between supply and demand for teams is at least partially responsible for the expanding role of the public sector in the financing of facilities. Part of the risk associated with a private investment in a professional sports team has been transferred to and accepted by the public sector. However, this observation does not address the key analytical issues, which are: (1) who is ultimately paying for the cost of the facilities when taxes are increased to finance the public sector's investment; (2) are those payments in excess of the benefits received; and (3) how do any changes in who pays influence the distribution of the benefits from sports? To address these questions, and to understand their dynamics, it is best to initially consider the most direct and simple model. That model is the one that existed prior to the extensive involvement of the public sector in the financing of facilities, but it might be one that fails to distribute the costs appropriately in relationship to the benefits produced.

Value for the Team

Before the public sector began participating in the financing of arenas, ballparks, and stadia, team owners paid for facilities and the cost of their maintenance – solely and in entirety. Owners were also responsible for player salaries, franchise fees, and costs relating to team operations, spring training (summer for football and late summer and early fall for basketball and hockey), player development (minor leagues), and travel. If revenues met projections, then one would observe that the costs for the ballpark were covered by revenue from fans' ticket purchases. This would imply that demand was sufficient to sustain the needed price to generate a profit after all costs were paid. In instances where teams were unable to generate a profit that would cover all costs, owners could choose between relocating or ending operations. Whichever of these scenarios played out, the transaction for a facility was confined to economic exchanges between a team's fan base, the players, and the owner. For some, this seems only appropriate as spectator sport is essentially a private good that should be sustained by market transactions.

Turning attention to a venue, owners will add amenities as long as the marginal revenue generated exceeds the costs. In recent years, owners have seen it beneficial to add entrances and enhanced architectural features to attract sponsors. Large concourses can make it possible to have more points for retail sales. Wider seats can also lead to fans' willingness to pay more to attend games. Regardless of the amenity, it is also clear that a team's revenue position would be enhanced if the public sector paid for some or all of the cost of these amenities, permitting the team to retain all or most of the revenue generated. As negotiations take place between a team and the public sector, the franchise's objective is to ensure that an ever-growing share of the capital cost for a venue is paid by taxpayers. At the same time, the public sector's position usually includes a focus on having more of a venue's costs paid by fans and the team through the prices paid for tickets or the fees charged to sponsors.

Value for the Public Sector

Treating sport as a private good might ignore externalities that create other benefits that should be considered as value for the public sector from the existence of a venue and the presence of a team. Should the public sector intercede to protect that welfare as it does when other types of public goods are not produced as a result of market inefficiencies? It should be recognized that sport generates positive externalities for people who do not attend games or "consume" them through broadcasts. As will be discussed further, those benefits include the enjoyment of a team's success and any of the conversations or exchanges that occur when fans discuss recent games. If the team did not exist, these benefits would not exist.

Goods and services, as well as the actions of people, can create two different types of externalities. Those that improve life or another person's welfare are considered positive externalities, and those that make an individual's situation worse are described as negative externalities. If you drive a car, for example, initially you paid all the costs associated with the benefits you received. Those costs include those associated with ownership of the vehicle as well as the cost of building and maintaining roads (financed through gasoline taxes paid when you purchased fuel for the vehicle). In this manner, then, the transaction was limited to drivers (consumers), auto workers, those people who built the streets (labor), those who owned the manufacturing plants for cars (capital), and those who owned the companies that paved the streets and roads (capital). When your vehicle was driven, however, an externality was generated (air pollution), which creates costs in the form of reduced air quality, which can lead to breathing difficulties as well as the destruction of property (vegetation could be poisoned, property values could decline if pollution levels are too high, etc.). To reduce this negative externality, new costs were imposed on consumers (air purification systems built into cars). Another example of a negative externality is when someone throws some waste material on the road or sidewalk or on park grounds. The cost of that negative externality is evident in the expense society must allocate to clean the streets and parks. If the park or street is not cleaned, then all future users suffer the inconvenience of cleaning the area or fewer benefits from having to use a public space that is now dirty.

Sport generates externalities, too. Some see a negative externality in the form of traffic that might be generated when a large number of spectators converge on a facility or seek parking nearby, and others might see a negative outcome from society's preoccupation with sports and competition. To be sure, there are people who see these same negative externalities as having positive effects. For example, traffic and congestion increases parking revenues for some property owners and others believe the competition produced by games teaches important values to participants and fans. It seems an endless debate would ensue if one tried to conclude whether or not the positive effects outweigh the negative, or if some negative externalities are offset by the positive elements seen by others from the same effect. We consider a set of positive externalities that result from sport that several scholars have isolated. Four broad categories of positive externalities have been identified.

Social capital is the first of the positive externalities that should be considered. These benefits were best described by Putnam (2000: 411) in his popular book, *Bowling Alone: The Collapse and Revival of American Community*: "To build bridging social capital requires that we transcend our social and political and professional identities to connect with people unlike ourselves. This is why teams provide good venues for social capital creation." When does this form of social capital exist? One can point to any of the community-wide celebrations that occur after key victories or when people from dissimilar backgrounds are able to talk about the team and, as Putnam observes, get to know people in their community who are unlike them and may well disagree with them on many other points. The shared common interest in the team establishes a basis for compromise but also for recognizing that even with those with whom there are different positions or values there is still a degree of commonality and agreement. When a team wins, there is a palatable excitement "in the air," or a sort of civic celebration that is evident even if it is difficult to quantify. Everyone can remember their feelings of unity or "social capital" in New England when the Red Sox finally buried the "curse of the Bambino" in 2004, when the Cleveland Cavaliers ended Cleveland's decades of frustration with the winning of an NBA title in 2016, and when the Chicago Cubs finally won a World Series in the same year. Each of the winning teams was feted at a parade where millions of residents and fans rejoiced.

Canadian fans know where they were when Sidney Crosby's overtime goal against the USA netted Canada the Olympic gold medal in 2010, just as many Americans still recall what they were doing when Team USA upset the Soviet Union in the 1980 Olympics. Clearly, at each celebration and on the days when the teams won, extraordinary social benefits were created for residents. Those who have lived in college towns or are vocal alumni also know the benefits of the social capital created by a victory against an arch rival or a national championship.

A team's performance also can elevate a city's image nationally and make residents proud to live in the area. The Cavaliers and Cleveland, the Mets and Yankees in New York, and the Red Sox and Boston are each examples of how a team can come to define its host city. When teams lose, they also have the potential to create a negative impression of an area and that also must be taken into account. Yet, many residents in a large number of communities believe that the "major league status" conveyed by a team's presence is an externality that has a clear value.

While there might not be a monetary benefit from the social capital of attracting more than one million residents to downtown Cleveland to celebrate the Cavaliers' championship win, such an event does build bridges between people in divergent societies and engender a sense of unity, even if only for a short period of time. Social capital unites people across social classes and races. This is what Putnam meant by "bridging" capital. For any society to survive and advance a common agenda, there must be a set of institutions and activities that build bridges across economic classes and races. Without that "common ground," compromise, cooperation, and solidarity may never exist. Their absence would generate substantial costs or losses from a lack of progress to, in the most extreme examples, social disintegration and conflict. Bridging capital is regarded by many social scientists as the glue that holds cities, counties, and countries together. If they are correct, ensuring that this form of social capital exists represents a substantial collective benefit and, in its absence, a society is worse off. Therefore, some form of collective payments to ensure the potential for bridging social capital exists may well exceed the costs of a tax for a ballpark. It is also instructive to look at the social capital at a time of severe political conflict or contested elections. At those times people look to social institutions that can be the bridge between people with very intense political differences.

Teams and the facilities they use contribute to and, in some instances, help to define the identity of a city region. Some sport facilities **create a synecdochic effect**, which can enhance the city's image. A synecdoche is an image (or figure of speech) that creates an entire image. Telling someone that it is "the top of the ninth" or that to pass a test you need a "Hail Mary" creates well-understood meanings or word images. Similarly, a picture of the Eiffel Tower creates an image of Paris and France. Sports facilities can also be synecdochic, like the "the Green Monster" in Boston or Lambeau Field in Green Bay. The Packers and their venue have been synonymous with Green Bay and may well be the most distinctive aspect of that community's image.

Another benefit that can accrue to the public sector from the presence of a team is the **ability of teams to relocate regional economic activity**. That relocation can create important positive externalities. In many regions, the suburbanization of businesses and residential communities has weakened the tax bases of central cities where there is, frequently, an over-concentration of lower-income families. If teams also locate in suburban areas, the entertainment spending that takes place will generate tax revenues for suburban governments and the part-time or other jobs that are available may not be accessible to inner city residents. Conversely, teams located in downtown areas ensure that a certain level of the region's economic activity and the tax revenues produced by that spending (and the jobs related to that

Figure 5.1 Synecdochic Venues: *Boston's "Green Monster"*.

spending) are concentrated in central cities. To be clear, there will be losers with this economic relocation as less spending takes place in other parts of the region. However, relocating economic activity is a major public policy issue in several central cities, including Baltimore, Cincinnati, Cleveland, Detroit, Milwaukee, Pittsburgh, and St. Louis. If negotiated accordingly, a public investment can hinge on a city's ability to decide where a venue is located. In these instances, the public sector can choose to build the venue in a place that allows benefits to accrue to central cities from the redistribution of tax revenues, employment opportunities, and overall economic activity. As the urban economist Edwin Mills observed, *where* something happens (in terms of economic activity) is often just as important an issue as *if* economic development takes place at all (Mills and Hamilton, 1997). A public sector investment to ensure a team's facility is located where the benefits from fan spending and enhancements to the central city's finances are maximized could well be something a region should support.

In addition to relocating economic activity to an area, teams and facilities also have the **ability to attract residents and businesses** to an area. Economic development in the 21st century is driven and, in most instances, defined by the presence of a well-educated workforce and the people who are the "idea generators" behind the creation of new businesses, products, and processes. There is no debate that an educated workforce is important for a region's economic development. The needed labor force can be produced by educational systems that foster innovative thinking and creativity or a package of amenities that attract and retain the desired workers.

Companies often locate where they have the most confidence that they can attract and retain the labor force they need to innovate and lead their industry. Amenities assume a role in the choices made by people. It is not entirely clear if teams or sports attract people to a region, but there are some important indicators (attendance) and a few studies that now underscore the importance of amenity packages in attracting and retaining a highly skilled workforce (Beckstead, Brown, & Gellatly, 2008; Rosentraub & Joo, 2009; Rosentraub, 2010). The contribution by a team to a region's array of amenities and its attractiveness to high-skilled labor and entrepreneurs is another potential externality generating benefits. The loss of that benefit could create financial losses, and, therefore, there is collective interest in ensuring that a team remains in a region.

How much are these positive externalities worth to a region and its residents? If these intangible benefits were worth just $5 or $10 a year to every household in a region, the cumulative total would be sufficient to suggest (1) that a team's presence would create substantial value or ensure that welfare levels were not diminished and (2) that an investment by the public sector to ensure a franchise's presence would be appropriate and efficient (benefits exceed costs). Several scholars have tried to quantify the positive externalities that often emerge as intangible benefits and sometimes the amounts found exceeded the public sector's investment in a facility. We introduce these issues into the model not to minimize the costs imposed on fans and taxpayers as a result of a constrained supply of franchises maintained by team owners (usually described as monopoly rents by economists) but to point out that there are important reasons for an appropriate public investment to ensure that there is no loss of positive externalities.

Some might be tempted to argue that there are a number of other private transactions that produce positive externalities and that those externalities could occur without an investment by a government. There can be no objection to that point. What is critical, however, is that the positive externalities created by a team are known, and assuring their occurrence may warrant a level of payment. This observation does not mean the public sector should pay 100 percent of the cost of a facility allowing a team to retain 100 percent of the generated revenues. The challenge for a community is to provide the investment that matches the positive externalities without turning that investment into a subsidy that generates excess monopoly rents (excessive salaries and profits) for owners and players. To be sure, this is a difficult task and negotiation, but one which every city has to conduct to protect taxpayers while being sure that desirable positive externalities are not lost.

Regional or Single City Participation

An example of the difficulty in weighing positive externalities and their value to residents (coupled with the desire to be home to two professional teams despite the relatively small size of the region) is underscored by the Indianapolis metropolitan region's decision to build a new facility to ensure the presence of the Colts for 30 additional years. It was argued that if benefits from the Colts' presence accrued to residents in all of the cities in the metropolitan region, the public sector would make an investment paid by residents of each of these cities. As a result, local governments in central Indiana invested more than $750 million to build a domed stadium. Lucas Oil Stadium serves as the home for the Indianapolis Colts and hosts numerous NCAA events, Indiana youth sport events, and large-scale entertainment events. The annual payment on the bonds sold to finance the facility is $33.6 million, and the public sector is also responsible for maintaining the facility.

The region's investment, then, is secured by more than just the presence of an NFL franchise. The NCAA's headquarters are located in Indianapolis and, as a result, the city hosts a robust number of NCAA events. The Central Indiana market has fewer than 1.7 million residents. Despite this relatively small population base, the region is also home to an NBA franchise and the continent's largest sporting event, the Indianapolis 500, as well as other motor sport events at the Speedway. At the same time, the region helps support the financial success of the athletic teams at Purdue, Butler, and Indiana Universities.

Note that both of Indianapolis' major professional teams have encountered "troughs" where ticket sales slumped in response to poor performance. In the early 1990s, the Colts were the region's second team behind the Pacers, who were enjoying repeated runs for the Eastern Division championship in the NBA. In 2000, the Pacers lost in the NBA Finals. During the past several years, the Pacers' competitiveness has declined and so have ticket sales, while the popularity of the Colts has soared. There have also been periods when both teams have had substantial levels of success.

When the public sector made a substantial investment in Lucas Oil Stadium, the Colts' owner agreed to release the public sector from an earlier commitment to enhance the team's income and to remain in the city for 30 years. For the positive externalities of having the team play its home games in downtown Indianapolis, the public sector's annual investment could approach $40 million (principal and interest as noted is $33.6 million and annual maintenance costs could be as much as $5 million).

Are the externalities worth that much to Indiana's residents? Rosentraub, Swindell, and Tsvetkova (2009), using a contingent valuation survey research method, found that the annual value of the team's presence to the state's residents exceeds $66 million. If that measure of the benefits accruing to residents of the state from the team's presence is accurate, then even with a $40 million annual cost (and even one that is slightly higher), the investment by the public sector generates a positive return.

In larger markets (e.g., Boston, Chicago, Dallas, New York, Los Angeles) there is generally less need to pay for the positive externalities. The wealth and size of these markets are sufficient to generate substantial profits and opportunities that will attract investors willing to pay for a franchise and a facility. While owners in these areas will still try to negotiate and secure payments for the externalities their teams generate, public commitments in these markets are harder to come by and are considerably smaller when they do occur. For example, in 2016 the Rams secured permission to relocate to the Los Angeles region; the team's owner will pay 100 percent of construction and maintenance costs for the team's new domed stadium, which will likely cost upwards of $1.8 billion. It would be foolhardy to minimize the advantage larger markets have when negotiating with teams. In some instances, however, even in these areas, teams have received large inducements. The owners of the Phillies and Eagles were successful in convincing Pennsylvania and Philadelphia to each contribute to the cost of building new facilities for their teams. Those investments seem excessive given the size of the Philadelphia market (7.2 million people in the combined statistical area, 8th largest in the in the United States).

In several large markets, the public sector has assumed responsibility for the infrastructure required to have a sport venue built. Should those expenses be a public or private responsibility? There is no straightforward answer to that question. Cities provide streets, sewers, and other forms of civil infrastructure to sustain business development. In other instances, special development impact fees have been assessed. Would those be appropriate for sport venues or are positive externalities generated by teams deserving of public support for the needed infrastructure enhancements? This question must be answered by each community.

Financing College Sports Venues

There a few collegiate football and basketball programs that are sufficiently popular to be able to finance their venues through donations, ticket prices, and personal seat licenses. At universities such as Michigan, Ohio State, Stanford, Penn State, Alabama, and Texas, alumni donations have been integral to the financing of athletic venues.

At other universities, student fees and specific allocations from state legislatures have been used to pay for venues. Some universities have also entered into partnerships with local governments to build venues. For example, the University of Louisville and the City of Louisville joined together to build an arena in 2010 (KFC Yum! Center). There have also been partnerships between universities and professional teams to build venues. For example, in Frisco, Texas, the City, school district, and Dallas Cowboys joined together to build a venue, dubbed "The Star," that is used by the local high school football and soccer teams for games and the Dallas Cowboys for training and practice. Other universities and professional teams have also been known to share the same venue, as well. The Carolina Hurricanes (NHL) and North Carolina State University use the same arena, just as the Pittsburgh Steelers and University of Pittsburgh share Heinz Field.

Notes

1 It is important to double-check calculator settings when making these calculations. Some common mistakes are that the payment per year (P/Y) equals 1 and, in this case, the payments should be end-of-the-year payments because a firm would start paying off the bond at the end of the first year. Furthermore, the calculator separates cash inflows and outflows. Therefore, to get a positive net present value, the outflows need to be negative.
2 A typical loan might have monthly payments, but because the number of periods and interest rates are in years, this represents a yearly payment. Financial calculators can be adjusted to make monthly payments (P/Y = 12).
3 In Canada, a community revitalization levy (or CRL) is similar to a TIF.

References

Beckstead, D., Brown, W. M., & Gellatly, G. 2008. The left brain of North American cities: Scientists and engineers and urban growth. *International Regional Science Review* 31 (3): 304–338.

Buchanan, J. M. 1965. An economic theory of clubs. *Economica* 32 (125): 1–14.

Cantor, M., & Rosentraub, M. S. 2012. A ballpark and neighborhood change: Economic integration, a recession, and the altered demography of San Diego's Ballpark District after 8 years. *City, Culture, and Society* 3 (3): 219–226.

Mason, D., & Rosentraub, M. S. 2010. *Financing a new arena in downtown Edmonton.* Unpublished report. City of Edmonton, Alberta: University of Alberta, Faculty of Physical Education and Recreation.

Mikesell, J. 2009. *Fiscal administration: Analysis and applications for the public sector.* Boston: Wadsworth Publishing.

Mills, E. S., & Hamilton, B. 1997. *Urban economics.* New York: Basic Books.

Mills, B. M., Rosentraub, M. S., Winfree, J. A., & Cantor, M. B. 2014. Fiscal outcomes and tax impacts from stadium financing strategies in Arlington, Texas. *Public Money & Management* 34 (2): 145–152.

Monevator. 2010. Bond default probabilities: by rating, *Monevator*, April 9. Retrieved from http://monevator.com/bond-default-rating-probability/ (accessed April 9, 2010).

Musgrave, R. A., & Musgrave, P. B. 1973. Public finance in theory and practice. New York: McGraw Hill.

Ostrom, V., Tiebout, C .M., & Warren, R. 1961. The organization of government in metropolitan areas: A theoretical inquiry. *American Political Science Review* 55 (4): 831–842.

Putnam, R. D. 2000. *Bowling alone: The collapse and revival of American community*. New York: Simon and Schuster.

Rosentraub, M. S. 1997. *Major league losers: The real cost of sports and who's paying for it*. New York: Harpercollins.

Rosentraub, M. S. 2010. *Major league winners: Using sport facilities and cultural centers for economic development*. Boca Raton, FL: CRC Press/Taylor and Francis.

Rosentraub, M. S., & Joo, M. 2009. Tourism and economic development: Which investments produce gains for regions? *Tourism Management* 30 (5): 759–770.

Rosentraub, M. S., Swindell, D., & Tsvetkova, S. 2009. Justifying public investments in sports: Measuring the intangibles. *Journal of Tourism* 9 (2): 133–159.

Tiebout, C. M. 1956. A pure theory of local expenditures. *Journal of Political Economy* 64 (5): 416–424.

University of Michigan. 2007. Michigan Stadium story, *Bentley Historical Library*, April 15. Retrieved from http://bentley.umich.edu/athdept/stadium/stadtext/bonds.htm (accessed July 31, 2010).

Appendix I

This appendix shows more of the mathematics behind the time value of money. First, there are three types of cash flows: lump sums, annuities, and mixed streams. Lump sums are simply one payment, while an annuity is a constant payment that is made each period. A mixed stream of payments is non-constant or is made in uneven intervals. We will first focus on lump sums, which is the same technique used to find mixed stream cash flows. To find the value of a mixed stream cash flow, each payment must be treated like a lump sum.

When making an investment with a fixed interest rate, an investor will want to know how much money they will have at the end of the investment, which is the future value. The equation for calculating the future value of a lump sum, given the principal and interest rate, is

$$FV = principal(1 + r)^N$$

where the principal is the investment, r is the interest rate, and N is the number of periods of the investment. This assumes that there is a yearly compound interest rate. We also can calculate what is called a future value interest factor. The future value interest factor tells us the future value of each dollar invested in the principal. The future value interest factor is calculated by:

$$FVIF = (1 + r)^N$$

Rearranging these equations, we can also find the present value of a future lump sum,

$$PV = \frac{principal}{(1+r)^N}$$

where principal in this case is a future lump sum.

The present value interest factor (the present value of one future dollar) is calculated by:

$$PVIF = \frac{1}{(1+r)^N}$$

Annuities include bonds, loan payments, and many other contracts. Companies also may want to know how much money they will have if they invest a certain amount each year. The future value of an annuity is given by:

$$FV_{Annuity} = payment(1+r)^1 + payment(1+r)^2 + \ldots$$

$$+ payment(1+r)^{N-1} + payment(1+r)^N$$

$$= \sum_{t=1}^{N} payment(1+r)^t$$

The future value interest factor for an annuity, which is the future value of one dollar invested each time period, is equal to:

$$FVIF_{Annuity} = (1+r)^1 + (1+r)^2 + \ldots + (1+r)^{N-1} + (1+r)^N = \sum_{t=1}^{N}(1+r)^t$$

It also is important to know the present value of an annuity because firms often pay or receive annuities. The present value of an annuity is given by:

$$PV_{Annuity} = \frac{payment}{(1+r)^1} + \frac{payment}{(1+r)^2} + \ldots + \frac{payment}{(1+r)^{N-1}} + \frac{payment}{(1+r)^N} = \sum_{t=1}^{N} \frac{payment}{(1+r)^t}$$

The present value interest factor for an annuity is

$$PVIF_{Annuity} = \frac{1}{(1+r)^1} + \frac{1}{(1+r)^2} + \ldots + \frac{1}{(1+r)^{N-1}} + \frac{1}{(1+r)^N} = \sum_{t=1}^{N} \frac{1}{(1+r)^t}$$

This discussion of future and present value for annuities has glossed over the difference between beginning of the year payments and end of the year payments. When calculating the future value of an annuity, beginning of the year payments were assumed, and when calculating the present value of an annuity, end of the year payments were assumed. This was done because it would be somewhat rare to calculate a future value when the first payment is in one year or calculate a present value when there is an immediate payment. For example, if a business takes out a loan, it would be odd to make the first payment at the exact same time they received the loan. So, if a calculator is being used to solve for both future values and present values of annuities, this setting must often be switched. If for some reason one is calculating the future value of an annuity with end of the year payments, the formula is

$$FV_{Annuity} = payment + payment(1+r)^1 + \ldots + payment(1+r)^{N-2}$$

$$+ payment(1+r)^{N-1} = \sum_{t=0}^{N-1} payment(1+r)^t$$

The present value of an annuity with beginning of the year payments is given by:

$$PV_{Annuity} = payment + \frac{payment}{(1+r)^1} + \ldots + \frac{payment}{(1+r)^{N-2}} + \frac{payment}{(1+r)^{N-1}}$$

$$= \sum_{t=0}^{N-1} \frac{payment}{(1+r)^t}$$

Notice that the only difference is that time periods go from 0 to $N-1$ instead of 1 to N.

A perpetuity is simply an annuity with an infinite life. In this case, $N = \infty$. While infinite payments might be unrealistic, there are annuities with a very long lifespan which continue until the payments cannot be made. The future value of a perpetuity is incalculable; however, the present value of an annuity is

$$PV_{Perpetuity} = \frac{payment}{(1+r)^1} + \frac{payment}{(1+r)^2} + \frac{payment}{(1+r)^3} + \ldots = \frac{payment}{r}$$

and the present value interest factor is:

$$PVIF_{Perpetuity} = \frac{1}{(1+r)^1} + \frac{1}{(1+r)^2} + \frac{1}{(1+r)^3} + \ldots = \frac{1}{r}$$

The succinctness of this mathematical formula makes valuing perpetuities easy. Also, while realistically perpetuities might not have an infinite life, this valuation technique can be very close if the annuity has a long lifespan of, say, 30 years or more.

Sometimes money is compounded more than annually. Occasionally, money is compounded semiannually or monthly. If money is being compounded M times a year, then this effectively increases the interest rate. This means that money is being compounded MN times and the interest gained in between compounding is at a rate of r/M. Therefore, the future value of a lump sum is

$$FV = principal\left(1 + \frac{r}{M}\right)^{NM}$$

The present value of a lump sum is

$$PV = \frac{principal}{\left(1 + \dfrac{r}{M}\right)^{NM}}$$

The future value of an annuity is

$$FV_{Annuity} = \sum_{t=1}^{N} payment\left(1 + \frac{r}{M}\right)^{tM}$$

And the present value of an annuity is

$$PV_{Annuity} = \sum_{t=1}^{N} \frac{payment}{\left(1 + \dfrac{r}{M}\right)^{tM}}$$

Often, interest is constantly being compounded so that it is immediately added to the principal. Daily compounding is approximately the same as continuously compounding. The future value of a lump sum payment with continuous compounding is given by:

$$FV = principal(e^{rt})$$

where e is the exponential function, often labeled exp on calculators.

The present value of a lump sum payment with continuous compounding is

$$PV = \frac{principal}{e^{rt}}$$

An annuity with continuous compounding can be difficult because there is not a simple equation. There are a couple of ways of circumventing this problem. One is simply treating an annuity as a mixed stream cash flow and finding the future or present value of each payment. This can be extremely tedious for an annuity with many payments. Another way is to adjust the interest rate.

All interest rates can be classified into nominal and effective annual rates. A nominal annual rate is the actual interest rate charged. Thus far, we have been assuming interest rates have been nominal annual rates. The effective annual rate is the actual amount of interest that is paid over one year. For yearly compounding, nominal rates are the same as effective rates. If the interest is compounded more than once a year, the effective annual rate is higher than the nominal annual rate. For semiannual compounding, the effective annual rate is given by:

$$EAR = \left(1 + \frac{r}{m}\right)^{m} - 1$$

If the interest is being compounded continuously, then the effective annual rate is

$$EAR = e^{r} - 1$$

Therefore, if an annuity is continuously compounded, it is appropriate to first find the effective annual rate and then use that in the previous equations. For example, suppose there is a nominal annual rate of 10 percent, but it is continuously compounded. The effective annual rate is 10.52 percent ($e^{1} - 1 = .1052$). This rate can then be used in the equations above, or using a financial calculator, to solve for the future value or present value of an annuity.

The annual percentage rate (APR) is equal to the nominal annual rate of interest and the annual percentage yield (APY) is equal to the effective annual rate of interest. These rates must often be disclosed by banks or credit cards companies.

Chapter 6

Teams, Venues, and Real Estate Development

Introduction

Attributed to William Dillard, founder of Dillard's department stores, one of the most common terms in real estate is "location, location, location." As noted in Chapter 4, the phrase is also very relevant to the business of sport; the availability and location of land are the two most important factors that guide site selection for sport venues. Sport venues, when complemented by additional development and other amenities, can contribute to the revitalization of urban neighborhoods and enhance adjacent property values. That enhanced value has motivated many team owners to change their business models to include real estate development as part of their team's business activities.

Oriole Park at Camden Yards (opened 1992) was the first venue designed to both complement and facilitate adjacent real estate development and the horizontal integration of sport and entertainment. Its design, led by Janet Marie Smith and team president Larry Lucchino, illustrated for the sport industry what could be accomplished with the land surrounding a venue if a team attracted millions of visits and had control of adjacent land. From their pioneering effort, two development approaches emerged. The first involved real estate outside venues, on adjacent land. When sufficient acreage could be secured, new neighborhoods were built (e.g., San Diego Ballpark District; Columbus Arena District; The District Detroit). Other owners focused on building new types of entertainment complexes when smaller amounts of acreage were available and market conditions favored a focus on restaurants, pubs, and live performance spaces instead of residential buildings, hotels, or offices.

Even when an owner was not interested in developing adjacent real estate or including other entertainment venues into his or her sport business model, there was still a need for a far larger "footprint" for the new venue. As discussed in Chapter 4, the larger footprint did not affect the size of the playing field and often the seating capacity was also smaller; rather, the extra space was needed for the various amenities built into the new venues, which were designed to encourage fans to spend far more time (and money) at the venues. The second approach to real estate involved developing the space within venues. To expand the revenue streams at these new facilities, space was needed for luxury seating and to deliver higher quality food and beverages in expansive concourses where fans could linger while receiving service in a relatively short period of time. Video displays in the concourses and other entertainment spaces ensured fans would not miss any of the action while they made their purchases or talked with clients, friends, or colleagues. This chapter focuses both on the management of the real estate *inside* facilities and that which *surrounds* them.

The Increasing Value of Downtown Locations for Sport Facilities

With ballparks and arenas attracting between 750,000 and 3 million visits each year, sport and entertainment venues have become the most visited spaces in many urban areas. Even in larger urban centers with many tourist attractions that also attract millions of visits, sport venues still retain their allure. At least four factors have contributed to the enhanced value of sport venues. First, arenas, ballparks, and stadia are often located at the nexus of many transit systems, meaning it is easy to get to and from the area from many parts of a region. Second, sport facilities now routinely include amenities that are available before, during, and after games and events, and in some areas on non-event days. Third, horizontal integration of sport with entertainment operations is now increasingly popular. Fourth, sport has sustained its popularity across several decades.

In the early years of spectator sport, most fans relied on public transportation to commute to games. To make the commute as inexpensive as possible (to encourage more fans to attend games), facilities were built at the nexus of public transportation lines or in urban neighborhoods where many could bike or walk to games. When fans shifted their preference from public transit to automobiles, team owners sought locations where they could surround their venues with a vast number of parking spaces. The post-1960 era saw millions of fans relocating from central cities to the suburbs, all of whom preferred to drive to games. As a result, team owners followed their customers to these newly emerging cities and built facilities with acres of adjacent parking spots. The teams that stayed in urban centers were met with demands for ample parking to meet their customers' preference for private as opposed to public transportation. As leagues expanded in the west and south in the 1950s, 1960s, and 1970s, the provision of ample parking became a necessity.

Then, demonstrated in the last several decades, the advent of luxury seating and the inclusion of other in-facility amenities enhanced the value of downtown locations. The allure of downtown locations for new venues with luxury seating came from the large concentration of businesses likely to be interested in suites and other luxury seating options. The Cleveland Cavaliers, Washington Wizards (previously the Baltimore Bullets), San Francisco Giants, Detroit Lions, and Detroit Pistons had moved to suburban locations and then relocated back to downtown areas. Despite the decentralization of economic activity, banks, law firms, real estate corporations, and other related firms have maintained offices in financial districts. Ensuring that this portion of a team's fan base has easy access to new facilities has become a financial necessity. This change in the ways teams earn money has created new development opportunities for many cities, including Baltimore, Cleveland, Denver, Indianapolis, Los Angeles, Philadelphia, Pittsburgh, and St. Louis. In each of these markets, downtown revitalization strategies were enhanced by the presence of sport venues and adjoining entertainment and cultural centers. Placing these other amenities near sport venues helped attract fans to the downtown area before games for pre-game activities and convinced them to stay longer afterwards, essentially enlivening downtown areas. In many cities, new residential properties attracted people to live in downtown areas that in the past had seen a substantial decline in demand.

Aside from businesses located in central business districts, who has actually raised the demand for real estate adjacent to sport and entertainment venues? Which individuals? Across the past 20 years, there has been an increasing interest in urban living and lifestyles from two different market segments. Young professionals just beginning their careers have become primary tenants in downtown neighborhoods across the country. Having decided to postpone child-rearing, this growing market segment has created a demand for apartments and condominiums that offer easy access to nearby restaurants and entertainment. Capitalizing on this trend, developers (and in some cases, team owners interested in real estate) have built condominiums, townhouses, and apartments in downtown areas near sport venues. Demand for this urban lifestyle also comes from the baby boomer generation. Having completed their child-raising responsibilities, this large cohort of empty nesters has created a strong demand for condominiums and townhouses in downtown neighborhoods. Several team owners have focused on downtown locations for new facilities and used those locations to anchor related real estate investments (e.g., Brooklyn, Columbus, Denver, Los Angeles, Newark, San Diego). This is but one example of horizontal integration that has now changed the definition of which land is the most valuable for a sports facility.

In-Facility Real Estate

It might seem unusual to use real estate management terms to describe sport facilities, but at their core, ballparks, stadiums, and arenas are quite similar to other large-scale real estate projects. Similar to malls, for example, these venues offer teams large tracts of space, and maximizing revenues requires managers to realize the potential each offers to enhance the bottom line. It is important to think of just a few examples before discussing the management issues and revenue potential that is available within a facility. The 60-yard video/scoreboard that hangs across the Dallas Cowboys' AT&T Stadium provides 25,000 square feet of space across which messages can be delivered to as many as 100,000 people. For scale, comfortable three-bedroom houses typically have approximately 2,500 square feet of living space. One could think of the Cowboys' scoreboard as being the equivalent of ten of these houses. Managing these houses, if they were to be rented, would create enormous revenue potential. If the space created by the giant video board did not offer sufficient new revenue possibilities for the Cowboys' business model, the new stadium also offers 11,000 square feet of ribbon board space: electronic message boards that form a giant ring around the entire facility. That would add another four houses worth of revenue potential to the inventory. AT&T Stadium itself encloses 3 million square feet, complete with concourses that are 15,000 and 20,000 square feet in size. Yankee Stadium, though smaller than the Cowboys mega-facility, is 63 percent larger than its predecessor, encompassing 714,384 square feet. MetLife Stadium, where the Giants and Jets play, encompasses 2 million square feet. While in every instance the playing fields account for a large proportion of the available area, there remain numerous opportunities to enhance revenues in the space surrounding the playing surface.

It is best to think of any sport venue as having six distinct pieces of real estate that must be managed to maximize revenue flows:

1 Luxury seating
2 Seating deck
3 Concourses and entrances
4 Scoreboard and other electronic displays
5 Playing surface(s)
6 Naming rights

Within each of these six broad categories there are component parts. Those teams that are able to effectively manage the complete array of their real estate holdings will enjoy far more profits. Each of these real estate assets, their revenue potential, and the management issues are described below in greater detail.

A quick look at revenue earned by some selected MLB teams in new facilities illustrates the importance of managing internal real estate (see Figure 6.1). The data in Figure 6.1 include team revenues from all sources, so it is possible that income from local media sources influence the outcome. Despite that reservation, the pattern is clear. New facilities have additional revenue possibilities and, as teams enhance their abilities to manage

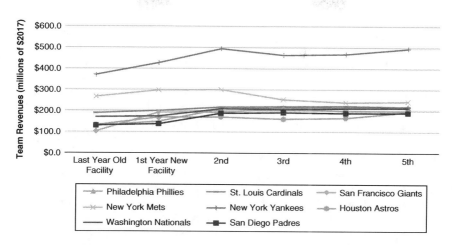

Figure 6.1 Revenues Earned by Select MLB Teams During the Last Season in an Older Facility and the Years After in a New Facility (millions of $2017).

all aspects of the expanded real estate and assess market demand, revenues increase. Notice that the elevated revenue levels are sustained even after the "honeymoon phase" of new facilities pass. By including several different teams in the analysis, it also becomes evident that while winning matters relative to escalating revenues, even teams that were less successful were able to sustain their elevated revenue levels (e.g., San Diego Padres). Revenue earned from real estate operations outside the facility are not included, as those funds accrue to other businesses that may be owned by the same individuals that own the teams but are distinct and separate from the operations of the franchise.

Luxury Seating

The largest single change in facility management has involved the incorporation of suites, club seats, and other luxury configurations such as special moveable seating, theatre box or opera seating, bar rail and other social seating or standing areas, and loge seating. It should come as no surprise that people would be interested in watching games in surroundings that are more luxurious or in seating configurations that permit socializing with several people.

When thinking about how team owners have begun including new experiences and amenities in venues, it can be helpful to look to the experiences of other industries. Changes in amenities offered in automobiles, for example, seem to parallel those in the sport industry. There was a time when people did not care about amenities in their cars; consumers' primary interest was in function – transportation – and safety. However, as people's incomes increased, additional amenities (automatic transmission, electronic windows, heat and air-conditioning, AM/FM and eventually HD satellite radios, enhanced sound systems, backseat video systems, rear-view cameras etc.) became popular.

In some ways, it is probably a bit surprising how long it took for team owners to realize that fans (both individuals and businesses) would be willing to pay more for improved amenities. Some of these include exclusive areas that offered an excellent view of play, meeting places with private bathrooms, closets for clothing and personal belongings, temperature-controlled areas, and a wide choice of premium food and beverage options. Deciding on the number of suites and club seats to include in a venue becomes an important issue when designing a facility for each team. The situation involving the Cleveland Indians and Progressive Field (previously Jacobs Field) underscores the critical nature of the design decisions that must be made.

Suites, Club Seats, and Designs for Flexibility

A new ballpark for the Cleveland Indians opened in 1994. The team owner, Richard Jacobs, was in the midst of substantially increasing his investment in players, and the team began to dominate the Central Division, winning five consecutive titles and appearing in two World Series. During this spectacular run (which extended into the tenure of the team's new owners, the Dolans), the team sold every ticket for 494 consecutive games. Anticipating the explosion in demand for tickets, Jacobs insisted on building 122 suites and 2,024 club seats. The inclusion of an additional tier of suites increased the size of the ballpark and changed the elevation of the upper deck. As a result, the seats in the third deck are 10 to 12 feet higher and 20 to 24 feet farther back from the playing field than what would have existed had the extra tier of suites not been added. If all or most of the 122 suites were consistently sold, the increased revenue from the luxury seating would offset any losses from the reduced quality of the view from the upper deck. With these seats farther from the field, however, their revenue potential was significantly reduced from what would have existed if the seats were closer to the field.

In the years after the team's robust success, attendance declined. To be sure, the team's losing record was a major factor in the lower level of fan interest. In 2007, however, the team won the American League's Central Division and defeated the Yankees in the first round of the playoffs before losing to the Red Sox in seven games in the AL Championship series. Despite that success, the team only attracted

2,275,913 fans to their home games, far less than the 4 million+ who turned out for games in the late 1990s. Northeast Ohio was in the midst of a substantial economic contraction that included the loss of numerous residents and businesses. The team's market had contracted and the remaining fans and businesses had less money to spend on tickets. The success of the Cleveland Cavaliers also had a role in explaining Indians fans' level of spending during a period of constrained discretionary income in the region.

By 2010, it had become clear that it was unlikely that the team would ever again be able to lease 122 suites (or it would take a decade of growth for the number of fans to rise back to the number present in the 1990s). As a result, the team decided to hire an architectural firm and a designer to present the team with ideas on how best to utilize an entire level of suites. Jacobs' decision to build an extra tier left the Indians with a "dark" area of unsold suites and thousands of square feet of real estate that was not producing revenue. The new owners' options were constrained by irrevocable design decisions made once an additional level of suites was added. The critical lesson from Cleveland's experience is how important it is to carefully consider long-term demand for suites. It is important that team owners carefully assess the potential that exists within a market and then design a facility that fits best with an appropriate mix of luxury and non-luxury products. Sport managers must look carefully at the demand for luxury seating in a market and the long-term prospects for growth and demand.

The question remains: how many suites should be built? In measuring the demand for luxury seating, conducting market surveys or producing ratios that permit a consideration of the levels of supply available in other markets (and the relative success of selling that product in the other markets) can be valuable. It can also be beneficial to produce a database enumerating the total number of luxury seats in a market (as a result of the existence of facilities for other teams or potential facilities) as compared to the number of larger companies and wealthier individuals. Table 6.1 illustrates the number of large firms (those with at least 500 employees), as well as the number of suites and club seats to produce two interesting statistics: (1) the number of large firms per suite and (2) the total payroll dollars per club seat in each market.

It is easier to sell suites in markets where there are a larger number of firms with 500 or more employees. Markets with fewer teams typically have less competition for the entertainment dollars firms are willing to spend. For example, in Sacramento, which has only an NBA team, there are 49.6 large firms per available suite in the market. In Atlanta, with the relocation of

Table 6.1 Available Demand for Luxury Sport Products in Selected Markets (NFL, MLB, NBA, and NHL)

Region	Firms with 500+ Employees[1]		Teams in Market[2]	Suites in Market[3]	Firms per Suite	Club Seats in Market[4]	Payroll Dollars per Club Seat ($millions)
	Number	Payroll ($billions)					
Atlanta–Sandy Springs–Roswell, GA	3,400	$73.4	Atlanta Falcons (NFL), Atlanta Braves (MLB), Atlanta Hawks (NBA)	321	10.6	13,266	$5.5
Baltimore–Columbia–Towson, MD	1,984	$32.4	Baltimore Ravens (NFL), Baltimore Orioles (MLB)	200	9.9	13,316	$2.4
Boston–Cambridge–Newton, MA–NH[5]	2,745	$92.9	New England Patriots (NFL), Boston Red Sox (MLB), Boston Celtics (NBA), Boston Bruins (NHL)	314	8.7	14,676	$6.3
Buffalo–Cheektowaga–Niagara Falls, NY	1,010	$10.8	Buffalo Bills (NFL), Buffalo Sabres (NHL)	224	4.5	9,378	$1.2
Charlotte–Concord–Gastonia, NC–SC	2,250	$31.7	Carolina Panthers (NFL), Charlotte Hornets (NBA)	217	10.4	13,621	$2.3
Chicago–Naperville–Elgin, IL–IN–WI	4,017	$133.2	Chicago Bears (NFL), Chicago Cubs (MLB), Ch-icago White Sox (MLB), Chicago Bulls (NBA), Chicago Blackhawks (NHL)	597	6.7	16,707	$8.0
Cincinnati, OH–KY–IN	1,931	$26.5	Cincinnati Bengals (NFL), Cincinnati Reds (MLB)	178	10.8	11,835	$2.2
Cleveland–Elyria, OH and Akron, OH[6]	2,651	$32.8	Cleveland Browns (NFL), Cleveland Indians (MLB), Cleveland Cavaliers (NBA)	357	7.4	12,825	$2.6
Columbus, OH	1,881	$25.8	Columbus Blue Jackets (NHL)	52	36.2	1,450	$17.8

Table 6.1 Continued

Region	Firms with 500+ Employees[1]		Teams in Market[2]	Suites in Market[3]	Firms per Suite	Club Seats in Market[4]	Payroll Dollars per Club Seat ($millions)
	Number	Payroll ($billions)					
Dallas–Fort Worth–Arlington, TX	3,657	$94.4	Dallas Cowboys (NFL), Texas Rangers (MLB), Dallas Mavericks (NBA), Dallas Stars (NHL)	788	4.6	23,904	$3.9
Denver–Aurora–Lakewood, CO	2,565	$38.5	Denver Broncos (NFL), Colorado Rockies (MLB), Denver Nuggets (NBA), Colorado Avalanche (NHL)	385	6.7	16626	$2.3
Detroit–Warren–Dearborn, MI; Ann Arbor, MI; Jackson, MI; and Toledo, OH[7,8]	3,974	$61.4	Detroit Lions (NFL), Detroit Tigers (MLB), Detroit Pistons (NBA), Detroit Red Wings (NHL)	351	11.3	10,290	$6.0
Green Bay, WI and Milwaukee–Waukesha–West Allis, WI[9]	2,043	$25.9	Green Bay Packers (NFL), Milwaukee Brewers (MLB), Milwaukee Bucks (NBA)	276	7.4	9,520	$2.7
Houston–The Woodlands–Sugar Land, TX	3,143	$96.8	Houston Texans (NFL), Houston Astros (MLB), Houston Rockets (NBA)	366	8.6	16,697	$5.8
Indianapolis–Carmel–Anderson, IN	1,923	$24.5	Indianapolis Colts (NFL), Indiana Pacers (NBA)	208	9.2	17,340	$1.4
Jacksonville, FL	1,569	$15.2	Jacksonville Jaguars (NFL)	75	20.9	11,000	$1.4

(continued)

Table 6.1 Continued

Region	Firms with 500+ Employees[1]		Teams in Market[2]	Suites in Market[3]	Firms per Suite	Club Seats in Market[4]	Payroll Dollars per Club Seat ($millions)
	Number	Payroll ($billions)					
Kansas City, MO–KS	1,984	$26.4	Kansas City Chiefs (NFL), Kansas City Royals (MLB)	105	18.9	12,744	$2.0
Las Vegas–Henderson–Paradise, NV[10]	1,702	$19.4	Las Vegas Golden Knights (NHL)	52	32.7	undisclosed	
Los Angeles–Long Beach–Anaheim, CA[11]	3,879	$154.5	Los Angeles Rams (NFL), Los Angeles Chargers (NFL), Los Angeles Angels (MLB), Los Angeles Dodgers (MLB), Los Angeles Clippers (NBA), Los Angeles Lakers (NBA), Los Angeles Kings (NHL), Anaheim Ducks (NHL)	848	4.6	17,349	$8.9
Memphis, TN–MS–AR	1,478	$14.6	Memphis Grizzlies (NBA)	59	25.1	1,642	$8.9
Miami–Fort Lauderdale–West Palm Beach, FL	2,552	$47.5	Miami Dolphins (NFL), Miami Marlins (MLB), Miami Heat (NBA), Florida Panthers (NHL)	409	6.2	16,545	$2.9
Minneapolis–St. Paul–Bloomington, MN–WI[12]	2,336	$59.0	Minnesota Vikings (NFL), Minnesota Twins (MLB), Minnesota Timberwolves (NBA), Minnesota Wild (NHL)	299	7.8	8,102	$7.3
Nashville–Davidson–Murfreesboro–Franklin, TN	1,903	$22.2	Tennessee Titans (NFL), Nashville Predators (NHL)	249	7.6	13,100	$17
New Orleans–Metairie, LA	1,257	$12.1	New Orleans Saints (NFL), New Orleans Pelicans (NBA)	209	6.0	11,200	$1.1

(continued)

Table 6.1 Continued

Region	Firms with 500+ Employees[1]		Teams in Market[2]	Suites in Market[3]	Firms per Suite	Club Seats in Market[4]	Payroll Dollars per Club Seat ($millions)
	Number	Payroll ($billions)					
New York–Newark–Jersey City, NY–NJ–PA and Bridgeport–Stamford–Norwalk, CT[13][14]	5,505	$338.0	New York Jets (NFL), New York Giants (NFL), New York Mets (MLB), New York Yankees (MLB), New York Knicks (NBA), Brooklyn Nets (NBA), New York Rangers (NHL), New York Islanders (NHL), New Jersey Devils (NHL)	824	6.7	44,810	$7.5
Oklahoma City, OK	1,408	$12.0	Oklahoma City Thunder (NBA)	48	29.3	3,380	$3.5
Orlando–Kissimmee–Sanford, FL	2,015	$24.5	Orlando Magic (NBA)	70	28.8	1,428	$17.2
Philadelphia–Camden–Wilmington, PA–NJ–DE–MD	3,048	$85.1	Philadelphia Eagles (NFL), Philadelphia Phillies (MLB), Philadelphia 76ers (NBA), Philadelphia Flyers (NHL)	494	6.2	13,617	$6.2
Phoenix–Mesa–Scottsdale, AZ	2,713	$44.0	Arizona Cardinals (NFL), Arizona Diamondbacks (MLB), Phoenix Suns (NBA), Arizona Coyotes (NHL)	338	8.0	16,846	$2.6
Pittsburgh, PA	1,845	$31.6	Pittsburgh Steelers (NFL), Pittsburgh Pirates (MLB), Pittsburgh Penguins (NHL)	256	7.2	14,808	$2.1
Portland–Vancouver–Hillsboro, OR–WA	1,918	$28.1	Portland Trail Blazers (NBA)	50	38.4	2,397	$11.7

(continued)

Table 6.1 Continued

Region	Firms with 500+ Employees[1]		Teams in Market[2]	Suites in Market[3]	Firms per Suite	Club Seats in Market[4]	Payroll Dollars per Club Seat ($millions)
	Number	Payroll ($billions)					
Raleigh, NC and Durham–Chapel Hill, NC[15]	2,340	$22.9	Carolina Hurricanes (NHL)	75	31.2	2,000	$11.4
Sacramento–Roseville–Arden-Arcade, CA	1,687	$19.5	Sacramento Kings (NBA)	34	49.6	undisclosed	
Salt Lake City, UT	1,466	$15.8	Utah Jazz (NBA)	56	26.2	668	$23.6
San Antonio–New Braunfels, TX	1,838	$20.9	San Antonio Spurs (NBA)	50	36.8	2,018	$10.4
San Diego–Carlsbad, CA	2,098	$35.1	San Diego Padres (MLB)	58	36.2	5,000	$7.0
San Francisco–Oakland–Hayward, CA and San Jose–Sunnyvale–Santa Clara, CA[16,17]	4,351	$170.7	Oakland Raiders (NFL), San Francisco 49ers (NFL), Oakland Athletics (MLB), San Francisco Giants (MLB), Golden State Warriors (NBA), San Jose Sharks (NHL)	667	6.5	34,842	$4.9
Seattle–Tacoma–Bellevue, WA	2,379	$63.9	Seattle Seahawks (NFL), Seattle Mariners (MLB)	173	13.8	12,156	$5.3
St. Louis, MO–IL	2,124	$35.5	St. Louis Cardinals (MLB), St. Louis Blues (NHL)	152	14.0	5,456	$6.5
Tampa–St. Petersburg–Clearwater, FL	2,068	$26.6	Tampa Bay Buccaneers (NFL), Tampa Bay Rays (MLB), Tampa Bay Lightning (NHL)	334	6.2	18,616	$1.4
Washington–Arlington–Alexandria, DC–VA–MD–WV	3,069	$89.3	Washington Redskins (NFL), Washington Nationals (MLB), Washington Wizards (NBA), Washington Capitals (NHL)	541	5.7	23,615	$3.8

(continued)

1 Firm size data as of 2014.

2 Team locations as of 2017.

3 For venues shared by multiple teams, suite and club seat totals are doubled. For example, Chicago's United Center, which hosts both the Blackhawks and Bulls, has 150 suites. For each team, 150 suites have been allocated, for a total of 300.

4 For venues shared by multiple teams, suite and club seat totals are doubled. For example, Chicago's United Center, which hosts both the Blackhawks and Bulls, has 150 suites. For each team, 150 suites have been allocated, for a total of 300.

5 Club seat data unavailable for Fenway Park (home to Boston Red Sox).

6 The Cleveland–Elyria, OH and Akron, OH Metropolitan Statistical Areas have been combined due to their close proximity and overlapping market areas.

7 Club seat data unavailable for Little Caesars Arena (home to Detroit Pistons and Detroit Red Wings).

8 The Detroit–Warren–Dearborn, MI; Ann Arbor, MI; Jackson, MI; and Toledo, OH Metropolitan Statistical Areas have been combined due to their close proximity and overlapping market areas.

9 The Green Bay, WI and Milwaukee–Waukesha–West Allis, WI Metropolitan Statistical Areas have been combined due to their close proximity and overlapping market areas.

10 As noted, team locations are as of 2017; the Raiders had not yet moved to Las Vegas.

11 Data on Los Angeles Rams' stadium unavailable.

12 Club seat data unavailable for U.S. Bank Stadium (home to Minnesota Vikings).

13 Suite and club seat data unavailable for Madison Square Garden (home to New York Knicks and New York Rangers).

14 The New York–Newark–Jersey City, NY–NJ–PA and Bridgeport–Stamford–Norwalk, CT Metropolitan Statistical Areas have been combined due to their close proximity and overlapping market areas.

15 The Raleigh, NC and Durham–Chapel Hill, NC Metropolitan Statistical Areas have been combined due to their close proximity and overlapping market areas.

16 The NFL's Raiders anticipate a 2020 move to a new stadium in Las Vegas. This data reflects the current Oakland stadium location.

17 The San Francisco–Oakland–Hayward, CA and San Jose–Sunnyvale–Santa Clara, CA Metropolitan Statistical Areas have been combined due to their close proximity and overlapping market areas.

their NHL team to Winnipeg, Canada (Jets), the region has 10.6 large corporations per available suite, including the new venues for the Braves and Falcons. Excluding the Rams and Chargers' new stadium, the Los Angeles market has 4.6 large firms for each available suite. The Phoenix metropolitan region has 8.0 large firms per suite. These findings may seem perplexing, considering the financial success of Los Angeles franchises relative to the challenges that have been faced by teams in Phoenix. However, it is important to note that sport managers must consider a plethora of factors in measuring market viability; clearly there are other aspects of the Los Angeles market that allow that region to thrive and elements of the Phoenix market that pose challenges. The data in Table 6.1, specific to the four major professional sports (NFL, MLB, NBA, NHL), provides an overview of factors that can help guide the mix of seating products to be used in a venue.

Table 6.2 is similar to Table 6.1 but introduces MLS venues as well as collegiate teams. The college-level teams included have been identified as those at the Division I-A level in NCAA football and basketball, in a Power Five Conference (Atlantic Coast Conference, Big 12 Conference, Big Ten Conference, Pac-12 Conference, or Southeastern Conference). In order to be included in Table 6.2, the schools' football or basketball venue(s) must be located within the same market as an existing professional team. While many other factors could have been included in the selection of teams and venues – whether the school is a "football" or "basketball" school, for example – this approach allowed for a broad view of the entire supply of luxury sport product in each market. It is also important to note that the data in Tables 6.1 and 6.2 are limited to data availability.

The importance of the analysis in Table 6.2 is underscored in markets that have few professional teams but one or more collegiate teams, such as Raleigh, North Carolina. Table 6.1 indicates the market has 31.2 large firms for every available suite, but after adding Duke University, North Carolina State University, and the University of North Carolina's venues, Table 6.2 puts that figure at just 9.6 large firms per available suite. This perspective is perhaps most important in the Columbus region, where Ohio State University football reigns supreme. With the inclusion of OSU's football and basketball venues, as well as the Columbus Crew facility, the Columbus region drops from 36.1 large firms per suite and over $17 million payroll dollars per club seat in Table 6.1 to 8.8 firms per suite and under $5 million payroll dollars per club seat in Table 6.2.

While the methods described above can be informative, there is no iron rule of the desired ratio of companies to suites, or how many higher-income residents a region needs to ensure that suites will sell. What is important to understand, however, is that scarcity is valuable. As with any good or service, a lower supply of suites allows for a higher selling price, which in turn *could* produce more revenue than if a larger number were built (and sold at

Table 6.2 Available Demand for Luxury Sport Products in Selected Markets (NFL, MLB, NBA, NHL, MLS, and Division I-A Power Five Conference Teams in NCAAF and NCAAB)

Region	Firms with 500+ Employees[1]		Teams in Market[2]	Suites in Market[3]	Firms per Suite	Club Seats in Market[4]	Payroll Dollars per Club Seat ($millions)
	Number	Payroll ($billions)					
Atlanta–Sandy Springs–Roswell, GA[5]	3,400	$73.4	Atlanta Falcons (NFL), Atlanta Braves, (MLB), Atlanta Hawks (NBA), Atlanta United FC (MLS), Georgia Tech (NCAAF, NCAAB)	582	5.8	23,406	$3.1
Baltimore–Columbia–Towson, MD[6]	1,984	$32.4	Baltimore Ravens (NFL), Baltimore Orioles (MLB), University of Maryland (NCAAF, NCAAB)	284	7.0	13,552	$2.4
Boston–Cambridge–Newton, MA–NH[7,8]	2,745	$92.9	New England Patriots (NFL), Boston Red Sox (MLB), Boston Celtics (NBA), Boston Bruins (NHL), New England Revolution (MLS), Boston College (NCAAF, NCAAB)	465	5.9	20,552	$4.5
Buffalo–Cheektowaga–Niagara Falls, NY	1,010	$10.8	Buffalo Bills (NFL), Buffalo Sabres (NHL)	224	4.5	9,378	$0.2
Charlotte–Concord–Gastonia, NC–SC	2,250	$31.7	Carolina Panthers (NFL), Charlotte Hornets (NBA)	217	10.4	13,621	$2.3
Chicago–Naperville–Elgin, IL–IN–WI[9]	4,017	$133.2	Chicago Bears (NFL), Chicago Cubs (MLB), Chicago White Sox (MLB), Chicago Bulls (NBA), Chicago Blackhawks (NHL), Chicago Fire (MLS), Northwestern University (NCAAF, NCAAB)	639	6.3	17,811	$7.5
Cincinnati, OH–KY–IN	1,931	$26.5	Cincinnati Bengals (NFL), Cincinnati Reds (MLB	178	10.8	11,835	$2.2
Cleveland–Elyria, OH and Akron, OH[10]	2,651	$32.8	Cleveland Browns (NFL), Cleveland Indians (MLB), Cleveland Cavaliers (NBA)	357	7.4	12,825	$2.6
Columbus, OH[11]	1,881	$25.8	Columbus Blue Jackets (NHL), Columbus Crew SC (MLS), Ohio State University (NCAAF, NCAAB)	213	8.8	5,794	$4.5

(continued)

Table 6.2 Continued

Region	Firms with 500+ Employees[1]		Teams in Market[2]	Suites in Market[3]	Firms per Suite	Club Seats in Market[4]	Payroll Dollars per Club Seat ($millions)
	Number	Payroll ($billions)					
Dallas–Fort Worth–Arlington, TX[12]	3,657	$94.4	Dallas Cowboys (NFL), Texas Rangers (MLB), Dallas Mavericks (NBA), Dallas Stars (NHL), FC Dallas (MLS), Texas Christian University (NCAAF, NCAAB)	831	4.4	24,265	$3.9
Denver–Aurora–Lakewood, CO[13]	2,565	$38.5	Denver Broncos (NFL), Colorado Rockies (MLB), Denver Nuggets (NBA), Colorado Avalanche (NHL), Colorado Rapids (MLS), University of Colorado (NCAAF, NCAAB)	447	5.7	18,721	$2.1
Detroit–Warren–Dearborn, MI; Ann Arbor, MI; Jackson, MI; and Toledo, OH[14,15]	3,974	$61.4	Detroit Lions (NFL), Detroit Tigers (MLB), Detroit Pistons (NBA), Detroit Red Wings (NHL), University of Michigan (NCAAF, NCAAB)	432	9.2	13,490	$4.6
Green Bay, WI and Milwaukee–Waukesha–West Allis, WI[16,17]	2,043	$25.9	Green Bay Packers (NFL), Milwaukee Brewers (MLB), Milwaukee Bucks (NBA), University of Wisconsin (NCAAF, NCAAB)	384	5.3	10,447	$2.5
Houston–The Woodlands–Sugar Land, TX	3,143	$96.8	Houston Texans (NFL), Houston Astros (MLB), Houston Rockets (NBA), Houston Dynamo (MLS)	401	7.8	17,797	$5.4
Indianapolis–Carmel–Anderson, IN	1,923	$24.5	Indianapolis Colts (NFL), Indiana Pacers (NBA)	208	9.2	17,340	$1.4
Jacksonville, FL	1,569	$15.2	Jacksonville Jaguars (NFL)	75	20.9	11,000	$1.4

(continued)

Table 6.2 Continued

Region	Firms with 500+ Employees[1]		Teams in Market[2]	Suites in Market[3]	Firms per Suite	Club Seats in Market[4]	Payroll Dollars per Club Seat ($millions)
	Number	Payroll ($billions)					
Kansas City, MO–KS	1,984	$26.4	Kansas City Chiefs (NFL), Kansas City Royals (MLB), Sporting Kansas City (MLS)	141	14.1	16,144	$1.6
Las Vegas–Henderson–Paradise, NV[18]	1,702	$19.4	Las Vegas Golden Knights (NHL)	52	32.7	undisclosed	
Los Angeles–Long Beach–Anaheim, CA[19]	3,879	$154.5	Los Angeles Rams (NFL), Los Angeles Chargers (NFL), Los Angeles Angels (MLB), Los Angeles Dodgers (MLB), Los Angeles Clippers (NBA), Los Angeles Lakers (NBA), Los Angeles Kings (NHL), Anaheim Ducks (NHL), LA Galaxy (MLS), Los Angeles FC (MLS), UCLA (NCAAF, NCAAB), USC (NCAAF, NCAAB)	958	4.0	20,249	$7.6
Memphis, TN–MS–AR	1,478	$14.6	Memphis Grizzlies (NBA)	59	25.1	1,642	$8.9
Miami–Fort Lauderdale–West Palm Beach, FL[20]	2,552	$47.5	Miami Dolphins (NFL), Miami Marlins (MLB), Miami Heat (NBA), Florida Panthers (NHL), University of Miami (NCAAF, NCAAB)	650	3.9	26,754	$1.8
Minneapolis–St. Paul–Bloomington, MN–WI[21]	2,336	$59.0	Minnesota Vikings (NFL), Minnesota Twins (MLB), Minnesota Timberwolves (NBA), Minnesota Wild (NHL), Minnesota United FC (MLS), University of Minnesota (NCAAF, NCAAB)	398	5.9	8,952	$6.6
Nashville–Davidson–Murfreesboro–Franklin, TN[22]	1,903	$22.2	Tennessee Titans (NFL), Nashville Predators (NHL), Vanderbilt University (NCAAF, NCAAB)	274	6.9	13,300	$1.7

(continued)

Table 6.2 Continued

Region	Firms with 500+ Employees[1]		Teams in Market[2]	Suites in Market[3]	Firms per Suite	Club Seats in Market[4]	Payroll Dollars per Club Seat ($millions)
	Number	Payroll ($billions)					
New Orleans–Metairie, LA	1,257	$12.1	New Orleans Saints (NFL), New Orleans Pelicans (NBA)	209	6.0	11,200	$1.1
New York–Newark–Jersey City, NY–NJ–PA and Bridgeport–Stamford–Norwalk, CT[23,24]	5,505	$338.0	New York Jets (NFL), New York Giants (NFL), New York Mets (MLB), New York Yankees (MLB), New York Knicks (NBA), Brooklyn Nets (NBA), New York Rangers (NHL), New York Islanders (NHL), New Jersey Devils (NHL), New York City FC (MLS), New York Red Bulls (MLS), Rutgers University (NCAAF, NCAAB)	952	5.8	52,778	$6.4
Oklahoma City, OK[25]	1,408	$12.0	Oklahoma City Thunder (NBA), Oklahoma State University (NCAAF, NCAAB), University of Oklahoma (NCAAF, NCAAB)	268	5.3	11,590	$1.0
Orlando–Kissimmee–Sanford, FL	2,015	$24.5	Orlando Magic (NBA), Orlando City SC (MLS)	101	20.0	4,299	$5.7
Philadelphia–Camden–Wilmington, PA–NJ–DE–MD	3,048	$85.1	Philadelphia Eagles (NFL), Philadelphia Phillies (MLB), Philadelphia 76ers (NBA), Philadelphia Flyers (NHL), Philadelphia Union (MLS)	524	5.8	15,617	$5.4
Phoenix–Mesa–Scottsdale, AZ[26]	2,713	$44.0	Arizona Cardinals (NFL), Arizona Diamondbacks (MLB), Phoenix Suns (NBA), Arizona Coyotes (NHL), Arizona State University (NCAAF, NCAAB)	390	7.0	21,786	$2.0
Pittsburgh, PA[27]	1,845	$31.6	Pittsburgh Steelers (NFL), Pittsburgh Pirates (MLB), Pittsburgh Penguins (NHL), University of Pittsburgh (NCAAF, NCAAB)	402	4.6	22,108	$1.4

(continued)

Table 6.2 Continued

Region	Firms with 500+ Employees[1]		Teams in Market[2]	Suites in Market[3]	Firms per Suite	Club Seats in Market[4]	Payroll Dollars per Club Seat ($millions)
	Number	Payroll ($billions)					
Portland–Vancouver–Hillsboro, OR–WA	1,918	$28.1	Portland Trail Blazers (NBA), Portland Timbers (MLS)	80	24.0	3,123	$9.0
Raleigh, NC and Durham–Chapel Hill, NC[28,29]	2,340	$22.9	Carolina Hurricanes (NHL), Duke University (NCAAF, NCAAB), North Carolina State University (NCAAF, NCAAB), University of North Carolina (NCAAF, NCAAB)	243	9.6	5,813	$3.9
Sacramento–Roseville–Arden-Arcade, CA	1,687	$19.5	Sacramento Kings (NBA)	34	49.6	undisclosed	
Salt Lake City, UT[30]	1,466	$15.8	Utah Jazz (NBA), Real Salt Lake (MLS), University of Utah (NCAAF, NCAAB)	103	14.2	2,468	$6.4
San Antonio–New Braunfels, TX	1,838	$20.9	San Antonio Spurs (NBA)	50	36.8	2,018	$10.4
San Diego–Carlsbad, CA	2,098	$35.1	San Diego Padres (MLB)	58	36.2	5,000	$7.0
San Francisco–Oakland–Hayward, CA and San Jose–Sunnyvale–Santa Clara, CA[31,32,33]	4,351	$170.7	Oakland Raiders (NFL), San Francisco 49ers (NFL), Oakland Athletics (MLB), San Francisco Giants (MLB), Golden State Warriors (NBA), San Jose Sharks (NHL), San Jose Earthquakes (MLS), University of California – Berkeley, Stanford University (NCAAF, NCAAB)	690	6.3	40,818	$4.2
Seattle–Tacoma–Bellevue, WA[34]	2,379	$63.9	Seattle Seahawks (NFL), Seattle Mariners (MLB), Seattle Sounders (MLS), University of Washington (NCAAF, NCAAB)	377	6.3	21,663	$3.0
St. Louis, MO–IL	2,124	$35.5	St. Louis Cardinals (MLB), St. Louis Blues (NHL)	152	14.0	5,456	$6.5

(continued)

Table 6.2 Continued

Region	Firms with 500+ Employees[1]		Teams in Market[2]	Suites in Market[3]	Firms per Suite	Club Seats in Market[4]	Payroll Dollars per Club Seat ($millions)
	Number	Payroll ($billions)					
Tampa–St. Petersburg–Clearwater, FL	2,068	$26.6	Tampa Bay Buccaneers (NFL), Tampa Bay Rays (MLB), Tampa Bay Lightning (NHL)	334	6.2	18,616	$1.4
Washington–Arlington–Alexandria, DC–VA–MD–WV	3,069	$89.3	Washington Redskins (NFL), Washington Nationals (MLB), Washington Wizards (NBA), Washington Capitals (NHL), D.C. United (MLS)	572	5.4	25,115	$3.6

[1] Firm size data as of 2014.
[2] Team locations as of 2017.
[3] For venues shared by multiple teams, suite and club seat totals are doubled. For example, Chicago's United Center, which hosts both the Blackhawks and Bulls, has 150 suites. For each team, 150 suites have been allocated, for a total of 300.
[4] For venues shared by multiple teams, suite and club seat totals are doubled. For example, Chicago's United Center, which hosts both the Blackhawks and Bulls, has 150 suites. For each team, 150 suites have been allocated, for a total of 300.
[5] Club seat data unavailable for Fenway Park (home to Boston Red Sox).
[6] Club seat data unavailable for the University of Maryland's NCAAB venue.
[7] Suite data unavailable for Georgia Tech's NCAAB venue.
[8] Club seat data unavailable for Boston College's NCAAF & NCAAB venues.
[9] Suite and club seat data unavailable for Northwestern University's NCAAF and NCAAB venues.
[10] The Cleveland–Elyria, OH and Akron, OH Metropolitan Statistical Areas have been combined due to their close proximity and overlapping market areas.
[11] Club seat data unavailable for Ohio State University's NCAAB venue.
[12] Suite and club seat data unavailable for Texas Christian University's NCAAB venue.
[13] Suite and club seat data unavailable for the University of Colorado's NCAAB venue.
[14] Club seat data unavailable for Little Caesars Arena (home to Detroit Pistons and Detroit Red Wings); suite and club seat data unavailable for the University of Michigan's NCAAB venue.
[15] The Detroit–Warren–Dearborn, MI; Ann Arbor, MI; Jackson, MI; and Toledo, OH Metropolitan Statistical Areas have been combined due to their close proximity and overlapping market areas.

(continued)

16 The Green Bay, WI and Milwaukee–Waukesha–West Allis, WI Metropolitan Statistical Areas have been combined due to their close proximity and overlapping market areas.

17 Club seat data unavailable for the University of Wisconsin's NCAAB venue.

18 As noted, team locations are as of 2017; the Raiders had not yet moved to Las Vegas.

19 Data on Los Angeles Rams and Los Angeles FC's stadia unavailable; suite and club seat data unavailable for UCLA's NCAAB venue; suite and club seat data unavailable for USC's NCAAF venue; club seat data unavailable for USC's NCAAB venue.

20 Club seat data unavailable for the University of Miami's NCAAB venue.

21 Club seat data unavailable for U.S. Bank Stadium (home to Minnesota Vikings).

22 Club seat data unavailable for Vanderbilt University's NCAAB venue.

23 Suite and club seat data unavailable for Madison Square Garden (home to New York Knicks and New York Rangers); suite data unavailable for Rutgers University's NCAAF venue; suite and club seat data unavailable for Rutgers University's NCAAB venue.

24 The New York–Newark–Jersey City, NY–NJ–PA and Bridgeport–Stamford–Norwalk, CT Metropolitan Statistical Areas have been combined due to their close proximity and overlapping market areas.

25 Club seat data unavailable for Oklahoma State University's NCAAB venue; suite and club seat data unavailable for the University of Oklahoma's NCAAB venue.

26 Suite and club seat data unavailable for Arizona State University's NCAAB venue.

27 Club seat data unavailable for the University of Pittsburgh's NCAAB venue.

28 The Raleigh, NC and Durham–Chapel Hill, NC Metropolitan Statistical Areas have been combined due to their close proximity and overlapping market areas.

29 Suite and club seat data unavailable for Duke University's NCAAB venue; suite and club seat data unavailable for University of North Carolina's NCAAB venue; club seat data unavailable for University of North Carolina's NCAAF venue.

30 Suite and club seat data unavailable for the University of Utah's NCAAB venue.

a lower price). If a facility appears to have so many suites that buyers can wait to see if the supply is consumed and prices lower, then too many have been built. It is therefore better to design a facility such that there are more firms in a market than there are suites to purchase.

Returning to the situation in Cleveland, with the building of a new ballpark (Progressive Field) and arena (Quicken Loans Arena) in 1994, the Indians and the Cavaliers were the first teams in the market with luxury seats. As the Indians were in the midst of a surge in their on-field success, Richard Jacobs, the team's owner, correctly guessed that he would be able to exploit short-term demand and lease a large number of suites. In later years, the Cleveland Browns entered the luxury seating market with their new stadium and the Cavaliers had their own run of success during LeBron James' two periods of play with the club. When the Indians entered a period of decline in terms of their on-field success and the regional economy contracted, there was suddenly a "glut" of unsold luxury seating.

Supply and demand issues impact large markets as well. Yankee Stadium, for example, has 56 suites and 6,000 club seats. Citi Field, the home of the New York Mets, has 54 suites and 7,800 seats in its club level. Given the size of the New York market in terms of large corporations and people, as compared to the size of the market in Cleveland, the lower number of suites at Yankee Stadium and Citi Field further underscores that the capacity built into the Indians' ballpark (126 suites) was excessive. Oriole Park at Camden Yards was built at about the same time as Progressive Field and has 72 suites. When Oriole Park opened, there was no team in Washington, D.C. As a result, the Orioles had a far larger market than did the Cleveland Indians. With the Nationals now in Washington, D.C., and given the change in the economy, the Orioles have considered a reduction in the number of suites and the conversion of the space in some suites to other uses to extract more revenue from that real estate. Some ideas for the space include all-you-can-eat accommodations with seating for a few dozen fans or areas where children can have play space while their parents enjoy the game.

The pricing of suites is frequently more complex than the sale of tickets. Clients interested in suites may want to take advantage of advertising opportunities in the facility. Their contract price for the suite may include a certain number of messages that appear on video boards or permanent signage, or a set of other incentives such as meet and greets, private events with players, or field passes to offer their guests a chance to watch practices. Suites are leased for multiple years and different payment schedules can be arranged that change the present value of the asking price. Suites also require the purchase of food plans that range from simple fare to far more elegant meal service. A variety of points are negotiated in the leasing of a suite, and the price agreed upon often includes different mixes of amenities for different clients. Suites at some arenas where there are numerous non-sport events are sometimes sold at an all-event or condominium pricing.

In these cases, suite owners receive tickets for all regular season games and for most or all of the non-sport entertainment events at the venue, although there are some events that cannot be included in these all-event packages, such as those owned by the NCAA.

In recent years, baseball teams have also offered luxury seating in the rows closest to the field and have provided these patrons with unlimited high-end food service. Yankee Stadium has several rows of these luxurious super club seats. Some of these seats were marketed as being "closer to the batter's box than the pitcher" (less than 60 feet from home plate). For these seats with unlimited premium food and beverage service, the Yankees were charging as much as $2,500 per game. Sales were quite slow, and televised games showed scores of empty seats. Even with their on-field success and brand reputation, the Yankees were unable to sell all of these high-priced seats. The image of unsold luxury seats convinced the Yankees to offer everyone an additional seat for each ticket purchased, dropping the price by 50 percent. Today the cost of renting a Legends Suite is closer to $1,600, though prices vary depending on the sales package. While the Yankees may have originally set a price point above what the market would support, the concept of first class seating and unlimited high-end food service was not an impractical or inappropriate use of the real estate closest to the field. Numerous other teams have copied the program and now make available premium club seats with exclusive food service to their fans.

Fans with club seating tickets have access to exclusive, club-member only areas where extensive food and beverage service is offered. Most modern venues design these areas so that the game is visible to patrons eating and socializing in the clubs, though older venues (e.g., the Calgary Flames' Scotiabank Saddledome or the now-vacant Palace of Auburn Hills, formerly home to the Detroit Pistons) did not include this design feature. In some instances, the food service may be included in the price of the club seat ticket. Several teams have experimented with buffet-style food service in their clubs with ticket holders permitted to eat as much as they want. Other teams require club seat ticket holders to pay for the food and beverages they consume. Increasingly, teams are offering a mix of both packages.

Some new arenas offer theatre boxes; this luxury product blends the concept of a suite and a club ticket into one. Theatre box packages include four to six seats in a semi-private area that is attached to an exclusive dining room where food and beverages are served before, during, and after each event. Loge seating is also increasingly common. These packages are similar to bar rails offered in the general seating deck, but are typically located on the premium level, and include two rows of high-top chairs with private tables for fans to entertain guests. Loge seats can be "bought by the table" in full- and partial-season ticket packages and come with higher-end catering options than general admission seats. The newest arenas also offer "gondola" seating areas, which appear to be suspended from the top of a venue. Gondola seating areas contain a great deal of glass to provide fans with a unique view of the action on the ice or on the court.

With all of these different seating packages, managers must consider dividing seat real estate into different tiers, much like the way an apartment building or a luxury condominium building would be designed. In most buildings, there are smaller and larger units, units with terraces and other amenities, and even penthouse units. Team owners now look at the real estate in their luxury inventory in a similar manner. This is a substantial change in the management of a facility's real estate. Many of these special seating areas are named for sponsors that seek to have their brand linked to the team. For example, at Citi Field, Delta Airlines chose to pay for the naming rights for two different seating areas. What is critical to appreciate is that by providing numerous club options, not only is the available real estate divided to ensure that separate market segments and demands are satisfied, but that numerous naming opportunities are also available for sponsors. Facilities and the available square footage are prime examples of the need for expertise in real estate management by sport managers.

Every team needs a supply of luxury seating packages to elevate team revenues. The challenge is to find the mix and number of luxury products that best fits in a team's market. The supply must be scaled to the wealth in the area, the number of other teams in the market (and the supply of luxury packages they offer their fans), and the demographic mix of fans for a particular team. Tables 6.3, 6.4, 6.5, and 6.6 list the luxury seating currently available at each NFL stadium, MLB ballpark, NBA/NHL arena, or MLS stadium in use today. Table 6.7 provides the same information, but for NCAA Division I-A football and basketball programs in Power Five Conferences. The tables also show how quickly the sport business has changed. Prior to the 1990s, luxury seating did not exist. Its popularity and profitability spread so quickly that some teams playing in relatively new arenas requested or demanded new facilities long before communities had finished paying for the ones that had become economically obsolete (e.g., Dallas Mavericks, Texas Rangers, Phoenix Suns, Minnesota Vikings).

That the demand for luxury products has shifted is not surprising; the "luxury product" itself was not introduced to consumers until the 1980s. That offering was focused on suites, which, at first, were relatively small in the sense that the entertainment and food service area within the suite was relatively modest. As this product became a staple in the design of venues, the supply was quite robust as it appeared that companies and very wealthy fans wanted to offer their clients and employees (as well as family members) the new unique experience. For example, when the Palace of Auburn Hills opened to host the Detroit Pistons in 1988, it had 180 suites. Beginning in 2017, the team will play its home games at Little Caesars Arena in downtown Detroit (opened in 2017), which has 60 suites.

Contrary to belief, including fewer suites does not lead to lower revenue levels. Instead, teams are now varying the mix of luxury products; rather than including 150 suites, for example, a team might choose to build 70

Table 6.3 Luxury Seating at NFL Stadia

Team	Facility	Suites	Club Seats
Arizona Cardinals	University of Phoenix Stadium	88	7,501
Atlanta Falcons	Mercedes-Benz Stadium	190	7,600
Baltimore Ravens	M&T Bank Stadium	128	8,196
Buffalo Bills	New Era Field	144	6,878
Carolina Panthers	Bank of America Stadium	153	11,321
Chicago Bears	Soldier Field	133	8,000
Cincinnati Bengals	Paul Brown Stadium	114	7,600
Cleveland Browns	FirstEnergy Stadium	143	8,801
Dallas Cowboys	AT&T Stadium	342	15,000
Denver Broncos	Sports Authority Field at Mile High	132	8,500
Detroit Lions	Ford Field	129	7,251
Green Bay Packers	Lambeau Field	168	6,260
Houston Texans	NRG Stadium	196	8,600
Indianapolis Colts	Lucas Oil Stadium	139	14,700
Jacksonville Jaguars	EverBank Field	75	11,000
Kansas City Chiefs	Arrowhead Stadium	80	10,199
Los Angeles Chargers	StubHub Center	43	1,500
Los Angeles Rams	Los Angeles Memorial Coliseum[1]	undisclosed	undisclosed
Miami Dolphins	Hard Rock Stadium	216	10,209
Minnesota Vikings	US Bank Stadium	131	undisclosed
New England Patriots	Gillette Stadium	89	5,876
New Orleans Saints	Mercedes-Benz Superdome	153	8,400
New York Giants, New York Jets	MetLife Stadium	218	10,005
Oakland (Las Vegas) Raiders	Oakland Alameda Coliseum[2]	143	6,300
Philadelphia Eagles	Lincoln Financial Field	172	8,740
Pittsburgh Steelers	Heinz Field	129	7,300
San Francisco 49ers	Levi's Stadium	176	9,000
Seattle Seahawks	CenturyLink Field	112	7,000
Tampa Bay Buccaneers	Raymond James Stadium	195	12,000
Tennessee Titans	Nissan Stadium	177	12,000
Washington Redskins	FedEx Field	243	15,044
NFL Average		**152**	**8,992**

[1] After leaving St. Louis, the Rams moved Los Angeles in 2016 and will share the L.A. Coliseum with the USC Trojans football team as they await the construction of their new stadium in Inglewood.
[2] The NFL's Raiders anticipate a 2020 move to a new stadium in Las Vegas.

Table 6.4 Luxury Seating at MLB Ballparks

Team	Facility	Suites	Club Seats
Arizona Diamondbacks	Chase Field	75	4,000
Atlanta Braves	SunTrust Park	32	3,800
Baltimore Orioles	Oriole Park at Camden Yards	72	5,120
Boston Red Sox	Fenway Park	45	undisclosed
Chicago Cubs	Wrigley Field	60	874
Chicago White Sox	Guaranteed Rate Field	104	1,833
Cincinnati Reds	Great American Ball Park	64	4,235
Cleveland Indians	Progressive Field	126	2,024
Colorado Rockies	Coors Field	63	4,526
Detroit Tigers	Comerica Park	102	3,039
Houston Astros	Minute Maid Park	63	5,197
Kansas City Royals	Kauffman Stadium	25	2,545
Los Angeles Angels	Angel Stadium of Anaheim	78	5,075
Los Angeles Dodgers	Dodger Stadium	68	2,098
Miami Marlins	Marlins Park	39	3,000
Milwaukee Brewers	Miller Park	66	2,760
Minnesota Twins	Target Field	54	3,400
New York Mets	Citi Field	54	7,800
New York Yankees	Yankee Stadium	56	6,000
Oakland Athletics	Oakland Alameda Coliseum	143	6,300
Philadelphia Phillies	Citizens Bank Park	70	1,277
Pittsburgh Pirates	PNC Park	61	5,558
San Diego Padres	PETCO Park	58	5,000
San Francisco Giants	AT&T Park	68	6,700
Seattle Mariners	SAFECO Field	61	5,156
St. Louis Cardinals	Busch Stadium	61	3,706
Tampa Bay Rays	Tropicana Field	70	2,776
Texas Rangers	Globe Life Park in Arlington[1]	126	5,704
Toronto Blue Jays	Rogers Centre	161	5,700
Washington Nationals	Nationals Park	78	2,571
MLB Average		**73**	**4,061**

[1] In late 2017, Arlington voters approved the use of up to $500 million toward the cost of a new ballpark for the Texas Rangers. The team anticipates playing in the new ballpark by 2020 or 2021.

suites, two levels of loge seating, four gondola seating sections, eight theatre boxes, and three exclusive clubs. Diversification, it seems, is one of the keys to success in 21st century facility design. By offering more choices, there can also be varying levels of product exclusivity. This allows consumers the ability to match their desired product and level of exclusivity with what they are willing to pay. The Minnesota Vikings followed this strategy in their new facility, U.S. Bank Stadium, offering more than 9,000 club seats in six clubs. A different sponsor names each of their clubs; there are six different price levels and six different sets of amenities. Those packages

Table 6.5 Luxury Seating at NBA and NHL Arenas

Team(s)	Facility	Suites	Club Seats
Atlanta Hawks	Philips Arena	99	1,866
Boston Celtics, Boston Bruins	TD Garden	90	1,100
Brooklyn Nets, New York Islanders	Barclays Center	101	4,400
Charlotte Hornets	Spectrum Center	64	2,300
Chicago Bulls, Chicago Blackhawks	United Center	150	3,000
Cleveland Cavaliers	Quicken Loans Arena	88	2,000
Dallas Mavericks, Dallas Stars	American Airlines Center	160	1,600
Denver Nuggets, Colorado Avalanche	Pepsi Center	95	1,800
Detroit Pistons, Detroit Red Wings	Little Caesars Arena	60	undisclosed
Golden State Warriors	Oracle Arena[1]	72	3,242
Houston Rockets	Toyota Center	107	2,900
Indiana Pacers	Bankers Life Fieldhouse	69	2,640
Los Angeles Clippers, Los Angeles Lakers, Los Angeles Kings	Staples Center	192	2,500
Memphis Grizzlies	FedexForum	59	1,642
Miami Heat	AmericanAirlines Arena	80	1,100
Milwaukee Bucks	BMO Harris Bradley Center[2]	42	500
Minnesota Timberwolves	Target Center	40	1,702
New Orleans Pelicans	Smoothie King Center	56	2,800
New York Knicks, New York Rangers	Madison Square Garden	undisclosed	undisclosed
Oklahoma City Thunder	Chesapeake Energy Arena	48	3,380
Orlando Magic	Amway Center	70	1,428
Philadelphia 76ers, Philadelphia Flyers	Wells Fargo Center	126	1,800
Phoenix Suns	Talking Stick Resort Arena	88	2,270
Portland Trail Blazers	Moda Center	50	2,397
Sacramento Kings	Golden 1 Center	34	undisclosed
San Antonio Spurs	AT&T Center	50	2,018
Toronto Raptors, Toronto Maple Leafs	Air Canada Centre[3]	154	3,600
Utah Jazz	Vivint Smart Home Arena	56	668
Washington Wizards, Washington Capitals	Capital One Arena	110	3,000
Anaheim Ducks	Honda Center	83	1,176
Arizona Coyotes	Gila River Arena	87	3,075
Buffalo Sabres	KeyBank Center	80	2,500
Calgary Flames	Scotiabank Saddledome	74	1,645
Carolina Hurricanes	PNC Arena	75	2,000
Columbus Blue Jackets	Nationwide Arena	52	1,450
Edmonton Oilers	Rogers Place	57	3,100
Florida Panthers	BB&T Center	74	2,236

(continued)

Table 6.5 Continued

Team(s)	Facility	Suites	Club Seats
Minnesota Wild	Xcel Energy Center	74	3,000
Montreal Canadiens	Bell Centre	135	2,656
Nashville Predators	Bridgestone Arena	72	1,100
New Jersey Devils	Prudential Center	76	2,200
Ottawa Senators	Canadian Tire Centre	139	2,376
Pittsburgh Penguins	PPG Paints Arena	66	1,950
St. Louis Blues	Scottrade Center	91	1,750
San Jose Sharks	SAP Center	65	3,300
Tampa Bay Lightning	Amalie Arena	69	3,840
Vancouver Canucks	Rogers Arena	88	2,200
Las Vegas Golden Knights	T-Mobile Arena	52	undisclosed
Winnipeg Jets	Bell MTS Place	57	918
NBA/NHL Average		**83**	**2,225**

[1] The Golden State Warriors anticipate moving to Chase Center in Mission Bay in 2019.
[2] The Milwaukee Bucks anticipate moving to a new arena in 2018.
[3] The Raptors' arena is anticipated to be renamed Scotiabank Arena in 2018.

Table 6.6 Luxury Seating at MLS Stadia

Team(s)	Facility	Suites	Club Seats
Atlanta United FC	Mercedes-Benz Stadium	190	7,600
Chicago Fire	Toyota Park	42	1,104
Colorado Rapids	Dick's Sporting Goods Park	22	192
Columbus Crew SC	MAPFRE Stadium	28	1,717
D.C. United	Audi Field	31	1,500
FC Dallas	Toyota Stadium	18	111
Houston Dynamo	BBVA Compass Stadium	35	1,100
LA Galaxy	StubHub Center	45	1,500
Los Angeles FC	Banc of California Stadium	undisclosed	undisclosed
Minnesota United FC	TCF Bank Stadium	39	300
Montreal Impact	Saputo Stadium	16	undisclosed
New England Revolution	Gillette Stadium	89	5,876
New York City FC	Yankee Stadium	56	6,000
New York Red Bulls	Red Bull Arena	30	1,000
Orlando City SC	Orlando City Stadium	31	2,871
Philadelphia Union	Talen Energy Stadium	30	2,000
Portland Timbers	Providence Park	30	726
Real Salt Lake	Rio Tinto Stadium	22	1,000
San Jose Earthquakes	Avaya Stadium	16	576
Seattle Sounders FC	CenturyLink Field	112	7,000
Sporting Kansas City	Children's Mercy Park	36	3,400
Toronto FC	BMO Field	50	1,500
Vancouver Whitecaps FC	BC Place Stadium	50	1,300
MLS Average		**46**	**2,303**

Table 6.7 Luxury Seating at Division I-A, Power Five Conference NCAA FBS Stadia

Team(s)	Facility	Suites	Club Seats
Arizona State University	Sun Devil Stadium at Frank Kush Field	52	4,940
Auburn University	Pat Dye Field at Jordan-Hare Stadium	80	2,200
Baylor University	McLane Stadium	45	1,200
Boston College	Alumni Stadium	54	undisclosed
Clemson University	Memorial Stadium	100	1,500
Duke University	Brooks Field at Wallace Wade Stadium	22	858
Florida State University	Bobby Bowden Field at Doak S. Campbell Stadium	94	undisclosed
Georgia Tech	Bobby Dodd Stadium at Grant Field	71	2,040
Indiana University	Memorial Stadium	10	732
Iowa State University	Jack Trice Stadium	49	3,542
Kansas State University	Bill Snyder Family Stadium	57	2,300
Louisiana State University	Tiger Stadium	70	3,200
Michigan State University	Spartan Stadium	24	838
Mississippi State University	Davis Wade Stadium at Scott Field	50	1,700
North Carolina State University	Carter-Finley Stadium	51	955
Northwestern University	Ryan Field	undisclosed	undisclosed
Ohio State University	Ohio Stadium	81	2,627
Oklahoma State University	Boone Pickens Stadium	123	4,000
Oregon State University	Reser Stadium	33	3,175
Penn State University	Beaver Stadium	60	11,500
Purdue University	Ross-Ade Stadium	35	1,541
Rutgers University	High Point Solutions Stadium	undisclosed	968
Stanford University	Stanford Stadium	7	400
Syracuse University	Carrier Dome	42	undisclosed
Texas A&M University	Kyle Field	97	2,300
Texas Christian University	Amon G. Carter Stadium	25	250
Texas Tech University	Jones AT&T Stadium	83	1,854
University of Alabama	Bryant-Denny Stadium	157	1,690
University of Arizona	Arizona Stadium	23	225
University of Arkansas	Donald W. Reynolds Razorback Stadium	132	8,950
University of California – Berkeley	California Memorial Stadium	undisclosed	3,000
University of California – Los Angeles	Rose Bowl Stadium	54	1,400
University of Colorado	Folsom Field	40	1,903
University of Florida	Ben Hill Griffin Stadium	82	2,900
University of Georgia	Sanford Stadium	77	750
University of Illinois	Memorial Stadium	49	3,500

(continued)

Table 6.7 Continued

Team(s)	Facility	Suites	Club Seats
University of Iowa	Kinnick Stadium	40	1,000
University of Kansas	Memorial Stadium	36	3,000
University of Kentucky	Kroger Field	40	2,300
University of Louisville	Papa John's Cardinal Stadium	70	2,550
University of Maryland	Capital One Field at Maryland Stadium	64	236
University of Miami (Florida)	Hard Rock Stadium (2)	216	10,209
University of Michigan	Michigan Stadium	81	3,200
University of Minnesota	TCF Bank Stadium	39	300
University of Mississippi	Vaught-Hemingway Stadium at Hollingsworth Field	58	2,500
University of Missouri	Memorial Stadium/Faurot Field	36	500
University of Nebraska	Memorial Stadium	101	3,000
University of North Carolina	Kenan Stadium	20	undisclosed
University of Notre Dame (3)	Notre Dame Stadium	undisclosed	undisclosed
University of Oklahoma	Gaylord Family-Oklahoma Memorial Stadium	83	4,210
University of Oregon	Autzen Stadium	40	4,000
University of Pittsburgh	Heinz Field (4)	129	7,300
University of South Carolina	Williams-Brice Stadium	18	2,595
University of Southern California	Los Angeles Memorial Coliseum	undisclosed	undisclosed
University of Tennessee	Neyland Stadium, Shiuelds-Watkins Field	122	800
University of Texas	Darrell K. Royal-Texas Memorial Stadium	110	3,262
University of Utah	Rice-Eccles Stadium	25	800
University of Virginia	Carl Smith Center, Home of David A. Harrison III Field at Scott Stadium	56	350
University of Washington	Alaska Airlines Field at Husky Stadium	92	2,507
University of Wisconsin	Camp Randall Stadium	72	927
Vanderbilt University	Vanderbilt Stadium	16	200
Virginia Tech	Lane Stadium/Worsham Field	15	1,200
Wake Forest University	BB&T Field	22	650
Washington State University	Martin Stadium	21	1,300
West Virginia University	Mountaineer Field at Milan Puskar Stadium	30	648
Division I-A, Power Five Conference NCAA FBS Stadia Average		**61**	**2,388**

can be adjusted to market conditions and any long-term changes in the demography of fans. The point to understand is that in every market, fans and businesses must be surveyed to identify the right mix of amenities. The team then needs to market-test pricing strategies. What has changed in the management of luxury real estate is that it is now tailored to each team's market.

As teams build new or renovate older venues, a frequent complaint is that, because the sight lines in older venues are still wonderful, there is no need for a new or renovated facility. Such an observation fails to appreciate how consumers' preferences change over time and how every business in any form of retail or entertainment must adjust to those trends.

Allen Sanderson, a senior lecturer in the University of Chicago's Department of Economics, was among the first who observed that sport fans, like other consumers, enjoy new products with enhanced amenities. He noted that many consumers enjoy shiny new cars with the newest amenities and technology. Just as automobile manufacturers responded to changing appetites among customers, teams must also change or risk losing their fans to other forms of entertainment. Sanderson does not criticize team owners for providing fans with what they want, nor does he belittle fans who want more comfortable seats and spaces within which they could entertain guests or enjoy higher quality and more varied food choices. The cornerstone of his observation was that, as people's discretionary income rises, it is common to find a demand for enhanced amenities and different experiences. Joseph Pine and James Gilmore initially introduced the observation that people were becoming more interested in consuming experiences rather than purchasing possessions in their book *The Experience Economy* (1999). Their advice to businesses was that they plan and present events so that the memory of the experience becomes the product. Collecting experiences has become just as important as consuming tangible goods. Enhancing the game-day experience, therefore, necessitates providing luxury seating and opportunities to enjoy different types of food and beverages and other forms of entertainment while at games. Those who can afford club seats or suites get to enjoy experiences that, if not offered at sport venues, they would consume elsewhere. An essential part of the sport business now is understanding that the game-day experience is paramount in terms of ticket sales and realizing all of the revenue potential that exists for franchises. Had new facilities with luxury seating and other amenities not been built, both players and owners would have lost the opportunity to realize a substantially enhanced level of revenues that have led to higher salaries and profit levels. They also might have lost fans to other forms of consumption that were more attentive to their demands. The issue in every market is to ensure that an adequate supply of luxury seating exists. Each team must also protect against an oversupply that leaves too much real estate unsold and, therefore, does not contribute to the overall revenue picture. As markets change, the demand for luxury seating can fluctuate, which is why, in the newest designs, owners are seeking plans that would permit luxury seating to be converted to other uses and the ability to add luxury seating when needed.

Seating Deck

Chapter 10, which focuses on pricing strategies, describes the various decisions and options that must be considered by team owners and business managers as they seek to optimize revenues and attendance levels. In this section, we focus on design decisions that influence the real estate management issues and ticket pricing involved with every facility's non-luxury seating, or "the deck," as the other seats are sometimes described.

The first management issue involves the lessons learned from the circular facilities that were built in the 1960s and 1970s to accommodate baseball and football teams in the same facility. While having two teams in a single facility is advantageous relative to the number of event dates the venue is used, it can also lead to compromised sight lines, which reduce the quality of a fan's experience. That reduced quality often means lower prices must be charged for those seats. Business managers must never lose sight of the need to deliver quality game experiences to each fan, and that begins with seating that provides excellent sight lines. When every seat offers fans excellent views of the playing surface, revenues rise from individual ticket sales as a result of higher and more persistent levels of demand. Simply put, people will pay higher prices for better sight lines and comfortable seats; facilities that are designed to cater to each individual sport (ballparks for baseball, stadiums for football, and so on) create better sight lines.

When arenas serve as a home for both an NBA and NHL team, certain design compromises are unavoidable. Most arenas are designed to accommodate both even though the size of the playing surfaces differ. Arenas built to offer basketball fans the best views of that court place the upper deck closer to the court, but to ensure that fans seated in the upper deck can see the entire rink (and both goals), the upper deck must be recessed. The case below outlines one such example.

The Problems Associated With Playing Hockey in an Arena Designed for Basketball

(Bondy, 2015)

Thirteen minutes into the first period, Artem Anisimov broke down ice and flipped a top-shelf backhander toward the Islanders' net past goaltender Thomas Greiss. It was the first regular-season goal ever scored at Barclays Center. From Section 201, however, there was only the sight of Anisimov's shot heading toward a black hole somewhere below.

Then silence. Then anger. The goal itself had been obscured by the Brooklyn building's quirky, asymmetric architecture.

"You got to be kidding," said Christopher Dabrowski, a Long Islander from Franklin Square, who had paid $125 for a seat that did not allow him to see the goal at his end of the building.

While it was true that Dabrowski had purchased a ticket featuring the explicit warning "Limited view," he had not expected his view to be quite so limited. He could not be blamed for expecting more from an arena that bills itself as "one of the most intimate seating configurations ever designed."

The Islanders' opener on Friday night received mixed reviews from the fans in attendance, whose experiences varied greatly according to ticket price and location. For one thing, the crowd was far quieter than those that filled Nassau Coliseum at times. The decibel level was far lower than those at the Islanders' playoff games last spring.

Many in the crowd had made the commute from Nassau and Suffolk Counties by train or car. These were old-style blue-and-orange loyalists, not Brooklyn hipsters in the team's alternate black jersey. Upon arrival, some of the more privileged supporters were wined and dined in the arena's fanciest niches, the clubs. They had a grand old time. Others – the fans sitting up by Denis Potvin's retired jersey in Sections 201, 202, 203, 229, 230 and 231 – found life far more frustrating.

The second goal also came at the wrong end. In the second period, John Tavares fired a shot from the crease that, like the others, disappeared into the darkness below. This time it was an Islanders goal. Once more, right below. Fans who had not been watching the scoreboard as it happened had to settle for a replay on the big screen.

"I'm getting madder and madder the more I think about it," said Kristie Rodgers of Merrick.

Rodgers remembered how she and her high school friends had worn hard hats to games at the Coliseum, goofing around with the notion that the ceiling might fall down upon them at any moment.

"The Islanders need to go back to Long Island," Rodgers said. "I'd rather be in the Coliseum wearing a hard hat than here with an obstructed view."

There have been obstructed views before at New York hockey games. Fans sitting along the side of the upper deck at the old Madison Square Garden often could not see the quarter of the ice closest to them, though they could see the goals. Pillars in Nassau Coliseum blocked some views, yet most of those were mere visual nuisances.

A pregame ceremony at Barclays Center, a celebration of the team's Long Island history, was enough to charm even some of the fans near the rafters. The most cynical among them had to admit that this was a more convenient new home for the Islanders than Kansas City, one potential location the owner Charles Wang had flirted with.

"It's a bit disappointing, but it's good to be here," said Dave Barbieri of Garden City. "People just have got to suck it up."

Some fans predicted that the Islanders would be back on Long Island within five years after attendance had faded in Brooklyn and the Coliseum site had been revamped. Others blamed their basketball-friendly sight lines on Jay Z. There were also suggestions for how to fix the arena, starting with the removal of a banner, advertising a sports fantasy website, that blocked the view of many rows.

"I'm no architect, but they could take out five rows on one end, shift the ice," said Patrick Drexler of Brooklyn. "They really botched this. It's not O.K. But in the end, it's about the product that's on the ice."

The league did the Islanders no favors in scheduling them against the Blackhawks, the Stanley Cup champions, who were coming off a tough opening loss to the Rangers and looking for a quick rebound.

Still, this was a marquee event at a clean, well-ordered arena. Rodgers, the fan from Merrick, eventually settled into her seat and tried to watch the game. Then things grew worse. A few minutes before the start, a large, loud man in a Blackhawks jersey took his seat directly in front of her, further blocking her view and disturbing her peace.

"Go, Hawks!" he screamed.

"Aargh," Rodgers said.

Another lesson learned is that those facilities that lack the amenities fans want lose revenue. Even in the general seating deck, people are willing to pay higher prices for improved surroundings. Newer venues offer the opportunity for fans to walk around an entire venue while still able to see action on the field, court, or ice, as well as social seating areas without fixed seating. These types of amenities are typically made available for fans seated in the deck, rather than on the luxury level, though they are made available to all fans in attendance. In effect, teams are now focused on offering unique experiences that cater to fans' interests and at varying price points. Customers respond positively to the availability of amenities, and new facilities that charge higher prices have, nonetheless, received uniformly favorable responses from consumers. What is important for managers to realize is that in most instances, higher-priced tickets are met with less market resistance if the conveniences and amenities are state-of-the-art and relatively unique in the market. This does not mean that there is no limit to what fans are willing to pay when amenities are offered; as discussed, the New York Yankees had to change their pricing policies with regard to their special seats adjacent the field. That was a vivid reminder that severe price escalations can result in unsold seats (although it is important to note the Yankees had the misfortune of unveiling their new seating and fan experience at the height of the Great Recession).

Scoreboard and Other Electronic Displays

Advertising on scoreboards began decades ago, but the advent of high definition video and the technology that allows the presentation of multiple images substantially increased the revenue potential of these assets. Managers must ensure scoreboards continue to fulfill their initial purpose – to inform spectators about the game – while also generating important revenue streams for the team.

Ribbon boards, first introduced in the 1970s and 1980s, are now standard fare in arenas and some ballparks and stadia. Ribbon boards usually surround an entire arena and in ballparks and stadiums run the length of the grandstands. In between plays and during time-outs, scoreboards and ribbon boards send out advertising messages. Because of the timing of advertisements' placement on these elements, attention to detail is crucial in the design of these features so that advertising messages are visible to everyone regardless of where they sit.

While filling scoreboards and electronic displays with sponsors' messaging can create a valuable revenue stream, covering the scoreboard and other surfaces with too much advertising can cause visual pollution and result in a backlash from customers and sponsors. Fans may become annoyed if they are bombarded with commercials at every turn. Similarly, lower revenues can result if there are too many commercials because sponsors become concerned that messages will simply be ignored. Figure 6.2 and Figure 6.3 provide two examples of visual pollution, the first of which is a view of the entrance to the Gila River Arena (home to the Arizona Coyotes); the second image is of the entertainment zone immediately adjacent to the Gila River Arena. The commercialization of the entrance to the venue compromises views of its architecture. The presence of so many large billboards in front

Figure 6.2 Visual Pollution at the Gila River Arena.

of the venue and across the street could dull consumers' attention, essentially lowering the value of each to less than what it would be if there were fewer visual messages. Every facility manager and team must balance the incremental value of an additional message board and its impact on the team's fans.

The balancing of advertising messages and game information to ensure that spectators do not become inured to advertising has become a major design issue. In planning for the use of the scoreboard and other electronic displays, managers must balance revenue potential with the information that fans want to see during a game (Figure 6.4).

Playing Surfaces

While there has been some reluctance to create an overly labeled environment, advertising on the playing field has increased steadily as teams seek additional revenue streams. If a sponsor has been secured for a facility or event (e.g., Air Canada Centre, Capital One Orange Bowl), it is increasingly common to find the sponsor's brand somewhere on the playing surface. While some team owners are less aggressive with regard to the placement of advertising on the playing surface, there remains an unmistakable

Figure 6.3 Visual Pollution at the Gila River Arena Entertainment Zone.

trend. The playing surface represents a substantial amount of real estate, and while it can be counted upon to drive the largest portion of revenue from the game itself, from a management perspective it seems unlikely that other income possibilities will be ignored. Electronically, television networks and teams already offer clients the possibility of imposing different graphical representations on the field and elsewhere that are only seen by viewers. Baseball fans routinely see advertisements on the backstop behind the catcher that are not visible in the ballpark. Different statistical boxes, replay windows, and strike zone projections are made available for advertising by the networks. Will teams and the leagues decide to adorn the playing surfaces with even more advertising in the future? That decision will probably be made relative to what fans will tolerate before becoming too alienated by the advertising messages or when sponsors believe the addition of one more message has no value as fans have become either alienated or numb to the content as a result of the bombardment of ads.

Concourses and Entrances

Facilities are now designed to provide myriad advertising opportunities. As recently as 30 years ago, the concept of naming an entire facility was seen as

Figure 6.4 Scoreboard Usage at Target Field, Minneapolis.

extraordinary. Twenty-first century facilities are now built with the intention of creating numerous distinct entrances (as well as entry points reserved solely for luxury clients), concourses, atriums, and gathering spaces, each with the ability to be bought and branded by distinct sponsors, while the venue itself is named by yet another sponsor (to be discussed in the following section). Including distinct entrances with special architectural themes creates an opportunity to offer companies an advertising deal that would cost far less than an opportunity to purchase a name for the entire facility. The number of teams that have sold naming rights to facilities, entrances, concourses, and even clubs underscores the popularity of named portions of a facility.

Naming Rights

If there is a "big banana" in the effort to secure revenue from advertising, it is the naming of the facility itself. Surprisingly, the concept of naming rights is not a new venture. In 1926 William Wrigley built a baseball stadium to house the team he owned and gave it his family's name, which also happened to be the name of his chewing gum company. However, the concept was not without controversy. When breweries wanted to expand their advertising at venues, there was some concern among MLB leadership. A proposal to name the St. Louis Cardinals' ballpark Budweiser Stadium was opposed by then-MLB Commissioner Ford Frick. A compromise ensued and the venue was named Busch Memorial Stadium (with an emphasis on the family's name). The venue has always been popularly known as Busch Stadium and there was never an effort to rename it for the family's beer. Since then, Coors Field became the home of the Colorado Rockies, and a similar outcome guided the naming of the Milwaukee Brewers' home, Miller Field.

The largest amount of money ever secured for naming rights that has been publicly disclosed was the $400 million Citi Financial agreed to pay for the name on the New York Mets' ballpark, Citi Field. The magnitude of this 20-year naming rights agreement was partially credited to the size of New York City. However, two other locational factors also contributed to the deal's high price tag. First, the Citi Field sign is adjacent and visible to all traffic on New York's Grand Central Parkway. Second, Citi Field is quite close to La Guardia Airport, and planes taking off and landing offer passengers a panoramic view of the ballpark. These two unique factors added value to the deal in a way no other sponsorship element in North America could; no other sport venue can access as many "eyeballs" as the Citi Field sign does from the Grand Central Parkway and La Guardia Airport.

It should be noted that owners of some of the most historically significant facilities have made the decision not to place corporate names on their venues. A corporate name preceding or replacing such venerable names as Fenway Park, Yankee Stadium, or Lambeau Field might engender a strong negative reaction from consumers. That possibility has likely reduced sponsors' interest in securing a naming right for the entire venue. As a result, the Yankees have not sold the naming rights to Yankee Stadium, nor have the Packers sold naming rights for Lambeau Field. Instead, at both venues, naming rights for entrances and concourses have been permitted. Managers should be aware that naming certain facilities and events can create a level of consumer backlash that reduces or eliminates any value from the advertising to consumers. When that happens, focusing on other naming rights opportunities can be far more profitable. For example, the Rose Bowl (stadium) remains with its historical name, but the game itself is now referred to as "The Rose Bowl Presented by" with a corporate sponsor's name inserted. This began in 1999 when AT&T became the game's initial sponsor. In recent years, Citi Financial (CitiBank) was a sponsor. For 2011, Vizio affixed its name to the game, while the facility remains "The Rose Bowl" (see Figure 6.5). And in 2018, the game was referred to as the Rose Bowl presented by Northwestern Mutual. The value of naming rights to teams is illustrated in Table 6.8.

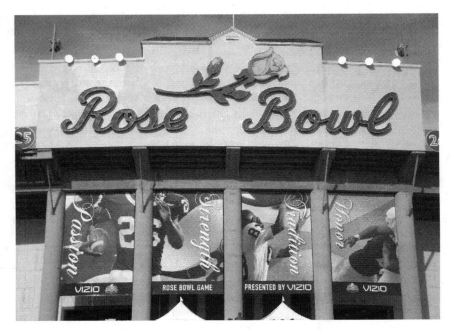

Figure 6.5 The Rose Bowl Stadium with Vizio Sponsorship Affixed.

A typical naming rights deal also usually includes more than just the adorning of a name on a facility. The corporate name usually appears in many different places throughout the facility and the deal might also include other benefits, such as the placement of cash machines throughout the facility in the case of a bank, or exclusive food or beverage services rights (Minute Maid products, for example) for sales in the facility. In other instances, advertisements also might range from a number of exposures on ribbon boards or static (billboard type) ads placed at strategic points.

Naming Rights and NCAA Events

An interesting advertising issue often arises when a facility is used for NCAA championship events and that facility is also part of a naming rights agreement. In the guidelines issued that cities must follow to submit bids to host a championship, the NCAA requires that the following practices be adhered to regardless of preexisting advertising, naming, or licensing agreements made by a venue's owners or the team that may control advertising inside the venue (NCAA, 2010).

Table 6.8 Naming Rights Deals for Selected Facilities

Facility Name	Sponsor	Average Annual Fee	Expires
TD Garden	TD Bank	$5,955,000	2025
Barclays Center	Barclays	$10,000,000	2032
United Center	United Airlines	$11,000,000	2034
American Airlines Center	American Airlines	$6,500,000	2030
Little Caesars Arena	Little Caesars	$625,000	2036
Oracle Arena	Oracle	$3,000,000	2016
Staples Center	Staples	$5,800,000	2019
FedexForum	FedEx	$4,090,909	2024
AmericanAirlines Arena	American Airlines	$6,500,000	2030
Moda Center	Moda Health	$4,000,000	2023
Golden I Center	Golden I Credit Union	$6,000,000	2035
AT&T Center	AT&T	$2,050,000	2022
Air Canada Centre[1]	Air Canada	$1,520,000	2019
Capital One Arena	Capital One	$10,000,000	2027
Honda Center	Honda	$4,030,000	2020
Nationwide Arena	Nationwide Insurance Company	$2,850,000	2021
Bell Centre	Bell Canada	$3,197,000	2023
Prudential Center	Prudential Financial	$5,265,000	2027
Canadian Tire Centre	Canadian Tire	$1,750,000	2021
Mercedes-Benz Stadium	Mercedes-Benz	$12,000,000	2042
Bank of America Stadium	Bank of America	$7,000,000	2023
Ford Field	Ford	$2,264,000	2026
EverBank Field	EverBank	$3,320,000	2024
US Bank Stadium	U.S. Bank	$8,800,000	2040
Gillette Stadium	Gillette	$16,000,000	2031
MetLife Stadium	MetLife	$21,000,000	2036
Heinz Field	Heinz North America	$2,800,000	2021
Levi's Stadium	Levi Strauss	$11,015,000	2034
CenturyLink Field	CenturyLink	$5,000,000	2018
Raymond James Stadium	Raymond James Financial	$3,051,111	2028
Chase Field	Chase Bank	$2,213,333	2028
SunTrust Park	SunTrust Banks	$10,000,000	2039
Guaranteed Rate Field	Guaranteed Rate	$2,040,000	2029
Progressive Field	Progressive Corp.	$3,600,000	2023
Comerica Park	Comerica Bank	$2,200,000	2030
Minute Maid Park	Minute Maid	$6,357,143	2029
Miller Park	Miller/Miller Lite	$2,060,000	2020
Citi Field	Citigroup	$20,000,000	2028
Citizens Bank Park	Citizens Financial Group	$3,800,000	2029
PNC Park	PNC Financial Services Group	$2,000,000	2021
PETCO Park	Petco	$2,727,273	2026
AT&T Park	AT&T	$2,083,333	2024
Tropicana Field	Tropicana Products	$1,533,333	2026
Globe Life Park in Arlington	Globe Life Insurance	$5,000,000	2024

[1] The Raptors' arena is anticipated to be renamed Scotiabank Arena in 2018.

NCAA Venue Guidelines

Advertising/Banners/Signs/Displays: No advertising, banners, signs, or displays of any kind may be hung, posted, or displayed anywhere within the general public seating/viewing area of the competition, practice, and ancillary events venue(s) (i.e., any place that can be seen from the playing surface or seats), including the scoreboard other than NCAA banners and television banners approved by the NCAA. Any permanently affixed (or previously leased) advertising banners, signs, cup holders, or displays shall be covered with décor elements by the competition, practice, and ancillary event venue(s) and at the expense of the venue(s) as specified by the NCAA.

External Signs: All exterior venue corporate and/or professional franchise identification must be covered and must be covered with décor elements as specified by the NCAA.

Commercially Named Competition Venues: Commercially named competition, practice, and ancillary event venue(s) may display two preexisting interior signs with the competition, practice, and ancillary event venue(s)' name at the top of the venue (excluding the scoreboard), with placement designated by the NCAA. The competition, practice, and ancillary event venue(s) sign-age design and placement must be approved by the NCAA.

NCAA Corporate Champion/Partner Banners: The NCAA shall have the right to display NCAA corporate champion/partner banners and NCAA signage inside and outside of the competition, practice, and ancillary event venue(s) in various locations, including but not limited to on the concourse, within the competition bowl and venue exterior without limitation. The NCAA shall have the right to display banners and the like (e.g., inflatables, projections, kiosks, decals, window clings, lighting, street teams, logos, etc.) on the concourse (without limitation) and in other areas designated by the NCAA inside and outside the competition, practice, and ancillary event venue, identifying its corporate champions/partners.

The NCAA's interest in controlling the advertising real estate for its championship events is obvious. The NCAA wants to offer advertising rights to sponsors and does not want any interference or conflicts that would reduce the revenue it can earn. In effect, the NCAA accepts bids and will place its events only in venues where it can be assured that it has full authority to sell advertising regardless of the agreements in place at the venue. Notice that the only compromise that is made regards limited exposure for a facility for which the naming rights have been sold.

Similar conflicts exist when the Olympics are involved. The International Olympic Committee (IOC) also has a set of stringent rules and only their approved sponsors may be associated with the event or any participating athletes. Olympic Charter Rule 51 governs advertising and is even more specific and demanding than those issued by the NCAA. Similar to the NCAA, the IOC also seeks to protect its interests and the revenues it can earn from any of the real estate it controls during the Olympic Games. That "real estate" is defined as the venues where the games are played, the areas where athletes live, train, or practice, and even the equipment used.

The International Olympic Committee's Rule 51

Advertising, Demonstrations, Propaganda
(*The Vancouver Sun*, 2009)

1   The IOC Executive Board determines the principles and conditions under which any form of advertising or other publicity may be authorised.
2   No form of advertising or other publicity shall be allowed in and above the stadiums, venues and other competition areas which are considered as part of the Olympic sites. Commercial installations and advertising signs shall not be allowed in the stadiums, venues or other sports grounds.
3   No kind of demonstration or political, religious or racial propaganda is permitted in any Olympic sites, venues or other areas.

By-Law to Rule 51

(*The Vancouver Sun*, 2009)

1   No form of publicity or propaganda, commercial or otherwise, may appear on persons, on sportswear, accessories or, more generally, on any article of clothing or equipment whatsoever worn or used by the athletes or other participants in the Olympic Games, except for the identification – as defined in paragraph 8 below – of the manufacturer of the article or equipment concerned, provided that such identification shall not be marked conspicuously for advertising purposes.

   1.1   The identification of the manufacturer shall not appear more than once per item of clothing and equipment.

1.2 *Equipment*: any manufacturer's identification that is greater than 10% of the surface area of the equipment that is exposed during competition shall be deemed to be marked conspicuously. However, there shall be no manufacturer's identification greater than 60 cm^2.

1.3 *Headgear* (e.g., hats, helmets, sunglasses, goggles) and gloves: any manufacturer's identification over 6 cm^2 shall be deemed to be marked conspicuously.

1.4 *Clothing* (e.g., T-shirts, shorts, sweat tops and sweat pants): any manufacturer's identification which is greater than 20 cm^2 shall be deemed to be marked conspicuously.

1.5 *Shoes*: it is acceptable that there appear the normal distinctive design pattern of the manufacturer. The manufacturer's name and/or logo may also appear, up to a maximum of 6 cm^2, either as part of the normal distinctive design pattern or independent of the normal distinctive design pattern.

1.6 In case of special rules adopted by an International Sports Federation, exceptions to the rules mentioned above may be approved by the IOC Executive Board. Any violation of the provisions of the present clause may result in disqualification or withdrawal of the accreditation of the person concerned. The decisions of the IOC Executive Board regarding this matter shall be final. The numbers worn by competitors may not display publicity of any kind and must bear the Olympic emblem of the OCOG.

2 To be valid, all contracts of the OCOG containing any element whatsoever of advertising, including the right or license to use the emblem or the mascot of the Olympic Games, must be in conformity with the Olympic Charter and must comply with the instructions given by the IOC Executive Board. The same shall apply to contracts relating to the timing equipment, the scoreboards, and to the injection of any identification signal in television programmes. Breaches of these regulations come under the authority of the IOC Executive Board.

3 Any mascot created for the Olympic Games shall be considered to be an Olympic emblem, the design of which must be submitted by the OCOG to the IOC Executive Board for its approval. Such mascot may not be used for commercial purposes in the country of an NOC without the latter's prior written approval.

4 The OCOG shall ensure the protection of the property of the emblem and the mascot of the Olympic Games for the benefit of the IOC, both nationally and internationally. However, the OCOG alone and, after the OCOG has been wound up, the

NOC of the host country, may exploit such emblem and mascot, as well as other marks, designs, badges, posters, objects and documents connected with the Olympic Games during their preparation, during their holding and during a period terminating not later than the end of the calendar year during which such Olympic Games are held. Upon the expiry of this period, all rights in or relating to such emblem, mascot and other marks, designs, badges, posters, objects and documents shall thereafter belong entirely to the IOC. The OCOG and/or the NOC, as the case may be and to the extent necessary, shall act as trustees (in a fiduciary capacity) for the sole benefit of the IOC in this respect.

5 The provisions of this by-law also apply, *mutatis mutandis*, to all contracts signed by the organising committee of a Session or an Olympic Congress.

6 The uniforms of the competitors and of all persons holding an official position may include the flag or Olympic emblem of their NOC or, with the consent of the OCOG, the OCOG Olympic emblem. The IF officials may wear the uniform and the emblem of their federations.

7 The identification on all technical gear, installations and other apparatus, which are neither worn nor used by athletes or other participants at the Olympic Games, including timing equipment and scoreboards, may on no account be larger than 1/10th of the height of the equipment, installation or apparatus in question, and shall not be greater than 10 centimeters high.

8 The word "identification" means the normal display of the name, designation, trademark, logo or any other distinctive sign of the manufacturer of the item, appearing not more than once per item.

9 The OCOG, all participants and all other persons accredited at the Olympic Games and all other persons or parties concerned shall comply with the manuals, guides, or guidelines, and all other instructions of the IOC Executive Board, in respect of all matters subject to Rule 51 and this By-Law.

Uniforms or "Kits"

European football (soccer) teams have placed corporate sponsorships on uniforms (or kits, as they are referred to) for years. Manchester United is currently sponsored by AON, and the Nike "swoosh" is prominently visible. Chelsea's uniform is adorned with both Samsung and Adidas' logos. And in the Korean Baseball League, where teams are owned by corporations, team uniforms proudly display the owning corporation's logos. The visibility of a team's uniform during games watched by millions of people can produce an important revenue stream. The revenue stream is enhanced by merchandise sales of replica jerseys (between 1.2 and 1.5 million are sold each year by the leading Premier League teams), which can become "walking billboards" for corporate sponsors (Miller, 2010). While the four major North American leagues have been reluctant to follow the practice of European soccer clubs, other North American sports have been more active in pursuing uniform sponsorships. The uniforms worn and cars driven by professional race car drivers are adorned with advertising messages, as is the equipment used and clothing worn by professional golfers. MLS, which has gained traction in recent years, also allows its teams to engage in this advertising practice. The Seattle Sounders, for example, have "XBOX 360" emblazoned on their jerseys. And while historically opposed to doing so, the NBA was the first of the four major North American leagues to permit advertising on team uniforms. The rule took effect in the 2017–2018 season.

Real Estate Outside Facilities: Sport Venues as Anchors for Development

As discussed in Chapters 1 and 4, Walt Disney recognized what Rome's city planners understood more than 2,000 years earlier. Spectacles and the facilities built to host those events attract crowds. And, as a result, the large numbers of people present create opportunities to develop adjacent properties. That development can revitalize downtown areas or create entirely new neighborhoods filled with amenities. In both settings, profits can be earned and the public sector's objectives for new development and tax revenues can be realized. So, if you knew that at least one million visits were going to take place at a single specific geographic place, what would you build in the immediate area that would appeal to these crowds and others? In other words, how can a real estate development plan capitalize on the presence of crowds attracted to games and other events hosted at facilities?

In the early days of spectator sport, team owners were not as focused on external real estate development as they were on maximizing in-facility revenues. Indeed, Disneyfication within the sport business in the late 1980s and early 1990s was focused on creating dining and shopping venues inside facilities to deflect spending away from adjacent locations controlled by other entrepreneurs. Team owners saw more profit potential from absorbing all of the entertainment and hospitality spending from fans' game day experiences. That could be accomplished by building larger facilities replete with restaurants and other retail outlets capable of driving spending into a facility to maximize a team's revenues. Pursuing that option, however, reduced the value of the facility to the city or neighborhood where the arena, stadium, or ballpark was located. Ironically, if owners followed their revenue maximization strategy and pushed all fan spending into a venue, a sort of economic black hole for a city would exist: crowds would come to a facility and spend all of their money inside, essentially creating a tourist bubble. In the black hole scenario, the area adjacent to the facility could be entirely devoid of activity, resulting in no discernible effect on the city and the adjacent neighborhood (Judd & Fainstein, 1999). Some point to the Texas Rangers' Ballpark in Arlington as an example. The lack of attention to external development or a plan to integrate the facility with the surrounding neighborhood led to no real improvements for the immediate area (Swindell & Rosentraub, 2009). When a proposal was made for a new ballpark, part of the proposal presented to voters involved a commitment to build a new set of mixed-use properties between the ballpark and AT&T Stadium.

The lack of results in Arlington stands in sharp contrast to impressions that Indianapolis and San Diego have made with substantial levels of success linking sport and entertainment facilities to comprehensive redevelopment strategies. In both cities, a portion of the downtown area benefitted from substantial private sector investments to complement those made by the public sector in sports, entertainment, and cultural centers. Indianapolis' sport strategy for its downtown area produced a redeveloped area about four square miles in size that featured a domed facility for football (Lucas Oil Stadium) and an arena for an NBA franchise and other entertainment events (Bankers Life Fieldhouse), a convention center, a new shopping mall, thousands of hotel rooms, and many restaurants. San Diego's Ballpark District is home to thousands of residents, park spaces, and numerous restaurants. There have been other successes, too. Eutaw Street, adjacent to Oriole Park at Camden Yards, has added more attractions to Baltimore's Inner Harbor, which includes numerous amenities. And in 2017 the Green Bay Packers opened Titletown adjacent to Lambeau Field. That project includes acres of public spaces as well as commercial and residential properties.

Sport managers should also be aware that there are critics of a focus on revitalization efforts that, while successful, might deflect attention away from other urban neighborhoods. These points, below, are made by Professor Marc Levine (2000). What should also be noted is that in many instances when sport venues have anchored revitalization efforts, there has also been a commitment to build below-market-rate housing to promote economic integration. The notable achievements on this score in San Diego, Los Angeles, and Indianapolis might be an example of policies and practices in other areas.

Baltimore, Its Sport Facilities, and the Inner Harbor

In noting that the Inner Harbor has been a success relative to the attraction of visitors and tourists and the anchoring of a new urban neighborhood, the challenges confronting Baltimore's overall development and the pervasiveness of decline in numerous other parts of the city are not minimized. Marc Levine has written extensively on the dichotomy of worlds that exists between the Inner Harbor and the other parts of Baltimore. His work also attempted to assess the effects of Oriole Park at Camden Yards as a tool for moving economic activity. Professor Levine observed, "Camden Yards cannot be considered a successful urban redevelopment catalyst. Despite hopes to the contrary, public investment in the Camden Yards sports complex did not catalyze a 'dramatic transformation' of the western edge of downtown." While it expanded the tourist bubble to the west, little development spilled into nearby areas desperate for an influx of investment and consumer spending. While bringing even larger crowds to the Inner Harbor area, the sports facilities "have done little in terms of catalyzing development in those areas most in need of it; the Howard Street corridor still sags, Pigtown and other western-edge neighborhoods remain economically and socially separated from the thriving downtown, and Sharp-Leadenhall still teeters at the precipice of gentrification and decline" (2000: 148). 6Levine noted that Baltimore's challenges were less severe than those facing Detroit and some other former industrial capitals of North America. He notes, though, the creation of a "Fantasy City" image and environment (Harrigan, 1998) in the Inner Harbor has not led to a successful attack on any of the "city's core difficulties ... with people, jobs, and businesses continuing to desert the city ... By the end of the 1990s, after three decades of 'fantasy city' redevelopment strategies, city policy makers seem to have run out of answers short of 'slum clearance' or 'planned shrinkage' to the problems of ghetto poverty and neighborhood decay" (Levine, 2000: 151).

The development of new facilities, commercial space, residential areas, public spaces, and new neighborhoods are robust indicators of success for many advocates of the use and value of sports, entertainment, and culture for redevelopment. Critics, however, have challenged a definition of success that relies on new buildings and public spaces. They point to important economic development goals that were not achieved (Rosentraub, 1999; Levine, 2000). For example, some of the goals included population growth (or a stabilization of population levels), the attraction and retention of residents with higher incomes to stabilize the tax base, the attraction of more job opportunities, an overall increment in the local tax base, and the improvement of neighboring communities. Progress on these points has been made by some cities with sport-anchored development strategies, while others have seen few benefits. Despite any shortcomings, the crowds and vibrancy that filled downtown areas as a result of sport-anchored revitalization strategies are seen by many public and community leaders as sufficiently valuable to warrant the investment of tax dollars. Debates have ensued regarding appropriate public/private funding mechanisms for these redevelopment efforts, and while this issue remains at the forefront of negotiations on new arenas today, an important consensus was reached. One of the most important factors to consider in planning a new venue is how a new arena, ballpark, or stadium can be incorporated into a redevelopment plan as a means to achieve public sector goals while also producing profits for team owners and other private sector investors. The case studies in Chapter 14 illustrate this change and its implications for sport managers and cities.

References

Bondy, F. 2015. Islanders fans came. They didn't see. They griped, *The New York Times*, October 9. Retrieved from https://www.nytimes.com/2015/10/10/sports/hockey/islanders-fans-came-they-didnt-see-they-griped.html (accessed July 30, 2018).

Judd, D. R., & Fainstein, S. S. eds. 1999. *The tourist city*. New Haven, CT: Yale University Press.

Hitchcock, M. n.d. Welcome to PETCO Park: Home of your Enron-by-the-sea Padres, *Berkeley Law, University of California Boalt Hall*. Retrieved from http://www.law.berkeley.edu/sugarman/PETCO_Park_and_the_Padres_____Mark_Hitchcock.pdf (accessed December 18, 2010).

Levine, M. V. 2000. A third world city in the first world: Social exclusion, racial inequality, and sustainable development in Baltimore, Maryland. In *The social sustainability of cities: Diversity and the management of change*, eds. M. Polese and R. Stren, 123–156. Toronto: University of Toronto Press.

Miller, A. 2010. Exclusive: Manchester United Lead Global Shirt Sales; Liverpool in chasing pack, *Sporting Intelligence*, August 31. Retrieved from http://www.sportingintelligence.com/2010/08/31/exclusive-manchester-united-lead-global-shirt-sales-list-liverpool-chase-as-england%E2%80%99s-second-best-310805/ (accessed July 30, 2018).

NCAA. 2010. *2011–2014 Championship host city bid specification*. Retrieved from http://www.ncaa.org/wps/portal/ncaahome?WCM_GLOBAL_CONTEXT=/ncaa/ncaa/sports+and+championship/general+information/championships+administration/general+bid+template+(oct+2010) (accessed July 31, 2018).

Pine, B. J., & Gilmore, J. 1999. *The experience economy: Work is theater & and every business onstage*. Boston: Harvard Business School Press.

Rosentraub, M. S. 1999 *Major league losers: The real cost of sports and who's paying for it*, New York: Basic Books

Swindell, D., & Rosentraub, M. S. 2009. Doing better: Sports economic impact analysis, and schools of public policy and administration. *Journal of Public Administration Education* 15 (2): 219–242.

The Vancouver Sun. 2009. Your 2010 free expression rights were sold, in 2003, *The Vancouver Sun*, July 29. Retrieved from http://vancouversun.com/news/community-blogs/your-2010-free-expression-rights-were-sold-in-2003 (accessed July 31, 2018).

Chapter 7

Media, Entertainment, and Sport Management

Introduction

There were many changes in the sport business beginning in the 1990s – many of which involved venues and the real estate within and around them. As discussed in Chapter 6, the inclusion of new types of luxury seating, improved sight lines, expanded retail outlets, and new advertising opportunities created new revenue streams, as well as new issues for sport managers to consider. These fundamental shifts have been matched and, in many instances, exceeded by the ways in which games and other team-related content are delivered to fans. The media have always been integral to the financial success of teams, but what was first merely a medium used to increase fans' interest in a team, or to convince them to attend games, has become *the* defining financial component for teams' profitability. A brief review will illustrate media's change from a tool to advertise teams' basic product, to a revenue source responsible for substantially escalating team values and player salaries. Some of the changes that have taken place across the past two decades include the formation of regional sport networks, the creation of sport networks by individual teams and college conferences, and the use of web-based platforms for the delivery of games and other content to fans. The aggregate impact of these seemingly minor changes has been significant. The growing prominence of web-based platforms, for example, seems to have cast doubt on the future success of traditional television networks, which rely on cable and satellite systems to deliver content. In turn, the future stability of the relationships between leagues and these networks has come into question.

To understand the dramatic changes in the relationship between sport and media, it is perhaps easiest to consider three phases (Figure 7.1). Initially, the media was used to advertise teams through stories about games and players as well as the publication of statistics. Next, with the expansive consumption of radios and then televisions, teams could have more income from fans who were not buying tickets (through the sale of broadcast rights) while also having more paying fans in the stands. This was followed by the complete vertical integration of media into team operations. An offshoot

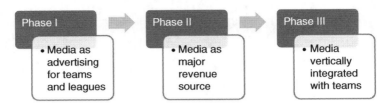

Figure 7.1 The Three Phases of the Media's Relationship with Teams and Sports.

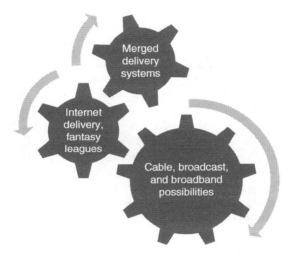

Figure 7.2 Future Media Issues and Revenue Potential from Phase III.

from this third phase, considered in the final parts of this chapter, is the rise of merged distribution systems (cable, airwave broadcast, and internet delivery systems) and advanced media that rely on the internet to deliver games to millions of fans across the globe in real time. In this context, there is also the emergence of fantasy sport, which creates new demand for viewing multiple games and having instant access to statistics on player performance (Figure 7.2). Each phase and the rise of revenue possibilities through the internet are considered in this chapter.

Sport and the Media: A Brief History

At first, the media was a vehicle for teams to publicize or advertise their sport and the entertainment value provided to fans. Teams relied on the media for publicity (through reports on the games and their outcomes and the reporting of player statistics on their prowess and accomplishments) and for maintaining fan interest in games. The means to these ends was to make it as convenient and profitable as possible for newspapers to report on a team. Teams built press boxes to provide reporters with excellent views of games and a convenient place to write their stories. Reporters also were provided with access to players and coaches in an effort to advance the team's interests. The initial goal for team owners was to ensure that newspapers would deliver favorable and exciting stories to readers, who would then become fans. The relationship with the media was designed to extend the image of the team and its players and describe the entertainment that sport provides. As people's interest grew, a demand emerged for game and player statistics, as well as insights into team management. Newspapers responded to this growing interest with the expansion of sport sections. Providing information and a positive image of players and the game was essential to the success of this form of entertainment. In the early years of the twentieth century, sport was in competition with the images and fantasy created by the movie industry, which routinely publicized the exploits of its stars and forthcoming movies and shows. Teams and leagues copied the successful media strategy that Hollywood created in the effort to be a prime choice for the emerging middle class' discretionary income. Publicity was essential for the success of the fledgling entertainment business of professional team sport, which is how the first phase of the relationship between sport and media came to be.

Phase I: Media and Team Relationships

In early years, there was a mutually beneficial link between teams and the media. Teams needed the media to deliver positive images to fans, and the media felt it was in their best interest to portray teams in a positive light, too. Owners feared negative reports might not attract fans and could even lead to some people losing interest in a team. The media feared a loss of interest would lead readers to ignore the sport section of the newspaper. This link ostensibly tempered the production of stories that failed to extol a team and its players.

As the popularity of sport grew, media became increasingly important to the profitability of newspapers. The growing importance of and interest in sport attracted more readers, and with more readers, newspapers enjoyed more advertising revenue. Sport was a high-profit area for newspapers because it was relatively low-cost to cover. Reporters could be hired to follow the team and, even though there were travel expenses associated with covering away games, teams readily provided access to players. A great deal of "copy" was generated at relatively low costs, and because readers were eager for statistics and insights, advertisers flocked to have their messages printed in the sport section of daily newspapers. Through the 1980s, it was not uncommon for newspapers to have their largest runs (number of copies of papers printed) prior to or after important games. Some papers would report their highest circulation days were those prior to or after a Super Bowl when the home team appeared in the game. Similar outcomes were noted for World Series games. Others noted their highest sales existed when special sections were included in the daily newspapers prior to the start of a season (Rosentraub, 1997).

With both sides benefiting from favorable stories, there were concerns that stories would minimize unfavorable topics or critical insights into team operations. If people's interest in a team declined, team and newspaper owners would both see lower profits. Today, the ubiquitous nature of internet-based news sources turns any positive or negative incident into an instant story. Looking back at the newspaper coverage of sport, however, most could observe that some of the questionable behavior of legendary players (e.g., Mickey Mantle) and even some issues (e.g., steroids) were largely ignored. During Phase I, when attention was directed at attracting customers, there were incentives for the media to minimize negative insights, and stories on sport were generally positive.

Returning to the central point, the initial relationship between teams and the media was one of financial reciprocity. Teams benefitted from the coverage provided, and, to achieve their goal, provided the media access to games, players, and managers. Newspapers benefitted from the increased advertising that was sold in response to their enhanced readership levels.[1] From a revenue standpoint, Phase I involved an indirect relationship between the media and teams. Teams did earn income from the media, but it was through the creation of new fans and the provision of information to all fans (and fans' subsequent decision to buy tickets) that revenues rose. The receipt of money from media distribution services begins in Phase II, which did overlap with Phase I, but soon emerged as a fountain of wealth.

Phase II: Large-Scale Revenue from the Sale of Media Rights

Phase II marked the advent of large amounts of direct revenue for teams from the broadcast of games. Perhaps surprisingly, this came well before games were broadcast on television, or even radio! Few people realize that before radios became common household amenities, teams received income from telegraphic transmissions. Western Union offered free telegraph service to teams in exchange for the right to transmit updates on games to saloons in the 1890s (Haupert, 2007). The popularity of these updates grew to the point where, in 1913, Western Union paid each team $17,000 per year over five years ($419,390 in 2017 dollars) for the right to transmit game descriptions. Of course, in those days, someone on the receiving end of the telegraph had to recount to those gathered what had happened. There are numerous stories of Western Union hiring readers to embellish what was received to create a degree of excitement from the mechanical descriptions that came through to fans as the telegraph's system of dots and dashes (Morse code). A monotonous process, indeed. Regardless, the key takeaway is that even in 1913, before fans could hear or see instantaneous reports about games, the value of sport to media firms was apparent.

Motion picture entrepreneurs bought the rights to film the 1910 World Series and then distributed those images for $500 in 1910 ($12,500 in 2017 dollars). By 1912 the cost of the rights had grown to $3,500 ($87,500 in 2017 dollars). Baseball's growing popularity and the demand for sport was ripe to explode into people's homes as soon as the technology expanded to permit the live transmission of games.

Radio broadcasts of baseball began in 1921 over the air waves of the first commercial radio station, KDKA, in Pittsburgh. As radio's popularity grew, so did the broadcasting of games. The 1921 World Series was transmitted to Pittsburgh (from New York) and in 1923 the station that would become WNBC broadcast the World Series. Chicago's baseball fans began enjoying baseball games in 1924, and in 1938 the New York Giants, Brooklyn Dodgers, and New York Yankees agreed their games could be broadcast on the radio. Some owners had feared that radio broadcasts might reduce attendance and that loss might not offset the revenues gained by allowing games to be broadcast. As that fear was eliminated (radio created more baseball fans), the number of broadcasts increased. Every team entered into a contract with local radio stations and MLB itself sold the rights to the World Series with revenues shared by all clubs. Revenues began to escalate, as did the value of franchises. The real bonanza, however, was on the horizon and, in the post–World War II years, televised games and television sharply increased revenues.

Even though the first telecast of a game took place in 1939 to a small audience in New York (Cincinnati Reds versus Brooklyn Dodgers televised in the New York area by the station that was the forerunner to WNBC), the 1950s marked the beginning of the television era. Later that same year, that same station also televised the first NFL game from Ebbets Field. That game, between the Brooklyn Dodgers and the Philadelphia Eagles, was played before 13,050 fans. Unfortunately, overcast skies reduced the available lighting and parts of the game were literally "blacked out." At the time of these first telecasts, there were approximately 500 television sets that had been purchased by households in the New York City region.

In 1947, the first World Series was televised, and in 1948, WGN in Chicago began televising White Sox and Cubs games. Again, some worried that the proliferation of televised games would lead to fewer fans buying tickets at the ballpark, but MLB's attendance increased even as more and more games were available to fans on television. By bringing games to a broader audience, television may have actually helped to expand the market for baseball. In 1951 the first baseball game was televised in full color, and those with televisions across America could actually watch the final game of the Dodgers–Giants legendary playoff series (Bobby Thompson's home run won the pennant for the Giants). The color telecast could be seen in a handful of laboratories with access to televisions that could reproduce those images.

In the post–World War II years, with the rising wealth of the middle class and the advancing technology that would lead to lower effective prices, televisions became a staple of life. The rapid spread of this technology in the United States is illustrated in Tables 7.1 and 7.2. Most importantly, in 1950, fewer than one in ten households had a television, but by 1960,

Table 7.1 The Rising Presence of Televisions in the United States, 1939–1959

Year	Total Televisions Sold	Cumulative Total of Televisions in Service
1939–1941	7,000	7,000
1942–1949	Not available	3,602,872
1950	6,132,000	9,734,872
1951	5,905,000	15,639,872
1952	6,144,989	21,784,861
1953	6,370,571	28,155,432
1954	7,317,034	35,472,466
1955	7,421,084	42,893,550
1956	6,804,783	49,698,333
1957	6,560,220	56,258,553
1958	5,140,000	61,396,000
1959	5,749,000	67,145,000

Source: www.tvhistory.tv/stats.htm

Table 7.2 Proportion of U.S. Households with Televisions, Selected Years, 1950–1975

Year	Households with at Least One Television	Percent of All Households with a Television
1950	3,880,000	9.0
1952	15,300,000	34.2
1954	26,000,000	55.7
1956	34,900,000	71.8
1960	45,750,000	87.1
1965	52,700,000	92.6
1970	59,550,000	95.2
1975	68,500,000	97.0

Source: www.tvhistory.tv/stats.htm

almost nine out of every ten households had at least one television. This rapid surge created a demand for content to be broadcast. With its supply of games, sport offered content that met the needs of emerging televisions stations; soon a strong and permanent relationship would form between teams and stations, and then between leagues and networks. The presence of televisions in almost 90 percent of all U.S. homes by 1960 (and virtually all by 1975), the large supply of content (games) controlled by teams and leagues, and the sustained popularity of sport created the opportunity for extremely profitable partnerships between teams, leagues, and networks. This profitability took a giant step forward with an idea presented to all NFL team owners by the league's young commissioner, Pete Rozelle, in 1961.

The Profitability of Television, the NFL, and Revenue Sharing

There are two football games that are usually identified as those that changed the profile and status of the NFL in the United States: the 1958 overtime championship game between the Baltimore Colts and New York Giants, and the 1960 championship game between the Philadelphia Eagles and Green Bay Packers. With the country's growing attachment to televisions, people found the games enticing and well-designed for at-home entertainment. There were sufficient timeouts for commercials that generated income and, yet, long periods of sustained play that were relatively easy to telecast and follow. Observing Americans' growing interest in sport, and eager to promote a unified league where each team would be profitable and competitive regardless of the size of the local market, NFL Commissioner Pete Rozelle proposed a unique idea. He suggested teams surrender their local television rights and permit the league to sell a package of all games to a single network. The teams would then equally share the revenue earned. If this concept would be approved, it would mean the team in the largest market (New York Giants) would receive the same amount of media income from television as the team in the smallest market (Green Bay). Rozelle argued that if all teams were financially stable, the league could deliver a large number of competitive games every week, which would make each team more money regardless of the size of their local media market. In essence, Rozelle believed that a truly competitive league where each team could win on any given Sunday would produce more revenue for the league's large market teams than they would earn from the telecast of games in a league where their teams were dominant. Table 7.3 provides insight into the success generated for the NFL from the Rozelle concept of shared revenues and a single media contract. Indeed, the popularity of the league has led ESPN to offer it an annual payment of approximately $1.9 billion for its package of Monday Night Football telecasts each year from 2014 through 2021. CBS is paying $1 billion per year through 2022, NBC pays $950 million annually for its nine-year contract, and Fox pays $1.1 billion

Table 7.3 Media Revenue and the NFL, 1960–2017 ($millions)

Year	CBS	NBC	ABC	FOX	Cable	ESPN	TBS	DirecTV	Twitter	Total Contract Value
1960	0.3	–	–	–	–	–	–	–	–	0.3
1961	0.3	–	–	–	–	–	–	–	–	0.3
1962	4.5	–	–	–	–	–	–	–	–	4.7
1963	4.8	–	–	–	–	–	–	–	–	5.8
1964	16.1	–	–	–	–	–	–	–	–	16.2
1965	16.8	–	–	–	–	–	–	–	–	16.8
1966	21.9	–	–	–	–	–	–	–	–	21.9
1967	25.7	–	–	–	–	–	–	–	–	25.7
1968	25.2	–	–	–	–	–	–	–	–	25.2
1969	25.7	–	–	–	–	–	–	–	–	25.7
1970	21.0	17.5	8.5	–	–	–	–	–	–	47.0
1971	22.5	16.0	8.5	–	–	–	–	–	–	47.0
1972	21.0	17.5	8.5	–	–	–	–	–	–	47.0
1973	22.5	16.0	8.6	–	–	–	–	–	–	47.1
1974	22.0	19.6	13.0	–	–	–	–	–	–	54.6
1975	25.0	16.6	13.0	–	–	–	–	–	–	54.6
1976	22.0	19.6	13.0	–	–	–	–	–	–	54.6
1977	26.0	16.6	11.5	–	–	–	–	–	–	54.1
1978	51.0	51.0	59.7	–	–	–	–	–	–	161.7
1979	57.0	45.0	59.7	–	–	–	–	–	–	161.7
1980	51.0	51.0	59.7	–	–	–	–	–	–	161.7
1981	57.0	45.0	59.7	–	–	–	–	–	–	161.7
1982	72.0	63.0	65.0	–	–	–	–	–	–	200.0
1983	108.0	94.0	98.0	–	–	–	–	–	–	300.0
1984	150.0	130.0	135.0	–	–	–	–	–	–	415.0
1985	150.0	140.0	160.0	–	–	–	–	–	–	450.0

Table 7.3 Continued

Year	CBS	NBC	ABC	FOX	Cable	ESPN	TBS	DirecTV	Twitter	Total Contract Value
1986						Strike year				
1987	150.0	120.0	160.0	–	46.0	–	–	–	–	476.0
1988	156.0	143.0	135.0	–	51.0	–	–	–	–	485.0
1989	194.0	146.0	135.0	–	56.0	–	–	–	–	531.0
1990	265.0	188.0	225.0	–	–	111.3	111.3	–	–	900.5
1991	265.0	188.0	225.0	–	–	111.3	111.3	–	–	900.5
1992	265.0	188.0	225.0	–	–	111.3	111.3	–	–	900.5
1993	265.0	228.0	225.0	–	–	111.3	111.3	–	–	940.5
1994	–	217.0	230.0	395.0	–	131.0	124.0	–	–	1,097.0
1995	–	217.0	230.0	395.0	–	131.0	124.0	–	–	1,097.0
1996	–	217.0	230.0	395.0	–	131.0	124.0	–	–	1,097.0
1997	–	217.0	230.0	395.0	–	131.0	124.0	–	–	1,097.0
1998	500.0	–	550.0	550.0	–	600.0	–	–	–	2,200.0
1999	500.0	–	550.0	550.0	–	600.0	–	–	–	2,200.0
2000	500.0	–	550.0	550.0	–	600.0	–	–	–	2,200.0
2001	500.0	–	550.0	550.0	–	600.0	–	–	–	2,200.0
2002	500.0	–	550.0	550.0	–	600.0	–	–	–	2,200.0
2003	500.0	–	550.0	550.0	–	600.0	–	–	–	2,200.0
2004	500.0	–	550.0	550.0	–	600.0	–	–	–	2,200.0
2005	500.0	–	550.0	550.0	–	600.0	–	–	–	2,200.0
2006	622.5	600.0	–	712.5	–	1,100.0	–	700.0	–	3,735.0
2007	622.5	600.0	–	712.5	–	1,100.0	–	700.0	–	3,735.0
2008	622.5	600.0	–	712.5	–	1,100.0	–	700.0	–	3,735.0
2009	622.5	600.0	–	712.5	–	1,100.0	–	700.0	–	3,735.0
2010	622.5	600.0	–	712.5	–	1,100.0	–	700.0	–	3,735.0
2011	622.5	600.0	–	712.5	–	1,100.0	–	1,000.0	–	4,035.0
2012	–	–	–	–	–	1,100.0	–	1,000.0	–	2,100.0
2013	–	–	–	–	–	1,100.0	–	1,500.0	–	2,600.0

(continued)

Table 7.3 Continued

Year	CBS	NBC	ABC	FOX	Cable	ESPN	TBS	DirecTV	Twitter	Total Contract Value
2014	1,000.0	950.0	–	1,100.0	–	1,900.0	–	1,500.0	–	6,450.0
2015	1,000.0	950.0	–	1,100.0	–	1,900.0	–	1,500.0	–	6,450.0
2016	1,225.0	1175.0	–	1,100.0	–	1,900.0	–	1,500.0	10.0	7,360.0
2017	1,000.0	950.0	–	1,100.0	–	1,900.0	–	1,500.0	–	6,450.0
2018	1,000.0	950.0	–	1,100.0	–	1,900.0	–	1,500.0	–	6,450.0
2019	1,000.0	950.0	–	1,100.0	–	1,900.0	–	1,500.0	–	6,450.0
2020	1,000.0	950.0	–	1,100.0	–	1,900.0	–	1,500.0	–	6,450.0
2021	1,000.0	950.0	–	1,100.0	–	1,900.0	–	1,500.0	–	6,450.0
2022	1,000.0	950.0	–	1,100.0	–	–	–	1,500.0	–	4,550.0
2023	–	–	–	–	–	–	–	1,500.0	–	1,500.0

Source: https://sites.google.com/site/rodswebpages/ (accessed January 15, 2018).

annually (2014–2022). DirecTV's satellite package costs the company $700 million per year (2006–2010).

At first glance, and realizing that the NFL will have earned nearly $115.2 billion in collective television revenues between 1960 and 2023, it would seem that Rozelle was correct. Pooled media rights and the creation of numerous competitive teams produced more revenue than most, if not all, owners realized was possible. Furthermore, selling media rights collectively creates a monopoly and eliminates competition between individual teams. Recognizing this revenue growth, however, does not answer the question of the value or benefit for larger-market teams. Would the Giants and Bears, among other larger-market teams, have earned more money if they controlled their media rights in a manner similar to what exists in other leagues? It is impossible to answer that question. The NFL remains committed to sharing its largest source of revenue equally among every team. The Jacksonville Jaguars, Indianapolis Colts, and Green Bay Packers play in the league's smallest markets, yet their share of the television contracts is equal to that received by teams in the largest markets. Does this mean that a league that does not divide its largest revenue sources equally between all teams will lead to domination by those franchises in the largest markets? And if that domination occurs, will both fan interest and media revenues decline? Perhaps surprisingly, the answer might well be "no."

In England's Premier League, there is little sharing of media revenues, and each club can spend as much as it wishes on players without incurring a penalty or a fine. Across the past 20 years, only once has the league championship not been won by one of five major teams (Manchester City, Manchester United, Arsenal, Chelsea, and Liverpool). One might then observe that the Premier League operates within a philosophy that is the antithesis of NFL's "on any given Sunday any team can win" philosophy. Yet, despite a very limited uncertainty parameter (some teams simply never compete for the title), Premier League games remain popular, earning billions of dollars in media revenue each year.

In MLB, there also are substantial differences in media earnings; there is a national package that is divided equally among the clubs, but each team retains the right to sell their games that are not nationally televised in their local markets. As a result, the Boston Red Sox, Chicago Cubs, Chicago White Sox, Los Angeles Dodgers, New York Yankees, New York Mets, and Texas Rangers earn far more than several other clubs.

The small scale of the national media package – compared to local media packages – has been altered by the success of MLB.com. Formed in 2000 (as Major League Baseball Advanced Media or MLBAM with an investment of $1 million a year from each of the 30 owners), it was agreed that the profits derived would be shared equally by all 30 teams. MLB's total revenue from MLBAM was reported to have reached $800 million in 2015 (Brown, 2016). MLB sold part of MLBAM to the Disney Corporation and also derives revenue from supporting the distribution of NHL games on the MLBAM platform. This revenue gain has created a level of parity on media revenues for all teams. That said, the larger market teams still earn more than smaller market teams.

Despite these differences, eight different teams have won the World Series in the last ten seasons and attendance levels for the league have remained robust throughout the recession. There is far more competitiveness than one might imagine given the different media markets available to teams. Chapter 12 provides a detailed discussion of each league's policies.

In comparing the differences in outcomes with regard to the effects of revenue sharing, the important point is that what fans want, and what attracts them, varies. The NFL's model of success, based on the sharing of media revenue, has contributed to its popularity, but different models have worked well for other leagues that also have maintained high levels of popularity. Yet, in every instance, media revenue is both vital and robust. While its direct effect on winning, uncertainty of outcome, and championships varies, its impact on the overall rise in team values and salaries has remained constant. Team owners and players have reaped substantial financial rewards from growing media contracts, and team values have increased as well. This is not an outcome that has shortchanged fans. In the United States, for example, every game played can be seen by any fan as long as they purchase an appropriate media package. This provides ample evidence that consumers, owners, and labor have each benefitted from the televising of games and that leagues have remained popular even when some teams consistently do not appear in the playoffs.[2]

An example of the benefits accruing to players is provided in Table 7.4, where the change in players' average salaries from 1989 to 2017 is analyzed. Two factors contributed to rising team revenues that supported the observed increases. New facilities produced more revenues, as did local and national media contracts. For each season, the actual (nominal) average salary is presented, followed by the value of the average salary in 2017 dollars. The year-to-year percent change and the percent change from each year to the average salary in 2017 is also included. From 1989 to 2017, average salaries increased more than 348 percent, meaning the average player in 2017 earned three times more than the average player in 1989. To be sure, there are many league policies that can change the percentage of revenue that goes to the players. However, this period is well after the advent of free-agency that started in MLB in the 1970s. So, while there are many factors contributing to player salaries, the massive increase in revenues over this time period clearly had a large impact on what players were paid.

To illustrate the benefits that have accrued to owners, the changing value of sport franchises is summarized in Tables 7.5 and 7.6; these figures will also be discussed in Chapter 8, but they are important to briefly consider here in terms of understanding the effect of revenue from media and

Table 7.4 Average MLB Salaries, 1989–2017

Year	Average Salary	Average Salary in $2017	Annual Percent Change	Percent Change from Year to 2017
1989	512,804	1,002,526	–	348.1%
1990	578,930	1,066,668	6.4%	321.2%
1991	891,188	1,593,178	49.4%	182.0%
1992	1,084,408	1,883,951	18.3%	138.5%
1993	1,120,254	1,894,167	0.5%	137.2%
1994	1,188,679	1,957,501	3.3%	129.5%
1995	1,071,029	1,720,094	−12.1%	161.2%
1996	1,176,967	1,829,449	6.4%	145.6%
1997	1,383,578	2,114,601	15.6%	112.5%
1998	1,441,406	2,168,036	2.5%	107.2%
1999	1,720,050	2,519,510	16.2%	78.3%
2000	1,998,034	2,830,824	12.4%	58.7%
2001	2,264,403	3,159,195	11.6%	42.2%
2002	2,383,235	3,247,787	2.8%	38.3%
2003	2,555,476	3,418,265	5.2%	31.4%
2004	2,486,609	3,221,276	−5.8%	39.5%
2005	2,632,655	3,297,828	2.4%	36.2%
2006	2,866,544	3,501,843	6.2%	28.3%
2007	2,944,556	3,456,092	−1.3%	30.0%
2008	3,154,845	3,699,531	7.0%	21.4%
2009	3,240,206	3,698,968	0.0%	21.5%
2010	3,297,828	3,709,268	0.3%	21.1%
2011	3,333,955	3,642,011	−1.8%	23.4%
2012	3,396,125	3,646,440	0.1%	23.2%
2013	3,920,370	4,147,048	13.7%	8.3%
2014	3,945,430	4,142,221	−0.1%	8.5%
2015	4,188,113	4,365,164	5.4%	2.9%
2016	4,307,487	4,398,335	0.8%	2.1%
2017	4,492,607	4,492,607	2.1%	0.0%

Source: *USA Today* MLB Team Payrolls (Accessed January 12, 2018).

facilities on franchise values. Again, it is important to remember that media and facility revenues have been increasing across the past two decades and both have contributed to increases in franchise values.

NFL franchises have enjoyed robust growth across the past two decades resulting from the revenues generated by new facilities and rapidly escalating contracts with broadcast networks, a satellite television service, and the development of the NFL network. In some instances, values increased tenfold since 1991. Teams worth approximately $250 million (2017 dollars) in 1991 are valued at more than $2.5 billion today. The value of the New England Patriots increased 1,922 percent in the 26 years from 1991 to 2017. While the chart does not isolate facility and media effects, suffice

Table 7.5 NFL Team Value Growth ($millions)

Team	Value in $2017	Value in 1991 or First Year ($2017)	Percent Change
Arizona Cardinals	2,150	218	886.2%
Atlanta Falcons	2,475	207	1,095.7%
Baltimore Ravens	2,500	320	681.3%
Buffalo Bills	1,600	229	598.7%
Carolina Panthers	2,300	232	891.4%
Chicago Bears	2,850	263	983.7%
Cincinnati Bengals	1,800	229	686.0%
Cleveland Browns	1,950	266	633.1%
Dallas Cowboys	4,800	329	1,359.0%
Denver Broncos	2,600	208	1,150.0%
Detroit Lions	1,700	212	701.9%
Green Bay Packers	2,550	366	596.7%
Houston Texans	2,800	218	1,184.4%
Indianapolis Colts	2,375	212	1,020.3%
Jacksonville Jaguars	2,075	232	794.4%
Kansas City Chiefs	2,100	224	837.5%
Las Vegas/Oakland Raiders	2,380	359	563.0%
Los Angeles/San Diego Chargers	2,275	208	993.8%
Los Angeles/St. Louis Rams	3,000	491	511.0%
Miami Dolphins	2,575	375	586.7%
Minnesota Vikings	2,400	218	1,000.9%
New England Patriots	3,700	183	1,921.9%
New Orleans Saints	2,000	227	781.1%
New York Giants	3,300	275	1,100.0%
New York Jets	2,750	229	1,100.9%
Philadelphia Eagles	2,650	258	927.1%
Pittsburgh Steelers	2,450	205	1,095.1%
San Francisco 49ers	3,050	275	1,009.1%
Seattle Seahawks	2,425	237	923.2%
Tampa Bay Buccaneers	1,975	209	845.0%
Tennessee Titans	2,050	490	318.4%
Washington Redskins	3,100	229	1,253.7%

Source: Forbes.

to note that the management of the real estate within facilities and income from the media combined to dramatically change the business of the NFL at what is likely an unprecedented rate relative to any sport franchise business. In addition, new facilities and the media have catapulted numerous NFL franchises into billion-dollar companies with each worth more than $1.5 billion (Table 7.5).

MLB franchises have seen very robust real growth rates as well, although the changes are far less than those enjoyed by NFL franchises (Table 7.6). Notice the increments in value enjoyed by teams that own (or are part

Table 7.6 Growth in Team Values in MLB ($millions)

Team	Value in $2017	Value in 1991 or First Year ($2017)	Percent Change
Arizona Diamondbacks	1,150	432	166.2%
Atlanta Braves	1,500	163	820.2%
Baltimore Orioles	1,175	191	515.2%
Boston Red Sox	2,700	249	984.3%
Chicago Cubs	2,675	259	932.8%
Chicago White Sox	1,350	220	513.6%
Cincinnati Reds	915	172	432.0%
Cleveland Indians	920	163	464.4%
Colorado Rockies	1,000	183	446.4%
Detroit Tigers	1,200	210	471.4%
Houston Astros	1,450	201	621.4%
Kansas City Royals	950	229	314.8%
Los Angeles Angels of Anaheim	1,750	278	529.5%
Los Angeles Dodgers	2,750	335	720.9%
Miami Marlins	940	135	596.3%
Milwaukee Brewers	925	163	467.5%
Minnesota Twins	1,025	182	463.2%
New York Mets	2,000	335	497.0%
New York Yankees	3,700	384	863.5%
Oakland Athletics	880	163	439.9%
Philadelphia Phillies	1,650	268	515.7%
Pittsburgh Pirates	289	163	77.3%
San Diego Padres	1,125	163	590.2%
San Francisco Giants	2,650	163	1,525.8%
Seattle Mariners	1,400	172	714.0%
St. Louis Cardinals	1,800	268	571.6%
Tampa Bay Rays	825	334	147.0%
Texas Rangers	1,550	191	711.5%
Toronto Blue Jays	1,300	278	367.6%
Washington Nationals	1,600	397	303.0%

Source: Forbes.

owners of) their own networks (New York Yankees, New York Mets, and Boston Red Sox).

Phase III: Vertical Integration of Teams and the Media

Demonstrated in the preceding tables, the dramatic increase in revenue earned by teams from media contracts in Phase II elevated both player salaries and team values. However, another change in the relationship between teams and the media would define Phase III: the vertical integration of teams and media networks. This shift is exemplified by a business decision by the New York Yankees and the New Jersey Nets.

In 1999, the Yankees and Nets agreed to what initially appeared to be an inconsequential merger of both teams' business operations. The goal of the merger was to improve the business offices of both clubs and, through the realization of some efficiencies and the removal of duplicate operations, increase profitability. There also was interest in unifying marketing efforts to leverage increased revenues from the local broadcast of both team's games. With business operations merged and a cooperative marketing agreement, both teams focused on enhancing revenues from the sale of their broadcast rights to New York City's largest cable television operator, Cablevision. Initially the teams simply wanted higher revenues, but in the course of discovering the real value of their broadcast rights, they began to consider the feasibility of establishing their own independent network. Cablevision enjoyed control of the distribution of local broadcast rights to all seven of the region's MLB, NBA, and NHL teams. Unified, the Yankees and Nets believed they would be able to entertain a variety of offers and opportunities when it came time to renew their contracts.

After considering all of their options, the two teams decided to form their own network with financing provided through an investment by Goldman Sachs. When the New Jersey Nets were sold to Bruce Ratner (Forest City Enterprises), the stake in Yankees–Nets was not included. The Steinbrenner family has wrapped their share of The Yankee Entertainment and Sports (YES) Network into Yankee Global Enterprises LLC, which operates the New York Yankees and the family's interest in the television network. The value of the network was placed at more than $3 billion in 2007 when Goldman Sachs expressed interest in selling their share (Davies, 2007). In 2017, *Forbes* estimated that the Yankees were worth $3.7 billion. In 2014, 21st Century Fox increased its ownership share of the YES network from 49 to 80 percent (YES Network, 2014). Then, in late 2017, the Disney Corporation proposed a $52.4 billion deal to purchase the majority of 21st Century Fox's assets – including the YES network (Barnes, 2017).

The notion that teams could form their own network begins a bit earlier than 1999. Some might argue that Ted Turner's linking of the Braves to his television empire was the first example of a team forming or being used to establish a network. The Braves were an important part of TBS and its success, but Turner acquired the local broadcast rights to the team's games in 1972, four years before acquiring complete ownership of the team. It seems more appropriate to conclude that Ted Turner acquired the team to bolster the network, rather than having a franchise and then forming a network with the team as its core product. What is clear, however, is that the owners of the Boston Red Sox and Boston Bruins established the New England Sports Network (NESN) in 1984, beginning in earnest the era of teams and then leagues creating their own television networks and media distribution systems. These networks would then negotiate with cable television operators and satellite providers to deliver their content as do ABC, NBC, Lifetime, CNN, or ESPN. The teams could use the popularity of their games as a way to entice the highest possible fees for the right to deliver the content to fans. The Red Sox own 80 percent of the NESN network and the Bruins retain the balance. In 2009, when the *New York Times* was interested in selling its stake in NESN (The Times Corporation is a minority owner of the Boston Red Sox and, therefore, owns a portion of NESN), the network was valued at $443 million (Farrell, 2009). The Red Sox's stake in NESN is actually owned by New England Sports Ventures, which owns the baseball team, the 80 percent share of NESN, FC Liverpool, Fenway Park, and the Fenway Sports Group, which is a marketing, management, and real estate company that also has ownership interests in an auto racing business. These collective interests make the Red Sox part of a business empire that, while less valuable than the one that includes the New York Yankees and the YES Network, is far more diversified.

Several teams have added media corporations to their holdings and have vertically integrated television and radio into their operations. The Yankees, Mets, Red Sox, Bruins, Rangers, and Knicks are no longer just teams. They are media corporations with teams, or teams intertwined with a media network such that where one ends and the other begins is indistinguishable. In addition, the fact that some baseball teams have created their own networks has helped others receive very lucrative contracts from Fox Sports. For example, the Los Angeles Dodgers' contract with Fox Sports involved payments of $35 million in 2011, $37 million in 2012, and $39 million in 2013. Then, in 2016, the Dodgers entered into a 25-year, $8.35 billion contract with Time Warner (Hiltzik, 2016).

As will be discussed in the section that follows, the first part of the twenty-first century also saw the advent of college conference networks. The prospect of additional revenues from media sales prompted realignments, with universities joining other conferences to ensure that conference championship games could be played and that additional media markets would be added to a network's inventory.

Phase III saw the merging of teams, leagues, and media networks, as well as substantial growth in profits, but the relationship between sport and media remains complex. For example, a debate over the use of media funds sat at the heart of the NFL's 2011 labor conflict. The scale and importance of the revenues earned by the league from its broadcast partners has made these contracts critical to the players, as they are the centerpiece of the revenue dedicated to player salaries. With their salaries inexorably linked to the size of the contracts negotiated by the league with its media partners, the players' union agreed with NFL owners in the White Stipulation and Settlement Agreement (SSA) that owners alone would be depended upon to negotiate the best possible contracts with their media partners to assure the richest possible pool of revenues for players' salaries (White, 1993). The intent of the agreement was to ensure that the NFL would act in accordance with the best interests of both the players and owners in terms of maximizing revenues from the broadcast partners. In exchange, the players agreed that the negotiations with the media partners would be left to the Commissioner's office and the owners. The players' perspective is that this agreement restrains the NFL and team owners from having individual interests in media corporations and then accepting lower broadcast fees to elevate the profits of their own media corporations. In addition, the agreement serves to ensure that the owners would never have any interest other than in maximizing the revenues received from the broadcast partners.

This agreement became a controversial centerpiece in the 2011 labor dispute when it was disclosed that the NFL would continue to receive payments from the broadcast partners even if games were not played in 2011 as a result of a "lockout" or a strike by the players. The NFLPA argued that by accepting this benefit, the value of the contracts was likely lower than what they would have been if prepayments tied to a lockout were not included. As noted in ESPN,

> In TV deals made while the SSA was in effect, the players contend, the owners failed to obtain the maximum revenues the agreement requires. Instead of using remarkable increases in television ratings to extract greater fees from the networks, the players assert, the owners accepted less money in return for payments during a lockout.
>
> (Munson, 2010)

The union's blunt assertion was that money had been left on the table that would lead to lower salaries for the players. The players filed a grievance against the NFL and the owners, arguing that accepting guaranteed payments even if games were not played was a violation of the SSA and constituted an unfair labor practice with regard to the maintenance of a fair environment in which negotiations would occur. If the owners receive media revenues even if games are not played, they clearly enjoy an economic benefit not available to the players. In April 2011, a court found the owners had indeed violated the SSA and the players were entitled to damages and additional compensation (White, 1993).

Another change unique to Phase III involves the way teams, players, owners, and leagues are portrayed in the media. Phase I and II saw generally positive stories on sport in an effort to engender consumer interest. However, the wide-ranging number of news outlets, pundits, and bloggers created by the internet has made the suppression of negative stories difficult in recent years. Difficult, but not impossible. Even though there was widespread evidence in the early 1990s that helmets either did not protect NFL players or were being used to inflict injuries, the issue was largely ignored by the media. There was little criticism of the NFL, the NCAA, or high school athletic associations for lax attitudes toward the diagnosis and treatment of head injuries and concussions. Complaints of concussions in the NHL were also sparsely discussed. Such injuries were often comically referred to as a player having "his or her bell rung." This underplayed the severity of the situation and many players were encouraged to return to play too soon after a "bell ringing," resulting in permanent and disabling conditions that emerged in later years. The issue of head trauma and its treatment did not become a centerpiece issue for the media or the major leagues until 2010 (Brain Injury Resource Center, 1997). While several players had suffered from head trauma, in January 2010, Sidney Crosby suffered a concussion that not only required him to miss the rest of the season – and significant playing time in the next two seasons – but at press conference in the fall of 2010 he detailed the effects of the concussion including his inability to drive or watch television (Baker, 2011). In the aftermath of his injury and several to NFL players, both leagues have developed new protocols to evaluate players and to restrict playing time if a concussion is diagnosed.

The relationship between sport and the media has continued to change the financial structure of team sport since its inception in 1913. Slightly more than 100 years after Western Union purchased broadcasting rights for baseball games – marking the first-ever purchase of sports broadcast rights – media rights now sustain teams and players at levels that were never dreamed of.

College Conference Networks

No discussion of Phase III of media and the sport business is complete without a review of the changes taking place in the NCAA. Unlike in the professional leagues, college sport never went through a period where the media was relied upon to expand the popularity or fan base for athletics. Decades before the NFL established its identity and dominance, college football was attracting large crowds to its games. Each of America's major universities had rivalry games that frequently attracted large crowds (e.g., Harvard–Yale, Army–Navy, Texas–Texas A&M, Texas–Oklahoma, Michigan–Ohio State, USC–UCLA) that required no additional exposure from the media to ensure fans would attend. Ohio State and Michigan each had attracted more than 70,000 fans to football games by the late 1920s and early 1930s, and the men's NCAA basketball tournament attracted sell-out crowds long before Brent Musburger employed the term "March Madness" in 1982 during the CBS telecast of tournament games (the term appears to have been used first to describe the state high school basketball tournament in Illinois in the 1930s). In fact, before the NCAA tournament was a staple on America's calendar, the National Invitational Tournament (NIT), with its final games hosted at Madison Square Garden in New York, was played before sellout crowds.

The initial issue for collegiate sport was not the role of the media in popularizing games, but rather the control the NCAA could exercise to regulate the number of times any one team could appear on television. Prior to 1984, the NCAA limited the number of appearances any team could make on national television and the number of games any university could televise of its football team. The NCAA would argue in court that too many televised games of any one team would lead to adverse effects on attendance. The NCAA had entered into contracts with CBS and ABC to televise football games, and it set the schedule with the networks. The University of Oklahoma challenged the NCAA's authority, claiming it violated the Sherman Anti-Trust Act. In 1984, the Supreme Court agreed with the University of Oklahoma that the NCAA's television plan violated the anti-trust law and that universities were free to televise as many or as few games as the market would demand and support, noting:

> The NCAA television plan on its face constitutes a restraint upon the operation of a free market, and the District Court's findings establish that the plan has operated to raise price and reduce output, both of which are unresponsive to consumer preference. Under the Rule of Reason, these hallmarks of anticompetitive behavior place upon the NCAA a heavy burden of establishing an affirmative defense that competitively justifies this apparent deviation from the operations of a free market. The NCAA's argument that its television plan can have no significant anticompetitive effect since it has no market power must be rejected. As a matter of law, the absence of proof of market power does not justify a naked restriction on price or output and, as a factual matter, it is evident from the record that the NCAA does possess market power … The record does not support the NCAA's proffered justification for its television plan that it constitutes a cooperative "joint venture," which assists in the marketing of broadcast rights and, hence, is pro-competitive. The District Court's contrary findings undermine such a justification.
>
> (NCAA, 1984: 468)

The ending of the NCAA's control on the telecast of collegiate events created a surge in the supply of televised games. The increase did not have a negative effect on attendance levels. Records maintained by the NCAA indicate that at least 38.1 million fans attended Division I-A or I-AA games in every year from 2003 through 2017 (Table 7.7). While recent years have seen a slight dip in college football attendance, it still remains high compared to historical standards.

Table 7.7 Annual Attendance at NCAA FBS and FCS
Football Games, 2003–2017

Year	Attendance
2003	41.2 million
2004	38.2 million
2005	38.1 million
2006	42.5 million
2007	43.0 million
2008	43.5 million
2009	43.0 million
2010	43.7 million
2011	43.8 million
2012	43.1 million
2013	44.4 million
2014	43.7 million
2015	43.5 million
2016	43.5 million
2017	42.1 million

Source: NCAA http://www.ncaa.org/championships/statistics/
ncaa-football-attendance (accessed March 6, 2018).

Just as the vertical integration of professional teams with television networks was a major change in the industry with regard to the revenues earned
by professional teams, a seemingly innocuous announcement by the Big Ten
Conference had a very similar effect on collegiate sports. In 2006, the Big Ten
Conference announced that while it would be extending its contract with
ABC/ESPN for football games, the conference would begin televising other
games not selected by ABC/ESPN on its own network (Big Ten Network,
2006). The network, created as part of a 20-year joint project with the Fox
Entertainment Group, would be called The Big Ten Network (BTN). The
Conference would own 51 percent of the network and provide all of its
programming, including games and matches not televised as part of any
national or league contract. This included, but was not limited to, football,
hockey, softball, volleyball, and lacrosse games as well as all other matches.
The Fox Entertainment Group would own 49 percent of the network and
provide the hardware and distributional mechanism required. Currently the
BTN is available in 60 million homes across North America (BTN, n.d.).
A document secured from the Ohio State University through a Freedom of
Information request by third parties disclosed that most of the universities
in the Big Ten Conference received $21.5 million from television rights and
the BTN in 2015 (Trahan, 2016). At a University of Michigan Regents open
meeting in 2017, it was disclosed that the Athletic Department received

$36.3 million in FY17 from the network and anticipates receiving a total of $51.1 million in media revenues in FY18 (Snyder, 2017).

The success of BTN attracted substantial interest from other conferences that either launched networks of their own or expanded their membership to enhance their media presence and create a football conference championship game. All of these activities expanded the number of televised games. Most notable was the PAC-10's expansion effort that initially seemed to focus on the University of Texas and other institutions in the Big 12 Conference. When Texas spurned both the Pac-10 and the Big Ten, the Pac-10 invited the University of Colorado and the University of Utah in 2011, creating the PAC 12. Utah's decision to leave the Mountain West Conference encouraged that league to invite Boise State University to be a member, and then the Big 12 reached out to both WVU and TCU in 2012. The Big Ten Network added the University of Nebraska in 2011, and Maryland and Rutgers joined in 2014.

The creation of collegiate networks set in motion a wide-ranging series of management and business changes that are still reverberating, creating issues and opportunities for athletic directors and university presidents. These potential opportunities make it more and more difficult for any aspiring or growing athletic program to avoid an alliance with one of these new networks. The Big Ten universities changed the game and profited from the creation of their own network, but the next few years may see even more innovations and media revenues generating an even larger portion of a university's total athletic budget.

Media, Sport, and the Future: Emerging Competition in the Delivery of Games

Escalating revenue figures might lead some to wonder if a media "bubble" exists. Real estate values plummeted in the aftermath of the collapse of the housing market and the Great Recession. Are escalating media deals yet another example of Shiller's irrational exuberance (Shiller, 2005)? If they are, is a massive market correction in values inevitable? It is certainly possible that prices will decline, but the escalating value of sport as a media product lies in (1) its ability to consistently attract large audiences, (2) the need of advertisers to place their product messages before large numbers of people, and (3) consumers' willingness to pay fees through their cable and satellite providers for the entertainment provided by sport.

As an advertising medium, sport has benefitted from the fragmentation and expansion of the number of video options available to consumers. Add to all of the cable and satellite options those available on the internet, and it seems more appropriate to describe the televising of entertainment as "narrowcasting" rather than broadcasting. The fragmentation and expanding number of entertainment choices has elevated the value of sport given its continuing popularity. Of all televised events, games continue to attract some of the largest viewership figures. That ability is what continues to pique the interest of advertisers. As long as the popularity of sport endures, televised or internet-streamed games will continue attract a multitude of viewers and encourage consumers to pay cable and satellite fees. Their consumption of sport will make games the most valuable medium from which to distribute advertising messages. It is imprudent to suggest that media rights for sports will never decline. In fact, ESPN has seen a decline in ratings in recent years leading to financial problems. Part of the problem stems from an increase in competition from other media outlets. Nonetheless, evidence shows that the popularity of sport has weathered economic cycles and, as a product consumed through the media, will continue to enjoy considerable popularity.

It should also be noted that the major media networks have taken notice of recent trends and updated their strategies. The actions and reactions of these media giants will shape the next phase of the relationship between sport and media. Changes could signal that the landscape in the decades ahead will be dramatically different from what traditional media networks know today.

One observation is that two of the original three major networks (ABC, NBC, and CBS) are now part of much larger media corporations. In 1996, the Disney Corporation acquired ABC, as well as 80 percent of ABC's stake in ESPN. Disney's acquisition of ESPN and ABC gives it control of 23 network ventures involving ESPN and two involving ABC that can be used to distribute games and programs. If Disney's acquisition of assets from 21st Century Fox is approved (2018), there will likely be some reorganization of the 20 owned networks and five affiliated networks that are included as part of the purchase. Comcast acquired NBC in 2013, giving the company its own movie studio as well as several other networks (CNBC, Bravo, Telemundo, and Oxygen). CBS remains an independent network. The strategy for distribution giants such as these is to essentially control as many of the platforms by which consumers access sport content as possible. Comcast is the nation's largest cable television company, serving almost 22.3 million households and 23.3 internet users (Brodkin, 2016). With 22.3 million video subscribers, Comcast has a huge base of customers that rely upon it for internet connections.

This next phase of sport and the media, then, will involve the competition for games between integrated cable providers and networks and the individual networks created by teams and leagues. That competition will lead to higher revenues for teams and leagues and, over time, elevated player salaries. The advent of internet-based platforms should also be carefully monitored. There will be an increasing availability of games and content on the internet, and that could change the reliance on more traditional forms of distribution. Verizon entered the broadcast business in 2017 when it paid more than $1.5 billion for the rights to stream NFL games on mobile platforms (Kafka, 2017). Twitter and Facebook have begun experimenting with streaming services as well. Given the improved images delivered by HD video devices, the quality of the fan experience from watching games in their homes seems poised to enjoy considerable increments. The growing financial returns to teams and the media outlets may well be based on sound supply and demand factors and not an irrational exuberance.

Notes

1 The advent of the internet has not substantially altered this relationship. Reporters who distribute their stories electronically are accorded the same or similar access as those reporters from the print media; the relationship is still considered financially reciprocal.
2 Certainly policies such as the salary cap affect competitive balance in the NFL. This leads to factors other than payroll that create team success. For example, management also matters given the high level of success across time of franchises such as the Pittsburgh Steelers and Indianapolis Colts. When their success is contrasted with the lack of success of some larger market teams (e.g., New York Jets), it is apparent that something other than equal revenues contributes to on-the-field success.

References

Baker, K. 2011. The timetable: Sidney Crosby's lost year, *Grantland*. Retrieved from http://grantland.com/features/sidney-crosby-lost-year/ (accessed August 1, 2018).

Barnes, B. 2017. Disney makes $52.4 billion deal for 21st Century Fox in big bet on streaming, *New York Times*, December 14. Retrieved from https://www.nytimes.com/2017/12/14/business/dealbook/disney-fox-deal.html

Big Ten Conference. 2006. The Big Ten Conference announces media agreements increasing national coverage of Big Ten sports, *B1G*, June 21. Retrieved from http://www.bigten.org/genrel/062106aad.html (accessed August 1, 2018).

Brain Injury Resource Center. 1997. Brain injury in sports, *Brain Injury Resource Center*. Retrieved from http://www.headinjury.com/sports.htm (accessed February 14, 2018).

Brodkin, J. 2016. Comcast shrugs off years of cord-cutting losses, adds 89K TV customers, *arstechnica*, February 3. Retrieved from https://arstechnica.com/information-technology/2016/02/comcast-shrugs-off-years-of-cord-cutting-losses-adds-89k-tv-customers/ (accessed August 1, 2018).

Brown, M. 2016. 2016 MLB Advanced Media revenues projected to reach $1.1–$1.2 billion, *Forbes*, March 3. Retrieved from https://www.forbes.com/sites/maurybrown/2016/03/03/mlb-advanced-media-projected-revenues-to-be-1-1-1-2-billion-in-2016/#4e84ca5454cc (accessed August 1, 2018).

BTN. n.d. About us, *Big Ten Network*. Retrieved from http://btn.com/about/ (accessed February 15, 2018).

Farrell, M. 2009. New York Times puts NESN on block, *Multichannel News*. Retrieved from http://www.multichannel.com/article/162920-New_York_Times_Puts_NESN_Stake_On_Block.php (accessed January 3, 2011).

Davies, M. (2007). Yankees' YES Network stakeholders test market value, *Reuters*, August 2. Retrieved from https://www.reuters.com/article/industry-yankees-yes-dc/yankees-yes-network-stakeholders-test-market-value-idUSN0243190420070802 (accessed August 1, 2018).

Haupert, M. J. 2007. The economic history of Major League Baseball, *Economic History Association*, December 3. Retrieved from https://eh.net/encyclopedia/the-economic-history-of-major-league-baseball/ (accessed February 14, 2018).

Hiltzik, M. 2016. Time Warner Cable and the Dodgers finally discover the limits of greed, *Los Angeles Times*, April 1. Retrieved from http://www.latimes.com/business/hiltzik/la-fi-hiltzik-dodgers-greed-20160401-snap-htmlstory.html (accessed August 1, 2018).

Kafka, P. 2017. Verizon will pay more than $1.5 billion to stream NFL games, *Recode*, December 11. Retrieved from https://www.recode.net/2017/12/11/16760394/verizon-nfl-games-stream-football-1-5-billion (accessed August 1, 2018).

Munson, L. 2010. NFL's lockout-likelihood plot thickens, *Courtside Seat*. Retrieved from http://sports.espn.go.com/espn/commentary/news/story?page=munson/100617 (accessed January 17, 2011).

NCAA v. Board of Regents of Univ. of Okla. 83-271 U.S. Supreme Court of the United States. 1984. Retrieved from http://caselaw.findlaw.com/us-supreme-court/468/85.html (accessed August 1, 2018).

Rosentraub, M. S. 1997. *Major league losers: The real cost of sports and who's paying for it*. New York: Basic Books.

Shiller, R. 2005. *Irrational exuberance*. New York: Random House.

Snyder, M (@Mark__Snyder). 2017. "That new Big Ten TV deal is working out. U-M projects a $51.1 million distribution for FY 2018 [image]" June 15, 12:52 PM. Retrieved from https://twitter.com/mark__snyder/status/875440948431421440 (accessed June 16, 2017).

Trahan, K. 2016. Big Ten schools will see media revenues skyrocket thanks to new TV deal, *Awful Announcing*, April 20. Retrieved from http://awfulannouncing.com/2016/big-ten-schools-will-see-media-revenues-skyrocket-thanks-new-tv-deal.html (accessed August 1, 2018).

White v. *National Football League*. 836 F. Supp. 1458 (D. Minn. 1993)

YES Network. 2014. 21st Century Fox acquires majority stake in YES, *YES*, January 24. Retrieved from http://web.yesnetwork.com/news/article.jsp?ymd=20140125&content_id=67106176&fext=.jsp&vkey=news_milb (accessed August 1, 2018).

Chapter 8

What Are Teams Worth?
Team Valuation

Introduction

Financial analysts spend a good portion of their time valuing companies. Using financial data and industry knowledge, analysts can estimate future profits and firm value. In the case of the sports industry, there can be many complicating factors, including a lack of data or complicated ownership structures. For example, the value of a college sports team is nearly impossible to estimate since it is tied to so many other aspects of the university. Further complicating matters is that sometimes the valuation of a sports team has a political component. Franchise values are often cited or called into question during negotiations with players' unions for collective bargaining agreements, or those with local governments for assistance in funding the construction or renovation of venues. Team owners often claim annual losses or weak returns to justify implementing salary caps or to leverage public investments in venues, while players' unions and public actors point to *Forbes*' and other valuation estimates as evidencing the contrary.

There are countless examples where valuation estimates have been used to leverage deals, so the importance of this skill for sport managers is virtually undeniable. This chapter focuses on the private valuation of sport franchises. While the financial techniques used in this chapter can be applied to find the value of bonds used to finance facilities, preferred stock, or common stock, most of this chapter applies time-tested techniques to the valuation of teams.

It can be difficult to estimate firm values and future profits in any industry. To start, valuing an entire firm is very different from valuing an individual financial asset for which all cash flows are known. Because firms entail much more risk and uncertainty than bonds, future profits are difficult to estimate. This increased level of risk should, reasonably, increase the required return for investors. Alternatively, if a firm faces more risk, its value will be seen as lower than another firm with the same expected profits and less risk. It should also be noted that future discount rates can be difficult to estimate because they are constantly changing. Finally, an investor's perspective of a company's value depends on how much of the company that investor owns. For example, investors will often purchase 51 percent of a company – a "controlling interest" – and that investor will have complete control of the firm's decisions. This could drastically increase the value to that majority owner.

One way to value a company is to derive a total value figure from the company's stock price. After all, stock prices – which represent an estimated net present value of all future dividends – are a tangible representation of how the market values a company's shares. For the most part, teams are no different. Therefore, team valuations should represent all of the franchise's discounted future profits.[1]

The following section discusses several factors for consideration with regard to team valuation. An overview of financial theory precedes the actual assessment of valuation techniques to provide an understanding of how to approach team valuation. Even if the available data make it difficult to use the equations introduced below, the different models illustrate the crucial factors that enter into a valuation estimate. Lastly, the values of the major professional leagues and some college teams are examined.

Team Valuation: Factors to Consider

The task of valuing teams is noticeably different from the work required to project most firms' worth and presents unique obstacles. These issues are outlined below.

First, it can be difficult to obtain accurate financial data for most teams; teams are under no legal obligation to share their financial records, so estimates are commonly used. Although some data are available, these are usually estimates, meaning the resulting valuations are approximations. Furthermore, when accurate data are available, the full value may still be unclear as money and profits can be shifted between related businesses (e.g., the Lakers and AEG Worldwide, the Detroit Tigers and Olympia Entertainment). If a media company owns a team, it could choose to pay too much (or too little) for broadcast rights fees so that the team's financial statements show either artificially inflated or deflated revenues. Typically, team owners have an incentive to show a financial loss or low levels of operating profits to prepare for negotiations with the players' unions. Claiming a loss is one way owners can portray players as greedy or that greater support is needed from local governments. Disclosures of the financial records of the Florida Marlins and Los Angeles Dodgers illustrated that some owners entered their own salaries and salaries of family members as expenses, thereby lowering profits (and illustrating operating losses). It is often very difficult to estimate profits as teams can obscure costs and shift revenues to other entities.

Second, some have argued that owners might view owning a team as consumption: something acquired to gain prestige. That means that the owner did not buy the team solely to maximize profits or for financial returns on the investment. Rather, the buyer is seeking to maximize intangible but valuable gains. If an individual buys a team because he/she thinks it is useful for a community, creates prestige, or is simply fun, then it can be hard to put a price tag on the team using financial tools. If that is true, this welfare benefit could account for a substantial portion of the team's value and could be far greater than the future value of anticipated profits. Even if that is the case, the financial value should still be affected by the discounted value of future profits.

Third, because teams are becoming part of larger conglomerates, it is not always easy to know how the team contributes to the profits of an owner's related businesses. For example, some team owners own multiple teams as well as media, food, or other entertainment companies. If this is the case, there can be efficiencies to owning multiple teams. If a media company owns the team, it may be easier to get the team's games on television, which could help both the media company and the team. A food or beverage company might sell their products in the facility, or if an entertainment company owns a team, they might utilize the facility for other entertainment events. Because of this, it can be difficult to determine the team's contribution to the related corporations' bottom lines. This also means that the team can have a different value depending on who buys the team.

Along the same lines, the value accruing to a team's majority owner could increase if he/she is involved in other businesses related to the team. That could mean a franchise's value might be greater for someone who also owns other businesses that capitalize on the team's operations – including other teams – but less valuable to minority owners. In addition, because many teams have become anchors for entertainment complexes, much of the value of these teams can come from ensuring the success or value of other capital assets. For example, the Yankees increase the value of the YES network and numerous teams increase profits for businesses around their facilities. The Lakers and Kings create value for L.A. LIVE, for example. These values may or may not show up on the team's income statements, but these are very real values that can be leveraged by owners. Given teams' extraordinary public image, platform, and footprint, and the increasingly complex ownership structures, a team's value can be derived from multiple uses.

Fourth, given league structure, policies can dramatically affect team values. Salary caps, luxury taxes, revenue sharing, and player drafts all have a large impact on team value. Each of these policies is intended to help small-market teams, though some might increase franchise values of all teams. Revenue sharing in the NFL is but one example.

Individual team revenues in the NFL are somewhat homogeneous. With salary caps and a high amount of revenue sharing, there is less variance in the relative values of NFL franchises. Therefore, it is harder to find team-specific determinants. Alexander and Kern (2004) found that team performance is still important for NFL franchise values. Variables such as regional population and acquiring a new stadium do not significantly increase values in the NFL to the extent that they do in other professional leagues. Revenues are comparatively more heterogeneous in other leagues. In the NBA, NHL, and MLB, there is a large difference between the most valuable team and least valuable team in the league. In addition, the NFL prohibits its owners from owning other teams in NFL cities. Other leagues do permit cross-ownership, so owners can use the same infrastructure to operate multiple teams, which decreases cost and increases franchise value (Fort, 2006).

And, fifth, there are countless other benefits to team owners that do not show up on financial statements. Tax shelters from owning a team are one such benefit. For example, the roster depreciation allowance is clearly worth quite a bit to owners, but the financial statements show this as a depreciation of the players. In other words, while they might show losses on their tax forms, they might actually be making quite a bit of profit.

It should also be remembered that the relationship between value and profits implies one of three things. First, the team's profits may not include all of the benefits of owning a team (consumption value, effect on other related businesses, etc.). Second, owners and potential buyers may expect profits to dramatically increase in the future. That may not be a bad assumption and, in some cases, that has happened with teams. The third explanation is that owners are simply paying too much for franchises. While this explanation may seem appealing to some, owners tend to be successful business operators. They did not become wealthy enough to purchase a team by making bad investments, so the notion that they would willingly overpay for a franchise doesn't sit well. Keep each of these elements in mind as you read through the sections that follow.

Valuation Models

If the profits generated by a team were known and it also was clear how the team affected other businesses owned by the same individual, partners, or conglomerate, then with the application of an appropriate discount rate, an accurate value could be established. The one exception to this is if an owner is buying the team to secure intangible benefits (e.g., prestige, fun, or to advance a community without any pecuniary gain for the team owner). Assuming the team is bought as a financial investment, the value of the team is equal to the present value of all future profits the team expects to gain over an infinite horizon. This equation is given by:

$$Value = \frac{\pi_1}{(1+r)^1} + \frac{\pi_2}{(1+r)^2} + \ldots + \frac{\pi_\infty}{(1+r)^\infty} = \sum_{t=1}^{\infty} \frac{\pi_t}{(1+r)^t}$$

where π is the team's profit's in year t and r is the required return. The required return represents the owner's discount rate and can vary depending on the type of asset. Of course, the problem with this model is that an analyst does not know exactly what future profits will be. Therefore, typically financial models are used that assume certain things about future profits. Another possibility is that firms are valued by using some kind of industry standard. What follows are a few of the more common valuation techniques.

Multiple Earnings

One basic valuation model that is occasionally discussed in the sport industry is the multiple earnings approach. This approach is rarely, if at all, mentioned in general finance texts because it is not very useful. The only reason to use this is when there is very little data available, which is often the case for teams. Even in sport, however, while there is little information disclosed to observers, potential buyers may have far more information. Therefore, this method is typically used to simply generate a gross estimate of the team's value. Using the multiple earnings approach, the value of a team is considered to be some multiple (an industry rule of thumb) of revenue. The formula for the multiple earnings approach is

$$Value = Multiple \cdot Revenue$$

where *Multiple* simply represents some number.

The limitations of this approach are clear. Most obviously, costs are not taken into account. Also, the growth of future revenues or profits is not considered. In order for this method to be remotely accurate, the analyst must be comparing two very similar teams. For example, suppose the revenue for the New York Islanders was $100 million last year and they were sold for $600 million. In this case, the multiple is 6. Now suppose the New York Rangers had revenues of $150 million last year. The best guess might be that the Rangers were worth $900 million (150 × 6). This would assume, however, that costs were proportional for both teams and their future growth rates are expected to be identical. It is clear as well that the *Multiple* changes for leagues over time. So, while this approach might yield an approximate value with additional financial data, a more accurate franchise value could be projected.

Zero Growth Model

The zero growth model is only slightly more sophisticated than the multiple earnings approach. For some assets, however, it is more appropriate. As the name implies, this model assumes that any cash flow (in our case, profits) does not change. As with the multiple earnings approach, there are clear drawbacks with using this model to value a firm. There are some assets that produce a constant annual return, such as annuities. Annuities can include bond payments or some stock dividends. These assets have a fixed payment. The problem is that a team's profits are usually not constant. On the other hand, one's best guess might be that, on average, a team's profits might not change much from year to year in the foreseeable future. Or, even if one expects profits to change, it is completely unclear if profits will increase or decrease. If this is the case, the following equation can be used:

$$Value = \frac{\pi}{(1+r)^1} + \frac{\pi}{(1+r)^2} + ... + \frac{\pi}{(1+r)^\infty} = \sum_{t=1}^{\infty} \frac{\pi}{(1+r)^t} = \frac{\pi}{r}$$

The big advantage of using a zero growth model is that mathematically, it is very simple to use. The value equals the yearly profits divided by the discount rate (or required return). If the discount rate is 10 percent (.1), then the value of a firm will be 10 times their yearly profits. If the discount rate is 5 percent, the value will be 20 times yearly profits.

Establishing Discount Rates and Value

Risk-free discount rates are typically (but not always) around 5 to 10 percent. This means that 1 divided by the discount rate is roughly 10 to 20. If we know the value and profits for a firm or team, then that tells a financial manager something about what people expect future profits to be. If the value divided by profits is less than 10, then people expect profits to decrease (either that or it is undervalued). If value divided by profits is more than 20, profits are expected to grow.

For example, there have been spikes and declines in oil prices in previous years. When the price of oil rises sharply, profits for many oil companies increase. When this has happened, however, the price to earnings ratio (analogous to value divided by profits) was approximately 3 or 4 for some of the oil companies. This implied that the market did not expect high profits to last and there would be a negative growth rate of profits in the future. So, even though the price of these stocks increased, they did not increase proportionately to the increase in profits.

Historically, the average price to earnings ratio for the S&P 500 since 1871 has been approximately 15.7 (9Multpl.com, 2018). But, in 1917, the average price to earnings ratio hit a low of 5.31 and in 2009 reached 123.73. This means that either investors expected very high growth rates in 2009 or stocks were overpriced. At this time, profits had dropped sharply, and investors ostensibly expected profits to at least partially rebound. This issue was at the forefront of some people's concerns as the stock market soared to levels never seen before in late 2017 and early 2018. The Dow Jones Industrial Average set its highest closing record at 26,616.71 on January 26, 2018 (Amadeo, 2018). Those who fear this valuation is an expression of an "irrational exuberance" are predicting a severe market correction (or collapse of values). This same pessimism can be applied to the purchase price of different franchises or the expansion fees being charged for NHL and MLS franchises, which are now at historically high levels.

Constant Growth Model

A useful approach to valuing stocks or firms is the constant growth model, otherwise known as the Gordon model. The reason this is so useful is that a financial analyst can use it to try and predict the future growth of profits. This methodology might not be as useful for very young firms, but it works quite well for more established businesses. The zero growth model is actually a special case of the constant growth model; it assumes that the profit growth is zero. Growth estimates of profits are almost always wrong, but, more often than not, they should be more accurate than assuming a growth rate of zero. If profits grow at a constant rate, the value of a firm can be given by:

$$Value = \frac{\pi(1+g)}{(1+r)^1} + \frac{\pi(1+g)^2}{(1+r)^2} + \ldots + \frac{\pi(1+g)^\infty}{(1+r)^\infty} = \sum_{t=1}^{\infty} \frac{\pi}{(1+r)^t} = \frac{\pi}{r-g}$$

where g is the expected growth rate of profits.[2] Using a constant growth rate, the value is the profits divided by the difference of the required return and the growth rate. If a team can grow their profits close to the required rate of return, their franchise value would be very high.

One drawback of this model is that it does assume one growth rate. This model is not as useful if the growth rate varies a lot from year to year, and it can be difficult to predict average future growth rates. Another drawback is that it is not very useful if a team is currently experiencing a financial loss. It is not uncommon for teams to experience a loss in the short term but expect profits in the future.

Capital Asset Pricing Model (CAPM)

The most sophisticated model examined in this chapter is the CAPM. This model is often used for stocks, which represent a firm's value. The model can also be used to find a team's value. Furthermore, even if the exact equations of the CAPM are not used, there is value in understanding how risk affects value. The benefit of this model is that it illustrates the relationship between risk and value. Essentially, if risk is higher, then the required return (discount rate) also should be higher. In other words, investors or potential buyers do not like assets that have highly variable returns. If a team's profits are very different year to year, then that team's value will be smaller than a team with constant profits (assuming their average profits are the same).

The drawback is that estimating risk can be more difficult than estimating future profits. If the level of risk for an asset or firm is known, the CAPM works well. If the level of risk is hard to determine, then other models might work better. Risk is usually measured by past performance. If a financial analyst knows past profits, then they should also know the variation of those profits. Research has shown that a company's past returns often have little correlation with their historical risk level (Fama & French, 1992). But again, at the very least, this model helps us understand the relationship between risk and value.

The CAPM model is somewhat similar to the constant growth model, but the difference is in the required return. In the CAPM, the required return is given by:

$$r_{required} = r_{risk\,free} + \beta(r_{market} - r_{risk\,free})$$

where $r_{required}$ is the required return, $r_{risk\,free}$ is the risk-free rate, β is the beta value, and r_{market} is the market rate. The risk-free rate is the return that investors can get with no risk to themselves. Investments with the least amount of risk are usually bonds or treasury bills. Therefore, the risk-free rate is equal to the returns on these types of investments. The market rate is the return on the market portfolio of all traded securities. This represents the average return on all investments in a market. Sometimes this can be represented by some stock market index.

The beta value represents risk. Specifically, the beta value indicates how risky an investment is compared to the market average. For example, if an investment's beta value is 2, then that asset is twice as variable (risky) as the market average. The return of an investment that is twice as responsive as the market should change 2 percent for every 1 percent change in the market's return. If the market increases by 3 percent, then an investment with a beta of 2 should increase by 6 percent. By definition, the average beta value is 1. If an investment has a beta value of less than one, then it is not as risky as an average investment. A risk-free investment has a beta value of 0. Some investments have negative beta values. That is, they are countercyclical. When the market increases, some investments decrease. Countercyclical investments are good to have if the economy is in decline. The CAPM shows that if returns or profits are risky, then the required return is higher. In other words, investors need to expect a higher return if they are taking on more risk. This model helps us understand the tradeoff between risk and reward.

Now that we know what determines the required return, we can use that to find a team's value. We simply use the required return and put it into the constant growth model so the value is determined by:

$$Value = \frac{\pi}{r_{risk\,free} + \beta(r_{market} - r_{risk\,free}) - g} = \frac{\pi}{r_{required} - g}$$

As stated before, if the risk increases, the required return increases. Because the required return is in the denominator, if the required return goes up, the value of the firm decreases. More risk means lower value. This implies that teams should try to decrease their risk as much as possible in order to increase the value of their franchise.

Free Cash Flow Model

Another valuation technique is the free cash flow model. Free cash flow is defined as the available cash flow that investors can access. "Investors" include all providers of debt and equity. More formally, free cash flow is the difference between cash flows from operations and capital expenditures. This method might be preferred over the others if a team is not as established. Older teams have a history of profits, which can be used to estimate valuations (although outside analysts have a hard time getting reliable profit values). The free cash flow is similar to other models that use profit or dividends in that it estimates the present value of money, but it uses free cash flows instead of profits. Mathematically, the free cash flow models are similar to models that use profits.

What Are Professional Teams Worth?

The price of franchises has certainly increased across the past few decades. This is true for all NFL, MLB, NBA, and NHL teams; the cost of expansion franchises has also increased. Furthermore, when the changes in valuation are analyzed, it should be noted that most analysts must disregard any profits taken out of the company. Just because team value increases or decreases does not imply that the team was a good or bad investment. In other words, if owners are receiving a profit every year, then an increase in franchise value is only part of the return on their investment. Still, it is certainly worthwhile to look at how values have changed.

Most teams have enjoyed large increases in revenue streams, especially media contracts that have created elevated franchise values and sale prices. A smaller percentage of facility-based revenue is coming from the typical ticket sales and more revenue is coming from luxury seating, advertising, sponsorships, food and beverage sales, and retail activity. And as noted earlier, owners are making additional money from the hosting of entertainment events. As the theoretical models show, revenues and profits are key in determining franchise values. Therefore, everything that affects revenues affects values.

As noted earlier, financial data for teams can be difficult to obtain. While much of the revenue that comes from national television contracts is known, there are other revenue streams that are not publicly disclosed. Without that data, only estimated values can be included in the financial models. Nonetheless, people are buying teams and their value must be determined. This chapter will compare four different ways of estimating a franchise's value. These methods are using actual sale data, *Financial World* and *Forbes* valuations, a multiple earnings approach, and present value models. As always, there are strengths and weaknesses with each of these methods.

Sale Prices

The obvious advantage of examining actual sale prices is that a sale price is literally the amount an individual is willing to pay to own a team. These values typically include any ancillary benefits as well as any consumption values realized by the new owner. Ultimately, any company is worth what investors are willing to pay. The drawback of using actual sale data is that teams are not sold frequently (small sample size), and the sale price of one team may not be transferable to other teams. Furthermore, the exact structure of the sale might not be known. Even if it is disclosed, it is difficult to separate the team from other entities, such as the facility and terms for its use, or land or other assets related to the team. To make matters even more complicated, even when elements of deals are disclosed, sometimes the dollar figures reported in the media are disputed.

The NFL has been relatively successful for more than 70 years. Supported by rapidly growing media contracts and the widespread construction of iconic new stadia, profits have increased dramatically over the past two decades. The league is known to be the most valuable in the world. As would be expected, NFL franchise sale prices indicate the league has been a robust financial success. Quirk and Fort (1992) give a useful history of sport franchise values from the 1920s through 1990 and show that franchise values have had extremely high growth rates since the league's birth. The average annual return from 1920 to 1990 was about 20 percent. In 1926, the Duluth Kellys (later the Washington Redskins) were bought for one dollar and the team's debts. While the team's debt may have been significant, buying the Redskins for a dollar was not a bad investment, since *Forbes* estimates the 2017 value of the franchise to be $3.1 billion. Given the extraordinary rate of return since 1926, financial theory is not needed to illustrate that values have dramatically increased, even compared with other investments. While one can find investments with higher growth rates – the stock value of UBER, Amazon, Google, and Microsoft have been extraordinary – a growth from $1 to $3.1 billion (even controlling for changes in the value of dollars across the past 100 years) indicates the Redskins franchise was a smart investment. Buying an NFL team in the 1920s was a good investment by any standard.

Table 8.1 shows there were 29 NFL franchise sales from 1991 to 2016. As the limited details of these transactions illustrate, NFL teams can be part of relatively complicated ownership structures. For example, regarding the 2009 partial sale of the Pittsburgh Steelers, the percentage sold is not even known. The values are therefore difficult to ascertain. Nevertheless, the fifth column in Table 8.1 creates an estimated value of the team by taking the sale price divided by the percentage of the team that was sold. Table 8.1 also compares the sale prices with *Financial World/Forbes*' estimated values; those numbers will be discussed later.

The growth rate in the value of MLB franchises was not quite as impressive as those for NFL franchises during the twentieth century, in part because the league was established earlier. Although MLB values did grow quite rapidly during the 1960s, 1970s, and 1980s, the average annual growth rate of from 1901 to 1990 was 7.5 percent (Quirk & Fort, 1992). While this seems paltry compared to the NFL, 7.5 percent is still a respectable growth rate, and it is for a longer time period. Across this time period, there are many instances of team values rapidly changing in both positive and negative directions. For example, it has been reported that George Steinbrenner bought the New York Yankees for $8.8 million ($49 million in 2017 dollars) in 1973. Given that in 2017, *Forbes* estimated the Yankees to be worth $3.7 billion, the growth rate (9.2 percent yearly growth rate after adjusting for inflation) has been extraordinary.

Table 8.2 shows MLB franchise sales across the past 27 years. Since 1990, there have been 48 sales (or partial sales). MLB teams, on average, are not quite as valuable as NFL teams. In addition, the values of MLB franchises seem to vary more than those of NFL teams. For example, in 2002, the Boston Red Sox were sold for almost six times as much as the Montreal Expos (now the Washington Nationals) were worth. The Los Angeles Dodgers were sold at a price nearly three times as much as the San Diego Padres in 2012.

The NBA historically has had growth rates more similar to the NFL, but it is not nearly as old. On average, franchise values grew at a rate of 16.5 percent from 1950 to 1990 (Quirk & Fort, 1992). Again, this is quite a remarkable rate of growth. At that rate, every dollar invested in a team in 1950 would be worth $450 dollars in 1990. Table 8.3 shows that NBA team prices are somewhat similar to those paid for MLB teams, but on average, they tend to be a bit higher.

Table 8.1 Sale Prices of NFL Teams, 1991–2016

Year	Team	Price ($millions)	Percentage Sold	Implied Value	Financial World/Forbes Estimate (Year if Different)	Percentage Difference
1991	New York Giants	75	50	150	150	0.0
1991	Minnesota Vikings	52	51	102	119	16.8
1993	Carolina Panthers	140	100, expansion fee	140	161 (1995)	15.0
1993	Jacksonville Jaguars	140	100, expansion fee	140	145 (1996)	3.6
1994	Miami Dolphins	109	85, some debt	128	161	25.5
1994	Philadelphia Eagles	185	100, some debt	185	172	−7.0
1994	New England Patriots	158	100	158	142	−10.1
1995	Tampa Bay Buccaneers	192	100	192	151	−21.4
1995	St. Louis Rams	60	30	200	186	−7.0
1997	Baltimore Ravens	32	9	356	235	−33.9
1997	Seattle Seahawks	200	100	200	171	−14.5
1998	Minnesota Vikings	206	96, some debt	215	232	7.9
1998	Cleveland Browns	476	100, expansion fee	476	557 (2000)	17.0
1998	St. Louis Rams	20	10	200	322	61.0
1999	Baltimore Ravens	275	49	561	408	−27.3
1999	Washington Redskins	800	100	800	607	−24.1
1999	Houston Texans	700	100, expansion fee	700	791 (2003)	13.0
2000	New York Jets	635	100	635	384	−39.5
2001	Atlanta Falcons	545	100	545	338	−38.0
2002	Atlanta Falcons	27	5	540	407	−24.6
2003	Washington Redskins	200	20	1,000	952	−4.8
2004	Baltimore Ravens	325	51	637	776	21.8
2005	Minnesota Vikings	600	100	600	658	9.7

(continued)

Table 8.1 Continued

Year	Team	Price ($millions)	Percentage Sold[1]	Implied Value	Financial World/Forbes Estimate (Year if Different)	Percentage Difference
2008	Miami Dolphins	550	45	1,222	1044	−14.6
2009	Pittsburgh Steelers	250	Unknown	Unknown	1020	–
2010	St. Louis Rams	450	60	750	779	3.9
2011	Jacksonville Jaguars	770	100	770	725	−5.8
2012	Cleveland Browns	1,050	100	1,050	1005	−4.3
2014	Buffalo Bills	1,400	100	1,000	935	−6.5

Average −3.1
Correlation between sale price and estimate = .954

[1] Although this lists the percentage of the team bought, there are typically many more details that should be considered. For example, there are often team debts that are assumed. Often there are also land or stadium issues involved with the sale. Many times, owners are purchasing a larger percentage of a team of which they were already part owner. Sometimes there are also other estimates of the amount paid.

Table 8.2 Actual Sale Prices of MLB Teams, 1990–2017

Year	Team	Price ($millions)	Percentage Sold¹	Implied Value	Financial World/Forbes Estimate (Year if Different)	Percentage Difference
1990	Montreal Expos	86	100	86	100	16.3
1990	San Diego Padres	75	100	75	85	13.3
1991	Florida Marlins	95	100, expansion fee	95	81 (1994)	−14.7
1991	Toronto Blue Jays	60.3	45	134	178	33.1
1992	Colorado Rockies	95	100, expansion fee	95	110 (1994)	15.8
1992	Houston Astros	115	100	115	95	−17.4
1992	Seattle Mariners	106	60	177	79	−55.4
1992	San Francisco Giants	100	100	100	99	−1.0
1993	Baltimore Orioles	173	100	173	130	−24.9
1993	Detroit Tigers	80	100	80	97	21.3
1994	San Diego Padres	94	100	94	85	−9.6
1995	Oakland A's	85	100	85	101	18.8
1996	Pittsburgh Pirates	90	100	90	62	−31.1
1996	St. Louis Cardinals	150	100	150	112	−25.3
1998	Arizona Diamondbacks	130	100, expansion Fee	130	291 (1999)	123.8
1998	Los Angeles Dodgers	311	100	311	237	−23.8
1998	Tampa Bay Rays	130	100, expansion fee	130	225 (1999)	73.1
1998	Texas Rangers	250	100	250	253	1.3
1999	Anaheim Angels	140	75	187	195	4.3
1999	Cincinnati Reds	183	Unknown	Unknown	163	–
1999	Florida Marlins	158.5	100	159	153	−3.8
1999	Montreal Expos	50	35	143	84	−41.3
1999	New York Yankees	225	38	600	491	−18.2
2000	Cleveland Indians	323	100	323	364	12.7
2000	Kansas City Royals	96	100	96	122	27.1
2000	Toronto Blue Jays	112	80	140	162	15.7
2001	Colorado Rockies	35	24	148	334	125.7

(continued)

Table 8.2 Continued

Year	Team	Price ($millions)	Percentage Sold[1]	Implied Value	Financial World/Forbes Estimate (Year if Different)	Percentage Difference
2002	Boston Red Sox	700	100	700	428	-38.8
2002	Florida Marlins	158.5	100	159	137	-13.6
2002	Montreal Expos	120	100	120	108	-10.3
2002	New York Mets	150	50	300	483	61.2
2003	Anaheim Angels	184	100	184	225	22.3
2004	Los Angeles Dodgers	371	100	371	399	7.5
2004	Arizona Diamondbacks	Unknown	100	Unknown	276	–
2004	Cincinnati Reds	6.1	7	91	245	169.2
2004	Colorado Rockies	20	14	143	285	99.3
2005	Milwaukee Brewers	220	100, some debt	220	208	-5.5
2005	Oakland A's	180	Unknown	Unknown	185	–
2006	Cincinnati Reds	270	100	270	274	1.5
2006	Washington Nationals	450	100	450	440	-2.2
2007	Atlanta Braves	450	100	450	458	1.8
2009	Chicago Cubs	845	95	845	700	-17.2
2010	Texas Rangers	593	100	593	451	-23.9
2011	Houston Astros	610	100	610	474	-22.3
2012	Los Angeles Dodgers	2150	100	2150	1400	-34.9
2012	San Diego Padres	800	100	800	458	-42.8
2016	Seattle Mariners	1400	100	1400	1200	-14.3
2017	Florida Marlins	1200	100	1200	940	-21.7

Average 28.0
Correlation between sale price and estimate = 0.959

[1] Although this lists the percentage of the team bought, there are typically many more details that should be considered. For example, there are often team debts that are assumed. Often there are also land or facility issues involved with the sale. Many times, minority or majority owners are purchasing a larger percentage of a team. Sometimes there are also other estimates of the amount paid.

Table 8.3 Sale Prices of NBA Teams, 1991–2017

Year	Team	Price ($millions)	Percentage Sold	Implied Value	Financial World/Forbes Estimate (Year if Different)	Percentage Difference
1991	Denver Nuggets	70	100	70	41	−41.4
1991	Orlando Magic	85	100	85	61	−28.2
1992	Golden State Warriors	21	25	84	63	−25.0
1992	Sacramento Kings	140	53	264	63	−76.1
1993	Houston Rockets	85	100	85	58	−31.8
1993	San Antonio Spurs	75	100	75	65	−13.3
1995	Golden State Warriors	95	75	127	83	−34.6
1995	Miami Heat	60	Unknown	Unknown	88	–
1995	Minnesota Timberwolves	88.5	Unknown	Unknown	99	–
1995	New York Knicks	1,100	Unknown	Unknown	173	–
1996	Minnesota Timberwolves	6	10	60	110	83.3
1996	Philadelphia 76ers	125	100	125	93	−25.6
1997	New York Knicks	850	Unknown	Unknown	250	–
1998	New Jersey Nets	123	82	150	157	4.7
1998	Sacramento Kings	250	53	472	119	−74.8
1998	Toronto Raptors	408	100	408	121	−70.3
1999	Charlotte Hornets	80	35	229	136	−40.6
1999	New York Knicks	1,430	Unknown	Unknown	334	–
2000	Dallas Mavericks	280	54	519	167	−67.8
2000	Denver Nuggets	450	Unknown	Unknown	175	–
2000	Vancouver Grizzlies	170	100	170	118	−30.6
2001	Atlanta Hawks	184	100	184	199	8.2
2001	Seattle Supersonics	200	100	200	200	0
2002	Boston Celtics	360	100	360	274	−23.9
2003	Toronto Raptors	71	Unknown	Unknown	249	–
2003	Charlotte Bobcats	300	100	300	225 (2004)	−25

(continued)

Table 8.3 Continued

Year	Team	Price ($millions)	Percentage Sold[1]	Implied Value	Financial World/Forbes Estimate (Year if Different)	Percentage Difference
2004	Atlanta Hawks	208	100	208	232	11.5
2004	New Jersey Nets	300	100	300	296	-1.3
2004	Phoenix Suns	401	100	401	356	-11.2
2004	Charlotte Hornets	65	35	186	225 (2005)	21
2005	Cleveland Cavaliers	375	100	375	356	-5.1
2006	Seattle Supersonics	350	100	350	268	-23.4
2010	Charlotte Bobcats	300	Unknown	Unknown	281	–
2010	Golden State Warriors	450	100	450	363	-19.3
2010	New Jersey Nets	200	80	250	269	7.6
2010	Washington Wizards	170	56	304	322	5.9
2011	Philadelphia 76ers	330	100	330	330	0
2011	Detroit Pistons	325	100	320	360	12.5
2012	Memphis Grizzlies	377	70	539	269	-50.1
2012	New Orleans Pelicans	338	100	338	285	-15.7
2013	Sacramento Kings	534	65	822	525	-36.1
2014	Milwaukee Bucks	550	100	550	405	-26.4
2014	Los Angeles Clippers	2000	100	2000	575	-71.3
2015	Atlanta Hawks	850	100	850	825	-2.9
2017	Houston Rockets	2200	100	2200	1650	-25

Average -11.0
Correlation between sale price and estimate = 0.853

[1] Although this lists the percentage of the team bought, there are typically many more details that should be considered. For example, there are often team debts that are assumed. Often there are also land or facility issues involved with the sale. Many times, minority or majority owners are purchasing a larger percentage of a team. Sometimes there are also other estimates of the amount paid.

vWhile there is less information about historical sale prices of NHL teams, Table 8.4 shows sale prices for NHL franchises across the past couple of decades. The variation in franchise values looks more like MLB and NBA than for teams in the NFL. On average, the value of NHL teams is the lowest of the four major North American sport leagues. While this fact remains unchanged, the $500 million expansion fee recently paid for the Las Vegas Golden Knights eclipsed the league's previous average. The New York Islanders' $485 million sale value for 85 percent of the team (implying the team's total value was $571 million) was also notably high. Comparatively, 61 percent of the Carolina Hurricanes franchise was sold for $256 million, implying the total team value was $420 million.

It is easy to look at Tables 8.1 through 8.4 and observe that sales prices have increased over the years, but the amount by which these values grew is equally important. With only a few observations, it is difficult to obtain a robust analysis, but it is possible to estimate growth rates. A regression analysis provides an estimate of how much franchise values increased across the past two decades.[3]

Table 8.5 shows the estimated growth rates for each league. This basic analysis shows a 10.3 percent rate of growth for the NFL, 10.1 percent growth rate for MLB, and 8.8 and 7.6 percent growth rates for the NBA and NHL, respectively. One obvious problem is that only teams that were sold are included in the sample. This could give us flawed results. It is, however, interesting to see how the leagues compare with each other. A return of 10.3 percent (NFL) in nominal terms across a 23-year period is extraordinarily high.

Financial World and Forbes Data

Financial World provided valuation estimates for franchises from 1991 to 1997. *Forbes* has produced these estimates since 1998. The strength of the *Financial World/Forbes* data is that it estimates values for teams for each year. Also, the authors of these estimates have some information on facility-based revenue and then input that data into their proprietary formulae. The drawback is that much of the methodology of *Financial World/Forbes* analyses is unknown. Furthermore, it is not clear that the revenue data that *Financial World/Forbes* uses are reliable. As previously stated, revenue data can be difficult to find. Even if revenue data are found, they may not show all of the benefits of owning a team. Of course, the valuation estimates can be compared with sales data to see how accurate those estimates have been.

Table 8.6 shows the Forbes valuations for 2017 and various growth rates for each team in the NFL using both *Financial World* and *Forbes* data. This data indicates a 12.0 percent return across the 26-year period (compared to 10.3 percent using actual sale data). What is remarkable about the values is the lack of variability from team to team. The most valuable team is the

Table 8.4 Actual Sale Prices of NHL Teams, 1990–2018

Year	Team	Price ($millions)	Percentage Sold[1]	Implied Value	Financial World/Forbes Estimate (Year if Different)	Percentage Difference
1990	Minnesota North Stars	38.2	100	38	30 (1991)	−21.1
1990	Minnesota North Stars[2]	24.6	100	25	30 (1991)	20
1990	San Jose Sharks	45	100, expansion fee	45	43 (1993)	−4.4
1991	Ottawa Senators	45	100, expansion fee	45	50 (1994)	11.1
1991	Tampa Bay Lightning	45	100, expansion fee	45	39 (1994)	−13.3
1992	Florida Panthers	50	100, expansion fee	50	47 (1995)	−6.0
1992	Anaheim Mighty Ducks	50	100, expansion fee	50	108 (1995)	116
1994	Hartford Whalers	47.5	100	48	46	−4.2
1994	Toronto Maple Leafs	54.9	Unknown	Unknown	77	–
1995	Dallas Stars	84	100	84	50	−40.5
1995	Los Angeles Kings	113.3	100	113	81	−28.3
1995	Vancouver Canucks	80.2	Unknown	Unknown	87	–
1996	Philadelphia Flyers	250	100	250	102	−59.2
1997	Atlanta Thrashers	80	100, expansion fee	80	138 (2000)	72.5
1997	Columbus Blue Jackets	80	100, expansion fee	80	145 (2001)	81.3
1997	Minnesota Wild	80	100, expansion fee	80	135 (2001)	68.8
1997	Nashville Predators	80	100, expansion fee	80	130 (1999)	62.5
1997	New York Rangers	195	100	195	147	−24.6
1998	Edmonton Oilers	68.8	100	69	67	−2.9
1998	Buffalo Sabres	76	100	76	91	19.7
1999	Pittsburgh Penguins	70	100	70	99	41.4

Table 8.4 Continued

Year	Team	Price ($millions)	Percentage Sold[1]	Implied Value	Financial World/Forbes Estimate (Year if Different)	Percentage Difference
1999	St. Louis Blues	100	100	100	137	37
1999	Tampa Bay Lightning	115	100	115	113	-1.7
1999	Washington Capitals	85	100	85	144	69.4
2000	Colorado Avalanche	450	Unknown	Unknown	198	–
2000	New Jersey Devils	175	Unknown	Unknown	163	–
2000	New York Islanders	190	100	190	139	-26.8
2000	Phoenix Coyotes	125	100	125	86	-31.2
2001	Florida Panthers	104.7	100	104.7	115	9.8
2001	Montreal Canadiens	183	80	228	182	-20.2
2002	San Jose Sharks	80	85, some debt	94	158	68.1
2003	Buffalo Sabres	92	100	92	95	3.3
2003	Toronto Maple Leafs	71	Unknown	Unknown	263	–
2003	Ottawa Senators	100	100	100	117	17
2004	Atlanta Thrashers	250	85, some debt	294	106	-63.9
2004	New Jersey Devils	125	100	125	124	-0.8
2005	Anaheim Mighty Ducks	75	100	75	157	109.3
2006	St. Louis Blues	150	100	150	144 (2007)	-4.0
2006	Vancouver Canucks	150	50	300	211 (2007)	-29.7
2007	Nashville Predators	193	100	193	143	-25.9
2007	Tampa Bay Lightning	206	100	206	199	-3.4
2008	Edmonton Oilers	200	100	200	175	-12.5
2008	Minnesota Wild	260	100	260	180	-30.8
2009	Montreal Canadiens	575	100	575	339	-41.0

(continued)

Table 8.4 Continued

Year	Team	Price ($millions)	Percentage Sold[1]	Implied Value	Financial World/Forbes Estimate (Year if Different)	Percentage Difference
2010	Tampa Bay Lightning	170	100	170	191	12.4
2011	Buffalo Sabres	189	100	189	169	-10.6
2011	Dallas Stars	240	100	240	227	-5.4
2011	Atlanta Thrashers	170	100	170	135	-20.6
2012	St. Louis Blues	120	100	120	157	30.8
2013	Arizona Coyotes	170	100	170	134	-21.2
2013	Florida Panthers	250	100	250	170	-32
2013	New Jersey Devils	320	100	320	205	-35.9
2016	Las Vegas Golden Knights	500	100	500	500 (2018)	0
2016	New York Islanders	485	85	571	325	-43.1
2018	Carolina Hurricanes	256	61	420	370	-11.9

Average = 22.8
Correlation between sale price and estimate = 0.863

[1] Although this lists the percentage of the team bought, there are typically many more details that should be considered. For example, there are often team debts that are assumed. Often there are also land or facility issues involved with the sale. Many times, minority or majority owners are purchasing a larger percentage of a team. Sometimes there are also other estimates of the amount paid.

[2] The Minnesota North Stars were sold twice in 1990.

Table 8.5 Estimated Franchise Value Growth Rates from Actual Sales

League	Growth Rate (Percent)	Number of Sales with Known Value
NFL	10.3	28
MLB	10.1	45
NBA	8.8	37
NHL	7.6	50

Table 8.6 Financial World/Forbes Valuation for the NFL

Team	2017 Value ($millions)	Growth Rates (Percent)				
		1 year	3 year	5 year	10 year	26 year
Arizona Cardinals	2,150	6.17	29.07	18.45	9.25	11.74
Atlanta Falcons	2,475	16.47	30.06	24.21	12.01	12.61
Baltimore Ravens	2,500	8.70	18.56	16.66	9.99	11.57
Buffalo Bills	1,600	6.67	19.61	14.73	6.90	10.28
Carolina Panthers	2,300	10.84	22.54	17.02	9.18	–
Chicago Bears	2,850	5.56	18.80	19.09	11.22	12.74
Cincinnati Bengals	1,800	7.46	22.05	15.62	7.04	10.80
Cleveland Browns	1,950	5.41	20.30	14.59	7.24	–
Dallas Cowboys	4,800	14.29	14.47	17.98	12.33	13.46
Denver Broncos	2,600	8.33	21.49	18.09	10.09	12.81
Detroit Lions	1,700	3.03	20.98	14.74	6.93	10.89
Green Bay Packers	2,550	8.51	22.86	17.04	10.65	10.29
Houston Oilers/Texans	2,800	7.69	14.81	16.50	10.24	–
Indianapolis Colts	2,375	9.20	19.26	15.53	10.06	12.31
Jacksonville Jaguars	2,075	6.41	29.07	21.93	9.85	–
Kansas City Chiefs	2,100	12.00	24.05	15.81	8.14	11.55
Los Angeles Chargers	2,275	9.38	31.74	19.44	10.66	12.23
Los Angeles Rams	3,000	3.45	47.76	30.92	12.69	12.67
Miami Dolphins	2,575	8.42	25.59	19.42	10.58	10.22
Minnesota Vikings	2,400	9.09	27.79	19.74	11.87	12.24
New England Patriots	3,700	8.82	12.48	17.74	11.93	14.91
New Orleans Saints	2,000	14.29	21.68	15.55	8.88	11.29
New York Giants	3,300	6.45	16.26	17.59	12.98	12.62
New York Jets	2,750	0.00	15.17	16.45	11.02	12.62
Oakland Raiders	2,380	13.33	34.88	24.84	11.35	11.67
Philadelphia Eagles	2,650	6.00	14.83	16.03	9.68	11.94
Pittsburgh Steelers	2,450	8.89	21.98	17.37	10.18	12.59
San Francisco 49ers	3,050	1.67	23.99	21.02	14.33	12.28
Seattle Seahawks	2,425	8.99	22.17	18.45	10.17	11.92
Tampa Bay Buccaneers	1,975	9.72	17.26	13.84	7.45	11.59
Tennessee Titans	2,050	2.50	20.90	15.19	8.32	11.56
Washington Redskins	3,100	5.08	8.91	14.14	7.77	13.14
Averages	2,522	7.90	22.23	17.99	10.03	12.02

Dallas Cowboys at $4.8 billion and the least valuable is the Buffalo Bills ($1.6 billion). While this range is larger than it has been in the past, the relative variation is much higher in other leagues. It is important to remember that most of the NFL's revenue comes from national broadcasting agreements that are shared equally among teams. The *Financial World/Forbes* data are also compared with actual sale prices in Table 8.1. While the values can be incorrect by as much as 61 percent (Stan Kroenke paid $20 million for 10 percent of the Rams in 1998 when it was valued at $322 million), the valuation estimates are generally fairly accurate. On average, the estimates were 3.1 percent less than the actual sale value.

Table 8.7 shows the *Financial World/Forbes* data for MLB teams. The average value ($1.3 billion) is quite a bit lower than $2.52 billion average valuation of NFL teams. What stands out is the variance between team values. For example, the New York Yankees' estimated value ($3.7 billion) is more than 348 percent larger than that of the Tampa Bay Rays ($825 million). Table 8.7 also shows that the average growth rate across the past 27 years has been less than the NFL, but the growth rate across the past ten, five, and three years, and even the last year alone, has actually been higher than the NFL. Comparing the *Financial World/Forbes* value estimates with actual sale prices shows that the estimates are typically 28 percent higher than the actual price.

Table 8.8 shows the value estimates for NBA teams. The average 2017 value of an NBA team is $1.36 billion, while the most highly valued team (New York Knicks) is estimated to be worth $3.3 billion. The least valuable team, the New Orleans Pelicans, were estimated to be worth $750 million. As in MLB, there is also substantial variation in NBA team values. NBA franchise values have had an average growth rate of 12.8 percent across the past 26 years, which is a high rate (slightly higher than the 8.8 percent estimated using sale data). Looking back at Table 8.3, what is striking is that the *Financial World/Forbes* data seem to consistently underestimate the value of NBA teams. On average, the estimates are 11 percent less than the actual sale value. Some of these deals include things like facilities, but that is true of the other leagues as well. It is not clear why these teams seem to be consistently undervalued.

Table 8.9 shows the valuations for NHL teams. The average value of an NHL team, in 2017, was $594 million. At the top of the league, the New York Rangers were valued at $1.5 billion; the Arizona Coyotes, as a result of their annual loss of $19 million, had a value of $300 million. Note that the value of the Rangers, despite being the highest in the NHL, is lower than the lowest-valued NFL team (the Buffalo Bills were said to be worth $1.6 billion). Compared to the other three leagues, NHL franchises are certainly the least valuable. The average growth rate for NHL teams across the last 26 years was 10.75 percent.

Table 8.7 Financial World/Forbes Valuation for MLB

Team	2017 Value ($millions)	Growth Rates (Percent)				
		1 year	3 year	5 year	10 year	27 year
Arizona Diamondbacks	1,150	24.32	25.27	20.80	12.99	–
Atlanta Braves	1,500	27.66	27.13	24.18	12.60	11.22
Baltimore Orioles	1,175	17.50	23.75	20.63	11.52	9.55
Boston Red Sox	2,700	17.39	21.64	21.98	14.07	11.89
Chicago Cubs	2,675	21.59	30.63	24.93	16.28	11.70
Chicago White Sox	1,350	28.57	24.77	17.61	13.49	9.55
Cincinnati Reds	915	1.10	15.10	16.63	11.54	8.97
Cleveland Indians	920	15.00	17.30	17.54	9.72	9.22
Colorado Rockies	1,000	16.28	20.26	16.60	12.17	–
Detroit Tigers	1,200	4.35	20.84	20.21	12.89	9.25
Houston Astros	1,450	31.82	39.86	21.44	12.61	10.21
Kansas City Royals	950	9.83	24.69	21.83	12.91	7.96
Los Angeles Angels of Anaheim	1,750	30.60	31.19	21.68	15.04	9.66
Los Angeles Dodgers	2,750	10.00	11.20	14.46	15.84	10.74
Miami Marlins	940	39.26	23.42	15.87	14.44	–
Milwaukee Brewers	925	5.71	17.86	15.60	12.42	9.24
Minnesota Twins	1,025	12.64	19.21	14.98	13.54	9.21
New York Mets	2,000	21.21	35.72	22.70	10.51	9.44
New York Yankees	3,700	8.82	13.96	14.87	11.92	11.41
Oakland Athletics	880	21.38	21.14	22.35	11.66	9.04
Philadelphia Phillies	1,650	33.60	19.17	17.94	13.70	9.57
Pittsburgh Pirates	1,250	28.21	29.77	30.05	16.39	10.47
San Diego Padres	1,125	26.40	22.30	19.69	11.85	10.04
San Francisco Giants	2,650	17.78	38.38	32.74	19.16	13.59
Seattle Mariners	1,400	16.67	25.40	19.07	12.37	10.70
St. Louis Cardinals	1,800	12.50	29.96	24.95	14.62	9.92
Tampa Bay Devil Rays	825	26.92	19.37	20.63	11.94	–
Texas Rangers	1,550	26.53	23.39	18.12	15.56	10.68
Toronto Blue Jays	1,300	44.44	28.69	25.78	14.22	8.46
Washington Nationals	1,600	23.08	31.73	27.23	13.60	10.81
Averages	1537	20.71	24.44	20.77	13.39	10.10

Figure 8.1 illustrates *Financial World/Forbes* estimates of league average team values for the four major leagues. In Figure 8.1 the valuations are all in 2017 dollars. Notice that values have doubled in real terms across the past several decades. Considering there are many industries that have not grown at all in these years, major professional teams have been quite successful. The NFL has clearly been the most successful, benefitting from large television contracts.

Figure 8.2 shows the growth rates of average teams over time from the *Financial World/Forbes* data, and Figure 8.3 illustrates a measure of relative

Table 8.8 Financial World/Forbes Valuation for the NBA

Team	2016–17 Value ($millions)	Growth Rate (Percent)				
		1 year	3 year	5 year	10 year	25 year
Atlanta Hawks	885	7.27	27.70	26.80	12.40	11.88
Boston Celtics	2,200	4.76	35.98	35.48	19.61	10.53
Brooklyn Nets	1,800	5.88	32.15	38.20	18.67	16.15
Charlotte Hornets	780	4.00	23.91	23.01	10.91	–
Chicago Bulls	2,500	8.70	35.72	33.03	18.42	13.74
Cleveland Cavaliers	1,200	9.09	32.57	29.54	12.19	12.65
Dallas Mavericks	1,450	3.57	23.76	23.88	12.09	14.03
Denver Nuggets	890	4.09	21.60	23.01	11.16	13.14
Detroit Pistons	900	5.88	25.99	22.07	7.69	7.43
Golden State Warriors	2,600	36.84	51.35	42.02	25.56	17.06
Houston Rockets	1,650	10.00	28.65	29.50	14.16	14.33
Indiana Pacers	880	4.76	22.82	25.47	9.98	13.99
Los Angeles Clippers	2,000	0.00	51.51	43.91	21.51	16.61
Los Angeles Lakers	3,000	11.11	30.50	27.23	18.11	11.44
Memphis Grizzlies	790	1.28	20.37	24.04	9.70	–
Miami Heat	1,350	3.85	20.58	24.19	12.68	13.37
Milwaukee Bucks	785	16.30	24.68	23.98	11.68	11.34
Minnesota Timberwolves	770	6.94	21.43	23.14	9.60	11.45
New Orleans Pelicans	750	15.38	21.32	21.35	11.70	10.66
New York Knicks	3,300	10.00	33.08	33.44	18.75	15.01
Oklahoma City Thunder	1,025	7.89	20.21	24.12	14.36	14.17
Orlando Magic	920	2.22	18.00	19.03	12.51	11.48
Philadelphia 76ers	800	14.29	19.48	20.57	7.87	9.93
Phoenix Suns	1,100	10.00	24.87	22.73	10.37	10.11
Portland Trailblazers	1,050	7.69	21.39	23.20	16.40	12.14
Sacramento Kings	1,075	16.22	25.03	29.08	10.99	13.14
San Antonio Spurs	1,175	6.82	21.20	22.96	11.66	13.79
Toronto Raptors	1,125	14.80	29.34	24.11	13.58	–
Utah Jazz	910	4.00	20.12	22.12	11.85	12.79
Washington Wizards	1,000	4.17	27.28	24.98	11.59	14.04
Averages	1,355	8.59	27.09	26.87	13.59	12.83

dispersion in team values for the four leagues. Specifically, it shows the coefficient of variation for each league. The coefficient of variation is the standard deviation of team values divided by the average value. This gives a measure of the relative variability of team values. The NFL consistently has the lowest coefficient of variation, meaning that the team values do not differ much from each other. This makes sense because they share a great

Table 8.9 *Financial World/Forbes* Valuation for the NHL

Team	2016–17 Value ($millions)	Growth Rate (Percent)				
		1 year	3 year	5 year	10 year	26 year
Anaheim Mighty Ducks	460	10.84	8.02	19.09	8.85	–
Arizona Coyotes (Winnipeg)	300	25.00	10.06	17.49	7.39	9.26
Boston Bruins	890	11.25	5.87	20.66	13.86	11.12
Buffalo Sabres	350	16.67	6.71	14.87	8.01	9.03
Calgary Flames	430	4.88	−1.58	11.91	10.12	8.46
Carolina Hurricanes (Hartford)	370	60.87	18.92	17.96	9.02	8.40
Chicago Blackhawks	1000	8.11	6.62	23.36	18.77	12.67
Colorado Avalanche (Quebec)	385	6.94	2.26	12.89	6.05	8.61
Columbus Blue Jackets	315	28.57	16.35	16.79	7.70	–
Dallas Stars (Minnesota)	515	3.00	7.03	16.50	7.32	11.55
Detroit Red Wings	700	12.00	7.09	15.13	9.10	11.26
Edmonton Oilers	520	16.85	3.06	18.24	12.72	9.29
Florida Panthers	305	29.79	17.09	12.40	7.28	–
Las Vegas Golden Knights	500	–	–	–	–	–
Los Angeles Kings	750	25.00	8.95	22.13	13.63	11.43
Minnesota Wild	440	10.00	5.95	15.08	9.35	–
Montreal Canadiens	1250	11.61	7.72	16.80	16.01	12.45
Nashville Predators	380	40.74	14.98	17.87	10.27	–
New Jersey Devils	400	25.00	6.62	14.30	7.45	9.82
New York Islanders	395	2.60	9.60	20.57	10.24	8.13
New York Rangers	1500	20.00	10.89	14.87	15.18	13.61
Ottawa Senators	420	18.31	1.64	13.81	8.49	–
Philadelphia Flyers	740	2.78	5.79	17.11	11.73	11.59
Pittsburgh Penguins	650	14.04	4.78	17.68	15.41	11.16
San Jose Sharks	490	4.26	4.86	17.05	11.50	–
St Louis Blues	450	45.16	24.18	28.19	12.07	10.76
Tampa Bay Lightning	390	27.87	19.25	17.52	6.96	–
Toronto Maple Leafs	1400	27.27	2.50	6.96	12.98	14.12
Vancouver Canucks	730	4.29	−3.01	16.37	13.22	11.65
Washington Capitals	625	8.70	7.72	20.11	15.73	11.37
Winnipeg Jets	375	10.29	1.56	13.40	9.74	–
Averages	594	17.76	8.05	16.90	10.87	10.75

deal of their revenue. MLB has historically had the highest coefficient of variation, but the NHL has had a higher coefficient in recent years.

When one looks at the *Financial World/Forbes* data compared to the actual sale prices, it is natural to ask: are *Financial World/Forbes* right, or

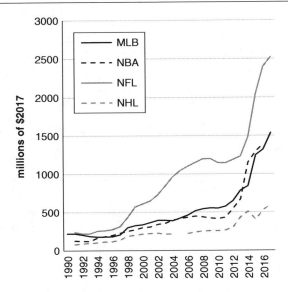

Figure 8.1 Average Franchise Values, All Leagues.

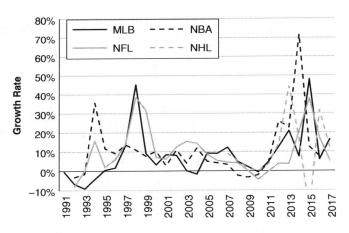

Figure 8.2 Real Growth Rates of Average Franchise Values.

do buyers have a better sense of the value? Often when buyers overpay relative to these estimates, pundits wonder why they paid so much. However, it is reasonable to assume potential buyers will have access to more information than the general public. It is also important to note that these deals are often complicated and can include related assets. For example, in acquiring majority control of the Carolina Hurricanes, the new owner also secured

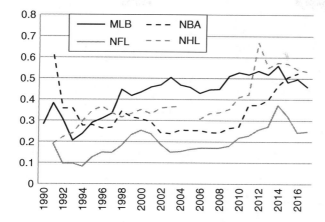

Figure 8.3 Coefficient of Variation of Franchise Values.

the right to operate the arena used by the team. That arena has the potential to host concerts and other entertainment events.

Multiple Earnings

Another valuation technique that is sometimes used in sport is the multiple of earnings approach. This approach simply multiplies revenue by some number to find the value of the firm. In 2001, when Bud Selig testified before the U.S. Congress, he gave values for all MLB franchises. Most baseball franchise values were quite close to twice their annual revenue. Also, on *Forbes*' website, Badenhausen, Ozanian, and Settimi (2009) reported that the 2009 economy had decreased "the average revenue multiple used to value teams from 4.7 to 4.4." The benefits of this approach are that it is quick and easy, and only revenue data are needed. The drawback is that costs and growth rates are not taken into account. Clearly cost, growth rates, and depreciation rates are important, but essentially this method assumes that costs (as a percentage of revenue) and growth rates are similar for all teams. Given that owners use their teams very differently and in different types of ownership structures, it is difficult to see how all teams can have the same ratio between value and revenue.

Using the *Financial World/Forbes* data, Figure 8.4 shows the ratios between franchise values and revenues for the four major leagues. In most instances, an average team is worth about two to three times its revenue, but there are a couple of exceptions. This ratio goes up when revenues are low due to a work stoppage. This makes sense because even though there may be a shortened season, analysts know this is not a long-term effect. If a league loses half of a season, and half of its revenues, this in no way means teams' values should be cut in half. If an analyst has some idea of what a

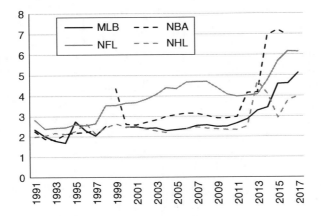

Figure 8.4 Multiples of Earnings.

typical multiple earnings value is for a league, it might be used to find future values of teams. Given what this technique omits, many financial analysts would shudder at using a multiple earnings approach to valuing teams.

Constant Growth Pricing Model

The final valuation method discussed is a constant growth present value model. Finding the net present value of future profits should give an investor the value of that asset. As stated earlier in the chapter, a basic constant growth model is as follows:

$$Value = \frac{\pi}{r - g}$$

where π is the team's profit, r is the required return, and g is the growth rate of the team's profit. Although, theoretically, this is a better valuation technique than the multiple of earnings approach, the main problem is getting reliable data. While estimates of team values, revenues, and costs are available for the past 25 years, there are still problems with using a constant growth pricing model. First, growth rates of profit are not realistically constant. Because growth rates are estimated anyway, this simplifying assumption is not too detrimental. Guessing what average growth rates are going to be in the foreseeable future is always extremely difficult. Second, while revenues and costs are available, they are not necessarily perfectly accurate, especially when those teams are part of a bigger entertainment complex. As noted, many revenues do not show up on the team's income statement. Third, the required return or depreciation rate is not always obvious. Analysts would like to include the level of risk in the depreciation rate, which implies the CAPM might be best to estimate values. Finding the level of risk compared to the market average is not always easy. In fact, even finding a risk-free depreciation rate can be difficult.[4] Finally, the net present value of a team also does not take into account any consumption value the owner may have or any assets or debt that are not a part of yearly profits. The expectation of higher future profits might explain some of the willingness of some investors to pay more for a team than its current value.

While realizing that valuing teams can be difficult, going through the process is still very useful. Furthermore, because our most reliable data are for values and profits, we can use that data to estimate the difference between the depreciation rate and growth rate. In other words, we can manipulate the model so that we estimate the following equation:

$$r - g = \frac{\pi}{Value}$$

This will allow an analyst to determine if the valuation estimates seem reasonable. One further complication is that the *Financial World/Forbes* data are actually an estimate of earnings before interest, taxes, depreciation, and amortization (EBITDA). Since EBITDA can be a fair amount larger than profits after interest payments, taxes, depreciation, and amortization, one has to try to figure out the comparison between the two. Some recent MLB financial documents have an average of profits equaling 36 percent of EBITDA (Fort & Winfree, 2013) In the interest of conciseness, we will show examples of profits equaling EBITDA and profits equaling half of EBITDA.

Table 8.10 shows various financial statistics for the NFL, MLB, NBA, and NHL. The average EBITDA ranges from 2.2 percent to 4.0 percent of the average franchise value. That means if profits are half of EBITDA, then profits range from 1.1 percent to 2.0 percent of value. Using the constant growth model, this implies that the difference between the expected future growth rate and the depreciation rate is roughly 1 to 2 percent (ignoring the other benefits of ownership that do not show up on income statements). Table 8.10 also shows nominal and real past growth rates of EBITDA, which should be similar to the growth rates for profits. While past growth rates do not guarantee future growth rates, this is used as the best guess for future growth rates. The final two columns provide estimates of the nominal and real depreciation rates.

If the depreciation rates in Table 8.10 seem high, this means the values might actually be too low. Conversely, if the depreciation rates seem too low, this means the valuations might be too high. What is interesting to note is that these implied depreciation rates are higher than when this analysis was done in the first edition in this book, meaning that profits have increased faster than team values, with the exception of MLB, which

Table 8.10 Average EBITDA ranges

League	Average Value[1]	Average EBITDA	EBITDA/ Value	.5 Times EBITDA/ Value	Nominal EBITDA Growth Rate[2]	Real EBITDA Growth Rate	Implied Nominal Depreciation Rate	Implied Real Depreciation Rate
NFL	2,522	101.4	0.0402	0.0201	12.94%	10.66%	14.95%	12.67%
MLB	1,536.8	34.2	0.0222	0.0111	12.20%	9.93%	13.31%	11.04%
NBA	1,355.3	32.4	0.0239	0.0119	13.21%	10.77%	14.40%	11.96%
NHL	594.4	19.5	0.0328	0.0164	15.08%	12.76%	16.72%	14.39%

[1] In $millions (2017 for NFL and MLB, 2016–2017 for NBA, 2017–2018 for NHL). *Forbes* gives the EBITDA for the previous season.
[2] The nominal and real EBITDA growth rates are past growth rates calculated from *Forbes* data from 2000 to the most recent year available.

is has a slightly lower implied depreciation rate. The most dramatic change is with the NBA, which has seen a remarkable increase in growth rates for profits. While NBA teams may have appeared overvalued a few years ago, this dramatic increase in profits seems to have at least partially justified high team values. What seems to be true of all leagues is that if teams see small increases in future profits, then the teams are overvalued. However, if they continue to increase profits as they have in recent decades, then they are probably undervalued.

If one knew exactly what depreciation rates should be, then a similar exercise calculating implied growth rates for teams could be performed. One must also remember that one bad or good year can significantly change these results. To make this analysis more robust, it would be useful to do the same exercise for different years. Again, it is important to remember that things like ancillary benefits are not captured in this analysis.

Other Sport

The focus on the four major North American leagues is not meant to dismiss the large values of teams in other leagues. Even though most NFL teams are among the most valuable sport franchises in the world, *Forbes* estimates that the English soccer team Manchester United is worth $3.69 million (2017). Ferrari Motorsports has been estimated to be worth $1.15 billion, while Hendrick Motorsports is estimated to be worth $350 million (2017). The Sacramento River Cats, a minor league baseball team, is valued at $49 million. *Forbes* estimated that the Los Angeles Galaxy is worth $315 million. Table 8.11 shows the valuations for all MLS teams.

It is clear that the various leagues have teams with incredibly high values, but *how* these teams generate their values can differ greatly. Some leagues,

Table 8.11 *Forbes'* 2008 Valuations of Major League Soccer Teams

Team	Valuation ($millions)
Chicago Fire	41
Chivas USA	24
Colorado Rapids	31
Columbus Crew	23
D.C. United	35
FC Dallas	39
Houston Dynamo	33
Kansas City Wizards	22
Los Angeles Galaxy	100
New England Revolution	27
New York Red Bulls	36
Real Salt Lake	30
Toronto FC	44
Average	37.3

like MLS, might get most of their value from potential growth. Most teams in MLS do not generate huge profits. If fan interest grows and is similar to what is found in other parts of the world, the value of MLS franchises will escalate. Minor league baseball teams, on the other hand, may not have the same growth potential because they will never offer fans the best athletes and, while some minor league teams have small media contracts, major league teams will always have far greater valuations because of their dominating media revenue streams.

College Sport

As alluded to earlier in the chapter, the value of college sport is almost impossible to calculate. As many analysts point out, a large number of college athletic departments operate at a loss. Virtually no college athletic department is a major source of profits for the school, and many are subsidized. While some athletic departments do have high revenues, their costs are typically just as high. If one looks at athletic departments separately, teams have very little financial value.

Just as in professional sport, college teams must be looked at as part of a larger organization. In fact, college teams are much more associated with a larger entity than professional teams. Universities and colleges use these teams as a marketing tool. It is an amenity used to attract students and donors to the school. Often young children know what university they would like to attend because their athletic loyalties have already been formed. But the question is: what is the value of this type of marketing? Since college sport is so much a part of the school, basic financial analysis is of little use. If one could estimate how many students come to a school because of its athletic program, then an analyst could try to make a financial calculation based on tuition rates. Sometimes the effect on enrollment is zero because enrollment is capped. Even in this case, there is still a benefit because if there are more student applications, then the school will end up with higher quality students. But, again, this is almost impossible to value.

College sports also have an impact on donations. Universities often try to generate donations by providing donors with tickets to games. The problem is that while it seems that athletics, especially successful teams, generate more in donations, it is not at all clear that they increase donations to the academic side of a university. In other words, if the point of an athletic department is to help a university's academic components, one drawback is that it could actually be siphoning away some donations.

While it is virtually impossible to correctly value athletic departments, it is clear that universities value them differently. Some schools, like the University of Chicago, have decided to pursue athletics without scholarship athletes and compete at a different level than the universities with major athletic programs. The leaders of institutions that followed the lead of the University of Chicago place less value on athletic departments than do the leaders of other universities with major athletic departments, such as the University of Texas and those at Big Ten Conference schools. At the end of 2016, for example, *Forbes* valued the football team at the University of Texas at $129 million. This value came from both direct and indirect contributions to the school and local area.

Even though some schools view athletic departments differently, this does not mean one side is wrong. It seems to be the case that some schools try to cater to students that do not need or want highly competitive teams while other schools are trying to entice students with the excitement of intercollegiate sport. It makes sense that each school has its own niche.

Notes

1 While there are various valuation techniques, including liquidation and accounting, relative, and contingent claim techniques, this chapter mainly focuses on discounted cash flow techniques.
2 Mathematically, it is important to note that the growth rate cannot be bigger than the required return. If this were the case, the firm or team would have an infinite value.
3 A regression was conducted using logged franchise value as the dependent variable and the year as the only independent variable. By logging the estimated franchise values, we can calculate the growth rate easily. Therefore, we will use the following model:

$$\ln(value) = \beta_0 + \beta_1 YEAR + \varepsilon$$

A basic OLS regression was done (assuming YEAR = 1 in 1991) and gives us the results in Table 8.5.

4 For more information regarding depreciation rates, see Damodaran, A. 2008. What is the risk-free rate? A search for the basic building block (working paper). Stern School of Business, New York University.

References

Alexander, D., & Kern, W. 2004. The economic determinants of professional sports franchise values. *Journal of Sports Economics* 5: 51–66.

Amadeo, K. 2018. Dow highest closing records, *the balance*, February 16. Retrieved from https://www.thebalance.com/dow-jones-closing-history-top-highs-and-lows-since-1929-3306174 (accessed July 31, 2018).

Badenhausen, K., Ozanian, M. K., & Settimi, C. 2009. Recession tackles NFL team values, *Forbes*, September 2. Retrieved from http://www.forbes.com/2009/09/02/ nfl-pro- football-business-sportsmoney-football-values-09-values.html(accessed May 13, 2011).

Damodaran, A. 2008. What is the risk-free rate? A search for the basic building block (working paper). Retrieved from Stern School of Business, New York University.

Fama, E. F., & French, K. R. 1992. The cross section of expected stock returns. *Journal of Finance* 47: 427–465.

Fort, R. 2006. The value of major league baseball ownership. *International Journal of Sport Finance* 1 (1): 3–8.

Fort, R. and Winfree, J. 2013. *15 sports myths and why they're wrong*. Stanford, CA: Stanford University Press.

Multpl.com. 2018. S&P 500 PE ratio, *Multpl.com*, February 16. Retrieved from http://www.multpl.com/ (accessed February 19, 2018).

Quirk, J., & Fort, R. D. 1992. *Pay dirt: The business of professional team sports*. Princeton, NJ: Princeton University Press.

Chapter 9

Demand and the Sport Business

Customers' Changing Expectations

Introduction

Every business owner understands that profitability depends on delivering to customers exactly what they want in the manner in which they want it. There are some elements unique to the sport business that make the assessment of consumer demand for sport unlike any other. For example, car manufacturers or computer makers would love to be the only purveyors of their product in a given market. If all competitors were eliminated from a particular market, it would become infinitely easier for the sole company to be profitable. While competition between companies might improve the quality of a product and lower the price, these benefits accrue more to consumers than to business owners. There are few, if any, benefits created for companies when competitors are introduced in the market. This is the major difference between most businesses and sport. Every team *and* every individual-sport athlete needs other competitors to exist in order to sell their product. Think about it: how exciting would it be to watch one team play against ... no one? For one race car driver to speed past ... no other cars? While no other computer maker or car company needs a competitor in the market to ensure their product is purchased, the sport business relies on competition for all revenues. This distinct quality has given rise to other issues for sport managers, namely, determining the appropriate level of competition to ensure profitability while also meeting the needs of fans.

Sport differs in another important way from many other businesses. When you buy a car, for example, its use or consumption is controlled by one person at a time. While you can drive others to different places, the driver controls the car's direction. Sport, on the other hand, can be enjoyed live by millions through the broadcast of a game, and each of these consumers is engaged in using the same product at the same time. The sport business, therefore, requires *conjoint production*, meaning it requires at least two producers. Sport fans also commonly engage in *conjoint consumption* (the experience is usually far better when one watches a game with others). Within this complex environment, the challenge for team owners and sport business leaders is to understand what will maximize the benefits received by fans (consumers). For example, proximity to the playing field and comfort (better seats and more comfortable seating environments) might be the most important benefits that fans seek. If that were the case, a sport manager would then measure the demand for these amenities and set the pricing accordingly.

This observation should focus sport managers on understanding what it is about the experience that can be differentiated, and priced, relative to demand, and what cannot be separated from the conjoint experience. Demand can change depending on the proximity to the field or different levels of luxury seating and services at the game. Luxury car makers also must understand the demand for amenities that are added to the basic transportation function of an automobile. That differs from the sport business in that no one else enjoys the car when it is driven besides the owner and his/her passengers. At a ballgame, however, there may be 30,000 fans in non-luxury seats and 3,000 in suites and club seats. Sport owners must create a private experience to satisfy the demand for luxury seating while still ensuring that other fans are willing to attend in non-luxury seating. Satisfying these different demand functions requires a deep understanding of the market as the facility design is impacted by the number of suites that are built. As discussed in previous chapters, including more luxury seating also means other seats are pushed farther and farther from the playing field, reducing their value. Balancing the different demand functions for the design of a facility is another unique element of the business of sport. In contrast, a car manufacturer can produce more luxury cars, but that number does not reduce the value of a less expensive car to others. More luxury seating in a venue, however, can have a negative impact on fans seated elsewhere as they may be more distant from the field or seated in areas with far less leg room.

While there are many differences between sport and most other businesses, one thing is clear. Teams are no different when it comes to increasing revenues and providing different consumer segments what they want. Every team owner seeks to understand what each of their fan segments desire, and to ensure that the appropriate number of products and services are available to satisfy all potential buyers.

Some components of the analysis of fans and their behavior are obvious – larger regions usually have more fans and more corporate clients. Both individual and corporate fans want to see a winning team, and both groups enjoy the amenities of new and well-maintained facilities. Some things, however, are not so obvious. Will fans pay to see a marquee player, even if he is past his prime playing years? Do fans care about the nationality of players? Do fans care about uncertainty in the sporting event (a close game), or would they prefer for their team to dominate? These are important questions that teams and leagues must ask, as each has an impact on the level of demand for the experiences offered by each team.

Defining Demand

Before delving too far into the case of sport, managers must be clear on the definition of the demand function. *Demand* is defined as the relationship between price and quantity of a product. The law of demand states that when prices increase, consumers will want less of a good. In Chapter 10, price changes are discussed, which implies a movement along the demand curve. This chapter focuses on consumer preferences that shift the demand curve up or down. Movements upward imply there is more demand for a good or service; movements downward highlight less consumer interest. This chapter focuses on things (besides price) that can help teams increase demand (either by creating new fans, or convincing existing fans to buy more tickets or buy better seats) and, therefore, pay more money to the team. But, first, what do teams produce? In other words, what is the quantity of each product that a team should produce?

This is not as straightforward as some people might think. At one level, teams produce games, merchandise, and fan "experiences." In this chapter, the focus is on the demand for games, which is reflected in attendance and television ratings. It must be underscored, however, that demand can be differentiated into different types of attendance. Even when simply considering overall attendance levels, a team actually produces many different components, including victories, exciting games, and fan experiences inside the facility. For example, the Chicago Cubs and Wrigley Field have provided fans with an extraordinary game day experience. The quality of that experience has contributed to high attendance levels even when the team was an "adorable" loser. Even in years of few wins, attendance levels remained robust. This is just one example of a team that has been able to offer fans something of extreme value besides winning that leads to high attendance levels and an elevated demand for tickets despite lower levels of on-field success.[1] Teams also offer a variety of seating plans from general seating to suites, which are marketed and sold to other fan segments seeking different products. It is important to remember that demand is not the same for all of the products teams offer, and there are several different fan segments to which a team must market. In addition, there are five factors that affect demand for any good:

1 Tastes and preferences
2 Income levels of consumers (individuals and businesses)
3 Population size
4 The price of substitutes
5 Future expectations

These components are impacted by long-term factors such as differences in regional wealth, market penetration (the popularity of the sport and team in their market), the presence of competing attractions (economic competition), and venue age, as well as other, short-term factors such as winning percentages, roster superstars, player performance, game-specific determinants (who is pitching, opposing team's quarterback, etc.), marketing, and competitive balance. This chapter also provides insight into which factors are most important and the magnitude of some of these effects. Empirical evidence is introduced to illustrate how different factors influence revenue streams.

Long-Term Demand Factors

Owners of existing teams and investors interested in bringing a new team to a community must understand the level of competition for discretionary income that exists. The biggest long-run factor for a team is its location, and the fundamental question is always: what will the market bear? To answer that question, one must first understand how much wealth exists to buy tickets, then place that demand in the context of the total supply of sports and entertainment produced for the region.

Population Size and Regional Wealth

The 2009 bankruptcy of the Arizona Coyotes, the financial problems encountered by the Columbus Blue Jackets and Indiana Pacers, and the declining attendance levels at Cleveland Indians' games each underscore the importance of considering demand. However, the issue of declining attendance and increasing competition for discretionary entertainment dollars is not limited to smaller markets or regions enduring particularly long and deep economic contractions. The issue is also present in larger markets. The New York City area, for example, is currently home to the Barclays Center, Madison Square Garden, the recently renovated Nassau Coliseum, and the Prudential Center (Newark). There will also be a new home for the New York Islanders in coming years, meaning that soon the market will host as many as five major arenas. Is there sufficient disposable income in the New York market to buy the entire supply of tickets for all events held at these and other, smaller venues (Radio City Music Hall, Carnegie Hall, Lincoln Center, etc.)? Understanding overall demand levels is critical, especially since Yankee Stadium, Citi Field, and MetLife Stadium can each host concert events during several months each year. At what point is a market even as large as New York saturated? The strains in smaller markets, such as Indianapolis, Minneapolis/St. Paul, and Phoenix are even greater, where there are also domed facilities that can compete with arenas for indoor events. In the Phoenix area, for example, there are two domed stadia and three arenas.

How does one measure the demand for sport and entertainment? While no one can accurately predict recessions or boom times, or the severity of a recession or how long an economic expansion will last, the *size of a market* and the *money consumers and companies* have for purchasing tickets can be measured. Wealth measurements indicate the size of the market and its potential to support teams and the entertainment events required to help pay for a venue.

One way to measure these factors is by accessing resources provided by the Federal government. The U.S. Department of Commerce's Bureau of Labor Statistics conducts an annual survey to understand what consumers buy and how much money they have available for entertainment and sports. The Department of Commerce also looks at annual changes in household income in an effort to understand how consumers are being affected by current economic trends. Other government agencies collect data on population growth, the number of businesses in a community and how many people they employ (larger firms, for example, might be more interested in entertaining clients at sporting events), and the overall payroll size (firms paying employees more might have larger entertainment budgets). Understanding how these different measures of wealth vary across numerous regions provides a careful assessment of the variety of opportunities for teams. It also illustrates the varying degrees of difficulty teams have in different markets due to such factors as rising levels of unemployment and reduced consumer spending.

To illustrate the factors that should be considered, a variety of these measures are used to describe the market for professional sport and the wealth available in several different regions (see Figure 9.1). The bars in the graph represent the total number of tickets to professional sports games available for sale, the supply in each region. This number was produced by multiplying the number of games home teams play by the number of seats in the venue used by the team. The regions with the most tickets for sale are New York, Los Angeles/Anaheim, and San Francisco/Oakland/San Jose. The line above or passing through each bar provides a broad measure of demand for tickets to professional sports (based only on the region's population size). The points within or above each bar where the line crosses the bar reflects the number of tickets that must be sold to every resident of the region *if* every ticket to every game is sold. Though entertainment events are excluded, Figure 9.1 provides a quick glance into the challenge each region's teams face as they sell tickets.

In New York, where the supply of tickets for professional sport exceeds 13.7 million, teams need to sell less than one ticket (0.68) to each resident to secure sellouts. Teams in this region have far less difficulty selling out their games because of the size of the market (at more than 20 million residents). This suggests that a team in New York would have an easier time selling tickets at a given price level than teams with similar records in most other

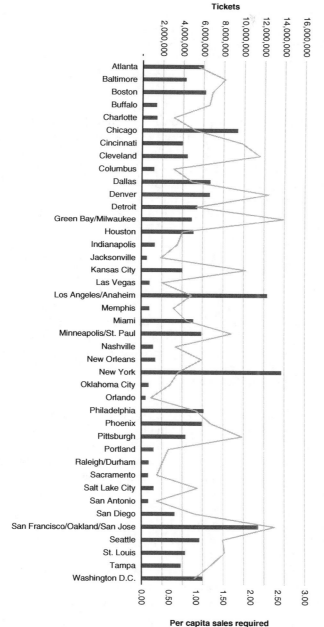

Tickets

2,000,000	
4,000,000	
6,000,000	
8,000,000	
10,000,000	
12,000,000	
14,000,000	
16,000,000	

Atlanta
Baltimore
Boston
Buffalo
Charlotte
Chicago
Cincinnati
Cleveland
Columbus
Dallas
Denver
Detroit
Green Bay/Milwaukee
Houston
Indianapolis
Jacksonville
Kansas City
Las Vegas
Los Angeles/Anaheim
Memphis
Miami
Minneapolis/St. Paul
Nashville
New Orleans
New York
Oklahoma City
Orlando
Philadelphia
Phoenix
Pittsburgh
Portland
Raleigh/Durham
Sacramento
Salt Lake City
San Antonio
San Diego
San Francisco/Oakland/San Jose
Seattle
St. Louis
Tampa
Washington D.C.

0.00 0.50 1.00 1.50 2.00 2.50 3.00

Per capita sales required

Figure 9.1 The Supply of Tickets and Per Capita Sales Required to Sell Out All NFL, MLB, NBA, NHL, and MLS Tickets in Selected Metropolitan Areas.

markets. Of course, championship teams tend to sell out in all markets. The value of having more wealth in a larger market is better illustrated when a team fails to win a championship. In these instances, a team in New York would likely be far more profitable than one from most other markets. Single-franchise regions also have fairly low per capita sales requirements. Orlando, San Antonio, Sacramento, Jacksonville, Las Vegas, and Raleigh must each sell fewer than 0.5 tickets per resident to sell out their entire supply of tickets to professional sports games.

The data in Figure 9.2 add the number of entertainment events held at each market's major concert venues to the mix, and Figure 9.3 adds collegiate football and basketball. Note that the regional supply levels provided in Figures 9.1 through 9.3 exclude a number of sports ticket options, including WNBA, NLL, and WHL games, among others. Figures 9.1 through 9.3 show, by introducing different competitors and substitutes, how difficult it can be for teams, entertainment groups, schools, and venues to sell out in each market. The figures also allow for discussion on which products should be considered as substitutes (do NCAA sports *really* compete with professional teams? What about concerts?).

Even after including concerts and other entertainment events (see Figure 9.2), the top five markets, with regard to lowest per capita sales required to sell the entire market's inventory, remain the same (Jacksonville, Orlando, Raleigh, San Antonio, and Sacramento). However, per capita sales requirements have shifted significantly. Orlando's per capita figure jumps 174 percent, from 0.18 in Figure 9.1 (sports only) to 0.49 (adding entertainment) in Figure 9.2. Numerous other markets saw spikes in their per capita sales requirements as well: Las Vegas' per capita requirement increased by 107 percent, New Orleans by 144 percent, Sacramento by 146 percent, and San Antonio by 128 percent.

Figure 9.3, with its inclusion of NCAA football and basketball tickets should also be considered. Jacksonville, Orlando, San Antonio, and Sacramento maintained their position as the least-stressed markets for sport and entertainment ticket sales, but others have fallen. Raleigh, for example, has three major NCAA Division I-A universities in its market, which already serves a professional team. The inclusion of Duke University, North Carolina State University, and the University of North Carolina raised the Raleigh market's per capita sales requirement by 213.5 percent. In order for Raleigh to sell its entire inventory of professional sports, entertainment, and NCAA football and basketball tickets, each resident would need to purchase 1.69 tickets!

Note that in this sample of markets for sports and entertainment, only Buffalo, Cleveland, Detroit, New Orleans, and Pittsburgh lost residents from 2000 to 2016. The Cleveland metropolitan area lost the greatest proportion of its 2000 population base, at more than 4 percent (see Table 9.1).

The next section of this chapter will discuss market penetration and provide a deeper understanding of factors that larger and smaller markets

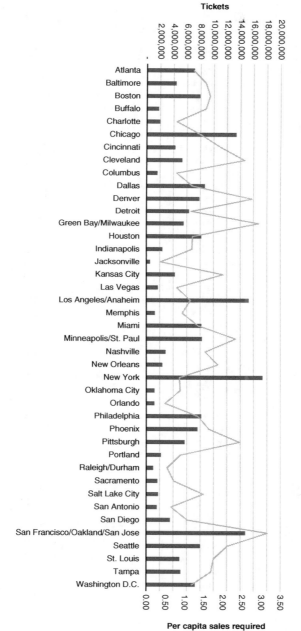

Figure 9.2 The Supply of Tickets and Per Capita Sales Required to Sell Out all NFL, MLB, NBA, NHL, MLS, and Entertainment Tickets in Selected Metropolitan Areas.

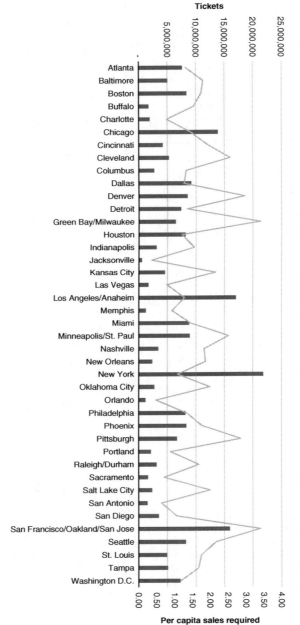

Figure 9.3 The Supply of Tickets and Per Capita Sales Required to Sell Out all NFL, MLB, NBA, NHL, MLS, NCAAF and NCAAB Division I-A Power Five Conference Games and Entertainment Tickets in Selected Metropolitan Areas.

Table 9.1 Population Changes in Selected Metropolitan Regions

Metropolitan Area	2000	2016	Percent Change
Atlanta–Sandy Springs–Roswell, GA	4,247,981	5,789,700	36.3%
Baltimore–Columbia–Towson, MD	2,552,994	2,798,886	9.6%
Boston–Cambridge–Newton, MA–NH	4,391,344	4,794,447	9.2%
Buffalo–Cheektowaga–Niagara Falls, NY	1,170,111	1,132,804	−3.2%
Charlotte–Concord–Gastonia, NC–SC	1,330,448	2,474,314	86.0%
Chicago–Naperville–Elgin, IL–IN–WI	9,098,316	9,512,999	4.6%
Cincinnati, OH–KY–IN	2,009,632	2,165,139	7.7%
Cleveland–Elyria, OH and Akron, OH	2,148,143	2,055,612	−4.3%
Columbus, OH	1,612,694	2,041,520	26.6%
Dallas–Fort Worth–Arlington, TX	5,161,544	7,233,323	40.1%
Denver–Aurora–Lakewood, CO	2,179,240	2,853,077	30.9%
Detroit–Warren–Dearborn, MI; Ann Arbor, MI; Jackson, MI; and Toledo, OH	5,593,062	5,426,007	−3.0%
Green Bay, WI and Milwaukee–Waukesha–West Allis, WI	1,783,340	1,890,718	6.0%
Houston–The Woodlands–Sugar Land, TX	4,715,407	6,772,470	43.6%
Indianapolis–Carmel–Anderson, IN	1,525,104	2,004,230	31.4%
Jacksonville, FL	1,122,750	1,478,212	31.7%
Kansas City, MO–KS	1,836,038	2,104,509	14.6%
Las Vegas–Henderson–Paradise, NV	1,375,765	2,155,664	56.7%
Los Angeles–Long Beach–Anaheim, CA	12,365,627	13,310,447	7.6%
Memphis, TN–MS–AR	1,205,204	1,342,842	11.4%
Miami–Fort Lauderdale–West Palm Beach, FL	5,007,564	6,066,387	21.1%
Minneapolis–St. Paul–Bloomington, MN–WI	2,968,806	3,551,036	19.6%
Nashville–Davidson–Murfreesboro–Franklin, TN	1,311,789	1,865,298	42.2%
New Orleans–Metairie, LA	1,316,510	1,268,883	−3.6%
New York–Newark–Jersey City, NY–NJ–PA and Bridgeport–Stamford–Norwalk, CT	18,323,002	20,153,634	10.0%
Oklahoma City, OK	1,095,421	1,373,211	25.4%
Orlando–Kissimmee–Sanford, FL	1,644,561	2,441,257	48.4%
Philadelphia–Camden–Wilmington, PA–NJ–DE–MD	5,687,147	6,070,500	6.7%
Phoenix–Mesa–Scottsdale, AZ	3,251,876	4,661,537	43.3%
Pittsburgh, PA	2,431,087	2,342,299	−3.7%
Portland–Vancouver–Hillsboro, OR–WA	1,927,881	2,424,955	25.8%
Raleigh, NC and Durham–Chapel Hill, NC	1,223,564	1,302,946	6.5%
Sacramento–Roseville–Arden–Arcade, CA	1,796,857	2,296,418	27.8%
Salt Lake City, UT	968,858	1,186,187	22.4%
San Antonio–New Braunfels, TX	1,711,703	2,429,609	41.9%
San Diego–Carlsbad, CA	2,813,833	3,317,749	17.9%
San Francisco–Oakland–Hayward, CA and San Jose–Sunnyvale–Santa Clara, CA	5,859,559	6,657,982	13.6%
Seattle–Tacoma–Bellevue, WA	3,043,878	3,798,902	24.8%
St. Louis, MO–IL	2,698,687	2,807,002	4.0%
Tampa–St. Petersburg–Clearwater, FL	2,395,997	3,032,171	26.6%
Washington–Arlington–Alexandria, DC–VA–MD–WV	4,796,183	6,131,977	27.9%

must consider. The latter issue is also relevant in the discussion of regional wealth. In other words, it might be possible for a smaller area with wealthier residents and a substantial number of large firms to be able to buy a sufficient number of tickets and luxury seating to allow a team to reach its financial goals. Note that some of the concepts in this chapter overlap with those discussed in Chapter 6.

Figure 9.4 provides data describing the total amount of money households in different regions spend on sports and entertainment, as well as the corporate payrolls in each market. The data in Figure 9.4 should be compared to that in Tables 6.1 and 6.2 from Chapter 6, which show the amount of corporate wealth and number of firms with more than 500 employees available for every luxury product in each market. Both of these data sets can be used to indicate the level of wealth available to purchase luxury suites and club seats in each market. There are some individuals who buy these products, but businesses are the primary clients that teams look to when selling their luxury seats. Teams in regions that have a larger number of businesses with robust corporate payrolls are typically better equipped to sell their entire inventory of tickets. While corporate payrolls were highest in New York, Los Angeles, Chicago, and Washington, D.C., the markets with the highest average household spending on sports and entertainment were Minneapolis, San Diego, Seattle, and Denver. Figure 9.4 underscores the variance that can exist within each market in the demand for general seating tickets (more often purchased by individuals and families) and luxury products (marketed to businesses). By these measures, Chicago is the market best suited to sell out *both* the general seating deck (7th highest household sports spending) and luxury products (3rd highest corporate payroll), followed by Minneapolis (1st/12th), Boston (6th/7th), and Washington, D.C. (9th/4th). Of course, a number of markets have much more variance. The New York/New Jersey market, for example, ranked 1st in total corporate payroll, but landed at number 18 out of 20 for average household spending on sports and entertainment. Los Angeles and San Diego saw similar discrepancies in the two measures. Los Angeles ranked 2nd in corporate payroll but fell to 17th in household spending on sports and entertainment. San Diego was just the opposite; the market ranked 17th in corporate payroll but had the second-highest average household spending on sports and entertainment. Teams in areas with fewer firms with large corporate payrolls will face a far more difficult challenge selling luxury seating and, as a result, have less available revenue to secure a desired return on their investment while also meeting the market prices for the best players.

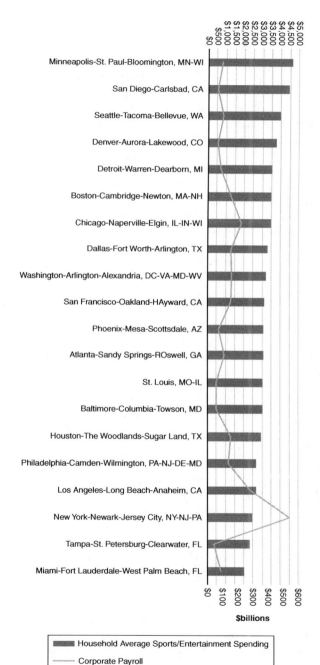

Figure 9.4 Household Spending for Sports/Entertainment and Corporate Payroll, Selected Markets ($2016).

Minneapolis-St. Paul-Bloomington, MN-WI

San Diego-Carlsbad, CA

Seattle-Tacoma-Bellevue, WA

Denver-Aurora-Lakewood, CO

Detroit-Warren-Dearborn, MI

Boston-Cambridge-Newton, MA-NH

Chicago-Naperville-Elgin, IL-IN-WI

Dallas-Fort Worth-Arlington, TX

Washington-Arlington-Alexandria, DC-VA-MD-WV

San Francisco-Oakland-HAyward, CA

Phoenix-Mesa-Scottsdale, AZ

Atlanta-Sandy Springs-ROswell, GA

St. Louis, MO-IL

Baltimore-Columbia-Towson, MD

Houston-The Woodlands-Sugar Land, TX

Philadelphia-Camden-Wilmington, PA-NJ-DE-MD

Los Angeles-Long Beach-Anaheim, CA

New York-Newark-Jersey City, NY-NJ-PA

Tampa-St. Petersburg-Clearwater, FL

Miami-Fort Lauderdale-West Palm Beach, FL

$billions

▨ Household Average Sports/Entertainment Spending

⸱⸱⸱⸱ Corporate Payroll

Market Penetration

Another helpful way to evaluate markets is to look at penetration rates across teams in the same sport. There are several slightly different definitions of market penetration rates. One definition focuses on one product's sale compared to the sale of all similar products in a market. Translated to a particular team, this could mean looking at its ticket sales relative to all tickets sold to sport and entertainment events in their market. Another measure of market penetration focuses on the volume of product sales in a particular market compared to the same product in different markets. This would involve looking at a team's total ticket sales as a percent of a measure of population (total population, all sports fans, etc.) in each region, then comparing that figure to other teams in the same league in other regions. Within this perspective, the concern is the extent to which the potential market of all consumers has bought a particular product compared to that product's performance in other regional markets.

To illustrate the usefulness of the concept, the analysis in Figures 9.5 and 9.6 looks at market penetration rates for all MLB teams from 2000 to 2016. In this exercise, market penetration was calculated by dividing the total number of tickets sold by each club by the population of the team's market, as defined by the metropolitan statistical area. With MSAs as the unit defining market sizes, the teams in Chicago and New York were each assumed to share the market equally. The populations of other regions with more than one team were not split, as each team plays in a separate MSA. Teams, of course, sell tickets to fans living outside of their MSA and to fans of other teams. This is expected to be the same for each team, although one could think of several differences related to tourism (e.g., far more tourists visit New York City than Kansas City), the presence of historic ballparks (e.g., Fenway Park, Wrigley Field), or the opening of a new facility. Each of those differences would impact total sales.

Figures 9.5 and 9.6 demonstrate how market penetration analyses can be useful in understanding demand. These data assess the relative popularity of a single product, MLB, in different markets, without controlling for any other factors. While Figures 9.1 through 9.3 investigated the number of tickets required to sell out all sports and entertainment tickets in the market, Figures 9.5 and 9.6 provide insight on actual consumer behavior in select MLB markets (excluding price differences and impacts to revenue, of course). The market penetration rates listed represent the number of tickets each person in a team's MSA bought, on average, each year. For example, the Kansas City Royals sold nearly 2.6 million tickets in 2016, despite their market population being only 2.1 million. They have a market penetration of 1.6, meaning that on average each Kansas City resident bought 1.2 Royals tickets in 2016. Of course, not *every* person living in Kansas City

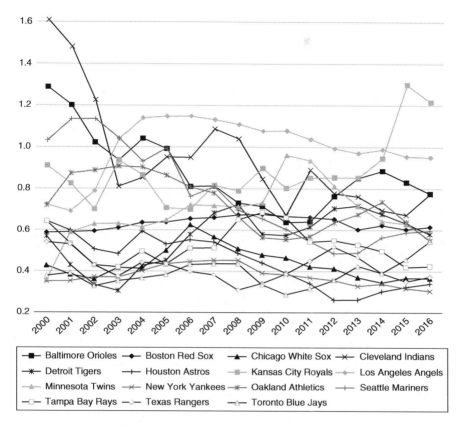

Figure 9.5 Market Penetration Rates of American League MLB Teams, 2000–2016.

is a baseball fan; the figure is an average. The figure also does not account for visiting teams' fans. The Los Angeles Angels, St. Louis Cardinals, San Francisco Giants, Pittsburgh Pirates, and Milwaukee Brewers each had a market penetration rate of 1.0 ticket per resident or higher in 2016.

Again, we underscore the simplicity of these two figures; no adjustments have been made to include price or revenue data. This limitation is significant in that teams often take very different approaches to "getting butts in seats." Looking back to Kansas City, the Royals' market penetration rate of 1.2 was helped by their low ticket price. The average price of a ticket to a Royals game was $43.48 – third lowest in the league. Contrastingly, the Yankees' market penetration was 0.3, despite an extraordinarily high average ticket cost ($106.05). Because the number of residents is larger in

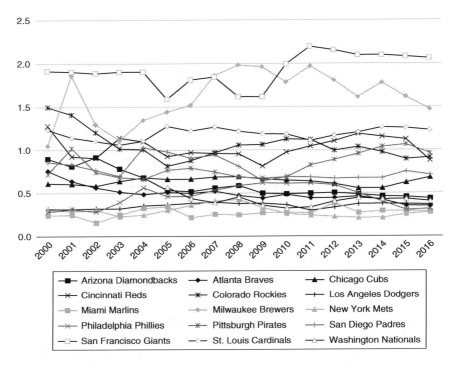

Figure 9.6 Market Penetration Rates of National League MLB Teams, 2000–2016.

New York, higher prices can be charged. The insights in Figures 9.5 and 9.6 remain helpful, however, because they demonstrate just how dedicated the fans of smaller market teams truly are to a particular team.

As you look at the figures, consider what happened to each team as their popularity changed over time. Some franchises, such as the Kansas City Royals, have had a consistently high market penetration rate despite some years with poor on-field performances. Clearly, it is easier to have a high penetration rate in a small market, but this could also indicate Kansas City is simply a "baseball market," where the sport remains popular regardless of on-field performance. Team owners in markets like these (small, with high, inelastic market penetration) must consider whether paying more for quality players and an improved on-field performance level would lead to the needed attendance levels to offset the sometimes-lower revenue streams that accrue to teams in smaller markets. Due to the size of the Kansas City market and the age of the Royals' ballpark (which does not offer as many new revenue streams to the team's owner), it is far more difficult to elevate demand (relative to asking residents to attend more games than their already-high average) and generate the revenue needed to pay the salaries of established star athletes. It is therefore not surprising to find lower expenditures for players. St. Louis, similar to Kansas City, also appears to be in "baseball country." The St. Louis Cardinals have long sustained a high level of on-field success, and consistently high market penetration rates have resulted, extending across the entire time period. The standard deviation for the Cardinals' market penetration rate, over the 16-year period measured, was a mere 0.07.

A third and final view of the penetration rates is provided in Table 9.2 and Table 9.3. In these tables, the penetration rates for each team are displayed together with the total attendance figures for each season. These data illustrate the value of large markets. In several large population centers, teams had penetration rates below those of franchises in smaller markets but often sold more tickets. Relative to the effort each team makes to attract fans, maintain profitability, maximize revenue streams, and ensure its product is affordable, there are important league-wide issues raised by these data. For example, if two teams in different-sized markets have similar penetration rates, but one attracts far more fans, should salary caps be instituted to equalize each owner's ability to attract the best players? Or do the owners of teams in larger markets effectively pay higher prices to own their franchise? If they did pay more for the franchise because of the larger market size and the resulting lower penetration rate needed to attract larger crowds, then the extra dollars earned from having more fans might merely offset the higher ownership costs, meaning no revenue sharing would be needed to equalize profitability. One can imagine the owners of teams in smaller markets, such as Kansas City or Tampa/St. Petersburg, taking exception to that logic and claiming the Yankees, Red Sox, and Dodgers have a clear advantage.

These figures also provide important insights into the challenges teams encounter in their efforts to remain profitable in the midst of a recession. There is evidence of financial stress in several markets, including Baltimore, Cleveland, Detroit, Minneapolis/St. Paul, Phoenix, and Seattle. Teams in the Los Angeles, New York, and Chicago regions would still be disadvantaged in a recession, but the impact of a recession would likely be less severe.

Economic Competition

Sport managers must understand the substitutes that exist in each region. For example, the Miami Heat may be the only NBA team in the Greater Miami area, but they are not the only professional sport experience. The Greater Miami area offers fans access to MLB, NFL, NHL, and MLS games, as well as numerous games played by various universities such as college bowl games. Each of these experiences are offered within a two-hour drive from the Greater Miami metropolitan area. As regions build more facilities, competition between venues to host teams and events increases. And when there

Table 9.2 American League MLB Teams' Market Penetration Rates (MPR, %) and Attendance (thousands), 2000–2016

Team	Measure	Season								
		2000	2002	2004	2006	2008	2010	2012	2014	2016
Baltimore Orioles	MPR	1.3	1.0	1.0	0.8	0.7	0.6	0.8	0.9	0.8
	Attendance	3.295	2.655	2.744	2.153	1.950	1.733	2.102	2.464	2.172
Boston Red Sox	MPR	0.6	0.6	0.6	0.7	0.7	0.7	0.7	0.6	0.6
	Attendance	2.586	2.650	2.837	2.930	3.048	3.046	3.043	2.956	2.955
Chicago White Sox	MPR	0.4	0.4	0.4	0.6	0.5	0.5	0.4	0.3	0.4
	Attendance	1.947	1.675	1.930	2.957	2.424	2.194	1.965	1.650	1.746
Cleveland Indians	MPR	1.6	1.2	0.9	0.9	1.0	0.7	0.8	0.7	0.8
	Attendance	3.456	2.621	1.814	1.998	2.169	1.394	1.603	1.437	1.591
Detroit Tigers	MPR	0.6	0.3	0.4	0.6	0.7	0.6	0.7	0.7	0.6
	Attendance	2.533	1.503	1.917	2.595	3.202	2.461	3.028	2.917	2.493
Houston Astros	MPR	0.6	0.5	0.6	0.6	0.5	0.4	0.3	0.3	0.3
	Attendance	3.056	2.512	3.087	3.022	2.779	2.331	1.607	1.956	2.306
Kansas City Royals	MPR	0.9	0.7	0.9	0.7	0.8	0.8	0.9	0.9	1.2
	Attendance	1.677	1.323	1.661	1.372	1.578	1.615	1.739	1.956	2.557
Los Angeles Angels	MPR	0.7	0.8	1.1	1.1	1.1	1.1	1.0	1.0	1.0
	Attendance	2.066	2.305	3.375	3.406	3.336	3.250	3.061	3.095	3.016
Minnesota Twins	MPR	0.4	0.6	0.6	0.7	0.7	1.0	0.8	0.6	0.6
	Attendance	1.059	1.924	1.911	2.285	2.302	3.223	2.776	2.250	1.963
New York Yankees	MPR	0.4	0.4	0.4	0.4	0.5	0.4	0.4	0.3	0.3
	Attendance	3.227	3.465	3.775	4.200	4.298	3.765	3.542	3.401	3.063
Oakland Athletics	MPR	0.7	0.9	0.9	0.8	0.7	0.6	0.6	0.7	0.5
	Attendance	1.728	2.169	2.201	1.976	1.665	1.418	1.679	2.003	1.521
Seattle Mariners	MPR	1.0	1.1	0.9	0.8	0.7	0.6	0.5	0.6	0.6
	Attendance	3.148	3.539	2.940	2.480	2.329	2.085	1.721	2.064	2.267
Tampa Bay Rays	MPR	0.6	0.4	0.5	0.5	0.7	0.7	0.5	0.5	0.4
	Attendance	1.549	1.065	1.274	1.369	1.780	1.843	1.559	1.446	1.286
Texas Rangers	MPR	0.5	0.4	0.4	0.4	0.3	0.4	0.5	0.4	0.4
	Attendance	2.800	2.352	2.513	2.388	1.945	2.505	3.460	2.718	2.710
Toronto Blue Jays	MPR	0.4	0.3	0.4	0.4	0.4	0.3	0.4	0.4	0.5
	Attendance	1.819	1.638	1.900	2.302	2.399	1.625	2.099	2.375	3.392

Table 9.3 National League MLB Teams' Market Penetration Rates (MPR, %) and Attendance (thousands), 2000–2016

Team	Measure	Season								
		2000	2002	2004	2006	2008	2010	2012	2014	2016
Arizona Diamondbacks	MPR	0.9	0.9	0.7	0.5	0.6	0.5	0.5	0.5	0.4
	Attendance	2.942	3.198	2.519	2.091	2.509	2.056	2.177	2.073	2.036
Atlanta Braves	MPR	0.8	0.6	0.5	0.5	0.5	0.5	0.4	0.4	0.3
	Attendance	3.234	2.568	2.327	2.549	2.532	2.559	2.420	2.354	2.020
Chicago Cubs	MPR	0.6	0.6	0.7	0.7	0.7	0.6	0.6	0.6	0.7
	Attendance	2.789	2.694	3.170	3.123	3.300	3.062	2.882	2.652	3.232
Cincinnati Reds	MPR	1.3	0.9	1.1	1.0	1.0	1.0	1.1	1.2	0.9
	Attendance	2.577	1.855	2.287	2.134	2.058	2.060	2.347	2.476	1.894
Colorado Rockies	MPR	1.5	1.2	1.0	0.9	1.1	1.1	1.0	1.0	0.9
	Attendance	3.285	2.740	2.338	2.105	2.650	2.875	2.630	2.680	2.602
Los Angeles Dodgers	MPR	0.3	0.3	0.4	0.4	0.4	0.4	0.3	0.4	0.4
	Attendance	3.010	3.131	3.488	3.758	3.730	3.562	3.324	3.782	3.703
Miami Marlins	MPR	0.2	0.2	0.3	0.2	0.2	0.3	0.4	0.3	0.3
	Attendance	1.218	0.813	1.723	1.165	1.335	1.535	2.219	1.732	1.712
Milwaukee Brewers	MPR	1.0	1.3	1.3	1.5	2.0	1.8	1.8	1.8	1.5
	Attendance	1.573	1.969	2.062	2.335	3.068	2.776	2.831	2.797	2.314
New York Mets	MPR	0.3	0.3	0.2	0.4	0.4	0.3	0.2	0.2	0.3
	Attendance	2.800	2.804	2.318	3.379	4.042	2.559	2.242	2.148	2.789
Philadelphia Phillies	MPR	0.3	0.3	0.6	0.5	0.6	0.6	0.6	0.4	0.3
	Attendance	1.612	1.618	3.250	2.701	3.422	3.647	3.565	2.423	1.915
Pittsburgh Pirates	MPR	0.7	0.7	0.7	0.8	0.7	0.7	0.9	1.0	1.0
	Attendance	1.748	1.784	1.580	1.861	1.609	1.613	2.091	2.442	2.249
San Diego Padres	MPR	0.9	0.8	1.0	0.9	0.8	0.7	0.7	0.7	0.7
	Attendance	2.423	2.221	3.016	2.659	2.427	2.131	2.123	2.195	2.351
San Francisco Giants	MPR	1.9	1.9	1.9	1.8	1.6	2.0	2.2	2.1	2.1
	Attendance	3.315	3.253	3.256	3.130	2.863	3.037	3.377	3.368	3.365
St. Louis Cardinals	MPR	1.2	1.1	1.1	1.2	1.2	1.2	1.2	1.3	1.2
	Attendance	3.336	3.011	3.048	3.407	3.430	3.301	3.262	3.540	3.444
Washington Nationals	MPR	0.0	0.0	0.0	0.4	0.5	0.3	0.4	0.4	0.4
	Attendance	0	0	0	2.153	2.320	1.828	2.370	2.579	2.481

are too many teams and too many facilities in a particular region, the risk of unprofitability – for all teams and venues – increases. This underscores the importance of understanding demand in a particular market, relative to other amenities and activities that compete for the discretionary income of residents. Along these lines, sport managers must also determine their team has a niche, such that its fans are only interested in attending games for that team, in that sport, in that region. In most cases, however, franchises compete with other professional teams and amenities for general sports fans. The number of substitutes and economic competitors can have a dramatic impact on a team's revenue potential. How many teams and entertainment options can a region support?

At one level, teams are substitutes for all other forms of entertainment spending undertaken by a household. If a family from Boston attends a Red Sox game at Fenway Park, then they are choosing to spend their entertainment dollars on an MLB game. In making this decision, they are not spending money for tickets to see the games of other teams in their region (sorry, Bruins and Celtics), nor are they enjoying any other form of entertainment with their discretionary income. Would these fans (and their spending) migrate from MLB to another form of consumption if the Red Sox left and the ballpark closed, removing MLB from the region? Are games interchangeable in the sense that fans want to enjoy competition, regardless of the sport? And what about other forms of entertainment?

Research has explicitly shown that MLB teams have less attendance if another team is nearby, especially if other nearby teams are successful (Winfree et al., 2004; Miller, 2008). This point was underscored earlier in this chapter by the graphs depicting the supply and demand of markets' professional sport event ticket inventory, which indicated stress existed in some markets. The effect of other teams' presence on the demand for a given team's tickets can best be illustrated by examining what occurs when teams enter or leave a market. Although all teams within a region compete economically, the effect is biggest when teams are in the same league (see Table 9.4). Table 9.4 indicates that when a new team enters a market, other franchises experience a decline in attendance. Note that when the Raiders first moved to Los Angeles in 1982, the league was in the midst of a strike during which team owners decided to use replacement players. As a result, the decrease in the Rams' attendance cannot be attributed to the presence of the Raiders.[2] Excluding that example, the introduction of a new team typically leads to a 10.3 percent decrease in the attendance of the existing franchise.

Table 9.5 shows the effect when teams from another league move into a market where another professional team (different sport) is already established. There is very little fan substitution when teams from different sport enter a market. It should be noted that the Los Angeles Rams are temporarily playing in the Los Angeles Memorial Coliseum until their new stadium

Table 9.4 Attendance Effects When an Additional Team Enters a Market (1950–2016)

League	Entry Year	New Team	Existing Team	Existing Team Att. Year Before Entry	Existing Team Att. Year After Entry	Percent Change
MLB	1954	Baltimore Orioles	Washington Nationals	880,242	1,039,698	18.1%
MLB	1961	Los Angeles Angels	Los Angeles Dodgers	2,253,887	1,804,250	−19.9%
MLB	1962	New York Mets	New York Yankees	1,747,725	1,493,574	−14.5%
MLB	1968	Oakland Athletics	San Francisco Giants	1,242,480	837,220	−32.6%
MLB	2005	Washington Nationals	Baltimore Orioles	2,744,018	2,624,740	−4.3%
NBA	1976–7	New Jersey Nets	New York Knicks	672,745	644,811	−4.2%
NBA	1984–5	Los Angeles Clippers	Los Angeles Lakers	622,398	613,826	−1.4%
NFL	1982	Los Angeles Raiders	Los Angeles Rams	493,964	258,421	−47.7%
NFL	1995	Oakland Raiders	San Francisco 49ers	516,808	518,928	0.4%
NFL	1996	Baltimore Ravens	Washington Redskins	413,150	427,750	3.5%

Average = −10.3%

Table 9.5 Attendance Effects When Competitors in a Different League Enter a Market (2000–2016)

Entering Team League	Entry Year	Entering Team	Existing Team League	Existing Team	Attendance Year Before Entry	Attendance Year After Entry	Percent Change
MLB	2005	Washington Nationals	NBA	Washington Wizards	628,159	705,069	12.2
			NFL	Washington Redskins	702,670	716,999	2.0
			NFL	Baltimore Ravens	558,594	563,076	0.8
			NHL	Washington Capitals	603,528	lockout	
NBA	2002–03	New Orleans Hornets	NFL	New Orleans Saints	560,472	542,796	-3.2
NBA	2004–05	Charlotte Hornets	NFL	Carolina Panthers	582,566	586,259	0.6
NFL	2002	Houston Texans	MLB	Houston Astros	2,904,277	2,512,357	-13.5
			NBA	Houston Rockets	481,227	565,166	17.4
NHL	2000–01	Minnesota Wild	MLB	Minnesota Twins	1,202,829	1,059,715	-11.9
			NFL	Minnesota Vikings	513,051	513,394	0.1
			NBA	Minnesota Timberwolves	655,999	717,371	9.4
NFL	2016	Los Angeles Rams	MLB	Los Angeles Dodgers	3,764,815	3,703,312	-1.6
			NBA	Los Angeles Lakers	768,244	776,917	1.1
			NBA	Los Angeles Clippers	785,892	782,609	-0.4
			NHL	Los Angeles Kings	748,893	747,858	-0.1
						Average =	0.9%

opens in Inglewood (estimated for 2020). Given the age of the Los Angeles Coliseum (built in 1923), it is reasonable to suggest that the minimal dip in attendance by existing Los Angeles franchises may be delayed until 2020 when the Rams and Chargers relocate and fans choose to purchase season tickets at the newer, more attractive facility in Inglewood.

What happens to attendance levels in a region when a team leaves? This is addressed in Table 9.6. When teams in the same league leave an area, there is a very slight effect on attendance; the remaining franchise, on average, had a 1.8 percent increase in attendance. There are too few examples to make a strong claim, but it does appear that reducing the competition elevates attendance.

Table 9.7 shows this same effect, but when the exiting team is from another league. Again, there are only a few examples of teams leaving within the past 16 years, but there does appear to be a significant attendance boost (9.4 percent, on average) when teams leave, even if they are in a different league. Other research suggests that between 5 and 15 percent of a team's fans will switch allegiances to another team in the same league if the original team leaves for a new city. Another 2 to 3 percent will switch their allegiances to minor league sports in the absence of major league teams (Winfree and Fort, 2008). These findings suggest few fans will switch their loyalties to other sports in the short-term.

Sport Venue Age

Another factor that can contribute to higher levels of attendance, and revenues, is a new venue. Frequently, there is also an increment in attendance in the last year of an old facility as fans capitalize on their memories. For example, both the Mets and Yankees enjoyed attendance surges in their last year at Shea Stadium and the original Yankee Stadium despite the fact that both teams failed to meet their fans' expectations for wins (or a division championship) in the 2008 season. Clapp and Hakes (2005) found that MLB teams that did not have a "classic" stadium had less in attendance during the last year of play at the venue. It also appears that new facilities have a "honeymoon" or "novelty" effect. The Mets certainly enjoyed that during their first season in Citi Field despite the team's poor on-field performance. New facilities will increase attendance in the short run, but attendance typically returns to lower levels after a number of years. It is at this point that the importance of winning and meeting or exceeding fans' expectations returns to explain variations in ticket sales.

Figure 9.7 shows the honeymoon effects for new facilities used by MLB, NBA, and NHL teams. Including NFL teams in this analysis would not add any explanatory power because these teams sell most, if not all, of their seats every year regardless of facility age. These estimates come from Clapp and Hakes (2005) for MLB (using years 1950–2002), Leadley and

Table 9.6 Attendance Effects When Economic Competitors in the Same League Leave a Market (1950–2016)

League	Exit Year	Exiting Team	Remaining Team	Remaining Team Att. Year Before Exit	Remaining Team's Attendance Year Before Exit	Percent Change
MLB	1953	Milwaukee Braves	Boston Red Sox	1,115,750	1,026,133	−8.0
MLB	1954	Baltimore Orioles	St. Louis Cardinals	880,242	1,039,698	18.1
MLB	1955	Kansas City Athletics	Philadelphia Phillies	738,991	922,886	24.9
MLB	1958	Los Angeles Dodgers San Francisco Giants	New York Yankees	1,497,134	1,428,438	−4.6
NFL	1952	Dallas Texans	New York Giants	174,076	203,090	16.7
NFL	1960	St. Louis Cardinals	Chicago Bears	270,000	278,843	3.3
NFL	1982	Los Angeles Raiders	San Francisco 49ers	435,182	274,837	−36.8
NFL	1984	Indianapolis Colts	Washington Redskins	416,512	421,500	1.2
					Average = 1.9	

* Not included were moves of American Football League teams out of markets and the effect on attendance at National Football League games. Those examples would be the Dallas Texans moving to Kansas City (Chiefs), leaving the Dallas Cowboys in the Dallas/Fort Worth region, and the Los Angeles Chargers moving to San Diego and leaving the Los Angeles market to the Rams.

Table 9.7 Attendance Effects When Competitors in a Different League Leave a Market (2000–2016)

Exiting Team League	Exit Year	Exiting Team	Remaining Team League	Remaining Team	Remaining Team's Attendance Year Before Exit	Remaining Team's Attendance Year After Exit	Percent Change
MLB	2005	Montreal Expos	NHL	Montreal Canadiens	842,767	lockout	
NBA	2000–1	Vancouver Grizzlies	NHL	Vancouver Canucks	600,313	697,717	16.2
NBA	2002–3	Charlotte Hornets	NFL	Carolina Panthers	573,377	572,015	-0.2
NBA	2008–9	Seattle Supersonics	MLB	Seattle Mariners	2,329,702	2,195,284	-5.8
NFL	2016	St. Louis Rams	NFL	Seattle Seahawks	545,551	543,965	-0.3
						Average = 9.4%	

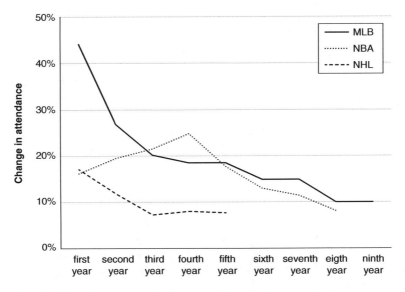

Figure 9.7 The "Honeymoon" Attendance Effects of New Facilities.

Zygmont (2005) for the NBA (using years 1971–2000), and Leadley and Zygmont (2006) for the NHL (using years 1970–2003).[3] Research suggests attendance increases of 44 percent during a newly built MLB stadium's first year of operation. This percentage gradually decreases until attendance is essentially the same as the old stadium after nine years. Contrastingly, it appears the effect of new NBA arenas are different in that while immediate effects in the first few years are minimal, there are statistically significant effects over the first eight years. The honeymoon effect only lasts for five years in the NHL.

Now that we know these effects, we can calculate the net present value of a new stadium (using a lot of assumptions). Table 9.8 translates the percent changes in attendance into additional ticket revenue over time using average attendance and ticket prices for all clubs. A new facility will, on average, increase regular season ticket revenue by $117 million for MLB teams, $47 million for NBA teams, and $21.5 million for NHL teams.

Despite the fact that ticket prices usually rise when a new facility opens, the figures above used the 2016 average ticket price for MLB and NBA games and the 2015 average for NHL, rather than adjusting for potential increases in price and the mix of luxury seating products. Managers are also reminded that a number of revenue streams have been excluded. The figures focus only on ticket sales and, as noted, that estimate was likely

Table 9.8 Expected Increase in Ticket Revenue from a New Facility

Year Team in New Ballpark	Percent Change in Attendance from Old Ballpark	Absolute Change in Attendance	Change in Ticket Revenue ($)	Discounted Revenue ($) at 5 Percent
Major League Baseball[1]				
1	44.1%	1,068,255	33,115,906	33,115,906
2	26.9%	651,611	20,199,952	19,238,049
3	20.2%	489,314	15,168,737	13,758,492
4	18.5%	448,134	13,892,160	12,000,570
5	18.5%	448,134	13,892,160	11,429,114
6	14.9%	360,930	11,188,821	8,766,734
7	14.9%	360,930	11,188,821	8,349,270
8	10.0%	242,235	7,509,276	5,336,702
9	10.0%	242,235	7,509,276	5,082,573
Totals	–	4,311,778	133,665,107	117,077,411
National Basketball Association[2]				
1	16.2%	118,667	6,631,115	6,631,115
2	19.5%	142,858	7,982,916	7,602,777
3	21.5%	157,880	8,822,311	8,002,096
4	24.9%	182,268	10,185,147	8,798,313
5	17.7%	129,814	7,254,032	5,967,910
6	13.0%	95,144	5,316,640	4,165,727
7	11.4%	83,627	4,673,076	3,487,121
8	8.1%	59,484	3,323,980	2,362,290
Totals	–	969,743	54,189,217	47,017,350
National Hockey League[3]				
1	17.1%	122,816	7,636,711	7,636,711
2	11.9%	85,036	5,287,542	5,035,754
3	7.3%	52,027	3,235,008	2,934,248
4	8.0%	57,432	3,571,139	3,084,884
5	7.7%	55,111	3,426,795	2,819,232
Totals	–	372,422	23,157,194	21,510,829

[1] MLB average attendance was 2,422,347 in 2017; average ticket price was $31.00 (2016).
[2] NBA average attendance was 733,263 in 2017; average ticket price was $55.88 (2016).
[3] NHL average attendance was 717,526 in 2017; average ticket price was $62.18 (2015).

highly conservative. Income from parking, concessions and merchandise sold at the facility, and the sale of tickets to postseason games or other entertainment events that the venue might host has been excluded. The increased costs of luxury seating products are also excluded from this analysis. In addition, the revenue estimates focus on changes in attendance, but not for increased ticket prices for different seating areas and higher levels of spending by fans and visitors for food, beverages, and other retail activities.

The analysis assumed that, if no new facility is built, the old facility would maintain a relatively constant attendance level. While this might be true in rare cases, it is typically an exception, rather than the rule. It is more realistic to expect that as a facility ages, there could be a slight decline in attendance. As venues age, they become more and more economically obsolete. As this occurs, all revenue streams become less profitable. The technology implemented in facilities at the time they were built, after a number of years, are rendered obsolete and must be replaced by newer technologies and amenities. Sometimes renovations can be made to older facilities in a way that allows the venues to access newer technology, but the cost could exceed the new revenues generated. In most cases, teams prefer to build a new venue. This is especially true if the older facility is already showing signs of age and is deteriorating in the absence of substantial investments to maintain or renovate it. In those situations, the new facility would be worth more than $117 million.

Short-Term Demand Factors

Attendance

Attendance can certainly change in the short-term, and the factors that affect attendance indirectly impact other revenue streams. If more people come to a game, concession and parking revenues increase. The value of in-venue advertising also increases with attendance, as many of those agreements are based on or indexed to attendance levels. Finally, businesses around the facility, often owned by the same individuals who own the team, also may enjoy increased revenues if more fans attend games. Variation in the pattern of sellouts is related to on-field performance and the economic situation of the market. It is not surprising that worse team performance, coupled with a declining economy, leads to lower ticket sales.

There are differences in demand related to the number of games played in each sport. Given that football teams play 10 home games (including preseason) and baseball teams play 81, for example, equally successful football and baseball teams in the same market might be expected to have very different demand functions. The effect of the additional games is illustrated by comparing attendance levels for MLB's Mets and the NFL's Jets; the Kansas City's Chiefs (NFL) and Royals (MLB); or the Minnesota Twins (MLB) and Vikings (NFL) (see Table 9.9). Numbers in bold refer to years that the teams qualified for the playoffs. The data illustrate that NFL teams more often play before sellout crowds than do baseball teams, regardless of win/loss records. Notice that when the Jets won just one-quarter of their games in 2014, they sold 94.7 percent of their tickets (they sold 97.9 percent of their tickets in 2007 in a season with the same winning percentage). Even in 2015, when the Mets went to the World Series and had a regular season

Table 9.9 Attendance and Win/Loss Records of Baseball and Football Teams in the Same Market

Season	New York Mets (MLB)			New York Jets (NFL)		
	Winning Percentage	Total Attendance	Percent Capacity	Winning Percentage	Total Attendance	Percent Capacity
2017	0.432	2,460,622	73.4%	0.313	620,496	94.0%
2016	0.537	2,789,602	83.2%	0.313	625,280	94.7%
2015	0.556	2,569,753	75.7%	0.625	625,280	94.7%
2014	0.488	2,148,808	64.1%	0.250	625,280	94.7%
2013	0.457	2,135,657	63.7%	0.500	615,656	93.3%
2012	0.457	2,242,803	66.9%	0.375	632,704	95.9%
2011	0.475	2,378,549	71.8%	0.500	631,888	95.7%
2010	0.488	2,559,738	77.3%	0.688	628,768	95.3%
2009	0.432	3,154,262	92.9%	0.563	616,420	96.0%
2008	0.549	4,042,047	122.0%	0.563	627,858	99.7%
2007	0.543	3,853,955	113.5%	0.250	616,855	97.9%
2006	0.599	3,379,551	103.4%	0.625	618,575	98.2%
2005	0.512	2,782,212	83.0%	0.250	619,958	96.6%
2004	0.438	2,313,321	69.0%	0.625	623,181	97.1%
2003	0.410	2,140,599	66.3%	0.375	622,255	96.9%
2002	0.466	2,804,838	85.8%	0.563	628,773	97.9%
2001	0.506	2,658,330	78.3%	0.625	627,203	97.7%
2000	0.580	2,820,530	85.2%	0.563	623,948	97.2%

(continued)

Table 9.9 Continued

Season	Minnesota Twins (MLB)			Minnesota Vikings (NFL)		
	Winning Percentage	Total Attendance	Percent Capacity	Winning Percentage	Total Attendance	Percent Capacity
2017	0.525	2,051,279	64.9%	0.813	533,769	100.1%
2016	0.364	1,963,912	61.4%	0.500	534,289	100.2%
2015	0.512	2,220,054	69.4%	0.688	419,440	81.8%
2014	0.432	2,250,606	70.3%	0.438	417,906	81.5%
2013	0.407	2,477,644	77.4%	0.344	448,135	87.4%
2012	0.407	2,776,354	86.8%	0.625	485,802	94.7%
2011	0.389	3,168,107	99.0%	0.188	502,529	98.0%
2010	0.580	3,223,640	100.7%	0.375	470,009	91.6%
2009	0.534	2,416,237	53.1%	0.750	510,203	99.5%
2008	0.540	2,302,431	50.6%	0.625	506,136	98.7%
2007	0.488	2,296,383	50.5%	0.500	506,046	98.7%
2006	0.593	2,285,018	50.2%	0.375	509,743	99.4%
2005	0.512	2,013,453	44.3%	0.531	511,960	99.8%
2004	0.568	1,911,418	42.0%	0.500	512,969	100.0%
2003	0.556	1,946,011	42.8%	0.563	513,437	100.1%
2002	0.580	1,924,473	42.3%	0.375	512,517	99.9%
2001	0.525	1,782,926	39.2%	0.313	513,344	100.1%
2000	0.426	1,000,760	22.0%	0.688	513,394	100.1%

(continued)

Table 9.9 Continued

Season	Kansas City Royals (MLB)			Kansas City Chiefs (NFL)		
	Winning Percentage	Total Attendance	Percent Capacity	Winning Percentage	Total Attendance	Percent Capacity
2017	0.494	2,220,370	73.2%	0.625	592,851	97.0%
2016	0.500	2,557,712	83.3%	0.750	586,624	96.0%
2015	0.586	2,708,549	88.2%	0.688	518,604	84.8%
2014	0.549	1,956,482	63.7%	0.563	599,743	98.1%
2013	0.531	1,750,754	57.0%	0.688	602,877	98.6%
2012	0.444	1,739,859	57.4%	0.125	548,070	89.7%
2011	0.438	1,724,450	56.2%	0.438	576,659	94.3%
2010	0.414	1,615,324	52.6%	0.625	541,380	88.6%
2009	0.401	1,797,887	54.6%	0.250	540,114	88.0%
2008	0.463	1,578,922	48.0%	0.125	592,622	93.2%
2007	0.426	1,616,867	49.1%	0.250	614,217	96.6%
2006	0.383	1,372,684	41.7%	0.563	623,275	98.1%
2005	0.346	1,371,181	41.7%	0.625	623,325	98.1%
2004	0.358	1,661,478	50.5%	0.438	623,010	98.0%
2003	0.512	1,779,895	54.1%	0.813	627,840	98.8%
2002	0.383	1,323,034	40.2%	0.500	625,503	98.4%
2001	0.401	1,536,101	46.7%	0.375	617,488	97.1%
2000	0.475	1,564,847	47.6%	0.438	626,974	98.6%

winning percentage of 0.556, they sold just 75.7 percent of the regular season tickets to their home games.

Similar observations can be made for the teams in Kansas City. The NFL's Chiefs have had winning percentages that have varied between 0.125 and 0.813, but attendance has never fallen below 93 percent of capacity. Conversely, the Royals only began to sell more than 55 percent of their tickets in recent years when their on-field performance improved. The Twins have appeared in the playoffs eight times since 2000 and yet have sold more than 70 percent of their tickets only five times. The Vikings appeared in the playoffs seven times since 2000 but have consistently sold out almost all of their games. The experiences of these six teams highlights the importance of the different number of games each team plays and the days of the week those games are played in assuring high levels of ticket purchases.

Winning

Short of moving to another area and attracting new fans or building a new facility, the fastest way to increase the demand for tickets is for a team to win more games. While a winning team might pick up some fans for the long-term, typically if a team starts losing, fans disappear. With few exceptions, winning cures all ills for a team. When a team wins, not only is there a clear, intangible benefit from an enhanced feeling of satisfaction in a community or region, but more fans attend games when teams win. This is even true, although to a much lesser extent, for minor league teams (Gitter & Rhoads, 2008; Winfree & Fort, 2008). In the four major leagues, however, the effect of winning on attendance can vary dramatically for different teams within a league (Davis, 2009). Winning can also create lasting effects that extend from one season to the next; a winning season typically creates high expectations for the following season, so attendance tends to be high at the beginning of the next season. Winning seasons also create more loyal fans who might follow a team across many years and that, too, can lead to higher revenue levels.

There are many studies that estimate the effect of winning on attendance. While every study shows that winning leads to elevated levels of demand for tickets, these studies have relied on different data and different specifications of the models used to test for the effects of winning, and many have focused on different time periods. The varying methods obscure the effects of outcomes that do not occur every year (such as winning a championship). As a result, some caution is required when looking for consistent patterns in an amalgamation of these studies. A basic analysis illustrates the relationship between winning and attendance. First, Figure 9.8 plots the team's attendance for the season with their winning percentage for each team in MLB, the NHL, the NBA, and the NFL for each year from 2000 to 2017.

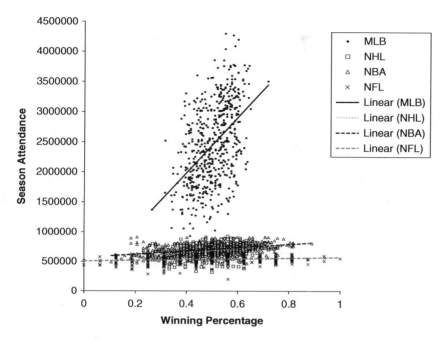

Figure 9.8 The Impact of Winning on Same-Season Attendance.

This figure illustrates several important points. MLB teams, for example, have a much higher seasonal attendance than the other leagues, a result of the many games played, so winning has a much larger effect on attendance for baseball teams compared to other sports. As noted earlier, winning also increases the next season's attendance (in part because fans often purchase tickets far in advance). Figure 9.9 illustrates the effect of winning on attendance for the current year and the next year. While the analysis could be improved,[4] it does show the basic relationship between winning and attendance from 2000 to 2017 and corresponds with the results with numerous studies (Schmidt & Berri, 2001; McEvoy, Nagel, DeSchriver, & Brown, 2005; Forrest & Simmons, 2002). The figure also shows the percentage change in regular season attendance resulting from additional wins, as compared to that of a team with a .500 winning record. Four of the lines in Figure 9.9 represent the added attendance likely in the subsequent year based on the team's performance in the preceding season.

Interestingly, in MLB, winning actually has a slightly larger effect on a team's attendance in the following season than it does in the year in which they won the games. This takes place because, if a team is good in one year, it creates high expectations for the next year (as long as the most important players return) and fans often base their future ticket buying habits on what

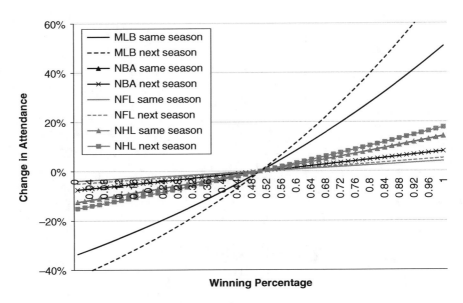

Figure 9.9 The Impact of Winning on Attendance in the Same Season and the Next.

took place in the preceding year. If the team does not get off to a good start when the new season begins, however, demand can be quickly lost and ticket sales can plummet.

Table 9.10 calculates the changes in attendance and revenue from the fitted line in Figure 9.9. This table uses 2016 average ticket prices for NFL, MLB, and NBA ($92.98, $31.00, and $55.88, respectively), and the 2015 average ticket price for NHL ($62.18) to calculate the change in ticket revenue. For example, if an MLB team has a winning percentage of .400, then winning an extra game would increase attendance that year by 10,981 fans and would increase attendance the next year by 14,491 fans on average. This would mean an increase in regular season ticket revenue of $786,249. For these calculations, we used an average MLB ticket price of $31.00 and then discount next year's revenue by 5 percent (10,981 × $31.00 + 14,491 × $31.00/1.05 = $786,249). If the team is better, has a winning percentage of, say, .600, then another win is worth an additional $935,672. This implies a win is actually worth more for a good team.

Some care has to be taken with the results in Table 9.10. The revenue estimate is for regular season ticket revenue only and does not include money earned from concessions, parking, playoff games, advertising, media outlets, or the sale of merchandise. Also, as will be discussed later in this chapter, television is very sensitive to winning. Furthermore, if a win means that a team makes the playoffs, that win could be worth millions of dollars in outside revenue streams. So, these numbers only show an increasingly

Table 9.10 Increments in Attendance and Ticket Revenues from an Additional Win

Winning Percentage	MLB			NFL		
	Additional Fans That Season from One Win	Additional Fans Next Season from One Win	Discounted (5%) Ticket Revenue ($) from One Win	Additional Fans That Season from One Win	Additional Fans Next Season from One Win	Discounted (5%) Ticket Revenue ($) from One Win
10	8,587	10,374	$572,487	2,579	3,291	$531,229
20	9,321	11,597	$631,322	2,600	3,325	$536,133
30	10,117	12,963	$696,354	2,620	3,359	$541,084
40	10,981	14,491	$768,249	2,641	3,393	$546,080
50	11,919	16,199	$847,747	2,662	3,428	$551,124
60	12,937	18,108	$935,672	2,684	3,463	$556,215
70	14,042	20,242	$1,032,935	2,705	3,499	$561,353
80	15,242	22,627	$1,140,550	2,726	3,535	$566,540
90	16,544	25,294	$1,259,641	2,748	3,571	$571,775
10	2,026	1,232	$178,752	1,938	2,347	$259,514
20	2,080	1,251	$182,816	1,990	2,425	$267,343
30	2,136	1,270	$186,978	2,043	2,506	$275,412
40	2,194	1,290	$191,240	2,097	2,589	$283,727
50	2,253	1,310	$195,605	2,153	2,675	$292,296
60	2,313	1,331	$200,075	2,211	2,764	$301,127
70	2,375	1,351	$204,654	2,269	2,856	$310,227
80	2,439	1,372	$209,342	2,330	2,951	$319,606
90	2,505	1,394	$214,145	2,392	3,049	$329,272

small part of a team's bottom line. For example, some economists claim that the winning of an extra game in MLB is worth about $2 million, maybe slightly less for an average team (Krautmann, 2009). This implies that the numbers in Table 9.10 represent about one-third of the effect that winning has on revenues. If we added other revenue streams, the numbers might indicate that a win is worth close to $2 million. In addition, our calculations were based on an average team. The numbers might be much larger for large-market teams and smaller for small-market teams. Furthermore, winning can have a very long-term effect if it creates fans for life, and they continue to spend for tickets and memorabilia. In addition, increasing numbers of fans will lead to more advertising revenue.

While it is important for team executives to have an idea of how much winning is worth, the point of this analysis is to show how winning affects demand and revenue, and what sports managers must study and assess for their team. It is not enough for managers to simply think that winning is better than losing. Winning comes at a financial cost (which we will explore later), and sports managers should understand how the financial benefit comes about. It also is useful to compare different leagues and how fans respond to winning.

Winning and Fan Loyalty

Interestingly, while winning does have a short-term effect (demand tends to drop off quickly if the teams starts losing), there does seem to also be a long-term effect. If a team wins, it tends to create more loyal, long-term fans. Using data from Facebook, Stephens-Davidowitz (2014) argues that if a baseball team won when a boy was 8 to 12 years old, they were more likely to be a fan of that team. The fandom of women seems to be less dependent on age. This coincides with some other related research. Janssen et al. (2012) asked people to name the five greatest soccer players of all time. Respondents consistently named players that played while the respondents were in adolescence or early adulthood. These results show that success can have a long-term impact on younger fans. So, while demand shifts up and down as the team wins and loses, winning will create some loyal, long-term fans. Since most analyses that estimate the financial benefit of winning use short-run data, their estimates probably underestimate the true, long-term financial benefit of winning.

Attendance: Other Factors

Many have argued that adding a "superstar" player to the roster dramatically increases attendance. While having big-name players does increase attendance, the effect is actually relatively small. It is true that teams with more superstars have higher attendance levels, but it is precisely because those teams also tend to win more. Conversely, teams with star players that lose typically do not draw very well, such as when the Chicago Cubs' attendance was sub-par during superstar shortstop Ernie Banks' tenure in the 1950s and 1960s. But of course, there are exceptions. When Michael Jordan was playing for the Washington Wizards, for example, they played in front of large crowds at home and away even though the team was not that successful (Berri & Schmidt, 2006; Hausman & Leonard, 1997).

Players from different countries can change attendance levels and create new fan segments as well. When Ichiro Suzuki first played for the Seattle Mariners, they enjoyed a huge following in Japan. Although having fans in another country will not dramatically increase attendance, it can bolster other revenue streams. It's also possible for foreign players to alienate fans who want to see domestic players on teams. Presumably this is the reason for limits on foreign players in the Canadian Football League as well as in other leagues. There is some evidence that foreign players were associated with decreasing levels of attendance for MLB teams, but that pattern has now been reversed (Tainsky & Winfree, 2010). The race of players also, at one time, changed attendance levels. MLB teams with a larger number of black players had lower attendance levels in the past (Scully, 1974). Research has found similar outcomes in the NBA using more recent data (Kahn & Sherer, 1988; Brown, Spiro, & Keenan, 1991). In the NHL, there is some evidence that English Canadians discriminate against French Canadians (Cranfield, Inwood, & Ross, 2016). While some research shows evidence of the race of players affecting demand, other research shows no effect (Druckman, Howat, & Rodheim, 2016). It appears that if there is some discrimination from consumers, the effect is now relatively small (Longley, 1995, 2006).

Teams that generate more offense also tend to have slightly higher attendance at their games even after win/loss records are taken into account. This is one reason why leagues might change the rules such that offense and scoring will increase, and why some have wondered if there was an interest in tolerating or ignoring the use of performance enhancement drugs. For instance, when scoring was too low in the NHL, the league reduced the size of the pads goalies could wear. While more scoring is preferred, fans do not want to alter the fundamental nature of the game. For example, after the 1961 season (a very prolific year for hitters), MLB raised the pitcher's mound. That advantage reduced scoring and led, in 1968, to a year in which pitchers dominated. After that season, MLB lowered the mound. Fans also want to see exciting plays; for that reason, the NBA and NCAA use shot clocks to reduce the possibilities that teams will waste time simply passing the ball. Before the advent of the shot clock, low-scoring games were commonplace. The NFL also has tried to limit touchbacks so there are more chances for returns for a touchdown. After injury rates increased, the NFL decided to modify its kickoff return rules.

Sport fans also like to see record-breaking performances. Many credit Mark McGwire and Sammy Sosa's race to set the season record for home runs as the decisive element that restored MLB's popularity after the 1994–1995 work stoppage. The excitement generated led some to ask if the league had begun to ignore the use of performance-enhancing drugs by players as the source of the sudden surge in home runs. There is no doubt that the home run chase, and eventual broken record, increased the demand for baseball (for St. Louis Cardinals and Chicago Cubs games in particular). Unfortunately, this proved to be a short-term effect, since in subsequent years the number of players hitting 50 home runs in a season substantially declined. Some have attributed the decline to the crackdown on steroid use, though there is likely a combination of factors. What is clear, however, is that when more home runs were hit, attendance soared. While record-breaking performances seem to be more important in MLB, record-breaking performances have also increased demand in other leagues, such as by Wayne Gretzky in the NHL and Brett Favre in the NFL. Fans also prefer to see the same players on their team from year to year (Kahane & Shmanske, 1997). It is certainly understandable that fans become attached to certain players, and, when a team is constantly changing its roster, fewer fans will attend games. It seems that this effect is not very large and there may not be any effect in the NBA (Morse, Shapiro, McEvoy, & Rascher, 2008).

Game-Specific Determinants of Attendance and Other Factors

Until now the discussion has focused on winning, players, market size, and competition issues as they affect attendance, but there are other short-term variables, often concerning marketing, that can bolster attendance as well. It should be no surprise that more fans attend weekend games or attend at more favorable times of day. Also, the home team's opponent makes a big difference. If there is high demand for the visiting team, this will help the home team's attendance. For instance, the Yankees draw large attendances wherever they play. Other times, home fans like to see rivalry games or visiting teams that have a high winning percentage.

One could argue that marketing is capable of having both long- and short-term effects on attendance. For instance, marketing can help build a brand that creates loyal fans and helps elevate ticket demand for many years. On the other hand, other kinds of marketing, such as game-day promotions, can increase demand for a particular game. Game-day promotions have a short-term effect because in order for consumers to know about the promotion, they typically need to be interested in attending a game in the first place. Although promotions clearly help increase attendance, the question is if it simply substitutes fans away from some other game in the same season. In other words, are fans who come for bobble head day simply coming on that day when they would have gone to a different game? Game-day promotions can also be used to get fans in their seats earlier, because some promotions (a free hat, for example) are only provided for the first several hundred fans to arrive. Although we do not focus on marketing, it can clearly have a big impact on demand.

Bill Veeck and the Birth of Sports Marketing

Bill Veeck (1914–1986) was a genius at increasing demand through marketing activities. His ideas are still practiced at most ballparks today. While working for the Chicago Cubs, he planted the famous ivy at Wrigley Field that now covers the outfield wall. As owner of the St. Louis Browns, he played 3 foot, 7 inch Eddie Gaedel, who walked on four pitches. Later, for one game, he let fans make all managerial decisions. He also developed the idea of "bat day" in St. Louis. As part owner of the Chicago White Sox, Veeck also started shooting fireworks when one of the White Sox players hit a home run and started putting player's names on the back of their jerseys. Of course, some of his marketing efforts, such as making the players wear shorts, did not work out so well.

Lockouts or work stoppages can also contribute to demand. Leagues lose money during a work stoppage, but the effect of a work stoppage on long-term demand is less clear. Even though fans and leagues are often highly concerned about long-term effects, the available evidence suggests resentment from fans is short-lived. Data do not typically show attendance losses after a lockout or strike. After the NHL lost an entire season due to a lockout, attendance levels were not substantially depressed. Fans may threaten that they will not return, but they typically do. Maybe the attendance is a result of "die hard" fans who could attend more games after being deprived of their ability to see their favorite team. Or, perhaps fans just have short memories. While some research shows there are not long-term losses (Schmidt & Berri, 2002; 2004), other research suggests that there are some losses from work stoppages that are being offset by new stadiums (Matheson, 2006).

Competitive Balance

An important aspect of the product that teams and athletes sell is the unpredictability of outcomes in games and matches. No matter how good any team or player is, each requires competitors who can defeat them or have sufficient talent to ensure there are exciting games. It is the uncertainty of outcome that attracts fans. When highly skilled teams or individual athletes play against noncompetitive squads or amateurs, the resulting exhibitions attract far fewer spectators than, say, when the Yankees play the Red Sox or when LeBron James and the Cavaliers played Steph Curry and the Golden State Warriors. Without exciting opponents, no team will be successful in its home market. It is crucial for the success of the sport business that fans believe upsets are possible. The issue is no different for individual sports.

Fans and pundits alike debate the impact of teams' competitiveness on attendance. Some argue that because fans desire uncertainty and exciting outcomes, if every team has a relatively equal chance of winning, more fans will attend. Does competitive balance lead to more fan interest and higher levels of attendance? It is difficult to answer that question because it seems people know competitive balance when they see it, but no one is quite sure of its meaning or definition.

In an abstract sense, competitive balance refers to the homogeneity of team quality. In practice, there can be many measures of competitive balance. If competitive balance means different teams win the championship every year, then both MLB and the NFL could sustain an argument that a high level of competitive balance has been achieved. Since 2000, 12 different teams have won the Super Bowl, and 12 different franchises have won the World Series.

Some think competitive balance should mean different combinations of teams with the highest winning percentages in different seasons, or that a team that does very poorly in one season has a chance to win in the next. For example, for many years, pundits lamented the yearly struggles of the Kansas City Royals, yet they won the World Series in 2015. Economists have grouped measures of competitive balance into three categories: game uncertainty, playoff uncertainty, and consecutive season uncertainty (Sloane, 1976).

It is not clear whether high levels of competitive balance are good for a league. While most fans might argue that uncertainty is needed, that does not necessarily mean that an abundance of uncertainty is required. At certain college football games, there is little doubt about the outcome, but demand is high nonetheless. Also, while small-market fans might lament the success of some large-market teams, leagues would rather make the large number of large-market fans happy as opposed to the smaller population bases in small markets. Some fans would also like to see the David versus Goliath games. During the NCAA's March Madness, for example, many college basketball fans want to see the low seeds win. Some fans love upsets. If a league was perfectly balanced, this could not happen. So, the optimal level of balance is ultimately a question left unanswered. The academic literature is somewhat mixed on the effect of uncertainty on demand. Most studies show that fans want some uncertainty, but it does not affect attendance significantly (Szymanski, 2003). Given that teams with smaller payrolls win some games against higher-payroll rivals each season, it is clear that some level of uncertainty exists. Most importantly, however, as the payrolls of larger-market teams have escalated in the past few years, so too has league-wide attendance levels, suggesting there is sufficient uncertainty to attract fans.

Television, Attendance, and Demand

For many teams, television revenue is more important than stadium revenue. Unfortunately, less academic research on the topic of television broadcast audiences exists because the data are more difficult to collect. Many demand factors for attendance are applicable for television. Hausman and Leonard (1997), studying television's effect on NBA viewership levels, found a "superstar" can attract television viewers, and noted that an increase in viewers did not translate to lower ticket sales (at least when the superstar is Michael Jordan). In an analysis of the 1996–1997 NBA season, Kanazawa and Funk (2001) showed that winning clearly affects local television ratings. While a high-quality visiting team will increase ratings, the biggest effect on viewership is the winning percentage of the home team. According to their study, if a team's winning percentage increases by .1, their ratings will increase by approximately 1.8 rating points. This represents an additional 11,600 to 121,000 households, depending on market size. The effect of a similar increase in the visiting team's winning percentage has about one-sixth of the effect (1,804 to 18,822 households). The study also found that games broadcast on weekends have higher ratings, and teams with more white players had higher television ratings than other teams. Tainsky (2010) produced an analysis of television ratings in the NFL. It is no surprise that high winning percentages increase ratings for both that season and the following season. Studies of the NBA and NFL also show that games have higher ratings when they are shown in primetime (Paul & Weinbach, 2015).

Many sport business leaders have grappled with finding the right balance of attendance and television viewership so that each are maximized without causing an adverse effect on the other. Sport managers, therefore, must understand how television viewership affects live attendance, and vice versa. Many owners have assumed that fans will switch between going to sporting events and watching them on television, but there is little evidence to support this. It's certainly possible that fans switch between watching a game on television or going to the game. On the other hand, it also could be the case that when fans go to some games, they have more fun later when they watch the team on television because of the memory created when they first watched a game live. Evidence on the substitution for attendance and television viewership has had varied results. It seems that attendance is not greatly affected if the game is televised. This research has focused on European football fans (Allan & Roy, 2008; Buraimo, 2008; Buraimo, Forest, & Simmons, 2006; Forrest, Simmons, & Szymanski, 2004; Baimbridge, Cameron, & Dawson, 1996; Allan, 2004), rugby fans (Carmichael, Millington, & Simmons, 1999; Baimbridge,

Cameron, & Dawson, 1995), college football fans (Kaempfer & Pacey, 1986; Fizel & Bennett, 1989), and National Football League fans (Putsis & Sen, 2000; Zuber & Gander, 1988; Siegfried & Hinshaw, 1979).

Notes

1 Of course, the Cubs' performance in the season leading up to their 2016 World Series Championship win turned the tide for the team and its fans. Nonetheless, the message indicated by franchise's ticket sales performance in less successful years remains valuable.
2 The Rams presided in Los Angeles from 1946 until 1994, before moving to St. Louis in 1995. The team returned to Los Angeles for the 2016 season.
3 See Coates and Humphreys (2005) for more stadium novelty effect estimates.
4 EGLS was used with the log of attendance as the dependent variable. Winning percentage, last year's winning percentage, year fixed effects, and team fixed effects were the only independent variables used.

References

Allan, S. 2004. Satellite television and football attendance: The not so super effect. *Applied Economics Letter* 11 (2): 123–125.

Allan, G., & Roy, G. 2008. Does television crowd out spectators? New evidence from the Scottish Premier League. *Journal of Sports Economics* 9 (6): 592–605.

Baimbridge, M., Cameron, S., & Dawson, P. 1995. Satellite broadcasting and match attendance: The case of rugby league. *Applied Economics Letters* 2 (10): 343–346.

Baimbridge, M., Cameron, S., & Dawson, P. 1996. Satellite television and the demand for football: A whole new ball game. *Scottish Journal of Political Economy* 43 (3): 317–333.

Berri, D., & Schmidt, M. B. 2006. On the road with the National Basketball Association's superstar externality. *Journal of Sports Economics* 7 (4): 347.

Brown, E., Spiro, R., & Keenan, D. 1991. Wage and nonwage discrimination in professional basketball: Do fans affect it? *American Journal of Economics and Sociology* 50 (3): 333–345.

Buraimo, B. 2008. Stadium attendance and television audience demand in English League Football. *Managerial and Decision Economics* 29 (6): 513.

Buraimo, B., Forrest, D., & Simmons, R. 2006. Robust estimates of the impact of broadcasting on match attendance in football (working paper). Retrieved from http://eprints.lancs.ac.uk/48824/4/BroadcastingFootball.pdf (accessed July 31, 2018).

Carmichael, F., Millington, J., & Simmons, R. 1999. Elasticity of demand for rugby league attendance and the impact of BskyB. *Applied Economics Letters* 6 (12): 797–800.

Clapp, C. M., & Hakes, J. K. 2005. How long a honeymoon? The effect of new stadiums on attendance in Major League Baseball. *Journal of Sports Economics* 6 (3): 237–263.

Coates, D., & Humphreys, B. R. 2005. Novelty effects of new facilities on attendance at professional sporting events. *Contemporary Economic Policy* 23 (3): 436–455.

Cranfield, J., Inwood, K., & Ross, A. J. 2016. Ethnic inequality in professional sport: A question of discrimination in the National Hockey League draft. In *Sports through the lens of economic history*, eds. R. Pomfret and J. K. Wilson, 128–146. Northampton, MA: Edward Elgar .

Davis, M. C. 2009. Analyzing the relationship between team success and MLB attendance with GARCH effects. *Journal of Sports Economics* 10 (1): 44–58.

Druckman, J. N., Howat, A. J., & Rodheim, A. 2016. The influence of race on attitudes about college athletics. *Sport in Society* 19 (7): 1020–1039.

Fizel, J., & Bennett, R. 1989. The impact of college football telecast on college football attendance. *Social Science Quarterly* 70 (4): 980–988.

Forrest, D., & Simmons, R. 2002. Outcome uncertainty and attendance demand in sport: The case of English soccer. *Journal of the Royal Statistics Society*, Series D, 51 (2): 229–241.

Forrest, D., Simmons, R., & Szymanski, S. 2004. Broadcasting, attendance and the inefficiency of cartel. *Review of Industrial Organization* 24 (3): 243–265.

Gitter, S., & Rhoads, T. 2008. If you win they will come: Fans care about winning in minor league baseball (working paper). Retrieved from http://citeseerx.ist.psu.edu/viewdoc/download?doi=10.1.1.571.577&rep=rep1&type=pdf (accessed July 31, 2018).

Hausman, J. A. and Leonard, G. K. 1997. Superstars in the National Basketball Association: Economic value and policy. *Journal of Labor Economics*, 15 (4) 586–624.

Janssen, S., Rubin, D., & Conway, M. 2012. The reminiscence bump in the temporal distribution of the best football players of all time: Pele, Cruijff or Maradona? *The Quarterly Journal of Experimental Psychology* 65 (1): 165–178.

Kaempfer, W., & Pacey, P. 1986. Televising college football: The complementarity of attendance and viewing. *Social Science Quarterly* 67 (1): 176–185.

Kahane, L., & Shmanske, S. 1997. Team roster turnover and attendance in Major League Baseball. *Applied Economics* 29: 425–431.

Kahn, L. M., & Sherer, P. 1988. Racial differences in professional basketball players' compensation. *Journal of Labor Economics* 6 (1): 40–61.

Kanazawa, M. T., & Funk, J. P. 2001. Racial discrimination in professional basketball: Evidence from Nielsen Ratings. *Economic Inquiry* 39 (4): 599–608.

Krautmann, A. C. 2009. Market size and the demand for talent in Major League Baseball. *Applied Economics* 41 (25): 3267–3273.

Leadley, J. C., & Zygmont, Z. X. 2005. When is the honeymoon over? National Basketball Association attendance 1971–2000. *Journal of Sports Economics* 6 (2): 203–221.

Leadley, J. C., & Zygmont, Z. X. 2006. When is the honeymoon over? National Hockey League attendance 1970–2003. *Canadian Public Policy/Analyse de Politiques* 32 (2): 213–232.

Longley, N. 1995. Salary discrimination in the National Hockey League: The effects of team location. *Canadian Public Policy* 21 (4): 413–422.

Longley, N. 2006. Racial discrimination. In *Handbook on the economics of sport*, eds. W. Andreff and S. Szymanski, 757–765. Northampton, MA: Edward Elgar.

Matheson, V. A. 2006. The effects of labour strikes on consumer demand in professional sports: revisited. *Applied Economics* 28 (10): 1173–1179.

McEvoy, C. D., Nagel, M. S., DeSchriver, T. D., & Brown, M. T. 2005. Facility age and attendance in Major League Baseball. *Sport Management Review* 8 (1): 19–41.

Miller, P. 2008. Major league duopolists: When baseball clubs play in two-team cities, (working paper). Retrieved from http://repository.stcloudstate.edu/econ_seminars/7/ (accessed July 31, 2018).

Morse, A. L., Shapiro, S. L., McEvoy, C. D., & Rascher, D. A. 2008. The effects of roster turnover on demand in the National Basketball Association. *International Journal of Sport Finance* (3): 8–18.

Paul, R. J., & Weinbach, A. P. 2015. The betting market as a forecast of television ratings for primetime NFL football. *International Journal of Sport Finance* 10 (3): 284–296.

Putsis, W., & Sen, S. 2000. Should NFL blackouts be banned? *Applied Economics* 32 (12): 1495–1507.

Schmidt, M. B., & Berri, D. J. 2001. Competitive balance and attendance: The case of Major League Baseball. *Journal of Sports Economics* 2 (2): 145–167.

Schmidt, M. B., & Berri, D. J. 2002. The impact of the 1981 and 1994–1995 strikes on Major League Baseball attendance: A time-series analysis. *Applied Economics* 34 (4): 471–478.

Schmidt, M. B., & Berri, D. J. 2004. The impact of labor strikes on consumer demand: An application to professional sports. *American Economic Review* 94 (1): 344–357.

Scully, G. W. 1974. Discrimination: The case of baseball. In *Government and the sports business*, ed. R. Noll, 221–273. Washington DC: The Brookings Institution.

Siegfried, J., & Hinshaw, C. E. 1979. The effect of lifting television blackouts on professional football no-shows. *Journal of Economics and Business* 32: 1–13.

Sloane, P. J. 1976. Restrictions on competition in professional team sports. *Bulletin of Economic Research* 28 (1): 3–22.

Stephens-Davidowitz, S. 2014. They hook you when you're young, *New York Times*. Retrieved from http://www.nytimes.com/2014/04/20/opinion/sunday/they-hook-you-when-youre-young.html?_r=0 (accessed July 31, 2018).

Szymanski, S. 2003. The economic design of sporting contests. *Journal of Economic Literature* 41 (4): 1137–1187.

Tainsky, S. 2010. Television broadcast demand for National Football League contests. *Journal of Sports Economics* 11 (6): 629–640.

Tainsky, S., & Winfree, J. 2010. Discrimination and demand: The effect of international players on attendance in Major League Baseball. *Social Science Quarterly* 91 (1): 117–128.

Winfree, J., & Fort, R. 2008. Fan substitution and the 2004–05 NHL lock out. *Journal of Sports Economics* 9 (4): 425–434.

Winfree, J., McCluskey, J., Mittelhammer, R., & Fort, R. 2004. Location and attendance in Major League Baseball. *Applied Economics* 36: 2117–2124.

Zuber, R., & Gandar, J. 1988. Lifting the TV blackout on no-shows at football games. *Atlantic Economic Journal* 16 (2): 63–73.

Chapter 10

Pricing Strategies

Introduction

One of the most important financial decisions that any team makes is the price charged for each of its products. The rules of basic economics tell us that if a team charges a high price for any of its products, it is likely that fewer units will be sold. If products have low prices, then more units are sold. As discussed in Chapter 9, demand is affected by many factors. This means that the optimal price also is affected by those same factors. For example, teams will charge a higher ticket price when they have a new facility. Those higher prices are a reflection of the improvements that range from better sight lines, to improved technology that enhances the fan experience, to wider seats and concourses that make it easier and far more pleasant to be at a facility.

Pricing in sport quickly becomes more complicated, however, when one thinks about the many different aspects of fan consumption and how those various avenues contribute to gross revenues and profits. For example, because revenues come from various sources, teams must decide on prices for many different components. A team could price tickets lower, hoping that fans impressed with "bargain" admission prices decide to spend more on food, beverages, and souvenirs sold at the facility, which have high profit margins. Managers must remember that sport products are not sold in a vacuum but are part of a fan's "game day experience" and their relationship to and with the team. The goal is always to ensure fans' long-term commitment to the team. That commitment is critical because there will be years when the team's on-field success wanes; it is imperative, even in those seasons, that fans still want to attend games.

At the same time, managers have to remember that those fans who are spending premium prices for seats or food and beverages may insist upon or expect segregated entrances, clubs, and seating that offers far better sight lines than those available to fans seated in areas with far lower ticket prices. Placing luxury seating too close to the grandstands reduces the value produced and, subsequently, the prices that can be charged. Simply put, premium seats must offer far better sight lines, exclusivity, and elevated amenities to protect the demand for that product. In addition, every team is focused on growing its fan base as ticket revenue has begun to decline as a percentage of teams' gross earnings. Sport managers have to be focused on efforts to attract or create new fans. Each league, for example, has developed programs designed to appeal to women, and new facilities often have improved women's restroom facilities. MLB has implemented a program to re-engage inner city youth in baseball in an effort to grow their fan base. Teams in each of the leagues are actively engaged in youth programs, and these community service activities not only create goodwill but new fans. Several MLB teams offer day game seats to youth groups at discount prices to build their fan bases.

Every team's ticket pricing structure is set in such a way that there is an appropriate mix of expensive premium seats, and an adequate supply of relatively inexpensive seats. In this way, far more people can afford to attend a game. Some NBA teams offer tickets that cost as little as $10 to ensure that the game is affordable to a large segment of its fan base. This chapter examines various pricing strategies and the factors that affect prices.

Ticket Prices

Setting ticket prices is a complex task because it requires understanding exactly how much fans are willing to pay. In most instances, prices are established by the team. Team executives estimate demand and then price tickets accordingly to be sure that the maximum number of fans can or will attend. This is also achieved through experience; prices are changed as team executives receive feedback from fans or as they observe attendance trends. Although not increasing as fast as some other revenue streams, the income earned from ticket sales can be a large factor in a team's financial stability and in determining its profitability. Over the years, it has become more expensive to attend a game. For example, in 2017, the average ticket price for a regular season Boston Red Sox game was $97. This is compared with an average ticket price of $9.33 in 1991 ($17.10 in 2017 dollars), increasing the cost by 467 percent. Average ticket prices in the NFL increased from $25 in the early 1990s ($45.82 in 2017 dollars) to approximately $85.83 in 2017 (an 87 percent increase in ticket cost). Fans are constantly describing how it is more and more difficult to bring a family to a game.

Team Marketing Report is a company that has produced a "Fan Cost Index" for teams in each of the four major leagues since 1991. Fan Cost Index, or FCI, measures the average cost to take a family of four to a single, regular-season game in an "average" seat. The MLB's league-wide average FCI during the 2016 season was $219.53 (Team Marketing Report, 2016). As one might expect, several popular and successful large market teams (Red Sox, Yankees, and Cubs, among others) have FCIs that are well above the league average; the FCI for each of these teams exceeded $300 in 2016.

The Arizona Diamondbacks, on the other hand, were the best bargain at $132.10. Figure 10.1 shows the FCI for all four major leagues across the past two decades.

This chart supports several important observations. First, MLB ticket prices are quite a bit less than tickets to games in the other leagues. Presumably this is because MLB has more games than the other leagues and cannot expect fans to pay as much when the supply is so much greater. NFL teams play ten home games (including preseason). MLB teams play eight times as many games at their home ballparks. Second, while ticket prices for NHL and NBA games were at the same level as the NFL through the 1990s, the NFL is now quite a bit more expensive. The reason for this divergence is not entirely clear. While the NFL has certainly been successful in recent years, it is unclear that there was a divergence of demand of the magnitude suggested by the price increase. Third, NFL and MLB teams have been increasing prices for the most part across the past few decades, even in real terms.

Figure 10.2 indicates the minimum and maximum ticket prices charged by NFL teams over the last 26 years. The league average ticket price is also included for comparison. Ticket prices (in real terms) have been increasing, and the maximum average ticket price is roughly twice the minimum average ticket price.

The same changes for MLB appear in Figure 10.3. While ticket prices are lower when compared to the NFL, maximum average ticket prices skyrocketed across the past decade, but minimum prices did not increase at the same rate. One might be tempted to credit (or blame!) the New York Yankees for this; however, for the 26 years that data are available, the Yankees have had the highest ticket prices only four times. It is true that they had the highest

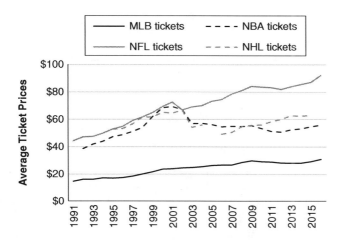

Figure 10.1 Average Ticket Prices ($2016), 1991–2016.

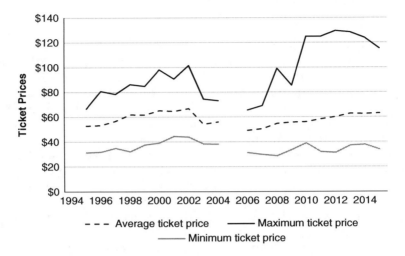

Figure 10.2 NHL Ticket Price Changes ($2016), 1996–2015.

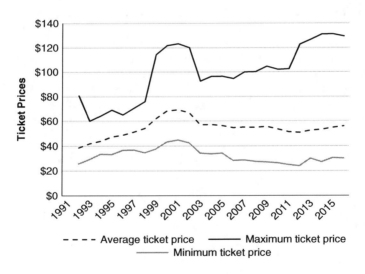

Figure 10.3 NBA Ticket Price Changes ($2016), 1991–2016.

ticket price in 2009 (the first year of their new stadium), but the other three years were all before 1998. For the most recent seasons, the Boston Red Sox have had the highest average ticket price as a result of the relatively small capacity of Fenway Park.

In the NBA (Figure 10.4), average ticket prices have remained somewhat low and are increasing about at the same rate as inflation. Premium NBA

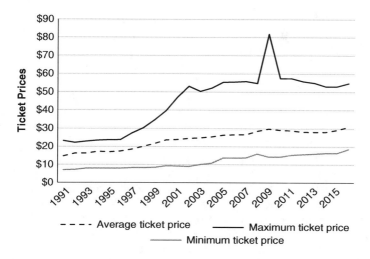

Figure 10.4 MLB Ticket Price Changes ($2016), 1991–2016.

tickets seem to oscillate up and down, but there does seem to be a general upward trend. The most expensive tickets are typically for the New York Knicks and the Los Angeles Lakers.

Finally, for the NHL (Figure 10.5), average ticket prices have been pretty flat over the last couple of decades. While there is some variation, ticket prices have not increased much once adjusted for inflation. What is particularly interesting is that ticket prices were low right before and after the 2004 lockout. Teams may have had to drop ticket prices the season before to lure

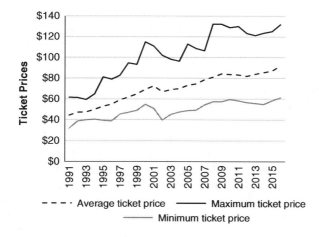

Figure 10.5 NFL Ticket Price Changes ($2016), 1991–2016.

fans who knew a work stoppage was eminent. They may have had lower ticket prices the year after to lure fans back to the league.

Are Ticket Prices Too High, Too Low, or Just Right?

The ticket prices charged by teams have been somewhat of a puzzle to economists, not because prices are too *high*, but because they are too *low*. While a number of fans will claim that prices are clearly too high from their perspective, virtually all research shows that, on average, professional teams actually set their ticket prices too low, at least if they are trying to maximize ticket revenue. Some teams might have prices that are high, and it is hard to argue otherwise with some of the previous examples. As a rule, however, teams set prices relatively low. That is, if teams increased their ticket prices, ticket revenue would increase. For those who doubt this observation, a quick check of any online ticket reselling service will illustrate that, for most teams and for most games, there is a vibrant market where tickets are sold for prices that exceed what the teams charge.

Basic economics suggests that raising ticket prices can have three effects on profits. The first is that an increase in price increases the cash inflow for each ticket sold. The second is that, at higher prices, a team will sell fewer tickets, which decreases cash inflow. The third is that higher prices will decrease costs because there are fewer fans. When there are large crowds, teams might spend more in the form of extra security or for janitorial services and maintenance. However, the cost to the team of one extra fan attending a game is not large, so marginal costs are negligible. Basically, teams weigh the per ticket gain from the price increase with the feared decrease in the number of tickets sold. Most businesses will raise prices until the benefit of increasing prices equals the cost of raising prices. In the absence of variable (marginal) costs, this means maximizing revenue. If teams are maximizing revenue from tickets, their ticket prices should be such that a 1 percent increase in prices leads to a 1 percent decrease in the number of tickets sold. At this point, it is impossible to get more revenue from ticket sales. If prices are above this point, not enough people are buying tickets. If prices are below this point, the team is not getting enough revenue from each sale.[1] The statistical analysis done to date argues that ticket prices are too low to be maximizing ticket revenue.

Although firms will always want to maximize profit rather than revenues, in sport these two things are almost the same. Because, as previously stated, the marginal cost of an extra fan is small, there is little difference between profit maximization and revenue maximization. Figure 10.6 shows the difference between a profit maximizing and revenue maximizing price.

Statistical analysis shows that when teams do raise ticket prices, it has very little effect on attendance. In the NFL, for example, almost every game is sold out. As a result, an increase in ticket prices has virtually no effect on

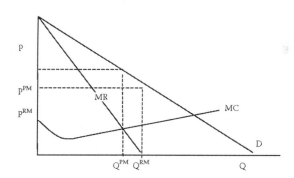

Figure 10.6 Profit Maximizing vs. Revenue Maximizing.

how many people attend the game. This, in and of itself, is evidence that ticket prices are too low. Certainly, if most NFL teams increased ticket prices by $1, they would still sell out. The only change is that the team's profit would increase at the expense of fans. In other leagues, where sell-outs are less common, raising ticket prices still doesn't change attendance levels very much. For example, in 2007 the Los Angeles Dodgers raised ticket prices by 26.9 percent. Their attendance actually increased by more than 1,200 fans per game even though they won six fewer games. There is example after countless example of this phenomenon in professional team sport. While few people would argue that raising ticket prices is the cause of an increase in attendance, it *does not* seem to have a large negative effect.

There also is other anecdotal evidence that ticket prices are too low. For instance, at many sporting events, ticket resellers offer tickets for much higher than face value. While teams do not like this practice, teams know that these resellers often enjoy robust profits, providing evidence that prices are too low. Every year Super Bowl tickets are sold for many times their face value. For example, in 2015, the face value for tickets to Super Bowl XLIX were between $500 and $1500. While most people would consider this a lot of money, many tickets ended up being sold online for more than ten times their face value. These unexpected prices created a problem for some ticket dealers. Many brokers had already sold tickets to fans before they actually had the tickets. While this is not entirely uncommon, the unexpected jump in ticket prices created a situation where brokers would have to pay much more for the ticket then they received from the fan. This caused some brokers to lose their business and some fans were not able to go to the game. The question that emerges, then, is why doesn't the NFL sell the tickets at that value in the first place? Furthermore, both fans and teams know certain games are virtually guaranteed to sell out, meaning that a marginal increase in ticket prices will not affect the size of the crowd in any way.

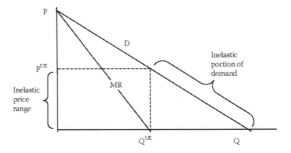

Figure 10.7 Inelastic Pricing.

When prices are too low, that is to say that a price increase will have a relatively small effect on quantity sold, the pricing is labeled *inelastic*. When prices are too high, a price increase will have a large effect on quantity sold, and that is an example of *elastic* pricing. If the price is such that a 1 percent increase causes a 1 percent decrease in quantity, the phenomenon is labeled *unit elastic*. This is the price that maximizes revenue. If additional fans increase a team's cost, then the team should actually have elastic ticket prices to maximize profits. As previously argued, the price for most tickets are actually low, so it is in the inelastic portion of demand.

Figure 10.7 illustrates inelastic pricing. As the figure shows, with inelastic pricing, not only are prices lower than the unit elastic price level (revenue maximizing prices are equal to the unit elastic price), the number of tickets sold is higher than the optimal level. Geometrically, a manager should think about the total revenue being the price multiplied by the quantity. As a result, revenue can be represented by the rectangle shown in Figure 10.7. The rectangle is the largest when the price and quantity are at the unit elastic levels.

Why are Ticket Prices Inelastic?

There are many potential explanations for inelastic pricing (Fort, 2004a). The different possibilities are defined below.

More Fans at the Game Mean Increased Concession Sales

While charging low ticket prices does not maximize ticket revenue, it does get more fans to the game. This would imply that teams have an incentive to get fans into their facility, even if it means decreasing ticket revenue. As noted, teams sell a variety of products. When more fans come to the game, this could help other sources of revenue. The most obvious source of revenue that a high attendance helps is parking and concessions (Zimbalist,

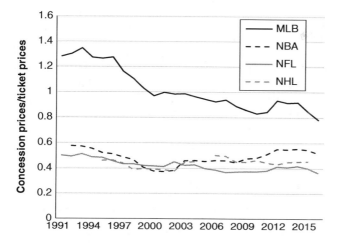

Figure 10.8 Ratio of Concession to Ticket Prices for the Four Major Sports Leagues.

1992; Krautmann & Berri, 2007; Coates & Humphreys, 2007). When there are more fans at the game, there are more consumers buying parking or concessions, both of which are often important sources of revenue for the team.

Figure 10.8 illustrates the ratio of concession prices and ticket prices. Of course, fans do not always buy the same concessions, but the graph gives us a sense of how important concessions are for each league. Concessions used in this graph are one-fourth of the Fan Cost Index with an average ticket price subtracted.[2] While the Fan Cost Index certainly overestimates what the average fan spends at a game, this does show us how leagues vary with each other and over time.

One clear conclusion from the graph is that MLB earns a higher percentage of its revenue from concessions compared to other leagues. This may be due to the fact that MLB has the lowest average ticket prices. Appendix 2 shows an economic model where the benefit of fans at the game is more than just ticket revenue.

More Fans at the Game Increase Advertising and Sponsorship Sales

Again, a low ticket price means more fans will attend the game. When more fans are at the game, it also is easier to find sponsors or advertisers that are willing to pay for ad space in the facility. If there are more fans at the game, there are more people looking at the advertisements. Therefore, demand for advertising increases and teams can charge a higher price for advertising space or sponsorship, which can be a very important source of revenue.

More Fans at the Game Lead to a Larger Fan Base

Bigger crowds also mean more potential fans. In particular, those fans that are not fervently committed to a team may be enticed by lower ticket prices and then more likely to return to a game or become more devoted fans of the team (Ahn & Lee, 2007; Lee & Smith, 2008). As friends and family of fans know, rooting for a team can be addictive. Sometimes getting somebody to the game can make them a fan for life. Not only does this mean a higher attendance in the future, it also means higher television ratings and more merchandise sales in the future. Therefore, getting more fans to the game with low ticket prices might provide increased revenue in the future.

More Fans at the Game Increases Television Audiences

If there are more fans at games, then it is likely that television ratings might also be enhanced as people are more interested in following the team. Most fans like watching games on television when there are a lot of fans in a venue. Larger crowds are more likely to create a more exciting feel to the game. Thus, if a lower ticket price leads to a larger crowd, this might help television ratings or the experience of every fan in attendance. In response, teams have made efforts to enhance the views of fans in their venues for television. Usually, if there are empty seats, television cameras try to hide it.

While the effect of attendance on television appears to be positive, the effect of television on attendance is less clear. Many team owners have indicated concern that televising games will reduce the number of people that are willing to go to the game. Universities, too, were worried that broadcasting games would lead to lower attendance. European football leagues have claimed that televising a game leads to a smaller crowd. Also, televising baseball games was once thought to have caused the dramatic decrease in minor league baseball teams in the 1950s. The data cannot sustain the fears of lower attendance. While attendance at televised European football matches is slightly lower, leagues that embrace television seem to do very well in the long run. While some fans might stay home and watch the game, more people become fans and might go to the game in the future.

Lower Prices Help a Team's Image and Reputation

The first four explanations of why ticket prices are inelastic each involve getting more fans to the stadium. However, there seems to be some other explanation needed with regard to the decision to raise prices because some teams sell out consistently. For example, the Green Bay Packers have a season ticket waiting list of more than 100,000 people. Their games have been sold out since 1960. The Toronto Maple Leafs have a waiting list that is "decades long." Certainly, these teams could sell the same number of tickets if they increased the price a little bit. In other words, a change in price would have absolutely no impact on attendance. But there is also value to having these waiting lists, or to having a remarkable number of consecutive sellouts.

Teams that sell out their games or have long waiting lists tend to advertise this fact. Even if the team does not advertise these things, other fans will. Most fans want to know if a team's games typically sell out. It gives the fan two signals. One is that the team's ticket is a "hot item" and they should want to go; the other is that they should get their ticket early. Those signals or perceptions are valuable marketing tools for a team.

Lower Prices Produce Goodwill

Another explanation unrelated to getting more fans to a facility is that low-ticket prices may give the team some goodwill with fans. If the fans believe they are being gouged, they are less sympathetic toward things like the public sector's investment in facility (Fort, 2004b). If facilities have already been built with public money, it may be a disservice to the community to have high ticket prices. Regardless of public money, because sports teams are very public businesses, managers certainly want the team thought of in a positive way. It is clearly important for sports teams to have a strong, positive public image.

Teams Actually Are Pricing in the Elastic Part of Demand

Why does statistical analysis show that ticket prices are too low? One final explanation is that the statistical analyses are incorrect. Economists try to understand the demand for tickets. They control for things such as the quality of the team, types of players, quality of the stadium, local population, average income, recent work stoppages, other sports teams in the area, day of the week, time of the game, quality of the opponent, and many other things that affect how badly fans want to watch the game live. It is possible, however, that economists are simply not doing a good enough job. For example, the New York Yankees have a higher ticket price and higher attendance than the Pittsburgh Pirates. In fact, teams with higher ticket prices tend to have a higher attendance. Does this mean that higher ticket prices cause a higher attendance? No. This means that other factors, such as market size, team quality, or team brand cause demand to be different for different teams. If demand is high for a team, prices and attendance also should both be high. This means that the challenge for researchers is to completely control for these other factors. If managers understand the dynamics of their markets, then researchers might mistakenly find that teams are pricing their tickets too low.

While it is possible that statistical analysis does not perfectly estimate the effect of ticket prices on attendance, in all likelihood, the analysis is correct in showing that ticket prices are low. Most researchers are diligent in their attempt to find correct estimates, and there is other evidence that ticket prices are too low. Remember, if ticket prices were optimizing ticket revenue, we would not see as much reselling, nor as many sellouts.

Price Discrimination

Price discrimination is when firms charge different customers different prices for identical goods. There are many types and degrees of price discrimination, and teams use most of them. Many franchises will sell identical seats at different prices, depending on who buys them. Although this might be less common with major professional teams, teams might give a senior citizen or child discount just like the zoo or the movies, for example. This is because senior citizens and children (or rather, families with children) typically have a lower demand than other fans. Because their demand is lower, teams can generate more revenue bringing these fans into the venue at a lower ticket price, as these fans are likely to spend money on other in-venue items such as concessions and merchandise. Remember, even though children might love to go to games, a reasonable substitute might be the zoo or the movies. If the price for admission to those activities is lower, their parents' willingness to pay higher prices for their tickets to a game will be understandably lower. From a financial standpoint, the more teams dissect the demand curve, the more revenue they can generate. In other words, if a team can better guess a customer's willingness to pay by some characteristic, then they can more efficiently set prices. Figure 10.9 shows this graphically. It is assumed that some groups (we will call them "fanatics") have a very high demand for sport. We refer to the people that have a lower demand as "casual fans." The team will get more revenue if it can charge fanatics and casual fans different prices.

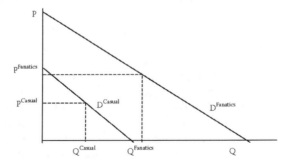

Figure 10.9 Price Discrimination.

Another common example of price discrimination is student discounts. Often, university students pay less for tickets than the general public. There are a few reasons for this, especially if students are paying for tickets at their own university. Because students are already paying for tuition, it may not seem fair to charge them the same price as other people. Also, the university might have an interest in getting students to the game so they develop a deep allegiance. Another reason is that they have less disposable income, so they might have a lower demand than others. Therefore, they are charged a lower price.

Luxury Seats and the "Deck"

To this juncture, pricing has been discussed as if a single product was being sold for every ticket to each game, but in reality, nothing could be further from the truth. As any fan knows, luxury seats and those in sections closer to the playing surface are more expensive than the "nosebleeds," far from the action. While luxury products and nosebleed seats are far from being identical goods, the difference between both products is similar, in some ways, to price discrimination. Offering both luxury seating products and more average, less expensive options in the seating deck is a way to separate fans on the high end of the demand curve with fans on the low end.

Bulk and Group Discounts

The price of a ticket is subject to change if tickets are bought for multiple games, or for multiple people. Many teams offer multiple-game packages at a slightly cheaper rate. All teams offer season ticket packages as well as other multigame packages. Again, bulk and group discounts are related to price discrimination. It might be the case that some fans get diminishing returns from attending games. That is, they would really like to go to one game, but after that they become less interested. Therefore, demand decreases for multiple games. Many teams offer a discount if fans attend multiple games in response to this phenomenon. In addition, large groups of fans might be able to get a discount for a particular game. Financially, this is similar to multiple-game packages. Many fans in a group may have a relatively low demand for attending a game and they may be more likely to attend if the tickets are cheaper, or if they can go with a large group of their friends, family, or colleagues.

Product Bundling

As with many service industries, teams often bundle goods with ticket purchases. Product bundling refers to offering multiple goods and selling them as one. The idea is similar to selling in bulk, but instead of selling a multiple number of one good at a time, it is selling multiple different goods at one time. Usually sellers are willing to sell at a discount if the buyers commit to buying multiple items. Sport seems to be an ideal situation for bundling because an empty seat is a perishable good (it is worthless after the game is over). As a result, the goal for many teams is simply to get fans to the game. Even though the cost is often very high to produce a big-time sporting event, it costs virtually nothing to have additional fans at the game. Therefore, if teams can offer other things to entice some fans, it can be worthwhile.

Items that are commonly bundled with tickets are parking and concessions. Often luxury seating comes with many complimentary items, such as food, beverages, or souvenirs (e.g., game-day programs, midgame statistics reports). Furthermore, sometimes teams can offer items to fans that no one else can. For example, only the franchise can offer some unique experience with the team (e.g., standing along the runway where players enter the field). Some teams offer season ticket holders special events with players or a former player. While these items or events are "free" with the purchase of the ticket, in reality, the tickets are priced higher because of these additional amenities. Ticket resellers also have used bundling with tickets, but for a different reason. While there may be a legal limit on resale price of a ticket, clever entrepreneurs circumvent these restrictions by bundling services into the tickets. These services (or extra goods) have included simple things like a pencil or coffee cup, or delivery services. Frequently there are no limits on the resale price of a ticket if it is attached to other goods and services provided by a reseller.

It is increasingly popular for teams to bundle other goods with tickets, but only if certain things happen during the game. Teams are also tying giveaways to game statistics. The example of the 2010 Seattle Seahawks is illustrative. When the Seahawks defeated the San Diego Chargers, fans received a free 7-Eleven slurpee and an Oberto beef jerky (because the team scored a touchdown in the red zone), six free toppings on a Papa John's pizza (they scored three touchdowns and won), a small stack of buttermilk pancakes at the International House of Pancakes (they scored 21 points), Jack in the Box Jumbo Jack burger (more than three sacks of the opposing quarterback), and Top Pot doughnuts (more than 100 yards passing). As if those inducements were not sufficient, 50 fans received a yearly Xbox subscription because there were two kickoff returns for touchdowns, and one fan won tickets from Seattle to Hawaii as the Seahawks scored with less than two minutes remaining in the half. If only the Seahawks would have scored a defensive touchdown, fans would have received a free haircut from Great Clips (Rovell, 2010).

Product bundling has strong marketing advantages. For example, product giveaways are simply bundling items together. Hats, bats, bobble head dolls, and posters are common examples. One of the more famous examples is the all-you-can-eat section at Dodger Stadium in Los Angeles in the Right

Field Pavilion (alcoholic beverages are not included). The obvious question is whether or not it is wise to offer an all-you-can-eat section. Most people's first thought is of the potentially unlimited cost of food that some fans might eat. But, how much could it really cost to produce a large number of Dodger Dogs? As with many of these pricing strategies, the real question is: what would these fans have spent if there were no all-you-can-eat section? The Dodgers hope that most of these fans would not have come to the game if it were not for these seats. In this case, each fan represents an additional $33 and maybe they will buy a beer or some souvenirs. Furthermore, if new fans have a good time and come back again, revenues increase, and they might become lifelong Dodger fans. The Dodgers' fear is that an unusually large number of Dodger fans, who would have attended the game without the all-you-can-eat offer, self-select themselves and purchase seats in the Right Field Pavilion. Maybe these fans were already spending $50 on a ticket and food before the promotion. If that is the case, then the Dodgers would gain few benefits from the promotion. Given that a number of teams are now offering all-you-can-eat seats, it seems likely that a large number of the people attending are new fans generating additional revenue for the team.

Like professional teams, universities also participate in product bundling by including admission to more than one sport if a ticket is purchased for a very popular team. The University of Michigan frequently offers free or discounted admission to soccer games with a ticket stub to a football game, for example.

Variable Ticket Pricing

More and more teams are charging different prices for different games. It has long been the case that playoff tickets were generally more expensive than regular season games. Some teams are now changing their regular season ticket pricing based on the opponent, which is known as *variable ticket pricing*. As discussed in Chapter 9, demand changes based on the opponent. Therefore, teams can maximize profit by charging different prices based on the opponent. Teams like the San Francisco Giants will charge a lower price if the visiting team is not a team that typically draws well. In MLB, having the Yankees as an opponent typically increases attendance between 20 and 30 percent compared with some other teams (Weinbach, Paul, & Melvin, 2004). Teams know this, and now many of them are charging a higher ticket price when the Yankees visit. This practice is increasingly popular in North American leagues. For example, some NHL teams have raised prices for games against popular teams (Wyshynski, 2008). While it might make economic sense to charge different prices for "premium games," if the practice aggravates fans, the additional revenue might generate other costs that lead to an overall decline in revenue levels.

Day of Game Pricing

When consumers buy a ticket on the day of an event, the price charged is sometimes less than the price paid by those who made their purchase far earlier. Some teams also raise the price of a ticket on game day to encourage advance purchases. Ultimately, the best pricing approach depends on the price elasticity of consumers who buy tickets early compared with consumers who buy tickets late. It might be the case that fans who buy tickets early are the most dedicated and do not want to take a chance on missing the game. If this is the case, then demand is very inelastic and a change in price will not result in a dramatic change in the quantity sold. Fans who buy tickets at the last minute might be more passive, and more likely to forego the game if prices were higher (more elastic). If this is the case, then a discount for fans who buy tickets on the day of the game would be appropriate.

Alternatively, it might be the case that fans are not worried about ticket availability, but rather they are worried about their own availability or desire to go to the game. There is a value to being able to wait to decide to attend a game. Fans might end up not wanting to go to a game because something else came up or maybe the team's performance has declined. If a fan can get the same ticket on game day as months earlier, one would think they would wait to make their purchase. In this case, demand for tickets could be higher or more inelastic on game day and prices should be slightly higher.

Also, if it is easier for teams logistically to have the tickets sold earlier, then there should be an additional charge on game day. In 2010, the Baltimore Orioles began charging slightly more for tickets on the day of the game. They ostensibly believed that fans were not as concerned about ticket availability as they were with being able to wait to buy their tickets. Or, it was better for them to have fans buy tickets early. Either way, charging fans more when they procrastinate and giving "early" fans a break could increase their revenue.

Dynamic Pricing

Several teams have started to use dynamic pricing. This means that prices change depending on shifts in demand. If sales are high for a particular game and there are few seats left, prices for that game will increase. If sales are lagging, prices will decrease. Not only does this method respond to changes in the demand fans have to attend a particular game, it also adjusts if demand was not estimated properly. For example, if a team starts to perform well, demand will increase, and in a dynamic pricing system, the cost for tickets will rise. Also, if demand is higher than previously thought at the beginning of the season, then dynamic pricing will increase and adjust to reflect demand. There is one drawback that is similar to variable ticket pricing: some fans resent the fact that others paid less for their ticket. This can be a common issue for sports teams when they issue discounts for certain seats or games.

Auction Pricing

Some teams are beginning to sell tickets using auctions. For example, Northwestern University has started to sell tickets using "Purple Pricing," which is type of Dutch Auction. This means that the university initially sets a high price for tickets and then lets the price fall until enough fans have purchased tickets. Once the auction is completed, everyone pays the final price of the auction, which is lower than the initial price. In this system, if fans are willing to pay at the current price, there is no reason for them to "game" the system by waiting.

Personal Seat Licenses

Another important trend in ticket pricing is personal seat licenses (PSLs). PSLs can cost from a few hundred dollars to tens of thousands of dollars. Although this mechanism can vary, fans buying a PSL have the right to buy future season ticket packages. Sometimes fans who buy a PSL receive a discounted price for each future ticket purchase. Those who do not buy a PSL pay a higher price. PSLs are often sold before a new facility is built so the team (or public sector, if there is a shared financing plan) has more "up-front" money and, therefore, needs to borrow less to pay for the cost of construction. NFL teams have most often sold PSLs.

The Utah Jazz, the Toronto Raptors and Maple Leafs (for the Air Canada Centre), and the Charlotte Bobcats also sold PSLs to help offset the cost of the arenas in which they play. The Carolina Panthers were able to raise $100 million in after-tax revenue from their sale of PSLs (Ostfield, 1995). Combined, the New York Giants and the New York Jets raised more than $500 million for their new stadium through PSLs.

Many things, including team quality and market size, affect the price of the PSLs (Salaga & Winfree, 2015). First, the scale of the investment has led to the creation of secondary markets as fans look at their PSLs as investments and assets that could be sold if they wanted to liquidate their investment. Of course, the value of their investment rises and falls with the quality of play. In some markets, however, where there are very long waiting lists to buy tickets, the value of a PSL could increase.

Second, the income generated by PSLs is nothing more than the present value of a per ticket surcharge. In other words, fans purchasing PSLs simply impute or add that value to the price of the ticket. The team could dispense with PSLs and charge higher ticket prices, or it could charge a PSL and a lower ticket price. The market that exists for the PSL and the ticket is the same. For the team or a city, the PSL generates more up-front cash. The value of the PSL does improve a team's cash flow and, therefore, can be seen as more beneficial. The risk or drawback is that asking in advance for money as opposed to a payment each year can alienate some fans.

Colleges and universities have also started issuing PSLs, although sometimes they are identified as contributions (donations or gifts). Often colleges will require fans to make an annual contribution that is a de facto PSL. Even when colleges do not have this system, those individuals who make large donations typically receive the opportunity to purchase the best seats for games. Thus, the donation becomes a PSL of sorts. Regardless of whether it is part of an official PSL program or not, a portion of these annual prepayment contributions is treated as a tax deduction (contribution to a nonprofit organization) under the existing U.S. Internal Revenue Code.

One question that arises is: why do teams have PSLs? In other words, why don't teams just simply raise ticket prices instead of making fans pay for a PSL and then also pay for their season tickets? There are a couple of possible explanations for this. One reason is that revenue generated from PSLs is often treated differently than other revenue. For example, in the NFL, revenue from PSLs is not shared with other clubs or the players. Ticket revenue, however, is included in the revenue sharing plan. Teams can only issue a PSL when they are building or renovating a stadium. Therefore, PSLs are a way for the NFL to give teams an incentive to build a new stadium, which helps the league.

Another possible explanation for the increase in PSLs is two-part pricing, also called a two-part tariff. Two-part pricing also is used by businesses, such as Sam's Club or Costco. Customers pay a membership fee and then get a discount on products. In sport, this happens at places like golf courses. Golfers can pay per round of golf, or they can pay an annual membership. Why would a store, golf course, or team do this? Because it can increase the quantity sold and the revenue that the firm or team receives. If there is no PSL, fans will pay for tickets until their willingness to pay is at least as great as the ticket price. With a PSL, however, teams can capture fans' willingness to pay for the entire season.

Suppose a team prices tickets at the optimal price and a fan is planning to buy three tickets, but the fan will buy eight tickets if they are sold at a discounted price. Clearly the fan will be happier and willing to attend more games if the tickets are discounted. To buy tickets at the discounted price, however, the team can charge for a PSL. The price of this PSL would be equal to the sum of the differences of willingness to pay and the discounted price. Therefore, the team receives more revenue with a PSL and lower ticket prices than with no PSL and higher ticket prices. Appendix 3 gives an example of this. Because most NFL games are sold out, the two-part pricing explanation seems unsatisfactory. As discussed, the NFL does not really need to sell more tickets, so the revenue-sharing explanation may be more appropriate.

Teams have tried different ways to initiate PSLs. One informative example involves the New York Jets/Giants stadium. Even though the Jets and Giants share the same stadium, they sold their PSLs in different ways. Like a vast majority of teams with PSLs, many Giants fans were unhappy with how the team set prices for their PSLs. Understandably, fans can get angry when they are required to pay for the right to buy a ticket. While some Jets fans may not have been happy about the PSLs, their club handled things differently. For some of the best seats, the Jets sold PSLs using an auction. Because demand for the PSLs was not entirely known, an auction gets fans to offer a bid at least close to their willingness to pay. Therefore, the Jets generated more revenue for some of the premium seats. Also, fans seemed less dissatisfied because the Jets let the market set the price.

In summary, PSLs should be thought of as a futures market for tickets. The PSL is itself an option. The fan buys the PSL or pays an option that means they secure seats for the future at a price that is lower than it would be if the PSL did not exist. If the team plays well and demand increases, the fan can sell the ticket or the PSL for a higher price and make a profit. If demand drops, the fan could own a PSL or tickets worth less than the face value of the investment.

Condominium Seats

For some arenas in Europe and newer arenas and stadia in North America, "condominium" or "all-event" seats have been sold in an effort to raise more revenue to reduce construction loans. One American university also sold condominium seats to pay for the cost of a facility's renovation. The price charged, usually several hundred thousand dollars, ensures the buyer that he or she can occupy a seat for every game or event that is held at the facility for a fixed period of time (that can range from one year, to 10 or 20 in some European venues). The condominium seat buyer does not have to pay for any ticket to any individual game or event during their period of tenure. In other words, just like a condominium in a building, the purchaser owns the seat for the entire duration of their "lease" and can attend every event. Managers have to carefully price these products because it commits them to provide the owner with tickets to every single event at the facility.

In the case of a university, loyalty to the institution might be a real inducement, but the purchase could make the buyer less likely to make other philanthropic gifts to the alma mater.

Futures Options

Another pricing strategy that has become more popular is selling futures options. This happens in the case of playoff tickets, which can often be hard to secure. In a manner similar to PSLs, teams and leagues have started to sell the right to buy playoff tickets for a particular team. The main difference from PSLs (or condominium seats) is that a team may or may not actually appear in the playoffs. If the team does not appear, then the buyer holding the futures ticket loses the value of his/her investment. If, however, the team does appear, then the buyer is guaranteed a seat. This has been done somewhat informally for Super Bowl tickets. Many fans would only like to purchase Super Bowl tickets if their favorite team is going to play. Once the Super Bowl teams are known, tickets often become very expensive. While the NFL sells the tickets at face value, secondary markets typically charge much more. Therefore, if one does not wish to purchase the tickets on the secondary market, it is possible to buy a futures option. That is, you can buy the right to purchase the ticket if your favorite team is playing in the Super Bowl or some other playoff game.

MLB has experimented with futures options on playoff tickets, as well. The main difference is that MLB sanctions the selling of the futures, instead of involving a third party. MLB calls this a "postseason ticket reservation." For the 2010 season, fans were able to buy these reservations for either a division series for $10, a league championship series for $15, or the World Series for $20. Given that each household was limited to one game, two tickets per series, this led to a maximum price of $90 for postseason reservations. Given what we know about demand, one would think that the optimal price would be different for different teams. For example, one would suspect that the value of such an option would be higher for the New York Yankees than the Pittsburgh Pirates. Not only are there more fans in New York, but the probability of the Yankees appearing in the playoffs is typically higher. Regardless, this difference in demand will clearly change the quantity demanded given that prices are constant and, in 2010, the Yankees sold out all of their postseason ticket reservations. Of course, MLB on their website tries to leverage small-market fan loyalty by asking: "How optimistic *are* you?" This is a clever marketing ploy designed to enhance revenues.

Ticket futures are a form of insurance. There is a certain probability that an event will happen, like your favorite team making the playoffs. If this happens, you want to be prepared. Therefore, if you buy this option, you will not be gouged by high ticket prices in secondary markets or, even worse, be without a ticket. On the supply side of the market, the sellers can sometimes make more money than just selling the ticket after the playoffs are known if they sell options to fans of different teams. As with many of these strategies, however, there could be a balance of short-term revenue weighed against customer dissatisfaction. With sport, though, as in many other industries, paying higher prices for things that were not charged for in the past might engender customer anger. Managers must balance the risk of fan resentment with the value of the additional revenue that can be generated.

Another type of futures options pricing comes from the Milwaukee Brewers. In 2015, they started selling "Timeless Tickets." For $1,000, fans would get nine tickets that they could use for any regular season game in the future, with the exception of opening day games, and one bronze ticket that could be used for any future Brewers game.[3]

Valuing a ticket that can be used for any future game is not trivial. Let's suppose that the owner of the bronze ticket decides to wait until the Brewers play a World Series game before redeeming the ticket. In this case, in order to value the ticket, you would need to know the value of a World Series ticket, the growth rate of the value of a World Series ticket, the discount rate, and the probability of the Brewers making the World Series each year. For simplicity's sake, let's assume that none of these values change.

In this case, the value of the ticket would be

$$V = pW + pW\frac{(1-p)(1+g)}{(1+r)} + pW\frac{(1-p)^2(1+g)^2}{(1+r)^2} + \ldots$$

$$= pW\sum_{n=0}^{\infty}\frac{(1-p)^n(1+g)^n}{(1+r)^n}$$

$$= pW\left[\frac{(1+r)}{(1+r)-(1-p)(1+g)}\right]$$

where V is the valuation of the ticket, p is the probability of making the World Series, W is the value of going to the World Series, g is the growth rate of the value of a World Series ticket, and r is the discount rate. If the team makes it to the World Series right away, which happens with probability p, then the value of the ticket is equal to the value of a World Series ticket. If the team first makes it to the World Series in a year, which happens with probability $p(1-p)$, the value of the ticket is equal to the current value of a World Series ticket, adjusted for one year of growth of the value of World Series tickets, $(1+g)$, and finally discounted by the discount rate.

Perhaps now we can make some reasonable guesses as the value of these parameters. Since there are 15 teams in the National League, a reasonable guess might be that the chance of the Brewers making the World Series in any given year is .06666 (1/15). The value of a World Series ticket depends on many factors, but let's say that it is about $1,000.[4] It is difficult to say how fast World Series ticket values are changing over time, in part because we do not have great data on market prices (i.e. scalping prices). For the sake of the calculation, we will suppose the growth is .03, or 3 percent. We will use a discount rate of 5 percent. With these parameter values, the value of the bronze ticket would be $789. When you add the other nine regular season tickets, this appears to be a pretty decent deal. If we value the bronze ticket at $789, then we would only need to value each regular season ticket at $24 in order to value this package at more than the $1,000 selling price.

We could try other strategies as well. For example, what if we waited for a National League Championship Series game? Often those tickets are only roughly one-fourth the cost of a World Series game, but the chances of playing in that game are twice as high. So, if we use $250 for W and .13333 for p, we get a valuation of $222. Obviously, this is not as good of a deal, so waiting for a World Series game seems to be the better option. Of course, one could wait for a World Series Game 7, but the chances of that seem quite low.

Note that if World Series ticket prices are increasing at a fast enough rate, the best strategy could be to just hold onto the ticket as an appreciable asset. Notice that if $(1-p)(1+g) > (1+r)$, then our valuation turns negative. What this is telling us, is that if the growth of ticket prices are high enough, then the best strategy is to not redeem the ticket until the growth of prices slows down so that $(1-p)(1+g) < (1+r)$. When prices are growing that rapidly, the value of a current ticket would be less than the option value of future tickets.

Pay What You Want

Another interesting phenomenon is letting fans or customers pay whatever they want. This may seem odd, but this is becoming a more attractive pricing strategy for some businesses. While some fans may take advantage of this pricing strategy and not pay much, many fans will actually pay more. If fans actually paid what they were willing to pay (probably not many fans would), this would be a form of price discrimination. Typically, this type of pricing has been limited to things related to fundraising or nonprofit activities, such as car washes or museum entrance fees. This has become more common, and some restaurants are letting customers pay what they want.

This happened in sport with the British soccer team Mansfield Town. For one game, the team allowed fans to pay what they wanted. Apparently, prices varied from "as little as three pence to as much as £50" (Etoe, 2010). The usual ticket price was £16. It is not clear whether the price per person was up or down, but the team did enjoy a large crowd for that game. There could be many effects of a pricing strategy such as this. On the negative side, fans might not pay much. Furthermore, even though the crowd was large, there may be a substitution between fans who would go to some other game with fixed prices, but instead went to the game with no set prices. On the positive side, many fans went to the game. This will increase concession sales and might create more long-term fans. It might also create some goodwill with fans.

In a similar fashion, the Florida Panthers have started selling season tickets by allowing fans to make an offer, which may or may not be accepted (Talalay, 2010). This is similar to the more known *Priceline* strategy. While this is different from Mansfield Town's strategy in that not all offers are accepted, they are selling tickets at a discount that fans chose. Again, even if this is a bad strategy in terms of maximizing ticket revenue, it may help concession revenue and advertising revenue. One downside is that it could anger season ticket holders who have already paid full price for tickets.

Media Prices

Revenues from media outlets are becoming more and more important for teams. In the United States, the Sports Broadcasting Rights Act of 1961 allows leagues to collectively sell their broadcasting rights. As discussed, college sports were not afforded this same right until the University of Oklahoma and the University of Georgia sued the NCAA (NCAA, 1984).

Pricing for broadcast rights and other media contracts is very different from ticket pricing. In fact, teams typically do not price media contracts. Instead, teams, or leagues, or conferences (sellers) sell rights to the highest-bidding media company (buyer). What makes pricing media contracts so different from pricing tickets is that there are very few parties involved. The number of teams, leagues, and conferences is quite limited, as is the number of vying media companies. The number of buyers and sellers in the market for any good is important. If there is only one buyer (monopsony), the price will be low. If there is only one seller (monopoly), the price will be high. This helps us understand why teams often prefer to sell rights collectively through the league as opposed to each team selling its rights individually.

Teams sell television broadcasting rights in two ways: nationally and locally. When thinking about major professional teams, most leagues have a national contract. Teams do not have to worry about negotiating these contracts because they are done by the league. National contracts are an important source of revenue for virtually all leagues, as well as professional golf and tennis. Local contracts also can be important for leagues like MLB, the NBA, and the NHL. The local contracts are negotiated by the team. In addition, web-based distribution rights are usually conducted by the leagues.

Selling rights collectively can have two effects. First, if teams sell rights collectively, there is an incentive to sell rights to fewer games. This is because if fewer games are televised, the price per game is higher. Basically, the market is moving up the demand curve. Selling collectively is essentially creating a monopoly, which means that teams can earn higher profits. Second, if the league is selling rights, they can charge whatever media companies are willing to pay. If teams are selling rights, media companies can buy rights from the team with the best deal.

A vast majority of college teams negotiate media contracts through their conference. A select few teams do not belong to a conference and negotiate their own contracts.[5] The NCAA men's basketball tournament provides another interesting example of how broadcast rights for collegiate sport can be sold collectively, by the NCAA. In 2016, the NCAA sold broadcasting rights to the tournament for $8.8 billion for an eight-year extension to their existing agreement. Previously the NCAA was receiving $740 million per year; the extension raised the annual payment to $1.1 billion per year (Tracy, 2016).

There are also many differences in the way European football teams sell their media rights. Some leagues sell their rights through individual teams (La Liga, Serie A), while some rights are collectively sold. The English Premier League sells media rights collectively, but there are differences with the North American leagues that collectively sell rights. For example, for many years the English Premier League sold exclusive rights to BSkyB, a European network. The European Commission forced the league to sell rights to more than one network starting in 2007. Also, the league does not share the rights equally. The large-market teams (more specifically, teams that are on television more often and/or teams that win more often) receive a larger share of the revenue. With the contract for the 2016–2019 seasons, the English Premier League receives approximately £1.76 billion (about $2.5 billion) per year (PA Sport, 2015).

On average, teams are better off if they can collectively sell broadcasting rights. It gives the teams and league more market power. The only teams that might be worse off with collectively sold media rights are the large-market teams. Typically, collectively sold broadcasting fees are divided evenly among teams (the English Premier League is an exception). Even though fees will be higher on average, large-market teams might be able to individually negotiate more money than they would get through the league. Sometimes a large slice of a small pie is bigger than an equal slice of a bigger pie.

Merchandise Pricing

The process of creating optimal prices for merchandise has elements similar to both ticket and media pricing. Merchandise is no different from tickets in that there is a demand for merchandise and there is an optimal price that balances increasing prices with selling more of the product. In theory, the elasticity of merchandise is similar to the elasticity of ticket sales. The number of buyers and sellers in the market also is important. Teams have a monopoly with regard to selling merchandise for their team.

To the extent that fans choose between buying merchandise from different teams in the same league, they gain more market power if they collectively sell merchandise. For example, there is a demand for LeBron James' jersey. There is also a demand for Steph Curry's jersey. If teams are individually selling merchandise, the Cleveland Cavaliers would be competing against the Golden State Warriors to sell jerseys. However, if the NBA is selling jerseys, they will raise the price of both jerseys and increase revenue for each team.

It should also be noted that what constitutes sport merchandise has actually changed over time. Today, even tickets could be considered merchandise. For example, on May 19, 2010, Roy Halladay of the Philadelphia Phillies threw a perfect game against the Florida Marlins. A perfect game is very rare, and this was only the 20th in MLB history. What is interesting about this, from a financial standpoint, is what the Marlins did with the tickets. Because tickets to this event became a collector's item, the team sold tickets even after the event had happened. They were able to sell tickets to the game, after the game, at the original prices. One drawback from this is that it may not be good publicity to sell tickets to an event that has already happened, especially when it is marketing a performance of a visiting player. During the same season, Matt Garza threw a no-hitter for the Tampa Bay Rays. The Rays did something similar by offering fans tickets to the game, after the game had been played, but only to fans who attended a charity event.

Notes

1 The mathematics of the profit/revenue maximization problem are shown in Appendix 1.
2 The Fan Cost Index is available at www.teammarketingreport.com and represents the cost of four people attending a game. Included in the Fan Cost Index is the price of two adult average-price tickets, two child average-price tickets, two small draft beers, four small soft drinks, four regular-size hot dogs, parking for one car, two game programs, and two least expensive, adult-size adjustable caps.
3 There are other details that we will ignore in our analysis. For example, the tickets are subject to availability. Also, Timeless Ticket owners can buy up to three companion tickets for the game at the single game box office price.
4 In 2013 and 2014, exactly one World Series game had an average ticket transaction price above $1,000 (Roeder, 2014). Of course, the valuation of the tickets also greatly depends on where the seats are located in the stadium.
5 For example, Notre Dame football does not belong to a conference and has its own national contract with NBC for its football games.

References

Ahn, S., & Lee, Y. H. 2007. Life-cycle demand for Major League Baseball. *International Journal of Sport Finance* 2: 25–35.

Coates, D., & Humphreys, B. R. 2007. Ticket prices, concessions, and attendance at professional sporting events. *International Journal of Sport Finance* 2 (3): 161–170.

Etoe, C. 2010. Attendance doubles as Mansfield fans pay what they want, *BBC*, February 6. Retrieved from http://news.bbc.co.uk/sport2/hi/football/teams/m/mansfield_town/ 8502204.stm (accessed April 10, 2011).

Fort, R. 2004a. Inelastic sports pricing. *Managerial and Decision Economics* 25 (2): 87–94.

Fort, R. 2004b. Subsidies as incentive mechanisms in sports. *Managerial and Decision Economics* 25 (2): 95–102.

Krautmann, A., & Berri, D. 2007. Can we find it at the concessions? Understanding price elasticity in professional sports. *Journal of Sports Economics* 8 (2): 183–191.

Lee, Y. H., & Smith, T. 2008. Why are Americans addicted to baseball? An empirical analysis of fandom in Korea and the U.S. *Contemporary Economic Policy* 26 (1): 32–48.

NCAA v. Board of Regents of Univ. of Okla., 468 U.S. 85. 1984.

Ostfield, A. 1995. Seat license revenue in the National Football League: Shareable or not? *Seton Hall Journal of Sport Law* 5: 599–610.

PA Sport. 2015. Premier League reveals £5 billion British TV rights deal, *ESPN*, February 10. Retrieved from http://www.espn.com/soccer/league-name/story/2291898/headline (accessed July 31, 2018).

Rovell, D. 2010. The Seattle "Freehawks" show teams future of sports marketing, *CNBC*, September 28. Retrieved from http://www.cnbc.com/id/39398351/The_Seattle_Freehawks_Show_Teams_Future_Of_Sports_Marketing (accessed April 10, 2011).

Roeder, O. 2014. The average cost of World Series tickets has gone up, *FiveThirtyEight*, October 25. Retrieved from http://fivethirtyeight.com/datalab/the-average-cost-of-world-series-tickets-has-gone-up/ (accessed July 31, 2018).

Salaga, S., & Winfree, J. A. (2015). Determinants of secondary market sales prices for National Football League personal seat licenses and season ticket rights. *Journal of Sports Economics* 16 (3): 227–253.

Talalay, S. 2006. Florida Panthers: Name your own price for tickets, *Sun Sentinel*, September 25. Retrieved from http://blogs.trb.com/sports/custom/business/blog/2010/08/florida_panthers_name_your_own.html (accessed July 31, 2018).

Team Marketing Report. 2016. MLB FCI 2016, *Team Marketing Report*. Retrieved from https://www.teammarketing.com/public/uploadedPDFs/MLB_FCI_2016.pdf (accessed February 25, 2018).

Tracy, M. 2016. N.C.A.A. extends basketball deal with CBS Sports and Turner through 2032, *New York Times*, April 12. Retrieved from https://www.nytimes.com/2016/04/13/sports/ncaabasketball/ncaa-extends-basketball-deal-with-cbs-sports-and-turner-through-2032.html (accessed July 31, 2018).

Weinbach, A. P., Paul, R. J., & Melvin, P. C. 2004. The Yankees effect: The impact of interleague play and the unbalanced schedule on Major League Baseball attendance, *New York Economic Review*. Retrieved from https://www.researchgate.net/publication/227356065_The_Yankees_Effect_The_Impact_of_Interleague_Play_And_The_Unbalanced_Schedule_On_Major_League_Baseball_Attendance (accessed January 29, 2018).

Wyshynski, G. 2008. Why NHL teams price gouge fans for premium home games, *Yahoo Sports*. Retrieved from https://sports.yahoo.com/nhl/blog/puck_daddy/post/Why-NHL-teams-price-gouge-fans-for-premium-home-?urn=nhl,97847 (accessed January, 29, 2018).

Zimbalist, A. 1992. *Baseball and billions: A probing look inside the big business of our national pastime.* New York, NY: Basic Books.

Appendix I

In this section we illustrate pricing that maximizes revenue. In general, firms maximize the following profit function:

$$\pi = QP(Q) - C(Q)$$

where π is the profit, Q is the quantity sold, P is the price of the product, which is a function of the quantity sold, and C is the cost function, which is also a function of the quantity sold. $QP(Q)$ represents the total revenue and $C(Q)$ represents the total cost. Using calculus, we can find that firms maximize profit when marginal revenues equal marginal cost:

$$MR = QP'(Q) + P(Q) = C'(Q)$$

where $P'(Q)$ is the change in price when quantity increases, or the slope of the demand curve, and $C'(Q)$ is the change in the cost from additional quantity.

For sports, a simplifying assumption is possible. When more fans arrive at a game, the costs are not that much more. It is true that more fans may mean higher custodial or maintenance costs, but usually these additional costs are minimal. Therefore, it can be assumed that $C'(Q) = 0$, and teams only need to worry about maximizing revenue. If marginal costs are not minimal, this would lead to higher optimal prices and lower optimal quantities.

Therefore, it is optimal for teams to set prices where marginal revenue equals zero, or when $QP'(Q) + P(Q) = 0$. This shows that there are two effects of changing quantity (or price) on revenue. If the number of fans who show up increases by one person, then the team will get additional revenue equal to the price of the ticket, but they also will lose money on all of the fans they already had because they had to decrease prices to get that additional fan.

An analogous way to think about this would be using the price elasticity. Rearranging the equation in the previous paragraph produces:

$$\frac{-P(Q)}{QP'(Q)} = 1.$$

The left half of the equation is known as the price elasticity. The elasticity shows what percent of consumers or fans will not come if prices are increased 1 percent. Revenues are maximized when the elasticity equals 1. In other words, revenues are maximized if you are at the point where a 1 percent increase in price will lead to a 1 percent decrease in quantity. If elasticity is equal to more than 1, it is said to be elastic. This means consumers are sensitive to price and prices should be decreased to maximize revenue. If elasticity is less than 1, it is inelastic. In this case, consumers are not sensitive to price and prices should increase to maximize revenue.

In this case, an example can be very useful. Suppose that demand for some sporting event is given by:

$$P = 80 - 4Q$$

and the cost is given by:

$$C = 20$$

Note that the cost does not change depending on how many people show up to the game. In this case profit is given by:

$$\pi = 80Q - 4Q^2 - 20$$

which is just price multiplied by quantity minus the cost. Using calculus, we can show that the marginal revenue is equal to:

$$MR = 80 - 8Q$$

(if demand is linear so that it is in the form of $P = a - bQ$, then marginal revenue can be written as $P = a - 2bQ$). If marginal revenue is set equal to zero, then the optimal quantity is 10. To find the optimal price, the optimal quantity of 10 in the demand curve is used to show that $P^* = 80 - 4(10) = 40$. Therefore, the optimal price is $40, which will bring in 10 people. Plugging this back into the profit function yields:

$$\pi = 80(10) - 4(10)^2 - 20 = 380$$

At most, the team can earn $380 profit.

An analyst can also can use the elasticity. In this example, elasticity equals:

$$\frac{-(80 - 4Q)}{QP'(Q)}$$

Using calculus, $P'(Q) = -4$. Even without calculus, one can still think about its interpretation. What this is saying is that when quantity increases by 1, price goes down by 4 (if demand is linear so that it is in the form of $P = a - bQ$, then $P'(Q)$ is equal to $-b$). Therefore, the elasticity becomes:

$$\frac{-(80 - 4Q)}{-4Q}$$

which can be reduced to:

$$\frac{(20 - Q)}{Q}$$

If the elasticity is set equal to 1, the optimal quantity is 10, which means that the optimal price is \$40. If the price is set at \$41, the price is elastic. If price is set at \$39, the price is inelastic.

Appendix 2

This section analyzes pricing with multiple revenue streams. Assume, as in Appendix 1, that demand for tickets is given by:

$$P = 80 - 4Q$$

and the cost is given by:

$$C = 20$$

However, now assume that each fan at the game is worth an average of \$16 because they might buy concessions or park a car. In this case, profit is given by:

$$\pi = 80Q - 4Q^2 - 20 + 16Q$$

which is price multiplied by quantity minus the cost plus ancillary benefits from extra fans. Using calculus, it can be seen that the marginal revenue is equal to:

$$MR = 96 - 8Q$$

This time, if marginal revenue is zero, then the optimal quantity is 12. To find the optimal price, we use the optimal quantity of 12 in the demand curve to show that:

$$P^* = 80 - 4(12) = 32$$

Therefore, the optimal price is $32, which will bring in 12 people. In this case, if ticket prices are $40, then 10 people go to the game and the team earns $540, but if ticket prices are $32, the 12 people go to the game and the team earns $566.

The price elasticity is the same as in the last example:

$$\frac{(20 - Q)}{Q}$$

If quantity is 12, then elasticity equals .667, which means that the prices are in the inelastic range.

Appendix 3

This section examines two-part pricing. Again, as in Appendix 1, it is assumed that demand for tickets is given by:

$$P = 80 - 4Q$$

In this case, though, it is assumed this is the demand for one individual and that that individual may buy multiple tickets. Now, suppose the team could charge the fan the exact price the fan would be willing to pay for each ticket. If the team could do this, they would charge the fan $800 for a bundle of 20 tickets. The value $800 can be found by finding the area under the demand curve or by integrating the demand function. However, it is not likely that the team will be able to charge the fan a price equal to their willingness to pay. They could, however, charge a PSL fee of $800 and then give the tickets to the fan for free. Clearly teams are not likely to give tickets away, but this happens in this model because no marginal costs are assumed. What is key in this example is that the team has generated $800 in revenue. If there are fixed costs of $20, profits are $780. This is an increase of $400 when compared to the example in Appendix 1. Furthermore, the team sold a total of 20 tickets.

Chapter 11

Capital Budgeting and Team Investments

Introduction

This chapter focuses on capital budgeting techniques and the benefits and costs of different types of financial investments that teams make. Capital budgeting is the process of evaluating and selecting long-term investments that are consistent with a firm's goal. Almost every firm's goals, at least in a financial sense, include the generation of profits. Although there are myriad financial decisions that teams constantly make, the focus in this chapter is on the longer-term commitments that include (1) the purchase of the franchise, (2) the building of a facility, and (3) investments in players. Managers must understand the fundamental financial concepts and apply them to these investments. There are also a few financial concepts that are unique to the sports business which are addressed in this chapter. At the heart of this book is the observation that the sports business has become dominated by large-scale investments in real estate, entertainment, and media. When this happens, teams become part of a larger conglomerate. These other investments must be considered when analyzing teams' financial returns. In a sense, the team is at the center of the conglomerate, but some of the other activities could actually account for more of the profits produced by the overall set of businesses linked to each other because of the team's existence. In addition, when a team is involved with the building of a new facility, ownership must estimate the new revenue streams that will be created. These revenue streams must increase profits to the point where the investment in the facility makes financial sense. If a facility costs too much, a team's financial position could, in theory, be stronger in an older facility. In a similar manner, when investing in players it is important to consider the amount of additional revenue that could be raised by adding these players to the roster. These funds should exceed the cost of acquiring the player. Team owners and management staff must also consider the effect a "star" has on the other players on the team. If the star is seen as taking too much of the team's revenues, jealousies can arise, leading to discontent. In terms of owning a team, building a new facility, or signing players, it is essential to assess each investment as it affects an owner's complete portfolio. The end of this chapter includes an analysis of the cost of some of these investments, using a cost of capital approach.

Team Investments

Chapter 8 discussed franchise valuation. In that chapter, historical and current values were analyzed using different financial models. Profits taken out of the team's operations were largely ignored in the valuation process. In contrast, in this chapter, the different investments are compared in terms of their rate of return and risk level. Correlations also are assessed to understand how various assets are related and what might be a particular team's optimal strategy for producing profits. In sports, as with any industry, it is important to understand that the value of investments, relative to profit levels, can change depending on what else an investor owns.

Like any investment, team owners and their managers need to focus on expected profits and the level of risk assumed when they buy a team or make any other long-term commitment related to the franchise. One way to assess that return is through an estimate of value, but typically it makes more sense to assess rates of return and some quantitative measures of risk. To do this, it is imperative to know what is meant by rate of return (a manager must also understand his/her owner's expected rate of return). While "return" can mean the amount of profit earned across a certain period of time, "rate of return" compares profit with the initial investment. The rate of return is then expressed as a percentage of the investment made. Calculating a rate of return for an asset can be slightly more complex, as it is necessary to account for both an increase in the value of an asset as well as any cash flow that was received from the asset. The rate of return across a given year can be calculated by:

$$k_t = \frac{C_t + V_t - V_{t-1}}{V_{t-1}}$$

where k_t is the rate of return in period t, C_t represents any cash flows in period t, and V_t represents the value of an asset in period t. V_{t-1} is the value of the asset in the previous period (a period is almost always a year so that an annual rate of return is presented). If the asset is a publicly traded stock, the value would simply be the price of the stock. In the case of sports teams, it is the price or value of the franchise. Cash flow is a general term that could represent dividend or profits. In the context of buying sports teams, the rate of return of the team would be any profits that owners received plus the increase in value, all divided by the value of the team in the preceding year.

Calculating a return is usually straightforward if reliable data are available. The difficult part is estimating expected future returns. Finding the expected return can be very difficult, and it always helps to have some institutional knowledge. For example, is the league going to receive a big media contract in the future? If so, one would expect profits to increase. Also, trends are very important. As noted in Chapter 8, the value of all major professional sports teams in North America has increased over the past several decades. If one thinks that the economy will enter into a prolonged contraction, then future returns will not be as robust. For the purposes of this chapter, the focus is on averages of past results. While this might be a somewhat crude measure, it is a convenient starting point. Expected return of an investment as the average of past results is given by the formula:

$$\bar{k} = \frac{\sum_{j=1}^{n} k_j}{n}$$

where $\bar{k}$ represents the expected return and k_j is the return in year j, across the last n years.

If we had more information about the chances of different outcomes, a weighted average could be found. For example, if there were some prior knowledge about the probabilities of certain outcomes, or if we wanted to put more weight on more recent outcomes, we could then use those probabilities to find a better expectation about future returns. The weighted average is calculated by:

$$\bar{k} = k_j p_j$$

where k_j is the return for outcome j and p_j is the probability of outcome j.

Past rates of return are not always the best measures of future rates of return. If a team won the championship, one would expect profit levels to increase not only for that year, but probably the year after. But, because most teams do not win the championship every year, it could be expected that returns could decrease in future years. If, on the other hand, the team experienced some bad luck in the past, returns might be expected to increase. Good financial analysts show some foresight into the revenues and costs of the firm. It is not uncommon to offer projections based on different scenarios and to offer a range of expected outcomes.

Risk

Once future returns are estimated, the next factor to be considered is risk. One definition of financial risk is the variability of returns of an asset. If the expected returns are for the most part known with little variability, then there is little risk. On the other hand, if future returns are very unclear and dependent upon numerous factors, then there is a high level of risk (or uncertainty). Nearly all investors are risk averse and try to minimize it. Some financial managers are willing to assume larger levels of risk when there is an expectation of higher returns. When there is greater risk, there is usually the opportunity for far more earnings and profits. Historically, investments with low risk (bonds, U.S. Treasury Bills) have had low average returns over the long run. Investments with high risk (small companies) have had high average returns, although the journey to a long-run average can involve numerous peaks and valleys (a bumpy ride). In terms of teams, it is not necessarily clear what constitutes a risky investment. In a major sports league, most teams have relatively similar risks, especially when revenue is shared. An expansion team might be considered risky because it is often hard to estimate demand in a market until a team is in the region. Maybe a team in a new startup league would be considered risky; one can imagine situations where future returns on sports teams were somewhat easy to calculate and situations where future returns were difficult to project.

Risk can come from a variety of sources. Because the biggest investments for teams are players and the facilities used, that is where assessments must be initially made. Probably the most common type of risk is player performance. Often player or team performance is highly variable across time. Furthermore, team revenue changes drastically depending on how players perform. There is also some risk associated with the team's facility. If a facility is not popular or does not work in terms of enhancing the fan "experience," money is lost.

There are also many general types of risk that can be associated with most industries. A general type of risk is *business risk* or the need for a firm to support its operating costs. *Financial risk* deals with satisfying *all* financial obligations. All firms face *market risk*, which comes from the uncertainty in consumer preferences and needs, which are dynamic. When thinking about market conditions and changes, it also must be remembered that some businesses actually thrive in a poor economy (and enjoy less risk). How is this possible? Many consider localized entertainment to be countercyclical, for example, meaning they have high returns in a bad economy. While most teams and businesses prefer a good economy (anticipating less risk and higher prices when the economy is robust), some minor league teams might be somewhat indifferent, meaning that attendance does not wane during an economic contraction.

Market risk also involves political or social events that could change demand. *Event risk* is another common type of risk. While many events could take place to adversely affect teams, a common worry among owners (and fans) is a work stoppage. A lockout or strike will lead to a sharp decline in short-term revenues. *Tax risk* is the risk that tax laws could change. While analysts can often foresee tax law changes into the near future, long-term decisions can be dramatically changed by changes in tax law. Some leagues (e.g., the NHL and NBA) encounter *exchange rate risk* when teams in the same league play in more than one country. Because some teams earn revenue in the United States and some teams earn revenue in Canada, a quick change in the exchange rate can elevate or depress the purchasing power of teams. As noted in Chapter 8, interest rates are critical in calculating team values, so teams face *interest rate risk*. Furthermore, when the interest rate increases, the value of investments decrease. *Liquidity risk* is the risk that firms will not have enough liquid assets to meet their obligations, and *purchasing power risk* is the risk of inflation. These are just a few types of risk.

Risk and Uncertainty

People often use *risk* and *uncertainty* interchangeably and, in some ways, there is no problem with that. Be aware, however, they do not measure exactly the same phenomenon. Financially, risk can be defined as the variability of returns associated with a given asset. Uncertainty is a concept that deals more with *unknown* chances. In other words, risk is randomness with known probabilities and uncertainty is randomness with unknown probabilities (Knight, 1921). If the chances of various outcomes are known, then an accurate measure of risk exists. If the chances of various outcomes are unknown, there is great uncertainty. It is possible for an investment to be risky, but not uncertain. It also is possible for an investment to not be risky, but very uncertain.

For example, the NBA uses a lottery system for their player draft. They use what is called a weighted lottery system, meaning that poor performing teams have better chances at getting a higher draft pick than better performing teams. People can and do calculate the probabilities of various teams getting the first overall pick. In other words, the risks regarding which team will get which draft pick can be calculated. There is no uncertainty about those risks. There can be great uncertainty regarding the drafted players. Some Number 1 draft picks have met expectations, but others have not. While people can still estimate performance measures for drafted players, it is not an exact science. There may be things about the player that the team does not know and, as a result, there is some uncertainty (and risk) regarding the drafted players.

Again, a financial analyst *might* use previous returns to estimate the risk of the investment. It is possible that better information is available than historical returns. To keep consistent with the calculation of expected value, it can be assumed that past returns are the best measure for expected returns. One measure of risk is the standard deviation of the returns, which is given by:

$$\sigma_k = \sqrt{\frac{\sum_{j=1}^{n}\left(k_j - \bar{k}\right)^2}{n-1}}$$

The standard deviation represents a measure of dispersion or, in the case of investments, risk.[1] On average, the return will be one standard deviation away from the average return. The standard deviation is most useful when different investments are compared.

Because investors almost always want less risk, they would rather buy an investment with a small standard deviation of returns. A financial analyst's job is sometimes straightforward. If two investments have the same expected rate of return, but one has a smaller standard deviation, then the preferred choice is obvious. The investment with the smaller standard deviation is clearly better. Conversely, if two investments have the same standard deviation and one has the higher expected return, then it is the better investment. The problem comes when one investment has a higher expected return and a higher standard deviation.

In most markets, there is a tradeoff between risk and reward. If investments have a high risk, there should be a high average reward. How does an analyst compare an investment with high risk and high reward with another investment that offers lower risks and returns? One way is by using the coefficient of variation. While the coefficient of variation is quite crude, it does provide some valuable insight. The coefficient of variation is given by:

$$cv_k = \frac{\sigma_k}{\bar{k}}$$

In other words, the coefficient of variation is the standard deviation divided by the average return. Because a good investment has low risk and high reward, a low coefficient of variation is ideal. Just because an investment has a low coefficient of variation, however, does not mean it is a good investment. There may be other metrics that are useful as well, or there could be circumstances that make that investment unwise. If an investor is not very risk averse, he/she will care more about the expected return than the standard deviation. Conversely, if he/she is very risk averse, he/she will care more about the standard deviation.

The Green Bay Packers' financial statements provide some context for the analysis of returns. Table 11.1 illustrates the Packers' operating profit (profit level before interest payments, dividends, and taxes) from 1997 to 2003. The figure shows that, on average, the Packers made $7.3 million in operating profit for the seven years reported. The standard deviation was $7.6 million, making the coefficient of variation just over 1. The rule of thumb is that most of the time values will fall inside two standard deviations of the

Table 11.1 Green Bay Packers' Operating Profit, 1997–2003

Year	Operating Profit ($)
1997	7,099,031
1998	8,047,411
1999	6,993,945
2000	−419,517
2001	2,769,928
2002	3,268,025
2003	23,198,367
Average	7,279,599
Standard deviation	7,635,631
Coefficient of variation	1.049

average.[2] So, while it depends on distributional properties, a rough confidence interval would be from a loss of $8 million (the mean minus two times the standard deviation) to a gain of $22.6 million (the mean plus two times the standard deviation). To analyze it a different way, if the coefficient of variation is more than about .5, then there is certainly a possibility of a loss.

The best use of these data would be in predicting the 2004 operating profit. The data can be used to determine if profits increased. While a more sophisticated approach involving a regression or time-series analysis might be ideal, a casual assessment indicates that there is no obvious growth, up or down. While 2003 was a more robust year financially, the three years prior to that were not. The graph in Figure 11.1 also shows no clear trend.

While this graph may show that profits might be growing (a trend line does have a positive slope), it is hard to make a firm statement with one data point that is high. The Milwaukee *Journal Sentinel* did report that the Packers had a profit, *after taxes*, of $18 million in 2005 and $22 million in 2006. So, an analysis showing that profits were increasing would have been prescient. *Forbes* estimated that the value of the Packers more than doubled from 2001 to 2005, which illustrates what can happen when profits dramatically increase (Forbes, 2017).

Diversification and Correlation

Many financial analysts preach diversification or having unrelated assets. If a portfolio[3] has investments that are completely unrelated and, thus, is quite diversified, then risk will normally not be as high as a portfolio dominated by correlated assets. Diversification in sports could mean owning a basketball team and a NASCAR team. Diversification is often more difficult that it would appear. Even in the case of a basketball team and a NASCAR team, there could be things that affect both in the same way. For example, maybe

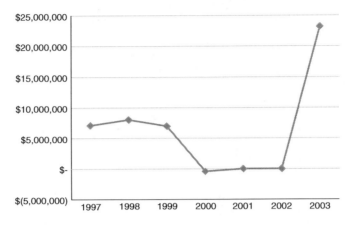

Figure 11.1 Packers' Operating Profit

both are dependent upon the national economy. One strategy to diversify would be to invest internationally. Occasionally, owners do own teams on different continents. In any case, it is usually safer to make investments that diversify a portfolio.

Diversification must be balanced against having too many unrelated business investments. It is common for investors to own firms that are related to each other, and as financial experts know, correlated investments can be managed to decrease risk. Owning two risky investments that are negatively correlated can be very effective in decreasing risk. For instance, there could be sports teams that are countercyclical, that is, they thrive in a weak economy. In a recession, many fans might go to minor league sporting events. Therefore, owning minor league teams might be a hedge against a bad economy that reduces demand for major league events.

Owning multiple teams in the same region could be another way to decrease risk by having negatively correlated assets. Using an extreme example, suppose that a fixed number of fans will attend games during the basketball/hockey season in Detroit. In other words, fans will go to exactly one game and they will decide between a Detroit Pistons or Detroit Red Wings game. If this is the case, there would be some risk and uncertainty with owning either the Pistons or Red Wings. If jointly owned, that risk is eliminated.

On the other hand, there might be factors that will affect both the Pistons and Red Wings in the same way, which will create some positive correlation between the two. If the Detroit regional economy declines, there might be fewer fans for both the Pistons and Red Wings. If this is the major effect, then owning both the Pistons and Red Wings would be very risky. Of course, this is ultimately an empirical question to be answered with data. Some teams might be positively correlated while others are negatively correlated.

The extent to which the Red Wings and Pistons are substitutes (negatively correlated) or complements (positively correlated) can be measured. Ideally, an analyst would look at profits of the two teams, but as a proxy, what is assessed here are attendance levels across 17 years (Table 11.2). Other things, such as media contracts, are clearly important for profits and many things affect attendance. As a result, looking only at attendance is not sufficient, but some important insights are possible.

On average, the Pistons have a slightly lower attendance and a much higher standard deviation. With the exception of the lockout year, the Red Wings had the same attendance from 2003 to 2007, and again from 2014 to 2017 due to sellouts. Because the Pistons average only a slightly lower attendance, but have much more risk, their coefficient of variation is quite a bit higher than that of the Red Wings. In this case, the Red Wings seem to be the better investment since they have both a higher average and a lower standard deviation. Keep in mind, this assumes the same price of the investment and we are analyzing attendance, which is certainly an imperfect proxy for profits.

The correlation is also important. With unemployment levels rising in Southeast Michigan throughout the Great Recession, attendance declined. However, when the teams won more games, attendance rose. The correlation

Table 11.2 Detroit Pistons and Detroit Red Wings Attendance, 2000–2017

Season	Pistons Attendance	Red Wings Attendance	Total
2000–2001	607,323	819,785	1,427,108
2001–2002	760,807	822,373	1,583,180
2002–2003	839,278	822,378	1,661,656
2003–2004	872,902	822,706	1,695,608
2004–2005	905,119	*lockout*	905,199
2005–2006	883,040	822,706	1,705,746
2006–2007	905,116	822,706	1,727,822
2007–2008	905,116	775,394	1,680,510
2008–2009	896,971	814,474	1,711,445
2009–2010	768,826	781,847	1,550,673
2010–2011	683,080	806,892	1,489,972
2011–2012	475,638	824,706	1,300,344
2012–2013	606,094	481,584	1,087,678
2013–2014	615,238	908,131	1,523,369
2014–2015	625,917	821,107	1,447,024
2015–2016	677,138	821,107	1,498,245
2016–2017	655,141	821,107	1,476,248
Average	746,044	799,313	1,535,414
Standard deviation	137,715	89,126	172,153
Coefficient of variation	0.185	0.112	0.112
Correlation of Pistons and Red Wings (excluding 2004–2005)			0.13451

is mildly positive, meaning that when the Pistons are doing well, typically so are the Red Wings.

Suppose the owner of the Pistons is considering buying the Red Wings. The standard deviation of fans for the Pistons is 137,715. If the Pistons' owner also bought the Red Wings, the standard deviation would increase to 172,153. So, this would be a way to increase the investment with only a moderate increase in risk. There are other reasons to own multiple sports teams in the same city (which the NFL does not allow). For example, because teams are seasonal, owning multiple teams might cut costs. An NBA team's marketing department might be very busy in the fall, but an MLB team's marketing department might be busy in the spring. So, it might make sense to have one marketing department for both teams. There also could be institutional knowledge that is useful for both teams. Teams also could advertise to sports fans more easily by using other teams in the market. Teams could also increase their market power by owning multiple teams in a market. Another reason for owning two teams could be that sports teams are negatively correlated and this decreases the risk of the owner.

Facility Investments

Financial analysts have to focus on the net present value (NPV) and the internal rate of return (IRR) from a new facility. As illustrated in Chapter 9, a new facility will increase attendance *ceteris paribus* (with all other factors remaining the same).[4] A successful new facility should produce financial benefits that exceed the costs. The benefits, as well as the costs, are not always straightforward and easy to calculate. First, what is the counterfactual to a new facility? In other words, what would happen if a new facility were not built? Maybe the old facility would continue to be used and attendance would remain unchanged; attendance could also decrease if fans were disappointed with the experience produced during their visits. Perhaps a new facility should be compared to an alternative new facility. Furthermore, a new facility can affect more than just attendance. It is not always clear what exactly the benefit of a new facility will be. The cost side can be complicated as well. Often there is a mix of private and public funding, so the private cost is not always the total cost.

Even though benefits and costs of a new facility are not always obvious, the NPV of Oriole Park at Camden Yards can be estimated. Finding the NPV of an investment is similar to finding the value of a team. The discounted value of all cash flows has to be found. The NPV of an investment can be given by:

$$NPV = CF_0 + \frac{CF_1}{(1+r)^1} + \frac{CF_2}{(1+r)^2} + \ldots + \frac{CF_3}{(1+r)^N} = \sum_{t=0}^{N} \frac{CF_t}{(1+r)^t}$$

where CF_i is the cash flow in year t, r is the discount rate, and the investment lasts for N years. Note that, in other similar equations in the book, the first value is discounted. In this NPV formula, the first value is not discounted. Often when an NPV is calculated for an investment, there is one large outflow that is relatively immediate and should not be discounted. After the initial investment is made, often future cash flows are inflows.

One difficulty with estimating NPV is finding the appropriate discount rate, which was discussed in Chapter 8. Often some type of interest rate can be used, but the amount of risk involved with the cash flows also should be taken into account. One way to do this would be to use the Capital Asset Pricing Model discussed in Chapter 8. Another difficulty with estimating NPV beforehand is that cash flows are not always easy to predict. The number of additional fans a new facility generates is not always easy to calculate even after the facility is built, let alone before it opens. Another difficulty is that the depreciation rate is not always known, but if the cost of capital is known (cost of capital is discussed at the end of the chapter), it might be a reasonable depreciation or discount rate.

Another common technique is to calculate the IRR. The internal rate of return is simply the depreciation rate that gives the investment a net present value of zero. A high internal rate of return means the investment is profitable. The formula for IRR is given by:

$$NPV = \sum_{t=0}^{N} \frac{CF_t}{(1+r)^t} = 0$$

This equation implies that there is some rate, r, that makes the NPV of an investment zero. That rate is the IRR.

Table 11.3 provides some data pertaining to Oriole Park at Camden Yards. The first seven columns (Season, Finish, Wins, Losses, Attendance, Average Ticket Price, and Ticket Revenue) can all be found in Chapter 1. Given these data, the first thing for a financial analyst to do is adjust for inflation and put the financial values into real or constant terms. The eighth column provides a measure of inflation (the Consumer Price Index) and the ninth column adjusts ticket revenue so that it is in real 2016 dollars.[5]

The tenth column then finds the increase in real ticket revenue compared to the ticket revenue in 1991, the last year the Orioles played in Memorial Stadium. This brings up the question as to whether the ticket revenue from Camden Yards should be compared to the last season in Memorial Stadium. This is difficult to say. In Chapter 9, previous academic research was used to estimate the average effect of a new stadium. In this case, because the focus is on one specific team, it might be better to analyze the Orioles' attendance pre- and post-play at Oriole Park at Camden Yards. Even though the team did perform poorly with a record of 67 wins and 95 losses in the last year of

Table 11.3 Impact of Oriole Park at Camden Yards on Attendance

Season	Division Finish	Wins	Losses	Attendance	Average Ticket Price ($)	Ticket Revenue ($)	Consumer Price Index	Real Ticket Revenue ($)	Change in Real Ticket Revenue ($)	Discounted Change in Real Ticket Revenue ($)	
										(r = 10%)	(r = 18.7%)
1991	6th	67	95	2,552,753	8.04	20,524,134	134.6	36,125,526			
1992¹	3rd	89	73	3,567,819	9.55	34,072,671	138.1	58,453,013	22,327,487	20,297,715	18,810,014
1993	3rd	85	77	3,644,965	11.12	40,532,011	142.6	67,339,985	31,214,459	25,797,074	22,154,114
1994	2nd	63	49	2,535,359	11.17	28,319,960	146.2	45,892,282	9,766,756	7,337,909	5,839,803
1995	3rd	71	73	3,098,475	13.14	40,713,962	150.3	64,176,906	28,051,380	19,159,470	14,130,299
1996	2nd	88	74	3,646,950	13.14	47,920,923	154.4	73,531,304	37,405,779	23,226,046	15,873,954
1997	1st	98	64	3,612,764	17.02	61,489,243	159.1	91,563,706	55,438,180	31,293,407	19,820,046
1998	4th	79	83	3,684,650	19.77	72,845,531	161.6	106,796,236	70,670,710	36,265,249	21,285,528
1999	4th	78	84	3,432,099	19.82	68,024,202	164.3	98,088,995	61,963,469	28,906,416	15,722,803
2000	4th	74	88	3,295,128	19.78	65,177,632	168.8	91,478,814	55,353,288	23,475,198	11,832,785
2001	4th	63	98	3,094,841	18.23	56,418,951	175.1	76,336,678	40,211,152	15,503,140	7,241,680
2002	4th	67	95	2,655,559	18.23	48,410,841	177.1	64,761,732	28,636,206	10,036,816	4,344,678
2003	4th	71	91	2,454,523	20.15	49,458,638	181.7	64,488,403	28,362,877	9,037,287	3,625,281
2004	3rd	78	84	2,744,018	22.53	61,822,726	185.2	79,086,354	42,960,829	12,444,222	4,626,082
2005	4th	74	88	2,624,740	22.53	59,135,392	190.7	73,466,810	37,341,284	9,833,127	3,387,499
2006	4th	70	92	2,153,250	22.53	48,512,723	198.3	57,959,860	21,834,334	5,226,966	1,668,703
2007	4th	69	93	2,164,822	22.45	48,600,254	202.4	56,883,733	20,758,208	4,517,591	1,336,529
2008	5th	68	93	1,950,075	23.85	46,509,289	211.1	52,201,983	16,076,458	3,180,641	872,023
2009	5th	64	98	1,907,163	23.42	44,665,757	211.1	50,117,847	13,992,321	2,516,642	639,406
2010	5th	66	96	1,733,018	23.42	40,587,282	216.7	44,376,342	8,250,816	1,349,074	317,639

(continued)

Table 11.3 Continued

Season	Division Finish	Wins	Losses	Attendance	Average Ticket Price ($)	Ticket Revenue ($)	Consumer Price Index	Real Ticket Revenue ($)	Change in Real Ticket Revenue ($)	Discounted Change in Real Ticket Revenue ($)	
										(r = 10%)	(r = 18.7%)
2011	5th	69	93	1,755,461	23.9	41,955,518	220.2	45,135,765	9,010,239	1,339,315	292,228
2012	2nd	93	69	2,102,240	23.89	50,222,514	226.7	52,493,843	16,368,318	2,211,860	447,238
2013	3rd	85	77	2,357,561	23.9	56,345,708	230.3	57,969,427	21,843,902	2,683,435	502,822
2014	1st	96	66	2,464,473	24.97	61,537,891	233.9	62,327,121	26,201,596	2,926,146	508,114
2015	3rd	81	81	2,320,590	24.97	57,945,132	233.7	58,740,769	22,615,244	2,296,026	369,474
2016	2nd	89	73	2,172,344	29.96	65,083,426	236.9	65,083,426	28,957,901	2,672,698	398,565
Camden Yards Avg		77.1	82.1	2,686,915	20.14	51,852,327	–	66,350,053	–	–	–
Total		–	–	–	–	–	–	1,658,751,334	755,613,192	303,533,469	176,047,306

[1] First season in Oriole Park at Camden Yards.

Memorial Stadium, the team enjoyed a record year relative to attendance. This may be due to the fact that there is often a jump in attendance during the last year of an old facility because fans want an opportunity to enjoy the nostalgia and memories. This tells us that, if anything, the impact of Oriole Park at Camden Yards could be underestimated because attendance and ticket revenue at Memorial Stadium may have been lower than what took place in its last year. With so many factors influencing attendance, a single year offers little insight as many things change each year.

The eleventh column in Table 11.3 discounts the change in real ticket revenue by 10 percent each year. In other words, this figure is the NPV of Camden Yards. If the discounted cash flows from Oriole Park are added together from 1992 to 2016, the resulting figure is $303.5 million. This figure is much larger than the estimated increase in ticket revenues noted in Chapter 9. Not only was this analysis done differently, but Oriole Park is considered one of the most successful ballparks ever built. Now, let's introduce the cost of the ballpark. It has been reported that in 1991, Camden Yards cost $100 million to build, which is $176 million in 2016 dollars. If the cost is subtracted from the estimated benefit, the NPV of the investment is $127.5 million. This is a remarkably positive net value, and the value produced in 2017 and in future years is not considered. Future ticket revenue will show that the NPV of this stadium will be even higher.

What is the IRR for Oriole Park? If the cash flows were constant, then a calculator could be used. As described in Chapter 5, financial calculators have five keys: PV is the present value, PMT is a constant payment made every period, N is the number of periods, I/Y is the depreciation rate, and FV is the future value. An analyst would simply solve for I/Y, which in this case represents the IRR, by inputting the other four values. Because the change in ticket revenues varies over time, a financial calculator cannot find the IRR.[6] Using other programs, the actual IRR is 18.7 percent (again a remarkable return). This also is a real rate of return (adjusted for inflation). Certainly, any investment with a real IRR of 18.7 percent should be considered a success. Without adjusting for inflation, the IRR is more than 24 percent. Notice that in the last column, when the values are discounted at 18.7 percent, the sum of the values equals the cost of the stadium with some rounding error. This indicates that if the discount rate was 18.7 percent across time, the NPV would be zero. Clearly, Oriole Park has been a success. This analysis does not even consider changes in concession, parking, and advertising revenues, or other benefits. The high NPV and IRR values illustrate why other MLB teams often copy Oriole Park.

Player Investments

As we saw in Chapter 3, player salaries are the highest cost faced by most teams. Clearly the value of the players is high as well. While some fans cannot fathom why some players make as much as they do, there is some basic economics behind player contracts. Players make as much as they do for the most part because that is how much value they bring to the team. While the same measures of expected value and risk pertain to the investment in players, we will examine some other basic financial concepts and how they are related to players.

Value of a Player

To understand the value of a player, financial managers must understand the marginal revenue product (MRP) of each athlete (Scully, 1974). MRP is an economic idea that is not always straightforward but can be applied to any worker. To understand MRP, two other terms have to be defined, *marginal product* and *marginal revenue*. A worker's marginal product is the additional units of output they create. For example, if a company is making footballs, then a worker's marginal product would be the additional number of footballs that are made because of that individual. Although probably no individual actually makes footballs from start to finish anymore, everyone at the football company helps create some number of footballs. The number of footballs made because of a specific worker is the marginal product of that specific worker. The goal of athletes is to win games. Therefore, a player's marginal product is the number of games that player helped the team win. While a player's marginal product is not exactly known, especially before the season starts, teams must make their best guess. If the Houston Astros win 100 games but would have won only 85 games without Jose Altuve (but with a replacement player that would play for a much smaller salary), then Jose Altuve's marginal product is 15 games. For baseball, a player's marginal product is similar to their wins above replacement (WAR) statistic. In basketball, it is similar to the term *wins produced* (for a mathematical explanation of wins produced, see Berri, 2008). In sports like football, where players are so dependent on each other, the marginal product is much harder to estimate.

Marginal revenue also is critical to understanding any particular player's value. If the team wins more games, the franchise earns more revenue. A team's marginal revenue is the additional funds earned from one more win. Remember, this is not just revenue from ticket sales, but revenue from all of the revenue streams that were discussed in Chapter 3. For example, if the Houston Astros receive $3 million in additional revenue for each game they win, then that is their marginal revenue. A player's marginal revenue product is then simply his/her marginal product multiplied by the marginal revenue. With these assumptions, a very talented player could have a marginal revenue product of $45 million (15 × $3 million). Remember that a player's marginal product might depend on how good the team is without that individual.[7] Players also might bring in more value than through their marginal product. For example, basketball icon Michael Jordan brought fans to the games late in his career when he was not helping the team win that many games. In 1998, Mark McGwire and Sammy Sosa increased demand for their teams as a result of their home run race. In 2017, Aaron Judge might have done the same for the New York Yankees.

Marginal Value of Wins

The marginal value of winning games is a function of many things. For example, because teams are becoming integral components of entertainment companies, the marginal revenue from winning is increasing. Today if a team wins, it does not just increase ticket sales, but also sales from concessions, parking, and souvenirs. A team's media revenue might depend on winning as well. Furthermore, if the team owner also has interests in restaurants, hotels, or casinos surrounding the facility, it will increase the marginal revenue of players even further. Not only does this ownership integration increase profits, it also increases the value of players. Therefore, all of these things have increased player salaries across the past decade or two.

People often do not make the connection between revenues and player salaries. Player salaries exploded during the 1990s and continued to escalate into the 21st century, but this is because revenues soared as well. For example, when owners receive large media contracts, a share of this goes to the players. Also, if teams start receiving sponsorship dollars, a share goes to the players. A much larger share of these revenues goes to the players if the revenues depend on how the team performs. For example, the NFL receives most of its revenue from national media contracts that are always shared. So, although financially the NFL might prefer if large-market teams win, whoever wins does not affect the bottom line that much. On the other hand, if a league receives most of its income from gate revenue, then the franchise is very dependent on winning and the players become more important. The escalating media contracts discussed earlier would not have been possible without the players that fans wanted to see compete.

Correlation of Players

Just like the financial performance of teams might be correlated, the performance of players could be correlated as well. Players can be complements or substitutes just like other investments. For example, when one position player plays well, this can affect the performance of others. If a quarterback has a good game, it is likely that the wide receivers also have a good game.

If a goalie has a good game, it might be due to the defensemen. Assume for a moment that when the quarterback has a good game, the running back tends to have a poor game. Teams should be thinking about how their players play together. If a football team has a good quarterback, is it better to invest in wide receivers or running backs? If a team's management believes it is in their best interest to focus on a passing game, then they should invest in wide receivers. This would be a riskier move. If the team wants to be balanced, they should invest in a running back. This would cause the team to have more average games and would be a more conservative strategy. It is hard to say which strategy is best, but team owners and managers should clearly be aware of how their investments are related to each other.

Option Value for Players

In finance, an option is something that gives an investment some flexibility. There are many types of options. For example, a *call* is the option to *buy* an investment at a specified price at a certain time in the future. A *put* is an option to *sell* an investment at a specified price at a certain time in the future. A call or a put does not force the investor to buy or sell the investment but allows the sale or purchase if it becomes a good business decision to do so. There are other types of options as well.

Many players have a type of option. In fact, nearly all players give teams some options. Because of the uncertain nature of sport, teams always like to have options. For example, suppose that a hockey team has an injury-prone starting goalie with a 30 percent chance of getting hurt during the season. Suppose that the same team has a defenseman who can play goalie if necessary. The uncertainty of the starting goalie's health can create an option value for the defenseman. Now, consider three possible outcomes. The first outcome is that the starting goalie remains healthy and gives up an average of one goal per game. The second outcome is that the starting goalie gets hurt and the defenseman must play goalie. With this outcome, the team gives up an average of two goals per game. That results from the loss of the starting goalie and the requirement to replace the defenseman. The third outcome is that the goalie gets hurt and nobody else on the team can play goalie very well. If the team is not able to find a reasonable replacement, this will hurt the team drastically and they will give up three goals per game. Table 11.4 shows the possible outcomes.

If the hockey team can use the defenseman as the backup goalie, then on average the team will yield 1.3 goals per game. If they have no reasonable replacement for goalie, they will yield 1.6 goals per game.[8] Therefore, the option value of a defenseman's ability to play goalie is the difference of the two averages or .3 goals per game.

If this is the case, it should be part of a player's marginal product. If we assume that the defenseman is worth .5 goals per game when he is playing

Table 11.4 Option Value of a Player

Goals Given Up Per Game		Backup Goalie	
		Defenseman	None
Goalie's health	No injury (70 percent chance)	1	1
	Injury (30 percent chance)	2	3
Expected value of goals yielded per game		1.3	1.6

as a defenseman, then his total benefit also should include the .3 goal option value, for a total value of .65 goals.[9] That value is worth a certain number of wins. If .65 goals produce 10 additional wins across the season, then the player's marginal product is 10 games. Most owners, managers, and fans have an intuitive understanding of option values. Certain "utility" players often are valuable just in case they are needed. Having options is always a benefit; if a team is hiring a player, it is helpful to be able to quantify these options.

Why Do Teams Take Risks with Players?

In finance, risk is always a crucial factor when dealing with investments. Typically, when an investment has a high risk, fewer investors will want to buy that investment, lowering the price. In other words, if there are two investments that have the same expected return, the riskier investment is typically cheaper because a majority of investors are risk averse and prefer not to gamble and to secure positive returns with the least possible risk.

Ironically, in sports, it has been shown that teams often prefer riskier players (Bollinger & Hotchkiss, 2003; Hendricks, DeBrock, & Koenker, 2003). What are risky players? One example is when baseball teams draft high school players instead of those who went on to play in college. Players characterized by the latter are older and have played more games. Alternatively, players fresh out of high school may have raw skills that are not yet fully developed and have not yet been challenged by high-level opponents. Another example of a risky player is one that is injury prone. Yet another example is a player whose performance varies greatly. Research has shown that given the same expected return, teams actually prefer riskier players. That is, if two players have the same expected performance but different variances of performance, the player with more variance (more risk) would get paid more.

So why do teams prefer risky players? Are sports teams less risk averse than other types of businesses? One possible explanation is that teams hire risky players because the team can bench them if they do not perform (Lazear, 1998). If players are very risky, meaning that they might perform very well or very poorly, teams can typically bench players as soon as their performance declines. Financially speaking, players have an option value. Teams have the option of not using that investment if the investment (player) does not perform well. A slightly different example than the previous option value example can prove illustrative. Suppose a team has 20 roster positions but can only play 10 players at a time. Further suppose that a team can either hire 20 players that they are certain will perform at an average level or 20 players that will perform very well half of the time and very poorly half of the time. If the team hires the 20 "risky" players, then, on average, 10 of them will perform well and those are the players that will get most of the playing time. Certainly, this option value for players has something to do with teams hiring or drafting riskier players.

There is another possible explanation for teams hiring risky players. It is possible that teams face a unique revenue structure. Typically, when a firm produces more goods, the additional revenue from producing the goods decreases, and there are diminishing marginal returns. If teams are producing wins, then this might not be the case. A traditional business would rather produce a certain amount of goods every year than produce a high amount one year and a small amount the next year. Again, teams might be different. Let's think of these alternatives. Would a team rather have a .500 record every year, or finish in last place half of the time and win a championship half of the time? Given how fans respond to team quality and the additional revenue from playoffs, their revenues might be higher if their win/loss record varied from year to year. Obviously, teams want to win every year, but given their constraints, they might be better off with a 50 percent chance of winning and a 50 percent chance of losing, rather than with a 100 percent chance of winning just half their games. In other words, there is a big difference between a first-place team and an average team compared to the difference between an average team and a bad team. This implies that teams might have an increasing marginal revenue curve. While economists typically do not like the idea of an increasing marginal revenue curve, there are reasons to think why this could be the case (Fort & Winfree, 2009). If teams do have an increasing marginal revenue curve, it might explain why teams have an incentive to hire risky players. This might be especially true for small-market teams. One can imagine that the only way small-market teams with small payrolls can win is by taking chances on players who might or might not pan out.

Player Contracts

What is the cost of hiring or signing a player? Different sports have different nuances concerning player contracts, but there are some common and basic aspects. Most contracts are multiyear. Therefore, what is critical is the contract's present value. To find the present value of a player's contract, future payments must be discounted:

$$Present\,Value = \frac{salary_1}{(1+r)^1} + \frac{salary_2}{(1+r)^2} + \ldots + \frac{salary_3}{(1+r)^N} = \sum_{t=1}^{N} \frac{Salary}{(1+r)^t}$$

where $salary_t$ is the player's salary in year t, r is the discount rate, and the contract is for N years. If the salary is the same for each year, then the present value can be calculated using a financial calculator.[10]

Looking at some surprising past deals, in 2000, many wondered how the Texas Rangers could sign Alex Rodriguez to a 10-year, $252 million contract. While this was certainly a large contract, it was not really a $252-million-dollar contract in present value terms. If the contract was for $25.2 million each year for 10 years, and a 10 percent discount rate is applied, the contract was actually only worth $154.8 million dollars (if the payment was at the end of the year). Because one dollar is worth less in the future than it is today, owners would prefer to delay payments to players (back-loaded contracts). That is, they would rather pay players farther into the future. Conversely, players would prefer to be paid as early as possible or to have their contracts "front-loaded." A lower discount rate would increase the present value of the contract.

For example, suppose Alex Rodriguez's contract was back-loaded so that he received $10.2 million a year for the first five years and $40.2 million for the next five years. The net present value of this contract is $133.3 million (at a 10 percent discount rate). On the other hand, if the contract was front-loaded so that he received $40.2 million a year for the first five years and $10.2 million for the next five years, then the net present value is $176.4 million. While these are all "$252 million contracts," clearly Alex Rodriguez would prefer a front-loaded contract and the Rangers would prefer a back-loaded contract. In reality, both sides know and understand the net present value of the contract. So, if for some reason, the team would prefer not to make large payments early, they would have to compensate the player by increasing the "back" end of the contract so that the net present value is the agreed amount. In other words, Alex Rodriguez and the Rangers agreed to a net present value of approximately $154.8 million for 10 years, but there are many different payment schemes that will give a net present value of $154.8 million. Remember, the value of a long-term contract is never what is reported in the news.

Back-loading or front-loading might be done for various reasons. For example, in leagues with salary caps (where back-loading is permitted), teams might not be able to pay players more than a certain amount in certain years. Therefore, their contracts are adjusted in years that the team has more salary cap space. So, while there might be some issues with things like guaranteed versus nonguaranteed money, or maybe a player needs the money early, in principle, it is the net present value of a contract that is important, not the actual amount of money paid.

Incentives in Contracts

Incentive clauses are another common occurrence in sports contracts. Of course, putting incentives in contracts is not unique to sports. Virtually every industry deals with what is called the *principal–agent problem*. The principal–agent problem is when two entities, the principal and the agent, have different incentives. The classic example is when a worker does not work hard. In some cases, the employer and employee can have differences of opinion about what is expected. This is not the only case of a principal–agent problem. Some people have blamed financial analysts for the drastic drop in housing prices in 2008 and 2009. Many have said that because some investors were not risking their own money, they took too many risks. In other words, investors did not have the correct incentives. To try to fix the principal–agent problem, workers often have incentive clauses in their contracts so that their goals are the same as the company's. One example is when employees receive a commission or a percentage of the profit they made for the company.

The story of Ken O'Brien, who played quarterback years ago, gives insight into the challenges faced by sports teams and their managers (Brown, 1990). When Ken O'Brien played for the New York Jets, he had an incentive in his contract linking his salary to his quarterback rating. This may sound like a good idea. A quarterback's rating is reduced by incomplete passes, but not by sacks. As all quarterbacks do, O'Brien had an option when all of his receivers were covered. He could throw the ball out of bounds for an incompletion or he could wait and get sacked. While under certain situations a sack might be helpful, more than likely the team would rather he throw the ball out of bounds. Because he lost money every time he threw the ball out of bounds, he might have decided to be sacked. Even former Jets quarterback Joe Namath noticed the flaws in his contract, saying,

> I'm amazed at [O'Brien's] accuracy, but I see him hold the ball more than he should. I always thought it was better to have second and 10 than second and 18. I don't like incentive contracts that pertain to numbers.
>
> (Anderson, 1988)

This situation – while dated – illustrates the conflict that can occur when contracts are laden with play-dependent incentives. It is not hard to think of other examples that might create problems. If an NBA player is paid based on how many points are scored, then that player is more likely to be selfish and shoot the ball all of the time. In baseball, performances are more individual and not dependent on teammates. This makes it easier to place mutually beneficial incentive clauses in contracts. For example, if a player gets a bonus for winning a Gold Glove Award, it is hard, but not impossible to see how that would hurt the team. The trick is that the team should give players incentives that are completely compatible with the team's goals. The team wants the players to win games. So, teams or leagues typically give a bonus if players reach the championship. If a player is paid based on how many games the team wins, much of that is out of the player's control. On the other hand, if the player is paid based on individual statistics, his/her selfish play could hurt the team.

Other incentive issues involve the length of a player contract. There are advantages and disadvantages to long-term contracts. While a longer-term contract provides some security for the player and team, there is also some risk that the performance of the player will change as the player ages. Also, there is some evidence that players perform slightly better on average in the last year of their contract (Berri & Krautmann, 2006). Presumably this is because players do not have guaranteed money for the next year and their future earnings depend greatly on their current performance. One should remember, though, that athletes already have a large incentive to perform well. Therefore, any changes in effort through contract incentives will probably be somewhat small.

Opportunity Costs

In economics, an opportunity cost is the cost of the next best thing you could have done with your money. If there is a situation where one investment does not preclude other investments, then the opportunity cost can be thought of as the cost of borrowing money, the interest rate. The opportunity cost of an investment is the second best use of the funds. While opportunity costs might seem like a straightforward idea, it can be enlightening. For example, think about the draft choices made by the Oakland Athletics as described in the book *Moneyball* (Lewis, 2003). Lewis noted the Athletics drafted catcher Jeremy Brown in the first round. The point here is not whether Jeremy Brown should have been a first round draft pick or not, a point debated by general manager Billy Beane and his scouts. While Billy Beane argued that the player was highly undervalued, he seemed to agree that Brown would have been drafted much lower had they not drafted him. Therefore, even if Jeremy Brown, in fact, was good enough to be a first-round draft pick, the Athletics should not have drafted him in the first round assuming they could have gotten him in later rounds. By picking him in the first round, he had a relatively high opportunity cost. Presumably, the Athletics could have picked him in a later round and drafted a different player in the first round, one they might not have had the opportunity to draft otherwise. Every time an investment is made, the opportunity costs should be considered.

Sunk Costs

A sunk cost is a cash outlay that has already been made. In the middle of an investment, the sunk cost is money that has already been paid. The important point is that sunk costs should have *no bearing* on future decisions. Again, this concept seems straightforward, but apparently some sports teams do not have a full grasp of this concept. For example, once a player's contract has been signed, the amount owed to the player is a sunk cost for the team. The player will earn that money regardless of whether or not he or she plays, so the player's salary should have no bearing on future team decisions. Most fans have heard teams or announcers say something to the effect of, "Well, he makes too much money to sit on the bench." If a player is not performing up to expectations, and there are other players who are playing better, it makes no sense to play the underperforming athlete. Teams should not compound mistakes by playing athletes simply because of their salary.

Players and Capital Budgeting

To discuss capital budgeting regarding players, managers must first understand *independent* and *mutually exclusive* investments. Independent investments are those that are completely unrelated and that do not eliminate alternatives. For example, the type of beer that Little Caesars Arena sells has no effect on which goalie the Red Wings sign. Mutually exclusive investments are those that are completely related and cannot both be executed. For example, if an NFL team signed Tom Brady (in his prime) as their quarterback, it would be virtually impossible to also sign Russell Wilson. With mutually exclusive investments, teams must choose one or the other, which may raise the opportunity cost of the investment. Some investments are related, but not necessarily mutually exclusive. Independent and mutually exclusive investments present the two extremes.

Independent investments are related to the idea of *unlimited funds*. If investments are independent, then choosing an investment has no bearing on other investments. The same might be true if an investor has unlimited funds. If an investor had unlimited funds, then a financial analyst should use an *accept–reject* method to judge investments. That is to say, if an investment meets a certain criterion, usually a certain rate of return, then the investment should be made. For example, if a team can borrow as much as they want from a bank, then each investment that will have a higher rate of return than the interest rate should be made.

In sport (as well as in many other industries), investors do not have unlimited funds and investments are not independent. In other words, if five different quarterbacks would help the team, the team cannot say, "Let's just sign all of them." The opposite of unlimited funds is *capital rationing*. With capital rationing, investors or firms must use a *ranking* method and only choose the best investments. That is to say, teams will choose the one quarterback that helps the team the most (financially).

There are many ways in which leagues impose a situation where capital rationing must be used. One example is roster limits. In most industries, firms hire workers as long as their MRP is higher than their salaries. In this situation, employees are judged based on the ratio of their MRP and wages. If employees of type A are only paid 50 percent of their MRP and employees of type B are paid 90 percent of their MRP, then firms will always prefer type A. Even if the productivity (MRP) of type A employees was only half of type B, the firm will simply hire twice as many type A employees.

Roster limits and limited playing time changes this. If an NBA team can only have 12 players, then they are now worried about the difference between MRP and wages, not the ratio. For example, suppose rookies have an MRP of $2 million, but are only paid $1 million. Suppose that a more talented player has an MRP of $10 million but gets paid $8 million. If there were no roster limits, teams would sign as many rookies as possible because they are only paying 50 percent of MRP instead of 80 percent.[11] With roster limits, teams have a fixed number of slots, so this means the profit maximizing strategy is to sign as many superstars as possible. In the hypothetical case above, the more talented player produces $2 million for the team as opposed to the $1 million generated by a less-talented rookie.

Salary caps also impact player decisions. When teams are constrained, they must rank players and choose the best ones. Many teams would like to invest more in player talent, but they are restrained by the salary cap. With the same MRPs and salaries of players in the previous paragraph, a salary cap might give an incentive to have more rookies as opposed to more talented and experienced players. Every league with a salary cap also has roster limits, so the net effect is ambiguous. Regardless, teams are forced to use capital rationing.

With an understanding of how the sport industry is different than others with regard to capital rationing, different valuation techniques for players can be compared. The first is the payback period. The payback period is simply the time that an investment takes to recover the investment cost. Sometimes firms use the payback period as a capital budgeting technique because it can be easy to calculate and it does give some implicit consideration of the timing of cash flows. The clear problem, however, is that the payback period does not consider the net present value of the investment, any kind of rate of return, or the risk of the investment. For example, one investment may recover its costs very quickly. If an alternative investment recovers its costs more slowly and then gains big returns after that, it might be a much better investment. Although the payback period might be a reasonable first method to use, especially if there is a high level of uncertainty dealing with the investments, it is usually considered an inferior technique.

Another capital budgeting technique is simply using net present value (discussed earlier). Most financial analysts consider net present value to be a superior method to the payback period. This is a very common method and for good reason. By depreciating future values, it gives an accurate measure of the investment in current dollars. Players also can be evaluated in terms of the team's IRR. Although calculating the internal rate of return can be useful, one disadvantage is that investors are forced into calculating one rate. Net present value, for example, is flexible enough that analysts can change the depreciation rate. This problem can be especially egregious if it is comparing investments of different length. Changing depreciation rates can be difficult to foresee and the limit of using one rate is an advantage in the sense that it boils down the investment to one metric.

A technique not yet discussed is the *risk adjusted discount rate*. As the name implies, this is a rate of return that takes into account some risk level. One drawback of NPV and IRR is that risk is not considered. The tricky part of determining a risk-adjusted rate is that the investor must put some value on risk. For example, an owner could say, "I need $100,000 to assume the risk of that player." In this case, the risk-adjusted discount rate is calculated the same way as an internal rate of return, except that, instead of being zero, the net present value should be –$100,000.

The final technique examined is the risk-adjusted net present value. This takes risk into account in the same way as the risk-adjusted discount rate and, therefore, has the same pluses and minuses. If one can easily value the risk of the investment, then the risk-adjusted net present value is a very attractive method. Table 11.5 presents five different players with varying signing bonuses, yearly salaries, marginal revenue products, and risk levels.

To sign player A, the team needs to offer a $1 million signing bonus and a yearly contract of $3 million. The player gives the team a marginal revenue product of $3.5 million. To remove any risk involved with the player, the team would be willing to pay $1 million and the length of the contract is four years. For each player, it is assumed that end of the year payments and a 10 percent depreciation value for the team owner. It is also assumed that the signing bonus is paid at the beginning of the first year. Therefore, using a financial calculator, the players have the values (in millions) shown in Table 11.6. Table 11.7 shows the results using the payback period, net present value, internal rate of return, risk-adjusted discount rate, and a risk-adjusted net present value.

As Table 11.7 illustrates, there are five different investments, and each one could be "best" depending on the capital budgeting technique. Thus, the obvious question is: which investment is best? As noted earlier, the payback

Table 11.5 Various Contracts for Hypothetical Players

Factor	Player A	Player B	Player C	Player D	Player E
Signing bonus	$1 million	$3 million	$1.1 million	$1.5 million	$3.1 million
Yearly salary	$3 million	$3 million	$1 million	$1 million	$3 million
Marginal revenue Product	$3.5 million	$4.1 million	$1.5 million	$1.6 million	$4.1 million
Risk adjustment[1]	$1 million	$1 million	$1 million	$0.2 million	$0.2 million
Length of contract	4 years[2]	5 years	5 years	5 years	5 years

[1] This represents how much owners need to be compensated due to the risk of the player. Remember it was noted earlier in this chapter that it appears that teams prefer risk. So, this could be looked at as a liability of having not enough risk.

[2] Because Player A only has a four-year contract, that would allow the team to sign another player for the 5th year, but we will ignore that for the purposes of this example.

Table 11.6 Financial Values of Players

Factor	Player A	Player B	Player C	Player D	Player E
N	4	5	5	5	5
I/Y	10%	10%	10%	10%	10%
PV[1]	−1/−2	−3/−4	−1.1/−2.1	−1.5/−1.7	−3.1/−3.3
PMT[2]	.5	1.1	.5	.6	1.1
FV	0	0	0	0	0

[1] The first value is the signing bonus and is subtracted from the present value to calculate the net present value. It also is used to calculate the internal rate of return. The second value is the signing bonus with the risk adjustment. This is used to find the risk adjusted discount rate and is subtracted from the present value to find the risk adjusted net present value.

[2] The yearly payment is the player's marginal revenue product minus his/her salary.

Table 11.7 Various Assessment Techniques

Technique	Player A	Player B	Player C	Player D	Player E
Payback period[1]	2 years	3 years	3 years	3 years	3 years
Net present value	$.584	$1.170	$.795	$.774	$1.070
Internal rate of return	34.90%	24.32%	35.51%	28.65%	22.75%
Risk adjusted discount rate	0%	11.65%	6.11%	22.50%	19.86%
Risk adjusted net present value	−$.416	$.170	−$.205	$.574	$.870

[1] If there are small constant payments throughout the year, the payback period can be calculated by dividing the present value (without any risk adjustment) by the yearly payment. However, since there are end of the year payments, the payback period represents the number of years needed to completely pay off the initial investment.

period is usually worse than finding the net present value or internal rate of return, so player A is not the best investment. If risk is factored into the decision making, then player B or C should be selected. If there is no capital rationing, then the investment with the highest risk-adjusted discount rate might be the best. If players were more like stocks, player D would be the best. That is because player D only costs approximately half the investment ($1.7 million versus $3.3 million) of player E. If these athletes were similar to traded stocks, investors would just buy two of player D. In sport, that is not an option as there are a fixed number of players and roster spots. In that case, the team would want to choose the player with the highest risk-adjusted net present value, player E. This shows the importance of understanding the investment environment. Because of the mutually exclusive nature of players, using net present value (or risk-adjusted net present value) is the more appropriate technique.

Is the Market for Players Efficient?

Economists and financial analysts are always trying to see if different markets are efficient. *Efficiency* can have different definitions, and many people argue whether financial markets are efficient. The *efficient market hypothesis* deals with financial markets and can have slightly different definitions. Many would say that the efficient market hypothesis holds if the price of assets accurately reflects all of the available information and immediately reacts to new information. Intelligent people can disagree on whether certain markets show "irrational exuberance" or whether they price investments with amazing precision. While the market for things like stocks can be very different than the market for players, there can be the same debate about whether player markets are efficient.

Professional teams and analysts are always trying to determine if the market for players is efficient. That is, do teams pay players the "correct" amount with regard to how much they help the team? For example, many have argued that statistics such as on-base percentage are, or at least were, undervalued in MLB (Lewis, 2003). If that is the case, teams with a given payroll could win more games if they signed players with a high on-base percentage as opposed to a high batting average. While there is evidence that the player market in MLB was inefficient in this regard, it is always easier to say that after the fact. For example, after the ".com" bust of the 1990s, analysts were saying that the market was clearly overvalued. Some have argued that, at the time, the market was not overvalued, just unlucky. Or maybe it was simply difficult to foresee the .com bust before the fact. Maybe some of the companies in fact did have high potential, but that potential was never realized. It is easy to say the stock market was overvalued after everything has played out.

While people can dispute whether player markets can be inefficient, research shows that while this may have been the case, the market for talent in MLB has corrected this (Hakes & Sauer, 2006). Typically, when there are inefficiencies in markets, they correct themselves. While some might argue that MLB owners and managers were slow to correct this inefficiency, once the inefficiency is known, sports player markets seem to quickly correct for any excessive payments. Because markets such as these are often efficient, this makes the risk and correlation of players very important.

It is important as well to remember that what can be perceived as an inefficiency may reveal something about fan or owner preferences. For example, some have argued that scoring points is overvalued in the NBA (Berri, Brook, & Schmidt, 2007). The argument is that players who do other things, such as get rebounds, make great passes, and play tough defense, help teams win more, but players are not paid enough for this. What if fans like to see fast-paced, high-scoring games? It is possible that the team's objective is not to maximize wins but to maximize fan satisfaction. This could mean that teams will pay certain types of players a premium for their type of play because this is what fans want to see. The old sayings "Drive for show, putt for dough" and "Offense sells tickets, defense wins championships" come to mind.

Cost of Capital

Because any investment should give returns higher than the costs, the cost of capital is the rate of return that a firm must earn on the projects in which it invests to maintain its market value. The target capital structure is the desired optimal mix of debt and equity financing that most firms attempt to maintain. An example proves useful in understanding why there sometimes needs to be an optimal financing mix of debt and equity financing. Suppose that someone purchases a team for $500 million (e.g., the Las Vegas Golden Knights). The team has an expected internal rate of return of 8 percent, and the cheapest financing for the owner is debt financing at 7 percent. Now suppose that, immediately after, a different team is for sale for $500 million (Carolina Hurricanes), but the owner has used all available debt financing. The new team has an expected internal rate of return of 12 percent and the cheapest financing is now equity financing at 13 percent. The problem for the owner is that there are limits to how much debt financing can be supported. Even if the first team's expected return was higher than the cost of financing, it may not have been a good decision because there is also a cost to using all of one's debt financing to sustain the investment. In other words, there may be an opportunity cost when using debt financing. Many investors always use a mix of debt and equity financing. If the investors had used 50 percent debt financing and 50 percent equity financing, the cost of financing would have been 10 percent (.5 × 7% + .5 × 13% = 10%). If the investors had thought of the cost of capital as being 10 percent, they would have foregone the first team and bought the second team. Not only would they have expected to make 2 percent more than the costs as opposed to 1 percent, but they would have also had more debt financing available to them because they only debt-financed $250 million instead of $500 million. The optimal mix of debt and equity financing may not be 50 percent of each, but usually using a mix of financing will help the firm use the best investments.

Before identifying the optimal mix of debt and equity financing, analysts need to be sure all costs have been included. There are often various costs associated with issuing and selling bonds and stocks called flotation costs. Flotation costs typically include administrative costs or underwriting costs. For example, suppose a team issues a 20-year bond with a $1,000 par value and a 5 percent coupon rate. Further, let us suppose that underwriting and administrative costs are 3 percent of the bond. Therefore, the net proceeds, or the money received from the sale of a security, is only $970, not $1,000. If we calculate the cost of capital after we include the flotation costs, we find that the cost of the bond is 5.25 percent (PV = 970, PMT = –50, FV = –1000, N = 20). The floatation costs increase the cost of capital in this case by one-quarter of a percent. It is important to note that for corporate bonds there are also taxes that need to be taken into account to find the cost of capital.

Calculating the cost of equity capital is different than the cost of debt capital, but the cost of issuing a preferred stock is somewhat similar. The cost of issuing preferred stock is simply the annual dividend divided by the net proceeds. For example, if a firm receives $100 from selling a share of preferred stock and the dividend is $4 per year, then the cost of obtaining the capital is 4 percent.

The cost of capital as it pertains to common stock is more unknown because it deals with the firm's future profits. Selling common stock to fund investments is somewhat more complicated because it deals with selling future dividends, which is unknown. Because companies can be valued by using the constant growth model, an analyst can use the same model to estimate the cost of capital for common stock. Rearranging the constant growth model indicates that the cost of capital for common stock is given by:

$$k = \frac{D}{P} + g$$

where k is the cost of capital, D is the dividend payment, P is the price of the stock, and g is the expected growth rate of the dividend. For example, if a firm sells a share of common stock for $100, the dividend is $4 per year, and it grows at 2 percent, then the cost of obtaining the capital is 6 percent.

What is the optimal mix for financing capital? In what some call a "perfect market," it does not really matter if firms use debt capital or equity capital, which is known as the *capital structure irrelevance principle* (Modigliani & Miller, 1958). This is because if the market is efficient, the prices of stocks and bonds should adjust so that investors are indifferent between buying stocks or bonds and firms are indifferent between selling stocks or bonds. In this "perfect market" there are no taxes, no flotation costs, symmetrical information, and one interest rate. These are the things that might make debt or equity financing more attractive. One of the benefits of debt financing is that issuing bonds often includes tax breaks. Because interest payments from bonds can be deducted from taxes, this often makes debt financing attractive. Using debt financing increases the possibility of bankruptcy because interest payments must be made. There also can be agency costs with debt finance, which means that the lender needs to make sure the borrower is using the funds appropriately. There also can be issues associated with investors not having full information. Especially with small firms, it is possible that the owner knows more about the future profits of the firm than other outside investors.

In Chapter 8, we did not focus on the depreciation rate when valuing teams. If an analyst can calculate the weighted cost of capital for the firm, this is a reasonable choice to use for the depreciation rate. If there is a mix of debt and equity financing, then the weighted cost of capital is given by:

$$k_W = w_D k_D + w_E k_E$$

where k_W is the weighted cost of capital, w_D and w_E are the percentages of debt and equity finance used, and k_D and k_E are the costs of debt and equity capital. If preferred and common stock were both used, the weighted cost of capital should account for their differentiation as well.

It should be underscored that when facilities are built, an owner typically uses bonds or cash. If a facility is completely financed with a bond, then all of the cost of capital comes from that instrument of debt. If cash is used, then the cost of capital could be considered the return the owner would have received from the next best investment. In most instances, owners rely on a mix of equity (cash) and debt financing, and if other investors are involved (minority owners), then the principal owner creates equity partners by selling portions of the team.

There are various methods to find the optimal mix of debt and equity financing, such as the EBIT–EPS (earnings before interest and taxes–earnings per share) method. There are typically a few shortcomings with these methods. Finding the optimal mix depends on the risk of various financing tools as well as the opportunity cost of utilizing too much of one type. As noted earlier, reliance on debt financing reduces the ability to borrow for other investments, and reliance on cash could leave the owner with too little liquidity. Finding the right mix relative to risk is an important management decision for an owner and the senior management of a firm.

Notes

1   If we know the probability of every outcome, the standard deviation is calculated by:

$$\sigma_k = \sqrt{\sum_{j=1}^{n} \left(k_j - \bar{k}\right)^2 p_j}$$

   Most programs, such as Excel, have a default setting that calculates a standard deviation assuming all probabilities are equal.

2   If the data follows a normal distribution, then values will fall within two standard deviations of the average 95.4 percent of the time. There is, however, no reason to assume that raw data will follow a normal distribution.

3   A portfolio is simply a group of investments.

4   Certainly it is possible for attendance to decrease with a new stadium if the team performs poorly, but almost certainly attendance will increase if all other factors are the same.

5   To put ticket revenue into 2016 dollars (the last available year for all of the data), the nominal ticket revenue data was multiplied by 236.9 (the 2016 value of the Consumer Price Index) and divided by the Consumer Price Index value of that year.

6   A program, such as Excel, can be used to find the IRR in this case. It can, however, still be relatively difficult. Using formulas in Excel, one can try various rates to see if the NPV is positive or negative and adjust accordingly. This will eventually give an accurate IRR. There are other programs that can more easily give the IRR on a given investment.

7   In baseball, there are different estimates of WAR. For example, fWAR and rWAR are estimates of marginal product. If two players had identical playing statistics, their fWAR would be the same, but their rWAR is dependent upon the team on which they played. For more information, see http://www.tangotiger.net/wiki/index.php?title=WAR

8   With the defenseman replacement, the expected value is equal to .7(1) + .3(2) = 1.3. Without the defenseman, the expected value is equal to .7(1) + .3(3) = 1.6.

9   Note that the defenseman is worth .5 goals per game when the regular goalie is healthy and the defenseman is worth 1 goal per game when the regular goalie is injured, so the expected value in terms of goal differential is .7(.5) + .3(1) = .65.

10 In this case, the financial key N would be equal to the number of years of the contract, I/Y would be the discount rate, PMT would be the amount of the salary, and FV would be equal to zero assuming there is no payment at the end of the contract. PV would then be solved for to find the present value of the contract. If there is a signing bonus that the player gets as soon as the contract is signed, that would be added to the present value of the contract because no discounting is necessary for the signing bonus.

11 A team can realistically only play so many players. This would imply that after a while, MRPs would dwindle. The example is simplified for illustrative purposes.

References

Anderson, D. 1988. "Super" Jets question today's Jets, *The New York Times*, August 7.

Berri, D. 2008. A simple measure of worker productivity in the National Basketball Association. In *The business of sport*, eds. B. Humphreys and D. Howard, 3 volumes, 1–40. Westport, CT: Praeger.

Berri, D., Brook, S., & Schmidt, M. 2007. Does one simply need to score to score? *International Journal of Sport Finance* 2 (4): 190–205.

Berri, D., & Krautmann, A. 2006. Shirking on the court: Testing for the incentive effects of guaranteed pay. *Economic Inquiry* 44 (3): 536–546.

Bollinger, C., & Hotchkiss, J. 2003. The upside potential of hiring risky workers: Evidence from the baseball industry. *Journal of Labor Economics* 21 (4): 923–944.

Brown, C. 1990. Firms' choice method of pay. *Industrial and Labor Relations Review* 43 (3): 165S–182S.

Forbes. 2017. Sports money: 2017 NFL valuations, *Forbes*, September. Retrieved from https://www.forbes.com/teams/green-bay-packers/ (accessed July 31, 2018).

Fort, R., & Winfree, J. 2009. Sports really are different: The contest success function and the supply of talent. *Review of Industrial Organization* 34: 69–80.

Hakes, J. K., & Sauer, R. D. 2006. An economic evaluation of the moneyball hypothesis. *Journal of Economic Perspectives* 20 (3): 173–185.

Hendricks, W., DeBrock, L., & Koenker, R. 2003. Uncertainty, hiring, and subsequent performance: The NFL draft. *Journal of Labor Economics* 21 (4): 857–886.

Knight, F. 1921. *Risk, uncertainty, and profit*. Boston: Hart, Schaffner, & Marx; Houghton Mifflin Co.

Lazear, E. P. 1998. Hiring risky workers. In *Internal labour market, incentives, and employment*, eds. I. Ohashi and T. Tachibanaki, 143–158. New York: St. Martin's.

Lewis, M. 2003. *Moneyball: The art of winning an unfair game*. New York: W. W. Norton.

Modigliani, F., & Miller, M. H. 1958. The cost of capital, corporation finance, and the theory of investment. *American Economic Review* 68 (3): 261–297.

Scully, G. W. 1974. Pay and performance in Major League Baseball. *American Economic Review* 64 (6): 915–930.

Chapter 12

League/Conference Policies and Taxes

Introduction

This chapter focuses on league and conference policies, taxes, and the relationship between the North American sport leagues and international organizations. Turning first to league and conference policies, each has guidelines that influence how teams receive money and how those funds can be spent. The policies adopted by professional leagues, in most instances, exist to achieve competitive balance or to ensure smaller market teams have more equitable opportunities to enhance their fiscal status. There are also several tax issues unique to professional teams, such as player taxes or the roster depreciation allowance, that will be discussed.

For colleges, the NCAA is critical to the governing process. But so too are the policies adopted by each conference. At the collegiate level there is also a concern that larger (more financially successful) athletic departments would leave less robust universities less able to attract high-quality athletes, thereby hurting competitive balance.

League Policies

League policies, such as player drafts, revenue sharing, luxury taxes, and salary caps, can be of tremendous importance for a team's bottom line and for the salaries of the players. Players' unions are constantly negotiating policies or seeking new ones that increase the share of sport-related revenue that becomes part of the pool of funds from which players are paid. At the ownership level, there is usually unified opposition to the unions' efforts to secure more revenue sources for player salaries and benefits. At the same time, there is usually disagreement among the owners with regard to the extent to which any single owner can seek revenues that might interfere with league-wide interests. The owners of smaller market teams also argue for greater revenue-sharing plans that equalize financial differences related to market sizes.

The conflicts between owners and players have led to work stoppages. For example, the 2004–2005 NHL season was canceled because players and owners could not agree on the implementation of a salary cap. MLB lost one of its World Series when owners and players could not agree on policies. During one labor conflict with the players' union in 1987, the NFL not only canceled some games, but for others used replacement players. The use of replacement players created conflicts since the union's players regarded the replacement players as opponents of the union, and therefore not "team players."

League policies are sometimes confusing because they are very complicated and affect various actors in unexpected ways. For example, while on the face of it, revenue sharing might seem to hurt the profit of large-market teams, economic theory suggests that it could actually help them because revenue sharing leads to lower player salaries. This is not always obvious to the casual observer. This chapter attempts to look deeper into the effect of various league policies.

In many ways, sport leagues can be thought of as a contest between franchise owners to secure a championship. That championship, in turn, can boost profits if an owner can raise ticket prices and secure more revenue from advertising and sponsorships and the sale of food and beverages. Of course, the level of new profits is a function of demand from fans living in the team's market area and the cost of securing the players who make winning possible. Owners make investments to improve their chances of winning, and the more they win, the higher the payoff – if the market can sustain higher prices or buy additional output from the team (tickets, luxury seating, etc.). From a financial standpoint, all of this might seem logical: win more games and enhance profitability, but leagues are not a winner-take-all contest. Remember, franchises need each other in order to exist. Teams depend on competition with other franchises in order to sell tickets to fans, so it is in owners' best interests to ensure the continued existence (and financial stability) of all franchises within the league.

Consider this example: if team A wins a championship, it will enjoy enhanced revenues, but, as a result, team B could see a loss of revenue with fewer wins and no championship. A limited number of teams will make it to the playoffs, and even fewer will play in championship games. This has led to agreements with winners, who have shared some of their enhanced revenues with other teams. When revenues are shared, there is less value in paying players higher salaries since player costs are not also shared.

Team owners, in charge of maintaining profitable franchises in dramatically different markets, are understandably drawn in different directions. In response, leagues have taken it upon themselves to impose measures meant to lead individual owners in the "right direction." There are two basic ways of manipulating this system. A league can try to change how teams invest in winning, or they can change the payoff structure.

League policies, such as salary caps, luxury taxes, and player drafts, aim to lower the investment that each team makes in its players. Think about the draft, in which a player's rights are controlled by a single team. If the best college player could auction their skills to all teams, then they would receive more money than what they earn under the current system. The ability to auction one's talent to all teams is reserved for those with a sufficient number of years of service when they can become free agents. The leagues have, in some instances, made the bidding for players a bit costlier. This has been achieved by requiring the team attracting a free agent to offer some level of compensation (another player) to the team that lost its player. In addition, there is always a suspicion among players that the owners could agree to not compete for free agents (Passan, 2018).

Revenue sharing, on the other hand, changes the payoff structure. Revenue sharing creates a financial situation that is more even between winning and losing teams. This also decreases the incentive to invest in winning, because losing teams are assured of receiving money from those franchises that are more successful. Note that revenue sharing is typically structured in a way that brings the lowest financially performing franchises up to a predetermined league average level with regard to revenues. The collective bargaining agreements (CBAs) never allow for teams on the receiving end of financial support to reach a point where their "bottom line" is above that of a team on the giving end of revenue sharing funds. The support from large-market teams for revenue sharing is based on the expectation that engaging in revenue sharing will ultimately lower the average player salary across the league. This could yield benefits for owners in large markets, even if they have to share some of their revenue. Of course, players do not want the incentive to invest in players decreased, which is why it is in their best interest to oppose revenue sharing plans.

Before focusing on these policies, a few essential concepts need to be understood. First, teams will invest in players and a facility to the point where the marginal return of that investment equals the marginal cost. In other words, if teams are profit maximizing, total revenues do not dictate how much they will invest. Owners and financial analysts always concentrate on marginal analyses. No matter how profitable a team is, when signing a new player, the issue of concern is whether or not that player has the potential to produce more money than the player will cost. Some league policies can change either the marginal revenue or marginal costs of an investment in talent (luxury taxes, etc.). This can change the competitive balance of a league[1] and/or player salaries.

Second, complete competitive balance (where all teams are of equal quality) is probably not an optimal financial outcome for a league. While fans and pundits typically want more balance,[2] there can be too much balance from a profit-maximizing perspective. Some fans prefer to watch games with favorites and underdogs. The NCAA's men's basketball tournament, March Madness, flourishes, in part, because there are underdogs who periodically upset favored teams. Casual fans who only follow the tournament and might not know who is an underdog are easily informed by the seeding process. In that way, almost everyone knows who is "supposed" to win the game. In this instance, then, a lack of competitive balance has helped create a sport phenomenon now worth hundreds of millions of dollars to the NCAA. Similarly, it could be reasonable argued that LeBron James and Steph Curry have been good for the NBA, or that Sidney Crosby is good for the NHL, but it should also be noted that, because of their skills, each reduced the competitive balance in their leagues. Although great athletes and teams distort competitive balance, they often create new fans for a league that might not have been there otherwise. Their presence also elevates the value of upsets, which, if and when they occur, generally attract a great deal of media attention. Some fans even like to root for continual underdogs, such as the Chicago Cubs (prior to their 2016 World Series win). Furthermore, there are more fans in bigger markets. For example, if the Royals started winning as much as the Yankees, year after year, this would be bad financially for MLB because a small fan base in Kansas City cannot generate as much revenue as the larger one in New York. As pundits often point out, leagues prefer to have large market teams in the championship series because it typically helps television ratings (and elevates earnings for the league). When the Yankees acquired Giancarlo Stanton to join Aaron Judge, while many groaned, the possibility of more and more fans watching MLB games because of the presence of the two sluggers on the same team could lead to higher profits for all teams.

Player Drafts

Player drafts have a long history in professional sports. The first draft appears to have taken place in 1915 when the Australian Football League instituted a metropolitan zoning program to stop owners from signing players from across the country. What their plan entailed was limiting teams to the players in their home geographic region. The NFL also had a type of geographical selection process when it became the first major North American league to formalize a draft in 1936. The professional team located in the area in which the athletes played their collegiate ball had the right to draft those players. This was done to capitalize on the stronger popularity of college football at the time and transfer some of that excitement into the fledgling NFL. The first player drafted, Jay Berwanger (University of Chicago), by the Chicago Bears, decided not to play professional football. The NBA followed with a draft for the 1949–1950 season; the NHL initiated its draft in 1963 and MLB followed suit in 1965. While a few domestic and many foreign players do not enter the professional ranks through a draft, a vast majority of athletes enter their professional careers through a selection process overseen by the leagues.

Player drafts are a good way to understand the actual effects of policies. Many believe that allowing teams with the least wins to draft first will somehow improve those teams' future on-field performance because they will then get the best new talent. The problem with this logic is that profit-maximizing teams should invest in talent to the point where marginal returns from that talent equals marginal costs. The player draft does not really change this relationship. If a smaller-market team acquired a player with substantial talent, the amount that an owner could earn from employing that athlete could be far less than the owner of a larger-market team could earn. Should that player receive less in compensation because of the differentials in income related to market size? In the end, teams in smaller markets often trade the rights to these players to larger-market teams, receiving some of the excess profits earned in the larger market. This is also seen throughout Europe when teams receive transfer payments to allow athletes to move to larger markets. Even if high draft picks are kept on the team, the team may decide to forgo signing a talented free agent. So, while it is certainly possible that there could be a short-term effect, the long-term quality of the team will likely not be impacted by a player draft.

With this observation in mind, managers must consider the effect player drafts have on competitive balance. After all, many see the purpose of drafts as achieving exactly that. In today's drafts, each of the leagues' lowest-performing teams get the earliest draft picks as a means to give lower-quality teams access to higher-quality players at low costs. Unfortunately, empirical findings suggest player drafts have very little effect on competitive balance. Consider the Cleveland Browns. Since 1999, the Browns have had 11 top-10 draft picks, seven of which were top-three picks. Yet, the team reached a winning record above .500 only twice. If drafts truly impacted leagues' competitive balance, we would be talking about the Browns a bit differently. After all, the Browns became the first NFL team to win only one game across two seasons (2016 and 2017) despite all of their high level draft picks.

Certainly, there are exceptions. For example, LeBron James changed the fortunes of the Cleveland Cavaliers in his initial years after being drafted. Though it should be noted the Cavs failed to win a championship during his first tenure with the team. James eventually decided to relocate to a larger market, Miami, and won two championships. He then returned to Cleveland and finally helped that city enjoy its first national championship in several decades.

Nonetheless, analysis seems to indicate that balance before a player draft is really no different than the balance after the draft. So, what is the point of the draft? Are leagues simply going through a meaningless process? Drafts do have one important component regarding team finances. Drafts are very effective at restricting player pay. They create a complete monopsony situation where there is only one team with which the player can negotiate, which limits players' bargaining power. Therefore, players will be paid less and team profits will increase.

If players' salaries decrease with a draft, one might wonder why each players' union has agreed to it. Player unions and owners agree to many policies and practices, but it is important to note that younger players do not have as strong a voice in the players' union as compared to veterans. One reason players might be willing to keep a draft is because it does not affect veteran players and their representatives. Further, pushing economic sacrifice onto rookie players to secure rewards for veterans appeals to the largest proportion of a union's members. A player draft might seem particularly appealing to veteran players when an alternative could be a salary cap.

Revenue Sharing

As with player drafts, many fans believe that revenue sharing is designed to increase competitive balance. After all, if a large-market team shares some of its revenue with a small-market team, total revenues should even out. A report from MLB's Blue Ribbon Panel, convened in 1999 and 2000 to assess the state of the business of baseball, endorsed expanded revenue sharing, arguing that smaller-market teams would have the resources to attract and retain better players. It was argued that, with those better players, these franchises would be able to more effectively compete for championships. It is true that revenue sharing evens out the funds available to different franchises (as it does in the NFL). However, this does not necessarily mean that small-market teams will invest more in talent. There are no restrictions on how the shared revenue can or should be spent, and it can be difficult to pinpoint exactly how owners are using the shared funds.

For example, if a team's payroll is $60 million and the team receives $40 million from shared revenue streams, there is no way to know if they are using the shared revenue on payroll costs. One could argue the team should use the excess funds to acquire more skilled players, upping payroll costs to $100 million. Alternatively, the team might argue that, without revenue shared funds from the league, their roster payroll would have been only $20 million, and that the $60 million they pay now is already more than enough. In addition, investing in talent includes much more than player salaries. There are often substantial player development costs to consider. Remember, if an owner does not believe spending money will produce a positive financial impact on a team's bottom line, it could well be a smarter business decision *not* to expend shared revenues.

Recently, the Miami Marlins and the Pittsburgh Pirates have come under criticism from the MLB players' association for not spending enough on player salaries. It is likely that it is in the teams' financial interest to not spend the money they received from revenue sharing on player salaries. Furthermore, the last thing that large-market owners want is for the

Marlins and Pirates to use that money to compete with them in the market for free agents.

Again, an obvious question is: why do leagues have revenue sharing if small-market teams may not use the funds to invest in player talent? One reason might be because some revenue is generated by the league, not individual teams, and, therefore, must be shared. Most of the NFL's revenue comes from national television contracts and is shared equally among teams. MLB's revenues from its web-based delivery of games involves every team. As a result, the league's owners agreed to equally share the profits from MLBAM and its related components.

Payments from larger to smaller market teams can also be seen as a way to discourage owners in smaller markets from demanding to be permitted to relocate into a larger market as the market's second team. For example, when the Dallas Cowboys were created, the Dallas/Fort Worth region had a population of approximately 2 million people (2.2 million in 1970). Today, the region's population is in excess of 7.4 million. An argument could be made that the region could easily support a second team. To ensure that the owner of the Jacksonville Jaguars, for example, currently in a market of 1.5 million residents, does not demand to be permitted to relocate, revenue sharing makes it possible for his team to remain profitable and valuable, despite its smaller market. The vast revenue opportunities for Jerry Jones and the Cowboys is clearly a function of the existence of a single NFL team in such a large market. *Forbes* estimates the team is worth $4.8 billion. In exchange for not relocating, revenues are shared, providing other owners with a benefit from the extra profits earned by the Cowboys and other large market teams.

Another reason why leagues participate in revenue sharing (despite its faults) is that just like player drafts, revenue sharing decreases player salaries. How? Revenue sharing decreases player salaries because teams only receive a percentage of any one player's marginal revenue product. All owners share the value of an Odell Beckham Jr. or a Dak Prescott in a larger market as a result of the NFL's revenue sharing policies. This means neither the Giants nor the Cowboys will pay these players their true market value since their owners cannot realize the full return on their performance in the New York metropolitan area or in the Dallas/Fort Worth region. This makes the players less valuable to any single owner, and because players only negotiate with one owner, their ultimate salary is lower, even if they produce more profits for the entire league. As a result, revenue sharing decreases salaries, and this helps all owners, not just those with franchises in small markets. Small-market teams benefit from revenue sharing because they can pay less for talent but still receive a transfer of money from larger-market teams. Large-market teams gain from the overall decrease in player costs but must make a monetary transfer to small-market teams.

This does not mean that revenue sharing has no effect on competitive balance. The effect is quite complicated and depends on exactly how talent investment affects team revenues. The interesting thing about this is that research actually shows that if revenue has any effect, it will probably hurt competitive balance, rather than improve it (Appendix 1 shows the mathematics behind this intuition).

Another issue that owners grapple with regarding revenue sharing is what should be shared. As noted, revenue sharing decreases the incentive to invest in assets that produce more income. Owners do not mind this change when dealing with player talent because it reduces their costs and, if it binds all teams, there is no large change in outcomes. Because it is unlikely that the overall talent level in a league will change from a decrease in average player pay (the players have no option other than to play in a league), the main net result is a decrease in player pay. Similarly, because owners are required to share revenues generated by in-venue spending, there is less incentive to build amenities from which owners receive only part of the marginal revenue produced. The NFL has addressed this possibility with a commitment to provide as much as $150 million towards the construction of new stadia when the facilities are privately financed (the G-3 program). The success of that program led to a G-4 plan, created in 2011. Its more detailed requirements achieved the same objective – all teams would share in some of the costs of a new venue to ensure that owners would have a greater incentive to offer amenities that increase overall revenue levels.

Luxury Taxes

A luxury tax is calculated as a percent of a team's payroll that exceeds a certain threshold. Some teams have found that in their markets, they can make more revenue with larger payrolls and star players (even if they are charged a luxury tax) than they could with a lower payroll below the threshold. For this reason, many owners are willing to exceed the payroll threshold. This makes the luxury tax the equivalent of a tax on high revenue (usually large-market) teams. Because this is structured differently than revenue sharing, there is a greater chance that this will in fact increase competitive balance.

MLB has a relatively straightforward luxury tax. Every year, MLB has a threshold, and if payrolls exceed that amount they are taxed. For 2016, for example, the threshold was $189 million. Several teams paid luxury taxes that year: Dodgers ($31.8 million), New York Yankees ($27.4 million), Boston Red Sox ($4.5 million), Detroit Tigers ($4 million), and Chicago Cubs ($2.96 million). The Yankees have paid more in luxury taxes than any other team and have paid the tax for 16 consecutive seasons. For that reason, the MLB's luxury tax is sometimes called the Yankees' tax. Although the Yankees' payroll dwarfs the MLB average every year, this luxury tax should give them some incentive to lower their expenditures. If that occurs, the players receive less money across the league because it lowers the league-wide average player salary. This then allows owners to keep a higher percentage of total revenues.

Luxury taxes are meant to improve competitive balance and promote parity. With this in mind, it is reasonable to wonder if the luxury tax actually helps large market teams like the Yankees. This creates somewhat of a "Yankee paradox." If fans' priority is competitive balance, the Yankees would be better off if they lost more often just to generate some uncertainty. As has been discussed, at least part of the draw for consumers to purchase tickets to games is the uncertainty of outcome. Empirical evidence, however, seems to suggest that competitive balance has a relatively small effect on demand in the short term. At the very least, it would be incredibly difficult to argue that it is in the Yankees' financial interest to lose more games. Although the long-term effect of competitive balance on a league is difficult to test,[3] it seems hard to imagine a team being "too" successful.

Salary Caps

The NFL, NHL, NBA, and MLS all have some form of a salary cap, and most of the teams in these leagues are financially stable and profitable. While each of these leagues do have a cap, teams can circumvent the established ceiling. Discussed in the previous section, luxury taxes are charged when teams spend over the league-imposed salary cap.[4] Furthermore, in each league, exceptions are provided if a team has to spend more money as a result of player's injury that might require the addition of a new player to the roster.

The logic behind a salary cap is fairly straightforward. The cap ensures that all teams have similar payrolls. This, in the long run, should equalize the chance of attracting and retaining quality players, as well as the chance of winning. Again, the long-term goal is to create more competitive balance. An effective salary cap can take market size and fan base out of the equation. However, the existence of a salary cap and floor does not mean that differences in team payrolls will not exist. There is flexibility in the space between salary caps and floors, and different owners will choose to spend at different levels within those bounds. In practice, though, salary caps seem to be the most effective policy tool for equalizing teams. The effect of various league policies on different teams is summarized in Table 12.1.

So, are salary caps good from a league standpoint? Even though caps clearly restrict player pay, it is not entirely clear if they increase profits. The NFL would undoubtedly prefer that the Dallas Cowboys, New York Giants, and Chicago Bears win more games than the Jacksonville Jaguars, Kansas City Chiefs, or Carolina Panthers. Why? Larger markets have more fans and higher incomes, meaning people in these markets will be more likely to pay higher prices for tickets. If they do pay more, then revenues will be

Table 12.1 Short-Term Effects of League Policies

Team Type	Player Draft	Revenue Sharing	Luxury Tax	Salary Cap
Large-market team's profit	Increases	Ambiguous	Decreases	Ambiguous
Small-market team's profit	Increases	Increases	Increases	Increases
Player salaries	Decreases	Decreases	Decreases	Decreases
Large-market team's win percentage	No effect	Possible small increase	Decreases	Decreases
Small-market team's win percentage	No effect	Possible small decrease	Increases	Increases
Competitive balance	No effect	Might decrease	Increases	Increases

higher. Salary caps promote competitive balance – a concept that is in conflict with the model described above, which promotes the on-field success of larger market teams. Essentially, even though a league will clearly save on player costs with a salary cap, a salary cap also might mean less revenue.

There are other management issues with a salary cap. For one thing, players do not like caps. Very few workers in any industry like the idea of having a limit on what can be earned. As a result, if players agree to a salary cap, owners might have to make other concessions to establish a collective bargaining agreement. Another problem is that teams can back- or front-load contracts across several years to manipulate salary caps.

Promotion and Relegation

Another league policy that seems to contribute to competitive balance is promotion and relegation, commonly used in European soccer. Promotion and relegation is the practice of having various levels of leagues and promoting some teams into better divisions, while relegating others to lower divisions. This process increases balance as lower quality teams are demoted and teams that are improving can be elevated from a lower league. Without promotion and relegation, last place teams will still compete in the same league the following year (as occurs in the United States). If a team is threatened with relegation, an owner might invest more in talent.

While this policy might improve competitive balance, it certainly does not help team profits. Any time the incentive for player investment increases, salaries rise (good for players) and costs increase (bad for owners). Generally, team owners, especially small-market owners, are in favor of policies that increase balance by decreasing marginal revenues for large-market teams. Although large-market owners might not like this, they benefit in that player salaries are decreasing for the larger-market team as well. In the case of promotion and relegation, competitive balance is improved as a result of increasing the marginal revenue earned by smaller-market teams. But this also means that while competitive balance is improved, player salaries will increase.

"Closed" and "Open" Leagues

There are some interesting differences between North American and European leagues. Economists often describe North American sport leagues as "closed" as there are no competing leagues in other countries offering similar salaries. This means the absolute talent level does not depend on salaries. In other words, if players' pay doubled for the NFL, it is likely the teams would still employ the same personnel. Therefore, if policies like player drafts, salary caps, luxury taxes, or revenue sharing decrease salaries, it will not decrease the overall talent level (because there is nowhere else for the players to go). Some policies might change the distribution of talent, but not the overall level of talent of the league. There might be slight exceptions to this rule, but, for the most part, the talent level is fixed.

This is certainly not the case for European leagues. European leagues are described as "open." The most popular European soccer leagues compete with each other for players. Great Britain, Germany, Italy, and Spain all have separate leagues, and it is not always clear which league is best. The best players in the world are distributed across many leagues. A salary cap might restrict costs, but it could also have a severe effect on the overall talent level of the league. The best players will simply leave for leagues where there is no salary cap and the policy will have a detrimental effect on the league.

Collective Bargaining

Why do leagues implement policies as opposed to allowing each team to function independently as they see fit? The answer has to do with leagues' cartel-like structure. Leagues consider themselves loosely coupled partnerships. In these partnerships, actions are sometimes needed to advance the league's collective self-interest – even if pursuing that goal interferes with some of the individual interests of particular owners. Many policies have also been the result of the strength of the players' union.

As in every industry, labor and management (players and ownership, in this instance) negotiate for a favorable division of the profits produced by their collection action. When labor gains strength through organized efforts (unions), a logical response for owners is to do the same.

The NFL Players Association (NFLPA) is considered by some to be relatively weak compared to those representing players in the other leagues. This is, at least in part, because NFL players do not typically have long careers and most players are members of the union for but a brief period of time. The result of the NFLPA's relatively weak union, today, has been the lack of guaranteed income for the full value of contracts. What that means is if a player signs a three-year contract – but is cut after two years – the team is not obligated to pay the final year. Other leagues' players' unions, on the other hand, have managed to negotiate guaranteed contracts. For example, the NBA's commissioner guaranteed players' contracts in exchange for the union's agreement to allow a salary cap to be established.

The story of the NHL cap is equally illustrative. Prior to the 2004–2005 lockout, wages were increasing in the NHL while revenues were stagnant. The NHL owners demanded a salary cap. While the players' union agreed to the cap, the "ceiling" they asked for was much higher than the owners would accept. When negotiations stalled, the owners cancelled the 2004–2005 season. A lost season is more difficult for labor than it is for an owner. While some of the players managed to join other leagues for the remainder of the season (where salaries were usually far lower), several NHL owners also owned minor league hockey teams, junior league hockey teams, NBA teams, and MLB teams, which continued to earn revenue during the lockout. Owners were also able to host other events in the arenas they owned or managed, and these produced some income as well. After a year, the players agreed to a salary cap that was actually lower than what the owners originally offered. While the power of any players' union depends on many factors, whatever strength it can manifest rests on the ability of its membership to forego a season of play.

League Specifics

NFL

The NFL might be the most egalitarian of all the leagues. The amount of money dedicated to pay player salaries is complicated, but is essentially based on 55 percent of media revenues, 45 percent of NFL Ventures/Post Season Revenue, 40 percent of local revenue. On balance, this means that approximately 48 percent of league revenues are dedicated to the players. These revenue streams have made it possible for each team to expend as much as $178 million for their 2018 rosters. Other new initiatives by the NFL could lead to even higher salary caps. For the 2017 season, it was estimated that, on average, teams spent 92.5 percent of the permitted funds. This means that in a year when the cap was $167 million, the average team spent $154.4 million. Table 12.2 shows the growth of the cap from 1999 to 2016.

Table 12.2 NFL Salary Cap

Year	Salary Cap
1999	$58.3 million
2000	$62.2 million
2001	$67.5 million
2002	$71 million
2003	$75 million
2004	$80.5 million
2005	$85.5 million
2006	$102 million
2007	$109 million
2008	$116 million
2009	$129 million
2010	Uncapped
2011	$120 million
2012	$120.6 million
2013	$123 million
2014	$133 million
2015	$143.28 million
2016	$155.27 million

MLB

MLB is somewhat unique compared to the other leagues in that it has no salary cap, but does have, as noted, a luxury tax. If the payroll of an MLB team exceeds a certain threshold, the team must pay a tax on the amount above that threshold. Over time, these thresholds have increased; it was at $197 million for the 2018 season. The tax paid by a team also depends on the amount by which they have exceeded the threshold and the number of times they have exceeded the threshold. For those teams that have exceeded the threshold more than three times, the tax is 50 percent of the amount that exceeds the threshold. Comparatively, teams breaking the luxury tax for the first time pay just 20 percent, and second-time offenders pay 30 percent (Brown, 2016). The league also added surcharges for those teams that exceed the luxury tax at astronomical levels. Teams that exceed the threshold by between $20 and $40 million pay a 12 percent surtax on top of their luxury tax penalties, while teams with payrolls in excess of $40 million above the threshold pay a surtax between 42.5 and 45 percent. Those funds are then distributed to low revenue teams.

This system can produce some incentives for lower revenue teams to actually gain by trading high-cost players to teams that regularly exceed the threshold. For example, in 2017, the Miami Marlins traded their highest paid star to the New York Yankees. If, as a result of the trade, the Yankees exceeded the payroll threshold in 2018 and had to pay a tax, that revenue would go to the league, and at least a small portion of that money would accrue to the Marlins. In that way, the Marlins reduced their total player costs and could receive a financial benefit in the form of a higher payment from MLB as a low revenue team from the tax paid by the Yankees.

NBA

The NBA has a salary cap, a luxury tax, and a modest level of revenue sharing. This can make revenue structures very complicated, but the NBA seems to be in between the NFL and MLB in terms of financial equality. *Forbes* reported that the New York Knicks, despite a losing record in 2016–2017, had a league-leading $141 million profit with revenue estimated to be $376 million (Forbes, 2017). The Los Angeles Lakers had an operating profit of $199 million based on an estimated $333 million of revenues. And at the other end of the revenue scale, the Minnesota Timberwolves had revenues of $154 million and the New Orleans Pelicans were estimated to have earned $156 million. There is then a 2:1 differential between the team that earned the most and the franchise that earned the least in this league.

NHL

The NHL's policies have changed dramatically since the 2004–2005 lockout. Before the lockout, team owners and the league's commissioner argued that costs were increasing and revenues were essentially flat. That combination of factors had made the league and many of its franchises, in their opinion, non-sustainable enterprises. To underscore their point, the league was prepared to cancel an entire season (which they did). This led to the owners successfully negotiating a salary cap with a salary floor. Table 12.3 shows the cap figures since the lockout. As Table 12.3 illustrates, in percentage terms, NHL payrolls have increased quite a bit since the lockout. While this trend indicates improvement, NHL payrolls are still far below those of other leagues.

Competitive Balance

The oft-stated goal of revenue-sharing programs is to enhance competitive balance; it is now time to look at the effect these policies have had on competitive balance. Competitive balance, itself, is a difficult concept to define. As a result, attention is focused initially on *within-season* competitive balance. In other words, how even are teams in a particular season? One popular metric of within-season competitive balance is the standard deviation of winning percentages at the end of the season. Figure 12.1 shows the

Table 12.3 NHL Salary Cap and Floor

Year	Salary Cap ($millions)	Salary Floor ($millions)
2005–2006	39.0	21.5
2006–2007	44.0	28.0
2007–2008	50.3	43.9
2008–2009	56.7	40.7
2009–2010	56.8	40.8
2010–2011	59.4	43.4
2011–2012	64.0	48.0
2012–2013	70.2	54.2
2013–2014	58.7	52.8
2014–2015	69.1	51.0
2015–2016	71.4	52.8
2016–2017	73.0	54.0

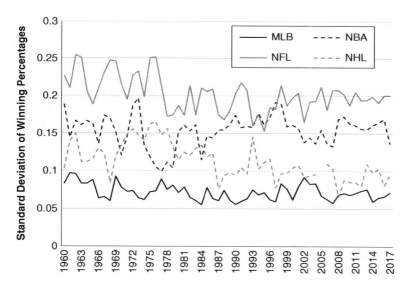

Figure 12.1 Within-Season Competitive Balance in the Four Major Leagues.

standard deviation of winning percentages for the four main leagues across the past five decades. What is interesting is that it appears that the NFL has the highest standard deviation (least balanced), followed by the NBA, the NHL, and MLB (most competitive balance), though there are exceptions. Over the past five decades, these leagues have seen many changes in league policies, but it might be hard to argue, using this graph, that these policies have changed balance at all. There might be slight differences when the NFL or NHL instituted salary caps, but these differences are small. This graph suggests that the biggest determinants in within-season balance are likely things that are inherent in the sport or league. For example, things like the number of games played or the very nature of the game seem to determine how close teams' winning percentages will be at the end of the season.

Another interesting question is how to best measure competitive balance *across seasons*. If a league is balanced across multiple seasons, then poorly performing teams have a better chance of improving the next season, compared to poorly performing teams in an unbalanced league. A basic metric that identifies this type of balance is the correlation of winning percentages from one season to the next. If the correlation is high, that means the league is unbalanced and the same teams tend to win year after year. Figure 12.2 shows the correlations of winning percentages for the NFL. Looking at the graph, it appears that the league has become more competitive over time, though the pattern is fairly erratic.

Figure 12.3 shows this metric for MLB. As with the NFL, there is no obvious trend. The correlation seemed to be relatively low in the 1990s, but then increased again. While MLB has had varying revenue-sharing and luxury tax policies, they have not had the dramatic shifts in policies of some other leagues. Still, it would be difficult to see a clear shift in balance due to policies. Figure 12.4 shows the correlation of winning percentages across seasons for the NBA. Again, there seem to be no trends or shifts. There was a period of relatively high turnover of quality teams in the late 1970s, but

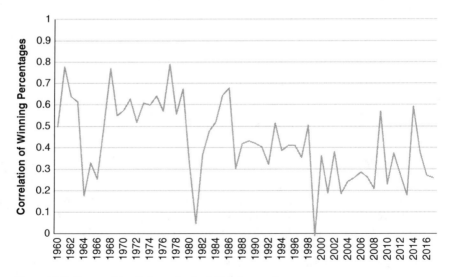

Figure 12.2 Competitive Balance in the NBA, Across Seasons.

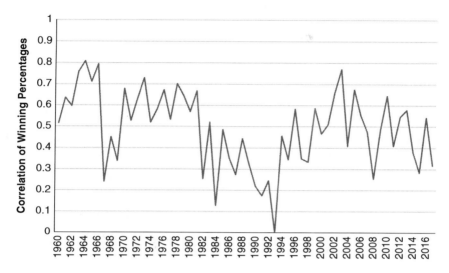

Figure 12.3 Competitive Balance in MLB, Across Seasons.

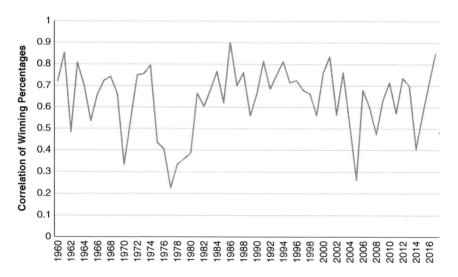

Figure 12.4 Competitive Balance in the NBA, Across Seasons.

it was short-lived. Figure 12.5 shows across-season balances for the NHL. As was the case in Figure 12.2 with the NFL, it appears that in recent years the correlation has been lower. This could well be a result of the 2004–2005 lockout and the 2012–2013 shortened season.

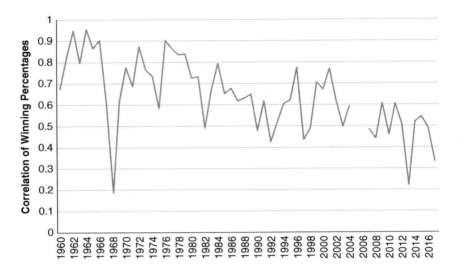

Figure 12.5 Competitive Balance in the NHL, Across Seasons.

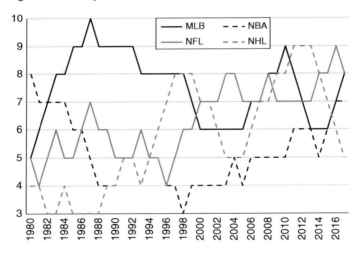

Figure 12.6 The Number of Different Champions in the Last Ten Championships.

Competitive balance also can be defined by championships. Figure 12.6 shows the number of different champions for each decade from the 1970s to 2016. From Figure 12.6, it is difficult to see any evidence of which league is the most balanced. It is interesting to see that many more NHL teams have won championships across the last several decades, as compared to the 1970s and 1980s. The NBA, on the other hand, has seen an opposite trend. It should be noted that this type of competitive balance depends on many variables, including the number of teams and playoff structure, which could change over time. The NHL and NBA are somewhat similar in these variables; the differences between the two leagues in Figure 12.6 are somewhat puzzling.

Taxes

Taxes impact expenditure decisions and profitability. However, managers must remember that an assessment of the effect of taxes focuses on the marginal tax rate, not the average. Just as with an investment in talent, managers need to consider marginal benefits and marginal costs. The average tax rate is equal to the total amount of taxes divided by taxable income, while the marginal tax rate is defined as the percent of taxes paid on one extra dollar of income. The United States, as well as most countries, has a progressive income tax system, and as of 2018, all federal corporate taxes are a flat rate of 21 percent.

The reason managers use the marginal tax rate for most decisions is because most financial decisions will have a small effect on income. For example, suppose a team is considering investing in talent to increase revenue. If the team calculates that this increase in investment will increase profits by $1 million, then the increase in taxes depends on their current marginal tax rate (unless the increase in income changes their tax bracket). Suppose the team currently has a 35 percent tax rate. Then the increase in the after-tax profits is only $650,000 ($1,000,000 × (1 − .35)). While after-tax profits still increase, it can alter investment strategies. Many times, whatever costs are incurred also will be included before taxes, so the financial analyst can simply look at benefits and costs before taxes. It is possible that this investment excludes the possibility of other investments in a different time period that might have increased after tax profits even more. In the example above, if the extra $1 million generated $650,000 after taxes, it is possible that the same investment would generate $800,000 before taxes the next year. If, for some reason, the marginal rate was lower the next year, possibly due to certain tax breaks or a decrease in profits, it might make sense to delay the investment. If tax rates are progressive, there is an incentive to smooth out profits over time instead of earning massive profits during one year.

Also, because many teams are often in complicated ownership structures, it is sometimes easy to move profits so that they are taxed at the lowest possible rate. Just as multinational corporations try to move profits to the country with the lowest tax rates, teams try to move profits where the lowest tax rates exist. Given the prominence of multifaceted corporations in contemporary sports, teams often have the opportunity to easily move funds. The differences in tax rates could be between different countries, personal and corporate taxes, or other tax discrepancies.

Below is a simplified example to illustrate this point. Let us suppose that an owner of a hockey team also owns a beer corporation. Let us further suppose that the beer corporation "sells" one million cans of beer to the team for $5 each. If the profits of the hockey team are reported on the owner's personal taxes, consider the outcomes if the personal tax rate is 25 percent. Furthermore, 16 percent of all hockey revenue is shared. This means that the owner gets to keep 63 percent $((1 - .25) \times (1 - .16))$ of all hockey revenue as the after-tax profit. In other words, 37 percent of revenue is either shared or taxed. If the beer company is a U.S. corporation and their taxable income is between $10 and $15 million, then according to Table 12.4, their marginal tax rate is 35 percent. In this case, the owner keeps more revenue from beer than hockey. Therefore, the owner might consider selling the beer to the hockey team for a higher price. If the price of the beer was an extra dollar, it would result in an extra $20,000 ($1,000,000 \times (.37 - .35)$) in after tax profits. While this is a simplified example, it illustrates that, with complicated ownership structures, it is possible to move profits to the lowest marginal tax rate.

Another major tax issue is capital depreciation. Depreciation occurs when capital loses value because it ages. Therefore, firms add the loss of the value of capital to their costs. The IRS allows firms to depreciate capital because it is a real cost of doing business even though it does not affect short-term cash flow. The *depreciable value* includes the total cost of an

Table 12.4 Example of Roster Depreciation Allowance

Year	Depreciable Value ($)	Depreciation Rate	Amount Depreciated ($)	Tax Rate	Tax Savings ($)	Net Present Value of Tax Savings ($millions) (5% Monetary Depreciation)
1	1 billion	6.67%	66.7 million	30%	20 million	19.05
2	1 billion	6.67%	66.7 million	30%	20 million	18.14
3	1 billion	6.67%	66.7 million	30%	20 million	17.28
4	1 billion	6.67%	66.7 million	30%	20 million	16.45
5	1 billion	6.67%	66.7 million	30%	20 million	15.67
6	1 billion	6.67%	66.7 million	30%	20 million	14.92
7	1 billion	6.67%	66.7 million	30%	20 million	14.21
8	1 billion	6.67%	66.7 million	30%	20 million	13.54
9	1 billion	6.67%	66.7 million	30%	20 million	12.89
10	1 billion	6.67%	66.7 million	30%	20 million	12.28
11	1 billion	6.67%	66.7 million	30%	20 million	11.69
12	1 billion	6.67%	66.7 million	30%	20 million	11.14
13	1 billion	6.67%	66.7 million	30%	20 million	10.61
14	1 billion	6.67%	66.7 million	30%	20 million	10.10
15	1 billion	6.67%	66.7 million	30%	20 million	9.62
Total	–	–	1 billion	–	300 million	207.59

asset, including any installation costs. Depending on the type of capital, there are many ways of depreciating assets. The length of time an asset is depreciated (its depreciable life) and the rate of depreciation vary. For instance, things like buildings depreciate very slowly and have a long depreciable life, while items like computers typically depreciate very quickly and have a short depreciable life. Also, straight-line depreciation means that the asset depreciates the same amount each year. However, because most assets depreciate more rapidly when they are new, sometimes double-declining, straight-line depreciation is used.[5]

Roster Depreciation Allowance

Many industries receive special tax exemptions, and the sport industry is certainly no different. In fact, one could argue that the sport industry has mastered tax loopholes. One of the more remarkable tax laws dealing with professional teams is the roster depreciation allowance. After he bought the Cleveland Indians in 1946, Bill Veeck convinced the U.S. Congress to allow baseball teams to depreciate their roster. There are several odd things about this. First, depreciation usually pertains to capital. Things like buildings, automobiles, or even cattle are generally depreciated for tax purposes. But players are clearly labor and not capital. Second, because players are labor, they should get paid according to their productivity. This means that teams should be paying players whatever they are worth and, if the players do lose value over time, their contract should reflect this. It could be argued that it is the responsibility of team owners to account for player depreciation in player contracts, rather than writing them off during tax season. Third, depreciation implies that an asset's value decreases across time. As any fan knows, players often get better before their productivity declines. Fourth, player costs are already considered when calculating profit. Because team owners do not literally own the players, the cost of players is counted against profit and depreciated. And, finally, one of the more remarkable features of the roster depreciation allowance is that once the team is sold to new owners, the roster depreciation allowance starts all over again. Typically, when a firm depreciates capital, it can do it only once. Normally, capital actually is depreciating in value, so if a building depreciates to zero, it cannot be depreciated a second time. Furthermore, if capital is sold at a value higher than its legal depreciable value, then the firm must pay taxes on the difference. This does not seem to be the case for teams. Teams are allowed to depreciate the value for a second time once the team is sold. So, the "Veeck loophole" began when Veeck sold the Indians in 1949.

While Veeck began the roster depreciation allowance, the Milwaukee Braves may have perfected it in 1964 (Leeds & Von Allmen, 2008). The Braves claimed that more than 99 percent of the purchase price of the team was represented by the value of the players. As a result, they used the entire value of the team as the amount that should be depreciated. The Braves also depreciated their players using straight-line depreciation across a ten-year span. This means that they deducted 10 percent of the depreciable value from their taxable income for ten years. In 1964, corporate tax rates went from 52 percent to 48 percent, so the team was able to save about half of the value of the team in taxes (approximately 5 percent of the team value for 10 years).

Across the years, the specifics of the roster depreciation have changed. In 1976, U.S. Congress declared that owners could depreciate 50 percent of the team over five years, which came about after Bud Selig successfully depreciated 94 percent of the Seattle Pilots in 1970 before he moved the team to Milwaukee. In 2004, the Internal Revenue Code was changed to allow owners to depreciate 100 percent of the value of the team over 15 years (Coulson and Fort, 2010). Although the depreciable value increased, the depreciable life decreased, which has an offsetting impact.

This special tax allowance increases not only profits, but also the value of the team. Because future after-tax profits are higher, the value of the team is also higher. Today when people buy teams, the roster depreciation allowance is built into the price. When the roster depreciation allowance started initially, it would have increased profits as well as the value of a team.

Again, an example is illustrative. Assume an owner depreciates 100 percent of the sale price of a team over 15 years, just as Congress changed the law in 2004. Suppose a team is purchased for $1 billion and makes $100 million a year in profit. Suppose also that the tax rate is 30 percent. Then each year, for 15 years, after-tax profits are increased by $20 million ($1 billion × .3/15). Over the 15 years, this is a total of $300 million. Assuming a 5 percent depreciation rate, the present value is $207.6 million. While we know that the value of money changes over time, the nominal value of this tax loophole is equal to the value of the team multiplied by the tax rate. Even assuming a 5 percent depreciation rate, the value is still more than two-thirds of the tax rate times the value of the team. It should be remembered that in our example the team's profits would have to be at least $66.7 million per year in order to take full advantage of this depreciation. Table 12.4 illustrates the change in cash flows from the roster depreciation allowance.

While Table 12.4 is somewhat redundant in that the only column that changes is the net present value of the savings, other methods of depreciation, such as double-declining and straight-line depreciation, change the amount depreciated from year to year. It also must be noted that teams are becoming large entertainment complexes that can easily move profits. Therefore, teams can typically earn enough profit to fully take advantage of this depreciation. Furthermore, because a future owner can renew the roster depreciation, the current owner should be able to increase the sale value.

Player Taxes

Player taxes, or jock taxes, are also a bit unique, in that players are taxed in the cities they play games in, even as a visiting player. This means that when LeBron James plays a game in Detroit against the Pistons, he is charged an earnings tax on the income he earned while playing in Detroit. The idea is that, because the players are earning their income in various states, they must pay various state taxes on that income. In fact, most states have passed laws requiring visiting players to pay taxes on their income earned in that state.[6] While these taxes are usually relatively low, given the salaries of players, they can generate substantial amounts. Everyone making income in a different locality is subject to that state and local government's income taxes. In the United States, only Florida, Texas, Washington state, and Washington D.C. have no player tax.

Tax Incentives and Disincentives

Tax incentives affect athletes just like any other workers. For example, sprinter Usain Bolt skipped a race in the United Kingdom because of their tax laws. Organizers of the race were willing to pay Bolt an appearance fee, but according to the U.K.'s tax laws, the sprinters in the race would have to pay "a 50 percent tax rate on their appearance fee as well as a proportion of their total worldwide earnings" (BBC Sport, 2010). Because there would actually be a tax on Bolt's worldwide income, he could have actually lost money from running the race. One might wonder how the United Kingdom can tax "worldwide" income. Essentially, the U.K. taxes pro-rated endorsements from athletes. If an athlete has 20 percent of his/her events in the United Kingdom, then the country will tax 20 percent of his/her endorsements. These taxes also have prevented golfers from playing in the United Kingdom and stopped soccer games from being played there as well. The country gave an exemption (tax incentive) to enable the London Olympic bid to go forward. The incentive offsets the disincentive applied to Bolt.

In 2010, former MLB commissioner Fay Vincent wondered why star players were not taking advantage of tax laws (Vincent, 2010). Vincent argued that players with large contracts could save millions of dollars in taxes if they negotiated for a percentage of ownership in the team. This way, the player's income would be in the form of capital gains, which is taxed at a lower rate than ordinary income. As Vincent points out, there have been player/owners in the past, such as Mario Lemieux with the Pittsburgh Penguins. The NBA currently prohibits people from being both a player and an owner, while MLB does not. While there are certainly some issues with having players being part owners, Vincent is correct that there are certainly possible tax savings for the players, and it may become more common in the future.

State Taxes

There is certainly nothing unique to the sport industry with regard to state taxes; all but seven states have some form of an income tax. Nonetheless, state taxes are crucial to consider because they tend to affect the bottom line for certain teams. One example involved LeBron James. When James left the Cleveland Cavaliers for the Miami Heat, he left for less money. However, the magnitude of the difference in his salary might not be as large as one might think. As some have pointed out, the highest state income tax in Ohio, at the time LeBron left, was 5.9 percent, while Florida had no state income tax (Windhorst, 2010). Furthermore, Cleveland had a 2 percent earnings tax yielding a state and local tax rate of approximately 8 percent. Players for the Miami Heat might have to pay taxes on the income they earned during their away games because of player earnings taxes, but they do not have to pay taxes on the income they earn from home games. While these taxes directly affect players, this also gives teams from states with no or low state income taxes a slight advantage to sign players.

Ticket Taxes

Ticket taxes essentially increase the cost of sports and entertainment tickets by adding an additional fee. The cost initially falls to fans, who are forced to pay higher prices, but because higher ticket prices can deter fans from attending games, the buck is eventually passed on to the team. It is clear that ticket taxes can be detrimental to teams' bottom lines. However, ticket taxes also ensure that users of the venue are paying for its construction and maintenance, as opposed to the general public (which would be the case if there were a tax levied to pay for venue construction or maintenance). In this way, city officials can remind their constituents that they are not being forced to pay for amenities they don't use; only fans and concert-goers are paying the fee.

Tax Exempt Status for Universities

Colleges and universities enjoy tax-exempt status, which means that, for *some* of their income, taxes are not paid. In the past, this meant that university donors could write off donations to the school and the athletic department (particularly those paid for tickets). This was changed by the 2017 tax law, and universities will have to adjust their pricing policies accordingly. When athletic donations were tax deductible, it was common for schools to require season ticket holders to make a sizable donation, especially if fans wanted to purchase the best seats. Essentially, athletic departments gained more revenue since they had a mechanism to allow fans this tax deduction. While some might argue university donations are good for society and should be tax deductible, it was not clear that it should have been seen as a donation. This illustrates the gray area of altruistic giving and simply purchasing a product. The new tax law will presumably change the way college athletic tickets are sold and revenues will decrease. Colleges and universities also receive revenue from commercial activities outside of sports, and those may be subject to federal and state taxes, too.

Profits

As noted earlier, knowing what the actual profits are for teams can be difficult. Given the different ownership structures in sport, and the lack of public data, it is not always clear how much was earned. Data are available for a few teams (e.g., Green Bay Packers). A snapshot of the Arizona Coyotes' financial standing also exists from documents that were made public during the team's 2009 bankruptcy. But, for the most part, analysts only have access to estimates of revenues and costs. There is an incentive for teams to try to avoid statements that might illustrate that there are substantial profits. Teams might move revenues depending on the marginal tax rates for their various related companies, but there are other considerations as well. Because of the public nature of teams, owners are usually better off if they can claim they are losing money. This is because owners often negotiate with local governments for subsidies to build new facilities and with the players' unions for salary caps. In 2004, just before the 2004–2005 NHL lockout, the owners hired an accounting firm to perform a financial analysis of every NHL team. The report concluded that NHL owners lost a combined $273 million during the 2002–2003 season. This certainly strengthened the owners' argument for a salary cap. The report recognized the difficulties of finding profits for all hockey teams. As page 4 of Arthur Levitt's (a former chairman of the Security Exchange Commission) report stated,

> The 30 teams represent 30 different businesses with different histories and unique business arrangements. For example, the teams have different owners and ownership structures, different financing arrangements, different contract terms with the municipalities and facilities in which they play, and different sponsorship and media arrangements. It should be noted that all teams play in venues used also for nonhockey events, including college basketball (e.g., Carolina Hurricanes and North Carolina State Wolfpack), professional basketball (e.g., Los Angeles Kings and the Los Angeles Lakers and Los Angeles Clippers), rodeos (e.g., Calgary Flames and the Calgary Stampede), and concerts. The

relative significance of hockey to nonhockey events varies widely from arena to arena. In some instances, such as in Columbus, the facility is owned by an independent unrelated third party. In other instances, a municipality may own the facility, while in still other instances, the team owner may own either a controlling interest or a minority interest in the facility. Because of the economic and business circumstances unique to each of the teams, the UROs[7] and URO instructions are designed to include all hockey-related revenues and expenses of each team, regardless of how that team is legally structured, operates or the ownership of the facility it plays in. The goals of the URO are to provide instructions to the teams so they report their business activities on a comprehensive basis using standard instructions and enable the compilation and presentation of a full and accurate statement of the League's combined financial results based upon a comprehensive picture of the entire business of hockey, including all revenues and expenses related to operating an NHL franchise.

(Levitt, 2004)

While the owners certainly did nothing illegal, it is impossible to know if $273 million represented the total losses of NHL owners.

Leverage

It is often useful to know how sensitive profits are to a change in revenues. The amount of leverage that a firm has represents how much of their revenues or assets are tied up in costs or liabilities. Analysts should think of a firm's leverage in terms of how narrow its profit margin is over the course of a year, or how much net wealth a firm has compared to its liabilities. They must also understand how leverage and revenues generate profit. This can be broken down further into operating leverage and financial leverage. The degree of operating leverage is defined as the percentage change in operating income (earnings before interest and taxes)[8] divided by the percent change in sales. If sales increase by 1 percent, then operating income will increase by the degree of operating leverage multiplied by 1 percent. The degree of operating leverage is calculated by:

$$Degree\ of\ Operating\ Leverage = \frac{Revenue - Total\ Variable\ Cost}{Revenue - Total\ Variable\ Cost - Fixed\ Cost}$$

The reason that variable costs are included in the numerator is because, if revenues or sales increase, variable costs must increase as well. Revenue could be considered quantity times price and the total variable cost is quantity times variable costs per unit. If more units are sold and quantity goes up, both revenues and total variable costs will go up. The denominator is simply operating income.

An example is illustrative. Suppose revenue is $200, total variable costs are $100, and fixed costs are $50. In this example, the operating leverage is 2. Another way of looking at it is if revenue increases 1 percent (so that revenue is $202 and total variable cost is $101), then the operating income increases 2 percent (operating income goes from $50 to $51). For this firm, whatever gain it sees in sales, it will be twice the increase, in percentage terms, for operating income.

The degree of financial leverage is defined as the percentage change in earnings (after taxes and financial payments) divided by the percent change in operating income. If operating income increases by 1 percent, then earnings will increase by the degree of financial leverage multiplied by 1 percent. The degree of financial leverage is calculated by:

Degree of Financial Leverage =

$$\frac{Revenue - Total\ Variable\ Cost - Fixed\ Cost}{Revenue - Total\ Variable\ Cost - Fixed\ Cost - Interest\ Payments - \left(\dfrac{Preferred\ Stock\ Dividends}{1 - Tax\ Rate}\right)}$$

In the case of financial leverage, operating income is in the numerator and net income is in the denominator.

Continuing with this example, if a company has operating income of $50, interest payments of $10, pays $14 in preferred stock dividends, and is subject to a tax rate of 30 percent, net income is $20. Because the operating income is $50 and the net income is $20, the firm's financial leverage is 2.5. Again, going back to the definition, if operating income increases 1 percent (from $50 to $50.5), then earnings will increase 2.5 percent (from $20 to $20.5).

Using both operating leverage and financial leverage, a manager can find the firm's degree of total leverage, which is defined as the percentage increase in earnings divided by the percentage increase in sales. The degree of total leverage is given by:

Degree of Total Leverage =

$$\frac{Revenue - Total\ Variable\ Cost}{Revenue - Total\ Varialble\ Cost - Fixed\ Cost - Interest\ Payments - \left(\dfrac{Preferred\ Stock\ Dividends}{1 - Tax\ Rate}\right)}$$

Notice the degree of total leverage is simply degree of operating leverage times financial leverage. In this example, if the firm's sales increased 1 percent (revenue minus total variable cost would go from \$100 to \$101), then the firm's earnings would increase 5 percent (from \$20 to \$21). Another way of looking at it is if operating leverage is 2 and financial leverage is 2.5, then total leverage is 5. This means that whatever the percentage increase in sales, it will increase earnings by 5 times as much. Alternatively, if sales decrease, then earnings decrease by fivefold in percentage terms. It is easy to see how highly leveraged firms are risky because they are sensitive to changes in sales. Firms or teams that have high leverage are riskier because they are sensitive to sales. Breaking the leverage down into operating leverage and financial leverage allows a firm or team to see what part of the business creates the risk.

As noted, leverage also could be examined in terms of assets and liabilities, which is known as *accounting leverage*. The formula for accounting leverage is relatively straightforward:

$$Accounting\ Leverage = \frac{Total\ Assets}{Total\ Assets - Total\ Liabilities}$$

This shows, in terms of the firm's wealth, how sensitive stockholder equity or the firm's net worth is to a change in assets. If a firm has a high degree of accounting leverage, then a small change in assets can have a big impact on the firm's net worth.

Like most industries, the degree of leverage can vary depending on the sport organization. For operating leverage, it depends on the profitability of the team. Because a new stadium is expensive and would probably be considered a fixed cost, this can increase the operating leverage for many teams. For example, the return on a new stadium depends very much on attendance levels. The profitability can be very sensitive to any changes in attendance.

The degree of financial leverage might be team dependent, but typically there is no reason why teams should be borrowing inordinate amounts of money relative to other industries. In 2015, the NFL restricted owners from borrowing more than \$250 million by using the team as collateral. This means that interest payments are essentially capped for NFL teams. While teams in other leagues might have fewer restrictions, it simply depends on the particular team owner.

Accounting leverage is also team dependent. Some teams have assets far greater than liabilities. This means there is little chance of insolvency or bankruptcy. Other teams might have a very small net worth and any change in assets, without changing liabilities, would greatly impact the team.

The Importance of Leverage

The importance of leverage became apparent during the 2008 Great Recession. After all, leverage is one of the key differences in the severity between falling housing prices around 2007 and 2008 and the "dot.com" bubble that burst from 2000 to 2002. Total stock market losses from the beginning of 2000 to the end of 2002 were about $7.5 trillion. While the "dot.com" crash was substantial, it seemed to have a relatively minor effect on the greater economy. In other words, the financial system seemed to absorb these losses fairly well. Falling housing prices tell a different story. From their peak in 2006, home prices fell roughly 35 percent, which meant total losses of $7.7 trillion. There were also substantial losses for the financial sector and closing of several banks.

One main reason the financial sector could not easily handle these losses is leverage. Liabilities of financial firms were nearly as much as their assets. Stockholder equity was small compared to assets. For example, Morgan Stanley, Bear Stearns, and Merrill Lynch all had a leverage ratio of over 30:1 at the end of 2007. This meant that total liabilities were around 97 percent of total assets. In this instance, financial firms did not have a lot of capital, but instead investments were all intertwined between different financial investments. This degree of leverage typically works well in a good economy, but clearly does not during a poor economy. When the financial sector had to absorb losses, their absolute magnitude might have been more than the company's net worth. Furthermore, any bankruptcies of financial firms might put pressure on the other interconnected financial firms. Because financial firms had little capital and were all highly leveraged, a crisis for the industry resulted.

Notes

1 Competitive balance can mean the variation of team quality within a season, across seasons, or variation of who wins championships. The standard deviation of winning percentages is a common metric of within-season balance. The standard deviation of a team's winning percentage over time could be one measure of balance across seasons. A Herfindahl index or Gini coefficient are sometimes used to measure balance in terms of championships.
2 For example, much of MLB's Blue Ribbon Panel Report was aimed at helping the leagues balance.
3 The problem with testing long-term effects on leagues is that many factors are always going on at the same time. Furthermore, parity is not a simple thing to measure and it typically does not dramatically change quickly. So, although some leagues see increases or decreases in overall demand, it is difficult to know the long-term effect of competitive balance.
4 Luxury taxes might be thought of as a "soft" salary cap.

5 Double declining and straight-line depreciation are examples of depreciation rates. Many methods of depreciating capital entail front-loading value to enhance the present value of the taxes saved.

6 Technically, this is referred to as an earnings tax. An earnings tax is an income tax paid based on where one works, not where one lives.

7 A URO is a unified report of operations.

8 Operating income is the same as earnings before interest and taxes as long as there is no non-operating income.

9 As noted, there is a difference here between "open" and "closed" leagues. In "open" European leagues, teams can invest in talent and not affect the talent level of other teams. In "closed" North American leagues, teams must increase their talent by decreasing the talent level of some other team. Nonetheless, in either type of league, teams invest in talent, which determines the winning percentage.

10 One common contest success function that is often used is

$$w_i = \frac{z_i}{z_i + z_j}$$

11 Here it is assumed that a percentage of revenue simply goes to the other team. Sometimes leagues split pool sharing, where revenues go into a pool and then the revenue is shared. If the revenue in the pool was split evenly between the two teams, then teams would be sharing exactly half of the revenue in the pool.

References

BBC Sport. 2010. Usain Bolt snubs London meeting over tax laws, *BBC Sport*, July 12. Retrieved from http://news.bbc.co.uk/sport2/hi/athletics/8812123.stm (accessed June 1, 2012).

Brown, M. 2016. Breaking down MLB's new 2017–21 Collective Bargaining Agreement, *Forbes*, November 30 Retrieved from https://www.forbes.com/sites/maurybrown/2016/11/30/breaking-down-mlbs-new-2017-21-collective-bargaining-agreement/#4910e12f11b9 (accessed July 31, 2018).

Coulson, N. E., & Fort, R. 2010. Tax revisions of 2004 and pro sports team ownership. *Contemporary Economic Policy* 28 (4): 464–473.

Forbes. 2017. Forbes releases 19th annual NBA team valuations, *Forbes*, February 15. Retrieved from https://www.forbes.com/sites/forbespr/2017/02/15/forbes-releases-19th-annual-nba-team-valuations/#1ee537397f03 (accessed July 31, 2018).

Leeds, M. A., & von Allmen, P. 2008. *The economics of sports*, 3rd ed. Boston: Pearson Publishing.

Levitt, A. 2004. Independent review of the combined financial results of the National Hockey League 2002-2003 season, *NHL*, February 5. Retrieved from http://www2.nhl.com/images/levittreport.pdf (accessed March 1, 2015).

Passan, J. 2018. Here's why baseball's economic system might be broken, *Yahoo! Sports*. Retrieved from https://sports.yahoo.com/heres-baseballs-economic-system-might-broken-224638354.html (accessed February 6, 2018).

Vincent, F. 2010. Albert Pujols's capital opportunity. *Wall Street Journal*, November 29. Retrieved from http://online.wsj.com/article/SB10001424052748704462704575590600879687646.html (accessed May 14, 2011).

Windhorst, B. 2010. LeGone: LeBron James announces he's leaving Cleveland Cavaliers for Miami Heat. *The Plain Dealer* online edition, July 8, http://www.cleveland.com/cavs/index.ssf/2010/07/legone_lebron_james_confirms_h.html (accessed May 14, 2011).

Further Suggested Reading on League Policies

El Hodiri, M. & Quirk, J. 1971. An economic model of a professional sports league. *Journal of Political Economy* 70: 1302–1319.

Fort, R., & Quirk, J. 1995. Cross-subsidization, incentives and outcomes in professional team sports leagues. *Journal of Economic Literature* 33: 1265–1299.

Rottenberg, S. 1956. The baseball players' labor market. *Journal of Political Economy* 64: 242–258.

Szymanski, S. 2003. The economic design of sporting contests. *Journal of Economic Literature* 41: 1137–1187.

Szymanski, S. 2004. Professional team sports are only a game: The Walrasian fixed-supply conjecture model, contest-nash equilibrium, and the invariance principle. *Journal of Sports Economics* 5: 111–126.

Szymanski, S., & Kesenne, S. 2004. Competitive balance and revenue sharing in team sports. *Journal of Industrial Economics* 52: 165–177.

Vrooman, J. 2009. Theory of the perfect game: Competitive balance in monopoly sports leagues. *Review of Industrial Organization* 34: 5–44.

Winfree, J., 2015. This game is being played under protest. *International Journal of Sport Finance* 10: 88–100.

Winfree, J., & Fort, R., 2012. Nash conjectures and talent supply in sports league modeling: A comment on current modeling disagreements. *Journal of Sports Economics*, 13: 306–313.

Appendix I

In this appendix, the math behind league policies and how they affect profits, player salaries, and competitive balance is presented. For simplicity, a model for a two-team league is used. Obviously, virtually all leagues have more than two teams, but it helps to make some generalizations about policies. First, an investment in talent leads to winning. This relationship is known as the contest success function and mathematically is represented by $w_i(z_i, z_j)$. That is, team i's winning percentage, w_i, is a function of the talent investment by team i, z_i, and j, z_j.[9] Thankfully, leagues do not simply calculate the investment in talent for each team and then calculate winning percentages. In other words, more goes into winning than just a team's investment. Nonetheless, when teams invest more, they win more,

$$\frac{\partial w_i}{\partial z_i} > 0,$$

and when the other team invests more, the winning percentage goes down,

$$\frac{\partial w_i}{\partial z_j} > 0.$$

Additionally, the two winning percentages have to add up to one, $w_i(z_i, z_j) + w_j(z_j, z_i) = 1$, which also means[10]

$$\frac{\partial w_i}{\partial z_i} = -\frac{\partial w_j}{\partial z_i}.$$

The reason that teams invest in talent is because if they win more, they will get more revenue. Team i's revenue function, denoted by R_i, is given by $R_i\big(w_i(z_i, z_j)\big)$, where

$$\frac{dR_i}{dw_i} > 0.$$

It is important to note that the revenue function is different than the contest success function in that it differs depending on the market size of the team. For example, if both teams won half of their games, the large-market team would have a higher revenue than the small-market team. The profit function of team i is given by:

$$\pi_i = R_i\big(w_i(z_i, z_j)\big) - z_i$$

Taking the derivative of that function means the team will invest in talent until the marginal benefit of investing equals the marginal cost of talent,

$$\frac{dR_i}{dw_i}\frac{\partial w_i}{\partial z_i} = 1,$$

which holds for both teams. This implies that:

$$\frac{dR_i}{dw_i}\frac{\partial w_i}{\partial z_i} = \frac{dR_j}{dw_j}\frac{\partial w_j}{\partial z_j}.$$

We assume that for any given winning percentage,

$$\frac{dR_l}{dw} > \frac{dR_s}{dw}$$

where l denotes the large-market team and s denotes the small-market team; then, if the further common assumption is made that talent investment has positive but decreasing returns,

$$\frac{\partial^2 R}{\partial z^2} < 0,$$

and because the contest success function is the same for both teams, the large-market teams will invest more in talent, $z_l > z_s$ and will have a higher winning percentage, $w_l > w_s$.

Salary Cap

The simplest policy to consider is a salary cap. Talent investment and team payroll or salary are not completely the same thing, but for our purposes it is assumed that a league is limiting all talent investment. It is assumed that the cap is restrictive on both teams. In this case, $z_i = z_j$ and $w_i = w_j$. Therefore, the model says that both teams should be of equal strength, implying that competitive balance is maximized. Furthermore, player salaries are lower than in the absence of a policy. The effect on profits is ambiguous at least for the large-market team. If the decrease in costs (talent investment) outweighs the decrease in revenues from a lower winning percentage, then large-market teams will enjoy increased profits with a salary cap. For the small-market team, talent investment decreases and winning increases and, therefore, profits increase.

Revenue Sharing

Thus far it has been assumed that teams keep all of their revenue, but in the case of revenue sharing, a team's profit is given by:

$$\pi_i = (1-\alpha)R_i(w_i(z_i, z_j)) + \alpha R_j(w_j(z_i, z_j)) - z_i$$

where α is the proportion of revenue that is shared.[11] Again, taking the derivative so that teams invest until the marginal benefit equals marginal cost indicate that the following equation will hold:

$$(1-\alpha)\frac{dR_i}{dw_i}\frac{\partial w_i}{\partial z_i} + \alpha\frac{dR_j}{dw_j}\frac{\partial w_j}{\partial z_i} = 1.$$

And, again, because this is true for both teams, that means that:

$$(1-\alpha)\frac{dR_i}{dw_i}\frac{\partial w_i}{\partial z_i} + \alpha\frac{dR_j}{dw_j}\frac{\partial w_j}{\partial z_i} = (1-\alpha)\frac{dR_j}{dw_j}\frac{\partial w_j}{\partial z_j} + \alpha\frac{dR_i}{dw_i}\frac{\partial w_i}{\partial z_j}$$

and because

$$\frac{\partial w_i}{\partial z_i} = -\frac{\partial w_j}{\partial z_i},$$

this implies that in equilibrium:

$$\frac{dR_i}{dw_i}\left[(1-\alpha)\frac{\partial w_i}{\partial z_i} + \alpha\frac{\partial w_j}{\partial z_j}\right] = \frac{dR_j}{dw_j}\left[(1-\alpha)\frac{\partial w_j}{\partial z_j} + \alpha\frac{\partial w_i}{\partial z_i}\right].$$

If this equation is invariant of α, then revenue sharing has no effect on competitive balance. This would be the case if winning is a linear function of talent investment. In other words, if talent investment has a constant effect on winning, then revenue sharing has no effect on competitive balance. If, however, talent investment has a decreasing return to winning,

$$\frac{\partial^2 w}{\partial z^2} < 0,$$

then revenue sharing actually decreases competitive balance. If i is the large-market team and

$$\frac{\partial^2 w}{\partial z^2} < 0,$$

then the bracketed term on the left-hand side will increase and the bracketed term on the right-hand side will decrease as α gets larger. In equilibrium,

$$\frac{dR_i}{dw_i}$$

must decrease and

$$\frac{dR_j}{dw_j}$$

must increase to maintain equilibrium. If it is assumed that winning increases revenues at a decreasing rate,

$$\frac{d^2 R}{dw^2} < 0,$$

then the winning percentage of the large-market team must increase and the winning percentage of the small-market team must decrease.

Revenue Sharing and Player Salaries

From this point forward, another simplifying assumption is made. The marginal benefit of talent investment on revenue is unaffected by the other team's talent investment,

$$\frac{d^2 R_i}{dz_i dz_j} = 0.$$

Although this cross derivative is probably not equal to exactly zero, it is not unreasonable to assume that it is sufficiently small. Also, just to simplify the math, w is suppressed such that revenue is a function of the two teams' investment, $R_i(z_i, z_j)$, analyzing the effect of revenue sharing on player salaries. Implicitly differentiating the equilibrium condition with respect to α yields:

$$\frac{dz_i}{d\alpha} = \frac{\dfrac{dR_i}{dz_i} - \dfrac{dR_j}{dz_i}}{(1-\alpha)\dfrac{d^2 R_i}{dz_i^2} + \alpha \dfrac{d^2 R_j}{dz_i^2}} < 0$$

so that overall expenditure on talent by the league is given by:

$$\frac{d(z_i + z_j)}{d\alpha} = \frac{\dfrac{dR_i}{dz_i} - \dfrac{dR_j}{dz_i}}{(1-\alpha)\dfrac{d^2 R_i}{dz_i^2} + \alpha \dfrac{d^2 R_j}{dz_i^2}} + \frac{\dfrac{dR_j}{dz_j} - \dfrac{dR_i}{dz_j}}{(1-\alpha)\dfrac{d^2 R_j}{dz_j^2} + \alpha \dfrac{d^2 R_i}{dz_j^2}} < 0$$

Therefore, revenue sharing will unambiguously decrease player salaries.

Revenue Sharing and Profits

In this section, the effect of revenue sharing on profit for the large-market team and the small-market team is analyzed. Most analysts assume that revenue sharing is bad for the large-market team's profits. Certainly, one effect is that the large-market team is sharing more revenue than the small-market team. Earlier, it was argued that revenue sharing decreases spending for players. Furthermore, if anything competitive balance will worsen, which means more revenue for the large-market team.

For the small-market team, their profit will increase from the direct effect of sharing less revenue than the large-market team. Similarly, the small-market team enjoys increased profit from the decrease in players' salaries.

The worsening in balance, however, hurts the profit of the small-market team. Mathematically, the effect of revenue sharing on profits at the equilibrium is given by:

$$\frac{d\pi_i}{d\alpha} = -R_i + R_j - \frac{dz_i}{d\alpha} + (1+\alpha)\left[\frac{dR_i}{dz_i}\frac{dz_i}{d\alpha} + \frac{dR_i}{dz_j}\frac{dz_j}{d\alpha}\right] + \alpha\left[\frac{dR_j}{dz_j}\frac{dz_j}{d\alpha} + \frac{dR_j}{dz_i}\frac{dz_i}{d\alpha}\right]$$

where $-R_i + R_j$ is the direct effect of sharing the revenue,

$$-\frac{dz_i}{d\alpha}$$

is the effect on profits of decreasing player salaries, and the rest of the equation represents the change in profits from the change in competitive balance. While the effects of revenue sharing on profits are ambiguous, if revenue sharing does not greatly change the winning percentages of the teams, then it will have a positive effect on small-market teams. The effect on large-market teams would still depend on the magnitude of the differences in the revenue of the two teams and the decrease in the investments made in talent.

The Effects of a Luxury Tax

In this section, the effect of a luxury tax is analyzed. There is an important distinction between this model and the model dealing only with revenue sharing. The team is being taxed on investment in players, and typically luxury taxes are placed on a team's payroll. Therefore, this model is not quite as general. Note that it still assumes

$$\frac{d^2R_i}{dz_i dz_j} = 0$$

and revenue is only a function of the two teams' investment, $R_i(z_i, z_j)$. If team i is the large-market team, and there is no revenue sharing, then the profit functions for the large and small market are

$$\pi_i = R_i(w_i(z_i, z_j)) - \bar{z} - (1+\tau)(z_i - \bar{z})$$

$$\pi_j = R_j(w_j(z_j, z_i)) - z_j$$

where $\bar{z}$ is the limit of investment that is not taxed and τ is the tax rate. Note that it is assumed that the large-market team is taxed and the small-market team is not. Therefore, the first order conditions are

$$\frac{d\pi_i}{dz_i} = \frac{dR_i}{dw_i}\frac{\partial w_i}{\partial z_i} - 1 - \tau = 0$$

$$\frac{d\pi_j}{dz_j} = \frac{dR_j}{dw_j}\frac{\partial w_j}{\partial z_j} - 1 = 0$$

Luxury Tax, Player Salaries, and Competitive Balance

Here the effect of a luxury tax on player salaries is analyzed. Implicitly differentiating those equations with respect to τ gives us:

$$\frac{dz_i}{d\tau} = \frac{1}{\dfrac{d^2 R_i}{dz_i^2}} < 0$$

$$\frac{dz_j}{d\tau} = 0$$

Thus, the overall expenditure on talent by the league is negative; therefore, player salaries decrease. Because the large-market team is the only team that is taxed and only the large-market team will change payroll by decreasing talent investment, competitive balance will be improved.

The Luxury Tax and Team Profits

Again using implicit differentiation, the following effect of a luxury tax on profit is identified:

$$\frac{d\pi_i}{d\tau} = \frac{dR_i}{dz_i}\frac{dz_i}{d\tau} - \left(z_i - \bar{z}\right) < 0$$

$$\frac{d\pi_j}{d\tau} = \frac{dR_i}{dz_i}\frac{dz_i}{d\tau} > 0$$

Therefore, under reasonable assumptions, the luxury tax will decrease profits for the taxed teams and increase profits for the small-market team.

Chapter 13

Facility Management

Public Authorities/Corporations and Real Estate Development

Michael B. Cantor and Sierra R. Bain[1]

Introduction

The vast majority of sport venues in North America involve a partnership between a team and a unit of government, be it at the city, county, or state level. While some venues are privately financed, for those venues that are built with public sector investments, an organization to represent the governmental entity, as well as public interests, is often utilized. At the forefront of these partnerships are independent public authorities, development corporations, and/or special districts. Often, a new public entity is created to assist in building and managing a facility owned by the city or county; these independent authorities are usually necessary, as there are limits on the amount of debt local governments can assume. Teams' financial interest in a public entity's ownership of a venue lies in the ability to (1) secure tax-exempt status of the bonds sold to finance the venue and (2) ensure the venue's exemption from local property taxes.

The structure of these organizations determines the actions they may undertake; in order for a partnership to achieve goals set by both the public and private sectors, advantages and limitations of different organizational designs must be considered. This chapter is designed to provide sport managers with an overview of the potential administrative structures of organizations created to build, maintain, and operate venues. After exploring the benefits these independent authorities create for both the public and private sectors, several examples of the management structures created are reviewed. First, the need for public authorities in building sport venues and the status of tax-exempt bonds used to finance stadiums are presented.

The Need for Public Authorities for Sport Venues

In forging a public–private partnership to build and finance a sport venue, ideally, benefits accrue to all parties involved. A team's interest in having a public sector partner, as briefly noted, is straightforward. In addition to reduced (or even zero) property taxes owed, the public sector's direct investment in a venue reduces private sector construction costs and enables the use of tax-exempt bonds to repay the cost of a venue. The interest rates from bonds subject to federal and state income taxes are higher than those for tax-exempt bonds; therefore, tax-exempt bonds sold to finance a venue, with their lower interest rates, save money for an owner. In partnering with the public sector to build a venue, the combination of reduced construction costs and tax exemptions create financial benefits for team owners. Before discussing the potential benefits for the public sector, an overview of tax-exempt bonds will be presented.

Sport Venue Bonds and the Exemption from Federal Taxation

For decades, the interest paid on bonds sold to pay for the building of a sport venue has been exempt from federal income taxes. Under existing law, for bonds to be tax-exempt (1) a public sector entity must participate in the financing of the venue and (2) the team's lease cannot contribute more than 10 percent of the debt service needed to repay the bonds. In order to satisfy the second element, teams and local governments must construct financing plans to ensure revenues from other sources are used to repay the majority of the debt.[2] This condition creates the potential for political issues – voters might object to a general tax increase to finance a venue unless tangible benefits from its existence are clear.

Many believe it is not appropriate for the interest for bonds sold to build sport venue to be "tax free." In June 2017, Senators Cory Booker and James Lankford introduced bipartisan legislation to eliminate the tax exemption for interest paid to bondholders if a sport venue used by a professional team is involved. The bill ultimately was not passed, and the Tax Cuts and Jobs Act of 2017 (passed by the Congress and signed into law by the President in December 2017) sustained the use of tax-exempt bonds for sport venues.

The benefits to the public sector from investing in a venue have been, and will be, discussed in other chapters of this book, but can be summarized by the potential for downtown revitalization, development of related real estate, elevation of surrounding property values, and/or a series of other intangible benefits. If a community decides the potential benefits exceed the cost of the investment in a venue, a public corporation, special district, or authority is usually created. This is because in the United States, state governments set debt limits for every unit of local government. These limits – usually a percentage of the value of taxable property in a jurisdiction (a city or county) – have been created to minimize the likelihood of local governments becoming insolvent.[3] For example, if a state establishes a debt limit of 6 percent, units of local government could borrow up to 6 percent of the taxable value of real estate within its jurisdiction. The debt limits are also an attempt to ensure annual tax collections are sufficient to meet a government's responsibilities for its ongoing operations.[4]

These debt limits exist for each unit of government, even if their boundaries overlap. For example, if a city and its independent school district have identical boundaries, the property assessed within each is the exact same and property owners in the jurisdiction may be responsible for paying property taxes to both entities.[5] There might also be other units of the local government (e.g., library district, community college district) collecting a property tax within the same jurisdiction. However, each unit of government is still entitled to an authorized debt limit. If a state establishes a 6 percent debt limit, the unit of local government, say, at the city level, could borrow up to 6 percent of the taxable value of real estate within its jurisdiction. In addition, a special district created to build a sport venue within the city could also borrow up to 6 percent of the taxable value of real estate within its boundaries. Therefore, the total debt assumed within the city could be greater, as a percentage of taxable property, than the state-established limit.

Because it is possible for a group of local governments in an area to assume debt that far exceeds the limit set for it, some may wonder why municipal bankruptcies are not more common. First, only a portion of the market value of a building or home is considered taxable; this reduces the overall debt limit, somewhat. Second, in most states, property tax to support operations, or a new project, must be approved by property owners through a vote. Third, and most importantly, even if the voters approve an additional bond issuance, the unit of government must find a willing lender. A request for an additional loan in an area supporting too much debt might not be accepted. Both referenda – in asking voters to approve property tax increases – and the opinion of prospective lenders are effective "checks" on excessive borrowing by units of local governments. Where bankruptcies have occurred, it has usually been the result of unprecedented economic collapses or demographic shifts.[6]

In addition to increasing overall borrowing power, public authorities permit flexibility for local governments in borrowing for other capital assets. Because local governments must assume debt for many crucial capital projects (roads, buildings, etc.), cities and counties that decide to borrow money for a sport venue generally create an authority or special district to oversee the building and maintenance of a venue. Public authorities are single-purpose organizations, focused on one major objective, while partially insulated from electoral politics. These characteristics make them well-suited to build and operate sport venues. Because authorities' commissioners often are appointed to periods of service that extend beyond a single election cycle, appointees are responsible to elected officials, but have a degree of independence. Additionally, authorities are responsible only for a venue and/or nearby real estate development; therefore, team owners can be assured that the venue's success is the organization's primary focus. In order to give sport managers an in-depth understanding of public corporations, a brief history of the broad use of authorities is included.

The Broad Use of Public Authorities

Many governments have an extensive history of utilizing public authorities with long-term success. While building and managing sport facilities has only been a relatively recent application of public corporations, authorities have long been a vital tool in facilitating economic development. In fact, most large cities have an independent authority for an airport, port, or both. For example, the Port Authority of New York, and Massport, of Boston– often regarded as the "pioneers" of public corporations – both ensure the adequacy of transportation infrastructure in their cities in order to facilitate economic and real estate development. Before focusing on authorities created to build and oversee sport venues, a brief description of the successes of these two authorities, as well as the lessons that can be learned from each, is presented.

The Port Authorities of New York and Massport, Boston

Founded in 1921, the Port Authority has been instrumental in constructing and maintaining the bridges, tunnels, and mass transit systems in New York City and New Jersey for nearly a century. As the region grew, the need to expand the existing airports, and construct better mass transit between them, became clear. Achieving this would require the participation of numerous local governments; an authority, as a single-purpose entity, is well-suited to facilitate cooperation between involved parties. The Port Authority has been successful in accomplishing what it was created to do, as today, the area's several airports and transit systems are vital economic engines for the region and its 22 million residents. A recent assessment of the Port Authority highlighted its numerous accomplishments but also underscored the need to ensure that the public's interest is protected (5Moss & O'Neill, 2014). Public officials must clearly stipulate an authority's responsibilities, and what can and cannot be undertaken in the pursuit of its mission.

In the 1960s, the Port Authority expanded its original mission to assist in developing lower Manhattan. The authority assumed responsibility for the Port Authority Trans-Hudson (PATH) – a rail line that connects several cities in New Jersey with Manhattan – as well as the building of the World Trade Center. While PATH has been vital for economic activity, the Port Authority's original mission did not include the management of fixed-rail systems. Why a public authority was needed to help develop lower Manhattan, and how the Port Authority was able to extend its control beyond its initial purpose, remains unclear. In addition, in the 1970s, the Port Authority built mixed-use waterfront developments and industrial parks throughout the region. Each of these endeavors clearly enhanced economic development but may have been outside the authority's original mission (O'Neill, 2014: 17). A lesson learned from the assessment of the Port Authority is that it is in the public's best interest for an authority to have a single, clearly defined purpose.

While the responsibilities of the Port Authority in New York now include a broadened span of economic development initiatives, contrastingly, the structure of Boston's Massport illustrates a single purpose authority. As such, Massport, while also created to develop and manage transit assets, has not been as gregarious in economic development activities as the Port Authority. Hogarty (2002) assessed elements of Massport's success and shortcomings, noting the building and operation of Boston's Logan Airport as the authority's most substantial achievements.[7] Strahinich (1989) noted that Massport was created to do the work that the public sector is ill-suited to perform.

Airports and ports commonly interface with privately owned companies, many with longevity in their field. Authorities have a permanency that facilitates long-term relationships with private businesses that are vital to a region's development and are well-suited to be the linkage between the public and private sectors.

In summarizing the value of authorities, Strahinich (1989) noted that some of these organizations behaved as rogue governments seeking to extend their existence even when activities were at cross purposes with public policies. However, public authorities in the hands of careful stewards of both economic activity and the public's goals can accomplish a great deal. Meyer and Rowan (1977) also stress that authorities should be designed to accomplish the goals sought by a government. The powers given to an authority must align with the expectations of the sanctioning government. Authorities must infuse business practices with public values, but like any other business, there must be a plan that defines success so that the achievement of goals and objectives can be measured. The potential structures, scopes of responsibility, and access to revenue streams will be discussed in the following section.

Creating Authorities for Sport-Anchored Districts and Venues

In creating a public authority, the enabling legislation should define the structure and responsibilities, as well as the expected accomplishments, with a framework to evaluate success (Brooks & Pallis, 2008). Sometimes the creation of an authority involves more than a single governmental entity. For example, the Port Authority in New York is the creation of the City of New York, the State of New York, and the State of New Jersey. The building of Lucas Oil Stadium, home of the Indianapolis Colts, involved several counties and the State of Indiana. And the Gateway Economic and Redevelopment Authority involved Cuyahoga County and the City of Cleveland in building an arena for the Cleveland Cavaliers and a ballpark for the Cleveland Indians. Regardless of the parties involved, the objectives of all organizations should inform the structure, responsibilities, and level of independence of the new corporation.

The governments authorizing the existence of these organizations select commissioners to lead a special district or authority. Sometimes, city governments choose members of its city council to be the commissioners of special districts. In San Diego, *all* members of the city council and the mayor led the central city redevelopment. It is far more common, however, for a city council, a city's mayor, county commissioners, or the state's legislature to select leadership from external sources. While the board of a special district is responsible to the government(s) that created it, commissioners are typically appointed for terms that extend beyond those involved in the selection process; this way commissioners can function without political interference. For example, the commissioners of the Gateway Economic Redevelopment Corporation, the organization that manages Progressive Field and the Quicken Loans Arena in Cleveland serve until they resign or relocate from the county.[8]

Once the structure is solidified, there are two essential dimensions to consider. The first consideration is an authority's access to a dedicated and/or reliable revenue stream. For example, port authorities can have numerous revenue streams, including landing fees at their airports, wharf/berth charges, leases for retail space operations, parking, etc. Authorities for sport venues could have access to revenue from ticket taxes, the leasing of retail space outside the venue, property taxes generated from real estate development, etc. The degree of independence an authority has is related to the control of its own "purse strings." Without fiscal independence, an authority will be less able to initiate activities without the express approval of the governments that created it.

Second is the scope of responsibility assigned to the newly created authority. The scope could be limited to a single venue, or could include the creation of a sports district, and/or the ability to participate in the development of adjacent real estate. Within each possible scenario, the authority could also be expected to manage the assets created. When there is growth in the scope of an authority's responsibilities, increased resources and/or access to revenue is often necessary. Numerous authorities for sport venues have been created at various scopes and scales. For example, the Santa Clara Stadium Authority was created to build and manage Levi's Stadium, home of the San Francisco 49ers. The Harris County–Houston Sports Authority is responsible for all sport venues in Houston. The Arizona Tourism and Sports Authority was created to oversee the stadium that is home to the Arizona Cardinals, several spring training sites for Major League Baseball teams, and other tourism infrastructure projects. In Columbus, an Arts and Entertainment District and Convention Center Authority was created to facilitate real estate development in the area and the adjacent Scioto River.

Next, three contrasting organizational structures of authorities created with a sport venue focus, as well as the implications of each structure will be examined: the Gateway Economic Development Corporation of Greater Cleveland (GEDC), Indianapolis' Capital Improvements Board (CIB), and the Downtown Development Authority (DDA) of Detroit.

Gateway Economic Development Corporation of Greater Cleveland (GEDC)

In early 1990, the city of Cleveland, which had suffered the loss of the Cavaliers when the team moved to Richfield in 1974, was at risk of losing yet another team. The Cleveland Indians threatened to leave if a new ball-park was not built. Cleveland's population had been declining since 1950 (see Table 13.1). In 1950, the city was home to more than 914,000 people, but it had just 505,000 residents by 1990. Elected and community leaders, in asking voters to approve a sales tax on alcohol and tobacco products to finance the venues, stressed not only the need to attract and retain the Cavaliers, but repurpose and revitalize the downtown area. In May of 1990, Cleveland and Cuyahoga County created the GEDC to oversee the building, operation, and maintenance of a new ballpark for the Cleveland Indians, and an arena intended to convince the Cleveland Cavaliers to return to the city.

The GEDC is an example of an authority with a limited scope and mini-mal autonomy, due to its structure, designated responsibilities, and finances. First, the structure and appointment of the five members of the GEDC's board of directors ensures the City of Cleveland and Cuyahoga County's control of the authority. Originally the city and county each appointed two commissioners, and the mayor and county commissioners appointed the board's chair. Voters have since changed the structure of Cuyahoga

Table 13.1 Cleveland's Population

Population		
Year	City	County
1950	914,808	1,389,532
1960	876,050	1,647,895
1970	750,903	1,720,835
1980	573,822	1,498,400
1990	505,616	1,412,140
2000	487,403	1,393,978
2010	396,815	1,280,122
2015	388,072	1,255,921

Source: US Census Bureau.

County, and today a county council, county executive, Cleveland's city council, and Cleveland's mayor each choose one commissioner, and the mayor and county executive jointly appoint the board's chair.

Additionally, the GEDC's defined scope of responsibilities limits the authority's influence. Despite the broad geographic scale of its name, the GEDC's jurisdiction was limited to the land upon which an arena, ballpark, parking garage, and two public plazas would be built. The GDEC was not given any role in economic development. The responsibility to leverage the venues for redevelopment was left to the City of Cleveland and the Historic Gateway Neighborhood Corporation. Neither team's owners were asked to contribute to development activities, even though the owner of the Cleveland Indians, Richard Jacobs, was a successful real estate developer. Richard Jacobs sold the Indians in 1999 to father and son Larry and Paul Dolan; they have not been involved with real estate development in the area.[9]

The GEDC's limited funds and lack of an independent revenue stream have severely restricted the authority's independence. As mentioned, to fund the construction of the venues, a county-wide tax on the sale of alcohol and tobacco products was approved by voters. Then, once built, the GEDC was to generate the revenues it needed to operate from the leases with the teams. When the tax on alcohol and tobacco products did not produce sufficient revenues to pay for the cost to construct both venues, additional funds were supplied by Cuyahoga County. Further, when the original leases with the teams did not produce sufficient revenues for GDEC to fulfill its financial responsibilities, the GDEC's board was required to renegotiate new terms of the leases with the teams in 2004. Each team assumed responsibility for all maintenance expenses of $500,000 or less, and the public sector's responsibilities were reduced to the arena's roof and heating and air conditioning systems, the arena and ballpark's foundations, and other large-scale infrastructure elements. The teams also agreed to provide the funds needed to pay the taxes owed to the Cleveland Public Schools and to pay for GDEC's staff.

As noted, the GDEC was not given any opportunity to participate in economic development, which limited the venues' potential to act as catalysts for revitalization in the area. However, according to the US Census Bureau, while population in the city overall has continued to decline, the number of residents in the downtown area has increased. As of 2016, Cleveland's downtown area was home to 13,886 people, opposed to only 4,651 people in 1990. Several residential development projects are underway and the downtown population base will soon surpass 15,000 (Sandy, 2016). In addition, the city has seen a growth in the number of higher income jobs, particularly in the health sector, and Cleveland's income tax base has continued to improve as a result (see Table 13.2). Between 2005 and 2015, Cleveland's annual income tax revenue increased from approximately $288 million to $347 million, an increase of more than 20 percent. While annual property tax revenues declined over the same period, property taxes account for a significantly smaller portion of Cleveland's general tax revenues. Additionally, the decline in property tax revenues during this period does not detract from the achievements of the GDEC because, as previously mentioned, the authority was not given any role in economic development. It is important to note that expansions to the Cleveland Clinic and University Hospitals do not generate any property taxes, as their facilities are tax-exempt.

While the GDEC had limited autonomy due to both its structure and lack of an independent revenue stream, it fulfilled its intended purpose: to build and operate two new sport venues in downtown Cleveland in order

Table 13.2 Cleveland's Tax Revenues, Selected Years

Cleveland Tax Revenues ($thousands)

Year	Income	Property
2005	288,191	64,390
2006	302,084	66,762
2007	317,268	69,313
2008	329,316	65,398
2009	296,507	63,573
2010	298,209	68,807
2011	311,492	63,839
2015	346,7973	55,017

Source: City of Cleveland annual comprehensive annual financial reports, various years.

to improve the city's amenity portfolio. In 2014, 56 percent of the voters approved an extension of the "sin" tax for 20 years, to meet the public sector's responsibilities in the lease extension, including improvements to the arena, ballpark, and the stadium used by the Cleveland Browns. It was estimated the Cavaliers and Indians would share in $135 million to repair and enhance the arena and ballpark. The Browns planned to request $23.7 million for the stadium, leaving of $100 million for the public sector's other responsibilities.

Indianapolis' Capital Improvements Board (CIB)

The rapid growth of surrounding suburban counties combined with decreasing residents in the downtown area highlighted the need to focus on revitalizing the core areas of Indianapolis. Despite the consolidation of Indianapolis with Marion County in the 1970s, suburban growth in adjacent counties has surged (see Table 13.3), and median incomes have remained substantially higher in the surrounding counties. Indianapolis' plan for the revitalization of a deteriorating downtown focused on professional teams, amateur sport, and cultural amenities. The scope, scale, and sustained commitment to the plan across five decades has led many to consider Indianapolis' plan to be a model for a successful revitalization of a downtown area and the rebranding of a central city.

Created in 1965 by the Indiana General Assembly to lead downtown economic development efforts and combat trends of suburban sprawl, Indianapolis' CIB was a key agent in the city's revitalization strategy. The CIB is similar in its structure to a port authority as it was created to finance, build, operate, and maintain facilities to promote conventions, culture, entertainment, sports, and recreational activities. While port authorities, as discussed, usually focus on transit-related development, the CIB was created

Table 13.3 Indianapolis Population Trends: Percentage Change by Decade

City/County	1940 to 1950	1950 to 1960	1960 to 1970	1970 to 1980	1980 to 1990	1990 to 2000	2000 to 2010
Indianapolis	10.4	11.5	56.8	−4.7	4.3	5.4	4.9
Boone	8.7	14.8	12.1	18.1	4.7	20.9	22.8
Hamilton	15.8	40.9	35.9	50.4	32.8	67.7	50.3
Hancock	17.5	31.1	31.6	25.2	3.6	21.7	26.4
Hendricks	22.0	66.3	32.0	29.3	8.5	37.5	39.7
Johnson	16.4	66.9	39.9	26.3	14.1	30.8	21.2
Marion[1]	19.7	26.4	13.8	−3.6	4.2	7.9	5.0
Morgan	19.8	42.8	30.4	17.7	7.5	19.3	3.3
Shelby	8.0	21.6	10.9	5.5	1.1	7.8	2.3

Source: US Census Bureau, various years.

[1] Population counts for Marion County include all independent cities in 1940–1960, and the four cities that did join the consolidated city/county from 1970 through 2010.

to oversee investments designed to enhance tourism and entertainment. In structuring the authority, the city's political leadership granted the CIB a wide scope of authority and autonomy to use sports and culture to enhance the downtown area and the local economy.

The appointment of the CIB's board members has led to a consolidated power structure. The members are appointed by the Mayor of Indianapolis (six members), the Marion County Board of Commissioners (two members), and the Indianapolis City–County Council (one member). Since a majority vote is required to authorize a project, the mayor, who appoints a majority of the board members, has a high level of control. The outcomes in Indianapolis, in terms of the number of projects initiated, are a result of the board's centralized power. While the rapid development that has occurred over the last 50 years has been crucial to the revitalization of the downtown, Cantor (2014) indicates the lack of public input in the process.

The CIB can issue revenue bonds, giving the authority a level of financial independence, but Indiana law limits the amount of indebtedness it can incur. In the past, when its debt limit had been reached, the CIB involved other authorities to assume issued debt for economic development activities. For example, the Marion County Convention and Recreational Facilities Authority (MCCRFA) is devoted to activities involving the convention center, and the Indiana Finance Authority was created to help finance other assets. The CIB worked with other authorities like these to build a minor league ballpark, Banker's Life Fieldhouse (home of the Indiana Pacers) and the adjoining parking garage, and part of the Indiana Convention Center.

Despite this level of debt, the City of Indianapolis and Marion County's fiscal condition was AAA in 2016. This evaluation, by Moody's, suggests that even though the financial mechanisms are complex, the county and city are still seen as financially sound. The bond market's ratings are an effective control on excessive or imprudent action by an independent authority. While the recent recession illustrated the inability of some lenders and rating agencies to properly evaluate exotic financial products, the debt sold by special districts was not a factor in the collapse of financial markets. The demand for the bonds in the market is used by the state as a fiscal oversight tool for the CIB's debt level. Simply put, the amount of debt the CIB can assume is a function of the confidence financial institutions have in the capacity of the organization to repay its obligations.

Although the city has been successful in taking on large amounts of debt to finance economic development projects, the building of Lucas Oil Stadium (a new venue for the Indianapolis Colts), required additional revenue to support the amount of debt. To sustain new bonds, the legislature approved increases in total tax rates and a redirection of state tax revenues produced within the Professional Sports Development Area (PSDA). The PSDA is a designated part of the downtown area, extending only for a few blocks between the arena, convention center, and stadium. Sales and income taxes,

Table 13.4 Select CIB Tax Collections,[1] 2011–2015 (in $2015)

Revenue Source/ Tax Rate	2011	2012	2013	2014	2015
Hotel (10%)	41,977,879	46,243,136	44,698,844	48,621,698	51,692,747
Food & Beverage (2%)	40,718,293	43,722,874	42,392,261	44,155,319	47,710,426
Admissions (6–10%)[2]	6,208,664	8,027,376	11,047,952	12,962,131	13,118,840
Auto Rental (4–6%)[2]	4,292,761	4,808,624	6,160,843	6,950,976	6,671,583
PSDA Allocation	26,259,285	24,598,704	25,508,258	24,433,664	25,400,848
Regional Food & Beverage (.5%)	5,637,470	5,314,763	5,255,956	5,375,289	5,167,191
Total	125,094,353	132,715,478	135,064,114	142,499,078	149,761,635

Source: CIB Comprehensive Annual Financial Reports.

[1] CIB Collections selected for Table 13-4 do not include revenues from Cigarette Tax, Specialty License Plate Fees, or Interlocal Agreement Funding (2010).
[2] The 4% Admissions and 2% Auto Rental Tax Increases are effective March 1, 2013.

as well as food and beverages taxes generated within the PSDA, accrue to the CIB. This financing tool was politically attractive to the Indiana legislature, as residents could avoid paying for the venues by spending their money elsewhere. But to further reduce the burden on the PSDA, each of the six counties adjacent to Marion County agreed to implement a tax on restaurant food and beverages to pay for the Indianapolis Colts' new stadium.

From 2011 to 2015, the CIB received more than $125 million, annually, from the various revenue streams dedicated to development opportunities (see Table 13.4). The taxes collected within the PSDA are used to repay part of the bonds sold for the arena and the stadium. The balance can be designated to facilitate economic development capital projects approved by Indianapolis' council. Although the CIB does not have the authority to ensure the development of mixed-use real estate, it has been effective in using a variety of sport and entertainment venues to enhance the downtown area and the local economy.[10] Many consider the scope, scale, and sustained commitment to Indianapolis' revitalization plan a model for success.

Detroit's Downtown Development Authority (DDA)

In March 2013, Michigan's governor announced the appointment of an emergency financial manager to oversee Detroit's finances. Three months later, the governor also authorized the Michigan Strategic Fund (MSF) to support a new arena for the Detroit Red Wings. MSF would contribute more than a quarter billion dollars of state aid to anchor the Catalyst Development Project (CDP) to stimulate real estate development throughout downtown and midtown Detroit (Cantor, 2014). The CDP is coordinated by Detroit's Downtown Development Authority (DDA), an entity created to sustain property values in the city, and whose members are appointed by the mayor. Per a concession management agreement with Olympia Development (the Red Wing's real estate development company), the DDA assumed full managerial, operational, and maintenance responsibilities of the new arena at its opening in 2017.

Development authorities in Michigan use Tax Increment Financing (TIF) and have the ability to leverage the increment in property taxes generated from new real estate development within its designated boundaries. The key to a TIF district's success is its ability to capture an increment from other taxing jurisdictions (Dye & Merriman, 2000). The additional property taxes can be used to support additional real estate development projects, giving authorities entrepreneurial motivation. The city of Detroit supports the success of the DDA by permitting investors to purchase foreclosed land and abandoned buildings at a cost of $1, then assigning the property taxes generated to the DDA through the TIF program.[11] Capital for future development must be generated by tax revenues collected from the projects in the district.

Additionally, the State of Michigan's support has ensured Detroit's public schools would not lose any revenues. In 1994, Michigan's voters approved a plan to transfer some property tax increments to the state. This was done to provide Michigan with the ability to redistribute property tax growth in suburban school districts to schools in central cities with far less economic growth. The CDP allows the DDA to continue the collection of school property tax revenue that otherwise would have been diverted to the state. The state's commitment to the project included a guarantee that Detroit's schools continue to receive their share of property taxes generated by new development.

Since Detroit's bankruptcy, and as a result of the competition with other urban areas in the polycentric region (Goetz, 2003), investments in downtown and midtown Detroit have been laden with risk. Part of the initial agreement required Olympia Development to contribute $200 million of private sector development, in addition to the venue. However, Olympia Development has since unveiled large-scale redevelopment plans, which would far exceed $200 million in additional real estate, if completed. At the arena's opening, Olympia Development announced plans for six additional residential developments, as well as $50 million for new buildings at nearby Wayne State University and the Detroit Medical Center. Additionally, with the Detroit Pistons' relocation to the new arena as a secondary tenant, further real estate development is likely.

As mentioned, Olympia Development's agreement with the DDA stipulated that the authority would assume full managerial, operational, and maintenance responsibilities of the facility, once opened. Ownership of the facility will flow through different, special-purpose governmental entities. The arena, but not the adjacent buildings, will be owned by the DDA. The DDA will transfer ownership of the arena to the Detroit/Wayne County Stadium Authority. Eventually, the DDA will develop a lease with the team; this complex arrangement is necessary to comply with the provisions of the 1986 Tax Act.[12]

Detroit's DDA generates revenue only if it is successful in attracting real estate development to the downtown and midtown areas. If anticipated TIF revenues are not produced, the DDA does not have access to other revenue streams to cover any shortfall in bond payments.[13] This structure encourages the authority to be entrepreneurial in pursuit of the goals established for it – in this case, to enhance property values in the downtown. Detroit has empowered an authority to aggressively promote development projects in the interests of the city, without committing any external revenues to the initiative.

Conclusion

The U.S. Census Bureau reported that there were more than 37,000 special districts in the United States in 2012. These special districts and/or authorities are at the center of public–private partnerships forged to facilitate many forms of economic development, including the oversight of professional sport venues. Of the examined authorities created for the development of sport venues, each has been successful in ensuring a sport venue (or several) was built. However, the organizational structures of each, and the outcomes each partnership saw as a result, were quite different. Because an authority's structure determines the actions it undertakes, it is crucial for sport managers to understand the history, culture, design, and responsibilities of the authority that will be part of a venue's building, operation, and maintenance. Because almost all recent venues are financed using public money, you will likely work with a public authority in the course of your career. For this reason, the ability to understand all aspects of an authority, as well as the expectations of elected officials, is vital.

Notes

1   Some of the material in this chapter is from "Protecting the public's interest: Options for structuring public authorities for sport venues," *The Physical Educator*," which appears in Volume 76. That material appears with the permission of *The Physical Educator*.
2   For example, repayment for bonds sold to build M&T Bank Stadium, the new home for the Baltimore Ravens, relies on lottery funds; additionally, Cleveland's Quicken Loans Arena and Progressive Field were both financed, in part, by a county-wide tax on the sale of alcohol and tobacco products.

3   While municipal bankruptcies are rare, as recently as July 2013, the City of Detroit had to file for bankruptcy protection as it could not repay its debts or meet other financial responsibilities.

4   A government's financial responsibilities could include, but are not limited to, government employee salaries and benefits, pensions owed former employees, delivery of publicly provided services, and the annual payments for the debt assumed.

5   For example, owners of homes or office buildings in Ann Arbor pay property taxes to both the City of Ann Arbor and the Ann Arbor Independent School District.

6   The City of Detroit's bankruptcy was a result of the outflow of people, economic activity, and wealth, beginning with the riots in 1967, and has continued into the 21st century. The city was impacted by a lengthy contraction of the manufacturing sector, the Great Recession (beginning in 2008), and the migration of almost one million residents to the suburbs, and/or out of the city.

7   This specialization did not prevent some criticism with regard to passenger safety in the aftermath of the 9/11 terrorist attacks. Two of the attacking planes left from Logan Airport, and a subsequent investigation of Massport's operations highlighted an insular personnel system that was insufficient in hiring the best professionals for airport operations (Hogarty, 2002).

8   If a commissioner were derelict in performing their roles, there are usually operational guidelines that specify how someone can be removed from the board.

9   Though the team owners did not initially play any role in additional development, in 2005, the Gund Brothers sold the Cavaliers to Dan Gilbert, who has been quite active in redeveloping downtown Cleveland.

10   Venues that have contributed to Indianapolis' downtown redevelopment strategy include a minor league ballpark, Banker's Life Fieldhouse (home of the Indiana Pacers), the Indiana Convention Center, and Lucas Oil Stadium.

11   The land at "no cost" provision was upheld when Detroit transferred 39 small parcels of land to the DDA and Olympia Development for the project.

12   To ensure that tax-exempt bonds were not primarily financing private assets, Congress established a two-pronged test. The 1986 Act established that an asset served "primarily private use" if more than 10 percent of its use was by a nongovernmental entity and if more than 10 percent of the costs of the bond were secured by property used directly or indirectly in a private business.

13   If revenues are not sufficient, the DDA would be dependent on additional support from the MSF.

References

Brooks, M. R., & Pallis, A. A. 2008. Assessing port governance models: process and performance components. *Maritime Policy & Management* 35 (4): 411–432.

Cantor, M. B. 2014. *Sports and real estate development as tools for changing patterns of regional economic activity: Managing the effects of teams and venues on local communities*. PhD dissertation.

Dye, Richard F. & Merriman, David F. 2000. The effects of tax increment financing on economic development. *Journal of Urban Economics* 47 (2) : 306 –328. https://doi.org/10.1006/juec.1999.2149

Goetz, E. G. 2003. *Deconcentrating the poor in urban America*. Washington, DC: The Urban Institute.

Moss, M., & O'Neill, H. 2014. *A port authority that works.* New York: NYU Wagner School, Rudin Center for Transportation Policy and Management.

Rosentraub, M S. 2014. *Reversing urban decline: Why and how sports, entertainment, and culture turn cities into major league winners.* Boca Raton: CRC Press/Taylor & Francis Group.

Sandy, E. 2016. The population boom in downtown Cleveland is very real and very good. But how long can it continue, *ClevelandScene.* Retrieved from http://www.clevescene.com/cleveland/the-population-boom-in-downtown-cleveland-is-very-real-and-very-good-but-how-long-can-it-continue/Content?oid=4700955 (accessed December 6, 2016).

U.S. Census Bureau. 2012. Census Bureau reports there are 89,004 local governments in the United States, *U.S. Census Bureau,* August 30. Retrieved from https://www.census.gov/newsroom/releases/archives/governments/cb12-161.html (accessed July 31, 2018).

Chapter 14

From Theory to Practice
Case Studies

Introduction

The preceding chapters have provided insights into the issues and skills that sport managers must understand and master to advance their careers. This final chapter's focus is on a few select cases that illustrate the complex elements that forged public/private partnerships and underscore the skills needed to analyze the impact of new venues on teams and cities. The purpose of including this chapter is to apply the insights detailed in the preceding chapters to several "real world" scenarios. In some instances, tools discussed in this book were prominent in the structuring of successful deals. In other deals, there was a reliance on intangible benefits that were left unquantified, or claims of improperly measured impacts. Every city, market, team, and project is unique in scale, scope, and makeup. Balancing these idiosyncratic differences to secure successful projects is an integral part of the sport business for the private and public sectors. In each case study, readers are encouraged to answer the questions at the end to discuss whether or not the negotiated deals were in the best interests of the team, the region's private sector, and the city that became the site of the new venue.

A $750 Million Public Sector Investment: The Raiders' Relocation to Las Vegas

It is widely understood that legalized gambling was the engine that initially fueled Las Vegas' growth, ultimately "putting the city on the map." And while gambling is still a vital contributor to the success of the region's mega-resorts, entertainment and other experiences are now equally, if not more, essential to the resorts' financial success. In 2013, the Las Vegas metropolitan area was one of three major urban centers in the United States that was *not* home to a large-scale stadium (capacity of 55,000 or more)[1]. The lack of this crucial amenity reduced the region's ability to compete with other tourism destinations for stadium-based events. An earlier effort to build an enclosed stadium failed. The possibility of attracting the Raiders, however, re-energized the discussion. A brief history is necessary to understand the context of the stadium's financing and the debate that preceded its construction.

Following the stock market crash of 1929 and the construction of the Hoover Dam, Governor Fred Balzar legalized all forms of casino gambling in Nevada by signing Assembly Bill 98 into law on March 19, 1931 (O'Reiley, 2011). Legalized gambling was seen as an asset to complement the state's natural environmental attractions and a catalyst to propel economic development. With no other state permitting legalized gambling, Las Vegas, Reno, and Lake Tahoe were able to attract large numbers of visitors. Nevada's monopoly on gaming weakened when other states and Canadian provinces issued licenses for casinos; for example, the State of Maryland gave several counties the right to offer gamblers the ability to play games on slot machines in the late 1940s (Cephas, 2015). In 1977, the State of New Jersey permitted the construction of full-scale casinos in Atlantic City (Star-Ledger Staff, 2010). Next, Florida, permitted the Seminole Tribe to build a 1,200-seat bingo hall on its Hollywood reservation (Gensler, 2016). By the 1980s and 1990s, Las Vegas' monopoly on legalized gaming ceased to exist. Today, casinos across the continent offer the same gaming activities that are available in Nevada, with the exception of betting on sport. New Jersey's efforts to permit sport betting at casinos, racetracks, and other athletic games suggests Las Vegas will continue to face competition for gaming in the years to come (Jackson, 2017).

Las Vegas' efforts to enhance its hospitality profile began with its entry into the convention business. Las Vegas, however, has always faced stiff competition from the meeting spaces built in other major urban and entertainment centers or cities with unique natural resources (e.g., Atlanta, Chicago, New York, Orlando, San Diego, Seattle). To meet these competitive challenges, Las Vegas needed to embellish its image as a unique event and entertainment center. As a result, numerous mega-resorts opened with unique attractions and theatres. Las Vegas became an entertainment center and a destination for the continent's largest conventions with an extraordinary concentration of entertainment, restaurants, and other amenities. As a convention hub, Las Vegas offered comfortable weather in the winter months, a very large convention center, numerous entertainment events, and virtually endless gaming activities. Eventually, some of the resorts constructed additional convention space on their own footprints, and with a concentration of live entertainment and gaming, the city was poised for substantial growth.

With the goal of enhancing the region's entertainment options, the public and private sectors worked with the University of Nevada Las Vegas (UNLV) to build an arena on the university's campus. When it opened in 1983, the Thomas & Mack Center (TMC), with seating for 19,500, was larger than any other indoor venue in Las Vegas. TMC's existence allowed concerts and shows that wanted to attract more than

15,000 spectators (depending on seating configurations) to be held in the region. Today, due to the dramatic improvements that have been made for "set" technology (set design, props, and other equipment used by entertainers during their performances), there are now many events that need even larger venues. In addition, some performers prefer to play at indoor stadia to avoid inclement weather. As will be described more thoroughly in the coming sections, concerts and other events with these needs bypassed Las Vegas to play in more temperate locations such as California, or to play in the covered stadiums available in Arlington (Dallas/Fort Worth area), Atlanta, Detroit, Houston, Indianapolis, and New Orleans. Leaders of the hospitality sector in Southern Nevada had long-identified the need for a domed or covered stadium to enhance the region's tourism infrastructure.

To adequately serve the Southern Nevada community, facilities must be covered so spectators can comfortably attend events in every season. As timing would have it, UNLV was also in need of a new home for its football team. By 1977, UNLV's growth had made it the state's largest university, surpassing the state's flagship campus, the University of Nevada Reno (UNR). UNLV began as an extension of UNR, but the prosperity of the Southern Nevada region led to large-scale population changes and steady enrollment growth. In 1970, just 13 years after the university's founding, Clark County supported the construction of a 40,000-seat stadium on the region's eastern edge, 7.7 miles from UNLV's campus to support the school's football team. The open-air stadium – still in use today – has no shade and as a result cannot be used for entertainment events during the region's long summer. Distant from the campus and the core of the city, the stadium contributed little to the life of students or the hospitality industry. As UNLV grew, so, too, did the demand for on-campus housing and student activities. The university's leadership began to explore the possibility of building a covered stadium that could be valuable to both the region and UNLV's future aspirations.

The University of Nevada Las Vegas: The Key to a Public Investment in a New Stadium

As noted, UNLV is Nevada's largest comprehensive university offering undergraduate, graduate, and doctoral-level education. Total enrollment reached 29,720 in fall of 2016. Relative to what this growth means, UNLV's total enrollment would rank fifth in the Big Twelve Conference, surpassing Baylor University, Kansas State University, Oklahoma State University, the University of Oklahoma, Texas Christian University, and the University of Kansas. UNLV hoped to use the new stadium to achieve its goal of reaching "Top Tier" status (UNLV, n.d.). UNLV's *Top Tier Initiative* sought to enhance student life on campus; the school's campus bloomed almost overnight. The school also hoped the new stadium would enhance their bid to join one of the NCAA's Power 5 Conferences.

In the aftermath of the Great Recession, Las Vegas recovered far more slowly than many other cities. It was clear that Southern Nevada was overly dependent on the financial success of its hospitality sector. As a result, community leaders put their energy toward diversifying the regional economy. Understanding this, UNLV added a new tenant to their Top Tier Initiative: graduating highly-skilled employees to help the region diversify and advance its economy. In doing so, UNLV accepted its role in steering the region towards its goal of economic diversification. In addition to proposals for a new stadium and several other on-campus improvements, the school's new medical program accepted its first class in 2017. These enhancements to campus life were seen as a step toward UNLV's effort to attract and retain the best students, who in turn could become part of a new labor force, furthering the economy's diversification.

Building the Case for a New Stadium

The importance of events to the growth and financial success of the Las Vegas economy is underscored by the sheer number of visitors needed to populate the city's hotels each day. As illustrated in Figures 14.1 and 14.2, the success of the Las Vegas economy is tied to very large daily attendance, and high occupancy rates. In order to sustain the needed flow of visitors, additional events are needed; this is especially true given the spread of gaming to other states and the increasing demand of consumers and their expectations.

Currently, there are 149,339 hotel rooms and 10,569 time-share units in Las Vegas. Together, this equates to 159,908 units that must be populated

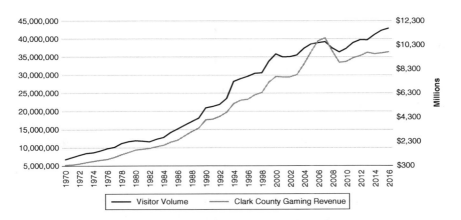

Figure 14.1 Las Vegas Visitor Volume and Clark County Gaming Revenue.

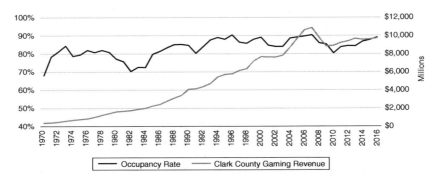

Figure 14.2 Las Vegas Occupancy Rate and Clark County Gaming Revenue.

to achieve full occupancy (LVCVA, 2016). While a team seeks to sell all of the seats in its venue, hoteliers hope to sell out their rooms as well. For Las Vegas to meet the goal of filling 90 percent of its room inventory, more than 42.9 million visitors must be attracted to the city each year. To fill seats at a sporting event, a team needs to win games. Similarly, for Las Vegas to continue to attract approximately 43 million visits each year, it must remain the "entertainment event capital" of the United States, if not the world. A state-of-the-art covered stadium would make it possible to host additional shows and games in the city, which would attract more and more visitors (filling more and more hotel rooms).

UNLV tried to reach out to the Las Vegas business community in an effort to unify its aspirations for a new covered stadium with the needs of the resorts and the regional economy. UNLV's goal was to replicate the successful coalition that led to the building of the TMC, which is home to the university's basketball teams and also hosts numerous shows, concerts, and events. Would a second public–private partnership be possible?

It is vital to underscore that UNLV's first proposal for a domed stadium did not include the presence of an NFL team. There was no indication in 2011 or 2012 that the NFL would consider Las Vegas as a viable location for a franchise. UNLV's sole focus was on a venue that could bring new concert and entertainment events to the region while also serving as the home for its football team.

UNLV's first proposal was for a covered stadium that would anchor the development of a new University Village that would enhance on-campus life for students, staff, and faculty. The planned University Village was meant to offer faculty and staff an amenity that could compete with what many other leading universities offer their employees. The University Village was expected to augment UNLV's image by providing a residential atmosphere that would attract undergraduate and graduate students from across the country. The additional amenities would also offer faculty and staff a better environment in which to work. The stadium, together with other new developments on campus, would allow UNLV to better position itself to attract and retain employees.

UNLV used an economic impact analysis to explain the value of a covered stadium to the campus community, political leaders throughout Southern Nevada, the resort industry, and residents of the region. An essential part of the report focused on the competitive disadvantage resulting from the absence of a venue capable of hosting events with more than 50,000 spectators. Without such a venue, some concerts and sporting events simply could not be held in the region, given Southern Nevada's long and very warm summer months. Other destinations (e.g., Dallas/Fort Worth, New Orleans, Phoenix, and Houston) did have covered stadia and, as a result, were able to host events that were not viable in Las Vegas.

Study #1: Methodology and Findings

UNLV's study identified the benefits that would likely accrue to the school if a partnership between the university and the resorts was created to build and manage a covered stadium. The economic impact analysis focused on the new visitors that would be attracted to the events and the resulting direct, indirect, and induced effects from their new, additional, or extended visits. The analysis also measured the incremental tax revenues from additional hotel nights and new or incremental visitor spending at the new stadium (excluding UNLV football games). Local governments and the state each benefit from the hotel taxes collected. The essential point of this report was to show that in the absence of this facility, large-scale events (e.g., Super Bowl, NCAA Men's Final Four) would not take place in the region. The report's methodology focused on *new* spending by visitors or tourists who would spend an additional day (or more) in the region. Spending by Nevada residents at the new stadium was not included in the analysis. As a result, the report only includes gains for the region that were *not* substitutions of one form of consumption for another.

In order to remain conservative, the economic study included only direct economic effects from additional spending at events that were unlikely to take place at the region's previously existing venues. It was conservatively assumed that indirect spending would not benefit the hospitality industry, as additional wages earned by workers would likely impact other parts of the regional economy. The indirect and induced spending effects would, however, enhance the regional economy and produce more tax revenues for the State of Nevada and local governments throughout the region. Regardless, a negligible amount of new income would be spent at the resorts.

Interviews with Las Vegas entertainment experts were conducted to identify events that could be attracted to the region by a new state-of-the-art facility with the capacity to host over 55,000 spectators:

1 PAC-12 Football Conference Championship Game (December)
2 NFL Exhibition game (August)
3 New College Football Bowl Game (December)
4 Neutral Site College Football Game (Fall)
5 Second Neutral Site College Football Game (Fall)
6 International Soccer Festival (Summer)
7 Electronic Music Festival (2 to 3 days, Summer)
8 Country Music Festival (either with ACM weekend or another time; 2-3 days)
9 UFC International Fight Week (Summer)
10 Tour Concert (Summer)
11 Second Tour Concert (Summer)
12 Winter Kick Soccer Festival (February)
13 Rock Music Festival (Summer)
14 X Games (Summer)
15 NFL Pro Bowl (January)
16 Mountain West Conference Football Championship Game (December)
17 NFR Closing Event (December)

In addition, Las Vegas entertainment experts identified the following events as potential new opportunities for Southern Nevada if the new covered stadium existed:

18 WrestleMania
19 Republican or Democratic National Convention
20 NCAA Final Four Basketball Championships
21 Comic-Con
22 Boxing
23 MLS All-Star Game
24 Corporate Events

It was determined that a new covered stadium with seating for at least 55,000 spectators, coupled with (1) the experience of organizations in the region that seek to attract events, (2) the existing resources of the hospitality industry (hotels, shows, retail centers, etc.), and (3) a pronounced marketing effort, hosting a total of 15 new events would be realistic. Projected impacts of these 15 new events, as well as other event scenarios, are displayed in Tables 14.1, 14.2, and 14.3.

The estimates of the number of spectators at an event was based on surveys conducted by the Las Vegas Visitors and Convention Authority (LVCVA), which focused on what visitors did during their stay in Las Vegas. Assuming

Table 14.1 Assumptions for Annual *Direct* Economic Value of Export-Based Events to the Las Vegas Regional Economy and the Region's Resorts

| Categories | Number of Export Events at Stadium | | | |
	15	20	25	30
Stadium capacity	55,000	55,000	55,000	55,000
Estimated event attendance	45,000	45,000	45,000	45,000
Tickets purchased by visitors (70%)	472,500	630,000	787,500	945,000
Tickets purchased by visitors who came only for event (85%)	401,625	535,500	669,375	803,250
Incremental visitors to Las Vegas	401,625	535,500	669,375	803,250
Visitors lodged in hotel/motel (95% of incremental visitors)	381,544	508,725	635,906	763,088
Length of stay (avg. # of nights)	3.7	3.7	3.7	3.7
Average # of people per room	2.1	2.1	2.1	2.1
Total number of room nights	672,244	896,325	1,120,406	1,344,488
Average lodging expenditures per night	$125.00	$125.00	$125.00	$125.00
Average food & beverage expenditure	$274.69	$274.69	$274.69	$274.69
Average local transport expenditure	$64.25	$64.25	$64.25	$64.25
Average retail expenditure	$129.34	$129.34	$129.34	$129.34
Average entertainment expenditure	$49.28	$49.28	$49.28	$49.28
Average gaming expenditure	$242.00	$242.00	$242.00	$242.00
Number of visitors participating in gaming (77% of incremental visitors)	309,251	42,335	515,419	618,503
Average sightseeing expenditure	$10.24	$10.24	$10.24	$10.24

that no event would attract more than 45,000 people (though it is likely some would surpass this estimate), the projected number of visitors, from outside the region, at any new event was 31,500 (70 percent of an average attendance of 45,000). Of course, if an event attracted 55,000 spectators, it is possible as many as 38,500 visitors would be in attendance.

The study found that if just 15 events were held, a total of 472,000 seats would be sold to visitors. Survey data suggested a total of $393.2 million in new spending would occur by way of these tourists. Of the $393.2 million in new spending, $66.2 million was expected to be spent at the new stadium, meaning the $327 million balance would be spent elsewhere in Las Vegas, such as at resorts or on shows (see Table 14.2).

Table 14.2 Annual Incremental Visitor Expenditures; Direct Economic Value of Export-Based Events to the Las Vegas Regional Economy and the Region's Resorts

Categories	Number of Export Events at Stadium			
	15	20	25	30
Lodging	$85,030,469	$112,040,625	$140,050,781	$168,060,938
Food and beverage	$110,332,371	$147,096,495	$183,870,619	$220,644,743
Retail spending	$51,946,178	$69,261,570	$86,576,963	$103,892,355
Entertainment (shows)	$19,792,080	$26,389,440	$32,986,800	$39,584,160
Gaming	$97,193,250	$129,591,000	$161,988,750	$194,386,500
Local transport	$25,804,406	$34,405,875	$43,007,344	$51,608,813
Sightseeing	$4,112,640	$5,483,520	$6,854,400	$8,225,280
Total annual benefit for the Las Vegas regional economy	$393,201,394	$524,268,252	$655,335,656	$786,402,788
Consumption on UNLV campus	$66,150,000	$88,200,000	$110,250,000	$132,300,000
Total annual direct economic benefit for resorts & retail centers in metro lv	$327,051,394	$436,068,525	$545,085,656	$654,102,788

Table 14.3 Annual Incremental Visitor Tax Revenues; Direct Economic Value of Export-
Based Events to the Las Vegas Regional Economy and the Region's Resorts

NV State Sales Tax	Number of Export Events at Stadium			
Categories	15	20	25	30
NV state sales tax	$13,037,862	$17,383,816	$21,729,770	$26,075,724
Clark County sales tax	$2,414,419	$3,219,225	$4,024,031	$4,828,838
Live entertainment tax	$4,329,863	$5,454,863	$6,579,863	$7,704,863
Hotel tax	$10,083,656	$13,444,875	$16,806,094	$20,167,313
NV general fund gaming tax	$6,560,544	$8,747,393	$10,934,241	$13,121,089
Car rental taxes and fees	$362,688	$483,584	$604,480	$725,376
Total tax revenues	**$36,789,032**	**$48,773,756**	**$60,678,479**	**$73,623,203**
LVCVA share of hotel taxes	$4,201,523	$5,602,031	$7,002,539	$8,403,047

As mentioned, the stadium would also produce new tax revenues for Nevada and Clark County's local governments. With 15 new events each year, it was projected that the State of Nevada, local governments throughout Southern Nevada, and the Clark County Department of Aviation would receive a total of $32.5 million in new tax revenues and fees. If the live entertainment tax were included, 15 events could potentially generate $36.8 million each year for the public sector (see Table 14.2).

While this estimate is conservative in some ways, it does assume that new visits would occur because of the events hosted in the stadium. In other words, if visitors decide to come to Las Vegas for other reasons and end up attending the event of the stadium (as a second thought), then the bulk of their spending is not new spending. A sporting event in Las Vegas might present a unique situation in this regard. Tourists come to Las Vegas for many reasons, so one could argue that stadium visitors from outside the region may have come to Las Vegas for other reasons. On the other hand, sport is unique in that it has events with loyal fans. No doubt many fans would attend the PAC-12 Football Conference Championship Game regardless of the location, so they would be additional visitors to the area.

Conflicts with the Hospitality Sector

As a result of its unique tourism and hospitality economy, Las Vegas' tax structure is unlike many other North American cities. For example, most American cities rely heavily on income and property taxes, paid by residents, to cover the cost of public services and government funding. Las Vegas is unique in that a substantial portion of its tax revenue is visitor-funded through transient occupancy taxes charged to those staying at hotels, motels, and other properties, and taxi taxes (primarily used by visitors). In addition, there are taxes on all gaming activities, on tickets to all live entertainment events, and, of course, a sales tax on all retail activity (including restaurants, pubs, and the consumption of beverages at any of the resorts). State and local governments and both campuses of the University of Nevada receive revenue from hospitality and gaming tax collections. The study produced for UNLV found that a large portion of the economic benefits from the existence of the stadium would accrue to the hospitality sector in the form of additional room nights and per diem spending (incremental revenue for resorts). This suggests that an investment in the new stadium by the resorts, through an increment in the Strip's transient occupancy tax, would be appropriate. The increment in the hotel or sales tax could be as small as one half of one percent, which equates to an increase of approximately $1.50 per visitor, per day. This very small increment in tourists' costs was not expected to have a significant impact on aggregate spending; it was not anticipated that a small increment would deter visitors from coming to Las Vegas.

The plans for financing the new stadium did not call for additional taxes to be levied on residents of the county or state unless they stayed in a hotel or spent money on the Strip. This meant the tax for the venue would have been exported almost entirely to visitors. Despite this, there was substantial resistance to the project from some hospitality sector organizations. One resort group feared competition from a new entertainment venue would reduce the number of shows it hosted at smaller venues in their resorts. Others believed that in the absence of a stadium with a larger capacity, performers would simply perform *more* shows at the Strip's existing (yet smaller) concert venues. Some industry leaders did not accept the perspective that some entertainers would bypass Las Vegas. Others believed that with hotel occupancy already exceeding 90 percent, an increase in the room tax was unjustified. These concerns derailed UNLV's first proposal.

Reinvigorated Efforts: Raiders' Interest in Las Vegas

UNLV's dreams of a domed stadium were suddenly revived when the Oakland Raiders decided to explore the option of relocating to Las Vegas. The team's owner visited Las Vegas after discussions for a new stadium in Oakland collapsed. The team was playing its home games in the aging Oakland–Alameda County Stadium, which it shared with the Oakland Athletics. While numerous renovations and improvements were made to the 1960s-built facility, several structural issues remained unresolved. Flooding issues that led to the seepage of raw sewerage into dugouts and other spaces in the stadium seemed to underscore the need for a replacement. Both teams reached the conclusion that a new venue was needed. The Raiders also resented their "tenant" status as the Athletics were permitted to receive some revenues generated by fans attending Raiders games. In late January 2016, ESPN reported that meetings were taking place between Raiders' owner, Mark Davis, and the CEO of the Las Vegas Sands, Sheldon Adelson. At the center of those conversations was a 65,000-seat domed stadium that would be built on or near UNLV's campus (Gutierrez, 2016).

Nevada Governor Brian Sandoval created the Southern Nevada Tourism Infrastructure Committee (SNTIC) in 2015 to assess the needs of the region's tourism economy. The SNTIC's purpose was to identify and prioritize tourism improvement projects in Southern Nevada, explore potential funding mechanisms to support new tourism-related initiatives, and make recommendations to the Governor regarding these matters (SNTIC, n.d.). The committee included elected officials, representatives from Las Vegas' major resorts, UNLV's president, and other community leaders. The SNTIC was expected to discuss the region's need for a new covered stadium as well as an expansion to the convention center. Other assets could also be evaluated. However, only after the Oakland Raiders' owner expressed interest in relocating from Oakland did a domed stadium became a central priority for the SNTIC.

The SNTIC and the community's renewed interest in developing a new stadium that could benefit UNLV encouraged the university to produce an updated study of the economic impact of a new stadium for UNLV, the State of Nevada, Clark County, and local governments in Southern Nevada. The section that follows outlines the methodology and findings of the second study, noting some key differences between the original and updated versions. The results of the study were presented at a convening of the SNTIC in April 2016.

Why Las Vegas? Raiders in the Dessert

So, what did the Raiders see in Las Vegas that provided a business opportunity enticing enough to relocate from Oakland? Given that the Oakland market is far larger than Las Vegas, there had to have been other factors at play. One element was that the team would receive public funding to help pay for a venue. Experts also speculate the Raiders believed a stadium in Las Vegas would earn more revenue from luxury seating, other in-facility revenue, and entertainment events than would a stadium in Oakland. Other relevant factors are detailed in the paragraphs that follow.

The Las Vegas tourism economy lends itself to the Raiders' goal of selling luxury products and enhancing in-facility revenue streams. Las Vegas had a record-breaking 42.9 million visitors in 2016. And while Las Vegas is associated with gaming, visitor spending on entertainment and restaurants accounts for a growing amount of the total amount of money spent by tourists. A recent study performed by the consulting firm Applied Analysis and the LVCVA found that "66 percent of the revenue generated on the famed Las Vegas Strip comes from non-gaming amenities and activities, and more than 25 percent of visitors chose not to gamble" (SNTIC, 2017). With visitors spending more money on other amenities than gaming, there was an undeniable window of opportunity for new forms of entertainment to grab market share on the Strip and in the region. The NHL saw this opportunity early, granting the city an expansion franchise. T-Mobile Arena, located on the Strip adjacent to the New York, New York resort, opened for concerts in April 2016, and the Las Vegas Golden Knights began play in 2017. After several months of deliberation, the NFL voted 31–1 on March 27, 2017 to approve the Raiders' relocation. The Raiders' new stadium will be built near the Strip, less than three miles southwest of UNLV's campus. The driving time between the stadium and campus is listed at seven minutes (comparably, the drive time between UNLV's current stadium and the campus is 20 minutes).

A comparison of Las Vegas to other destination markets underscores the unique dimensions of Southern Nevada. Las Vegas had 47.9 million room nights booked in 2015 (both domestic and international). In contrast, the Phoenix and Central Region of Arizona attracted just 22.1 million domestic overnight visitors (Coleman, Jr. & Floyd, 2016). It is also estimated that 15.5 million visitors spent at least one night in Greater Miami (Greater Miami Convention and Visitors Bureau, 2016). Of all cities studied, New Orleans was most similar to Las Vegas, hosting 9.78 million visitors who stayed an average of 4.2 nights (which equates to approximately 41 million overnight visitors) in 2015 (Larino, 2016).

Those opposing the team's relocation pointed to Las Vegas' slow recovery in the years after the Great Recession. However, comparing Las Vegas with other markets may not be appropriate because economic contractions impact regions in different ways. For example, the technology sector lost just 64,000 jobs during the Great Recession, whereas 1.1 million technology jobs were lost during the dot-com bubble of 2001 (Wolf & Terrell, 2016). The dot-com bubble's impact on the Las Vegas economy was insignificant; the number of visitors to Las Vegas was sustained and actually increased from 1999 until the Great Recession[2] (see Figure 14.3). Simply put, every region is impacted differently by economic contractions. Some setbacks in one region have no substantive effect on other areas.

It should also be noted that Las Vegas' recovery from the Great Recession had many nuances. First, within two years, visitor numbers had returned to levels similar to those reported for the years preceding the contraction of the national economy. In fact, the LVCVA found that Las Vegas visitor volume has increased 18.1 percent since the post-recession low of 36.4 million (SNTIC, 2016). It should be noted that several resorts reduced the room rates charged during this time, which reduced hotel tax collections

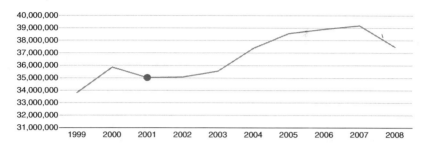

Figure 14.3 Historical Las Vegas Visitor Statistics.

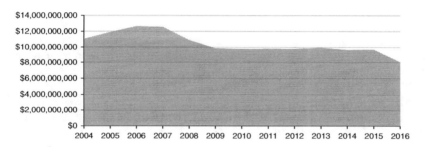

Figure 14.4 Annual Las Vegas Gaming Revenue ($2016).

Source: Las Vegas Convention and Visitors Authority.

Notes: 2016 Through October.

(Benston, 2009). Second, gaming revenues did decline during the recession (see Figure 14.4), but as the number of visitors increased, gaming activity recovered, and room rates returned to higher levels. That meant a quick recovery in the amount of hotel taxes collected by local governments, universities, and the LVCVA. Third, despite the stabilization of visitor levels, spending patterns in Nevada and Clark County, as measured by sales tax receipts and the volume of taxable sales, was not restored until 2014. This could have been a function of the recession, the changing characteristics of retail consumption, or a combination of several other factors. And fourth, the occupancy rate at the region's hotels was stable. Even in 2010, when visitor numbers were in decline, occupancy rates still exceeded 80 percent. By 2012, occupancy rates had climbed to 84.4 percent. These complex and conflicting indicators make it difficult to conclude exactly *when* the recession's effects receded in Las Vegas.

Other opponents claimed the tourist and gaming economy made for an unpredictable and inconsistent market for football and the NFL. Data from the LVCVA and U.S. Bureau of Labor Statistics, however, suggests otherwise. Figure 14.5 shows the number of visitors to Las Vegas every year from 2006 to 2015. While there were declines in 2008 and 2009 from previous

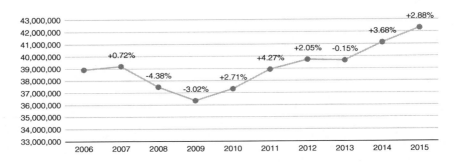

Figure 14.5 Las Vegas Visitor Statistics.

Source: Las Vegas Convention and Visitors Authority.

years, in 2010 and 2011 there were robust increases, indicating that within approximately two years, visitor levels were largely restored, even if hotel rates were the lure. Those data illustrate the nuances in trying to conclude when the recession ended.

Furthermore, additional evidence exists to suggest the Las Vegas economy has continued to diversify since the Great Recession. An aggressive strategy has been implemented to diversify the Las Vegas region's service economy, and success is already evident. There is a goal of increasing the number of jobs in the (1) information, (2) finance and insurance, (3) professional, scientific, and technical services, (4) management of companies and enterprises, (5) educational services, and (6) heath care and social assistance sectors of its economy. The recently approved new medical school for UNLV is one example of this diversification effort.

In 2011, Governor Sandoval worked with the Nevada legislature to help focus the region's economic development strategy. The Las Vegas Global Economic Alliance was formed at a conference hosted by UNLV called "Nevada 2.0" to build on initiatives that were started earlier in the century. Early success of the program has been observed through a 29.5 percent increase in the number of jobs in the professional, scientific, and technical services sector between 2002 and 2014. There has also been a 63.2 percent increase in the number of jobs in health care and social assistance. Perhaps most impressively, a 143.6 percent increase in the number of jobs in the management of companies and enterprises sector has been recorded across the same period. The changing nature of the Las Vegas economy is depicted in Table 14.4, clearly illustrating the success of the initiative.[3]

Study #2: Methodology and Findings

As with the earlier analysis, the revised study eliminated substitution effects to produce a conservative assessment of economic impacts. The following precautions support that effort:

Table 14.4 Las Vegas Metropolitan Area Job Market

NAICS Sector	2014	2002	%Change
Construction	40,020	59,517	−32.8
Manufacturing	19,836	19,916	−0.4
Wholesale trade	20,680	20,646	0.2
Retail trade	94,072	70,638	33.2
Transportation and warehousing	31,940	21,383	49.4
Information	10,214	12,263	−16.7
Finance and insurance	22,383	24,721	−9.5
Real estate and rental and leasing	17,498	14,931	17.2
Professional, scientific, and technical services	36,383	28,087	29.5
Management of companies and enterprises	16,336	6,707	143.6
Administration & support, waste management and remediation	56,705	42,274	34.1
Educational services	53,747	37,421	43.6
Health care and social assistance	72,353	44,344	63.2
Arts, entertainment, and recreation	16,561	15,086	9.8
Accommodation and food services	237,984	196,926	20.8
Other services (excluding public administration)	18,671	14,541	28.4
Public administration	31,993	24,613	30.0

Source: US Bureau of Labor Statistics.

1 The economic impacts projected in the report were based solely on events that (1) would bring new visits to the Las Vegas metropolitan area, (2) could only be held in a covered stadium, and (3) would attract more visits than would have taken place if the event was held at Sam Boyd Stadium.

2 A section of the report was dedicated to detailing new events and activities that would be attracted by a new covered stadium. However, these activities were not included in the measurement of the stadium's economic impact, as they would likely attract spending by residents of the region. Again, all substitution effects were excluded from the enumeration of economic benefits.

3 Adjustments were made to projected attendance levels at the new events to eliminate spending effects of residents. Of the estimated attendance of events at the stadium, it was estimated that visitors would account for only 65 percent of all tickets sold. It was anticipated that 35 percent of tickets sold for special events at the stadium would be sold to Nevada residents or visitors whose trip to the area did not constitute an additional trip to Las Vegas.

4 The construction of the new stadium will generate economic benefits for residents of the region and for several businesses in the area. Those benefits were excluded from the report.

5   Estimates on visitor spending were based directly on information produced by LVCVA, through its repeated surveys of visitors to Las Vegas.
6   The number of projected events was vetted with Las Vegas hospitality experts.
7   Calculations also did not include the economic value and associated contributions to the economy from the presence of an NFL franchise. The presence of an NFL team in Southern Nevada would likely lead to a small but valuable increase in the number of visits to the region from fans of both the visiting teams and of the Raiders (who live elsewhere). As that number is hard to predict, the potential contributions of that additional spending were excluded from the analysis.

The economic impacts reported were a function of the elevated attendance levels associated with the movement of five events from Sam Boyd Stadium to a state-of-the-art stadium, and ten new events likely to become part of Southern Nevada's entertainment calendar. In addition to the five existing events and ten new events, the analysis discussed the effects of five additional events. The report provided possible tax, economic impact, and quality of life outcomes for a range between 15 and 20 events.

The five events relocated from Sam Boyd Stadium and the enhanced attendance levels included USA Sevens Rugby (75,000 total for several games), Monster Jam World Finals (62,000), Monster Energy Super Cross Finals (24,000), Monster Energy Cup (24,000), and the Las Vegas Bowl (21,000). Many of these are multi-day events (see Table 14.5).

The ten new events included two concerts, two neutral site college football games, the Mountain West Football Championship game, the PAC 12 Football Championship game, an NFL exhibition game, an international rugby game, and one "friendly" soccer match involving teams from the English Premier League and/or other high-profile teams (see Table 14.6).

The other events that hospitality experts believe would be targets of opportunity (or "competitive bid" events) include UFC International Fight Week, a boxing program, WrestleMania, CONCACEF Gold Cup, NCAA college football playoff game, an additional iconic concert, and the NCAA

Table 14.5 Current Sam Boyd Stadium Events

Event Name	Date	Current Attendance	Projected Attendance
USA Sevens Rugby[1]	Feb	75,000	150,000
Monster Jam World Finals[2]	Mar	28,000	90,000
Monster Energy Supercross Finals	May	31,000	55,000
Monster Energy Cup	Oct	31,000	55,000
Las Vegas Bowl	Dec	35,000	55,000

[1]   Three-day event
[2]   Two-day event

Table 14.6 Projected New Events for New Las Vegas Stadium

Event Name	Date	Current Attendance	Projected Attendance
Stadium concert	Summer	0	60,000
Stadium concert	Summer	0	60,000
Neutral site college football game	Aug	0	55,000
Neutral site college football game	Fall	0	55,000
Friendly international soccer match[1]	July/Aug/Jan	0	55,000
MW Football Championship game[2]	December	0	45,000
PAC-12 Football Championship game[3]	December	0	45,000
NFL exhibition game	Aug	0	55,000
International rugby	Aug–Dec	0	55,000
Premier League Friendly	Summer	0	50,000

[1] Potential for multiple games (men's and women's)
[2] First weekend in December
[3] First weekend in December

Men's Basketball Final Four. To remain conservative, the economic impact analysis included just five of the nine possible "competitive bid" events provided by Las Vegas entertainment experts (see Table 14.7). A more aggressive projection would result in a more robust estimate of impacts. While that possibility is explored, the estimates used in this report illustrate more realistic valuations of the expected impact from a covered stadium to the Las Vegas economy.

It was estimated that a covered stadium hosting just 15 events would generate $314 million in direct, incremental visitor spending at the region's resorts (see Figure 14.6). The total annual economic impact of 15 events (including direct, indirect, and induced spending) would be $564.2 million. If as many as 20 events were held at the new stadium, direct spending rises to $429 million and total economic impact to nearly $770.7 million. Table 14.8 provides a detailed breakdown of incremental, direct visitor expenditures.[4]

The total amount of new tax dollars, generated by a covered stadium hosting just 15 events, would be $40 million (see Figure 14.7). This figure *does* include the additional sales tax revenues generated by indirect and induced spending effects. A complete breakdown of incremental tax revenue is available in Table 14.8. This figure does not, however, include any new tax revenue on the short-term rental of cars. There was no prudent way to make a valid estimate of that revenue.

Table 14.7 Projected New Competitive Bid Events (Five Anticipated Per Year)

Event Name	Date	Current Attendance	Projected Attendance
UFC International Fight Week[1]	July	14,000	40,000
Boxing[2]	September or May	14,000	40,000
Wrestlemania[3]	April	0	65,000
CONCACEF – Gold Cup[4]	July	0	50,000
World Cup Qualifiers[5]	July/August	–	–
College football playoff game[6]	January	0	55,000
Additional Stadium Concert[7]	–	0	50,000
Political Conventions	–	–	–
NCAA Final Four	March/April	0	55,000

[1] Second weekend in July
[2] Mexican Independence Day or Cinco de Mayo
[3] First weekend in April
[4] Every two years (men's and women's)
[5] Men's and women's
[6] Around January 1
[7] Led Zeppelin, Grateful Dead, Pink Floyd

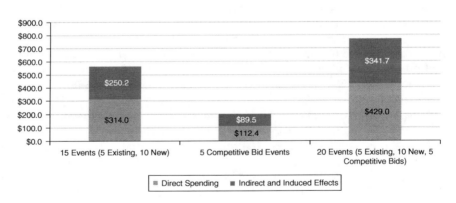

Figure 14.6 Projected Total Economic Impact (millions of $2016).

Critics have argued the study's attendance projections for entertainment events held at the stadium were too robust. However, Pollstar data underscores the ability of today's stadium venues to attract large numbers of visitors, even to non-NFL events. In 2016, MetLife Stadium, an uncovered stadium venue in the Meadowlands (New Jersey), attracted 540,852 people to non-NFL entertainment events. In the same year, Gillette Stadium,

Table 14.8 Projected Annual Incremental Direct Visitor Expenditures

	15 Events (5 Existing, 10 New)	5 Events (Competitive Bids)	20 Events (5 Existing, 10 New, 5 Competitive Bids)
Lodging	$58,327,776	$20,867,971	$79,670,873
Food and beverage	$77,852,843	$27,853,468	$106,340,484
Shopping (retail)	$68,129,451	$24,374,723	$93,059,142
Shows expenditure	$21,910,298	$7,838,863	$29,927,637
Gaming	$49,468,429	$17,698,356	$67,569,744
Local transport	$31,709,121	$11,344,595	$43,312,012
Sightseeing	$6,675,362	$2,388,249	$9,117,987
Total	**$314,073,278**	**$112,366,224**	**$428,997,879**

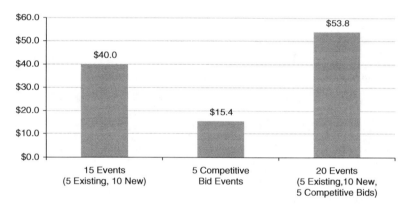

Figure 14.7 Projected Annual Incremental Tax Revenue (millions of $2016).

home of the New England Patriots, attracted 411,089 to non-NFL events. Chicago's Soldier Field, another open-air venue, attracted 252,114 spectators and the Dallas Cowboy's home, AT&T Stadium, welcomed 216,085 spectators to non-NFL events. Fenway Park in Boston also hosted 374,675 visitors for non-MLB events. Clearly, several stadium venues have managed to attract between 215,000 and 550,000 visitors to entertainment events each year. The UNLV study's attendance projection may be robust, but it is well within reach for a Las Vegas-based stadium venue. The issue to be evaluated in the future is whether these attendees extended their *existing* trips to Las Vegas or made a *special* visit for the purpose of attending an event at the stadium.

Table 14.9 Breakdown of Projected Annual Incremental Tax Revenue

	15 Events (5 Existing, 10 New)	5 Events (Competitive Bids)	20 Events (5 Existing, 10 New, 5 Competitive Bids)
State sales and use tax	$4,125,541	$1,475,998	$5,635,145
Local school support tax	$5,363,204	$1,918,797	$7,325,689
Supplemental city/county relief tax	$3,609,849	$1,291,498	$4,930,752
Basic city/council relief tax	$1,031,385	$368,999	$1,408,786
Public mass transportation tax	$515,693	$184,500	$704,393
Transportation/air quality tax	$515,693	$184,500	$704,393
Flood control	$515,693	$184,500	$704,393
Water and wastewater improvements	$515,693	$184,500	$704,393
Public safety tax	$618,831	$221,400	$845,272
Combined sales tax	*$16,811,581*	*$6,014,692*	*$22,963,217*
Additional sales tax (from I&I)	*$4,118,730*	*$1,473,561*	*$5,625,841*
Live entertainment tax	$8,097,503	$4,000,883	$10,431,593
Total hotel taxes	$6,999,333	$2,504,156	$9,560,505
State general fund gaming tax revenues	$3,833,803	$1,371,623	$5,236,655
Total tax revenues generated	**$39,860,950**	**$15,364,914**	**$53,817,811**

Conclusion

The Nevada legislature agreed to invest $750 million in the venue. The funds were raised by increasing the tax on hotel rooms by 0.88 percent per night (approximately $1.30 per night based on average hotel room rates). The present value of the anticipated incremental tax revenues produced by new visitors attending events at the stadium, across 30 years, is estimated to be $811.9 million. If there is a 10 percent error in the estimated annual tax collections, then the present value declines to $731 million (slightly less than what the public sector is investing in the venue). Data (year-to-year comparison of visitor levels to hotels in Las Vegas) for the first few months after the implementation of the tax showed no evidence of a decline in visitors. However, it is possible some of those visits were already planned in advance of the announced tax increase. Additional studies will be needed to assess if indeed the tax had any impact on the number of visitors to the city and their spending levels.

Questions for Discussion

1   The tax on hotel rooms is mostly paid by non-residents of Nevada. Does the use of an exported tax make the scale of the public sector's investment acceptable? Why, in your view, is it economically or politically acceptable to tax visitors? Is there any cost to businesses and residents of Las Vegas from increasing the taxes visitors must pay?

2   It is likely the new stadium in Las Vegas will cost $1.9 billion. The team will be responsible for approximately $1.2 billion in construction costs. The team will receive all revenue produced by the venue (except for revenues collected by UNLV for its home games). Is a public–private partnership where the public sector's investment is approximately 40 percent of the total project cost defensible when the team retains 100 percent of the revenues generated by the stadium? What does or does not justify this decision to the public?

3   Do the new hotel taxes (paid by visitors as a result of the events in the new stadium and used by governments to provide services to residents) create enough fiscal benefits to warrant your support of the financing plan? If the additional room nights produced by new visits to Las Vegas increase taxes, what is the return on the public sector's investment in the stadium?

4   All visitors staying in a hotel will be paying for the public sector's investment in the new stadium, but most of the visitors will not attend events in the new venue. Do you think it is acceptable for Las Vegas to administer a tax that is paid by people who do not benefit from the new venue?

5   If you were a member of the Nevada state legislature, would you have supported the 0.88 percent increase in the hotel to secure the relocation of the Oakland Raiders to Las Vegas? Why?

6   The NFL is a very profitable enterprise, with many teams valued at more than $2 billion. Given the economic success of the league and each team, is the public's investment in the venue appropriate and beneficial for the region?

Red Wings, Pistons, Little Caesars Arena, and The District: A New Future for Detroit

Ilitch Holdings, Integration, and Ownership Syndication

Ilitch Holdings, Inc. (IH) was established in 1999 in part to join together the many businesses founded or purchased by Mike and Marian Ilitch. Detroit-based companies under the IH umbrella include Little Caesars (pizza), Blue Line Foodservice Distribution, the Detroit Red Wings, Olympia Entertainment, the Detroit Tigers, Olympia Development, Little Caesars

Pizza Kit Fundraising Program, and Champion Foods. Additionally, Marian Ilitch owns the MotorCity Casino/Hotel.

The Ilitch family saw value in connecting each of their many assets, which makes IH an exemplary model of both horizontal and vertical integration (as described in Chapter 2). Both the Detroit Red Wings and the Detroit Tigers are owned by the Ilitch family (via IH), and while the two teams play in different seasons, they each compete for fans in the Detroit metropolitan area (horizontal integration). Little Caesars and Blue Line Foodservice Distribution are vertically integrated with the Red Wings, Tigers, and Olympia Entertainment. In addition, with control of two sport franchises and their venues, along with both Olympia Entertainment and Olympia Development, IH also serves as an example of an entity engaging in food services, entertainment, sport management, and real estate development.

The Detroit Red Wings began playing their home games in the Joe Louis Arena when the facility was built 1979. Owned by the city, "The Joe" offered excellent sight lines for fans and was a beloved destination for many metro-Detroiters. However, due to its aging infrastructure and technological limitations, the venue became economically obsolete. The Joe lacked many of the features that produced elevated revenues for hockey teams across the league. The Joe's location, approximately two miles from the neighborhood that was home to the Detroit Tigers' Comerica Park, the Detroit Lions' Ford Field, several live entertainment venues, and numerous restaurants, did little to support transit convenience or linkages to the downtown core. Furthermore, the arena's location on the Detroit River would likely have meant that extensive infrastructure renovations would be needed to protect the building from the river's pressure.

Recognizing these issues, IH began purchasing land west of Woodward Avenue near the Fox Theatre in 1997 (including the land upon which Comerica Park was built on in 2000) (Felton, 2014). As early as 1999, when the Detroit Free Press reported on the land purchases, many believed this land would eventually be used to build a new arena for the Red Wings. In 2000, Olympia Development announced plans to build a $15 million entertainment district adjacent to its Fox Theatre. The district, dubbed Columbia Street, was to include entertainment venues, restaurants, and shops – but was never built. Its development was postponed until work began on a new arena.

Despite Columbia Street's failure to launch, the 21st century saw Olympia Development refurbish the Fox Theatre and develop several other nearby entertainment and restaurant properties. The eastern edge of the entertainment district was defined by Comerica Park (built by Olympia Development in 2000 with an investment from the public sector) and the Detroit Lions' Ford Field, which opened in 2002. The aging arena, while adjacent to the convention center, was located two miles from the city's other two sport venues and various entertainment amenities. The need for a new sport and entertainment district in downtown Detroit was clear. Not surprisingly, in 2009, IH announced plans to renegotiate a shorter lease for the use of The Joe, sparking speculation that a new arena for the Wings would soon be discussed.

Issues Driving Detroit's Civic Leadership

Across roughly the same period of time, Detroit's civic leadership recognized a need to redefine the city's image and rebuild its deteriorated downtown area. There was an expectation that the city's two newly built sport venues, Comerica Park and Ford Field, would initiate a revitalization effort for the downtown and midtown neighborhoods. Midtown was anchored by Wayne State University and the Detroit Medical Center, but additional real estate development was needed to connect the neighborhood with the downtown area. Detroit's interest in a new image was driven by the staggering effects of the contraction of the manufacturing sector. In the seven years preceding the Great Recession, Michigan lost more than 417,000 jobs, almost 9 percent of its employment base. Michigan had the largest loss of total non-farm employment of all 50 states. In the midst of the recession, from 2007 to 2009, Michigan had the fourth-highest job loss in the United States (−9.46 percent, a loss of more than 401,000 jobs) (see Table 14.10) (Connaughton & Madsen, 2012). In addition to job losses, Detroit lost 234,209 residents between 2000 and 2010, a loss equal to 25 percent of the city's residential base in 2000 (MacDonald, 2016). With that depopulation, demand for residential properties declined and values shrank. As a result, there was little to no interest in major investments in real estate development by the private sector in Detroit's core area. The loss of jobs and residents also led to a predictable loss of tax revenue, causing the city's financial situation to deteriorate. Without sufficient funds to pay for urban services or to meet its other financial responsibilities (i.e., debt repayment and pensions), Detroit became the largest city in the United States to enter bankruptcy; the city filed for bankruptcy protection on July 18, 2013.

The city's instability resulted in a damaged reputation, closely followed by a lack of confidence from investors. In the midst of this social and financial freefall, two factors created the base for a recovery. First, Dan Gilbert made the decision to relocate Quicken Loans and his other holdings to newly purchased and renovated office buildings downtown. His real estate division invested $2.2 billion in purchasing and revitalizing more than 50 buildings in downtown Detroit. By 2016, Dan Gilbert reported that his businesses and suppliers employed more than 15,000 people in downtown Detroit (Aguilar, 2016). Second, in 2012, IH initiated plans for a new arena in the downtown area. That planning process culminated in a commitment to invest more than $1 billion in an arena, adjoining buildings, a new

Table 14.10 Michigan Job Changes Before and During the Great Recession (thousands)

Period	Job Losses/Gain	Percent Change	State Rank
2000–2007	−417.3	−8.95%	47
2007–2009	−401.8	−9.45%	50
2008–2009	−401.8	−9.46%	47
2000–2009	−819.1	−17.56%	50

Source: http://ageconsearch.tind.io//bitstream/143779/2/12-3-1.pdf

headquarters building for the Little Caesars Corporation, and new partnerships to build residential and commercial properties downtown.

A series of actions by the public sector also factored into Detroit's recovery. While the City was interested in providing support for the new arena and the efforts to revitalize downtown, financial strains limited the local government's options. After Detroit filed for bankruptcy, State government officials faced two crucial issues. First, should the State become involved in the attempts to restore Detroit's fiscal solvency? Secondly, if the State were to be involved, what would be politically acceptable to the legislature? While Governor Rick Snyder saw value in helping the city, the legislature was not as easily convinced. The resulting solution was a compromise: the State would support downtown development (crystalized around the arena) and provide a modest amount of help to the Detroit Public School System, but beyond that the Legislature's support would be limited.

Financing Little Caesars Arena

When the State government finalized the deal with IH, it was agreed that $250 million in public funds would be provided for the downtown arena. IH would also be responsible for all financing costs for the venue beyond the public sector's commitment and its long-term maintenance. The Michigan Strategic Fund (MSF)[5] sold $450 million in two series of 30-year variable rate bonds (maturity in 2045); $250 million in Series A bonds were backed by property taxes captured by the city's Downtown Development Authority (DDA)[6] and $200 million in Series B bonds were backed by Olympia Development (of IH).[7] If sufficient new real estate development took place, the funds would replace those guaranteed by the MSF.

The state agreed to replace any funds lost by the Detroit Public Schools as a result of the property taxes captured by the DDA. The public schools were essentially insulated from any adverse effects. In addition, the schools would likely benefit from enhanced property values resulting from new real estate development in the area.

Similar to many tax increment financing (TIF) districts used in municipalities across the country, the DDA captures property taxes in a designated area; in this instance that area includes the arena, all outbuildings, and five new downtown neighborhoods that Olympia Development has committed to redeveloping. The taxes paid by property owners are transferred to the DDA rather than the city, the city's school district, or any other public entities that would have been supported by the property taxes. The city, however, receives income taxes paid by people living or working in the DDA. The understanding is that by pumping a substantial amount of support into a single downtown district via development and other enhancements, property values of parcels in the district will rise. Higher property values equate to higher property tax payments and, thus, elevated property tax revenue for the local municipality. Furthermore, the residential, commercial, and retail establishments newly built by Olympia Development will be taxed (Shea, 2014).

The creation of a sport district, with three venues and three teams, was then expanded to four teams when the Detroit Pistons decided to relocate from the suburban Palace of Auburn Hills to Little Caesars Arena. It was also agreed that the Palace, which had sold 313,486 tickets to concerts in 2017, would transfer all of its entertainment business to Little Caesars Arena beginning in October 2017.

To help with the enhancements needed for the Pistons to play at Little Caesars Arena, the City of Detroit agreed to pay for $34.5 million of the more than $40 million of construction changes required. The Detroit Pistons agreed to spend more than $100 million to build a new practice facility and to move all of their corporate offices into the City of Detroit. The total public investment in the arena and surrounding neighborhood is $358.5 million. The bulk of this investment was made by the DDA through recapturing of property tax growth ($250 million for the arena and $74 million for real estate development). There will be more than $1 billion of investment and philanthropic donations by the private sector for the building of the arena, new commercial and retail spaces, and venues for Wayne State University and the Detroit Medical Center.

Conclusion

Critics of the financing plan and the State's decision to invest in the arena suggested that Detroit's needs for community development across deteriorating neighborhoods should have been a higher priority. The government's allocation of property taxes for improving Detroit's downtown core effectively meant that those funds could not be used in the other areas of the city that were in need. Further, the needs of the Detroit Public Schools, for many, represented a higher priority than the building of an arena. If the state was interested in enhancing Detroit as a place to live and work, many thought money should have been invested in public services and neighborhoods, rather than in a sport venue. The public sector's investment in the new arena, however, has ensured the redevelopment of five new downtown neighborhoods and the commitment of at least $1 billion from private sector investors. The long-term impact of the arena, the new entertainment district, and the revitalized downtown area for Detroit's future will unfold in the years ahead. Nonetheless, in an area of just 0.11 square miles, downtown Detroit now hosts four major league teams within three venues and is expected to generate more than 4 million visits per year. The next challenge for Detroit is to determine how to leverage this economic activity for future community development.

Questions for Discussion

1   The public sector's investment in a new arena was driven by the need to help Detroit recover financially and to ensure that the team would remain in downtown Detroit. Essentially, the public sector facilitated the construction of a sport venue and new residential areas in the downtown area. Is this the best course of action to help a city with the problems facing Detroit? Why or why not?

2   A large proportion of Detroit's residents are racial minorities, but studies have shown that hockey fans are largely white.[8] What does an investment by a government in a sport venue do to deal with the ever-present racial conflicts? Is such an investment adding to the racial and economic divides plaguing America's cities?

3   With the opening of Little Caesars Arena, the vast majority of the Detroit metropolitan region's live entertainment events will take place in venues owned or controlled by IH. The presence of more luxury seating options would also increase the team's revenues. Do you think the team's owner should have paid for more or all of the cost of the new venue without any public funds? What is the most appropriate way to evaluate the need for a public investment in an arena?

4   Do you think the public sector's investment in the new arena was prudent, given the importance of ensuring a site in downtown Detroit? If the arena were privately financed, how likely do you think it was that it would have been built in a suburban city?

5   The low-end estimate is that the private sector will have paid for 60 percent of the total project cost. If more new properties are developed, that percentage will increase from its current 2:1 ratio ($2 privately invested to every $1 publicly invested). Is that ratio of private to public dollars a sound policy approach in Detroit?

The San Diego Padres, JMI Realty, and the San Diego Ballpark District[9]

Qualcomm Stadium (then San Diego Stadium) opened in 1967 as the home of the San Diego Chargers (NFL); the franchise had relocated from Los Angeles. Soon after, MLB's San Diego Padres began playing at the venue

(1969). As the venue's primary tenants, the Chargers were given rights to nearly all in-facility revenues, even for non-NFL games. The Chargers also controlled parking revenue from all events held at the stadium. Each time the Chargers requested additional revenue streams to sustain parity with other teams, the public sector acquiesced. For example, the Chargers franchise was allowed to sell naming rights to the facility in the 1990s; the Qualcomm Corporation paid the Chargers $900,000 per year through 2017 (the public sector receives none of this income). The Padres, as the venue's second tenant, had very little control and only received in-facility revenue from ticket sales to their own games. These limitations would eventually lead to financial problems for the MLB franchise.

In addition to this fiscal constraint, fan support was also a challenge; the team lost 100 or more games in its initial six years in the National League. The tepid reception from fans almost convinced the Padres' owners to relocate the team to Washington, D.C. Ray Kroc saved the Padres for San Diego by acquiring the team in 1974. After Kroc's death, his widow controlled the team, but eventually sold the franchise to local business leaders. Financial problems continued to plague the franchise and after another change in ownership, John Moores acquired the franchise in 1996. Early on, he recognized that no business plan could make the team financially viable if the Padres continued to play at Qualcomm Stadium. Even in 1998 when the Padres advanced to the World Series, the team lost money. In order to be financially solvent, the Padres needed to move to a baseball-only facility where they could control all revenues and provide the appropriate amenity package (including excellent sight lines) to attract fans.[10]

During the time that the Padres were undergoing several ownership changes, the Chargers made a series of demands that ended with San Diego paying for a substantial renovation to the stadium and guaranteeing to purchase all unsold tickets. The public's negative reaction to these concessions intensified when stories surfaced in 1995 that the Chargers were interested in moving north to Los Angeles or Orange County.[11] With voters and community leaders skeptical of any deal with a professional team, a public investment in a new ballpark for the Padres would have to involve clear financial and public policy benefits for San Diego, as well as a substantial private sector investment from the team's owner.

As discussions between the team and the city's elected leaders began, the Padres' owner, John Moores, advocated for the new ballpark to be built in the Mission Valley area near Qualcomm Stadium. The location's appeal came mostly from its convenient access to an East–West freeway (Interstate 8 or the Mission Valley Freeway), and two North–South freeways (Interstate 15 and Interstate 805). However, it was also attractive because of surrounding population densities and fans' familiarly with the area.

The city's professional staff and many elected officials were open to the idea of a new ballpark in the Mission Valley area. However, because it was such desirable location, city planners understood that market forces would ensure that private investments would take place in the area even without a new sport venue. As a result, the city's staff and elected leaders became more interested in redeveloping the downtown area, specifically in the area adjacent to the San Diego Convention Center. The convention center, built in 1989 and expanded in 2001, had begun to successfully attract more conventions and tourists to the city, raising the demand for hotel rooms in the downtown area. The public sector's preferred location for a new ballpark was an area known as the East Village, southeast of the successful Gaslamp Quarter (entertainment and retail venues) and the convention center. The East Village is also adjacent to the downtown business district. Faced with the need to compromise and accept the idea of a downtown ballpark, the team's owner then asked for a waterfront site for the ballpark. Although San Diego did not agree to the building of a ballpark on the waterfront, they did offer a location across from the harbor and convention center. This location in the East Village neighborhood is where Petco Park was ultimately built.

The new ballpark needed to produce enough annual income to (1) support competitive salaries for players, (2) produce a financial return for the team's investment in the new ballpark, (3) pay rent for use of the facility, and (4) ensure that the team's revenues would exceed its operational expenses (or, more simply, generate a profit). With an anticipated cost of $411 million for the ballpark, John Moores wanted to limit his investment to $150 million. The team asked the public sector to invest $261 million in the venue. A public investment of that magnitude, with the team assuming responsibility for slightly more than one-third of the project's cost, was not politically viable. The years of conflict with the San Diego Chargers had soured voters on deals where it was seen that the public benefits were far less than those enjoyed by the team. If there was to be significant public investment in a new ballpark, Moores would be required to do much more than simply accepting the public sector's preferred location.

In the deal that emerged, which was unprecedented at the time, Moores guaranteed a level of real estate development that would be sufficient to generate the property tax revenues necessary to compensate San Diego for its investment in the ballpark. If the needed real estate was not developed, Moores agreed to be personally responsible for the shortfall. This new real estate would be built in an area designated as the Ballpark District (which surrounded the ballpark itself). That investment, together with the amount of money invested in the ballpark by the team, meant John Moores and his real estate development company (JMI), would be spending far more than the public entities.

The total cost for the new ballpark was $483.1 million; the Padres invested $187.4 million and the City of San Diego spent $191.6 million. The downtown redevelopment authority invested $83.1 million and the Port of

San Diego provided $21 million. In the Memorandum of Understanding that was signed between Moores and San Diego, Moores was required to build $487 million in new development in the area designated as the Ballpark District. That amount of real estate development was seen by San Diego officials and voters as a sufficient return for the public sector. In addition, if that that commitment was not fulfilled, Moores would be personally responsible for paying the taxes that new property would have generated. By the end of Phase II, however, JMI and its partners had built and sold more than $2.87 billion of new real estate. That's almost six times what had been guaranteed! The additional property taxes collected generated new funds for the public sector. As part of this investment, JMI also agreed to build a headquarters hotel for the convention center that would add at least 1,000 additional rooms to the immediate area's inventory.

While some have criticized the profits John Moores earned from the real estate developed and sold, those gains must be balanced by the risks taken. John Moores was the first team owner to guarantee a designated level of real estate development, and while he did profit from the building and sale of his real estate, he alone assumed the financial risk if the development did not occur. It should also be noted that without the public sector's agreement, John Moores would not have made such substantial changes to the landscape of downtown. The deal was monumental in that both sides took on risk, and as a result each party benefitted.

There are important policy questions that need to be addressed when analyzing the benefit of the Ballpark District. For example, if the real estate would have been built elsewhere in San Diego, should the $2.87 billion in development be considered incremental, or simply a transfer within the city? In response to the possibility of a transfer, it can be noted that San Diego wanted the East Village redeveloped to fulfill certain public policy goals and was willing to recognize that there could be some substitution effects (meaning that some of the new development would have likely taken place elsewhere within the City of San Diego). Seeking to reduce urban sprawl, with the goal of increasing the downtown residential population, the city's leadership was willing to accept that the transfer of development was a net gain relative to their vision for San Diego's future. From a sport management perspective, the real achievements in San Diego were (1) an owner's guarantee of a level of real estate development as part of the public–private partnership and (2) a test of using a sport venue to anchor an entirely new urban neighborhood. These goals were accomplished and the team owner was able to make a substantial profit from his real estate activities. While many had hypothesized that sport venues could anchor successful real estate development projects, the Ballpark District in San Diego tested the hypothesis and established firm proof.

Some have criticized that the Ballpark District development replaced older buildings that were a favored location for artists and the entrepreneurial community. They argued it would have been better for San Diego to let the area change slowly and naturally, which would ensure the presence of low-cost commercial space for start-up businesses as well as the region's local artist community. Others were disappointed with the size of the public sector's investment in the Padres' new home ballpark, and the politics surrounding the vote on the plan (Chapin, 2002; Erie, Kogan, & MacKenzie, 2010; Hitchcock, undated). Regardless of the project's criticisms, Petco Park and the San Diego Ballpark District demonstrate the value of a team and its venue as anchors for real estate development. This case also set the precedent for future sport venue projects. San Diego was not a case of "build it and they will come," but an example of an iron-clad guarantee from a team owner to generate property taxes for a local government.

Conclusion

The financial success of JMI's projects in the Ballpark District demonstrated to other team owners and investors the value of incorporating real estate development in plans for venues. The Ballpark District also illustrated the potential for a city's policy goals to be achieved, and, as a result, the tangible policy gains for the public sector from a public–private partnership. In a very real sense, John Moores' success changed sport organizations. The Ballpark District became a model for deals between teams and the public sector. In the past, public–private partnerships were assailed for the concentration of benefits for owners. Indeed, in the 1980s and early 1990s, public–private partnerships were routinely described as structures that merely subsidized team owners. The partnership in San Diego re-wrote the playbook for deals involving venues and proved that it is possible to create a partnership that creates real financial benefits for all parties. Those interested in evaluations and reviews of what was accomplished in San Diego should read the contrasting perspectives provided by Erie, Kogan, and MacKenzie (2010), Rosentraub (2010), and Newman (2006).

As a post-script, John Moores sold the San Diego Padres in 2012 and with the build-out of most of the Ballpark District, his company's footprint is now limited to one hotel and two remaining parcels in the Ballpark District. While the Ballpark District was being developed, Moores had invited the Chargers' ownership to negotiate for a new football stadium that would become a second anchor for the Ballpark District. Those conversations failed to gain traction and the Chargers continued to play their home games in the venue that the Padres vacated for Petco Park. Then, after decades of discussion and debate, in 2016, voters rejected a proposal from the Chargers to help finance a stadium that was proposed for the Ballpark District. The team's inability to form a partnership with San Diego's electorate led the Chargers to seek alternate locations. Originally from the City of Angels, the team resumed play in Los Angeles in 2017, after 56 years in San Diego. The Chargers will join the Los Angeles Rams in their new Inglewood stadium once construction is complete.

Questions for Discussion

1 When the public–private partnership was proposed for the Ballpark District, few, if any, thought it would be as successful as it became. Given the risks he was willing to assume, John Moores wanted a substantial investment from the public sector. Do you think the public sector's willingness to invest in the ballpark was prudent or necessary?
2 For real estate development near a sport venue to be profitable, it is necessary for many market-rate homes and apartments, along with attractive/luxury retail venues, to be built. Do you think this sort of development, often referred to as gentrification, is appropriate for local governments to support?
3 The success of areas similar to San Diego's Ballpark District require the attraction of wealthy people to live, work, and play in the area. Given that necessity for a project to be successful, how can or should the public sector advance the interests of the lower income households living in a central city?

The Staples Center, L.A. LIVE, and Downtown Los Angeles[12]

In 1993, Richard Riordan, a Republican, was elected mayor of Los Angeles. A Republican had not led the city for more than 30 years, but in the aftermath of police officers attacking Rodney King, numerous riots, and a fear that the Los Angeles police department was out of control, voters wanted change. The magnitude of the riots and violence, and the image of police officers unable to protect citizens caught amidst ransacking mobs, presented the world with an image of a city drowning in its own chaos. While some thought things could not become worse, downtown Los Angeles was seen as deteriorating, crime-laden, and overrun by the homeless. With downtown's shrinking role in the city's business life, Westwood, Hollywood, and Century City each became leading business centers. The city's decentralized (or multi-nucleated) urban structure led citizens and several leaders to question whether Los Angeles needed to invest in restoring the classic downtown area when other parts of the city were more desirable.

Despite the movement of offices, hotels, and residences to other parts of Los Angeles, the city and county had built a large convention center at the southern edge of the downtown area. In addition, the University of Southern California was still located south of the classical downtown area. With fewer and fewer meetings attracted to the convention center because of the inhospitable characteristics of the aging downtown area, the venue was losing money. The university's leadership was also concerned for its future if downtown Los Angeles continued to decline. These factors made it important to figure out a strategy to revitalize downtown Los Angeles despite the growth of other parts of the city.

In his mayoral campaign, Mr. Riordan painted himself as the only candidate "tough enough" to deal with the city's problems. A successful entrepreneur, Riordan spent several million dollars of his own money convincing voters he would deal with Los Angeles' problems. He defeated a Democratic member of the city council for the mayoralty in a city increasingly dominated by Asian, Black, and Hispanic minorities. The image he presented was that while white, he was a business leader who was too wealthy to be bribed, and tough enough to both clean up Los Angeles and reestablish its positive image.

To deal with the convention center and downtown Los Angeles, Mayor Riordan turned to Charles Isgar, a trusted aid with a doctorate in public administration. Isgar was given the seemingly impossible task of figuring out how to salvage the convention center and halt the annual revenue losses. If, along the way to reducing the public sector's operating losses for the convention center, he could also figure out a way to revive a portion of the downtown area, that too would be appreciated. Riordan was a Republican mayor pitted against a hostile city council led by members of the Democratic Party still annoyed by the loss of the mayor's race by one of their own. As local politics is a contact sport, the council was eager to portray Richard Riordan as just another (white) real estate developer primed to reward his wealthy friends at taxpayers' expense. Mayor Riordan needed solutions and a progressive way to improve downtown without using taxpayer subsidies.

Isgar was aware that the ownership of the Lakers and Kings was interested in a new arena. The teams played at the Great Western Forum (today the building is referred to as the Los Angeles Forum) in suburban Inglewood. The arena was popularly referred to as "The Fabulous Forum." The naming rights to the facility, however, had been sold and the formal name was the Great Western Forum. Built in 1967 with an exterior designed to recall the grandeur of ancient Rome, the facility was indeed fabulous, but lacked suites, club seats, and other revenue-generating amenities that were becoming common in the new arenas built by other NBA and NHL teams. Isgar approached the teams with the idea of building their new arena downtown, adjacent to the convention center. When his concept was soundly rejected (another suburban location was preferred), Isgar recruited a well-known local developer, Steve Soboroff, to serve as a volunteer deputy mayor ($1/year in salary) to help convince the Lakers and the Kings that their best destiny was to build a new arena in downtown Los Angeles. To many, it now seemed two dreamers had been chosen to implement an unworkable plan that was destined to fail.

Downtown Los Angeles, as uninviting a location as it must have appeared to many people, did have several assets. First, there was sufficient land available to build the exact sort of facility the teams wanted. The facility the teams ultimately constructed had more than three times the square footage or footprint of the Great Western Forum. Finding sufficient land in the suburbs for a facility of this scale with ample land for parking was no small challenge. While the teams might well have preferred a suburban location, the scarcity of available land elevated the value of downtown Los Angeles as a potential site. The advantage of having the land needed for a facility laden with revenue-producing luxury seats and other amenities was not lost on Isgar and Soboroff. Second, downtown Los Angeles had convenient freeway access. The excellent access to both an East–West (Interstate 10) and North–South (Harbor/Pasadena) freeway for fans accustomed to driving to athletic events made the downtown area an intriguing possibility. Downtown Los Angeles had two assets that few if any other sites anywhere else in the county could offer. The teams could have the land they needed to build the very large arena envisioned, and the facility would be adjacent to one of the main junctions for Los Angeles' network of freeways.

The advantages of what became the location for the Staples Center (visible at the corner of Chick Hearn Court and South Figueroa Street) and L.A. LIVE (the area immediately north of Chick Hearn Court) are evident in Figure 14.8. The intersection of Interstates 10 and 110 are visible, as is

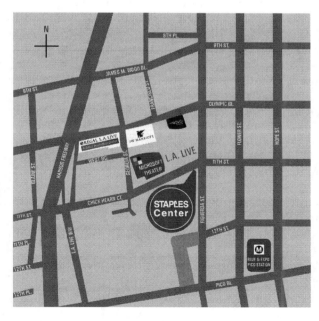

Figure 14.8 L.A. LIVE District Map.

the parking structure adjacent to Interstate 110 at Cherry Street and several surface parking lots along South Figueroa Street. The freeway access and the land to build the arena, a parking structure, and what came to be called L.A. LIVE suddenly turned everyone's attention toward downtown Los Angeles. Now what was needed was a plan where the teams' ownership would pay for the complete cost of the facilities and the taxpayers would be protected from any obligations.

To fulfill Mayor Riordan's objective of having the teams pay for the facilities, the City of Los Angeles did agree to permit the building of two advertising towers with exposures facing the I-110 and I-10 freeways. The average daily vehicle count at the juncture of these freeways was approximately 325,000. By allowing the business that would own the arena and L.A. LIVE the right to receive all advertising revenues from the two towers, it was agreed that (1) the private sector partners would spend not less than $325 million for the new arena and (2) a dedicated revenue stream from the facility would pay for the city's infrastructure investments. If that revenue stream were ever insufficient to repay the bonds sold by Los Angeles for its investment, the teams would provide the necessary funds to make up for the shortfall. That inevitability never arose and Los Angeles retired its obligation and then accepted a one-time payment from AEG for the revenue stream. In addition, the private sector partnership that owned and operated the Staples Center would be responsible for paying an annual fee for using the public lands upon which the arena stood. That fee is equal to the property taxes that would have been owed had the Lakers and Kings owned the land.

To pay for the infrastructure costs needed for L.A. LIVE, the owners of the complex agreed to pay all local property taxes. Los Angeles did not grant an abatement of any property associated with either the arena or the L.A. LIVE project.[13] A Los Angeles redevelopment corporation (Community Redevelopment Authority, CRA) also provided $12.6 million in support for the Staples Center; no revenue streams from the arena were pledged to offset that investment. The return for the CRA was in the form of incremental property tax gains from new residential construction in the area. With more than 7,000 units built in the downtown area, the property taxes generated offset the CRA's investment. Would the housing have been built without the Staples Center? The area had languished for years and it is unlikely new housing starts would have been as robust without the new arena. If that logic is accepted, then the public sector's investment was completely supported by new property taxes.

When the market for new hotels in the downtown area weakened, the owners of L.A. LIVE asked Los Angeles to agree to use the hotel tax revenue it would receive from the project for 25 years to pay for all of the needed infrastructure improvements. The present value of the public sector's investment in L.A. LIVE is $172.8 million. For this investment, the project's owner agreed their investment would be approximately $2.5 billion (or $2.6 billion in 2017 dollars). Los Angeles decided the public sector investment to offset the decline in the market was worthwhile as it was securing more than $2 billion ($2.1 billion in 2017 dollars) in private investments in the downtown area.

The most substantial accomplishment and innovation associated with the move of the Los Angeles Lakers and Kings (followed by the Clippers) to the downtown area was the building of L.A. LIVE. L.A. LIVE is an entertainment, retail, commercial, and residential complex that includes 22 restaurants, five different entertainment venues (including Staples Center), five hotels, luxury condominiums, and ESPN's West Coast broadcast center. The entire complex includes 5.6 million square feet of development across 27 acres of downtown Los Angeles. ESPN's broadcast center uses 12,300 square feet of space.

L.A. LIVE illustrated that teams can anchor large-scale entertainment centers that also include residential and commercial space. The Staples Center, with its three sport teams as tenants, ensures that there will be more than 2 million visits to the area each year. When the concerts and other entertainment events held at the arena or when the facilities at L.A. LIVE are added to the mix, there is a base of roughly 3 million visits to the area every year. That crowd now has the opportunity to spend pre- and post-event time (and money) in the area creating additional revenue potential. In this manner, entertainment and commercial development have become part of the horizontal integration of the sport business. The controlling entity for the Staples Center and L.A. LIVE is the Anschutz Entertainment Group (AEG), itself part of the Anschutz Company. Sport has become horizontally integrated into their business operations. As has been discussed in other chapters of this book, the holding company owns or operates facilities and teams across the United States and Europe and developed L.A. LIVE–type projects in China and Europe. They were joined by Comcast SPECTACOR, Forest City Enterprises, Patriot Place, Oak View Group and management companies, such as SMG, in integrating sport in large-scale entertainment and commercial projects that frequently include residential development. These large-scale projects provide insight into the revenue opportunities for teams that have revolutionized the business. Today numerous teams are purchased by real estate development firms, partner with real estate development companies, or create their own real estate development and entertainment divisions to capitalize on the opportunities created by the crowds attracted to sports.

John Moores, the Ballpark District, AEG, and L.A. LIVE redefined the sport business, and today most team owners are focused on the entertainment and real estate development opportunities created by their teams. Jerry Jones chose to build an extraordinary multipurpose stadium and the Dallas Cowboys now anchor a large entertainment corporation in AT&T

stadium. Forest City Enterprises acquired the New Jersey Nets to anchor their Atlantic Yards project in Brooklyn. Even after selling their assets to another entrepreneur, the team and the arena are part of a sport and entertainment corporation. The New England Patriots created an opportunity for Robert Kraft to build Patriot Place, a shopping mall and entertainment center with more than 60 different retail outlets adjacent to Gillette Stadium. Teams are no longer just franchises, and real estate development and management, as well as entertainment, are now an integral part of what is sport management in real time.

Conclusion

Today, downtown Los Angeles is home to more than 58,000 residents and more than 200,000 people now work in the area. Since the development of the Staples Center and L.A. LIVE and the subsequent turnaround of the city's downtown core, the University of Southern California has opened its own large-scale development north of its campus. A light-rail transit system also links the university with L.A. LIVE and the entire downtown area, and a new soccer stadium has been built near the university's campus. The extensive development that has taken place east and north of L.A. LIVE and the Staples Center has also helped to revitalize downtown Los Angeles. In effect, the vision that Mayor Riordan had in the 1990s for downtown Los Angeles has been achieved. Further, the revitalization of downtown Los Angeles has not inhibited additional growth and the vitality of Westwood, Hollywood, or Century City.

Three decades after the opening of Staples Center, the teams and the city are now confronted with the task of planning renovations that will be needed in the years ahead for both the Staples Center and L.A. LIVE. This time around, however, city planners will have the benefit of handling development tasks in an area that is no longer riddled with crime, deemed unsafe, or avoided by residents.

Questions for Discussion

1 The scale of the greater Los Angele market and the continual growth of the Southern California created market opportunities for a new and rather grand development project. Could an arena and entertainment district in a smaller market be as successful as Staples Center and L.A. LIVE? Why or why not?

2 The City of Los Angeles used its ability to offer advertising opportunities to offset AEG's investment in the arena and entertainment district. Can that approach – allowing team owners to sell advertising space on public buildings or on land in which the public sector has made an investment – work elsewhere? Is it appropriate for a government

to facilitate the development of advertising opportunities that generate revenues for a team? Why or why not?

Notes

1 Since that time, Mr. Stan Kroenke and the NFL made the decision to relocate St. Louis' Rams to Los Angeles, where Kroenke is building a new $3 billion stadium in Inglewood, California with a projected capacity of over 100,000 when configured for entertainment events.

2 There are other measures of tourist activity, including the purchase of taxable items, attendance at live shows, etc. A detailed assessment of the tourism market was beyond the scope of work that could be performed.

3 It is highly likely the loss of construction jobs observed in Table 14.4 was a result of the overbuilt housing market. The residential market has stabilized and the construction of the new stadium and expansion of the convention center will create thousands of new jobs for the regional economy.

4 Note that attendance assumptions shift slightly between models, so the sum of the impact of 15 [existing + new] events and the impact of five [competitive bid] events differs from the projected impact of 20 [existing + new + competitive bid] events. This is true in Tables 14.8 and 14.9, and Figure 14.8.

5 The MSF is a State-backed agency created to promote economic development and create jobs in the state of Michigan. The agency was created in 1984.

6 Created in 1978, the DDA is Detroit's economic development agency, promoting private investments and business growth within the city's central business district with loans, sponsorships and grants, capital improvements to public infrastructure, and other programs that increase economic activity.

7 Note that before the arena opened, IH privately repaid the Series B bonds in entirety, reducing the total public commitment to the venue and the District Detroit plan to $250 million.

8 An *Atlantic Monthly* survey found that 92 percent of NHL fans are white (Thompson, 2014).

9 A more detailed history and analysis of San Diego's Ballpark District, and the conflicting planning and development perspectives that surround the concept of extensive and rapid redevelopment is contained in Chapter 4 of Mark S. Rosentraub's (2010) *Major league winners: Using sports and cultural centers as tools for economic development*. Boca Raton, FL: CRC Press/Taylor and Francis.

10 These observations were made by John Moores in discussions with the author in October 2010.

11 In 2016 when the San Diego Chargers demanded a new stadium with a large investment by the public sector, voters rejected the proposal and the team made the decision to relocate to Los Angeles.

12 A more detailed history and analysis of the building of Staples Center and L.A. LIVE, and the conflicting planning and development perspectives that surround the concept of extensive and rapid redevelopment is contained in Chapter 2 and Chapter 5 of Mark S. Rosentraub's (2010) *Major League Winners: Using Sports and Cultural Centers as Tools for Economic Development*. Boca Raton, FL: CRC Press/Taylor and Francis.

13 The public sector owns the land upon which the Staples Center was built. The arena owners pay a fee for use of publicly owned land, and technically it is not a property tax, but a use of property fee or assessment. The owners of L.A. LIVE also own the land upon which it is built and are responsible for all property taxes.

References

Aguilar, L. 2016. Gilbert: 3,100 employees call Detroit home, *The Detroit News*, March 30. Retrieved from http://www.detroitnews.com/story/business/2016/03/30/gilbert-employees-live-detroit/82451352/ (accessed August 2, 2018).

Benston, L. 2009. Seduction by room rate, *Las Vegas Sun*, August 24. Retrieved from https://lasvegassun.com/news/2009/aug/24/seduction-room-rate/ (accessed May 2, 2018).

Cephas, A. 2015. A look at the history of gambling in Southern Maryland, *The Enterprise*, October 16. Retrieved from http://www.somdnews.com/enterprise/a-look-at-the-history-of-gambling-in-southern-maryland/article_ef96e692-4130-5a89-9864-0914e10fc620.html (accessed March 1, 2018).

Chapin, T. 2002. Beyond the entrepreneurial city: Municipal capitalism in San Diego. *Journal of Urban Affairs* 70 (2): 565–581.

Coleman, Jr., R., & Floyd, C. 2016. Phoenix & Central Region 2015 Year-End Data Review, *Arizona Office of Tourism*, September 7. Retrieved from https://tourism.az.gov/2015-year-end-data-review-phoenix-central-region (accessed February 28, 2018).

Connaughton, J. E., & Madsen, R. A. 2012. U.S. State and Regional Economic Impact of the 2008/2009 Recession. *Journal of Regional Analysis & Policy* 42 (3): 177–187.

Erie, S. P., Kogan, V., & MacKenzie, S. A. 2010. Redevelopment, San Diego style: The limits of public-private partnerships, *Urban Affairs Review* 45 (5): 644–678

Felton, R. 2014. New Red Wings arena — a timeline, *Detroit Metro Times*, May 6. Retrieved from http://www.metrotimes.com/detroit/new-red-wings-arena-a-timeline/Content?oid=2201888 (Accessed February 1, 2018).

Gensler, L. 2016. An alligator wrestler, a casino boss and a $12 billion tribe, *Forbes*, October 19. Retrieved from https://www.forbes.com/sites/laurengensler/2016/10/19/seminole-tribe-florida-hard-rock-cafe/#32fe56745bbc (accessed August 2, 2018).

Greater Miami Convention and Visitors Bureau. 2016. 2016 visitor industry overview, *Greater Miami Convention and Visitors Bureau*. Retrieved from http://partners.miamiandbeaches.com/~/media/files/gmcvb/partners/research%20statistics/annual-report-2016 (accessed August 2, 2018).

Gutierrez, P. 2016. Raiders owner Mark Davis to meet with Las Vegas magnate, *ESPN*, January 29. Retrieved from http://www.espn.com/nfl/story/_/id/14669152/oakland-raiders-owner-mark-davis-meet-las-vegas-officials-regarding-potential-stadium-sites-according-leaked-memo (accessed March 1, 2017).

Jackson, H. 2017. With New Jersey sports betting case, Supreme Court could affect wide array of issues, *USA Today*, December 26. Retrieved from https://www.usatoday.com/story/news/politics/2017/12/26/new-jersey-sports-betting-case-supreme-court-could-affect-wide-array-issues/977955001/ (accessed March 1, 2018).

Larino, J. 2016. New Orleans' 2015 tourism by the numbers, *NOLA.com*, May 3. Retrieved from http://www.nola.com/business/index.ssf/2016/05/new_orleans_tourism_by_the_num.html (accessed February 1, 2018).

LVCVA. 2016. Clark County Hotel/Motel Inventory, *Las Vegas Convention and Visitors Authority*, December 31. Retrieved from http://www.lvcva.com/includes/content/images/media/docs/16-Dec-Inventory.pdf (accessed February 21, 2018).

MacDonald, C. 2016. 58 Detroit population rank is lowest since 1850, *The Detroit News*, May 19. Retrieved from http://www.detroitnews.com/story/news/local/detroit-city/2016/05/19/detroit-population-rank-lowest-since/84574198/ (accessed August 2, 2018).

Newman, M. 2006. The neighborhood that the ballpark built. *The New York Times*, April 10.

O'Reiley, T. 2011. Legalizing casino gambling helped revive Nevada 80 years ago, *Las Vegas Review-Journal*, March 27. Retrieved from https://www.reviewjournal.com/business/casinos-gaming/legalizing-casino-gambling-helped-revive-nevada-80-years-ago/ (accessed February 1, 2018).

Rosentraub, M. S. 2010. *Major league winners: Using sports and cultural centers as tools for economic development*, Boca Raton, FL: Taylor & Francis.

Shea, B. 2014. On cost, financing of Wings arena: Here are answers, *Crain's Detroit*, September 21. Retrieved from http://www.crainsdetroit.com/article/20140921/NEWS/309219990/on-cost-financing-of-wings-arena-here-are-answers (accessed August 2, 2018).

SNTIC. n.d. Executive Order, *Southern Nevada Tourism Infrastructure Committee*. Retrieved from http://sntic.org/ (accessed February 21, 2018).

SNTIC. 2017. The economic impact of Southern Nevada's tourism industry and convention sector – 2016 update, *Southern Nevada Tourism Infrastructure Committee*, March. Retrieved from http://www.lvcva.com/includes/content/images/media/docs/EIS-Economic-Impacts-March-2017-FINAL.pdf (accessed December 20, 2018).

Star-Ledger Staff. 2010. Atlantic City: Timeline of events since casino gambling became legal, *NJ.com*, July 20. Retrieved from http://www.nj.com/news/index.ssf/2010/07/atlantic_city_timeline_of_even.html (accessed February 1, 2018).

Thompson, D. 2014. Which sports have the whitest/richest/oldest fans? *The Atlantic*, February 10. Retrieved from https://www.theatlantic.com/business/archive/2014/02/which-sports-have-the-whitest-richest-oldest-fans/283626/ (accessed December 19, 2017).

UNLV. n.d. Our Commitment, *University of Nevada Las Vegas*. Retrieved from https://www.unlv.edu/toptier (accessed February 21, 2018).

Wolf, M., & Terrell, D. 2016. The high-tech industry, what is it and why it matters to our economic future, *U.S. Bureau of Labor Statistics*, May. Retrieved from https://www.bls.gov/opub/btn/volume-5/pdf/the-high-tech-industry-what-is-it-and-why-it-matters-to-our-economic-future.pdf (accessed March 1, 2018).

Index